The
Good Hotel
Guide 2018

GREAT BRITAIN & IRELAND

Editors
M Astella Saw
Adam Raphael
Nicola Davies

Editor in Chief
Caroline Raphael

The Good Hotel Guide Ltd

This edition first published in 2017 by
The Good Hotel Guide Ltd

Copyright © 2017 Adam and Caroline Raphael
Maps © 2017 David Perrott

Chief executive: Richard Fraiman

Contributing editors:
Rose Shepherd
Emma Grundy Haigh
Bonnie Friend
Nora Mahony

Production: Hugh Allan
Managing editor: Alison Wormleighton
Designer: Lizzy Laczynska
Text editor: Daphne Trotter
Computer consultant: Vince Nacey
Website design: Matt Preston, Cotswolds Online Services
Researcher: Cristina Recio-Corral

A CIP catalogue record for this book may be found in the British Library.

ISBN 978 0 9932484 2 9

Cover photograph: Ballymaloe House, Shanagarry

Printed and bound in Spain by Graphy Cems

FSC
www.fsc.org

MIX
Paper from
responsible sources
FSC® C007507

THE GOOD HOTEL GUIDE LTD

'A good hotel is where the guest comes first'

Hilary Rubinstein, founding editor
(1926–2012)

Hotel Endsleigh, Milton Abbot

CONTENTS

www.goodhotelguide.com

Our website has many handy features to help you get the most out of your Guide.

- Explore offers and discounts
- View special collections
- Read the latest news
- Search for a hotel near you
- Search for a hotel near a particular destination
- Submit a review
- Join the Good Hotel Guide readers' club
- Order a copy of the printed Guide

DESKTOP

TABLET

SMARTPHONE

Make it even easier to get on the Good Hotel Guide website while you're on the go: add an icon to the home screen of your iPhone or iPad for one-touch smartphone access. Go to **www.goodhotelguide.com** on your mobile browser. Tap on the rectangle with an arrow pointing upwards, at the bottom of the screen. Then tap on the + sign ('Add to Home Screen') that pops up.

INTRODUCTION

Hilary Rubinstein launched the Good Hotel Guide 40 years ago as an informed companion for the discriminating traveller. Free-spoken yet reasoned, it was valued from the start for its personality and forthright independence.

For 40 years, we have upheld the values that shaped the first Guide. Personal recommendations, unbiased inspections and plain, old-fashioned research frame each entry in this book. Candid comments from our dedicated correspondents make a place stand out; frank observations temper over-enthusiastic reports. The Guide has never accepted payment or free hospitality from a hotel that wishes to be included, giving us the freedom to make an impartial judgement. Just four hotels have been in the Guide since the first edition, endorsed by readers who laud continued high standards: Ballymaloe House (whose wisteria-draped facade is on the front cover), Currarevagh House, Lastingham Grange and Rothay Manor.

Our 424 main entries and 416 Shortlist entries this year include hotels, inns, restaurants-with-rooms, guest houses and B&Bs in city and countryside and along the coast. Many are family owned and managed; at least one serves a fiendishly flavourful tangerine soufflé. Previous editions of the Guide retained César mentions indefinitely; from this year, César-winning hotels may hold on to their award for ten years, and could well win again after that time. There may appear to be no single unifying standard across the board, but one essential element holds: personable charm and character are what we champion.

Forty years on, we are forming new traditions. On the revamped Good Hotel Guide website, you can search for, and easily find, the most amenity-packed boutique B&B, the friendliest walkers' hotel or, handily, the Guide-approved hotel nearest you. (Most, but not all, of the hotels in this volume are well represented on our website. We ask our UK and Ireland hotels to pay a modest fee for their entry to appear online; if they choose not to pay, their listing remains, without the full content.) On our website, as well, discover more than 460 of our favourite hotels on the Continent and around the world, in addition to a slew of offers and special breaks to make a getaway even more memorable.

We're 40 years young. Come celebrate with us.

M. Astella Saw and Adam Raphael
July 2017

HOW TO USE THE GOOD HOTEL GUIDE

MAIN ENTRY

The 424 main entries, which are given a full page each, are those we believe to be the best of their type in Great Britain and Ireland.

Colour bands identify each country; London has its own section.

An index at the back lists hotels by county; another index lists them by hotel name.

Hotels are listed alphabetically under the name of the town or village.

This hotel is making its first appearance, is returning after an absence, or has been upgraded from the Shortlist.

We name readers who have endorsed a hotel; we do not name inspectors, readers who ask to remain anonymous, or those who have written a critical report.

The maps at the back of the book are divided into grids for easy reference. A small house indicates a main entry, a triangle a Shortlist one.

We try to indicate whether a hotel can accommodate wheelchair-users. It's always worth calling the hotel to check the details of wheelchair access.

The panel provides the contact details, number of bedrooms and facilities.

SCOTLAND 347

BALLANTRAE Ayrshire   Map 5:E1

GLENAPP CASTLE   NEW   25% DISCOUNT VOUCHERS

Enter through the 'splendid' wrought-iron gates and continue up a 'beautifully wooded' drive: in 'meticulously tended' grounds stands this 'impressive' 19th-century Scottish baronial castle. It is now owned by Paul and Poppy Szkiler; John Orr, the manager, is 'calm, kind, perceptive – very much a people person'. Within oak-panelled halls, all is 'refined', from the 'magnificent' staircases and Corinthian columns to a 'delightful flight of carved ivory elephants'. 'The spacious, immaculate lounge, with its deep, high-backed sofas, has the feeling of a grand entrance hall.' Traditionally decorated bedrooms have views of garden and woodland, or the wild Ayrshire coast. 'Our gracious room looked over lush gardens towards Ailsa Craig rising majestically in the sea. In the large period bathroom: soft towels and bathrobes. Housekeeping was excellent.' In the restaurant, 'high-quality' French-Scottish dishes (perhaps roast chicken, pommes purée, baby vegetables, black pudding bonbon) use produce from the Victorian greenhouse and the kitchen garden. Breakfast, 'served promptly', continues the feast: home-made muesli and yogurt, a wide selection of tempting hot dishes'. (Robert Gower)

Ballantrae
KA26 0NZ

T: 01465 831212
F: 01465 831000
E: info@glenappcastle.com
W: www.glenappcastle.com

BEDROOMS: 17, 7 on ground floor, some suitable for disabled.
OPEN: all year.
FACILITIES: lift, drawing room, library, 2 dining rooms, wedding facilities, free Wi-Fi, in-room TV (Freeview), 36-acre grounds (walled gardens, woodland, lake, tennis, croquet), boat for charter, access to local spa.
BACKGROUND MUSIC: none.
LOCATION: 2 miles S of Ballantrae.
CHILDREN: all ages welcomed.
DOGS: allowed in 2 bedrooms, not in public rooms.
CREDIT CARDS: Amex, MasterCard, Visa.
PRICES: [2017] per room B&B from £350, D,B&B from £450. 1-night bookings sometimes refused.

www.goodhotelguide.com

This hotel has agreed to give Guide readers a 25% discount off its normal bed-and-breakfast rate for one night only, subject to availability. Terms and conditions apply.

We give the range of room or B&B prices for 2018, or the 2017 prices when we went to press. The price for dinner is for a set meal, or the average cost of three courses from an à la carte menu.

HOW TO USE THE GOOD HOTEL GUIDE

SHORTLIST ENTRY

The Shortlist includes untested new entries and places we think should be appropriate in areas where we have limited choice. It also includes some hotels about which we have not had recent reports. There are no photographs; many of the hotels have chosen to be included, with pictures, on our website.

This hotel has agreed to give Guide readers a 25% discount off its normal bed-and-breakfast rate for one night only, subject to availability. Terms and conditions apply.

In some cases we list the entry under the nearest town.

These are abbreviated descriptions listing the essential facilities.

ENGLAND 533

and Wiltshire honey on the buffet; interesting cooked options. 8 miles NE of Bath. BEDROOMS 14. 1 in annexe. OPEN All year. FACILITIES Bar, restaurant, private dining rooms, free Wi-Fi, in-room TV (Freeview), garden, courtyard (alfresco dining), parking. BACKGROUND MUSIC In private dining areas and bar. CHILDREN All ages welcomed. DOGS Allowed in some bedrooms, bars, courtyard (£15 per night). PRICES Per room B&B £140–£240. À la carte £35. 25% DISCOUNT VOUCHERS

COVENTRY Warwickshire
Map 2:B2
BARNACLE HALL, Shilton Lane, Shilton, CV7 9LH. Tel 02476 612629, www. barnaclehall.co.uk. Rose Grindal's centuries-old farmhouse is a rustic refuge 20 minutes by car from the city centre. Enter by the old oak door: the house has much character in its low doorways, nooks and crannies, and steps of varying heights. B&B accommodation is in spacious, traditionally decorated bedrooms with dark beams and fresh flowers. There's fresh fruit and cereal at breakfast, plus hot dishes cooked to order. Dietary requirements can be catered for, with advance notice. The garden comes into full bloom in the spring and summer – ask to take a cup of tea in the country calm. The M6 motorway is within easy reach. BEDROOMS 3. OPEN All year except Christmas. FACILITIES Sitting room (wood-burning stove), dining room, free Wi-Fi, in-room TV, patio, garden. BACKGROUND MUSIC None. CHILDREN All ages welcomed (rates based on age, no special facilities). PRICES Per person B&B single £45–£55, double £75–£85. Credit cards not accepted.

COOMBE ABBEY, Brinklow Road, Binley, CV3 2AB. Tel 02476 450450, www. coombeabbey.com. Steeped in 'character, eccentricity and individuality', this atmospheric, history-rich hotel retains many traces of its past as a 12th-century Cistercian abbey. Watch for deer as you approach through a 'well-maintained' country park; cross a bridge into 'superb' formal gardens. Inside the 'stunning' building, there are wrought-iron chandeliers, a carved stone pulpit, antique armchairs in the high-vaulted reception. Long corridors displaying 'magnificent' antiquities and china lead to the sumptuous 'bed chambers'. Rooms may have a canopy bed, original moulding or leaded windows; bathrooms, some hidden behind a bookcase, have a Victorian bath or a richly tiled waterfall shower. Modern dishes (crispy lamb shoulder bon bon and breast noisette, sweetbread, wild garlic mash, spring greens) are served in the conservatory dining room, candlelit at night. BEDROOMS 119. FACILITIES Bar, restaurant, private dining rooms, free Wi-Fi, in-room TV, wedding/conference facilities, room service, medieval banquets, terrace, 500-acre grounds (formal gardens, parkland, lake, walking trails, wildlife), parking (£5 per day). BACKGROUND MUSIC In public areas. CHILDREN All ages welcomed. PRICES Per room B&B from £89, D,B&B from £159.

COVERACK Cornwall
Map 1:E2
THE BAY HOTEL, North Corner, nr Helston, TR12 6TF. Tel 01326 280464, www.thebayhotel.co.uk. Almost all the incoming calls come from the birds at Victoria and Nicholas Sanders's

www.goodhotelguide.com

Many readers tell us they find background music irritating. We tell you if music is played and where you might encounter it.

Dinner prices are either for a set menu or an estimate of the likely price of a three-course meal.

CÉSARS 2018

We give our César awards to the ten best hotels of the year. Named after César Ritz, the most celebrated of hoteliers, these are the Oscars of hotel-keeping.

🏆 NEWCOMER OF THE YEAR
The Mash Inn, Radnage
The superlative meals at Nick Mash's restaurant-with-rooms, in a Chiltern hills village, draw the crowds. Stay in simple, modern bedrooms in the refreshed 18th-century inn; toast your good fortune with turmeric ginger beer at breakfast.

🏆 LUXURY HOTEL OF THE YEAR
Hambleton Hall, Hambleton
Wonderfully spoiling, Tim and Stefa Hart's country house hotel overlooking Rutland Water has it all: delightful gardens; Michelin-starred dinners; exemplary breakfasts, complete with a hot cross bun or two.

🏆 SEASIDE HOTEL OF THE YEAR
Soar Mill Cove Hotel, Soar Mill Cove
The bedrooms come with binoculars at Keith Makepeace's family-friendly hotel on a Devon hillside – all the better to spot the dolphins in the sea. Lunch on chowder and fishcakes before walking to the beach, under the gaze of cows in neighbouring fields.

🏆 COUNTRY HOUSE HOTEL OF THE YEAR
Judges, Yarm
The Downs family's traditional hotel on the edge of the North York Moors wins fans for its professional yet friendly approach to hotel-keeping. Among the thoughtful touches guests love: a complimentary decanter of sherry in the lavishly decorated bedrooms.

🏆 B&B OF THE YEAR
St Cuthbert's House, Seahouses
A jug of monastery mead accompanies the morning porridge at this former church, in a coastal Northumberland village. Dedicated owners Jeff and Jill Sutheran serve the taste of the place at breakfast: village-bakery bread, local-smokehouse kippers.

♛ ROMANTIC HOTEL OF THE YEAR
Forest Side, Grasmere

In the Lake District, Andrew Wildsmith has created a
modern rustic setting to fall into – and fall for – at this
elegantly understated Victorian gothic mansion standing in
acres of landscaped gardens and dappled woodland.

♛ INN OF THE YEAR
The Red Lion Freehouse, East Chisenbury

Chef/patrons Guy and Brittany Manning run their thatch-
roofed inn in a village bordering the River Avon. Michelin-
starred dinners are followed by a magnificent sleep in a
bedroom decorated with flair.

♛ SCOTTISH HOTEL OF THE YEAR
Burrastow House, Walls

A peat fire burns at Pierre Dupont's laid-back small hotel
on the remote west side of Shetland – just right for the
library of books to read in front of it. The 18th-century
house stands on the bay; all around is extraordinary beauty.

♛ WELSH RESTAURANT-WITH-ROOMS OF THE YEAR
Llys Meddyg, Newport

In a coastal Pembrokeshire village, this affable restaurant-
with-rooms is run by owners Edward and Louise Sykes
with genuine charm and more than a dash of local flavour.
The food is sophisticated; the rooms are snug and serene.

♛ IRISH HOTEL OF THE YEAR
Viewmount House, Longford

Open fires, fresh flowers and Irish literature fill the rooms
of Beryl and James Kearney's Georgian mansion. Most
appealing are the congenial hosts, who encourage a relaxed
air throughout the house.

REPORT OF THE YEAR COMPETITION

Readers' contributions are the lifeblood of the Good Hotel Guide. Everyone who writes to us is a potential winner of the Report of the Year competition. Each year we single out the writers of the most helpful reports. These correspondents win a copy of the Guide and an invitation to our annual launch party in October. This year's winners are:

WENDY ASHWORTH OF LIGHTWATER
ANDREW AND HANNAH BUTTERWORTH OF BRADFORD-ON-AVON
PATRICIA HIGGINS OF ALEXANDRIA, VIRGINIA
CÉLINE LA FRENIÈRE OF LONDON
ALFRED LENNON OF PRENTON
RICHARD OSBORNE OF WILLOWBROOK
KEITH SALWAY OF LECHLADE
JANE THORNTON OF DORKING
SIMON AND MITHRA TONKING OF ABBOTS BROMLEY
MICHAEL WILLIAMS OF LONDON

JOIN THE GOOD HOTEL GUIDE READERS' CLUB

Send us a review of your favourite hotel.
As a member of the club, you will be entitled to:
- A pre-publication discount offer
- Personal advice on hotels
- Advice if you are in dispute with a hotel
- Monthly emailed Guide newsletter

The writers of the ten best reviews will each win a free copy of the Guide and an invitation to our launch party. And the winner of our monthly web competition will win a free night, dinner and breakfast for two at one of the Guide's top hotels.

Send your review via
our website: www.goodhotelguide.com
or email: editor@goodhotelguide.com
or fax: 020 7602 4182
or write to:
Good Hotel Guide
50 Addison Avenue
London W11 4QP
England

EDITOR'S CHOICE

A visit to a hotel should be a special occasion. Here are some of our favourite hotels in various categories. Turn to the full entry for the bigger picture.

NO. 15 GREAT PULTENEY
BATH

There's plenty to look at in this quirky, creative city hotel, from a collection of vintage apothecary bottles to fragments of ancient Georgian wallpaper. Every bedroom in the row of three imaginatively restored town houses is different and individual, and stocked with everything you could need. Peckish guests have free range in a shared pantry of tasty morsels.
Read more, page 89.

THE PIG AT COMBE
GITTISHAM

The boho chic atmosphere at this laid-back hotel in Devon's Otter valley (pictured) extends from well-equipped bedrooms in the Elizabethan manor house to the buzzy great-hall bar and extensive kitchen garden. In the chandelier-lit restaurant, the food has excellent pedigree. Fisherfolk have an extra draw: bring back your catch from the trout-packed River Otter and ask the chef to cook it for dinner.
Read more, page 167.

SIGN OF THE ANGEL
LACOCK

In a National Trust village in Wiltshire, wonky beams, flagstone passageways, huge fireplaces and doorways for hobbits lend this restored 15th-century coaching inn plenty of character. The cottagey, antique-filled bedrooms are delightful; at mealtimes, the refined cooking draws the crowds. Bordered by a stream, the garden is an ideal spot for a cream tea in the summer.
Read more, page 193.

THE CRAB & LOBSTER
SIDLESHAM

Surrounded by tranquillity, this whitewashed restaurant-with-rooms stands on the edge of a Sussex nature reserve. Seafood lovers are spoiled with choices including salt and pepper native cuttlefish, charred baby corn and pea purée; stone bass, steamed clams, sea vegetables. In the centuries-old inn, chic modern bedrooms overlooking fields and sea are supplied with binoculars.
Read more, page 288.

THE PIPE AND GLASS INN
SOUTH DALTON

James and Kate Mackenzie's friendly pub-with-rooms in a Yorkshire village may seem modest from the outside, though the Michelin-starred meals are anything but. (A bonus: vegetarians have their own menu.) Stylish bedrooms, most with a patio overlooking woodland, are set around a well-maintained herb garden. At breakfast, there are deep-yellow scrambled eggs on home-baked bread. Read more, page 293.

SHIELDAIG LODGE
GAIRLOCH

Peat, whisky and leather make up the heady aroma at this Highland former hunting lodge on the shores of Loch Gairloch. The atmosphere here is welcoming and wholly Scottish – Harris tweeds, tartan carpeting, judiciously picked antiques, the creamiest porridge at breakfast, even two rubber Nessies in a wood-panelled bathroom. A brass telescope in the lounge is trained on the water.
Read more, page 358.

THE INN AT LOCH TUMMEL
STRATHTUMMEL

The views stretch over loch and mountain from this old stone-built inn near Pitlochry. The 19th-century building has been given a new lease of life by Alice and Jade Calliva, the friendly owners. A crackling fire keeps things toasty; at mealtimes, kitchen garden produce shows up in the super-local dishes, several cuts above pub grub. Comfy bedrooms are supplied with shortbread and whisky.
Read more, page 398.

COES FAEN
BARMOUTH

An ultra-modern mix of glass and natural rock and stone, Sara and Richard Parry-Jones's 'spa lodge B&B' is on the edge of Snowdonia national park. Inside and outside appeal equally. Each bedroom was conceived with a spa feature in mind – a huge wooden bath; a cedar and Welsh slate steam room. Behind the house, the sloping woodland garden, lush with bluebells in season, is a treat to explore.
Read more, page 415.

LLANTHONY PRIORY HOTEL
LLANTHONY

Wild seclusion characterises this unpretentious hotel by the remains of a 12th-century Augustinian priory at the foot of the Black mountains. The accommodation is modest, and there's no Wi-Fi or mobile phone signal, but the character and spirit of the place are more than adequate. Book a room in the medieval tower, up Norman stone steps, for the best views over the green valley.
Read more, page 434.

RESTAURANT JAMES SOMMERIN
PENARTH

Good eating comes with a dose of glamour at this family-run restaurant-with-rooms on the esplanade of a Severn estuary town. Chef/patron James Sommerin has a Michelin star for his ambitious modern dishes – choose a tasting menu and have him create a custom line-up for your table. Most of the up-to-date bedrooms have floor-to-ceiling windows overlooking the water.
Read more, page 440.

BURGH ISLAND HOTEL
BIGBURY-ON-SEA
There's magic at work at this 1930s
Art Deco extravaganza, moored like
a liner on a tidal island. It might be
in the glamorous Palm Court bar, or
in the sea-view bedrooms, some with
a roll-top bath. It might be in the
ballroom dinners or live bands, the
secret Mermaid Pool, the shades of such
starry past guests as Noël Coward and
Josephine Baker. In all, the place cast
a spell on two readers who relate, 'We
got engaged!'
Read more, page 97.

OLD WHYLY
EAST HOATHLY
The gardens brim with flowers at
Sarah Burgoyne's Georgian manor
house. In summer, sit on a lily-scented
terrace, stroll through an adjoining
estate carpeted with wild orchids, take
tea under a rose-covered pergola, have
a dip in the outdoor pool. The Paris-
trained hostess cooks a candlelit dinner
and will supply a picnic for nearby
Glyndebourne. Country-style bedrooms
have Irish linens; at breakfast, honey is
from the bees in the orchard.
Read more, page 154.

PEN-Y-DYFFRYN
OSWESTRY
Everything enchants at this small
Shropshire hotel, a former rectory now
run by kind, caring hosts Miles and
Audrey Hunter. Outside is a tumult of
birdsong; inside, book a bedroom with
a double spa bath or private stone-
walled patio. Set off on a ramble in
sublime countryside with a view of the
Welsh hills, or take a boat ride across
the vertiginous Pontcysyllte aqueduct,
before returning for tea and home-
baked scones.
Read more, page 248.

THE PAINSWICK
PAINSWICK
In a pretty Cotswold village, this
splendid hotel is run with a sense of fun
against a backdrop made for flirtation:
gaze over the Slad valley through the
mullioned windows of the tastefully
updated late-Palladian stone mansion.
The terraced garden is the place for
dalliance; a loggia is just right for a fairweather dinner. A suite comes complete
with a wood-burner, a roll-top bath and
a stone balcony for sunset drinks à deux.
Read more, page 253.

DRIFTWOOD HOTEL
PORTSCATHO

Beautifully landscaped gardens surround this New England-inspired hotel overlooking Gerrans Bay. Book a room with a sea view or go for the seclusion of the weather-boarded cabin in the grounds. In fine weather, take a picnic hamper down the path to the private beach; on a clement evening, have an aperitif on the terrace by the light of hurricane lamps. Michelin-starred chef Chris Eden cooks dinners to remember.
Read more, page 264.

ARDANAISEIG
KILCHRENAN

A single-track road leads to this Scottish baronial mansion bordered on two sides by Loch Awe, with panoramic views across the water to Ben Lui. The antique-dealer owner has filled the place with a dazzling array of ornaments and artworks, kitsch and caprice. Some of the theatrical bedrooms have a four-poster bed, but go for the stylish honeymoon suite in a converted boatshed almost lapped by the water.
Read more, page 367.

THE AIRDS HOTEL
PORT APPIN

In a pretty hamlet on the shores of Loch Linnhe, with distant views of the Morvern mountains, this former ferry inn has an atmosphere of unpretentious luxury. From here, you can visit the island of Iona, drive through spectacular scenery for a mountain gondola ride, take a ferry and a packed lunch to Lismore island, and tour 13th-century Castle Stalker on its islet. Candlelit dinners bring the freshest seafood.
Read more, page 386.

KNOCKINAAM LODGE
PORTPATRICK

A perfect hideaway with a history of secret trysts – Churchill met with Eisenhower here during World War II – this stone hunting lodge stands in acres of gardens and woodland, surrounded by gorse-clad cliffs. Book the Bay bedroom, which has a window seat, a Victorian tester bed and a garden-view bathroom, and watch the sun set over the Irish sea. Landscaped gardens lead to a private sandy beach.
Read more, page 388.

GLIFFAES
CRICKHOWELL

On summer Sundays lunch may be served, Tuscan-style, on the stone terrace of this Victorian Italianate mansion, which stands in wooded grounds overlooking the River Usk – give in to la dolce vita. It's a pleasing place in cooler weather, too, as the log fire burns in the art-hung sitting room. Choose a bedroom with a wisteria-draped Juliet balcony or a four-poster bed with an embroidered canopy.
Read more, page 420.

GREGANS CASTLE HOTEL
BALLYVAUGHAN

Dramatically situated on the Wild Atlantic Way, this 18th-century mansion has views to Galway Bay. Antiques and garden blooms fill the house; bedrooms, some with their own private lawn, have no TV to distract from views of garden, bay or mountains. Dine in style, from exquisite amuse-bouche to delectable desserts. If you can bear to leave, explore the otherworldly limestone landscape of the Burren.
Read more, page 460.

THE CARY ARMS
BABBACOMBE

On a cliff-side above a secluded south Devon cove, this stylish hotel is just the place for seaside de-stressing. A sun terrace at the spa looks over Babbacombe Bay; inside, there's an aromatherapy shower, a hydrotherapy pool, a sauna and steam rooms. Algae-based beauty and well-being treatments are available for face and body – and a duo massage room means double the repose.
Read more, page 79.

PARK HOUSE
BEPTON

Luxurious and unstuffy, this Edwardian country house stands on the edge of the South Downs in a wide swathe of rural tranquillity. Decompress further in the chic spa, which has a mother-of-pearl swimming pool, men's and women's saunas and steam rooms, and a varied menu of body treatments including a sensory massage using muslin bags of orange, clove, ginger and seaweed.
Read more, page 95.

DORMY HOUSE
BROADWAY

Candles and comfy loungers are set around the indoor swimming pool at this cosseting hotel on the outskirts of a Cotswold village. Splash here, or step outside – even in cool weather, the hydrotherapy hot tub on the spa terrace is a pleasure. The spa also has a lavender-infused sauna, a salt steam room and a juniper-laced Finnish cabin, plus treatment rooms and a chilled-out café.
Read more, page 118.

CONGHAM HALL
KING'S LYNN

Green-fingered visitors come to stroll through the acclaimed herb gardens at this Georgian house, surrounded by orchards and woodland in Norfolk countryside. The modern spa – complete with a grounds-facing indoor swimming pool – makes full use of the herbal harvest, incorporating seasonal herbs and blossoming flowers into the massages and body treatments.
Read more, page 191.

LIME WOOD
LYNDHURST

There's naught to do but surrender to the serenity at this temple of tranquillity in the New Forest. Soak in the indoor swimming pool while gazing into the forest; mellow out in the alfresco hot tub or ozone-treated lap pool; check in to the mud house or one of the many treatment rooms; stretch into yoga positions in the rooftop herb garden. Superfood salads and picnic boards nourish, afterwards.
Read more, page 217.

THE SCARLET
MAWGAN PORTH

The tented treatment rooms are lit by lanterns at this sleek, adults-only hotel overlooking a Cornish beach. Indoor and outdoor swimming pools, cliff-top hot tubs and a cedar barrel sauna all take in views of the Atlantic, but close your eyes for a massage or a mud wrap, or simply to disappear into a cocoon-like pod swinging from the ceiling in the relaxation room.
Read more, page 223.

SEAHAM HALL
SEAHAM

In extensive gardens overlooking Durham's heritage coast, this Georgian mansion has a plush yet laid-back feel. The Asian-inspired spa menu enhances the sense of relaxation, with natural treatments (jasmine rice scrubs, sesame and coconut poultices, bamboo massages) that borrow from the Thai and Indian traditions. A hydrotherapy pool, hammam, sauna and outdoor hot tub are ideal for simply sitting in (pictured).
Read more, page 284.

CLIVEDEN HOUSE
TAPLOW

Hidden behind mellow-brick garden walls at this glorious Italianate mansion, the rejuvenated spa reopened in summer 2017 after a complete overhaul. The historic outdoor swimming pool still takes centre stage in the spa garden, but much else has been unveiled: more treatment rooms, new relaxation areas, a garden-facing restaurant and lounge for nutrition-focused meals indoors or out.
Read more, page 303.

ST BRIDES SPA HOTEL
SAUNDERSFOOT

The views over Saundersfoot Bay from this modern cliff-top hotel are tonic for the soul – and no more appreciated, perhaps, than from within the saltwater infinity hydro-pool at the low-key spa. Two steam rooms, a herbal rock sauna and an ice fountain make up the thermal suite; treatment rooms overlook the wide stretch of village, beach and sea.
Read more, page 443.

LONGUEVILLE MANOR
ST SAVIOUR

In a secluded setting within the extensive gardens surrounding this centuries-old manor house on Jersey, a bijou spa kneads all the right spots. Face and body treatments begin with a rose-scented hot towel and use plant-derived products; a holistic facial includes acupressure therapy and herbal compresses. Emerge to lounge under a parasol in the quiet courtyard, or to sit in the outdoor spa bath.
Read more, page 452.

THE CARY ARMS
BABBACOMBE

Yachts scud, white-sailed, across the Teign estuary, overlooked by Lana de Savary's hotel, which perches on the cliff-side, infused with the presence of the sea. There are deckchairs, binoculars, boating memorabilia, a marine spa, buckets and spades for children. You can even stay in a chic, luxuriously updated beach hut with a sun deck (pictured). Eat alfresco: choose from Devon crab, Lyme Bay lobster, Brixham scallops, fish and chips.
Read more, page 79.

THE BLAKENEY HOTEL
BLAKENEY

Explore the unspoilt beaches and salt marshes of north Norfolk from this well-established hotel on the quay of a coastal village. Children can paddle, go crabbing and mud-sliding. Seal-spotting boat trips are a highlight. Choose a bedroom with an estuary view, or one with a patio leading to the garden. Blakeney fish soup, potted shrimps, local crab, and cod and chips let hungry visitors savour the seaside.
Read more, page 100.

THE BEACH
BUDE

With boutique-chic bedrooms in coastal colours, a cool cocktail bar, and a decked terrace overlooking sandy Summerleaze beach and its sea pool, this hotel is a magnet for surfers and sybarites. The Victorian building has a fresh New England style and simply decorated seaview bedrooms. From classic Cornish mussels to prawn and spinach ravioli in a bouillabaisse sauce, the cooking has a strong sense of place.
Read more, page 122.

THE SEASIDE BOARDING HOUSE
BURTON BRADSTOCK

A once run-down B&B lives again as an artfully casual restaurant-with-rooms overlooking Lyme Bay, in the hands of escapees from London's Groucho Club. The bedrooms have views of Jurassic coast or countryside; the dining room opens on to the seaward terrace. From a sandwich of locally landed crab to moules marinière and cod in a shellfish bisque, the food is local and seasonal with a contemporary touch.
Read more, page 125.

IDLE ROCKS
ST MAWES

For more than a century, this family-friendly harbourside hotel has entertained happy holidaymakers. Smart bedrooms have a sea or village view, perhaps a freestanding bath set in a window overlooking the water. On sunny days, eat on the terrace – there's a dedicated oyster menu, plus Cornish crab, lime, Thai foam; roast hake, monk's beard, mussels. Go crabbing or kayaking; explore coast and countryside. Read more, page 282.

TRESANTON
ST MAWES

Olga Polizzi's nonchalant chic is evident in her laid-back hotel overlooking Falmouth Bay. Every bedroom, styled with antiques and Cornish art, has views over the water. Flop on a lounger in the new garden beach club, or head for high seas on the hotel's 1930s racing yacht, Pinuccia, with a picnic aboard. In the seaward dining room, classy cooking might bring brill on the bone, salt cod croquettes, cavolo nero. Read more, page 283.

THE PIG ON THE BEACH
STUDLAND

There's a fairytale quality to this 1820s neo-Gothic marine villa, in gardens looking towards Studland Bay and the Isle of Wight. The shabby-chic style within is typical of Robin Hutson's Pig hotels. Sleep in a shepherd's hut or a thatched bothy in the walled garden, explore miles of sandy beaches, then dine on whole Lyme Bay brill or Dorset venison 'stalker's pie' with home-grown vegetables, in the conservatory dining room. Read more, page 297.

THE NARE
VERYAN-IN-ROSELAND

Only the beautifully tended gardens stand between hotel and beach here on the Roseland peninsula. Traditional, country-style interiors and old-fashioned luxuries (such as a valet who unpacks for you) create a joyous sense of stepping back in time. Dress up to dine in the silver-service restaurant, or eat more casually in the Quarterdeck – the menu might include Portloe crab cakes, Fowey mussels, a lobster salad. Read more, page 320.

PORTH TOCYN HOTEL
ABERSOCH

Character abounds in this hotel overlooking Cardigan Bay, run by the Fletcher-Brewer family for 70 years. The interiors are traditional, but the food – served alfresco or amid a jolly atmosphere in the dining room – has a modern twist. Walk five minutes to the beach and the Wales Coastal Path, or stay put and enjoy the tennis court and open-air swimming pool. Read more, page 412.

THE WHITE HOUSE
HERM

A tractor brings your bags from the ferry to this former country house above the harbour on this car-free, carefree island. Bedrooms have neither television, clock nor telephone – choose a room with a balcony overlooking the water and watch the waves instead. Meals are casual in the Mermaid Tavern and Ship Inn brasserie; more formal in the Conservatory restaurant. Time slows, here: sit among the palm trees or take a dip in the outdoor pool. Read more, page 448.

LITTLE BARWICK HOUSE
BARWICK

No pleasures are skimped on in the shortbread-supplied bedrooms at Tim and Emma Ford's Georgian dower house, but food is the highlight. Eschewing foams and swooshes, Tim Ford focuses on the quality and seasonality of ingredients in such dishes as pan-fried Cornish red mullet, basil crushed new potatoes, saffron sauce. Exceptional wines are available by the glass. Breakfast is delicious, with sublime jams to spread.
Read more, page 83.

READ'S
FAVERSHAM

In the Garden of England, Rona and David Pitchford's Georgian manor is an enduring favourite. David Pitchford's seasonal dishes draw on produce from the kitchen garden, fish from Whitstable and local game. Menus are laced with foodie quotations and a sense of fun – consider 'lamb, lamb, lamb, lamb and lamb', fricassee of peas, broad beans, rosemary jus. The six spacious bedrooms have antiques and traditional decor.
Read more, page 163.

THE BLACK SWAN AT OLDSTEAD
OLDSTEAD

The extensive kitchen garden here gets nearly as much attention as the Michelin-starred restaurant. Local farmers Tom and Ann Banks own the former pub; their sons James and Tommy are front-of-house and in the kitchen. Home-grown produce stars on Tommy Banks's dishes, along with locally sourced, preserved and foraged ingredients in dishes like raw red deer, rhubarb-cured scallop, monkfish with hen-of-the-woods.
Read more, page 246.

THE CROWN AND CASTLE
ORFORD

Switch off your mobile and relax. Ruth and David Watson and Tim Sunderland want guests to focus on convivial company and the pleasures of the table (pictured). Ruth Watson is executive chef and driving force; in the kitchen, Robert Walpole and Charlene Gavazzi use a wealth of local produce in such dishes as slow-roast Dingley Dell pork belly; Orford-landed skate, sautéed grapes and almonds, black butter.
Read more, page 247.

JSW
PETERSFIELD

Chef/patron John Saul Watkins holds a Michelin star for cooking of elegant simplicity, at this former coaching inn. Carefully sourced produce is used in dishes to delight both carnivores and vegetarians – perhaps textures of lamb, shepherd's pie croquette; English truffle risotto, sea vegetables. Sleep in a cosy, contemporary bedroom and wake to a continental breakfast with pastries from Paris.
Read more, page 259.

TUDDENHAM MILL
TUDDENHAM

The accomplished modern cooking at this 243-year-old Suffolk mill is more than a fine match for the impressive bedrooms and Hobbity nooks spread out through the tranquil grounds. Chef Lee Bye cooks compelling yet accessible dishes such as sea trout, beetroot, smoked roe; Breckland lamb, St Edmunds ale. Breakfast while watching the swans on the stream, then borrow a bicycle to work off the feasting.
Read more, page 313.

THE THREE CHIMNEYS AND THE HOUSE OVER-BY
DUNVEGAN

In 1984, Shirley and Eddie Spear moved to Skye to open a modest bistro. Thirty-four years, a Michelin star and an OBE later (for Shirley Spear's services to food and drink), this is one of Scotland's most acclaimed restaurants. Nordic-inspired menus draw on produce fished, farmed and foraged on the island. Sample seaweed-cured salmon; Loch Harport oysters; Dunvegan langoustines, lightly smoked monkfish cheeks, sea dashi.
Read more, page 354.

THE PEAT INN
PEAT INN

Geoffrey Smeddle, Michelin-starred chef and food columnist, is kitchen supremo at this former coaching inn close to the Fife coast; his wife, Katherine, is front-of-house. The menus are a showcase of classical techniques with a modern spin: 12-hour braised daube of Scotch beef, smoked potato purée, wild garlic, tomato confit; roast brill, potato galette, samphire, wild asparagus, champagne velouté.
Read more, page 380.

THE HARDWICK
ABERGAVENNY

Having honed his skills in top kitchens, Stephen Terry, with his wife, Joanna, took on and transformed this one-time roadside pub. Local produce is the bedrock of menus short on drivel and long on dishes. Typical offerings: duck hash and fried local duck egg; roast plaice on the bone, monk's beard, capers, brown butter and shrimp. Bedrooms in a courtyard annexe are Scandi-smart, modern and comfortable.
Read more, page 411.

TYDDYN LLAN
LLANDRILLO

You'll find a relaxed atmosphere and Michelin-starred cooking at Bryan and Susan Webb's Georgian former shooting lodge in rural north Wales. The hostess presides over the pretty dining room while the chef/patron – 40 years at the stove – cooks such deceptively simple dishes as aged Welsh Black beef steak au poivre and chips; wild sea bass, laver bread butter sauce, samphire. Country-style bedrooms look over the garden.
Read more, page 430.

THE WENTWORTH
ALDEBURGH

'We understand that your four-legged friend is part of the family,' say the owners of this welcoming Victorian hotel on the Suffolk coast, who charge a modest £2 per dog-night. A reader's pooch this year loved the shingle beach opposite (open to dogs from October through April), as well as the canine-friendly beaches nearby and miles of trails to sniff out.
Read more, page 70.

THE TRADDOCK
AUSTWICK

The Yorkshire Dales and its peaks, rivers and hamlets have walks aplenty for active dogs, and this family-run hotel in its own gardens is the place to let tuckered pooches stretch out afterwards. Towels, scoop bags and washing facilities are provided; for a fee of £5 per dog, clean, well-behaved mutts are 'very much part of the ambience', the owners assure, in bedrooms and on a lead in the public rooms.
Read more, page 77.

THE MASTER BUILDER'S
BEAULIEU

Call room service: Sir would like the pork sausages with gravy and sprinkles; Madam will have a rump steak. Dogs are so welcome at this New Forest hotel on the Beaulieu river that they have their own menu, bed, bowl and treats in nine dog-friendly bedrooms. The restaurant is out of bounds, but there will be, everywhere else, no end of bounding.
Read more, page 93.

OVERWATER HALL
IREBY

Well-mannered dogs stay free and are 'genuinely welcome' at this 19th-century house amid large gardens and extensive grounds incorporating a woodland boardwalk. Beyond, there are the lakes and fells of the northern Lake District to explore. Canines are allowed in one bar and lounge; meals can be brought to the bedroom for guests wishing to eat with their pet. Dog-sitting services can be arranged.
Read more, page 187.

THE ARUNDELL ARMS
LIFTON

With Dartmoor almost on the doorstep, this fishing hotel is an ideal base for Rover. Friendly staff fuss over well-behaved dogs, who are allowed everywhere except in the restaurant and on the riverbank. The £15 nightly charge includes a bed, a bowl, waste bags and a welcome chew – perhaps even a sausage at breakfast. The hotel has plenty of ideas of pet-friendly places of interest nearby.
Read more, page 203.

MULLION COVE HOTEL
MULLION COVE

The dog-friendly lounge is the social hub of this traditional family hotel overlooking harbour and fishing cove. Canine guests stay free in the off season; in peak months pay £9 a night. Descend to the small, sandy beach: at low tide, a chink in the harbour rock leads to Porth Pyg, along the cove. Another day, walk (and scamper) the Coastal Path to Lizard Point, stopping at a pub along the way.
Read more, page 230.

PRINCE HALL
TWO BRIDGES

Fido has his fill of treats at this 18th-century manor on Dartmoor, from the pooch-friendly snacks at reception to the all-natural chews in the bedroom. Owners have a bucket, sponge and towels for mucky pups; scoop bags and a bin; access to refrigerated food storage; a torch for nighttime dog-walking. One or two dogs stay free; three or more are charged £15 each.
Read more, page 314.

COUL HOUSE
CONTIN

A Guide inspector's cockerpoo vouches for the friendliness at Stuart and Susannah Macpherson's Georgian house in the Highlands: 'the lovely people made a tremendous fuss'. Dogs are allowed in some bedrooms and all public rooms except the restaurant, at a charge of £7.50 a night. The wide outdoors sets tails wagging in the large grounds and on surrounding forest trails.
Read more, page 353.

TRIGONY HOUSE
THORNHILL

A gourmet box of treats awaits new arrivals to this 18th-century sporting lodge in gently rolling Dumfriesshire countryside. Beds, bowls, towels, walk maps and dog-sitters are available as well. A delicious bonus: the free breakfast sausage – or vegan alternative, if doggy dietary restrictions are made known in advance. Resident Retriever Roxy is in clover.
Read more, page 402.

THE FALCONDALE
LAMPETER

Chicken and gravy with a garden view are on the menu at this Italianate villa in wooded acres within west Wales – dogs can join their owner in the conservatory at mealtimes. A £10-a-night charge includes snacks and the use of a blanket and water bowl; upgrade to a 'doggy box' (£20) containing a rope toy, a chewy ear, more treats and a blanket for keeps. Veterinary help is forthcoming in case of collie wobbles.
Read more, page 429.

FARLAM HALL
BRAMPTON

The comforts of a much-loved private home fill the Quinion family's creeper-swathed manor house on the edge of the North Pennines. Bedrooms are large and individually styled, with comfy chairs and garden views. Afternoon tea is served in a sitting room hung with paintings; dinner, overlooking the ornamental lake, has a daily-changing menu. At breakfast, sit down to be served a kipper or full English on pretty china.
Read more, page 111.

GRAVETYE MANOR
EAST GRINSTEAD

Log fires burn in sitting rooms filled with flowers from the renowned gardens at this Elizabethan manor house on a 1,000-acre estate (pictured). Antique furniture and paintings decorate the bedrooms. Chef George Blogg's Michelin-starred dishes – served, from spring 2018, in the newly remodelled restaurant – showcase produce from the huge walled potager, plus more from the house's own orchards, glasshouses, smokehouse and chickens.
Read more, page 153.

LEWTRENCHARD MANOR
LEWDOWN

Sleep in a four-poster bed that once belonged to Charles I's queen, Henrietta Maria, at this wildly ambitious rebuild of a Jacobean manor, whose rescued architectural features were installed by the ebullient Reverend Sabine Baring-Gould. Family owned, the hotel has a special atmosphere, its rooms furnished with antiques, its walls hung with portraits. Fireside canapés precede a dinner cooked with home-grown ingredients.
Read more, page 201.

CHEWTON GLEN
NEW MILTON

In the New Forest, this 18th-century manor house has been welcoming guests for half a century. Modern bedrooms – including those in woodland tree-houses – are supremely comfortable; staff are friendly and attentive; children are made very welcome. Take afternoon tea on a terrace in sunshine; at dinner, eat in the conservatory dining room or in the new restaurant, stylish and unstuffy, overlooking the kitchen garden.
Read more, page 234.

GILPIN HOTEL AND LAKE HOUSE
WINDERMERE

Here you find not one but two country houses, both owned by the Cunliffe family and run, as a single enterprise, with warmth and friendliness. Choose a bedroom or spa lodge in the Edwardian Gilpin Hotel, or opt for a secluded suite at the Lake House, a mile away. No matter where you lay your head, first sample Hrishikesh Desai's inventive Michelin-starred cooking in the Gilpin dining room.
Read more, page 332.

GLENAPP CASTLE
BALLANTRAE

Come up a wooded drive to Paul and Poppy Szkiler's 19th-century Scottish baronial 'castle' on a sporting estate. You can take afternoon tea in the drawing room or library, gazing out to Ailsa Craig, then explore the Italian garden designed by Gertrude Jekyll. Gracious bedrooms have views of lawns, woodland or the Ayrshire coast. In the panelled dining room, feast on produce from the Victorian greenhouse and kitchen garden.
Read more, page 347.

THE GROVE
NARBERTH

Surrounded by lawns, meadows and trees, this newly refurbished 18th-century mansion is run as a small luxury hotel. A log fire burns in the panelled sitting room, where charming staff will bring you tea and a sweet pick-me-up. Bedrooms have home-made biscotti and smart toiletries. In the dining room, Michael Caines protégé Allister Barsby's cooking is commendable.
Read more, page 436.

LONGUEVILLE MANOR
ST SAVIOUR

One of Jersey's oldest manor houses stands in an 18-acre estate in a beautiful valley. It is a hotel and spa, today in the hands of the third and fourth generations of the Lewis family. Plush bedrooms have scented candles, smart toiletries, magazines and board games. After a swim or a game of tennis, dine on modern dishes in the oak-panelled Garden Room, with produce from the Victorian kitchen garden.
Read more, page 452.

HILTON PARK
CLONES

Fred and Joanna Madden's Italianate mansion stands amid the sheer beauty of nature – come in spring to admire the carpet of bluebells at the feet of ancient trees. Within the 18th-century house, gracious public rooms are filled with period furniture and family history. Eat within view of the swans on the freshwater lake; next day, row a boat across the water, perhaps even diving in for a spot of wild swimming.
Read more, page 466.

CURRAREVAGH HOUSE
OUGHTERARD

The easy-going hospitality at Henry and Lucy Hodgson's Victorian country house on the shores of Lough Corrib keeps guests coming back. So, too, do the lashings of the hostess's home-made Seville orange marmalade. There are plenty of books to borrow in the traditionally decorated, turf fire-warmed sitting rooms; at afternoon tea, a spread of cakes and cucumber sandwiches adds to the cosseting country house feel.
Read more, page 479.

BARNSLEY HOUSE
BARNSLEY

From the 1950s, Rosemary Verey, Queen of Horticulture, created the romantic gardens (pictured) that surround this 17th-century Cotswold stone manor house. She designed the knot garden, topiary and laburnum walk, and pioneered the ornamental fruit and vegetable gardens. Wander at will, admiring statues and fountain, then eat home-grown produce in the Potager restaurant.
Read more, page 82.

LINDETH FELL
BOWNESS-ON-WINDERMERE

Lake Windermere provides a glorious backdrop to this fine Edwardian country house, in seven acres laid out in 1907 by nurseryman and garden designer Thomas Mawson. He harmonised building, plantings and natural surroundings, with formality around the house opening on to the landscape. There are specimen trees, azaleas and rhododendrons, a private tarn. Have tea on the terrace; play croquet on the lawn.
Read more, page 108.

HOTEL ENDSLEIGH
MILTON ABBOT

Jeffry Wyatville built this cottage orné as a fishing lodge for the Duchess of Bedford in the early 1800s. Now run as a hotel by Olga Polizzi, it stands in an Arcadian, Humphry Repton-designed landscape of dells, streams and cascades, with the River Tamar running through. Discover a 100-metre arched rose walk, an arboretum of champion trees, a shell grotto and one of the UK's longest herbaceous borders.
Read more, page 227.

ASKHAM HALL
PENRITH

In the Lake District, pass between stone gate piers and beetle up the drive to this Elizabethan mansion, surrounded by Grade II listed gardens laid out more than 300 years ago. With views down to the River Lowther, the extensive grounds incorporate ponds, meadow and woodland; lawns, topiary and terraces. Follow animal trails to see rare-breed pigs, Boer goats, ducks, chickens and short-horn cattle.
Read more, page 254.

MILLGATE HOUSE
RICHMOND
Behind their Georgian house on the square, the owners of this exceptional B&B have created a plantsman's garden with terraces leading down to the River Swale. Within a walled third of an acre, voluptuous old roses and clematis, ferns and hostas grow in sweet profusion. There are shady nooks to sit in, and a balcony of iron lace from which to survey such beauty from above.
Read more, page 271.

TALLAND BAY HOTEL
TALLAND-BY-LOOE
Somewhere between the Mediterranean and Wonderland, the subtropical sculpture garden of this cliff-top hotel is full of surprises. Palms and umbrella pines wave in the breeze against the backdrop of a blue sea. Here you come upon a pixie, there a pig, a giant teapot, a white horse or a mermaid. Order a Cornish cream tea to enjoy on the terrace.
Read more, page 302.

LORDS OF THE MANOR
UPPER SLAUGHTER
Around a honeyed Cotswold stone former rectory, eight acres of landscaped gardens lead, by way of a wild flower meadow, to the River Eye. Discover an old skating pond; a 19th-century ice house in a bog garden; a walled garden of flowers, herbs and ancient, espaliered fruit trees. The site has been developed by Chelsea Flower Show gold medallist Julie Toll.
Read more, page 316.

BOATH HOUSE
AULDEARN
The grounds surrounding this late-Georgian classical mansion are a perennially changing work of nature and the gardener's art. Find yourself amid wild flower meadow or woodland; along a stream or in the orchard; strolling through parterres and herbaceous borders. Swans glide on an ornamental lake, hens forage, bees buzz in the hives. The restaurant is supplied with abundant organic produce.
Read more, page 346.

DOUNESIDE HOUSE
TARLAND
Seventeen acres of gardens surround this turreted and gabled house, built in the early 20th century around a Victorian core, on the edge of the Cairngorms national park. Find a wealth of botanical plants, an infinity lawn, a stream running through. Take a drink on the terrace, with views of the Grampians; eat organic fruit and vegetables from the walled kitchen garden.
Read more, page 401.

BODYSGALLEN HALL & SPA
LLANDUDNO
On the slopes of Pydew mountain, with views of Snowdonia, this historic manor house is surrounded by 200 acres of parkland and gardens. Long-serving head gardener Robert Owen leads tours of the 17th-century parterre, limestone rockery, walled garden, follies and lily pond. Follow the Pydew Village Walk to a Gothic tower and mountain-top obelisk.
Read more, page 431.

NANNY BROW
AMBLESIDE
Surmounting a crag in ancient
woodland, this Arts and Crafts house
overlooks the Brathay valley, with
Wrynose Pass in the distance. Through
leaded casement windows, gaze out on
the River Brathay and the Langdale
fells, or across the gardens to Ivy Crag.
Loweswater suite is a special-occasion
option, with patio doors that open on to
a private balcony.
Read more, page 72.

SHALLOWDALE HOUSE
AMPLEFORTH
On a south-facing hillside on the edge
of the North York Moors, this tranquil,
welcoming B&B has three bedrooms,
each with panoramic views over the
Howardian hills, an area of outstanding
natural beauty. Sit on the front terrace
to enjoy the flower-filled gardens and
wealth of birdlife; the garden reaches up
the slope behind, allowing still-more-
singular vistas.
Read more, page 74.

THE HENLEY
BIGBURY-ON-SEA
All five bedrooms are sea facing at this
Edwardian holiday cottage in an area of
outstanding natural beauty, with coastal
views across the Avon estuary to Burgh
Island and beyond. Below are gardens,
with a path leading down to the sandy
beach. Make a reservation for dinner,
and ask for a seat by the window to
contemplate Bigbury Bay.
Read more, page 98.

BELLE TOUT LIGHTHOUSE
EASTBOURNE
Stunning in its starkness, this
decommissioned lighthouse-turned-
B&B is in a remote situation on the
South Downs Way. It overlooks the
English Channel, with views to the
Seven Sisters chalk cliffs, Birling Gap
and the notorious lover's leap, Beachy
Head. Ascend to the lantern to enjoy
the panorama; on a dark night, watch
as the stars come out in hundreds
and thousands.
Read more, page 155.

HEDDON'S GATE HOTEL
MARTINHOE

In a valley on the north Exmoor coast stands this friendly hotel above the River Heddon, where the South West Coastal Path dips down to the sea. The views, to the west, are spectacular. Among bedrooms named after trees in the large wooded grounds, choose one overlooking gardens and valley – deluxe Beech has the most beautiful vantage. Read more, page 220.

STAR CASTLE
ST MARY'S

Long gone, the prospect of armadas approaching this Elizabethan building within star-shaped fortress walls, originally built to guard the coast against invasion. A hotel since 1933, this characterful place has sublime sea views from two castle bedrooms, and from garden rooms complete with a veranda. In summer, dine in the conservatory restaurant, where grapes ripen on the vine. Read more, page 281.

KYLESKU HOTEL
KYLESKU

In a fishing hamlet, this informal 17th-century coaching inn stands in a wild and wonderful location by the old ferry slipway on the shores of Loch Glendhu. Choose a bedroom overlooking the water: you can't do better than one in the extension, 'Willie's Hoose', with a sliding door on to a balcony. Deer roam, seals bask; keep your eyes peeled for otters and porpoises. Read more, page 373.

KILCAMB LODGE
STRONTIAN

Just remote enough, this peaceful small hotel on the Ardnamurchan peninsula stands on the wooded shores of Loch Sunart (pictured), with water and mountain views from the dining room and many of the country-style bedrooms. Some rooms have a dual aspect; one has patio doors that open on to a balcony. Head to the water and try to spot eagles, whales and dolphins. Read more, page 400.

BRYNIAU GOLAU
BALA

All the bedrooms overlook Bala lake at this friendly B&B amid the catch-your-breath beauty of Snowdonia national park, the Arenig mountain on the horizon. In the dual-aspect Aran room, take in lake views from the bathtub as well. The Victorian house, surrounded by landscaped gardens, faces west: sunsets can be sensational. Read more, page 414.

STELLA MARIS
BALLYCASTLE

A former coastguard headquarters on Ireland's rugged west coast, this hotel on the Wild Atlantic Way was built for scanning the sea. It looks out across Bunatrahir Bay towards Downpatrick Head, a vista best enjoyed from the 100-foot conservatory that runs the length of the building. Nearly every one of the bedroom windows frames an ocean view. Read more, page 458.

AUSTWICK HALL
AUSTWICK

Generosity of spirit and sheer individuality win honourable mention at Michael Pearson and Eric Culley's 16th-century manor house in Italianate gardens, in a Yorkshire Dales village. Theatrical interiors are filled with art and antiques to fascinate – there's much to look at while sitting down to a welcome tea and freshly baked scones. At breakfast order locally cured bacon, with eggs from the resident hens.
Read more, page 76.

NEWBEGIN HOUSE
BEVERLEY

Nuala and Walter Sweeney take real pleasure in welcoming guests to their Georgian mansion, a family home filled with personal treasures. Bedrooms are supplied with a cafetière, and fresh milk in a mini-fridge. Breakfast at the dining-room table includes deli sausages, prosciutto, local bacon. Help is readily provided with anything from a wake-up call to advice on eating out. The centre of the market town is steps away.
Read more, page 96.

DUKE HOUSE
CAMBRIDGE

It's the attention to detail that most impresses at Liz and Rob Cameron's well-situated, well-styled B&B, from the house-brand toiletries in the bathroom to the ethically sourced eggs, locally pressed apple juice, seasonal fruit compotes and pretty china at breakfast. In the guests' drawing room there are sweet treats, perhaps an evening drink, and occasional events and talks to enliven the atmosphere.
Read more, page 128.

BROWNBER HALL
NEWBIGGIN-ON-LUNE

New owners Amanda Walker and Peter Jaques have an infectious enthusiasm for their stylishly refurbished B&B between Lakes and Dales. The Victorian house (pictured) has been updated to great effect, say Guide inspectors, who arrived to find cakes on the sideboard with a gentle exhortation: 'Please eat me.' Breakfast brings a spread of buttery croissants, home-made bread and marmalade, eggs from free-range hens.
Read more, page 236.

JEAKE'S HOUSE
RYE
Jenny Hadfield's former wool storehouse on a cobbled street in this historic town is richly atmospheric, with oak beams, panelled walls, oil paintings and antiques. Literary associations abound: the building was once home to American writer Conrad Aiken; TS Eliot and Radclyffe Hall visited. In the morning, there are devilled kidneys, Rye rarebit, award-winning sausages and all-too-rare smoked wild salmon.
Read more, page 278.

STOBERRY HOUSE
WELLS
'An earthly paradise,' writes a Guide reader this year, of Frances Meeres Young's 18th-century coach house in well-tended gardens with wildlife ponds, a potager, a lime walk and a panoramic view of the city. Inside, there are book-lined shelves in the sitting rooms, and fresh fruit and flowers in the stylish bedrooms. Breakfast, served in the conservatory, is praised for its choice and quality.
Read more, page 322.

THE DOWER HOUSE
MUIR OF ORD
Mena and Robyn Aitchison's single-storey Georgian cottage orné in the Scottish Highlands is cosy and homey, with a log-burning stove, a baby grand piano, shelves of well-thumbed books, board games and ornaments, and a wide selection of malt whiskies. Guests can sit out by a fish pond or wander a wild flower meadow. Bedrooms have fresh flowers and garden views. At breakfast there are newly laid eggs from the house's hens.
Read more, page 377.

Y GOEDEN EIRIN
DOLYDD
A rustic base in rugged Snowdonia, this characterful, eco-friendly place is run by Eluned Rowlands with charm, genuine hospitality and a generous dose of Welsh culture. There are no frills or fancies here: the house, a converted cowshed, has squashy sofas with kilim cushions, and shelves packed tight with books; the bedrooms are spacious, with a sleep-inducing bed. Breakfast, at a chunky oak table, has an extensive menu.
Read more, page 423.

PENBONTBREN
GLYNARTHEN
Welcoming hosts Richard Morgan-Price and Huw Thomas have a winning formula at their fine conversion of a 19th-century farm: part B&B, part hotel, part holiday cottage, it is wholly recommendable. Each well-equipped suite has a private garden and separate sitting room, but do emerge for breakfast: award-winning sausages, smoked fish, cockles and laver bread are all sourced locally.
Read more, page 427.

SEA MIST HOUSE
CLIFDEN
Sheila Griffin is the smiling, relaxed hostess at this Georgian house near the centre of the coastal town. A peat fire burns in the cosy sitting room in cool weather; when temperatures rise, the garden (listen for bees buzzing and hens clucking) comes abloom. Breakfast, served on traditional Irish crockery, has much interesting choice; guests on special diets are more than capably catered for.
Read more, page 465.

FROG STREET FARMHOUSE
HATCH BEAUCHAMP

Louise and David Farrance skimp on nothing at their 15th-century longhouse, set amid farmland on the outskirts of a Somerset village. Fresh flowers, eggs from the hens, tomatoes from the greenhouse, home-baked bread and award-winning sausages show care and attention to detail. The cosy Willow bedroom, with its stone walls, beams, brass bedstead and espresso machine, is the best buy. Per room B&B £81–£130. Read more, page 178.

THISTLEYHAUGH FARM
LONGHORSLEY

Enid Nelless and her daughter-in-law, Zoë, welcome guests to their Northumberland farmhouse on an organic farm on the banks of the River Coquet. Pretty bedrooms are supplied with fresh milk and home-baked biscuits. An Aga-cooked three-course dinner costs just £25 (wines from £15 a bottle), so you can sleep in rural peace without worrying about the bill. Per room B&B £100.
Read more, page 208.

TRELASKE HOTEL & RESTAURANT
LOOE

Two miles from the south Cornish coast, Hazel Billington and Ross Lewin run their peaceful small hotel with grace and charm. Daily-changing dinner menus feature plenty of seafood; breakfasts are hearty. Bedrooms look over garden or open countryside – choose a room with a balcony or a patio. Rooms sleeping three or four would suit a family on a budget. Per room B&B from £130.
Read more, page 209.

THE NAGS HEAD
PICKHILL

A good base to tour moor and dale, Janet and Edward Boynton's 19th-century Yorkshire coaching inn is also a fine stopover for travellers between England and Scotland. The busy bar and restaurant are popular locally – there are real ales in the tap room, plus generous helpings of pub favourites. Some of the no-nonsense bedrooms may be compact, but all are clean and perfectly comfortable. Per room B&B from £80.
Read more, page 262.

THE BLACK SWAN
RAVENSTONEDALE

Louise Dinnes's Victorian pub-with-rooms is in a conservation village in the Eden valley – and a canny Dales choice for those who prefer not to pay top Lake District dollar. Dine on seriously good cooking, off a reasonably priced menu; to drink, there are real ales, Cumbrian spirits, and wines from £16 a bottle. The well-maintained bedrooms are supplied with organic toiletries. Per room B&B from £100.
Read more, page 268.

LAKE ISLE HOTEL & RESTAURANT
UPPINGHAM

There's no lake here, just a popular town-centre restaurant with 12 smart, contemporary bedrooms, and owners with a penchant for Yeats. Breakfast is a feast, while three courses at night might set you back £35 – and, a local reader avers, you won't get better food at the price anywhere else. Bedrooms vary in size, so pick one to suit the budget. Per room B&B from £90.
Read more, page 317.

DALSHIAN HOUSE
PITLOCHRY

In secluded woodland and gardens, guests get more than just an excellent bed and breakfast at Martin and Heather Walls's Georgian house on the edge of town. A guest lounge warmed by a log burner is supplied with magazines and nibbles; the grounds are a haven for wildlife – look out for resident red squirrels. Add to this the genuine welcome, and the price seems almost a steal. Per person B&B £37.50–£45.
Read more, page 382.

THE CEILIDH PLACE
ULLAPOOL

You could sleep in the bunkhouse for just £24 a night at Jean Urquhart's bookshop-with-restaurant-with-rooms in this Highland fishing village. But you won't break the bank if you opt for a proper bedroom with books, a radio and the use of a pantry and honesty bar. Dine for not much more – though not for a song, as you could have done when the place first opened as a café/music venue nearly 50 years ago. Per room B&B from £132.
Read more, page 405.

CNAPAN
NEWPORT

Personable hosts Judith and Michael Cooper run their relaxed B&B in a coastal village close to Pembrokeshire national park. Newly renovated bedrooms are modern and airy, and are supplied with books and a Welsh wool blanket. The garden is bliss on a sunny day – prosecco optional. At breakfast: pancakes, Glamorgan sausages and all the friendly local advice you could need. Per room B&B £95.
Read more, page 437.

INCH HOUSE
THURLES

In Tipperary countryside, the Egan family's farmhouse – indeed, a Georgian mansion – is filled with antiques and original features. The price is modest for bedrooms of some grandeur. Sit down in the deep-red dining room in the evening: exemplary dinners use locally grown produce, including potatoes from the family farm. Take breakfast as the sun shines through stained-glass windows. Per room B&B €120–€140.
Read more, page 483.

RED LION INN
BABCARY

Flagstone floors, exposed beams and a log fire create a cosy ambience at Clare and Charlie Garrard's 17th-century thatched inn, while bedrooms in a converted barn are contemporary and stylish. Sophisticated gastropub dishes bring visitors to the Somerset village: venison tortellini; pan-fried gurnard, saffron potatoes, braised fennel, crab bisque. Happy hours, pub quizzes and curry nights encourage the convivial air. Read more, page 80.

THE KING'S HEAD INN
BLEDINGTON

A brook runs through the village green in front of Nicola and Archie Orr-Ewing's Cotswold-stone inn. Inside: hefty beams, high-backed settles, horse brasses and all the trappings of an ancient country pub, plus Giles Lee's emphatically modern cooking. Characteristic dishes: fillet of sea trout, crisp gnocchi, pickled shallots; wild garlic leaf, pea and spinach risotto. Cottage-style bedrooms are above the inn and around a quiet courtyard. Read more, page 103.

BEECH HOUSE & OLIVE BRANCH
CLIPSHAM

There's plenty to be cheerful about at Ben Jones and Sean Hope's well-liked village pub/restaurant, from the smart bedrooms in Beech House to the superlative cooking in the Olive Branch. Home-grown and locally farmed and foraged ingredients take pub grub to a higher level, with such dishes as warm duck salad, paddock beetroot; roast lamb chump, pearl barley tabbouleh, pomegranate. Read more, page 142.

THE STAR INN
HAROME

Chef/proprietor Andrew Pern rescued and revamped this 14th-century thatched inn (pictured) in a north Yorkshire village and filled it with surprises. Modern plates of local produce have a Michelin star and some intriguing inverted commas: saddle of local deer 'cooked over charcoal', coffee bean carrot, pistachio cake, pickled cherries, 'Twiglets'. Bedrooms are quirky and quirkier – one has a piano. Read more, page 174.

THE BROWNLOW ARMS
HOUGH-ON-THE-HILL
Share a board of superior snacks in
the lively bar at Paul and Lorraine
Willoughby's 17th-century Lincolnshire
village inn, or eat in the stylish dining
room, where Ruaraidh Bealby creates
such modern classics as pan-roast
cannon of lamb, seared liver and
shepherd's pie; cep-crusted pork
tenderloin, wild mushroom faggot,
Portobello purée. Quiet bedrooms are
plush, cosy and traditional.
Read more, page 183.

THE FEATHERED NEST
NETHER WESTCOTE
A log fire still burns at this Cotswold
village real-ale pub, which was
rebuilt, refurbished and reinvented
as a gastronomic destination by Tony
and Amanda Timmer. Chef Kuba
Winkowski uses local produce in
seasonal dishes that read like a foodie's
shopping list: scallop, pig belly, carrot,
miso; sea bass, passion fruit, aji chilli,
pisco. Eat inside or alfresco. Sleep in an
excellent room with countryside views.
Read more, page 232.

THE ROCK INN
NEWTON ABBOT
Rock up to the Graves family's village
inn on the edge of Dartmoor for real
ales and hearty pub food cooked with
flair. Typical offerings: pan-roasted local
lamb rump, fondant potato, celeriac
purée; stone bass, sweet potato, king
prawns, chorizo butter. Traditionally
and cosily furnished bedrooms are
thoughtfully equipped, down to the
teapot on the hospitality tray.
Read more, page 239.

THE ROSE AND CROWN
ROMALDKIRK
Beside the Saxon church in a North
Pennines village, Cheryl and Thomas
Robinson's 18th-century inn has a
welcoming atmosphere. Seasonal four-
course menus, served in the candlelit,
oak-panelled restaurant, list beautifully
presented modern dishes such as
tomato and asparagus salad, cucumber
gazpacho; black bream, samphire,
brown shrimp, almonds. Characterful
bedrooms have antiques and locally
made furniture.
Read more, page 273.

THE BECKFORD ARMS
TISBURY
Patio doors open to the garden on a fine
day at Dan Brod and Charlie Luxton's
updated stone-built inn on the edge of
Wiltshire's Fonthill Estate. The food is
pub grub par excellence, from home-
made game pie with a pint of Butcombe
bitter, to weekend pizzas from the
wood-fired oven, and suckling pig
roasted over a fire in the bar. Modern
country-style bedrooms have natural
toiletries and vintage Welsh blankets.
Read more, page 308.

THE FELIN FACH GRIFFIN
FELIN FACH
There's a carefree feeling at the Inkin
brothers' pitch-perfect gastropub
between the Black mountains and
the Brecon Beacons. Find a spot on
a squashy sofa by the log fire in a bar
packed with locals; in the shabby-chic
dining room, unfussy dishes might
include cod, creamed leeks, crab,
cauliflower; lamb breast, white bean
mash, salsa verde, sweetbreads. Smart
bedrooms have many creature comforts.
Read more, page 425.

MOONFLEET MANOR
FLEET
Parents relax as the children are kept
endlessly amused at this Georgian
manor house amid peaceful countryside.
The hotel is geared to families, with
a crèche, heated swimming pools, an
indoor play area and a cinema; Chesil
Beach is nearby – a fossil hunt beckons.
Older children will thrill to read
Moonfleet, Falkner's 18th-century
tale of smugglers and ghosts in this
little village.
Read more, page 165.

FOWEY HALL
FOWEY
Kenneth Grahame, a frequent visitor
to this Italianate Victorian pile, took it
for his model of Toad Hall. Bring The
Wind in the Willows for the children
to read – when they're not painting,
bouncing on trampolines, walking
Bramble the dog, collecting eggs from
the hens or messing about in boats
in the estuary. With free childcare,
baby-listening facilities and children's
dinnertime, this is a break for grown-
ups, too.
Read more, page 166.

AUGILL CASTLE
KIRKBY STEPHEN
In sprawling grounds on the edge
of the Lake District, this Victorian
fantasy castle easily captivates a child's
imagination. It's an unstuffy place
where grandparents and tiny tots feel
equally at home. There are no house
rules – 'It's a castle – who needs rules?'
the owners say. Instead, there are games,
dressing-up clothes, film nights and
a Little Cooks club, plus more in the
gardens: a tree house, playground and
tennis court.
Read more, page 192.

BEDRUTHAN HOTEL AND SPA
MAWGAN PORTH
Family fun is on the schedule year
round at this cliff-top hotel overlooking
a north Cornish beach. Half-term is
packed with special activities – a Punch
and Judy show, say, or circus training
– but children can choose from a kids'
club, three outdoor pools (and a poolside
snack bar), a games room, and indoor
and outdoor play areas in any season.
Grown-ups have their own child-free
relaxation zone.
Read more, page 222.

CHEWTON GLEN
NEW MILTON
In the New Forest, a stroll from the sea, this luxurious yet laid-back country house hotel has plenty of activities to please young and old. With indoor and outdoor swimming pools, beach picnics, pony trekking, mountain biking and a children's club, there's never a dull moment. Astonishing for all ages, too, are the tree-house suites in a woodland setting, with outdoor hot tub and galleried bunk-bed area.
Read more, page 234.

CALCOT MANOR
TETBURY
Young guests are particularly well catered for at this converted Cotswolds farmhouse in beautifully kept grounds. The smallest visitors benefit from a crèche, plus babysitting and baby-listening facilities; children eight and up have an entertainment area stocked with video games, board games and books. Dedicated child-friendly swimming-pool times mean everyone gets to take a turn.
Read more, page 307.

THE COLONSAY
COLONSAY
The adventure begins with the ferry crossing to this island hotel where children are warmly welcomed. Books and board games are supplied for indoor amusement, but it's in the open air that young guests have the greatest time. There are unspoilt beaches for picnics, caves to explore, bicycles to hire and wildlife to watch; days are spent on kayaking, kite-flying, shell-seeking and the simpler pleasures of life.
Read more, page 352.

TREFEDDIAN HOTEL
ABERDYFI
For an idyllic, sand-in-the-sandwiches sort of getaway, families head for this friendly hotel overlooking Cardigan Bay. Buckets and spades are provided; children can spend the day paddling, building sandcastles and taking donkey rides before returning for an early supper, leaving adults free to linger over dinner. On site, there's a family lounge, an outdoor play area and a games room.
Read more, page 409.

THE WHITE HOUSE
HERM
The pace of life slows down on this small, car-free island, and children have a rare freedom to roam. There's an outdoor swimming pool here, and tennis and croquet in the garden, but all of Herm is ripe for exploration. Sandy beaches are ideal for shell-collecting, rock-pooling, snorkelling and crabbing; Shell Beach and Belvoir Bay have kiosks for ice creams, and deckchairs for hire.
Read more, page 448.

BALLYVOLANE HOUSE
CASTLELYONS
The name means 'the place of springing heifers', and children, too, jump for joy at this 18th-century country house, where they are invited to help feed the farm animals and collect the eggs for breakfast. There's a tree-house in the garden, and woods to explore, plus a seven-a-side soccer pitch, bicycles, trampolines, and high tea for the early-to-bed. For something completely different, try glamping in a fully serviced bell tent.
Read more, page 463.

TUDOR FARMHOUSE
CLEARWELL
Ask for a packed lunch, and hike
to Offa's Dyke from this former
farmhouse, now a chic hotel in the
Forest of Dean. Hari and Colin Fell,
the owners, have lots of ideas for walks
nearby, including 14 acres of ancient
woodland and winding pathways in
Puzzlewood, or a sculpture trail for
gentler exercise. Explore more than
35 square miles of Forestry Commission
land on the doorstep, then head back for
an in-room massage.
Read more, page 140.

HAZEL BANK
KESWICK
Walks start at the door of this Victorian
country house in the Borrowdale valley.
Breakfast sets you up for a not-too-
strenuous ascent of Castle Crag or
an easy descent to Grange for a stroll
around Derwentwater; another day,
ramble to see 1,500-year-old yews
– Wordsworth's 'Fraternal Four of
Borrowdale' (reduced now to three). A
more challenging climb, with boots and
maps, brings you to High Spy, Maiden
Moor and Catbells.
Read more, page 189.

EES WYKE COUNTRY HOUSE
NEAR SAWREY
Beatrix Potter once holidayed at this
Georgian house overlooking Esthwaite
Water. Today's guests can potter about
in her footsteps. Have a drink in the
Tower Bank Arms, pictured in the
Tale of Jemima Puddle-duck; set off
on a circular walk via Claife Heights,
taking in Moss Eccles Tarn and Wise
Een Tarn; wander through woodland
and countryside to Windermere. A
daily-changing dinner menu awaits
your return.
Read more, page 231.

THE PEACOCK AT ROWSLEY
ROWSLEY
Bring your dog to this 17th-century
manor house on the edge of the Peak
District national park. The dramatic
landscape of limestone and gritstone,
valleys and uplands, is a walkers'
paradise. Make a scenic circuit of
Stanton Moor, taking in the Nine
Ladies stone circle, and a pint and a
ploughman's at the pooch-friendly
Flying Chidders in Stanton village. Back
at base, wind down in the cosy, beamed
bar or in one of the chic bedrooms.
Read more, page 275.

THE INN AT WHITEWELL
WHITEWELL
Sitting beneath the fells in the Forest of Bowland, with the River Hodder running by, this relaxed, friendly hotel is a comfortable base for days of serious upland walking, an amble through the valley or a stroll through a wild flower meadow closer to home. Books, maps and advice are readily offered. Long-serving chef Jamie Cadman cooks superb local meals that taste of the landscape just roamed.
Read more, page 327.

CROSSWAYS HOTEL
WILMINGTON
From this popular restaurant-with-rooms in a Georgian house at the foot of the South Downs, you might follow the AA's 'Mystery of the Long Man' walk to investigate the enigmatic figure carved into the hillside, or hike the South Downs Way national trail – the old drovers' route along chalk escarpment and ridges. Book one of the spotlessly clean bedrooms with a bath to soak away the efforts of the day.
Read more, page 329.

THE GURNARD'S HEAD
ZENNOR
Be on the South West Coast Path within minutes of stepping out of this informally stylish roadside pub-with-rooms. Strike out for St Ives: it's a spectacular but rugged route – you'll need boots. From Zennor Head, spy dolphins or listen for the song that entranced the Mermaid of Zennor in Pendour Cove. Sleep in a splendid bedroom and wake to views of ocean or gorse-covered moorland. Guided foraging walks are also offered.
Read more, page 341.

MOOR OF RANNOCH HOTEL
RANNOCH STATION
At the end of the road, this cosy 19th-century hotel built for railway engineers is a relaxed, laid-back base in a vast moorland wilderness that offers serious walking for the well-prepared enthusiast. Drive or cycle to the Black Wood of Rannoch, to spot red deer, pine martens, venerable native trees; stride out on the old Road to the Isles, returning for a hearty dinner. Sally forth well prepared – there's no mobile signal in case of difficulty.
Read more, page 390.

PORTH TOCYN HOTEL
ABERSOCH
A perennial Guide favourite, this friendly hotel overlooks Cardigan Bay – if you want to stretch your legs on the shore, the beach is just a five-minute stroll away. To go further, follow the Wales Coastal Path, scanning the waves for seals and bottlenose dolphins. There are Celtic hill forts to discover, the lovely Lleyn peninsula to explore, a home-away-from-home to come back to.
Read more, page 412.

CURRAREVAGH HOUSE
OUGHTERARD
Rain gear and boots in the hall speak of walking opportunities at the Hodgsons' manor house in Connemara countryside. A breakfast of Edwardian proportions sets guests up to wander the estate, or to follow a number of scenic way-marked trails. Pick up the Western Way right at the front gate: it follows the western shore of Lough Corrib and leads through a wilderness of mountain, moorland and bogs – challenging at times.
Read more, page 479.

THE ZETTER TOWNHOUSE CLERKENWELL
LONDON

Behind the artful idiosyncrasy – past the winged armchairs and witty knick-knacks – the highest standards of hotel-keeping are evident at this sumptuously decorated Georgian town house. Everything for guests' comfort is in place, from interesting antique furniture and crisp Egyptian linens to ground coffee, rare teas and a retro radio. Accept a complimentary cocktail on arrival.
Read more, page 66.

THE QUEENSBERRY
BATH

Contemporary chic, original features and traditional hospitality blend together within four terraced Georgian town houses in a central, yet quiet, location in the busy city. From the smallest double bedroom to the four-poster suite, all rooms are individually styled. Sip a cocktail in Old Q Bar, then eat in the Olive Tree restaurant, where the modern cooking packs a gastronomic punch.
Read more, page 90.

DRAKES
BRIGHTON

Twin Georgian town houses form one top-rated hotel on the seafront. Come for the ambitious modern cooking, and the bespoke drinks in a seaward bar; stay in one of the modish bedrooms, each supplied with smart toiletries, waffle robes, glossy magazines and cafetière coffee. Book a room with a freestanding bath by triple-aspect windows and have a languid soak while the lights come on over the pier.
Read more, page 114.

NUMBER THIRTY EIGHT CLIFTON
BRISTOL

Overlooking the green space of Clifton Down, this Georgian merchant's house at the top of the city has been immaculately refurbished. B&B accommodation is in smart bedrooms stocked with posh toiletries and waffle robes – stay in one of the loft suites for the bonus of panoramic city and park views. A roof terrace is a treat at teatime on a sunny day; good local restaurants are easily reached.
Read more, page 116.

BANK HOUSE
KING'S LYNN

Most of the bedrooms at this Grade II* listed Georgian house on the quayside of the market town have views over the water; all have period features, a cool, uncluttered style, and a modern bathroom supplied with high-end toiletries. Tea, coffee and cakes are available all day; brasserie lunches and dinners may be taken in the popular drinking and dining areas or on the riverside terrace.
Read more, page 190.

2 BLACKBURNE TERRACE
LIVERPOOL

On a cobbled drive behind a screen of lime trees in the cultural quarter, this Georgian house has been made over with designer chic and a dash of wit. B&B bedrooms have striking colours and modern artwork; perhaps a velvet ottoman, or a slipper bath in a marble-floored bathroom. All have sloe gin, sweet treats, a coffee machine and fluffy slippers. Theatre, concert hall and cathedral are nearby.
Read more, page 204.

CHAPEL HOUSE
PENZANCE

Modern decor and contemporary art sit well with the original features of Susan Stuart's restful Georgian house, in which she runs this voguish B&B. Seaview bedrooms are airy and inviting, and stocked with up-to-date technology: a smart TV; an iPad loaded with personal recommendations for local exploration. Families choose the top floor, with its three bedrooms and retractable glass roof.
Read more, page 257.

BROCCO ON THE PARK
SHEFFIELD

With jazzy Sunday lunches, summer barbecues and delicious small plates in the 'neighbourhood-kitchen' restaurant, there's a real buzz about this good-natured city hotel. Style-conscious, Scandi-chic bedrooms (pictured) have many comforts: robes, organic toiletries, wool blankets, an espresso machine. Every room is different; one of the best has a deep copper bath and a Juliet balcony.
Read more, page 287.

PRESTONFIELD
EDINBURGH

Art and antiques fill this richly decorated stately pile by Royal Holyrood Park. Opulent bedrooms and suites with views of parkland are highly individual – they might have velvet-lined walls, an antique chaise longue or a gothic day bed – and the amenities are faultless: fruit and flowers, robes and slippers, a fully stocked minibar and nightly turndown service. Modern dinners are taken in the atmospheric restaurant.
Read more, page 356.

NO. 1 PERY SQUARE
LIMERICK

In the Georgian quarter, this modern hotel occupies a skilfully refurbished Grade I listed terraced house overlooking the People's Park. There are cocktails and sharing platters in the turf fire-warmed sitting room. In the first-floor restaurant, sit by the window to eat bistro-style dishes while watching life go by in the street below. The best bedrooms have huge sash windows and plenty of period character.
Read more, page 474.

HIPPING HALL
COWAN BRIDGE
A brook runs through the 12-acre grounds of this Lancashire country house at the foot of Gragareth; a stream, ponds and woodland add to the splendid setting. Tie the knot in the oak-beamed, 15th-century Great Hall, which has a minstrels' gallery and a large open fire, or book the Old Stables, with its views of the landscaped gardens. Exclusive use of the hotel can be arranged, with accommodation for up to 30 overnight guests.
Read more, page 144.

LANGAR HALL
LANGAR
Small, informal celebrations are a speciality at this lovely apricot-washed historic house, approached down an avenue of lime trees, in the Vale of Belvoir. If you choose to walk down the aisle, Langar church stands right beside the entrance. Invite up to 50 guests and book the whole house; any one of the country-style bedrooms, some pretty, some utterly romantic, is ideal for falling into after the reception.
Read more, page 194.

GOLDSTONE HALL
MARKET DRAYTON
'I want to get married at Goldstone Hall. If I can't… I don't want to get married at all.' So, it is said, runs the old Salopian folk song. An experienced team at this 18th-century manor house – they've been hosting weddings here for 30 years – will help couples plan the day and roll out the red carpet to the oak pavilion, where vows may be exchanged. Before and after, pose for photographs in the lovingly kept walled garden.
Read more, page 219.

BUDOCK VEAN
MAWNAN SMITH
In gardens and wooded acres on the banks of the Helford river, this tastefully refurbished hotel makes a refined setting for a Cornish wedding. There's a choice of wedding plans, with an option of champagne cream teas; most romantically, a commemorative tree may be planted in the grounds. To calm the nerves, bride and groom may book in to the spa for pre-wedding day pampering.
Read more, page 224.

BINGHAM
RICHMOND-UPON-THAMES

Arrive by boat to this stylish hotel on a scenic stretch of the River Thames. Celebrations here can take exclusive or semi-exclusive use of the Georgian town house; in either case, the atmosphere – as guests mingle on the river terrace and in the garden, perhaps over a wedding barbecue – is one of laid-back chic. A honeymoon suite takes in views over the water.
Read more, page 272.

THE HORN OF PLENTY
TAVISTOCK

The wooded Tamar valley makes a spectacular backdrop to weddings at this 19th-century stone manor house standing in large, well-tended gardens. It's an award-winning events venue; amiable staff tailor each wedding to the couple, whether the affair is an intimate gathering or a marquee party for 200. Ask for fireworks or falcons – either can be arranged.
Read more, page 304.

GLENFINNAN HOUSE HOTEL
GLENFINNAN

On the idyllic shores of Loch Shiel, with views of Ben Nevis, this old stone mansion has a traditional, romantic air. Panelled walls are hung with paintings; there are log fires, fresh flowers, and Scottish meals cooked with a French twist. Whether you want a small civil ceremony, a sit-down meal for 50 or a marquee on the lawn, a coordinator will help plan the day. Book a cruise on the loch, bring the band, and make a floating ceilidh of it.
Read more, page 361.

LLANGOED HALL
LLYSWEN

Birdsong fills the air around this 17th-century manor house in the Wye valley – a glorious setting for a wedding day. Filled with art and antiques, the country house stands in large gardens that stretch down to the river. Start a reception with drinks on the terrace, plan a meal in the orangery or book a marquee. The celebratory feast makes good use of Welsh produce and ingredients grown in the organic kitchen garden.
Read more, page 435.

PENALLY ABBEY
PENALLY

Modern and elegant, this marvellously updated 18th-century Gothic house looking out to sea is a happy place run with an easy charm. The hotel specialises in small weddings of up to 40 people; a high-ceilinged, stone-floored courtyard chapel is ideal for a homespun ceremony and rustic wedding feast. Any one of the chic bedrooms is a fine place to start married life.
Read more, page 439.

TEMPLE HOUSE
BALLYMOTE

Wedding parties are urged to stay more than just a day at this Georgian mansion on a private estate overlooking a lakeside Knights Templar castle. 'The house loves a celebration,' the owners say. An ancestral home rich in history, the house has huge rooms, terraced gardens and a casual grandeur in its portraits and antiques. The flexible hosts can cater for anything from 12 seated guests to a buffet for 200.
Read more, page 459.

Each of these hotels has
a tennis court (T) and/or
a swimming pool (S)

ENGLAND

Hartwell House & Spa,
  Aylesbury (T,S)

Park House,
  Bepton (T,S)

Burgh Island Hotel,
  Bigbury-on-Sea (T,S)

The Blakeney Hotel,
  Blakeney (S)

Woolley Grange,
  Bradford-on-Avon (S)

Dormy House,
  Broadway (S)

Hell Bay Hotel,
  Bryher (S)

Brockencote Hall,
  Chaddesley Corbett (T)

Tor Cottage,
  Chillaton (S)

Corse Lawn House,
  Corse Lawn (T,S)

Dart Marina,
  Dartmouth (S)

Fingals,
  Dittisham (S)

Old Whyly,
  East Hoathly (T,S)

The Grand Hotel,
  Eastbourne (S)

Starborough Manor,
  Edenbridge (T,S)

Moonfleet Manor,
  Fleet (S)

Fowey Hall,
  Fowey (S)

Hambleton Hall,
  Hambleton (T,S)

The Pheasant,
  Harome (S)

Congham Hall,
  King's Lynn (S)

Augill Castle,
  Kirkby Stephen (T)

The Feathers,
  Ledbury (S)

Lime Wood,
  Lyndhurst (S)

Bedruthan Hotel and Spa,
  Mawgan Porth (T,S)

The Scarlet,
  Mawgan Porth (S)

Budock Vean,
  Mawnan Smith (T,S)

Mullion Cove Hotel,
  Mullion Cove (S)

Hotel TerraVina,
  Netley Marsh (S)

Chewton Glen,
  New Milton (T,S)

The Old Rectory,
  Norwich (S)

Askham Hall,
  Penrith (S)
Star Castle,
  St Mary's (T,S)
Seaham Hall,
  Seaham (S)
Soar Mill Cove Hotel,
  Soar Mill Cove (T,S)
Plumber Manor,
  Sturminster Newton (T)
Cliveden House,
  Taplow (T,S)
Calcot Manor,
  Tetbury (T,S)
The Royal Hotel,
  Ventnor (S)
The Nare,
  Veryan-in-Roseland (T,S)
Gilpin Hotel and Lake House,
  Windermere (S)
Holbeck Ghyll,
  Windermere (T)
Middlethorpe Hall & Spa,
  York (S)

SCOTLAND
Glenapp Castle,
  Ballantrae (T)
Shieldaig Lodge,
  Gairloch (T)
Douneside House,
  Tarland (T,S)

WALES
Trefeddian Hotel,
  Aberdyfi (T,S)

Porth Tocyn,
  Abersoch (T,S)
Gliffaes,
  Crickhowell (T)
Bodysgallen Hall & Spa,
  Llandudno (T,S)
The Lake,
  Llangammarch Wells (T,S)

CHANNEL ISLANDS
The White House,
  Herm (T,S)
The Atlantic Hotel,
  St Brelade (T,S)
Greenhills,
  St Peter (S)
Longueville Manor,
  St Saviour (T,S)

IRELAND
Killiane Castle,
  Drinagh (T)
Castle Leslie,
  Glaslough (T)
Marlfield House,
  Gorey (T)
Rosleague Manor,
  Letterfrack (T)
Currarevagh House,
  Oughterard (T)
Rathmullan House,
  Rathmullan (T,S)
Coopershill,
  Riverstown (T)
Ballymaloe House,
  Shanagarry (T,S)

Each of these hotels has at least one bedroom equipped for a visitor in a wheelchair. You should telephone to discuss individual requirements

LONDON
The Goring
The Zetter
The Zetter Townhouse
  Marylebone

ENGLAND
The Wentworth,
  Aldeburgh
Rothay Manor,
  Ambleside
Hartwell House & Spa,
  Aylesbury
Red Lion Inn,
  Babcary
Barnsley House,
  Barnsley
No. 15 Great Pulteney,
  Bath
The Master Builder's,
  Beaulieu
Park House,
  Bepton
The Lord Crewe Arms,
  Blanchland
The Crown Hotel,
  Blandford Forum
Leathes Head Hotel,
  Borrowdale
The Millstream,
  Bosham
Lindeth Fell,
  Bowness-on-
  Windermere
Woolley Grange,
  Bradford-on-Avon
The White Horse,
  Brancaster Staithe

Brooks Guesthouse,
  Bristol
Dormy House,
  Broadway
Hell Bay Hotel,
  Bryher
Northcote Manor,
  Burrington
Pendragon Country House,
  Camelford
Brockencote Hall,
  Chaddesley Corbett
Crouchers,
  Chichester
Captain's Club Hotel,
  Christchurch
Kings Head Hotel,
  Cirencester
Beech House & Olive Branch,
  Clipsham
Clow Beck House,
  Croft-on-Tees
Dart Marina,
  Dartmouth
Dedham Hall,
  Dedham
The Red Lion Freehouse,
  East Chisenbury
The Grand Hotel,
  Eastbourne
Eckington Manor,
  Eckington
The Carpenters Arms,
  Felixkirk
Fowey Hall,
  Fowey

The Pig at Combe,
  Gittisham
Forest Side,
  Grasmere
Castle House,
  Hereford
Battlesteads,
  Hexham
No. 33,
  Hunstanton
Congham Hall,
  King's Lynn
Northcote,
  Langho
Lewtrenchard Manor,
  Lewdown
The Clive,
  Ludlow
Lime Wood,
  Lyndhurst
Sands Hotel,
  Margate
Bedruthan Hotel and Spa,
  Mawgan Porth
The Scarlet,
  Mawgan Porth
Hotel TerraVina,
  Netley Marsh
Chewton Glen,
  New Milton
Jesmond Dene House,
  Newcastle upon Tyne
The Packhorse Inn,
  Newmarket
Beechwood Hotel,
  North Walsham
The Assembly House,
  Norwich

Hart's Hotel,
  Nottingham
Old Bank,
  Oxford
Old Parsonage,
  Oxford
Tebay Services Hotel,
  Penrith
The Pig near Bath,
  Pensford
The Yorke Arms,
  Ramsgill-in-Nidderdale
The Black Swan,
  Ravenstonedale
The Coach House at
  Middleton Lodge,
  Richmond
Idle Rocks,
  St Mawes
Seaham Hall,
  Seaham
St Cuthbert's House,
  Seahouses
Brocco on the Park,
  Sheffield
Hotel Riviera,
  Sidmouth
The Rose & Crown,
  Snettisham
The Pipe and Glass Inn,
  South Dalton
Plumber Manor,
  Sturminster Newton
The Royal Oak,
  Swallowcliffe
The Horn of Plenty,
  Tavistock
Calcot Manor,
  Tetbury
Briarfields,
  Titchwell
Titchwell Manor,
  Titchwell
Tuddenham Mill,
  Tuddenham
The Royal Hotel,
  Ventnor
The Nare,
  Veryan-in-Roseland
The Inn at West End,
  West End

The Hare and Hounds,
  Westonbirt
The Crescent Turner
  Hotel,
  Whitstable
Holbeck Ghyll,
  Windermere
The George,
  Yarmouth
Middlethorpe Hall & Spa,
  York

SCOTLAND
Loch Melfort Hotel,
  Arduaine
Boath House,
  Auldearn
Glenapp Castle,
  Ballantrae
Coul House,
  Contin
The Three Chimneys
  and The House Over-By,
  Dunvegan
The Bonham,
  Edinburgh
Prestonfield,
  Edinburgh
The Glenelg Inn,
  Glenelg
Ballathie House,
  Kinclaven
Kylesku Hotel,
  Kylesku
Langass Lodge,
  Locheport
Craigatin House and
  Courtyard,
  Pitlochry
The Green Park,
  Pitlochry
Viewfield House,
  Portree

WALES
Harbourmaster Hotel,
  Aberaeron
Trefeddian Hotel,
  Aberdyfi
The Hardwick,
  Abergavenny

Coes Faen,
  Barmouth
The Bull,
  Beaumaris
Gliffaes,
  Crickhowell
Penbontbren,
  Glynarthen
Tyddyn Llan,
  Llandrillo
Bodysgallen Hall & Spa,
  Llandudno
The Lake,
  Llangammarch Wells
Restaurant James
  Sommerin,
  Penarth
St Brides Spa Hotel,
  Saundersfoot

CHANNEL ISLANDS
Greenhills,
  St Peter

IRELAND
The Mustard Seed at Echo
  Lodge,
  Ballingarry
Stella Maris,
  Ballycastle
Gregans Castle Hotel,
  Ballyvaughan
The Quay House,
  Clifden
Castle Leslie,
  Glaslough
Brook Lane Hotel,
  Kenmare
No. 1 Pery Square,
  Limerick
Sheedy's,
  Lisdoonvarna
Viewmount House,
  Longford
Rathmullan House,
  Rathmullan

LONDON

LONDON

Map 2:D4

ARTIST RESIDENCE

♔ Previous César winner

A smart red-and-white awning fronts this
'youthful, modern' hotel on a quiet street of
Regency terraces. Arrive to 'a cheerful greeting
– a model of its kind'. Charlotte and Justin
Salisbury, the owners, have created a space
that is 'quirky and full of character', from the
tin ceiling tiles in the basement cocktail bar to
the individually designed bedrooms decorated
with a shrewd mix of vintage pieces, auction
finds, original art and recycled materials. 'Our
first-floor room had a metal-framed bed with
good linen, and stools as bedside tables. A large
sash window overlooked neighbouring houses.
The details were well thought through: excellent
lighting, a well-stocked minibar, bathrobes
and slippers, a fine rain shower.' (Two suites
and a large bedroom have a roll-top bath.) The
ground-floor Cambridge Street Kitchen serves
food all day, perhaps lamb rump, aubergine
purée, goat's curd, salsa verde, cooked by Elliot
Miller, the new chef. On Sundays, jostle with the
locals at a popular weekend brunch. Art lovers,
delight: you're but a stroll to Tate Britain and
the Saatchi Gallery.

52 Cambridge Street
Pimlico
London
SW1V 4QQ

T: 020 7828 6684
E: london@artistresidence.co.uk
W: artistresidencelondon.co.uk

BEDROOMS: 10. 2 suites.
OPEN: all year.
FACILITIES: bar, restaurant, club
room, games room, small 'hidden'
garden, free Wi-Fi, in-room TV
(Freeview), unsuitable for disabled.
BACKGROUND MUSIC: in public areas.
LOCATION: Pimlico, underground
Pimlico.
CHILDREN: all ages welcomed.
DOGS: not allowed.
CREDIT CARDS: Amex, MasterCard,
Visa.
PRICES: [2017] room from £210.
Cooked breakfast from £8, à la
carte £40.

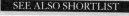

SEE ALSO SHORTLIST

LONDON

Map 2:D4

THE CAPITAL

♔ Previous César winner

Look out for the Union flag, and the doorman in suit and hat: this 'intimate luxury hotel' is all about 'old-fashioned London hospitality' – and is well loved for it. After 46 years in the hands of founder David Levin, the hotel is still managed by the founding family despite new ownership. Kate Levin, who worked alongside her father for many years, continues as manager; head chef Tom Brown, under the guidance of Nathan Outlaw, still turns out 'exceptional cuisine' at the Michelin-starred, sustainable seafood-focused restaurant. Bedrooms of varying sizes have a touch of the English, with antique furniture and pretty floral prints. (Young guests will find bathrobes and slippers in their size, along with a small gift.) While the hotel is 'ideally located' for the neighbourhood's chic shops and museums, guests staying in are rewarded with freshly baked scones with home-made jam at afternoon tea, or a whisky-and-cheese-pairing session in the bar. And if the modern cooking in the restaurant doesn't appeal, consider an informal meal at sister hotel The Levin, next door (see entry). (NK)

22–24 Basil Street
Knightsbridge
London
SW3 1AT

T: 020 7589 5171
F: 020 7225 0011
E: reservations@capitalhotel.co.uk
W: www.capitalhotel.co.uk

BEDROOMS: 49.
OPEN: all year.
FACILITIES: lift, sitting room, bar, restaurant, free Wi-Fi, in-room TV (Sky), access to nearby health club/spa, only restaurant suitable for disabled.
BACKGROUND MUSIC: none.
LOCATION: central, underground Knightsbridge, private car park.
CHILDREN: all ages welcomed.
DOGS: not allowed.
CREDIT CARDS: all major cards.
PRICES: [2017] per room B&B from £300, D,B&B from £400. À la carte £62 (plus 12½% discretionary service charge).

SEE ALSO SHORTLIST

LONDON

Map 2:D4

DURRANTS

❦ Previous César winner

With gilt-framed paintings, a panelled dining room and 'quiet corners and pretty public spaces to sit and chat in', the Miller family's hotel steeps in an 'old-worldly Edwardian club atmosphere' in the 'restless heart of the town'. Despite the traditional feel, time hasn't stood still: a return visitor was 'impressed by the improvements they've made over the years, including refurbished bathrooms and bedroom decor, and more generous lounge areas'. Guide readers in 2017 praise the attention to detail throughout: the silver-plated teapots, the 'gleaming brass rails', the 'neat period uniforms' for chambermaids, the 'very welcome tea' after a day in town. 'How splendid that such a place lives on!' Follow 'winding corridors' to the 'well-appointed bedrooms' – the quietest overlook a mews at the rear. In the restaurant, the cooking 'speaks of older, comforting verities', perhaps roast duck, purple kale, orange and golden raisin sauce. (A set menu is 'sufficient, and well priced'.) At an 'extensive, tasty breakfast', find 'good healthy options and plenty of cooked delights'. (Keith Salway, Max Lickfold, Ralph G Wilson)

26–32 George Street
Marylebone
London
W1H 5BJ

T: 020 7935 8131
F: 020 7487 3510
E: enquiries@durrantshotel.co.uk
W: www.durrantshotel.co.uk

BEDROOMS: 92. 7 on ground floor.
OPEN: all year, restaurant closed 25 Dec evening.
FACILITIES: lifts, bar, restaurant, lounge, function rooms, free Wi-Fi, in-room TV (Freeview), use of nearby fitness club.
BACKGROUND MUSIC: none.
LOCATION: off Oxford Street, underground Bond Street, Baker Street.
CHILDREN: all ages welcomed.
DOGS: allowed in George bar.
CREDIT CARDS: Amex, MasterCard, Visa.
PRICES: [2017] room from £175. Set menus £19.75–£22.75, à la carte £45 (plus 12½% discretionary service charge).

SEE ALSO SHORTLIST

LONDON

Map 2:D4

THE GORING

'For the quality of service, elegance and comfort, this fine hotel sits among the top rank,' writes an admirer of London's last grand Edwardian-era hotel, family run for more than a century. Long a favourite of the royal family – it stands a ten-minute walk from Buckingham Palace – the hotel is 'elegant and immaculate', with 'beautiful' floral arrangements to catch the eye. A doorman in a bowler hat and tails welcomes guests 'with great courtesy'. From the smallest queen rooms to the best garden rooms, each bedroom comes with bathrobes and slippers, complimentary newspapers and a bed dressed in Italian linen; 24-hour room service and a shoeshine are standard. (Ask to be talked through the 'incredibly complicated electronic controls that govern mood lighting, curtains, heating and air-conditioning'.) In the chandelier-lit dining room, Michelin-starred chef Shay Cooper's menus are devised around prime seasonal ingredients: salt-marsh lamb; Clarence Court eggs for the signature lobster omelette; roast rib of beef from the carver's silver trolley. Most delicious, perhaps: a private garden, dreamy for croquet and afternoon tea. (I and CM)

15 Beeston Place
Belgravia
London
SW1W 0JW

T: 020 7396 9000
F: 020 7834 4393
E: reception@thegoring.com
W: www.thegoring.com

BEDROOMS: 69. 2 suitable for disabled.
OPEN: all year.
FACILITIES: lifts, lounge, bar, restaurant, private dining rooms, free Wi-Fi, in-room TV (Sky), civil wedding licence, business centre, fitness room, veranda, 1-acre garden (croquet).
BACKGROUND MUSIC: none.
LOCATION: Belgravia, mews parking, underground Victoria.
CHILDREN: all ages welcomed (welcome programme, little ones' library).
DOGS: not allowed.
CREDIT CARDS: all major cards.
PRICES: [2017] room from £395, breakfast £26 (continental), £32 (cooked). À la carte £80.

SEE ALSO SHORTLIST

LONDON

Map 2:D4

THE GRAZING GOAT

On a narrow street lined with independent shops and restaurants, this voguish pub-with-rooms is equal parts bustle (downstairs in the busy pub) and calm (upstairs in the 'thoughtfully furnished' bedrooms). Coir carpets, pale woods and old London prints give the place a pleasing contemporary feel; bedrooms on the upper floors – there is no lift – continue in this modern-rustic vein. 'Our beautiful top-floor room looked down over rooftops to a small mews. There were proper sash windows that we could open; noise wasn't a problem. The bathroom was excellent, with especially good toiletries. On the tea tray: fancy teas, a large bottle of filtered water, a jar of ground coffee for the cafetière (they gave me decaf when I asked).' Stay in for dinner in the ground-floor bar or the first-floor dining room, and order off the 'largish menu' of bistro-style dishes, perhaps Lyme Bay mackerel, nettle dumplings; artichoke fritter, charred broccoli, courgettes. Breakfast, charged separately, might include home-baked pastries and a 'splendid bacon and eggs'. 'A great location': Marble Arch and Oxford Street are minutes away. The Orange, a sister inn, is in Pimlico (see entry).

6 New Quebec Street
Marble Arch
London
W1H 7RQ

T: 020 7724 7243
E: reservations@thegrazinggoat.co.uk
W: www.thegrazinggoat.co.uk

BEDROOMS: 8.
OPEN: all year.
FACILITIES: bar, dining room, patio, free Wi-Fi, in-room TV, unsuitable for disabled.
BACKGROUND MUSIC: all day in bar.
LOCATION: central, underground Marble Arch.
CHILDREN: all ages welcomed.
DOGS: allowed in public rooms, not in bedrooms.
CREDIT CARDS: Amex, MasterCard, Visa.
PRICES: [2017] room £210–£250. Cooked breakfast from £7, à la carte £35.

SEE ALSO SHORTLIST

LONDON

HAZLITT'S

There's romance and genteel decadence to be found in these three finely refurbished Georgian houses – Peter McKay and Douglas Blain's 'stunningly original' hotel. 'It remains an oasis of civilisation among the stream of maddening hordes that flock into central London.' It is named after the essayist William Hazlitt, who lived here when it was a boarding house; today, lavishly furnished rooms have fresh flowers, pictures and antiques, afternoon tea is served on proper china, and an honesty bar is tucked in among shelves of leather-bound books. Bedrooms and suites – some with sloping floorboards, all with restored period plumbing fixtures and fittings – are different as can be. Richly decorated junior suites have a private sitting room and, in the bathroom, a vintage roll-top bath and a throne loo, but even the snuggest single room overlooking neighbouring houses has a characterful antique bed and interesting artwork. The restaurants and the animation of Soho are on the doorstep; in the morning, breakfast may be served in the room. The owners ('two old gits', they call themselves) also run the east London Rookery (see entry).

6 Frith Street
Soho Square
Soho
London
W1D 3JA

T: 020 7434 1771
F: 020 7439 1524
E: reservations@hazlitts.co.uk
W: www.hazlittshotel.com

BEDROOMS: 30. 2 on ground floor.
OPEN: all year.
FACILITIES: lift, library (honesty bar), private lounge/meeting room, free Wi-Fi, in-room TV (Sky), unsuitable for disabled.
BACKGROUND MUSIC: none.
LOCATION: centre of Soho (front windows triple glazed, rear rooms quietest), underground Tottenham Court Road, Leicester Square.
CHILDREN: all ages welcomed.
DOGS: not allowed.
CREDIT CARDS: Amex, Mastercard, Visa.
PRICES: [2017] per room B&B from £288, D,B&B from £338. À la carte (from limited room service menu) £25.

SEE ALSO SHORTLIST

LONDON

Map 2:D4

THE LEVIN

Between Harrods and Hyde Park, this well-established small hotel is ideally located for visitors seeking culture, commerce and the calm of one of the city's largest green spaces. With its fine-heeled sister hotel, the Capital (see entry), it was until 2017 in the hands of founder David Levin; now under new ownership, it continues to be managed by his daughter, Kate. Help yourself from the fruit bowl in the lobby; peer at the spectacular light installation cascading through the stairwell. Upstairs, uncluttered modern bedrooms, each with a marble bathroom, are individually furnished. Bathrobes and slippers are supplied, as are a capsule coffee machine, fine teas and a champagne minibar. An iPad may be provided on request. Superior rooms have an alcove seating area; street-facing junior suites have a sofa bed to accommodate a child. Light bites and informal meals are served all day in the basement café; fancier food is just next door, at Nathan Outlaw's Michelin-starred restaurant. Sweet and savoury options at breakfast include French toast and bagel sandwiches; croissants and pastries from a sibling bakery are 'especially good'.

28 Basil Street
Knightsbridge
London
SW3 1AS

T: 020 7589 6286
F: 020 7823 7826
E: reservations@thelevinhotel.co.uk
W: www.thelevinhotel.co.uk

BEDROOMS: 12.
OPEN: all year.
FACILITIES: lobby, library, bar/brasserie, free Wi-Fi, in-room TV, access to nearby health club/spa, unsuitable for disabled.
BACKGROUND MUSIC: in restaurant.
LOCATION: central, underground Knightsbridge.
CHILDREN: all ages welcomed.
DOGS: allowed at extra cost.
CREDIT CARDS: all major cards.
PRICES: per room B&B (continental) from £335. À la carte £28.

SEE ALSO SHORTLIST

LONDON

NUMBER SIXTEEN

♀ Previous César winner

Guests bestow 'top marks for the perfect mattress' at this chic hotel on a residential street of white stucco town houses. Much else is praiseworthy, too: the 'helpful, courteous staff', the 'convenient location', the 'home-away-from-home feel'. Part of Tim and Kit Kemp's Firmdale group, it is decorated in the family way: with elan. Beyond the ionic portico and balconies of iron lace, the Victorian building is lively with colour, prints and patterns. Floor-to-ceiling windows fill the drawing room with light; through the conservatory hung with original artwork, the leafy patio garden is a treat in this busy part of town. Every bedroom is decorated differently, and supplied with good amenities: fine bedlinen, garden-scented bath products, a fully stocked minibar; books, board games and mini-bathrobes for the youngest guests. A short menu of uncomplicated food (crab and chilli spaghetti; grilled hake, brown shrimp, parsley butter) is available all day. On a fine morning, ask to have breakfast surrounded by garden greenery. The museums are within a ten-minute walk; the Royal Albert Hall is just an amble further.

16 Sumner Place
South Kensington
London
SW7 3EG

T: 020 7589 5232
E: sixteen@firmdale.com
W: www.firmdalehotels.com

BEDROOMS: 41. 1 on ground floor.
OPEN: all year.
FACILITIES: drawing room, library, conservatory, free Wi-Fi, in-room TV (Sky), civil wedding licence, garden.
BACKGROUND MUSIC: none.
LOCATION: Kensington, underground South Kensington.
CHILDREN: all ages welcomed.
DOGS: not allowed.
CREDIT CARDS: Amex, MasterCard, Visa.
PRICES: [2017] per room B&B single from £174, double from £276. À la carte £32.

SEE ALSO SHORTLIST

LONDON

Map 2:D4

THE ORANGE

Arrive to the 'warmest of welcomes' at this 'bustling' pub- and restaurant-with-rooms, whose elegantly weathered interiors and airy, high-ceilinged rooms attract a well-heeled crowd in this upmarket neighbourhood. (There's an organic deli down the street and a high-end florist across the road; Sloane Square is a five-minute walk away.) Find a spot at the bar for a real ale or a seasonal cocktail – the shabby-chic look matches the informal ambience. In the first-floor dining room, 'enjoyable, well-presented' modern British dishes might include heritage beetroot, sheep's curd, hazelnut, whisky; grass-fed beef rib-eye, smoked chilli and garlic butter, fries. Pizzas from the wood-fired oven are a crowd-pleaser. 'We were pleased we'd decided to eat in, though there's no lack of choice in the area.' 'Beautifully crafted' bedrooms are up narrow stairs. Two may be compact, but all rooms have a king-size bed and are supplied with bottled water, cafetière coffee and top-quality toiletries. Lots of interesting choices at breakfast. The inn is owned by the family-run Cubitt House group; sister establishment The Grazing Goat (see entry) is across Hyde Park.

37 Pimlico Road
Pimlico
London
SW1W 8NE

T: 020 7881 9844
E: reservations@theorange.co.uk
W: www.theorange.co.uk

BEDROOMS: 4.
OPEN: all year.
FACILITIES: restaurant, 2 bars, private dining rooms, free Wi-Fi, in-room TV, unsuitable for disabled.
BACKGROUND MUSIC: in public areas.
LOCATION: Pimlico, underground Sloane Square.
CHILDREN: all ages welcomed.
DOGS: not allowed.
CREDIT CARDS: Amex, MasterCard, Visa.
PRICES: [2017] per room B&B £205–£240. À la carte £35.

SEE ALSO SHORTLIST

LONDON

Map 2:D4

THE PORTOBELLO

Once known for its celebrity shenanigans, this west London bolthole, in two neo-classical mansions, is 'the opposite of bland'. Its rock 'n' roll history is well reflected in the 'quirky, unconventional' decor, from the Audubon-esque murals to the Victorian steampunk bathtub to the antique four-poster bed that users need steps to get into. 'The result is a delight.' Owners Peter and Jessica Frankopan – whose Curious Group of Hotels includes the Canal House, Amsterdam (see the Good Hotel Guide website) – have kept the hotel's original features and eccentricities, including vintage crockery from nearby Portobello Road market. Overlooking private gardens or the quiet residential street, bedrooms range from 'tiny but beautifully coloured' attic singles to generously sized 'Exceptional' rooms – one of them the very place where the theatrical singer-songwriter Alice Cooper once kept his boa constrictor in the bath. A continental breakfast of pastries, yogurts, meats and cheeses is taken in the 'large, light' drawing room (cooked dishes are available at extra charge); after-hours, pour yourself a drink in one of the crystal glasses from the honesty bar.

22 Stanley Gardens
Notting Hill
London
W11 2NG

T: 020 7727 2777
E: stay@portobellohotel.com
W: www.portobellohotel.com

BEDROOMS: 21.
OPEN: all year.
FACILITIES: lift, drawing room/breakfast room with honesty bar, free Wi-Fi, in-room TV, unsuitable for disabled.
BACKGROUND MUSIC: 'chill-out' in drawing room.
LOCATION: Notting Hill, underground Notting Hill Gate.
CHILDREN: not under 16.
DOGS: not allowed.
CREDIT CARDS: Amex, MasterCard, Visa.
PRICES: [2017] per room B&B (continental) from £195.

SEE ALSO SHORTLIST

LONDON

Map 2:D4

THE ROOKERY

In the buzz and hustle of trendy Clerkenwell, step back in time and enjoy a slice of Georgian London – though with air conditioning, Wi-Fi and better-than-decent bathrooms. Peter McKay and Douglas Blain's singular hotel (a sister to Hazlitt's in Soho, see entry) occupies three finely refurbished 18th-century houses, the whole filled with 'a soothing ambience and club-like calm'. The walls are painted in heritage shades, the windows hung with thick drapes; there are stone-flagged floors, open fires, polished wood panelling, gilt-framed paintings, antiques. French doors in the cosy conservatory (newspapers, leather armchairs, an oriental carpet) open to a small, leafy patio – a nice spot for a drink from the honesty bar. Every 'solidly soundproofed' room is judiciously decorated with period pieces – a 17th-century carved-oak bed, a Georgian four-poster, vintage bathroom fittings or a throne loo – and kitted out with modern amenities, including a minibar, bathrobes and top-end toiletries. At dinner time, powder your wig and head out to one of many good hostelries close by. Breakfast may be brought to the bedroom.

12 Peter's Lane
Cowcross Street
Clerkenwell
London
EC1M 6DS

T: 020 7336 0931
F: 020 7336 0932
E: reservations@rookery.co.uk
W: www.rookeryhotel.com

BEDROOMS: 33. 1 on ground floor.
OPEN: all year.
FACILITIES: conservatory lounge, meeting rooms, free Wi-Fi, in-room TV (Sky), small patio garden, unsuitable for disabled.
BACKGROUND MUSIC: none.
LOCATION: Clerkenwell, underground Farringdon, Barbican.
CHILDREN: all ages welcomed.
DOGS: not allowed.
CREDIT CARDS: Amex, MasterCard, Visa.
PRICES: [2017] per room B&B from £258. À la carte (from limited room-service menu) £28.

SEE ALSO SHORTLIST

LONDON

Map 2:D4

SAN DOMENICO HOUSE

Take tea on the sunny roof terrace above a quiet residential street at this 'luxurious, inviting hotel' – or, better yet, have an espresso and imagine you're in Italy. Built in 1887 as private residences, these adjoining Victorian red brick-and-stone town houses have been owned since 2005 by Pugliese hotelier Marisa Melpignano. Beyond the marbled entrance lobby, the interiors are lavishly styled. There are ornate door cases and fireplaces, oil paintings and gilt-framed mirrors, antiques and display cabinets of collectables; everywhere, seemingly, silk, stripes, ormolu and putti. The individually decorated bedrooms, all with air conditioning, have a marble bathroom; several have a balcony or terrace. Among the grander rooms, the gallery suites have a mezzanine seating area, perhaps even a bespoke four-poster bed – but, to feel like you're in your own palazzo, book a junior suite with a positively regal bed and a walk-in wardrobe. Breakfast, with freshly squeezed orange juice and good pastries, may be taken in the basement dining room or on the terrace in good weather. The Royal Court Theatre and the King's Road are minutes away. More reports, please.

29–31 Draycott Place
Chelsea
London
SW3 2SH

T: 020 7581 5757
F: 020 7584 1348
E: info@sandomenicohouse.com
W: www.sandomenicohouse.com

BEDROOMS: 19.
OPEN: all year.
FACILITIES: lounge, breakfast room, roof terrace, free Wi-Fi, in-room TV (Freeview), unsuitable for disabled.
BACKGROUND MUSIC: varied in lounge and breakfast room.
LOCATION: Chelsea, underground Sloane Square.
CHILDREN: all ages welcomed.
DOGS: not allowed.
CREDIT CARDS: all major cards.
PRICES: [2017] room from £228.60 (excluding VAT). Breakfast from £15.

SEE ALSO SHORTLIST

LONDON

Map 2:D4

THE VICTORIA

'We love the feel of the place,' writes a Guide reader in 2017 of this lively pub-with-rooms in a 'magnificent location' between Richmond Park and Kew Gardens. It is owned by Greg Bellamy and chef Paul Merrett, who stepped back from Michelin stardom to enjoy the relaxed gastropub style at this jollied-up Victorian inn. Encouraged by 'excellent staff', the vibe is buzzy all day: 'post-school drop-off coffees in the morning, great food and pub atmosphere at night'. Choose from a good-value bar menu (perhaps an Angus burger or a Caesar salad), or sample modern dishes in the conservatory restaurant and terrace. Typical offerings: radicchio and pear salad, salt-baked beetroot, walnut and labneh cheese balls; chargrilled Gloucestershire Old Spot pork chop, smoked apple ketchup, thrice-cooked chips. In the walled garden, the outdoor kitchen fires up for a summer cook-out. Well-priced, modern bedrooms are supplied with an espresso machine and home-baked cookies. 'Our ground-floor room had noise from the guests above, but was adequate otherwise.' More than adequate: the fruit, cereal and 'tasty local bread' at breakfast. (Gregory Powick)

10 West Temple Sheen
Mortlake
London
SW14 7RT

T: 020 8876 4238
E: reservations@victoriasheen.co.uk
W: victoriasheen.co.uk

BEDROOMS: 7. 3 on ground floor.
OPEN: all year.
FACILITIES: bar, lounge, restaurant, free Wi-Fi, in-room TV (Freeview), garden, play area, unsuitable for disabled.
BACKGROUND MUSIC: in pub and dining room, occasional live music events.
LOCATION: Mortlake, 10 mins' walk from Waterloo/Clapham Jct, car park.
CHILDREN: all ages welcomed.
DOGS: allowed in pub and garden.
CREDIT CARDS: MasterCard, Visa.
PRICES: [2017] per room B&B (continental) from £135. À la carte £33 (plus discretionary 12½% service charge).

SEE ALSO SHORTLIST

LONDON

THE ZETTER

Heralded as the ultimate in cool when it opened in 2004, this modish hotel, in a converted Victorian warehouse, remains 'on good form'. Locals and passers-by drop in at any time of day for food and drinks in the open-plan café/co-working space: its gallery of work by a roster of artists-in-residence makes an inspiring backdrop for mid-morning smoothies, afternoon-slump coffees and breakfasts of American pancakes or avocado-topped sourdough toast. At any time of day, too, the staff are 'exceptionally nice'. Uncluttered bedrooms have personality in their splashes of colour, and host of thoughtful touches: Penguin paperbacks, chic toiletries, a hot-water bottle in a hand-knitted cosy. Live the high life in one of the spacious rooftop studios, which have sun loungers on a private patio. At sundown, the atrium coffee shop transforms into a wine bar, with a menu of craft ales, cocktails, sharing platters, small plates and bar snacks to match. A short three-course menu might include beetroot salad, goat's curd, apple; chicken and chanterelle pie, cauliflower purée, hispi cabbage. Sister hotels are across the square or across the city (see next entries). (BB)

St John's Square
86–88 Clerkenwell Road
Clerkenwell
London
EC1M 5RJ

T: 020 7324 4444
E: info@thezetter.com
W: www.thezetter.com

BEDROOMS: 59. 2 suitable for disabled.
OPEN: all year.
FACILITIES: 2 lifts, café/wine room, function/meeting rooms, free Wi-Fi, in-room TV (Freeview, some with Smart TV), in-room spa treatments, reduced rates at local gym, bicycles to borrow.
BACKGROUND MUSIC: none.
LOCATION: Clerkenwell, NCP garage 5 mins' walk, underground Farringdon.
CHILDREN: all ages welcomed.
DOGS: only guide dogs allowed.
CREDIT CARDS: Amex, MasterCard, Visa.
PRICES: [2017] room £150–£475. Breakfast buffet £15.50, full English £12.

SEE ALSO SHORTLIST

LONDON

THE ZETTER TOWNHOUSE CLERKENWELL

♔ Previous César winner

'We've been raving about it to everyone!' A Guide reader this year extolled this 'brilliantly quirky hotel' in a Georgian town house across the cobbled square from the original Zetter (see previous entry). The owners conceived of the place as the imaginary home of an eccentric Great Aunt Wilhelmina: the walls are crowded with paintings; a fire crackles in the hearth of her parlour crammed with winged and button-back armchairs, knick-knacks and oddities. Throughout, 'the staff are wonderful'. Bedrooms have surprises among their antique furnishings, but most welcome are the homely comforts supplied: ground coffee, novels, fluffy robes, good toiletries. From aperitif o'clock, join locals for creative cocktails mixed with home-made cordials and infusions in the apothecary-inspired bar. A menu of superior snacks devised by chef Bruno Loubet (potted smoked mackerel and pickled cucumber, say, or parsnip crisps) may be taken here or ordered for room service at any time. For dinner, there are many popular restaurants on the doorstep. 'We'd go back in a heartbeat.' (Peter MacRobert)

49–50 St John's Square
Clerkenwell
London
EC1V 4JJ

T: 020 7324 4567
E: reservations@thezetter.com
W: www.thezettertownhouse.com

BEDROOMS: 13.
OPEN: all year.
FACILITIES: cocktail lounge, private dining room, games room, free Wi-Fi, in-room TV.
BACKGROUND MUSIC: none.
LOCATION: Clerkenwell, underground Farringdon.
CHILDREN: all ages welcomed.
DOGS: none.
CREDIT CARDS: Amex, MasterCard, Visa.
PRICES: [2017] room £234–£522. Continental breakfast Mon–Fri £15.50; cooked breakfast delivered by room service Sat, Sun, £10.50.

SEE ALSO SHORTLIST

LONDON

THE ZETTER TOWNHOUSE MARYLEBONE

Decked out in an opulent, eccentric style befitting the one-time home of Edward Lear, this seven-storey Georgian pile has a 'warm, inclusive atmosphere' and more than a touch of character. Enter via the deep-red cocktail bar – 'there's always something to catch the eye'. 'Every surface and inch of wall is busy: architectural plaster mouldings, Chinese ceramics, a sculpted nose.' There are 'decadent cocktails' to be had here, and afternoon teas with unusual options (black pudding Scotch eggs with Indian spiced mayonnaise, perhaps, or sandwiches of sloe gin-glazed ham). A short menu of 'perfect comfort food' (sharing boards; sausage rolls; Old Fashioned-cured salmon on rye) is available till late. 'Every detail has been carefully considered' in the lavish bedrooms – ground coffee and organic teas; slippers and bathrobes; a hot-water bottle; a selection of novels. 'Our rear room faced a mews – wonderfully quiet for London.' Even the smallest rooms have large sash windows and fine antiques, but consider booking Lear's Loft, which has a private roof terrace – ideal for dancing by the light of the moon.

28–30 Seymour Street
Marylebone
London
W1H 7JB

T: 020 7324 4544
E: reservations@thezetter.com
w: www.thezettertownhouse.com/
marylebone

BEDROOMS: 24. 3 suitable for disabled.
OPEN: all year.
FACILITIES: lift, cocktail lounge, free Wi-Fi, in-room TV (Freeview).
BACKGROUND MUSIC: all day in cocktail lounge.
LOCATION: central, underground Marble Arch.
CHILDREN: all ages welcomed.
DOGS: not allowed.
CREDIT CARDS: Amex, MasterCard, Visa.
PRICES: [2017] room £245–£798, continental buffet £14, cooked breakfast from £4.50.

SEE ALSO SHORTLIST

www.goodhotelguide.com

ENGLAND

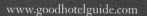

Norfolk Broads

ALDEBURGH Suffolk

THE WENTWORTH

Across a quiet road from the shingle beach, this 'delightful, warmly welcoming' Victorian hotel has been in Michael Pritt's family since 1920. It has built up a loyal following that appreciates its comfort, traditional values and 'accommodating staff'. 'A bonus: the welcome Pimm's and, later, cream tea on the terrace.' 'It has become a real friend,' says a Guide reader this year, a returnee who visits 'once or twice (sometimes thrice!) a year'. 'The owner always shows concern for the guests.' The hotel is popular with older visitors in the off-season and families in the summer months; all year long, dogs are made 'very welcome' ('our mutt loved the beach in February and many nice walks'). Many of the 'elegant, well-appointed' bedrooms in the main house have a sea view; four have their own lounge. Rooms in Darfield House, behind, have access to a courtyard garden. 'We liked the electronic controls in the shower that let us choose the precise temperature and pressure.' In the sea-facing restaurant, chef Tim Keeble's 'beautifully presented' dishes use much local produce, 'some from the fishing boats right outside'. 'We felt well cared for.' (Ashley Walton, Simon Rodway, and others)

25% DISCOUNT VOUCHERS

Wentworth Road
Aldeburgh
IP15 5BD

T: 01728 452312
F: 01728 454343
E: stay@wentworth-aldeburgh.com
W: www.wentworth-aldeburgh.com

BEDROOMS: 35. 7 in Darfield House opposite, 5 on ground floor, 1 suitable for disabled.
OPEN: all year.
FACILITIES: 2 lounges, bar, restaurant, private dining room, conference room, free Wi-Fi, in-room TV (Freeview), 2 terrace gardens overlooking sea, courtyard garden (Darfield House).
BACKGROUND MUSIC: none.
LOCATION: seafront, 5 mins' walk from centre.
CHILDREN: all ages welcomed.
DOGS: welcomed (£2 per dog per night), not allowed in restaurant.
CREDIT CARDS: all major cards.
PRICES: [2017] per room B&B £136–£303, D,B&B £166–£340. Set dinner £27.25. 1-night bookings refused Sat.

ALLERFORD Somerset

Map 1:B5

CROSS LANE HOUSE

Picture postcard it may be, but there is nothing twee about this 15th-century farmhouse, 'beautifully restored, and with lots of character', on a National Trust estate. It is run as a stylish guest house by 'great hosts' Max Lawrence and Andrew Stinson, with 'charming staff'. There are deep armchairs and sofas and a wood-burning stove in the lounge; on fine days, a parasol on the lawn marks the place for an alfresco drink or meal. Up the stairs, bedrooms are generously equipped with an espresso machine, Cornish-grown tea, home-made biscuits and a complimentary minibar; robes and smart toiletries in the bathroom. 'I thought my room – with an ancient wig cupboard! – very good, though I would have liked a chest of drawers.' Two nights a week, Max Lawrence cooks a short, seasonal menu of 'tasty' modern British dishes, perhaps beetroot salad, Somerset goat's cheese; duck breast, heritage carrots, potato terrine, broccoli. 'Breakfast has the lot': locally pressed apple juice, porridge with clotted cream and brown sugar, smoked haddock, local bacon. Ask for a picnic in a wicker hamper, and have the hosts point you in the direction of their favourite picnic spots. (Zara Elliott)

Allerford
TA24 8HW

T: 01643 863276
E: info@crosslanehouse.com
W: www.crosslanehouse.com

BEDROOMS: 4.
OPEN: Feb–Dec, open Christmas and New Year, restaurant closed Sun, Mon.
FACILITIES: lounge/bar, restaurant, free Wi-Fi, in-room TV (Freeview), 1-acre garden (alfresco dining), unsuitable for disabled.
BACKGROUND MUSIC: in lounge and dining room in late afternoon and evening.
LOCATION: 4¼ miles W of Minehead.
CHILDREN: not under 16.
DOGS: allowed in bedroom (£8 per night), not in public rooms.
CREDIT CARDS: Amex, MasterCard, Visa.
PRICES: [2017] per room B&B from £150, D,B&B from £223. 2-night min. stay preferred.

AMBLESIDE Cumbria

Map 4: inset C2

NANNY BROW

Sue and Peter Robinson's Arts and Crafts house stands on a crag in ancient woodland, the views tumbling down the Brathay valley. The owners have 'sympathetically restored' the Lakeland stone house, which was built in 1904 by the architect Francis Whitwell: there are polished wood floors and fine oak panelling; the walls are hung with architectural drawings, photographs and paintings. B&B accommodation is in individually styled bedrooms furnished with antique and contemporary pieces. They vary in size and aspect: a superior room has a bay window looking toward the Langdale Fells; a suite has a private balcony; two rooms that share a lounge are ideal for a family. In the original dining room, with its fireplace and Shapland and Petter sideboard, award-winning breakfasts use plenty of produce sourced from within a 20-mile radius of Ambleside. Spread home-made jams on local bakery bread or a freshly baked butter croissant; choose from locally smoked salmon, boiled eggs and soldiers, home-made drop scones with maple syrup and berries. This is walkers' country – the hosts can arrange for guided treks, taking in country pubs along the way.

Clappersgate
Ambleside
LA22 9NF

T: 01539 433232
E: unwind@nannybrow.co.uk
W: www.nannybrow.co.uk

BEDROOMS: 14. 2 in annexe, sharing a lounge.
OPEN: all year.
FACILITIES: lounge, bar, breakfast room, free Wi-Fi, in-room TV (Freeview), civil wedding licence, 6 acres of formal garden (sun terrace, croquet) and woodlands, unsuitable for disabled.
BACKGROUND MUSIC: 'at low volume' in breakfast room and bar.
LOCATION: 1½ miles W of Ambleside.
CHILDREN: not under 12.
DOGS: not allowed.
CREDIT CARDS: Amex, MasterCard, Visa.
PRICES: [2017] per room B&B £130–£280. 1-night bookings refused weekends.

AMBLESIDE Cumbria

Map 4: inset C2

ROTHAY MANOR

New brooms Jamie and Jenna Shail have refreshed this Georgian manor house since taking over in 2016, but traditional values have not been swept away. 'We were impressed,' say regular Guide correspondents in 2017. 'It's good to see this long-established hotel being maintained at a high standard, and updated with significant investment.' Some of the 'comfortable, well-equipped' bedrooms have a balcony with views to Wansfell Pike across landscaped gardens. In the refurbished dining room, 'adventurous, accomplished' chef Brandon Shepherd builds menus around seasonal and local ingredients; he has already started a vegetable garden. 'The food here has always been good, but this time it was exceptional: modern, delicious, stimulating.' Recently praised: lamb with peas puréed, foamed and au naturel; a 'stunning' lavender and vanilla panna cotta. By day there may be a hum of cars on the nearby road, 'but by night all is quiet'. Besides, 'you can easily escape the traffic and walk along the river, past the remains of a Roman fort, to the top of Lake Windermere'. (Stephanie Thompson, Keith Sutton, Pauline and Stephen Glover, and others)

Rothay Bridge
Ambleside
LA22 0EH

T: 015394 33605
F: 015397 33607
E: hotel@rothaymanor.co.uk
W: www.rothaymanor.co.uk

BEDROOMS: 19. 2 in bungalow in the grounds, 2 suitable for disabled.
OPEN: all year except 3 weeks Jan.
FACILITIES: lounge, drawing room, bar, 2 dining rooms, meeting/conference facilities, free Wi-Fi, in-room TV (Sky), civil wedding licence, 1-acre garden (croquet), free access to local leisure centre.
BACKGROUND MUSIC: all day in bar and restaurant.
LOCATION: ¼ mile SW of Ambleside.
CHILDREN: all ages welcomed.
DOGS: allowed in 4 rooms and drawing room, not in bar or restaurant.
CREDIT CARDS: Amex, MasterCard, Visa.
PRICES: [2017] per room B&B from £135, D,B&B from £215. À la carte £42.50. 1-night bookings sometimes refused at busy times.

AMPLEFORTH Yorkshire

SHALLOWDALE HOUSE

Standing in flower-filled gardens on the edge of the North York Moors national park, Phillip Gill and Anton van der Horst's 'tranquil, immaculate' B&B 'remains excellent', say returning guests this year. The hosts' 'great kindness' has won them many fans, who come to be 'greeted as old friends'. 'In 15 years of annual visits, we've never been disappointed.' Sit by the fire in the drawing room for afternoon tea with home-baked cakes; in the evening, tables are set for Phillip Gill's 'imaginative, delicious' four-course dinner, cooked using produce in season. Typical dishes: local asparagus; duck breasts, braised endives, marsala. Upstairs, the traditionally styled bedrooms are 'spacious and thoughtfully equipped'. 'All three rooms are equally delightful: comfortable beds, charming decoration, superb views across the Howardian hills. (What more can you ask for?)' At breakfast, there's freshly squeezed orange juice, local sausages and dry-cured bacon, Whitby kippers and home-made preserves. Rambles in the North Yorkshire countryside await; gardens and abbey ruins are within easy reach; John Vanbrugh's Castle Howard is a short drive away. (Richard Creed, AW)

West End
Ampleforth
YO62 4DY

T: 01439 788325
E: stay@shallowdalehouse.co.uk
W: www.shallowdalehouse.co.uk

BEDROOMS: 3.
OPEN: all year except Christmas/ New Year, 'occasionally at other times'.
FACILITIES: drawing room, sitting room/library, dining room, free Wi-Fi, in-room TV (Freeview), 2½-acre gardens, unsuitable for disabled.
BACKGROUND MUSIC: none.
LOCATION: edge of village.
CHILDREN: not under 12.
DOGS: not allowed.
CREDIT CARDS: MasterCard, Visa.
PRICES: [2017] per room B&B £125–£150, D,B&B £215–£240. Set dinner £45 (min. 48 hours' notice). 1-night bookings occasionally refused weekends.

ARUNDEL Sussex

Map 2:E3

THE TOWN HOUSE

Lee and Katie Williams run their restaurant-with-rooms in a Grade II listed Regency building close to the antique shops and historic sites in a bustling, riverside market town. The atmosphere is relaxed – 'like being at a dinner party with friends,' say the owners – and service is 'first class', a Guide reader reports. Served under a carved and gilded Renaissance Florentine ceiling ('worth a visit in its own right'), the chef/patron's menus are short, seasonal and accessible, without fuss, foam or swooshes. Try roast venison, beetroot, sauté potatoes, perhaps, or seared scallops, pork belly, spicy spring greens. There's an 'excellent and reasonably priced' wine list, too. Up 'steep stairs' (help with luggage is offered), bedrooms vary in size and style. A suite with a four-poster bed, an original fireplace and a moulded ceiling has a balcony overlooking Arundel Castle; a cheaper four-poster double shares the view. Gazing over the rooftops of the town, a top-floor suite of two bedrooms and a shared shower room suits a family. On a fine day, stroll to the banks of the River Arun, then into Sussex countryside. More reports, please.

65 High Street
Arundel
BN18 9AJ

T: 01903 883847
E: enquiries@thetownhouse.co.uk
W: www.thetownhouse.co.uk

BEDROOMS: 5.
OPEN: all year except 25/26 Dec, 1 Jan, 2 weeks Easter, 2 weeks Oct, restaurant closed Sun/Mon.
FACILITIES: restaurant, free Wi-Fi, in-room TV (Freeview), unsuitable for disabled.
BACKGROUND MUSIC: in restaurant.
LOCATION: top end of High Street.
CHILDREN: all ages welcomed.
DOGS: not allowed.
CREDIT CARDS: Diners, MasterCard, Visa.
PRICES: per room B&B £110–£150, D,B&B (midweek) £150–£190. Set dinner £25.50–£29.50. 1-night bookings refused weekends in high season.

AUSTWICK Yorkshire

AUSTWICK HALL

'A visit to this B&B is to be remembered, not just for the quirky, individual rooms, but also for the dedication and kindness of its owners, Michael Pearson and Eric Culley.' An inspector in 2017 was charmed by this 'fascinating, lovingly restored' 16th-century manor house, which stands in 'nurtured, cherished' Italianate gardens on the edge of the Yorkshire Dales. Arrive to tea in the 'grand', log fire-warmed hall, amid a collection of 'well-framed' art and ethnographic artefacts – 'a treasure trove for antique cognoscenti' – then swan about in one of the large bedrooms, each 'decorated with fine taste'. 'Ours had a brass chandelier, extravagantly thick curtains, an 18th-century Rococo-style bed (petite and creaky), and a beautiful Persian rug on the stained-wood floor. Two small carved tigers guarded the fireplace. The bathroom, with a freestanding bath, was entered through stained-glass doors.' In the morning ('an early breakfast was easily provided'), sit down to 'strong tea; a succulent fruit salad; beautifully prepared eggs on good toast'. Sculptures and wild flowers flourish along woodland walks through the grounds.

Townhead Lane
Austwick
LA2 8BS

T: 01524 251794
E: austwickhall@austwick.org
W: www.austwickhall.co.uk

BEDROOMS: 4.
OPEN: all year.
FACILITIES: hall, drawing room, dining room, free Wi-Fi, in-room TV (Freeview), 14-acre gardens, hot tub, unsuitable for disabled.
BACKGROUND MUSIC: none.
LOCATION: edge of village.
CHILDREN: not under 16.
DOGS: not allowed.
CREDIT CARDS: MasterCard, Visa.
PRICES: per room B&B single £110–£140, double £125–£155. 1-night bookings refused bank holiday weekends.

AUSTWICK Yorkshire

Map 4:D3

THE TRADDOCK

♀ Previous César winner

Come to Austwick in May for the Cuckoo Festival; come all year to the Reynolds family's 'lovely place', 'a welcoming hotel' in an 'excellent Dales location'. The Georgian house (with Victorian additions) has 'pleasant public areas' and a blazing fire in reception; the staff are 'attentive and helpful'. 'We were impressed when we stayed last year, and were glad, on a recent visit, to find high standards maintained,' say Guide readers this year. There are 'well-appointed bedrooms' to choose from (some 'on the small side'), supplied with fruit and biscuits. 'Our spacious loft room was stunning: tasteful furnishings, a large, comfortable bed, plentiful storage. Velux windows gave excellent natural light; a modern lighting system offered mood settings. The beautiful bathroom had a roll-top bath and separate shower.' At mealtimes, daily specials allow 'plenty of choice'. From new chef Thomas Pickard's 'imaginative menus', built around local and wild ingredients, choose, perhaps, 'perfectly roasted hake'. 'A wonderful meal, much enjoyed.' (Max Lickfold, John and Theresa Stewart, Peter Anderson, Robert Gower)

Austwick
LA2 8BY

T: 01524 251224
F: 01524 251796
E: info@thetraddock.co.uk
W: www.thetraddock.co.uk

BEDROOMS: 12. 1 on ground floor.
OPEN: all year.
FACILITIES: 3 lounges, bar, 2 dining rooms, function facilities, free Wi-Fi, in-room TV (Freeview), 1½-acre grounds (sun deck), unsuitable for disabled.
BACKGROUND MUSIC: in public areas except 1 lounge.
LOCATION: 4 miles NW of Settle.
CHILDREN: all ages welcomed.
DOGS: allowed on lead in public rooms, not in dining rooms.
CREDIT CARDS: MasterCard, Visa.
PRICES: [2017] per room B&B £110–£240, D,B&B £180–£310. À la carte £35. 1-night bookings refused weekends in season.

AYLESBURY Buckinghamshire

Map 2:C3

HARTWELL HOUSE & SPA

Swish up the drive through an Arcadian landscape to reach this Jacobean mansion. Enlarged and remodelled in the 1700s, it has 'extremely grand' interiors that have been 'kept in fine order'. 'The location and Georgian decor are everything you expect from a National Trust property,' writes a Guide insider, 'and the friendly staff work well as a family.' Bedrooms in the mansion and converted riding school are huge; bathrobes and home-made biscuits come as standard. 'We really appreciated our room in the main house – silent, comfy, with great views.' 'Royal rooms' with antiques and paintings recall the years when the house was home to the court-in-exile of Louis XVIII of France, who trashed the place. Today's more appreciative guests spend long afternoons in the spa and its swimming pool, then dress up to dine by candlelight, perhaps on roasted Chiltern Valley partridge or line-caught sea bass, truffled gnocchi, charred leeks. 'The food is up to the elegance of the surroundings,' said guests this year, though others wished for more variety. After a 'fine breakfast', 'formally served', head outside to the 'marvellous gardens'. (Francine and Ian Walsh, and others)

Oxford Road
Stone
Aylesbury
HP17 8NR

T: 01296 747444
E: info@hartwell-house.com
W: www.hartwell-house.com

BEDROOMS: 52. 16 in stable block, some on ground floor, 2 suitable for disabled.
OPEN: all year.
FACILITIES: lift, 4 drawing rooms, bar, 3 dining rooms, conference facilities, free Wi-Fi, in-room TV (Sky), civil wedding licence, spa (swimming pool, 8 by 16 metres), 94-acre grounds (gardens, parkland, tennis).
BACKGROUND MUSIC: pianist most Fri and Sat nights.
LOCATION: 2 miles W of Aylesbury.
CHILDREN: not under 6.
DOGS: allowed in dedicated suites, guide dogs in main house, dining areas.
CREDIT CARDS: Amex, MasterCard, Visa.
PRICES: [2017] per room B&B £200–£600. Set dinner £43–£49. 1-night bookings sometimes refused.

BABBACOMBE Devon

Map 1:D5

THE CARY ARMS

Step out of your yacht, if you have it, and on to the private jetty at Lana de Savary's cliff-face hotel, on a 'fabulously secluded' cove; the rest of us will descend the winding road and admire the wide vista over the Teign estuary. 'The exterior is unpretentious', but come in to 'a genuine, good-humoured welcome' and 'an appealing sense of domesticity'. Seasidey touches throughout include yachting memorabilia, binoculars for scanning the horizon, and buckets and spades for children, who are particularly welcome. (Dogs are liberally catered for, too, with a 'high-quality dog's dinner', and a 'well-produced guide of local walks' for mutt and master.) The by-the-seaside atmosphere carries through to the 'spacious, attractive' bedrooms. Choose to stay in one of the new, chic beach huts that have popped up, with a private terrace, in a sheltered, sunny spot in the grounds. In good weather, dine on local chef Ben Kingdon's Devon crab, West Country pork or Lyme Bay lobster on the 'extensive, layered terrace' ('blue-check tablecloths emphasise the informal dining'). When cooler air blows in, find a spot by the log stove in the rustic bar. (RG)

Beach Road
Babbacombe
TQ1 3LX

T: 01803 327110
F: 01803 323221
E: enquiries@caryarms.co.uk
W: www.caryarms.co.uk

BEDROOMS: 16. 2 on ground floor, 8 in beach huts and suites, 2 in cottages. Plus 3 self-catering cottages.
OPEN: all year.
FACILITIES: lounge, bar, restaurant, conservatory, free Wi-Fi, in-room TV, civil wedding licence, spa (treatment rooms, plunge pool, mini-gym, steam room, sun deck), garden, terraces.
BACKGROUND MUSIC: all day in bar.
LOCATION: by beach, 2¼ miles N of Torquay harbour.
CHILDREN: all ages welcomed.
DOGS: allowed in some rooms, not in conservatory.
CREDIT CARDS: Amex, MasterCard, Visa.
PRICES: per room B&B from £195. À la carte £30. 1-night bookings sometimes refused.

BABCARY Somerset

Map 1:C6

RED LION INN

'A hive of activity', Clare and Charlie Garrard's 17th-century thatched inn is well liked for its 'excellent accommodation', 'enjoyable food' and 'efficient, professional staff'. 'Certain O'Duigan, the energetic manager, capably divides his time between playing friendly host and managing the day-to-day affairs,' said a guest in 2017. Within old stone walls, there are flagstone floors, exposed beams, logs for the fire; visitors help themselves to newspapers and board games. Bedrooms are across the garden, in an 'immaculate, jaw-dropping' conversion of a former barn. 'Our ground-floor room, elegantly done out in pale grey and white, had stylish furnishings, abstract paintings and a generous hospitality tray with home-made biscuits. We slept well in the very comfortable bed.' Join the locals for dinner in the 'spacious, high-ceilinged' dining room, where modern gastropub dishes might include venison tortellini, charred tenderstem, blue cheese cream; pan-fried gurnard, saffron potatoes, braised fennel, crab bisque. In the morning, take to the country lanes that wind all around: gardens and galleries are within easy reach; Glastonbury Tor is 25 minutes' drive away.

Babcary
TA11 7ED

T: 01458 223230
E: info@redlionbabcary.co.uk
W: www.redlionbabcary.co.uk

BEDROOMS: 6. All in converted barn, 1, on ground floor, suitable for disabled.
OPEN: all year.
FACILITIES: 2 bars, restaurant, private dining room, meeting/function facilities, free Wi-Fi, in-room TV, farm shop, garden (play area, marquee for wedding parties).
BACKGROUND MUSIC: in bar area, regular live music nights.
LOCATION: 5 miles E of Somerton.
CHILDREN: all ages welcomed.
DOGS: allowed in bar only.
CREDIT CARDS: all major cards.
PRICES: [2017] per room B&B single £90–£100, double £110–£120. À la carte £28.

BAINBRIDGE Yorkshire

Map 4:C3

LOW MILL GUEST HOUSE `NEW`

'Full of character and quirkiness', Jane and
Neil McNair's 'wonderful guest house' is in a
'beautifully refurbished' 18th-century corn mill
on the River Bain. Thick stone walls and huge
beams 'add to the historic feel': ask for a tour of
the waterwheel – 'it was astonishing to see the
mill equipment turning through the house and
even in our room,' said a guess this year. Beyond
the marvel of engineering, however, 'it's Jane
and Neil's attention to detail that makes this
place so special'. A wood-burning range keeps
the homely lounge cosy in winter months; in
summer, the riverside garden appeals. Spacious
bedrooms decorated with vintage finds look on
to village, garden or river. 'Our huge Workshop
room had an emperor bed, an enormous copper
bath and a wood-burner; the home-made
fudge was a treat.' The hostess's rustic dinners,
sourced from the village butcher and other local
suppliers, are 'a delight'. A short menu, served
from 6 pm, might include pork chop, rhubarb
chutney, new potatoes. Much of the 'excellent
breakfast' is home made – bread, granola, jams
and yogurt. The Yorkshire Dales national park
is all around; the hosts have plenty of local
knowledge to share. (Adam Gibson, and others)

Low Mill
Bainbridge
DL8 3EF

T: 01969 650 553
E: lowmillguesthouse@gmail.com
W: www.lowmillguesthouse.co.uk

BEDROOMS: 3.
OPEN: all year except Christmas–27 Dec.
FACILITIES: lounge, dining room, free Wi-Fi, in-room TV (Freeview), ¼-acre riverside garden with seating, secure bicycle storage, unsuitable for disabled.
BACKGROUND MUSIC: none.
LOCATION: 5 miles E of Hawes.
CHILDREN: not under 12.
DOGS: allowed, not in dining room, on lead in other public areas.
CREDIT CARDS: MasterCard, Visa.
PRICES: [2017] per room B&B £110–£180, D,B&B £160–£230. Dinner £20–£25. 2-night min. stay preferred.

SEE ALSO SHORTLIST

BARNSLEY Gloucestershire

Map 3:E6

BARNSLEY HOUSE

Romance is in the air, along with the birdsong
of robins, nuthatches and chaffinches, at this
golden-hued manor house in a pretty Cotswold
village. Set in historic gardens, the 17th-century
stone house was once the home of Rosemary
Verey, grande dame of garden design. The
laburnum walk and ornamental fruit and
vegetable garden she created still flourish today.
Now part of the Calcot Hotels group, the whole
makes up a fine hotel and spa with 'an informal
atmosphere' and 'a nice country house feel'.
Traditional bedrooms are in the main house,
each individually decorated in soothing shades.
Duplex rooms are in a modern wing. All rooms
contain magazines, bottled water, hot drinks
and biscuits. Tables are dressed with sprigs
of rosemary and linen napkins in the Potager
restaurant, where Francesco Volgo's cooking
takes inspiration from the garden. His seasonal
menu might include chilled wild garlic velouté,
potato puff, ham hock; Barnsley lamb chop,
broad beans, tomato, black olive and anchovy
salsa. Up the road, the Village Pub (see Shortlist)
has more casual meals. Bicycles are available to
borrow for a rural ride. More reports, please.

Barnsley
GL7 5EE

T: 01285 740000
F: 01285 740925
E: info@barnsleyhouse.com
W: www.barnsleyhouse.com

BEDROOMS: 18. 7 in stableyard, 4 in
courtyard, 1 in cottage, 1 suitable
for disabled.
OPEN: all year.
FACILITIES: 2 lounges, bar,
restaurant, cinema, meeting room,
free Wi-Fi, in-room TV (Sky,
Freeview), civil wedding licence,
terrace, 11-acre garden (spa,
outdoor hydrotherapy pool).
BACKGROUND MUSIC: 'easy listening'
in lounge and restaurant.
LOCATION: 5 miles NE of
Cirencester.
CHILDREN: not under 14.
DOGS: allowed in stableyard rooms,
not in grounds or public areas.
CREDIT CARDS: Amex, MasterCard,
Visa.
PRICES: [2017] per room B&B from
£219, D,B&B from £299. À la carte
£40. 1-night bookings sometimes
refused.

SEE ALSO SHORTLIST

BARWICK Somerset

Map 1:C6

LITTLE BARWICK HOUSE

Tim and Emma Ford 'set the standard for fine country dining and impeccable hospitality' at their 'unpretentious, enchanting' restaurant-with-rooms, Guide readers agree. Approach the Georgian dower house down narrow country lanes: guests sip aperitifs on the sunny terrace or under the cedar tree on the lawn in good weather, and by the fire in the lounge when temperatures fall. 'The atmosphere is that of a friendly gathering at a modest, yet refined, country house.' Warm, 'tastefully decorated' bedrooms have 'all the accessories the modern guest expects', plus home-made shortbread and a bouquet of garden blooms. 'Ours had a superabundance of throw cushions, too.' (One dissenter this year was unhappy about her accommodation, but praised the cooking.) Younger son Olly now joins his father in the kitchen, turning out 'perfect food' for contented diners. 'Everything is presented with finesse. We enjoyed the seared scallop and red mullet starters; roe deer and a stuffed sole paupiette were fabulous.' In the morning, 'sublime jams' are part of a 'delicious breakfast'. (Alfred Lennon, Francine and Ian Walsh, Suzanne Lyons, Charles Goldie, and others)

Rexes Hollow Lane
Barwick
BA22 9TD

T: 01935 423902
F: 01935 420908
E: reservations@barwick7.fsnet.co.uk
W: www.littlebarwickhouse.co.uk

BEDROOMS: 7. 1 for week-long let.
OPEN: all year except 4 weeks post-Christmas, closed Sun, Mon.
FACILITIES: 2 lounges, restaurant, conservatory, free Wi-Fi, in-room TV (Freeview), 3½-acre garden (terrace, paddock), unsuitable for disabled.
BACKGROUND MUSIC: none.
LOCATION: ¾ mile outside Yeovil.
CHILDREN: not under 5.
DOGS: allowed in bedrooms, only assistance dogs in restaurant.
CREDIT CARDS: MasterCard, Visa.
PRICES: [2017] per room B&B £121–£190, D,B&B £240–£290. Set dinner £43.95–£49.95. 1-night bookings sometimes refused.

BASLOW Derbyshire

Map 3:A6

THE CAVENDISH

'Within lovely walking distance' of Chatsworth House, the Duke of Devonshire's 'very nice hotel' continues to please. Philip Joseph is the much-praised manager. 'The staff are some of the most helpful and welcoming we've come across.' Newly refurbished bedrooms overlooking parkland have kept their 'traditional theme' – they are 'delightful'. 'My room was magnificent, with a superb bathroom,' reports a correspondent this year. ('A slight criticism: the bedroom lighting could be better.') Among the 'welcoming touches' in the rooms: fresh milk and 'high-quality biscuits', thick bathrobes, 'a cute teddy bear – like them or loathe them'. Teatime brings 'the nicest, warm, home-baked scones' ('with a generous portion of clotted cream') – ask to eat them on the terrace in sunny weather. At dinner in the Gallery restaurant, chef Alan Hill earns plaudits for such dishes as 'salmon rillettes with unusual, delicious horseradish ice cream; tender, pleasantly gamey venison; flavourful wild sea bass with crisped skin'. A tasting menu may be taken at the Kitchen Table; simpler fare is on the menu in the Garden Room. (Richard Creed, Robert Gower, Susan Willmington)

Church Lane
Baslow
DE45 1SP

T: 01246 582311
F: 01246 582312
E: info@cavendish-hotel.net
W: www.cavendish-hotel.net

BEDROOMS: 24. 2 on ground floor.
OPEN: all year.
FACILITIES: lounge, bar, 2 restaurants, 2 private dining rooms, free Wi-Fi, in-room TV (Freeview), ½-acre grounds (putting), river fishing nearby, golf in Chatsworth grounds.
BACKGROUND MUSIC: none.
LOCATION: on A619, in Chatsworth grounds, on edge of village.
CHILDREN: all ages welcomed.
DOGS: not allowed.
CREDIT CARDS: Amex, MasterCard, Visa.
PRICES: [2017] per room B&B from £250, D,B&B from £349. Set menus £42.50–£62.50 (plus 5% service levy on all prices). 1-night bookings sometimes refused.

BASLOW Derbyshire

Map 3:A6

FISCHER'S AT BASLOW HALL

Fine dining is the order of the day at Max and Susan Fischer's Jacobean-style Edwardian mansion in 'prime Derbyshire countryside', approached by a chestnut tree-shaded drive. Chef Rupert Rowley's Michelin-starred cooking, including 'some simply conceived dishes and a few more conceptual ones', is 'outstanding in its quality', guests say. Dress for dinner in the dining room, or perch at the tasting bench in the kitchen if you prefer a buzz. Canapés and a 'surprise savoury' might be followed by oxtail ravioli; miso-glazed pork jowl, brown shrimp, coconut. Vegetarians, rejoice: fine menus use abundant produce from the kitchen garden. In the main house, spacious bedrooms are traditionally styled, with leaded windows overlooking mature landscaped acres. 'Modern, airy' Garden House rooms, grouped around a 'pleasant' walled courtyard and garden, are 'excellent'. All rooms have Egyptian cotton sheets, organic toiletries, comfy seating, fluffy towels and robes. After a breakfast of freshly squeezed juice, home-made granola, local bacon and sausages, perhaps toast with honey from the hives, take a stroll to Chatsworth House. (Richard Osborne, AB)

Calver Road
Baslow
DE45 1RR

T: 01246 583259
E: reservations@fischers-baslow
   hall.co.uk
W: www.fischers-baslowhall.co.uk

BEDROOMS: 11. 5 in Garden House, 4 on ground floor.
OPEN: all year except 25/26 Dec, 24/31 Dec evenings.
FACILITIES: lounge/bar, breakfast room, 3 dining rooms, function facilities, free Wi-Fi, in-room TV (Freeview), civil wedding licence, 5-acre grounds, unsuitable for disabled.
BACKGROUND MUSIC: none.
LOCATION: edge of village, 5 miles NE of Bakewell.
CHILDREN: no under-8s in restaurant in evening, no under-5s at lunch, all ages welcomed at Sunday lunch.
DOGS: not allowed.
CREDIT CARDS: Amex, MasterCard, Visa.
PRICES: [2017] per room B&B £230–£295, D,B&B £320–£451. Set dinners £62.50–£78, tasting menu £85.

BASSENTHWAITE LAKE Cumbria

Map 4: inset C2

THE PHEASANT

Wooded hillside forms a pleasing backdrop to this 'comfortable country hotel' in an 'optimal position' for exploring the northern Lakes. 'Our ideal spot for hunkering down has a log fire, comfortable chairs, and plenty of old editions of Country Life and similar magazines. The Pheasant met that requirement – though some updating wouldn't go amiss – and it was good to see the fire alight at breakfast each morning,' says a Guide reader in 2017. The garden appeals in good weather; inside the former coaching inn, locals and their dogs are welcomed in the oak-panelled bar. Traditionally furnished bedrooms are made homely with locally made biscuits and a china tea service. 'Our warm, spacious room in the main house had a separate sitting area and a really good bathroom.' Eat in the bar, the 'informal bistro' or the 'stylish, elegant restaurant', where new chef Jonathan Bell prepares 'well-cooked, artistically presented' dishes such as lamb loin, fondant potato, salt-roast celeriac. 'From the amuse-bouche to the petits fours with coffee, everything was delicious.' Bassenthwaite Lake and its nesting ospreys are a stroll away. (John Saul, Alan and Edwina Williams)

25% DISCOUNT VOUCHERS

Bassenthwaite Lake
CA13 9YE

T: 01768 76234
F: 01768 76002
E: reception@the-pheasant.co.uk
W: www.the-pheasant.co.uk

BEDROOMS: 15. 2 on ground floor in lodge.
OPEN: all year except 25 Dec, restaurant closed Sun eve and Mon.
FACILITIES: 2 lounges, bar, bistro, restaurant, private dining room, free Wi-Fi, in-room TV (Freeview), 40-acre grounds, lake 200 yds (fishing), access to nearby spa, pool and treatment rooms, unsuitable for disabled.
BACKGROUND MUSIC: none.
LOCATION: 5 miles E of Cockermouth, ¼ mile off A66 to Keswick.
CHILDREN: not under 8.
DOGS: allowed in some bedrooms (£10 charge), public rooms.
CREDIT CARDS: MasterCard, Visa.
PRICES: [2017] per room B&B £125–£180. Set menu (restaurant) £42.50, à la carte (bistro) £30. 1-night bookings sometimes refused Sat.

BATH Somerset

Map 2:D1

ABBEY HOTEL

'All kinds of interesting art and quirky touches' bring cheer to this lively modern hotel, which sprawls across three Georgian town houses on busy North Parade. It is owned by Bath hoteliers Christa and Ian Taylor, whose No. 15 Great Pulteney and Villa at Henrietta Park (see main and Shortlist entries) share the same flair. Andrew Foulkes manages 'upbeat, super-friendly' staff. 'Down hallways, round corners, up and down short flights of stairs', recently refurbished bedrooms of varying sizes (some have easier lift access) are well supplied with 'posh toiletries and thick, soft towels'; 'excellent bedside lights by a comfortable bed'; current magazines and an iPad loaded with local information. Discuss room choices before booking: a rear room was thought 'blissfully quiet'; one overlooking the main road had late-night noise from weekend partygoers. In the 'smartly decorated' restaurant, chef Rupert Taylor's modern dishes – perhaps pan-fried stone bass, Jerusalem artichokes, herb gnocchi – are 'delicious'. The morning meal is 'exemplary', with 'a fine buffet spread' and a cooked-breakfast menu of 'all the classics'. (Carol and Geoffrey Jackson, and others)

1–3 North Parade
Bath
BA1 1LF

T: 01225 461603
E: reception@abbeyhotelbath.co.uk
W: www.abbeyhotelbath.co.uk

BEDROOMS: 62.
OPEN: all year.
FACILITIES: lift, bar, restaurant, private dining area, function facilities, free Wi-Fi, in-room TV (Freeview), front terrace (alfresco meals and drinks).
BACKGROUND MUSIC: all day in bar.
LOCATION: central.
CHILDREN: all ages welcomed.
DOGS: allowed in bedrooms and bar, not in restaurant.
CREDIT CARDS: Amex, MasterCard, Visa.
PRICES: [2017] per room B&B from £115. À la carte £38. 1-night bookings sometimes refused.

SEE ALSO SHORTLIST

BATH Somerset

APSLEY HOUSE

In a Georgian country house said to have been built by the Duke of Wellington for his mistress, Claire and Nicholas Potts's elegant B&B is run with 'friendliness' and a fair number of egg dishes at breakfast. Managers Miro Mikula and Kate Kowalczyk, 'a delightful young couple', 'make guests feel welcome'. Newly refurbished public rooms are filled with antiques, paintings and original features. 'Well-proportioned' bedrooms (some snug) have a modern bathroom and individual period character. Choose a room with a carved four-poster bed and French doors leading to the garden, or one on the top floor, with views towards Beckford Tower and the Cotswold Way. Biscuits, coffee and a choice of teas are provided; fresh milk is available on request. In the morning, have an 'excellent breakfast' overlooking the pretty garden, 'with surrounding hills forming the horizon'. Fresh fruit and glass jars of cereals are set on the large dresser; cooked dishes, including a daily special, are served on tables laid with crisp white linens. The city centre is a half-hour's downhill walk away; alternatively, a regular bus service will take you there. (RG, and others)

141 Newbridge Hill
Bath
BA1 3PT

T: 01225 336966
E: claireypotts@btinternet.com
W: www.apsley-house.co.uk

BEDROOMS: 12. 1 on ground floor, plus 1 self-catering 2-bedroom apartment.
OPEN: all year except 24–26 Dec.
FACILITIES: drawing room, dining room, free Wi-Fi, in-room TV (BT, Freeview), ¼-acre garden, parking, unsuitable for disabled.
BACKGROUND MUSIC: Classic FM in drawing and dining rooms.
LOCATION: 1¼ miles W of city centre.
CHILDREN: all ages welcomed.
DOGS: not allowed.
CREDIT CARDS: Amex, MasterCard, Visa.
PRICES: [2017] per room B&B £99–£280. 1-night bookings refused Sat in peak season.

SEE ALSO SHORTLIST

BATH Somerset

Map 2:D1

NO. 15 GREAT PULTENEY NEW

'There's plenty to look at' in this 'eclectic, imaginative' hotel, say visitors in 2017, 'from prize-winning artwork to collections of glass, Victorian calling cards and Beswick dogs.' Spread across three Georgian town houses, the 'quirky, modern' hotel is owned by Ian and Christa Taylor, local hoteliers who also run the Abbey Hotel and Villa at Henrietta Park (see main and Shortlist entries). The staff are 'fabulous – helpful and happy'. Sip tea and cocktails in the small bar ('champagne came in the tallest, thinnest flutes imaginable'); a short seasonal menu is served in the café. From snug to spacious, 'highly individual' bedrooms are like no other. 'Ours had everything we could have wanted (except a luggage rack); tea and coffee things were hidden in a doll's house. There were big pillows on the comfy bed; velour dressing gowns; a super walk-in shower. In a shared larder, we could help ourselves to juices, sodas and ice creams.' Breakfast brings tea in a silver-plated teapot; a buffet with cereals, yogurt, cheeses and hams. 'I had scrambled eggs with smoked salmon and mashed avocado on sourdough toast – all good.' (Carol and Geoffrey Jackson)

13–15 Great Pulteney Street
Bath
BA2 4BR

T: 01225 807015
E: enquiries@no15greatpulteney.co.uk
W: no15greatpulteney.co.uk

BEDROOMS: 40. 8 in coach house, 1 suitable for disabled.
OPEN: all year, café closed Mon/Tues.
FACILITIES: lift, lounge, bar, café, private dining room, free Wi-Fi, in-room TV (Sky), spa, small garden terrace, limited parking (charge).
BACKGROUND MUSIC: all day in public areas.
LOCATION: central.
CHILDREN: all ages welcomed.
DOGS: allowed in bedrooms, bar, not in restaurant.
CREDIT CARDS: Amex, MasterCard, Visa.
PRICES: [2017] per room B&B from £169. À la carte £24. 1-night bookings sometimes refused.

SEE ALSO SHORTLIST

BATH Somerset

Map 2:D1

THE QUEENSBERRY

The city centre is an easy walk from Helen and Laurence Beere's 'near-faultless' hotel, in an 'unsurpassed situation' within reach of museums, shops and heritage spots. Spread across four freshly refurbished Georgian town houses on a quiet residential street, the hotel strikes a light-hearted note – there are Union flag cushions on velvet club chairs in the bar, and quirky prints in the restaurant. The staff are 'happy and helpful'; the modern bedrooms 'nicely proportioned and well equipped'; the cocktails 'very good indeed'. 'And the valet parking is a boon.' Accommodation ranges from club rooms ideal for solo travellers to a junior suite with an enormous four-poster bed, and a chaise longue in the spacious bathroom. There's no tea tray in the room, but hot drinks are served in the 'comfy drawing room' throughout the day. On a sunny afternoon, choose to sit in the 'charming courtyard garden' instead. In the basement restaurant, chef Chris Cleghorn's keenly modern tasting menus might include torched and confit trout, avocado, pink grapefruit; barbecued lamb cutlet, peas, morels, ewe's cheese. 'The cooking rightly has a very good reputation among locals.' (PJ, and others)

4–7 Russel Street
Bath
BA1 2QF

T: 01225 447928
F: 01225 446065
E: reservations@thequeensberry.
co.uk
W: www.thequeensberry.co.uk

BEDROOMS: 29. Some on ground floor.
OPEN: all year, restaurant closed Mon evening.
FACILITIES: lift, 2 drawing rooms, bar, restaurant, meeting room, free Wi-Fi, in-room TV (Freeview), 4 linked courtyard gardens, car-parking service, unsuitable for disabled.
BACKGROUND MUSIC: in restaurant and bar.
LOCATION: near Assembly Rooms.
CHILDREN: all ages welcomed.
DOGS: not allowed.
CREDIT CARDS: Amex, MasterCard, Visa.
PRICES: [2017] per room B&B £125–£460. Tasting menus £67.50–£80, à la carte £55. 1-night bookings sometimes refused.

SEE ALSO SHORTLIST

BATH Somerset

Map 2:D1

THE ROYAL CRESCENT HOTEL & SPA

Amid the sublime sweep of a Grade I listed Georgian crescent, two converted town houses combine as one 'very pleasant' hotel affording 'magical vistas' over lawns and public parkland. 'The most striking feature is the ambience created by engaging staff who appear only too happy to provide a service,' says a guest in 2017. 'Elegant, comfortable' public rooms are filled with antiques, paintings and fine fabrics. 'Fresh, stylish' accommodation ranges from snug bedrooms with a queen-size bed and comfy seating, to extravagant suites whose picture windows look onto the private garden. Have a glass of fizz with fish and chips in the bar, or eat in the Dower House restaurant, where chef David Campbell's 'outstanding menus' include such modern dishes as roast halibut, salt cod potato, charcoal emulsion. (Vegetarian options are no less imaginative.) Take tea in the garden on a fine day, or relax in the recently renovated spa in dour weather. If you can tear yourself away, step out into the city: the concierges are 'helpful in arranging a day of exploring'. 'Not cheap, but worth every penny.' (Robert Cooper, and others)

16 Royal Crescent
Bath
BA1 2LS

T: 01225 823333
E: info@royalcrescent.co.uk
W: www.royalcrescent.co.uk

BEDROOMS: 45. 10 in Dower House, 14 in garden annexes, 8 on ground floor.
OPEN: all year.
FACILITIES: lift, bar, drawing room, library, restaurant, function facilities, free Wi-Fi, in-room TV (Freeview), civil wedding licence, 1-acre garden, spa and bath house (12-metre 'relaxation' pool, gym, sauna, treatment rooms).
BACKGROUND MUSIC: in library and restaurant.
LOCATION: ½ mile from High Street.
CHILDREN: all ages welcomed, no under-12s in spa.
DOGS: allowed in some bedrooms, not in public rooms.
CREDIT CARDS: Amex, MasterCard, Visa.
PRICES: [2017] per room B&B from £330. À la carte £65, tasting menu £75.

SEE ALSO SHORTLIST

BEAMINSTER Dorset

Map 1:C6

BRIDGE HOUSE

'The welcome is always friendly' at Joanna and Mark Donovan's 'likeable' country hotel in a former priests' house dating back to the 13th century. 'It's nicely informative, too, with a guided tour of the facilities,' says a return guest this year. The 'immaculate interiors' are 'charming' – 'low-ceilinged and nicely furnished'; a beamed lounge with a huge inglenook fireplace and 'squashy sofas' is an 'enjoyable' spot for afternoon tea or a pre-dinner drink. Bedrooms in the main house and converted coach house are individually styled, with fine linen on the bed; two suites can accommodate a family. 'Our comfortable coach house room had a modern bathroom supplied with good toiletries, robes and fluffy towels.' At dinner in the Georgian panelled dining room ('we loved the high-back rattan-style chairs and spotless tablecloths'), chef Geraldine Gay focuses on Dorset venison, game birds, fish, and garden vegetables in season. 'Everything was beautifully cooked, especially the scallops and the sirloin steak served with triple-cooked chips.' The morning meal, in the 'light and airy' garden-facing breakfast room, is 'just as good'. (Ian Malone, MW)

25% DISCOUNT VOUCHERS

3 Prout Bridge
Beaminster
DT8 3AY

T: 01308 862200
F: 01308 863700
E: hello@bridge-house.co.uk
W: www.bridge-house.co.uk

BEDROOMS: 13. 4 in coach house, 4 on ground floor.
OPEN: all year.
FACILITIES: hall/reception, lounge, bar, sun room, conservatory, restaurant, free Wi-Fi, in-room TV (Freeview), civil wedding licence, ¼-acre walled garden, terrace (alfresco dining).
BACKGROUND MUSIC: light jazz/classical at lunch and dinner.
LOCATION: 100 yards from centre.
CHILDREN: all ages welcomed.
DOGS: allowed.
CREDIT CARDS: Amex, MasterCard, Visa.
PRICES: [2017] per room B&B £99, D,B&B from £169. À la carte £40.

BEAULIEU Hampshire

Map 2:E2

THE MASTER BUILDER'S

The lawn stretches down to Beaulieu river from this 18th-century shipbuilder's house. It's a fine place, today, to watch the boats on the water, as those once-upon-a-time shipwrights did. At the end of a tree-lined lane in the New Forest national park, the hotel is 'nice and relaxed', with 'lovely staff', say guests this year. Bedrooms in the main house, decorated, perhaps, with an oriental carpet or carved-wood four-poster bed, have a pleasing, eclectic air; those in the Henry Adams wing are brighter and more modern, with a breezy coastal feel – 'cute,' one visitor said. Light sleepers might discuss options before booking – an annexe room was found to hear noise from a late-night function. At mealtimes, try 'very good' modern dishes (perhaps River Test trout, tomato and anchovy pressing, black olive tapenade) in the restaurant; in the smartly refurbished Yachtsman's bar and on the wide terrace, staff in Breton stripes serve salads, sharing boards, pub classics and pizzas. On a sunny day, take a 'pleasing walk' along the river to pretty Beaulieu village, watching out for wildfowl. A sweet reward: tea rooms and a chocolate shop await. (LR)

Buckler's Hard
Beaulieu
SO42 7XB

T: 01590 616253
F: 01590 616297
E: enquiries@themasterbuilders.
   co.uk
W: www.themasterbuilders.co.uk

BEDROOMS: 27. 17 in Henry Adams wing, 1 suitable for disabled.
OPEN: all year.
FACILITIES: lounge, bar, restaurant, free Wi-Fi, in-room TV, civil wedding licence, ½-acre garden (alfresco dining).
BACKGROUND MUSIC: in bar and restaurant.
LOCATION: 6 miles NE of Lymington.
CHILDREN: all ages welcomed.
DOGS: allowed in 9 bedrooms, not in restaurant.
CREDIT CARDS: Amex, MasterCard, Visa.
PRICES: [2017] per room B&B £110–£200, D,B&B £140–£255. À la carte £32.

BEAULIEU Hampshire

Map 2:E2

MONTAGU ARMS

Two stone dogs guard the entrance of this country hotel in between High Street and the high waters of Beaulieu river. The traditional ambience and professional staff please its fans, who think it 'very special'. Its 'charming garden' ('where we like to sit before dinner') is another attraction. Sunil Kanjanghat is the long-serving manager. Many original features (oak panelling, an old brick fireplace) have been retained throughout the 19th-century house; there are armchairs, stuffed bookcases – a 'country house feel' throughout. 'The bedroom in which we choose to stay may not be the latest in design, but it's very comfortable, and we enjoy the views over the green.' In the restaurant, chef Matthew Tomkinson's refined menus showcase produce from the organic kitchen garden. Characteristic among his modern dishes: honey-roasted free-range duck breast, caramelised endive tart, celeriac purée. For something completely different, visit the popular, family-friendly Monty's Inn ('heaving on a sunny Sunday'), where locals and passers-by gather for the hand-pulled ales and posh, provenance-proven pub grub. Renewed, head out on any of the forest walks or bicycle trails nearby. (MC)

Palace Lane
Beaulieu
SO42 7ZL

T: 01590 612324
F: 01590 612188
E: reservations@
montaguarmshotel.co.uk
W: www.montaguarmshotel.co.uk

BEDROOMS: 22.
OPEN: all year, Terrace restaurant closed Mon, Tues lunch.
FACILITIES: lounge, conservatory, bar/brasserie, restaurant, free Wi-Fi, in-room TV (Freeview), civil wedding licence, 3-acre garden, access to spa at nearby Careys Manor, unsuitable for disabled.
BACKGROUND MUSIC: all day in reception.
LOCATION: village centre.
CHILDREN: all ages welcomed, not under 11 in restaurant.
DOGS: assistance dogs allowed.
CREDIT CARDS: Amex, MasterCard, Visa.
PRICES: [2017] per room B&B from £219, D,B&B from £359. À la carte £28 (Monty's Inn), £70 (Terrace restaurant). 1-night bookings sometimes refused.

BEPTON Sussex

Map 2:E3

PARK HOUSE

The day is one long round of pleasure at this 'luxurious but unstuffy' Edwardian country house beneath the South Downs, where classic lawn sports and garden games make jolly the 'gorgeous, well-maintained' grounds. Lawn tennis, croquet, bowls and golf are on offer; there are heated swimming pools indoors and out, plus a sleek spa for the weary of limb. Sixty years after Michael and Ioné O'Brien first opened their house to paying guests, the hotel retains a 'home-away-from-home' feel – 'intimate and relaxed', yet just right for celebrations and special occasions, a trusted Guide reader says this year. Bedrooms in the main house and in cottages in the grounds are prettily, traditionally styled, with 'a fabulous bed' and views over the lawn. After cucumber sandwiches at afternoon tea, country-house dinners suit the surrounds: chef Callum Keir's 'first-class' modern dishes might include chard and tomato chutney tart, rarebit; beef Wellington, shimeji mushrooms, celeriac. And if you hear murmurs of 'hired assassins' from fellow diners, never fear – that's just polo talk among the players from nearby Cowdray Park. (Mary Woods, and others)

Bepton
GU29 0JB

T: 01730 819020
E: reservations@parkhousehotel.com
W: www.parkhousehotel.com

BEDROOMS: 21. 5 on ground floor, 1 suitable for disabled, 9 in cottages in grounds.
OPEN: all year, except 25/26 Dec.
FACILITIES: drawing room, bar, dining room, conservatory, function rooms, free Wi-Fi, in-room TV (Sky), civil wedding licence, 10-acre grounds, spa, heated swimming pools, tennis, pitch and putt, six-hole 18-tee golf course.
BACKGROUND MUSIC: in dining room/conservatory.
LOCATION: village, 2½ miles SW of Midhurst.
CHILDREN: all ages welcomed.
DOGS: allowed in some bedrooms (charge), not in public rooms.
CREDIT CARDS: Amex, MasterCard, Visa.
PRICES: [2017] per room B&B from £95, D,B&B from £150. Set dinner £33–£42, à la carte £42. 1-night bookings refused weekends.

BEVERLEY Yorkshire

Map 4:D5

NEWBEGIN HOUSE

'A welcoming home-away-from-home', Nuala and Walter Sweeney's 'remarkable' B&B is but one of the 'delightful pleasures of the lovely town'. 'All the main requirements are well covered: excellent beds, linen and bathrooms; superb breakfasts; peace and quiet despite being close to the centre. The Sweeneys are a truly hospitable family, and we felt as if we were staying with great friends.' In large, 'lived-in gardens' with two ponds, a waterfall and a potager, the Georgian house is 'full of family life'; there are paintings, photographs and fine furniture, 'some clearly antique'. Choose among 'spacious bedrooms', each traditionally decorated and well stocked with hot drinks and treats. Appleton is 'very peaceful'; 'huge' Drawing Room is 'like being in a great, fun nursery or library'; Iveson, with a claw-footed bath, has 'wonderful garden views and lots of birdsong'. Much at breakfast is sourced at the local markets: 'proper bacon and black pudding; beautiful fruit; great coffee'. There's plenty to see in the town, and the hosts are helpful with recommendations; Westwood is a stroll away. 'One would be hard pushed to find a more perfect place to stay.' (S and JJ, and others)

10 Newbegin
Beverley
HU17 8EG

T: 01482 888880
E: wsweeney@wsweeney.karoo.co.uk
W: www.newbeginhousebbbeverley.co.uk

BEDROOMS: 3.
OPEN: all year except 'when we are on holiday'.
FACILITIES: sitting room, dining room, free Wi-Fi, in-room TV (Freeview), walled garden, unsuitable for disabled.
BACKGROUND MUSIC: none.
LOCATION: central.
CHILDREN: all ages welcomed.
DOGS: not allowed.
CREDIT CARDS: none accepted.
PRICES: [2017] per room B&B single £60, double £85. 1-night bookings sometimes refused.

BIGBURY-ON-SEA Devon

Map 1:D4

BURGH ISLAND HOTEL

❦ Previous César winner

'A place to dress up, to dream, to luxuriate', this 'one-of-a-kind hotel' on a tidal island charms Guide readers with its 'magical setting' off the south Devon coast. 'The surroundings, the history, the food and the secret pool are marvellous – a complete joy.' 'Romantic and timeless', it steeps in an atmosphere that, for some, inspires grand gestures: 'We got engaged!' At high tide, arrive by sea tractor to discover an Art Deco extravaganza. The hotel 'remains true to its 1930s roots'; every bedroom, from small doubles to sumptuous suites, is 'sophisticated'. (A standalone suite straddling rocky projections of the cliff edge was in planning as the Guide went to press.) 'Our large room opened on to a long balcony. In bed or in the roll-top bath, we took in the panorama of the sea.' Ballroom dinners – black-tie affairs, with a live band twice a week – kick off with cocktails and canapés; informal meals may be taken under the glass ceiling of the Palm Court bar. One day, follow the cliff path to the Mermaid Pool; another, order a crab baguette in the centuries-old Pilchard Inn while the waves break on the rocks outside. (Bonnie Friend, Elizabeth Cule)

Burgh Island
Bigbury-on-Sea
TQ7 4BG

T: 01548 810514
E: reception@burghisland.com
W: www.burghisland.com

BEDROOMS: 25. 1 suite in Beach House, apartment above Pilchard Inn.
OPEN: all year.
FACILITIES: lift, bar, restaurant, ballroom, sun lounge, billiard room, private dining room, spa, free Wi-Fi, civil wedding licence, 17-acre grounds on 26-acre island (30-metre natural sea swimming pool), unsuitable for disabled.
BACKGROUND MUSIC: 1920s and 1930s in bar, live music Wed, Sat with dinner in ballroom.
LOCATION: off Bigbury beach; private garages on mainland.
CHILDREN: not under 5, no under-13s at dinner.
DOGS: not allowed.
CREDIT CARDS: MasterCard.
PRICES: [2017] per room D,B&B £400–£665. 1-night bookings refused Sat, some bank holidays.

BIGBURY-ON-SEA Devon

Map 1:D4

THE HENLEY

'We cannot fault The Henley – it is one of the best traditions of our lives,' write regular visitors to Martyn Scarterfield and Petra Lampe's Edwardian holiday cottage, from which a cliff path leads to the beach. 'Indeed a home away from home,' concur other Guide readers. 'We felt like house guests rather than hotel clients.' 'Martyn has just the right approach, and Petra is so charming at all times.' Public areas ('a great environment for friendly chats with the other guests') are filled with 'many homely touches': potted palms, rattan chairs, a wood-burning stove, and plenty to read – if you can tear your eyes away from the 'fabulous views' of the sea and the Avon estuary. The bedrooms are traditionally styled. 'Ours was large, with a sea view and ample light for reading.' 'Inventive and delicious', the host's three-course, limited-choice dinners, using freshly landed fish, are served in the conservatory (veggie options on request). Breakfast is 'beautifully presented'. 'Our spaniel was thrilled to be with Caspar, the owners' Labrador, who waited outside the bedroom to be greeted each morning.' 'A special place.' (Simon Rodway, Geoffrey and Sue Bignell, Steven Hur)

Folly Hill
Bigbury-on-Sea
TQ7 4AR

T: 01548 810240
F: 01548 810240
E: thehenleyhotel@btconnect.com
W: www.thehenleyhotel.co.uk

BEDROOMS: 5.
OPEN: Mar–end Oct.
FACILITIES: 2 lounges, bar, conservatory dining room, free Wi-Fi, in-room TV (Freeview), small terraced garden (steps to beach, golf, sailing, fishing), Coastal Path nearby, unsuitable for disabled.
BACKGROUND MUSIC: jazz/classical in the evenings in lounge, dining room.
LOCATION: 5 miles S of Modbury.
CHILDREN: not under 12.
DOGS: not allowed in dining room.
CREDIT CARDS: Amex, MasterCard, Visa.
PRICES: [2017] per room B&B single £95, double £127–£160, D,B&B (2-night min.) single £125, double £188–£210. Set dinner £36. 1-night bookings sometimes refused weekends.

BIGGIN-BY-HARTINGTON Derbyshire

Map 3:B6

BIGGIN HALL

In a 'marvellous Derbyshire Dales setting', supporters of James Moffett's rustic, laid-back hotel find much to like: 'a warm welcome', 'decent home-cooked dinners', 'quiet, comfortable rooms'. It may not be to all tastes. 'A curious place' – 'slightly chaotic', some say – 'it has undeniable charm, despite the odd niggle.' Simple bedrooms are spread out across the rambling property. 'In winter, our spacious, nicely appointed top-floor room was chilly when we arrived, but it quickly warmed up. There was a chaise longue to relax on; masses of hot water in the small, recently refurbished bathroom. Good to have fresh milk in the fridge, too.' Complimentary aperitifs are served before a 'fine, if unexciting' country dinner ('rather too efficiently served' between 6.30 pm and 8 pm) – perhaps a 'tasty salad of sweet tomatoes; tender braised beef'. In the morning, help yourself to 'a good selection' of yogurt, fruit and cereals. 'The self-service hot buffet didn't appeal, but our special order of scrambled eggs and smoked salmon was freshly prepared.' A walker's heaven – hills and dales are all around; 'we were offered a free picnic lunch – a nice touch'. (Peter Anderson, Sara Price, and others)

Main Street
Biggin-by-Hartington
SK17 0DH

T: 01298 84451
E: enquiries@bigginhall.co.uk
W: www.bigginhall.co.uk

BEDROOMS: 21. 13 in annexes, some on ground floor.
OPEN: all year.
FACILITIES: sitting room, library, dining room, meeting room, free Wi-Fi (in sitting rooms, some bedrooms), in-room TV, civil wedding licence, 8-acre grounds (croquet), River Dove 1½ miles, unsuitable for disabled.
BACKGROUND MUSIC: none.
LOCATION: 8 miles N of Ashbourne.
CHILDREN: not under 12.
DOGS: allowed in courtyard and bothy bedrooms, not in public rooms.
CREDIT CARDS: MasterCard, Visa.
PRICES: [2017] per room B&B £70–£170, D,B&B £115–£215. Set dinner £25. 1-night bookings sometimes refused.

BLAKENEY Norfolk

Map 2:A5

THE BLAKENEY HOTEL

♔ Previous César winner

The view is one of marshes and moored boats, of creeks and children crabbing, from Emma Stannard's well-established, family-friendly hotel on the quayside of a coastal village. 'It has maintained its standards,' writes a returning visitor this year. Other regular guests agree: 'It's an attractive, welcoming place – no wonder we drive 300 miles for our annual visit. Many of the staff are long stayers, and it's a joy to experience their charm, cheerfulness and efficiency.' Several of the well-equipped bedrooms overlook the estuary; some others have a patio leading to the garden. 'My beautiful Granary room opened, through double doors, on to the green lawn, with a few steps along for a sea view.' 'Top-class' food is served all day inside or out; in the newly refurbished restaurant, the seasonal menu of 'good local food' might include grilled fillet of plaice, mashed potatoes, roast fennel, steamed courgettes. From day to night, children are well catered for, with flexible dining options, a games room, board games at the ready; the indoor swimming pool is particularly attractive on a rainy day. (Minda Alexander, Clive T Blackburn)

The Quay
Blakeney
NR25 7NE

T: 01263 740797
E: enquiries@blakeneyhotel.co.uk
W: www.blakeneyhotel.co.uk

BEDROOMS: 64. 16 in Granary annexe opposite, some on ground floor.
OPEN: all year.
FACILITIES: lift, lounge, sun lounge, bar, restaurant, free Wi-Fi, in-room TV (Freeview), function facilities, heated indoor swimming pool (15 by 5 metres), steam room, sauna, mini-gym, games room, terrace, ¼-acre walled garden.
BACKGROUND MUSIC: none.
LOCATION: on the quay.
CHILDREN: all ages welcomed.
DOGS: allowed in some bedrooms, not in public rooms.
CREDIT CARDS: Amex, MasterCard, Visa.
PRICES: [2017] per person B&B £92–£175, D,B&B (2-night min.) £104–£193. Supplement for single occupancy of double room. À la carte £32. 1-night bookings sometimes refused weekends, bank holidays.

BLANCHLAND Co. Durham

Map 4:B3

THE LORD CREWE ARMS

Previous César winner

The flagstone floors, cavernous fireplaces, labyrinthine corridors and barrel-vaulted crypt bar 'reek of history' at this cheerfully updated medieval abbot's lodge in a conservation village on the North Pennine moors. It is part of the Calcot group, whose Gloucestershire siblings are in Tetbury and Barnsley (see entries). 'The place has had a successful make-over – it's very stylish, but retains its heritage and the feeling of a locality,' say Guide readers this year. Smart bedrooms (some in adjacent cottages and at The Angel across the road) vary in size from 'canny' to 'champion', plus suites to suit a family. Each is different: one may have a roll-top bath or log-burner, another, stained-glass windows. 'Our room was lovely – large, well appointed, with good storage and a splendid bed.' Eat spit-roasted meats from the fire in the basement Hilyard, or mount stone steps to the Bishop's dining room, where chef Simon Hicks cooks accessible fare (perhaps chargrilled flat-iron steak with chips and 'naughty sauce') using local produce and home-grown vegetables. 'Breakfast was as good as I've seen – fresh, well chosen and well served.' (Tony Ayers)

The Square
Blanchland
DH8 9SP

T: 01434 675469
E: enquiries@
lordcrewearmsblanchland.co.uk
W: www.lordcrewearmsblanchland.
co.uk

BEDROOMS: 21. 7 in adjacent cottages, 10 in The Angel across road, some on ground floor, 1 suitable for disabled.
OPEN: all year.
FACILITIES: 3 lounges, restaurant, Gatehouse events space, free Wi-Fi, in-room TV (Freeview), civil wedding licence, beer garden.
BACKGROUND MUSIC: none.
LOCATION: in Blanchland village on the B6306, 9 miles S of Hexham.
CHILDREN: all ages welcomed.
DOGS: 'well-behaved dogs' allowed in some bedrooms, not in dining room.
CREDIT CARDS: MasterCard, Visa.
PRICES: [2017] per room B&B £129–£192. À la carte £30. 1-night bookings refused Fri/Sat Mar–Oct.

BLANDFORD FORUM Dorset

Map 2:E1

THE CROWN HOTEL   **NEW**

Between the High Street and the River Stour, this informal inn occupies a 'handsome' Georgian house, well placed for exploring Hardy country. It is owned by local brewers Hall & Woodhouse. Town residents come for coffee mornings and disco nights in the 'large, well-patronised' pub – oak-floored, panelled, with a 'relaxed atmosphere'; in summer, the parasol-shaded beer garden is the place to be. A fire is lit in the book- and bibelot-lined lounge in cooler weather. Lunch- and dinnertime bring 'pleasing, well-presented' British dishes, perhaps confit duck, buttered mash, red cabbage, Blandford Flyer gravy; there are small plates, sharing plates, sandwiches with a side of fries. ('The breakfast buffet could have been more imaginative, though.') Recently revamped bedrooms vary in size, but each is 'outstandingly decorated' with 'design quirks' like 'vintage luggage; interesting portraits; antique, or faux-antique, lamps'. Light sleepers, choose wisely: there may be noise from the pub across the street. 'Plenty of nice touches in my spacious, stylish room: Spode-lookalike cups, fine teas, a Roberts radio, Travelman Short Stories by the bedside.' (Richard Osborne)

West Street
Blandford Forum
DT11 7AJ

T: 01258 456626
E: crownhotel.blandford@
   hall-woodhouse.co.uk
W: crownhotelblandford.co.uk

BEDROOMS: 27. Some suitable for disabled.
OPEN: all year.
FACILITIES: lift, bar, common room, restaurant, function suite, free Wi-Fi, in-room smart TV (Freeview), civil wedding licence, garden terrace.
BACKGROUND MUSIC: none.
LOCATION: edge of town centre, 1 min. from High Street.
CHILDREN: all ages welcomed.
DOGS: allowed in some bedrooms, not in restaurant.
CREDIT CARDS: Amex, MasterCard, Visa.
PRICES: [2017] per room B&B £80–£180. À la carte £40.

BLEDINGTON Gloucestershire

Map 3:D6

THE KING'S HEAD INN

'Completely serene', Nicola and Archie Orr-Ewing's 'sweet Cotswold-stone inn' stands on the village green, a brook trickling by – here's 'a good spot for reading in sunny weather'. Within the honey-hued walls, 'ancient wooden beams and old wood settles give the place an authentic feel as a cosy country getaway', Guide inspectors found in 2017. Beyond the 'relaxed bar' ('sipping a pre-dinner cocktail by the large open fireplace was ideal'), the restaurant serves Giles Lee's 'excellent menu' of pub classics and more inventive dishes. 'The venison carpaccio was particularly worthy of praise; the cod fillet, with gnocchi and brown shrimp, came apart in succulent flakes.' Cottage-style bedrooms are above the inn or set on the rear courtyard. 'Our elegant annexe room was well lit and warm, with a firm, comfy bed, and Persian rugs covering the stone-flagged floor. In the small, well-finished bathroom: an efficient shower; large bottles of locally made natural bath products.' Wake to an 'outstanding' breakfast ('you could taste the freshness of the eggs'), then pull your boots on: a network of paths leads to neighbouring villages. The Orr-Ewings also manage the Swan Inn, Swinbrook (see entry).

The Green
Bledington
OX7 6XQ

T: 01608 658365
F: 01608 658902
E: info@kingsheadinn.net
W: www.thekingsheadinn.net

BEDROOMS: 12. 6 in annexe, some on ground floor.
OPEN: all year except 25/26 Dec.
FACILITIES: bar, restaurant, courtyard, free Wi-Fi, in-room TV, children's play area, unsuitable for disabled.
BACKGROUND MUSIC: none.
LOCATION: on village green.
CHILDREN: all ages welcomed.
DOGS: not allowed in bedrooms, restaurant.
CREDIT CARDS: MasterCard, Visa.
PRICES: [2017] per room B&B £100–£130. À la carte £32. 1-night bookings refused Sat.

BORROWDALE Cumbria

Map 4: inset C2

LEATHES HEAD HOTEL   **NEW**

'Beautiful views' of the Borrowdale valley and
fells – and the 'lovely walks' to go with them –
surround this 'enjoyable hotel' near Derwent
Water. Jamie Adamson and Jane Cleary
manage a team of 'friendly, accommodating and
professional staff', report Guide correspondents
this year. Parasols open on the 'pretty terrace' in
sunshine; inside the 'smart, well-kept' former
country house, sofas are gathered around the
fireplace in the lounge. 'Some might consider
the decor a little old-fashioned in parts', but
the recently renovated oak and slate bar is
'very "boutique hotel"' – and just the spot for
sampling local gin. Individually styled bedrooms
in varying sizes overlook countryside or garden.
'Our room was of a good size, with a brand-new
bathroom.' Ask for a window seat at dinner,
all the better to soak up the 'superb setting'
over chef Noel Breaks's 'innovative, delicious'
dishes. 'The food was a major delight, with
some of the best puddings we've ever eaten.'
Cumbrian produce is showcased: sample,
perhaps, asparagus, sourdough, crispy egg yolk,
mushroom ketchup; duck, pickled turnip, spelt,
artichoke, candied endive. 'Breakfast was very
good, too.' (Sarah Tier)

Keswick
Borrowdale
CA12 5UY

T: 01768 777247
F: 01768 777363
E: reservations@leatheshead.co.uk
W: www.leatheshead.co.uk

BEDROOMS: 11. Some on ground
floor, 1 suitable for disabled.
OPEN: Mar–end Nov.
FACILITIES: lounge, conservatory, bar,
dining room, free Wi-Fi, in-room
TV (Freeview), drying room,
terrace, 3-acre grounds.
BACKGROUND MUSIC: in bar and
dining room.
LOCATION: 4½ miles S of Keswick.
CHILDREN: not under 18.
DOGS: not allowed.
CREDIT CARDS: MasterCard, Visa.
PRICES: [2017] per room B&B
£145–£200, D,B&B £170–£300. Set
dinner £39.50.

BOSCASTLE Cornwall

Map 1:C3

THE OLD RECTORY

Literary pilgrims follow narrow single-track lanes to this Victorian rectory in a 'magical setting' in the Valency valley, where Thomas Hardy met and courted his first wife, Emma Gifford. It is run as a B&B by Sally and Chris Searle, whose kindness is 'beyond praise'. The house stands in large gardens, 'alive with birds and butterflies'; inside, there are cottage-style bedrooms, and flowers freshly cut from the grounds. Modest, homely, each room has its own charm: Emma's Room has armchairs by the window overlooking the lower lawn and woodland garden; dog-friendly Old Stables, with a log-burner and pull-out sofa bed, is ideal for a family. Organic fruit and vegetables find their way from kitchen garden to table, along with eggs from the house's hens and honey from the hives. At breakfast there are home-produced sausages and bacon, Cornish rarebit, locally smoked fish; supper, served in the restored greenhouse by arrangement, is 'delicious'. On the daily-changing menu, perhaps: chicken and mushroom pie; stuffed Mediterranean vegetables. Hardy came to restore St Juliot's church, 'three fields away, by footpath'; the sea is within reach.

St Juliot
Boscastle
PL35 0BT

T: 01840 250225
F: 01840 250225
E: sally@stjuliot.com
W: www.stjuliot.com

BEDROOMS: 4. 1 in stables (connected to house via conservatory).
OPEN: normally Feb–end Oct, 'but please check'.
FACILITIES: sitting room, breakfast room, conservatory, free Wi-Fi, in-room TV (Freeview), 3-acre garden (croquet lawn, 'lookout', walled kitchen garden), unsuitable for disabled.
BACKGROUND MUSIC: none.
LOCATION: 2 miles NE of Boscastle.
CHILDREN: not under 12.
DOGS: up to 2 allowed, only in stable room (£10 per stay).
CREDIT CARDS: MasterCard, Visa.
PRICES: [2017] per room B&B £100–£115 (single-occupancy discount 10%–20%). 2-course dinner (by arrangement; bring your own bottle) £17.50. 1-night bookings refused weekends and busy periods.

BOSHAM Sussex

Map 2:E3

THE MILLSTREAM

A stone footbridge leads across a rushing stream to the Wild family's traditional hotel, its front garden, in warm weather, dotted with tables for afternoon tea in the sunshine. In a 'lovely location' in a pretty village of thatched cottages near Chichester harbour, this 'friendly, relaxing' place has a 'nice, cosy atmosphere' that attracts many return guests. 'The combination of good food, comfy rooms and fabulous walks by the bay is impressive. And the long-standing staff always extend an enthusiastic welcome,' says a Guide reader in 2017. The building grew from three 17th-century workmen's cottages; individually styled bedrooms vary in size. Ask for one of the refurbished rooms: many look on to the gardens, or have patio doors opening on to the lawn. Smaller or more spacious, each room is supplied with biscuits, bathrobes, and fresh milk in the fridge. Snacks and casual meals (perhaps duck rillettes; an 'enjoyable' sea bream) are taken in Marwick's brasserie; in the restaurant, Neil Hiskey's modern dishes might include beef fillet, wild mushroom gratin, shallot purée, bone marrow. 'The cooked breakfast is a treat.' (Ian Marshall, Michael Gwinnell, Diana Goodey, Alec Frank)

25% DISCOUNT VOUCHERS

Bosham Lane
Bosham
PO18 8HL

T: 01243 573234
F: 01243 573459
E: info@millstreamhotel.com
W: www.millstreamhotel.com

BEDROOMS: 35. 2 in cottage, 7 on ground floor, 1 suitable for disabled.
OPEN: all year.
FACILITIES: lounge, bar, restaurant (pianist Sat eve), brasserie, conference room, free Wi-Fi, in-room TV (Freeview), civil wedding licence, front lawn (alfresco dining), residents' garden (stream, gazebo).
BACKGROUND MUSIC: all day in bar, lounge and restaurants.
LOCATION: 4 miles W of Chichester.
CHILDREN: all ages welcomed.
DOGS: not allowed.
CREDIT CARDS: MasterCard, Visa.
PRICES: [2017] per room B&B single from £79, double from £135, D,B&B from £174 (for 2 people, 2-night min. stay). À la carte £35. 1-night bookings refused Sat.

BOURTON-ON-THE-HILL Gloucestershire Map 3:D6

THE HORSE AND GROOM

The log fires still burn within the old stone walls, the mismatched furnishings still stand; the vegetable patch continues to push up fresh ingredients for lunch and dinner. This honey-hued Georgian inn is now under new ownership (as part of the Cirrus Inns group), but previous high standards have been maintained. 'We enjoyed good service from the same friendly staff, and the rooms were as we'd remembered. In fact, we had no idea the business had changed hands,' said regular Guide correspondents on a return visit in 2017. 'Comfortable, well-equipped bedrooms' are individually decorated in contemporary country style; one has French doors opening to the garden. (Rear rooms most removed from the main road are quietest.) Eat in one of three dining areas, or find a spot in the large garden on a sunny day: the 'pleasant, knowledgeable' staff bring out 'such good food'. On the 'interesting' pub menu: feta cheese, roasted beetroot, spinach and frisée salad; grilled Tamworth pork sausages and bacon, braised Puy lentils. In the morning, freshly baked croissants still show up at breakfast – 'but now there's brioche as well!' (Jill and Mike Bennett, Michael and Margaret Cross)

Bourton-on-the-Hill
GL56 9AQ

T: 01386 700413
E: enquiries@horseandgroom.info
W: www.horseandgroom.info

BEDROOMS: 5.
OPEN: all year except Christmas/New Year, restaurant closed Sun eve except on bank holiday weekends.
FACILITIES: bar/restaurant, free Wi-Fi, in-room TV (Freeview), 1-acre garden, unsuitable for disabled.
BACKGROUND MUSIC: none.
LOCATION: village centre.
CHILDREN: all ages welcomed.
DOGS: allowed in garden, guide dogs allowed in pub.
CREDIT CARDS: MasterCard, Visa.
PRICES: [2017] per room B&B £110–£185. À la carte £30. 1-night bookings refused weekends.

BOWNESS-ON-WINDERMERE Cumbria Map 4: inset C2

LINDETH FELL

⊘ Previous César winner

Enter through the wood-panelled hall at mid-afternoon to be greeted with a cream tea at this upmarket B&B overlooking Lake Windermere. 'Charming and friendly', the Kennedy family has owned the Edwardian country home for 34 years. With daughters Sheena, Joanna and Kate, matriarch Diana Kennedy runs the show. And what a show it is: take in 'wonderful views over Lakeland scenery' from the large, lush garden; inside, flop into an armchair in one of the spacious lounges, or settle into an individually designed bedroom made homey with sherry and an espresso coffee machine. Local gastropubs and restaurants are within an easy drive, but guests hankering after a lazy evening should pre-order a soup of the day or a supper platter (perhaps with chicken goujons and a country pâté, or a twice-baked cheese soufflé and grilled vegetables) to eat in. Breakfast, with freshly squeezed juice, home-made marmalade and granola, and 'a wide choice' of cooked dishes, is praised. Pack your boots – circular walks start from the doorstep; Bowness is a half-hour's downhill stroll around the lake.

25% DISCOUNT VOUCHERS

Lyth Valley Road
Bowness-on-Windermere
LA23 3JP

T: 01539 443286
E: kennedy@lindethfell.co.uk
W: www.lindethfell.co.uk

BEDROOMS: 14. 1 on ground floor, suitable for disabled.
OPEN: all year except Christmas, Jan.
FACILITIES: 2 lounges, bar, dining room, free Wi-Fi, in-room TV (Freeview), 7-acre grounds (terrace, gardens, croquet, putting, bowls, tarn, fishing permits), complimentary access to local gym, spa and pool, 5 mins' drive away.
BACKGROUND MUSIC: classical music in dining room at breakfast, evenings in bar.
LOCATION: 1 mile S of Bowness on A5074.
CHILDREN: all ages welcomed.
DOGS: only assistance dogs allowed.
CREDIT CARDS: MasterCard, Visa.
PRICES: [2017] per person B&B £66.50–£125. 1-night bookings sometimes refused weekends, bank holidays.

SEE ALSO SHORTLIST

BRADFORD-ON-AVON Wiltshire
Map 2:D1

WOOLLEY GRANGE

'There's lots of room to play and run around' at this 'pretty, rambling manor house' in 'fantastic grounds' on the edge of the Cotswolds. Part of Nigel Chapman's Luxury Family Hotels group, the hotel is run with 'care and empathy, and scores of considerate touches that make it perfect for parents of young children', say trusted Guide correspondents this year. In the 'cosy sitting rooms' in the Jacobean mansion, there are wood fires, squashy sofas, a hidden glockenspiel, books, magazines and Rex, the resident King Charles spaniel. The staff are 'laid-back and relaxed', the children, 'thrilled'. Individually styled bedrooms come in scores of different configurations. 'Ours, in the old laundry, was ideal for our family, with a large bed downstairs and two camp beds in the living room upstairs.' Flexible meal options include children's high teas, early family suppers, and grown-up candlelit dinners. 'The food was good – simple and hearty – but the service, though friendly, could have been sharper (long waits).' Read the morning newsletter over an 'excellent breakfast' to discover the adventures dreamed up for the day ahead.

Woolley Green
Bradford-on-Avon
BA15 1TX

T: 01225 864705
E: info@woolleygrangehotel.co.uk
W: www.woolleygrangehotel.co.uk

BEDROOMS: 25. 11 in annexes, 2 on ground floor, 1 suitable for disabled.
OPEN: all year.
FACILITIES: 2 drawing rooms, 2 restaurants, cinema, meeting rooms, free Wi-Fi, in-room TV (Freeview), crèche, play room, spa, heated indoor and outdoor swimming pools (12 by 5 metres), civil wedding licence, 14-acre grounds (kitchen garden, children's play areas).
BACKGROUND MUSIC: all day in restaurants.
LOCATION: 1 mile NE of Bradford-on-Avon, 8½ miles SE of Bath.
CHILDREN: all ages welcomed.
DOGS: not allowed in restaurants.
CREDIT CARDS: Amex, MasterCard, Visa.
PRICES: [2017] per room B&B £120–£580, D,B&B £190–£650. À la carte £40. 1-night bookings sometimes refused.

SEE ALSO SHORTLIST

BRAITHWAITE Cumbria

Map 4: inset C2

THE COTTAGE IN THE WOOD

'Perfectly positioned' on Whinlatter Pass, and with 'stunning views' towards Skiddaw from the curving conservatory restaurant, Kath and Liam Berney's restaurant-with-rooms is surrounded by England's only true mountain forest. Rich Collingwood is the new chef, but the kitchen's principles haven't changed: the daily menus, particularly the Cumbria-themed tasting menus, are based on seasonal produce from sea, shore, woodland, fell and farm. Among the modern dishes: asparagus, morels, wild garlic, quail's egg; Herdwick hogget, purple sprouting broccoli, merguez. Five cosy bedrooms in the oldest part of the house are small, 'but then, this is a cottage-style 17th-century coaching inn'. Guests wanting more space to stretch out could book one of the larger mountain-view rooms, which have a whirlpool bath and separate shower in the bathroom, or the garden room, spacious enough for a seating area with a leather sofa. Wake to birdsong, then breakfast on award-winning Waberthwaite sausages, Craster kippers or a free-range-egg omelette with forest mushrooms. The market town of Keswick, on Derwentwater, is a short, scenic drive away. (Richard Osborne, ST, and others)

Magic Hill
Whinlatter Forest
Braithwaite
CA12 5TW

T: 017687 78409
E: relax@thecottageinthewood.co.uk
W: www.thecottageinthewood.co.uk

BEDROOMS: 9. 1 in the garden with separate entrance.
OPEN: all year except 25/26 Dec, 2nd and 3rd week Jan, restaurant closed Mon.
FACILITIES: lounge, restaurant, free Wi-Fi, in-room TV (Freeview), drying room, secure bicycle storage, terraced garden, 2 acres of woodland, only restaurant suitable for disabled.
BACKGROUND MUSIC: none.
LOCATION: 5 miles NW of Keswick.
CHILDREN: not under 10.
DOGS: not allowed.
CREDIT CARDS: MasterCard, Visa.
PRICES: [2017] per room B&B £110–£205. Set menu £45, tasting menus £55–£65. 1-night bookings refused weekends.

BRAMPTON Cumbria

Map 4:B3

FARLAM HALL

'A quintessential country house hotel.' The Quinion family's creeper-covered manor house in mature grounds 'combines the familiar features and decor of an earlier age with exceptional service', writes a Guide reader, a frequent guest, in 2017. 'Barry Quinion, his wife, Lynne, and sister, Helen, are true innkeepers who take pride in their hotel. Barry presides over the kitchen, producing wonderful food; Helen and Lynne welcome guests as long-lost friends returning home.' Traditionally furnished sitting rooms are filled with the comforts of a cherished private house: paintings, wide sofas, a careful selection of ornaments. Generously sized bedrooms, each different, have comfy seating and garden views. Tall windows in the dining room look over lawns to an ornamental lake. A single dinner sitting, at 8 pm, brings a daily-changing menu of 'beautifully cooked and presented' dishes, perhaps smoked chicken, wild mushroom and spring onion risotto, white truffle; wild sea bass fillet, crushed new potatoes, green olives, pesto. Breakfast – a sit-down affair – offers plenty of choice, from half a grapefruit to the full English, via kippers, smoked salmon and omelettes. (Chris Savory)

25% DISCOUNT VOUCHERS

Hallbankgate
Brampton
CA8 2NG

T: 01697 746234
F: 01697 746683
E: farlam@farlamhall.co.uk
W: www.farlamhall.co.uk

BEDROOMS: 12. 2 on ground floor, 1 in stables.
OPEN: all year except 24–31 Dec (restaurant open Christmas eve), 7–25 Jan.
FACILITIES: 2 lounges, restaurant, free Wi-Fi, in-room TV (Freeview), civil wedding licence, 6-acre grounds, unsuitable for disabled.
BACKGROUND MUSIC: none.
LOCATION: on A689, 2½ miles SE of Brampton (not in Farlam village).
CHILDREN: not under 5.
DOGS: allowed in bedrooms (not unattended), not in restaurant.
CREDIT CARDS: Amex, MasterCard, Visa.
PRICES: [2017] per room B&B £216–£276, D,B&B £310–£370. Set dinner £49.50. 1-night bookings sometimes refused.

BRANCASTER STAITHE Norfolk

Map 2:A5

THE WHITE HORSE

Previous César winner

Wide, tranquil views of salt marshes add to
the relaxing atmosphere at the Nye family's
'first-rate' Norfolk inn. 'Cheerful, pleasingly
confident' staff, 'modern, well-equipped'
rooms and 'tasty, varied' menus seal the deal.
In the main building and sedum-roofed garden
annexe, each bedroom is different: some rooms
suit a family, others, with a private terrace
leading to the Coastal Path at the bottom of
the garden, are ideal for outdoorsy sorts. 'Our
spacious room at the top had great views over
the marshes; a large bed even more comfortable
than the one we have at home. Additional
pluses: a flask of fresh milk; a quality coffee
machine.' 'Splendid seafood meals' are served
in the conservatory restaurant – Brancaster
oysters get a special mention – but chef Fran
Hartshorne's vegetarian dishes are worth paying
attention to, perhaps wild garlic tart; roast
aubergine, bulgur wheat ('all good – the first
time I'd ordered a veggie meal!'). Go out at low
tide to watch the fishermen gathering mussels
and oysters; 'excellent coastal walks' beckon
beyond. (PA, ML, I and VA)

Main Road
Brancaster Staithe
PE31 8BY

T: 01485 210262
F: 01485 210930
E: reception@whitehorsebrancaster.
co.uk
W: www.whitehorsebrancaster.co.uk

BEDROOMS: 15. 8 on ground floor in
annexe, 1 suitable for disabled.
OPEN: all year.
FACILITIES: open-plan lounge areas,
bar, conservatory restaurant, dining
room, free Wi-Fi, in-room TV
(Freeview), ½-acre garden (covered
sunken garden), harbour sailing.
BACKGROUND MUSIC: 'subtle' in
restaurant.
LOCATION: centre of village just E of
Brancaster.
CHILDREN: all ages welcomed.
DOGS: allowed in garden rooms (£10
per night), bar.
CREDIT CARDS: MasterCard, Visa.
PRICES: [2017] per room B&B
£110–£240, D,B&B (Sun–Thurs in
low season only, except bank hols
and school hols) £160–£240. À la
carte £29.

BRIGHTON Sussex

Map 2:E4

ARTIST RESIDENCE BRIGHTON

'Laid-back and bohemian', Charlotte and Justin Salisbury's hip town house hotel brings a youthful air to a street of Regency terraces. The 'eye-catching' decor puts vintage pieces, industrial fittings, found objects and 'a range of fun art' to good use: 'There was a studenty feel, which we liked.' The cocktail bar and relaxed café attract locals (and not just for the ping-pong table). In the restaurant ('very nice, with bare bricks and distressed wood'), a choice of modern set menus might include such briefly described dishes as mackerel, cauliflower, capers; mushroom, miso, marjoram. Bedrooms, several with sea views, continue the freewheeling attitude. Many rooms are decorated with artists' prints; others were decorated by the artists themselves. 'Our room, with a comfy double bed, had plenty of nice touches: Anglepoise bedside lamps, a pink TV, a travel trunk tipped on its side to serve as a wardrobe. The compact, shabby-chic bathroom was well thought out, with piping-hot water and a deep bath.' Wake to a 'good' breakfast, with home-made smoky beans, perhaps, or a stack of pancakes. (David Berry, and others)

33 Regency Square
Brighton
BN1 2GG

T: 01273 324302
E: brighton@artistresidence.co.uk
W: www.artistresidence.co.uk

BEDROOMS: 23.
OPEN: all year, restaurant closed for 3 days over Christmas.
FACILITIES: lift, lounge, café, restaurant, ping-pong/meeting room, free Wi-Fi, in-room TV (Freeview), unsuitable for disabled.
BACKGROUND MUSIC: in public areas.
LOCATION: town centre.
CHILDREN: not under 16.
DOGS: not allowed.
CREDIT CARDS: Amex, MasterCard, Visa.
PRICES: [2017] per room B&B £99–£310. 1-night bookings refused at weekends.

SEE ALSO SHORTLIST

BRIGHTON Sussex

Map 2:E4

DRAKES NEW

At dusk, the lights come on over Brighton Pier – a view best taken in, perhaps, from a freestanding bath by floor-to-ceiling windows in the bedrooms of this stylish boutique hotel. 'It may be expensive, but it's exquisite,' says a Guide correspondent this year, who found the youthful place, which spans two Georgian town houses, 'on top form'. Order a cocktail at any time of day in the small, sleek bar facing the sea. In the evening, though the town may have plenty to entice, stay in for dinner: 'The restaurant is the best in Brighton,' a reader reports. Served in the dining room on the lower ground floor, chef Andy Vitez's modern dishes might include pan-fried scallops, Sussex Mangalitza lardo, pea velouté, scallop roe sabayon; beef fillet, bone marrow cappuccino, wasabi pomme purée, spinach. Afterwards, spend the night in one of the modern bedrooms, each supplied with magazines, ground coffee, robes and slippers. The sultriest are the most spacious (and have that in-room bath with those sea views), but some of the smaller bedrooms share the watery vista – and two, up four flights of stairs, have a private balcony so you can breathe in the sea air, too. (David Berry)

43–44 Marine Parade
Brighton
BN2 1PE

T: 01273 696934
F: 01273 684805
E: info@drakesofbrighton.com
W: www.drakesofbrighton.com

BEDROOMS: 20.
OPEN: all year.
FACILITIES: lounge/bar, restaurant, meeting/private dining room, free Wi-Fi, in-room TV (Sky), civil wedding licence, off-road parking, unsuitable for disabled.
BACKGROUND MUSIC: in bar and restaurant.
LOCATION: ½ mile from centre, on seafront.
CHILDREN: older children welcomed, 'but we are primarily a couples-only hotel'.
DOGS: not allowed.
CREDIT CARDS: Amex, MasterCard, Visa.
PRICES: [2017] room £160–£360. Breakfast £8.50–£15, tasting menu £60, à la carte £45. 2-night min. stay at weekends.

SEE ALSO SHORTLIST

BRISTOL

Map 1:B6

BROOKS GUESTHOUSE

In 'a great location' in the old city centre, a stroll from harbourside restaurants, Carla and Andrew Brooks have converted a 1960s office block into a contemporary B&B with a difference. 'Beautifully sleek and shiny' Airstream camper vans are parked on the AstroTurfed roof. Each has controllable heating, a hospitality tray and retro radio, a small bathroom and bird's-eye views over the town: 'very clever and cool.' (There's birdsong, too – guests may wake to gulls calling.) 'We stayed with our children in the largest caravan, comfortably done up with a double bed and two small singles. In the bathroom were a strong shower and lots of fluffy towels.' Visitors looking for more conventional accommodation find it in neat, modern bedrooms below. Mornings, an 'excellent breakfast' is taken in the 'friendly-feeling' open-plan kitchen. Besides organic yogurts, home-made muesli and granola, and 'lovely jams, marmalade and juices', 'great cooked options' (perhaps French toast, egg dishes, a full English) are 'efficiently served'. 'Grab-and-go' breakfasts are a bonus – ask for a smoked salmon bagel or a sausage sandwich before rushing off.

Exchange Avenue
St Nicholas Market
Bristol
BS1 1UB

T: 0117 930 0066
F: 0117 929 9489
E: info@brooksguesthousebristol.com
W: www.brooksguesthousebristol.com

BEDROOMS: 27. 4 in Airstream caravans on roof, 1 on ground floor suitable for disabled.
OPEN: all year except 23–27 Dec.
FACILITIES: lounge/breakfast room, free Wi-Fi, in-room TV (Freeview), courtyard garden.
BACKGROUND MUSIC: contemporary in lounge and breakfast area.
LOCATION: central, next to St Nicholas Market.
CHILDREN: all ages welcomed.
DOGS: not allowed.
CREDIT CARDS: MasterCard, Visa.
PRICES: [2017] per room B&B £80–£149.

SEE ALSO SHORTLIST

BRISTOL

Map 1:B6

NUMBER THIRTY EIGHT CLIFTON

♛ Previous César winner

In a popular neighbourhood with 'plenty of interesting local amenities' – the Saturday farmers' market, just down the hill, gives a fine flavour of the place – this upmarket B&B is 'highly recommended' by Guide readers. 'Pleasing and excellently located', it is liked for its 'well-appointed bedrooms' and 'commendable breakfasts'. It is owned by Adam Dorrien-Smith. 'It seems popular with regular guests on business trips, and it's easy to see why.' A cosy sitting room is just right for coffees and cream teas; contemporary artworks (a Leaper on the staircase, a Hockney in the bathroom) catch the eye. Bedrooms vary in size. Pick a suite overlooking parkland, or a 'very quiet' smaller rear bedroom with 'superb views over the rooftops of Clifton'; in every case, rooms are supplied with high-end toiletries and waffle dressing gowns. The house is unstaffed after 8 pm, but the neighbourhood's many restaurants ('the hotel provides a useful list') are 'an easy walk away'. In the morning, breakfast, with 'super-fresh croissants' and 'plenty of fresh fruit', is praised. (JP, and others)

38 Upper Belgrave Road
Clifton
Bristol
BS8 2XN

T: 0117 946 6905
E: info@number38clifton.com
W: www.number38clifton.com

BEDROOMS: 9.
OPEN: all year.
FACILITIES: lounge, breakfast room, free Wi-Fi, in-room TV (Freeview), terrace, limited number of parking permits on request, unsuitable for disabled.
BACKGROUND MUSIC: in public areas.
LOCATION: 2½ miles from city centre.
CHILDREN: not under 12.
DOGS: not allowed.
CREDIT CARDS: all major cards.
PRICES: [2017] per room B&B £115–£235.

SEE ALSO SHORTLIST

BROADWAY Worcestershire

THE BROADWAY HOTEL

Behind a facade of half-timbering and honeyed stone, this 'friendly, professionally run' hotel by the village green 'successfully combines an imaginative, glossy-magazine look with olde-worlde Cotswold charm'. Part of the Cotswold Inns and Hotels group, it pleased Guide inspectors in 2017 with its 'high standards of housekeeping and service'. The double-height Jockey bar has an open fireplace and plenty of seating; 'in fine weather, many guests congregate for drinks and snacks by the yew trees in the garden – a social hub for the smarter set'. Bedrooms are styled to an equestrian theme (Cheltenham Racecourse is not far). 'Our room was reached via creaky stairs and through numerous doors. All was smart and well thought out, if not luxurious – sensible lighting, adequate seating and storage space. A drawback: the tiny en suite. But we forgave some quirks on the grounds of charming authenticity.' Dine on 'fairly elaborate' dishes in the 'voguish brasserie' – perhaps saddle of local rabbit, pistachio farce, Iberico ham, pickled mushrooms; in the morning, an 'adequate buffet', with 'tempting bread', precedes eggs Florentine, Cotswold cheeses and more.

The Green
Broadway
WR12 7AA

T: 01386 852401
F: 01386 853879
E: info@broadwayhotel.info
W: www.cotswold-inns-hotels.
co.uk/the-broadway-hotel

BEDROOMS: 19. 1 on ground floor, 1-bed cottage a 2-min. walk away.
OPEN: all year.
FACILITIES: sitting room, bar, brasserie, free Wi-Fi, in-room TV (Freeview), garden.
BACKGROUND MUSIC: occasionally in public areas.
LOCATION: village centre, 'best to request a parking space before you arrive, especially in summer'.
CHILDREN: all ages welcomed.
DOGS: well-behaved dogs allowed.
CREDIT CARDS: Amex, MasterCard, Visa.
PRICES: [2017] per room B&B from £190, D,B&B from £258. À la carte £38.

SEE ALSO SHORTLIST

BROADWAY Worcestershire

Map 3:D6

DORMY HOUSE

Countryside chic fills this 17th-century farmhouse on a ridge above vast fields beyond the Cotswold village. 'An enjoyable place' with 'charming, helpful staff', it has been owned by the Sorensen family for more than 40 years. Large vases of flowers in the public areas bring the outside in; there are open fires, stone walls, a 'very special spa', deep sofas and the glossy magazines to read on them. Children are made welcome, too: 'Three generations of our family felt well taken care of.' From snug, country-cottage-style rooms to spacious contemporary suites, bedrooms are 'comfortable and relaxing'; all have an espresso machine, 'fancy teas', biscuits, bathrobes and slippers. Eat casually in the Potting Shed, or sample chef Ryan Swift's menus in the Garden Room facing the lawn – 'the food is very good', confirms a Guide reader in 2017. Typical offerings: stone bass, hand-rolled macaroni, coastal herbs; Tamworth pig, apple, black pudding, Cotswold cider. 'We thought the tasting menu and wine match good value. A gripe: the restaurants' popularity sometimes leads to slow service.' At the leisurely breakfast: 'first-class' cooked dishes; a 'memorable' buffet.

Willersey Hill
Broadway
WR12 7LF

T: 01386 852711
E: reservations@dormyhouse.co.uk
W: dormyhouse.co.uk

BEDROOMS: 38. 8 in Danish Court, 5 in Lavender Lodge, 2 suitable for disabled.
OPEN: all year.
FACILITIES: 4 lounges, Garden Room and Potting Shed restaurants, free Wi-Fi, in-room TV, civil wedding licence (for pagoda in garden), gardens, spa (16-metre indoor swimming pool, gym, treatment rooms).
BACKGROUND MUSIC: 'laid-back' in public areas.
LOCATION: 1½ miles E of Broadway.
CHILDREN: all ages welcomed.
DOGS: allowed in 4 bedrooms, lounges, not in restaurants.
CREDIT CARDS: Amex, MasterCard, Visa.
PRICES: [2017] per room B&B £255–£575. Set menu (Garden Room) £49, à la carte (Potting Shed) £35. 1-night bookings sometimes refused.

SEE ALSO SHORTLIST

BROADWAY Worcestershire

Map 3:D6

RUSSELL'S

In a village known as the 'jewel of the Cotswolds', Andrew and Gaynor Riley's restaurant-with-rooms occupies Sir Gordon Russell's former furniture showroom facing the grass-fringed, chestnut-shaded 'broad way'. The English designer brought together a craftsman's values with a modern aesthetic – a quality that has carried through to this more contemporary affair. Within the 17th-century mellow-stone building, the bedrooms – 'most of them special in their own way' – marry beams and joists with air conditioning, a modern bathroom, all the expected technology. Each room is supplied with bathrobes and smart toiletries; superior rooms also have a comfortable seating area. Dine on the front terrace or in the restaurant, where chef Neil Clarke wins praise for his 'excellent' modern cooking, perhaps spiced carrot and coconut soup; whole lemon sole, salsa verde, saffron potatoes. If you fancy a fish fry, the Rileys' 'delicious, good-value' chippy nearby gets the thumbs up. Breakfast, 'cooked accurately and well', is served in the front of the restaurant, 'where the view across the High Street and the village green launches one nicely into each new day'. (T and SM, CR)

The Green
20 High Street
Broadway
WR12 7DT

T: 01386 853555
F: 01386 853964
E: info@russellsofbroadway.co.uk
W: www.russellsofbroadway.co.uk

BEDROOMS: 7. 3 in adjoining building, 2 on ground floor.
OPEN: all year, restaurant closed Sun night and bank holiday Mon.
FACILITIES: residents' lounge, bar, restaurant, private dining room, free Wi-Fi, in-room TV (Freeview), patio (heating, meal service), unsuitable for disabled.
BACKGROUND MUSIC: in restaurant.
LOCATION: village centre.
CHILDREN: all ages welcomed.
DOGS: allowed in 2 bedrooms, public rooms.
CREDIT CARDS: Amex, MasterCard, Visa.
PRICES: [2017] per room B&B £130–£300. Set dinner (Mon–Fri) £24, à la carte £45. 1-night bookings refused weekends.

SEE ALSO SHORTLIST

BROCKENHURST Hampshire

Map 2:E2

THE PIG

The first in the parcel of Pigs, sunning itself in the New Forest, this 'relaxed, gorgeously rustic' hotel remains a favourite of Guide readers. 'You're positively encouraged to chill out over books, drinks and board games in the stunning public rooms. And the staff are flawless – friendly and exceptionally well trained.' Guests who stayed over Christmas had 'a perfect stay'. 'There was a real sense of festivity. With open fires burning in every lounge, the place couldn't have been more enticing.' Bedrooms of varying sizes are 'beautifully warm and cosy'. 'The huge bed in our forest cabin was the comfiest we've slept in. We enjoyed our own wood-burning stove, and the window-side roll-top bath looking into the woods.' In the 'attractive, buzzy' conservatory restaurant, forager and kitchen gardener work with the chefs to create an 'exceptional, adventurous' menu. 'We were blown away by the food, most notably a pigeon dish with dauphinoise potatoes and Russet apples, and pig's cheeks with girolles.' Bring the litter: 'It's clearly a family destination, which adds to the jovial atmosphere. We've booked to come back with the new baby!' (Anna and Bill Brewer)

Beaulieu Road
Brockenhurst
SO42 7QL

T: 01590 622354
E: reservations@thepighotel.com
W: www.thepighotel.com

BEDROOMS: 31. 10 in stable block (100 yds), some on ground floor, 2 lodges and a cabin in the garden.
OPEN: all year.
FACILITIES: lounge, library, bar, restaurant, free Wi-Fi, in-room TV (Freeview), civil wedding licence, Potting Shed spa, kitchen garden, 6-acre grounds.
BACKGROUND MUSIC: in public areas.
LOCATION: 1 mile E of Brockenhurst village.
CHILDREN: all ages welcomed.
DOGS: not allowed.
CREDIT CARDS: Amex, MasterCard, Visa.
PRICES: [2017] room £155–£420. Breakfast £10–£15, à la carte £35. 1-night bookings refused at weekends, Christmas, New Year.

SEE ALSO SHORTLIST

BRYHER Isles of Scilly

Map 1: inset C1

HELL BAY HOTEL

♔ Previous César winner

Hardly hellish, Robert Dorrien-Smith's island hotel, perky in a protected cove in the Atlantic Ocean, is 'well worth the trip'. 'The location is simply stunning, possibly the best and most isolated that we've ever stayed in,' write Guide readers this year. 'We had morning cups of tea in bed, gazing at the crashing Atlantic waves – a perfect start to the day.' This is a 'friendly place': 'the staff are charming and thorough, and do everything with a smile'.Bedrooms are spread out among a cluster of clapboard cottages, some with a balcony and sea views, all well conceived and decorated in breezy coastal shades. A short walk through 'beautifully tended' gardens leads to the restaurant, where chef Richard Kearsley turns out 'innovative, consistently excellent' dishes on a daily-changing menu. 'How the chef does this on a tiny island that gets cut off in bad weather, heaven knows, but he does.' The hotel's 'unrivalled' collection of Cornish art is not to be missed, nor is the summertime Crab Shack, where just three seafood dishes are served convivially and communally. 'Such fun, really different – one of the highlights of our trip.' (Fiona Foster, BW)

Bryher
TR23 0PR

T: 01720 422947
F: 01720 423004
E: contactus@hellbay.co.uk
W: www.hellbay.co.uk

BEDROOMS: 25 suites. In 5 buildings, some on ground floor, 1 suitable for disabled.
OPEN: mid-Mar–mid-Oct.
FACILITIES: lounge, games room, bar, 2 dining rooms, free Wi-Fi, in-room TV (Freeview), gym, sauna, large grounds (heated swimming pool, 15 by 10 metres, children's playground, par-3 golf course), beach 75 yds.
BACKGROUND MUSIC: none.
LOCATION: W coast of island, boat from St Mary's (reached by boat/plane from mainland).
CHILDREN: all ages welcomed.
DOGS: allowed (charge), not in public rooms.
CREDIT CARDS: MasterCard, Visa.
PRICES: [2017] per person B&B £95–£310, D,B&B £135–£350. Set dinner £45, à la carte bar menu £33.

BUDE Cornwall

THE BEACH

25% DISCOUNT VOUCHERS

Exchange lace-ups for flip-flops and train times for tidal tables at this popular surfing spot on the Cornish coast. Returning guests this year were wowed by the breezy, modern public spaces, and owners Susie and Will Daniel's 'innovative style'. A zinc-topped bar, blond wood furniture and muted colours set a cool New England air that carries through to the individually decorated bedrooms. (Ask for a room with a private terrace or Juliet balcony to make the most of the broad beachy views.) The upbeat bar and decked terrace overlooking the fine sandy beach are just right for a cocktail or two; in the restaurant, chef Joe Simmonds's contemporary menu includes the products of Cornish land and sea, perhaps sea trout, salsify chips, pickled samphire, smoked mussel fritters. 'On a Friday evening, we enjoyed live music over dinner. The service is excellent; every member of staff was helpful, pleasant, eager to please.' In the morning, breakfast on yogurts, muffins, fresh fruit salads; a selection of smoothies. 'The highlight of breakfast was making our own toast on a toaster conveyor belt!' (Frank G Millen)

Summerleaze Crescent
Bude
EX23 8HJ

T: 01288 389800
F: 01288 389820
E: enquiries@thebeachatbude.co.uk
W: www.thebeachatbude.co.uk

BEDROOMS: 16. 1 on ground floor.
OPEN: all year except Christmas.
FACILITIES: lift, 2 bars, lounge area, restaurant, free Wi-Fi, in-room TV (Freeview), terrace, unsuitable for disabled.
BACKGROUND MUSIC: all day in public areas.
LOCATION: above Summerleaze beach.
CHILDREN: all ages welcomed.
DOGS: not allowed.
CREDIT CARDS: Amex, MasterCard, Visa.
PRICES: [2017] per room B&B £150–£250, D,B&B £207–£307. À la carte £28.50.

BURFORD Oxfordshire

Map 3:D6

THE LAMB INN   NEW

'Here's a taste of Cotswold heritage: mullioned windows, beamed ceilings, flagstone floors, the sweet smell of wood smoke.' Guide inspectors this year were impressed by this 'well-managed hotel with a wonderful atmosphere'. 'Full marks, too, for the attentive staff.' Part of the small Cotswold Inns and Hotels group, the 18th-century inn has a series of log fire-warmed lounges that are just the spot for board games, afternoon teas and pre-dinner drinks. Modern, country-style bedrooms are decorated with antique furnishings. 'Our well-proportioned ground-floor room had striking wallpaper, a huge bed, a compact bathroom. A capsule coffee machine and home-made cookies had been supplied; shame about the captive hangers. The windows faced a pavement so we had to draw the curtains – fine in November, but I'd ask to be put upstairs in the summer.' Eat informally in the walled garden, lounges or bar; in the restaurant, 'beautifully presented' modern dishes might include 'stand-out sea bream' and 'a memorable lobster ravioli'. At breakfast: freshly squeezed orange and grapefruit juices, a tasty fruit compote, 'excellent bacon and sausage'. (Mary Coles, and others)

Sheep Street
Burford
OX18 4LR

T: 01993 823155
F: 01993 822228
E: info@lambinn-burford.co.uk
W: www.cotswold-inns-hotels.
   co.uk/lamb

BEDROOMS: 17. 1 with private garden.
OPEN: all year.
FACILITIES: 2 lounges, bar, restaurant, free Wi-Fi, in-room TV (Freeview), courtyard, ½-acre walled garden, unsuitable for disabled.
BACKGROUND MUSIC: none.
LOCATION: 500 yds from High Street.
CHILDREN: all ages welcomed.
DOGS: allowed in some bedrooms, bar, lounges, not in restaurant.
CREDIT CARDS: Amex, MasterCard, Visa.
PRICES: [2017] per room B&B £130–£300, D,B&B from £177. Set menu (lunch) £29.50, à la carte £45.

SEE ALSO SHORTLIST

BURRINGTON Devon

Map 1:C4

NORTHCOTE MANOR

In springtime, wisteria festoons Jean-Pierre Mifsud's 18th-century manor house, an 'oasis of tranquillity' set amid orchards and woodlands in the Taw valley. The atmosphere is one of 'peace, comfort and relaxation' – 'yet it's reasonably close to places of interest for active days'. There are oriental rugs on wood floors, and books to borrow by the log-burning stove; larky murals in the drawing room and restaurant add personality. Throughout, 'universally charming staff make you feel welcome'. Overlooking the terrace and garden, bedrooms vary in size. Each room has individual (traditional or more modern) style, and every one is supplied with 'all the necessities', plus mints, fresh fruit and home-made shortbread. At dinner, sample chef Richie Herkes's 'excellent' three-course menu (including, perhaps, crab cakes, smoked salmon boudin, tomato concassé; loin of Ryeland Mendip lamb, dauphinoise potatoes, asparagus) or go for broke: 'the unmissable tasting menu, the best we've had, is very special for lovers of fine food'. In Wales, the owner's Lake, Llangammarch Wells (see entry), shares the same cosseting feel. (MC)

Burrington
EX37 9LZ

T: 01769 560501
F: 01769 560770
E: rest@northcotemanor.co.uk
W: www.northcotemanor.co.uk

BEDROOMS: 16. 5 in extension, 1 suitable for disabled.
OPEN: all year.
FACILITIES: 2 lounges, bar, 2 restaurants, free Wi-Fi, in-room TV (Freeview), civil wedding licence, 20-acre grounds.
BACKGROUND MUSIC: classical in public areas after midday.
LOCATION: 3 miles S of Umberleigh.
CHILDREN: all ages welcomed, no under-9s in restaurant in evening (early teas for children).
DOGS: allowed in some bedrooms, not in 1 lounge or restaurant.
CREDIT CARDS: Amex, MasterCard, Visa.
PRICES: [2017] per room B&B £170–£280, D,B&B £260–£340. Set dinner £45, gourmet menu £90 (incl. wines).

BURTON BRADSTOCK Dorset

Map 1:D6

THE SEASIDE BOARDING HOUSE

Mary-Lou Sturridge and Tony Mackintosh (late of London's Groucho Club) run their 'laid-back but sophisticated' restaurant-with-rooms within sound of the waves. Fronted by a terrace with tables and chairs, the white-painted edifice stands above Lyme Bay and its beach – 'a wonderful location', writes a reader this year after an 'enjoyable stay'. Interiors are pared-down chic and 'in good taste' – pale walls, bare floorboards ('tread softly!'). In the 'elegant, unfussy' bedrooms overlooking Jurassic coast or gentle countryside, find books, a Roberts radio, a TV on request. 'Our room was spacious and airy, with a comfortable bed and a nicely kitted-out bathroom.' Dine on modern dishes rich in West Country produce in the sea-facing dining room – home-cured beef fillet, celeriac remoulade, perhaps, or hake fillet, smoked mussels, rainbow chard. On a balmy day, French doors are thrown open to the watery vista. 'It's not a cheap meal, but it's entirely pleasing, and served by friendly staff.' After breakfast the next day, ask for a greaseproof paper–wrapped crab sandwich, then follow the path to the beach. (Fiona Clifton, and others)

Cliff Road
Burton Bradstock
DT6 4RB

T: 01308 897 205
E: info@theseasideboardinghouse.com
W: theseasideboardinghouse.com

BEDROOMS: 9.
OPEN: all year.
FACILITIES: bar, restaurant, library, function facilities, free Wi-Fi, civil wedding licence, terrace, lawn, unsuitable for disabled.
BACKGROUND MUSIC: 'classic music' in bar.
LOCATION: ½ mile from village centre; 3½ miles SE of Bridport.
CHILDREN: all ages welcomed (1 family room).
DOGS: allowed in 2 bedrooms, bar, not in restaurant.
CREDIT CARDS: Amex, MasterCard, Visa.
PRICES: [2017] per room B&B £200–£250. À la carte £35. 1-night bookings sometimes refused.

BUXTON Derbyshire

Map 4:E3

THE ROSELEIGH `NEW`

On a pedestrianised street across from the
Victorian Pavilion Gardens, this 'elegantly
decorated' B&B stands in 'an attractive,
convenient location' in the old spa town.
Maggi and Gerard Heelan are the 'pleasant,
attentive' owners – 'and helpful to boot, as
we discovered during Buxton's busy Festival
period,' say trusted Guide correspondents this
year, who were impressed by their stay. The
traditionally styled 19th-century house faces
the lake in the public park; come in to find
potted plants, leather armchairs and a wealth
of books, magazines and travel guides in the
'very comfortable' lounge. Most of the bedrooms
are on the upper floors (pause to browse the
book-swapping library on the landing). 'Lots of
nice details in our room: proper coat hangers;
an elaborate towel arrangement of swans on our
bed. Facecloths, too, in the bathroom – always a
good sign.' There's 'excellent bacon' at a 'good
breakfast' ('just two niggles: foil-wrapped
pats of butter; canned, though quiet, muzak').
Chatsworth House is a half-hour's drive away;
the Heelans can arrange discounted tickets to
visit the stately home and gardens. (Stephen and
Pauline Glover)

19 Broad Walk
Buxton
SK17 6JR

T: 01298 24904
E: enquiries@roseleighhotel.co.uk
W: roseleighhotel.co.uk

BEDROOMS: 14. 1 on ground floor.
OPEN: all year except Dec–mid-Jan.
FACILITIES: lounge (computer for
guests' use), breakfast room, free
Wi-Fi, in-room TV (Freeview),
parking, unsuitable for disabled.
BACKGROUND MUSIC: classical/
baroque in breakfast room.
LOCATION: central.
CHILDREN: not under 6.
DOGS: not allowed.
CREDIT CARDS: MasterCard, Visa.
PRICES: [2017] per person B&B single
from £42, double £35–£50.

CAMBER Sussex

THE GALLIVANT

California beach motel meets the great British coast in 'plenty of good spirit' at Harry Cragoe's 'fun, likeable' hotel across the dunes from Camber Sands. The place lives up to its name, and jaunty exploration is encouraged: beach bags await in the bedrooms; bicycle hire can be arranged; there are flip-flops to borrow – a walk on the 'seemingly endless sandy beach' is 'one of the hotel's great assets'. Hot drinks and cake are laid out for a teatime return; at any time, raid the Larder of Guilty Pleasures, the in-house tuck shop stocked with everything from popcorn to champagne. Snug or with space to spread out, bedrooms have a breezy coastal air (cool hues, pale sanded floors); the best open on to a semi-private deck leading to the landscaped coastal garden. 'Ours had a comfy bed with crisp linen; a huge bathtub in the bathroom. There were books, a transistor radio, plenty of local information.' Chef Oliver Joyce's modern British cooking is 'exceptional'. His 'ten-mile menu' features the best local produce in dishes such as smoked haddock, Rye bay cockles, spring onion, curried mayo. At breakfast, honey and apple juice are local; granola bars, pastries and sausages are all home made.

New Lydd Road
Camber
TN31 7RB

T: 01797 225057
E: enquiries@thegallivant.co.uk
W: www.thegallivant.co.uk

BEDROOMS: 20. All on ground floor.
OPEN: all year.
FACILITIES: bar, restaurant, free Wi-Fi, in-room TV, civil wedding licence, function facilities, beach hut spa treatment room, terrace, coastal garden.
BACKGROUND MUSIC: in bar and restaurant.
LOCATION: 3¾ miles SE of Rye.
CHILDREN: all ages welcomed, no children in restaurant after 8 pm.
DOGS: allowed in some bedrooms, bar.
CREDIT CARDS: Amex, MasterCard, Visa.
PRICES: [2017] per room B&B from £135, D,B&B from £205. À la carte £35.

CAMBRIDGE Cambridgeshire

Map 2:B4

DUKE HOUSE

'A refreshing choice', Liz and Rob Cameron's 'delightful, well-located' B&B is minutes from the colleges and the Grand Arcade. Downstairs, the sitting room is stocked with books, newspapers and magazines; a sweet treat is served here every afternoon ('plus something stronger in the evening,' the hosts say). On the upper floors and in the cottage next door, 'quiet, beautifully presented' bedrooms, each a different size, are styled in cool shades, and supplied with waffle robes and a goose-down duvet. 'My room was small but warm, well lit and nicely finished, with good bedlinen. In the lovely big bathroom: bottles of their in-house brand of shower gel and body lotion. A slow-draining washbasin was quickly dealt with.' 'Liz is helpful in every way' and can offer restaurant recommendations and give advice on trip planning. In the morning, a 'first-rate breakfast' is served in a 'snug', rustic room (painted brick walls, a Shaker-style sideboard). Wake hungry: there's 'an abundance' of 'fresh, organic' produce, including 'beautiful breads' and 'marvellous' home-made compotes and jams, all of it served on pretty crockery. (Viv Tunstall, Susan Willmington, and others)

1 Victoria Street
Cambridge
CB1 1JP

T: 01223 314773
E: info@dukehousecambridge.co.uk
W: www.dukehousecambridge.co.uk

BEDROOMS: 5. 1 in adjacent cottage, plus self-catering apartment.
OPEN: all year.
FACILITIES: sitting room, breakfast room with courtyard, balcony, free Wi-Fi, in-room TV (Freeview), limited parking (by arrangement), unsuitable for disabled.
BACKGROUND MUSIC: none.
LOCATION: city centre.
CHILDREN: babies, and over-10s welcomed.
DOGS: not allowed.
CREDIT CARDS: Diners, MasterCard, Visa.
PRICES: [2017] per room B&B £130–£195. 1-night bookings sometimes refused.

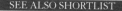

SEE ALSO SHORTLIST

CAMELFORD Cornwall

Map 1:C3

PENDRAGON COUNTRY HOUSE

25% DISCOUNT VOUCHERS

In an 'ideal position' between coast and moorland, guests enthuse about the 'attentive, professional service', 'warm and gracious hospitality' and home-baked in-room treats at Nigel and Sharon Reed's guest house. The former Victorian rectory is made inviting with board games and books, packs of cards at the antique card table, leather sofas, an honesty bar, and a log fire in cool weather. Decorated with 'taste and character', bedrooms have antiques, oil paintings and many 'individual touches' – choose one with a large French-style sleigh bed, or another with a cast iron roll-top bath. Book ahead for the set dinner, served most evenings (guests' likes and dislikes are readily accommodated). The meal is 'a nightly tour de force of Nigel's culinary skills', but 'leave room for Sharon's desserts!' In the morning, breakfast, with home-baked bread and home-made jams and marmalade, is 'elegantly served'. 'The kippers, dressed table-side, were a highlight of the morning.' Coastal villages and wide countryside are 'within easy reach'; the Reeds have plenty of ideas to share. 'Their pride in all things Cornish is inspiring.' (Richard Saunders, John Walters, Chris Rusbridge)

Old Vicarage Hill
Davidstow
Camelford
PL32 9XR

T: 01840 261131
E: enquiries@pendragoncountryhouse.com
W: www.pendragoncountryhouse.com

BEDROOMS: 7. 1 on ground floor suitable for disabled.
OPEN: all year except Christmas, restaurant closed Sun eve.
FACILITIES: sitting room, lounge/bar, Orangery breakfast/dining room, games room (pool table), free Wi-Fi, in-room TV (Freeview), civil wedding licence, 1½-acre grounds.
BACKGROUND MUSIC: none.
LOCATION: 3½ miles NE of Camelford.
CHILDREN: all ages welcomed.
DOGS: allowed in 1 bedroom, sitting room (£5 per night).
CREDIT CARDS: all major cards.
PRICES: [2017] per room B&B single £65, double £95–£150, D,B&B £145–£200. Set menu £25–£35.

CANNINGTON Somerset

Map 1:B5

BLACKMORE FARM

'There are no flashy bits, just a friendly atmosphere and good, old-fashioned hospitality' at Ann and Ian Dyer's rural B&B on the family farm at the foot of the Quantock hills. 'It's one of the best places (maybe the best) I've stayed in,' a Guide reader says. In countryside where native ponies, deer and wild fowl roam and graze, the Grade I listed 15th-century manor house retains character in its ancient beams, stone archways, leaded windows and medieval garderobes. In the Great Hall, where breakfast is taken at a carved-oak refectory table, a log fire burns in the massive stone fireplace. Bedrooms (some 'amazingly large') are in the main house, the converted barn and cider press, plus a quirky shepherd's hut in secluded gardens. All rooms are supplied with fresh milk on the tea tray. Breakfast gives a taste of the place: home-made muesli; bread from the village baker; eggs from the farm's free-range hens; organic milk and cream from a Somerset dairy. Local walks take in village, field and stream; on your return, visit the farm shop/café for home-baked cake, Blackmore Farm ice creams, perhaps one of Ian Dyer's specials of the day. (ME)

25% DISCOUNT VOUCHERS

Blackmore Lane
Cannington
TA5 2NE

T: 01278 653442
E: dyerfarm@aol.com
W: www.blackmorefarm.co.uk

BEDROOMS: 10. 6 on ground floor in annexes, 1 in shepherd's hut in grounds.
OPEN: all year.
FACILITIES: lounge/TV room, Great Hall/breakfast room, free Wi-Fi, in-room TV (Freeview), 1-acre garden (stream, coarse fishing), farm shop/café.
BACKGROUND MUSIC: none.
LOCATION: 3 miles W of Bridgwater.
CHILDREN: all ages welcomed.
DOGS: not allowed.
CREDIT CARDS: Diners, MasterCard, Visa.
PRICES: [2017] per person B&B £60–£75. 1-night bookings refused bank holiday weekends.

CARLISLE Cumbria

Map 4:B2

WILLOWBECK LODGE

In a leafy setting within easy reach of the city, this modern B&B stands in its own mature grounds with weeping willows and a duck pond – look out for the resident kingfisher. It is run by Andrew McGrillis and his wife, Sarah, who seamlessly took over when his parents, the former hosts, retired. 'Andrew is a young man blessed with interpersonal skills,' says a Guide inspector in 2017. 'He greeted us warmly, offering help with cases. Later, he arranged for us to have dinner in nearby Wetheral.' Enter via the 'imposing' timber-and-glass extension – 'a mixture of the ecclesiastical and Danish hygge' – and step straight into the open-plan lounge/restaurant: it has a log-burning stove, comfy sofas, magazines and a wall of well-thumbed paperbacks. Upstairs, uncluttered bedrooms, with underfloor heating, look over the pond. 'Simply but comfortably furnished, my room had a spacious, well-lit bathroom.' Two nights a week, an ambitious, home-cooked dinner might include honey-roasted duck breast, fennel and orange salad. Breakfast on pancakes with maple syrup, a bacon sandwich or 'eggs scrambled to perfection'. The M6 is a mile away.

Lambley Bank
Scotby
Carlisle
CA4 8BX

T: 01228 513607
F: 01228 501053
E: info@willowbeck-lodge.com
W: www.willowbeck-lodge.com

BEDROOMS: 4.
OPEN: all year except over Christmas and New Year period, restaurant open Fri and Sat.
FACILITIES: lounge, bar, restaurant, free Wi-Fi, in-room TV (Now, Freeview), 1½-acre garden (stream, pond), unsuitable for disabled.
BACKGROUND MUSIC: in public areas.
LOCATION: 3½ miles E of Carlisle, just off A69.
CHILDREN: babies and toddlers, and over-12s.
DOGS: not allowed.
CREDIT CARDS: MasterCard, Visa.
PRICES: [2017] per room B&B £120–£150. À la carte £30.

CARTMEL Cumbria

Map 4: inset C2

AYNSOME MANOR

Guests are assured of 'friendliness and an outstanding welcome' from second-generation owners Christopher and Andrea Varley at this 'lovely hotel in quiet countryside'. Its loyal following, who consider it 'a home away from home', return regularly, drawn by the 'pleasant atmosphere'. 'It may be old-fashioned, but it's none the worse for that.' There are lounges upstairs and down (just right for afternoon tea), with prints, log fires, deep armchairs, a grandfather clock; 'space to keep to oneself' if desired. Bedrooms may need an update, but they have all the usual comforts. Beneath a moulded ceiling in the panelled dining room (added in 1842 for a visit by the Duke of Devonshire), chef Gordon Topp cooks an 'excellent' daily-changing menu of country house fare, perhaps including roast sirloin of beef, creamed potato; breast of Gressingham duck, caramelised apple, Calvados and thyme. Work up an appetite by climbing Hampsfell to the 19th-century travellers' refuge built by Aynsome Manor resident John Remington, vicar of Cartmel, who was up there every day at 6 am, monarch of all he surveyed. (David Reed, and others)

25% DISCOUNT VOUCHERS

Aynsome Lane
Cartmel
LA11 6HH

T: 01539 536653
F: 01539 536016
E: aynsomemanor@btconnect.com
W: www.aynsomemanorhotel.co.uk

BEDROOMS: 12. 2 in cottage (with lounge) across courtyard.
OPEN: all year except 23–27 Dec, 2–30 Jan, lunch served Sun only, Sun dinner for residents only.
FACILITIES: 2 lounges, bar, dining room, free Wi-Fi, in-room TV (Freeview), ½-acre garden, unsuitable for disabled.
BACKGROUND MUSIC: none.
LOCATION: ¾ mile N of village.
CHILDREN: all ages welcomed, no under-5s in dining room in evening.
DOGS: allowed, not in public rooms or unattended in bedrooms.
CREDIT CARDS: Amex, MasterCard, Visa.
PRICES: [2017] per room B&B £95–£150, D,B&B £162–£195. Set dinner £30. 1-night bookings occasionally refused weekends.

CHADDESLEY CORBETT Worcestershire   Map 3:C5

BROCKENCOTE HALL

Views of parkland and surrounding countryside stretch out from this Victorian manor house, where 'the ambience exudes comfort and encourages total relaxation'. It stands by its own lake in extensive grounds; inside the grand mansion, all is refined, with open fires, oil paintings and fresh flowers. Take afternoon tea by the marble fireplace in the wood-panelled library, amid ornately framed artwork and leather-bound books; in sunshine, the terrace is the place to be (ask for a glass of home-made lemonade). 'Lovely' bedrooms, from classic doubles to feature suites, are plush: all have estate views, an immaculate bathroom, good toiletries. 'Housekeeping is excellent.' At lunch and dinner, tables are laid with white linens in the elegant Chaddesley restaurant. Former sous-chef Tim Jenkins has stepped up to run the kitchen; his market menu, inspired by the seasons, might include pan-roasted monkfish, spiced cauliflower, brassicas, mussel velouté. More straightforward options (a club sandwich, a charred sirloin steak) may be taken in the high-ceilinged bar. Nearby, the Malvern hills, Worcestershire son Elgar's great inspiration, regally stand. (G and EC)

25% DISCOUNT VOUCHERS

Chaddesley Corbett
DY10 4PY

T: 01562 777876
F: 01562 777872
E: info@brockencotehall.com
W: www.brockencotehall.com

BEDROOMS: 21. Some on ground floor, 1 suitable for disabled.
OPEN: all year.
FACILITIES: lift, hall, lounge bar, library, restaurant, function facilities, free Wi-Fi, in-room TV (Freeview), civil wedding licence, 72-acre grounds (gardens, lake, fishing, croquet, tennis).
BACKGROUND MUSIC: all day in public areas.
LOCATION: 3 miles SE of Kidderminster.
CHILDREN: all ages welcomed.
DOGS: not allowed.
CREDIT CARDS: Amex, MasterCard, Visa.
PRICES: [2017] per room B&B from £135, D,B&B from £225. Set dinner £47.50, à la carte £60.

CHESTER Cheshire

Map 3:A4

EDGAR HOUSE

Listen to the 'wonderful sound of water rushing over the weir' at Tim Mills and Michael Stephen's 'beautifully refurbished' Georgian villa on ancient city walls along the River Dee. 'The staff are charming and enthusiastic, and the decor is refreshingly different (a great deal more colourful than the Farrow & Ball we've come to expect),' say Guide inspectors who had 'a highly enjoyable stay'. Large bedrooms, some with a balcony overlooking the river, are individually designed. 'Our stunning junior suite had a huge copper bath against an exposed-brick wall. There was a chesterfield sofa in the sitting area; the good-sized bed had top-quality bedding. On the hospitality tray: a large jug of iced water, chic teas, little treats of intense chocolate and fruit cubes.' At lunch and dinner, join locals and passers-by at Twenty2 restaurant, where chef Christopher Hobley's modern menus might include tournedos of plaice, scallop mousse, smoked roe, rainbow chard. Breakfast, served by 'attentive, chatty' staff in a garden-facing room, is 'delightful': 'delicious yogurt, granola and fruit cups; perfectly poached eggs with a superb hollandaise'. 'We left with warm feelings.'

22 City Walls
Chester
CH1 1SB

T: 01244 347007
F: 01244 310147
E: hello@edgarhouse.co.uk
W: www.edgarhouse.co.uk

BEDROOMS: 7.
OPEN: all year.
FACILITIES: garden lounge, mini-cinema, restaurant, free Wi-Fi, in-room TV, terrace, riverside garden (alfresco meals), unsuitable for disabled.
BACKGROUND MUSIC: Classic FM in lounge.
LOCATION: central, on the river.
CHILDREN: not under 14.
DOGS: not allowed.
CREDIT CARDS: MasterCard, Visa.
PRICES: [2017] per room B&B from £210, D,B&B from £270. À la carte £30–£45. 1-night bookings sometimes refused in some bedrooms at weekends.

SEE ALSO SHORTLIST

CHETTLE Dorset

CASTLEMAN

'Set in large gardens, this lovely old house feels like a big family home, with many pictures, books and magazines.' Trusted Guide correspondents this year enjoyed Barbara Garnsworthy's 'relaxing' hotel, in a former dower house within Cranborne Chase. 'We love it in many ways,' concur other regular visitors. Some guests raise caveats – 'too-hasty housekeeping'; 'a mishmash of hangers' in the bedroom wardrobes – but it remains 'an agreeable, quiet place to stay', 'especially in the summer, when we take tea on the lawn'. Choose carefully among the individually decorated bedrooms: the largest have antiques, and a roll-top bath in the bathroom. 'Our huge room overlooking the garden had a comfortable, but very high, four-poster bed. A welcome flask of fresh milk appeared in the room each day.' Dine in: the 'interesting' daily-changing menu has 'a wide range of choices', perhaps English asparagus, Old Winchester cheese; pork medallions, glazed shallots, port. ('We would have loved to see more fresh, seasonal veg, though.') At breakfast: 'We can vouch for the excellent scrambled eggs.' (Jill and Mike Bennett, and others)

25% DISCOUNT VOUCHERS

Chettle
DT11 8DB

T: 01258 830096
F: 01258 830051
E: enquiry@castlemanhotel.co.uk
W: www.castlemanhotel.co.uk

BEDROOMS: 8. 1 family room.
OPEN: Mar–end Jan, except 25/26, 31 Dec, restaurant closed midday except Sun.
FACILITIES: 2 drawing rooms, bar, restaurant, free Wi-Fi, in-room TV (Freeview), 2-acre grounds (stables for visiting horses), riding, fishing, shooting, cycling nearby, only restaurant suitable for disabled.
BACKGROUND MUSIC: none.
LOCATION: village, 1 mile off A354 Salisbury–Blandford, hotel signposted.
CHILDREN: all ages welcomed.
DOGS: not allowed.
CREDIT CARDS: MasterCard, Visa.
PRICES: [2017] per room B&B £105–£120, D,B&B (midweek only) £135–£155. À la carte £32.

CHICHESTER Sussex

Map 2:E3

CROUCHERS

Between artsy Chichester and the sandy beaches of West Wittering, Lloyd van Rooyen and Gavin Wilson's hotel 'exceeds expectations'. In a former life, it was known locally as Crouchers Bottom; now, bless thee, Bottom, thou art translated, from farm buildings to modest B&B to today's pleasingly modern enterprise, filled with 'cheerful, charming staff'. Despite the road running by, a blissful midsummer night's dream, in converted outbuildings, is assured. 'Our bedroom was totally quiet in the dark hours, and filled with birdsong at dawn.' Some rooms have a four-poster bed; several have a private patio overlooking fields. All have 'quality furnishings and a state-of-the-art bathroom'. Tables are 'smartly laid' in the restaurant for lunch and dinner, where the 'interesting' menu might include 'generous portions' of textures of carrot, candied feta cheese, pickled ginger; pan-fried stone bass, salt-baked beetroot, oyster mayonnaise, kale. 'This is extremely competent classic English cooking, and it's obviously popular with local diners.' Breakfast has an 'adequate buffet'; 'the scrambled eggs and smoked salmon were just right'. (F and IW)

Birdham Road
Chichester
PO20 7EH

T: 01243 784995
E: enquiries@croucershotel.co.uk
W: www.croucershotel.co.uk

BEDROOMS: 26. 23 in converted coach house, barn and stables, 10 with patio, 2 suitable for disabled.
OPEN: all year.
FACILITIES: lounge, bar, restaurant, free Wi-Fi, in-room TV, civil wedding licence/function facilities, courtyard, 2-acre garden.
BACKGROUND MUSIC: in public areas.
LOCATION: 3 miles S of town centre.
CHILDREN: all ages welcomed.
DOGS: allowed in some bedrooms, bar, not in restaurant.
CREDIT CARDS: Amex, MasterCard, Visa.
PRICES: [2017] per room B&B £124–£159. Set menus £18–£23.50, à la carte £37.

SEE ALSO SHORTLIST

CHILLATON Devon

Map 1:D3

TOR COTTAGE

'Bridlepath,' cautions the sign, 'no vehicular access.' Press on regardless to reach Maureen Rowlatt's Arcadian B&B in gardens and woodland on the edge of Dartmoor. Bedrooms include one in an ancient cart house and two in a former craftsman's workshop; Laughing Waters, a cosy, New England-style cottage, has a rocking chair on the veranda, a barbecue area and steps leading to the stream. Each room is thoughtfully supplied with a trug of organic Devon cream fudge, sparkling wine and fruit. (Garden rooms also have their own log fire in winter.) On a fine day, walk along the bridleways into the Tamar valley; if the summer night turns balmy, ask about a starlight swim in the heated outdoor swimming pool. Eat in come dinnertime (each room has a well-equipped kitchenette), or follow the hostess's recommendations of local pubs; Guide entries in Tavistock, Lewdown and Milton Abbot are easily reached. In the morning, breakfast is taken alfresco or in the conservatory: home-made muesli; a wide selection of fruit; a full English, vegetarian grill or kedgeree cooked to order. More reports, please.

Chillaton
PL16 0JE

T: 01822 860248
F: 01822 860126
E: info@torcottage.co.uk
W: www.torcottage.co.uk

BEDROOMS: 5. 4 in garden.
OPEN: Feb–mid-Dec.
FACILITIES: sitting room, large conservatory, free Wi-Fi in conservatory, in-room TV (Freeview), 28-acre grounds (2-acre garden, heated outdoor swimming pool (12 by 6 metres, May–Sept) with pool house, barbecue, stream, bridleway, walks), river (fishing ½ mile), unsuitable for disabled.
BACKGROUND MUSIC: none.
LOCATION: ½ mile S of Chillaton, 6½ miles N of Tavistock.
CHILDREN: not under 14.
DOGS: no dogs allowed.
CREDIT CARDS: MasterCard, Visa.
PRICES: [2017] per room B&B single £98, double £150–£170. Normally min. 2 nights, 'but check availability'.

CHRISTCHURCH Dorset

Map 2:E2

CAPTAIN'S CLUB HOTEL

'Stylish and modern', Robert Wilson and Tim Lloyd's 'welcoming' hotel gleams on the banks of the River Stour, shipshape inside and out. Arrive via wheels or water (there are moorings for guests), and head straight for the popular riverside terrace, where drinks and meals may be taken in the summer. Within the purpose-built hotel, every one of the sleek bedrooms looks on to the water through floor-to-ceiling windows. Each room is kitted out with up-to-date technology – a smart TV, a Bluetooth-communicating audio system, a capsule coffee machine, a DVD-player on request. Spacious family suites also have a fully equipped kitchen. 'Our comfortable junior suite had interesting river views and plenty of space for lounging around. Shame the sofa was positioned with its back to the window.' Ring to discuss room choices before booking: a guest this year was troubled by noise from a function room. At lunch and dinner, Andrew Gault's 'well-cooked, unfussy' dishes might include double-baked Cheddar soufflé, spinach and shallot salad; roast turbot, samphire, chunky chips. Breakfast includes omelettes, smoked haddock, waffles with maple syrup – 'extensive, and enjoyable'.

Wick Ferry
Christchurch
BH23 1HU

T: 01202 475111
F: 01202 490111
E: enquiries@captainsclubhotel.com
W: www.captainsclubhotel.com

BEDROOMS: 29. 2 suitable for disabled.
OPEN: all year.
FACILITIES: lifts, open-plan bar/lounge/restaurant, function facilities, free Wi-Fi, in-room TV (Sky, Freeview), civil wedding licence, terrace, spa (hydrotherapy pool, sauna, treatments), moorings for guests.
BACKGROUND MUSIC: in public areas, live music some evenings.
LOCATION: on the river.
CHILDREN: all ages welcomed.
DOGS: allowed in suites, on terrace and small area of lounge.
CREDIT CARDS: MasterCard, Visa.
PRICES: [2017] per room B&B £279–£319, apartment/suite accommodating 3–6 people £379–£659. À la carte £30. 1-night bookings normally refused Sat.

CIRENCESTER Gloucestershire

Map 3:E5

KINGS HEAD HOTEL

Charles II is said to have slept here, and medieval beams and Georgian panelling attest to a long history, but this former coaching inn couldn't be more ready for the 21st century. Owners Mark and Alison Booth spent millions on the transformation, which turned up the Roman mosaic displayed in reception. Beyond, modish bedrooms varying in size and style are handsomely appointed, and supplied with dressing gowns, an espresso machine, fresh milk, and a Mac Mini computer. Larger rooms can accommodate an extra bed for a child. An inner courtyard houses the 'informal, friendly' restaurant (leather banquettes, a large wood-burning stove, a 'serendipitous collection' of prints, photos and artwork). Sit here for 'enjoyable' modern meals – perhaps market fish stew, saffron potatoes, rouïlle; flame-cooked meat from the Robata grill – accompanied by a glass from the 'comprehensive wine list'. Salads, sandwiches, small plates and large dishes are served in the lounge all day. There's freshly squeezed orange juice at breakfast, plus 'succulent bacon and tasty Gloucester Old Spot sausages'. The city bustles; take refuge in the vaulted spa.

24 Market Place
Cirencester
GL7 2NR

T: 01285 700900
E: info@kingshead-hotel.co.uk
W: kingshead-hotel.co.uk

BEDROOMS: 50. 1 suitable for disabled.
OPEN: all year.
FACILITIES: lifts, lounge/bar, restaurant, study, meeting/private dining rooms, free Wi-Fi, in-room TV (Freeview), civil wedding licence, spa (treatments, steam room, sauna), roof terrace.
BACKGROUND MUSIC: various in public areas.
LOCATION: town centre, limited secure parking (£15 a day), 24-hour pay-and-display 4 mins' walk.
CHILDREN: all ages welcomed.
DOGS: allowed by arrangement in some bedrooms, lounge, not in restaurant.
CREDIT CARDS: MasterCard, Visa.
PRICES: [2017] per room B&B £124–£265. À la carte £35. 1-night bookings sometimes refused.

CLEARWELL Gloucestershire

Map 3:D4

TUDOR FARMHOUSE

Live life close to the land at Hari and Colin Fell's 'refreshing, very special' hotel, on a one-time farm in the Forest of Dean. The former farmhouse, barn and cider house, 'renovated to a high standard', stand in acres of ancient grassland surrounded by fields grazed by sheep and ponies – it's a landscape best explored, perhaps, under the tutelage of Raoul, the in-house forager, who leads guests in search of wimberries and other wild treats. Closer to home, orchard and potager supply chef Rob Cox's super-local 20-mile menu of 'imaginative, well-presented and tasty' dishes, perhaps 'excellent' guineafowl, boulangère potato, or roasted carrots, raisins, lime, nasturtium. (Just leave room for a 'substantial' dessert.) Modern bedrooms are 'attractive and calming', with original beams, wool blankets and home-made shortbread, perhaps an espresso machine or a roll-top bath. 'We had one of the smaller rooms, but it was perfectly adequate – well equipped and quiet, with a comfy bed, a good walk-in shower and plenty of storage space.' In the morning, a 'very good' breakfast fuels walks among the wild flowers. (Jane Bailey, Peter Anderson, Josie Mayers)

High Street
Clearwell
GL16 8JS

T: 01594 833046
F: 01594 837093
E: info@tudorfarmhousehotel.co.uk
W: www.tudorfarmhousehotel.co.uk

BEDROOMS: 20. 8 on ground floor, 9 in barn, 7 in cider house.
OPEN: all year.
FACILITIES: lounge, bar, 2 dining rooms, free Wi-Fi, in-room TV (Freeview), 14-acre grounds (garden, ancient grassland), unsuitable for disabled.
BACKGROUND MUSIC: in restaurant and lounge at lunch and dinner.
LOCATION: 7 miles SE of Monmouth.
CHILDREN: all ages welcomed.
DOGS: allowed in 3 bedrooms, grounds, not in public rooms.
CREDIT CARDS: Amex, MasterCard, Visa.
PRICES: [2017] per room B&B £130–£250, D,B&B £210–£330. Tasting menu £60, à la carte £40. Min. 2-night stay at weekends.

CLEE STANTON Shropshire

Map 3:C5

TIMBERSTONE

Deep in Shropshire countryside, Tracey Baylis and Alex Read's B&B, in a quiet hamlet, is 'a total joy', say admirers. Natural materials come to the fore in the extended stone cottage, with bedrooms named Oak, Slate, Clay and Dhustone. Each is different, though all provide shortbread, hot chocolate and herbal infusions on the coffee/tea tray, and organic toiletries in the bathroom. Garden-view Oak, in the older part of the house, has handsome oak beams, plus a sofa bed to accommodate young guests; Clay has a double-ended slipper bath under the bedroom's sloping ceiling, and French doors that open to a balcony with views of the surrounding fields. On cool days, gather round the wood-burning stove in the open-plan lounge/dining room (the hosts are ready with tea and biscuits); when the weather turns warm, there's a lawn to play on, and an outdoor eating area. A fuss-free dinner (perhaps lentil and aubergine moussaka; duck breast, red wine, blackcurrants) may be provided by request. Breakfast – a source of pride – is a generous affair: choose among buttered kippers, local sausages, omelettes, organic porridge and more.

25% DISCOUNT VOUCHERS

Lackstone Lane
Clee Stanton
SY8 3EL

T: 01584 823519
E: timberstone1@hotmail.com
W: www.timberstoneludlow.co.uk

BEDROOMS: 4. Plus summer house retreat in summer.
OPEN: all year.
FACILITIES: lounge/dining room, conservatory, free Wi-Fi, in-room TV (Freeview), ½-acre garden, treatment room, unsuitable for disabled.
BACKGROUND MUSIC: none.
LOCATION: 5 miles NE of Ludlow.
CHILDREN: all ages welcomed.
DOGS: allowed by arrangement, not in dining room.
CREDIT CARDS: MasterCard, Visa.
PRICES: [2017] per room B&B £98. Set menus £25–£30.

CLIPSHAM Rutland

BEECH HOUSE & OLIVE BRANCH

🏆 Previous César winner

Apple. Berry. Biscuit. Double Cream… Ben Jones and Sean Hope clearly had food on their mind when they named the bedrooms in Beech House, which stands across the 'quiet road' from their 'lively, enjoyable' village pub/restaurant. The setting is scrumptious, too ('simply tops!' a fan says), from the honey-coloured facade to the 'warm, friendly interior', and cushion- and blanket-supplied ivy-covered pergola. 'What struck me was how cheerful all the staff are,' says a regular correspondent in 2017. 'I never witnessed one frump.' The popular dining room has a reputation for Sean Hope's 'tasty' modern cooking, a culinary round-up of the home-grown and local. Dine on 'fantastic grub' (perhaps an 'outstanding wild mushroom and smoked celeriac lasagne') before retiring to one of the handsome bedrooms, each provided with 'proper coffee and a decent selection of tea bags'; 'luxurious-feeling bedlinen'. Breakfast, served by 'obliging staff', is 'excellent': leaf tea, local bakery bread, 'the plumpest, tastiest kipper eaten in a long while'. (Mary Milne-Day, GC, Robert Sandham)

Main Street
Clipsham
LE15 7SH

T: 01780 410355
E: beechhouse@theolivebranchpub.com
W: www.theolivebranchpub.com

BEDROOMS: 6. 2 on ground floor, family room (also suitable for disabled) in annexe.
OPEN: all year, pub closed evening 25 Dec and 1 Jan.
FACILITIES: pub, dining room, breakfast room, free Wi-Fi, in-room TV (Freeview, Netflix), small terrace, garden.
BACKGROUND MUSIC: classical/jazz in pub.
LOCATION: in village 7 miles NW of Stamford.
CHILDREN: all ages welcomed.
DOGS: allowed in ground-floor bedrooms and bar.
CREDIT CARDS: MasterCard, Visa.
PRICES: [2017] per room B&B £115–£205, D,B&B £210–£260. Set dinner £32.50, à la carte £33.

CORSE LAWN Gloucestershire

Map 3:D5

CORSE LAWN HOUSE

'An ideal place to slow down and relax.' It is almost 40 years since Baba Hine and her late husband, Denis, took over an 18th-century coaching inn and opened their 'graceful hotel'. The hostess remains at the helm with 'ebullient' son Giles, attracting a loyal following of guests who return for the 'old-fashioned values', 'friendly, uniformly efficient staff', 'very comfortable rooms' and 'excellent food and wine'. 'We don't normally go back to the same hotel, but Corse Lawn is so reliable that we've returned three times.' Even standard bedrooms are spacious, with tall windows, and walls hung with pictures; all the rooms are supplied with leaf teas, 'proper coffee', shortbread, fruit, fresh milk. 'Our capacious room had a large bed and a settee; a pleasant sitting area; windows peering into the trees.' Downstairs, the bistro lounge looks out over pond and weeping willow. Eat here or in the restaurant, where long-standing chef Martin Kinahan wins praise for such dishes as trio of Cotswold lamb; chargrilled Orkney salmon, chive beurre blanc. ('Leave room for the interesting cheese trolley!') (William Wood, Michael Mayer-Jones, RE Greenhill)

Corse Lawn
GL19 4LZ

T: 01452 780771
F: 01452 780840
E: enquiries@corselawn.com
W: www.corselawn.com

BEDROOMS: 18. 5 on ground floor.
OPEN: all year except 24–26 Dec.
FACILITIES: 2 drawing rooms, snug bar, restaurant, bistro, private dining/meeting rooms, free Wi-Fi, in-room TV (Sky, BT, Freeview), civil wedding licence, 12-acre grounds (croquet, tennis, indoor heated swimming pool, 20 by 10 metres).
BACKGROUND MUSIC: none.
LOCATION: 5 miles SW of Tewkesbury on B4211.
CHILDREN: all ages welcomed.
DOGS: allowed in bedrooms, on lead in public rooms, not in eating areas.
CREDIT CARDS: Amex, MasterCard, Visa.
PRICES: [2017] per room B&B from £180, D,B&B from £215. Set dinner (restaurant) £33.50, (bistro) £22.50, à la carte £35.

COWAN BRIDGE Lancashire

HIPPING HALL

🏵 Previous César winner

In green grounds at the foot of Gragareth, this 'friendly, unstuffy' hotel makes a cushy base for travellers exploring the Yorkshire Dales and the southern Lakes. It is owned by Andrew Wildsmith; the staff are 'attentive and good humoured'. Parts of the 18th-century house date back to medieval times (an old well is embedded in the orangery's flagstone floor), but a contemporary country house atmosphere reigns. 'Comfortable, well-appointed' bedrooms (some newly refurbished) are in the main house, the converted stables and a cottage across the courtyard. In the 15th-century great hall, Oli Martin's seasonal menus of 'artfully arranged' modern dishes are 'cooked with flair'. (Rather too much flair, say some guests, who would have preferred heartier portions of humbler food.) Among his 'great flavours': artichoke, seaweed, curd; bream, oyster, kohlrabi. 'Pity the limited menu doesn't change more regularly, however.' Breakfast, guests agree, is 'very good'. Wildsmith Hotels' Forest Side, Grasmere, and The Ryebeck, Bowness-on-Windermere (see main and Shortlist entries), share the same easy air. (JP, and others)

Cowan Bridge
LA6 2JJ

T: 01524 271187
E: info@hippinghall.com
W: www.hippinghall.com

BEDROOMS: 15. 3 in cottage, 5 in converted stables.
OPEN: all year.
FACILITIES: lounge, orangery, restaurant, 'chef's kitchen', wedding/function facilities, free Wi-Fi in lounge only, in-room TV (Freeview), civil wedding licence, 4-acre garden, unsuitable for disabled.
BACKGROUND MUSIC: in lounge, restaurant.
LOCATION: 2 miles SE of Kirkby Lonsdale, on A65.
CHILDREN: not under 12.
DOGS: allowed in 2 bedrooms and orangery.
CREDIT CARDS: MasterCard, Visa.
PRICES: [2017] per room B&B from £169, D,B&B from £269. À la carte £55.

CROFT-ON-TEES Yorkshire

Map 4:C4

CLOW BECK HOUSE

Heather and David Armstrong have transformed an old farmhouse – in the family for more than a century – into a 'fascinating and unusual hotel' spilling over into converted outbuildings and a bungalow. Run with 'humour and charm', the place brims with personality; the owners 'go out of their way to oblige every request'. Eclectic bedrooms have antique pieces and surprising touches – gold-painted cornices, a shell-shaped loo seat, an old cast iron fireplace surround fixed to the wall as decoration. Each is well supplied with all sorts of amenities, from fresh milk in a mini-fridge to sweets, postcards, an umbrella, shaving kit and wine bible. Choose a book from the selection and sink into an armchair in the lounge; another day, pick out a tune on the piano. In good weather, sit in the landscaped gardens – the views over surrounding fields are 'beautiful'. The hostess, a 'friendly, bubbly presence', serves drinks and canapés before dinner; the ebullient host cooks hearty dishes, perhaps home-made spinach and ricotta tortellini; rack of local lamb, blackcurrant and port jelly. Next day, fill up on a Yorkshire breakfast, then stroll along the beck to the River Tees. (CLH)

Monk End Farm
Croft-on-Tees
DL2 2SP

T: 01325 721075
F: 01325 720419
E: david@clowbeckhouse.co.uk
W: www.clowbeckhouse.co.uk

BEDROOMS: 13. 12 in garden buildings, 1 suitable for disabled.
OPEN: all year except Christmas and New Year.
FACILITIES: lounge, restaurant, free Wi-Fi, in-room TV (Freeview), small conference facilities, 2-acre grounds on 100-acre farm.
BACKGROUND MUSIC: classical, 'easy listening' in restaurant.
LOCATION: 3 miles SE of Darlington.
CHILDREN: all ages welcomed.
DOGS: not allowed.
CREDIT CARDS: Amex, MasterCard, Visa.
PRICES: [2017] per room B&B single £90, double £145. À la carte £37.

DARTMOUTH Devon

Map 1:D4

DART MARINA

'Crumbly scones' make this chic, river-facing hotel 'probably the best tea place in town', but there's much more for its fans to enjoy: 'a lovely setting, good food and well-appointed bedrooms'. Some guests consider the atmosphere 'sedate' in the off-season, but 'it's my idea of paradise', said a regular visitor this year. It is owned by Richard Seton (himself a sailor); Paul Downing is the 'remarkable' manager. Every bedroom takes in views of the water – watch out for the occasional grey seal. Consider discussing rooms before booking: a guest this year judged his room 'fairly small, though comfortable, with a less-than-full view of the river'. Others were 'delighted' with their accommodation: 'Our deluxe room, with a huge, weather-protected balcony, was fabulous – contemporary, spacious, with quality furnishings. The superb bathroom had a double-ended bath and a drench shower; robes and slippers; fluffy towels. Bonus points for the binoculars, too.' Dinner in the restaurant, with its 'pleasant outlook and attentive staff', is thought 'excellent'. 'And the delicious home-made breads deserve a special mention!' (CR, IM, Mary Woods)

Sandquay Road
Dartmouth
TQ6 9PH

T: 01803 832580
E: pauld@dartmarinahotel.com
W: www.dartmarina.com

BEDROOMS: 49. 4 on ground floor, 1 suitable for disabled, plus 4 apartments.
OPEN: all year.
FACILITIES: lounge/bar, restaurant, free Wi-Fi, in-room TV (Freeview), river-front terrace, small garden with seating, spa (heated indoor swimming pool, 8 by 4 metres, gym).
BACKGROUND MUSIC: in restaurant and lounge/bar during the day.
LOCATION: on waterfront.
CHILDREN: all ages welcomed.
DOGS: allowed in ground-floor rooms, not in restaurant.
CREDIT CARDS: MasterCard, Visa.
PRICES: [2017] per room B&B from £180, D,B&B from £250. À la carte £40. 1-night bookings usually refused Sat.

SEE ALSO SHORTLIST

DEDHAM Essex

Map 2:C5

DEDHAM HALL & FOUNTAIN HOUSE RESTAURANT

'Describing it as "quirky" is a hole-in-one.' There's 'a pleasant, rural tranquillity' to Wendy and Jim Sarton's 15th-century manor house in large gardens where wild rabbits scamper. Fans like the informal approach and 'comforting, relaxing', lived-in feel. 'We arrived with our four children in the late afternoon and were shown to our own cosy parlour, where a bright fire, home-made brownies and tea awaited. It was nothing chi-chi, but was nicely decorated, with paintings and squashy sofas.' Hand-woven rugs and intricate furnishings add an eclectic air to the bedrooms, some in converted barns. 'My room had a comfortable bed with high-quality linen; an extraordinary bathroom basin. No guide to hotel facilities, though.' Wendy Sarton cooks 'simple, generous' dinners, served by 'prompt, courteous' staff; in the morning, a 'first-class' breakfast might include 'home-made marmalade served in vintage dishes; buttery scrambled eggs; home-baked bread'. 'Few places are better for a country retreat with children.' Residential painting courses are held from February to November. (Robert Gower, Thomas and Sybille Raphael)

Brook Street
Dedham
CO7 6AD

T: 01206 323027
E: sarton@dedhamhall.demon.co.uk
W: www.dedhamhall.co.uk

BEDROOMS: 20. 16 in annexe, some on ground floor, suitable for disabled.
OPEN: all year except Christmas–New Year.
FACILITIES: 2 lounges, bar, dining room, restaurant, studio, free Wi-Fi, in-room TV, 6-acre grounds (pond, gardens).
BACKGROUND MUSIC: none.
LOCATION: end of village High Street (set back from road).
CHILDREN: all ages welcomed.
DOGS: not allowed.
CREDIT CARDS: MasterCard, Visa.
PRICES: per person B&B £60–£75, D,B&B £95–£105. À la carte £30.

DEDHAM Essex

Map 2:C5

THE SUN INN

'A warm-hearted spot with obliging staff, good food, gracefully homey rooms and a genial community feel', Piers Baker's 15th-century inn is 'a good place in which to find oneself', say Guide inspectors in 2017. 'This is what pubs were meant to look like: low-beamed ceilings, wide wooden floorboards, red banquettes, the comforting smell of log fires merrily burning; in the oak-panelled lounge, a comely mishmash of sofas and armchairs. Behind the curving elm bar, the barman was a young, tattooed, flannelled chap with an enormous ear piercing and an easy disposition.' Bedrooms are individually designed. 'Dovecot, our well-lit room, smallish but sufficient, had crisp bedlinens, puffy pillows, a deep armchair, ground coffee, chic teas – all you could wish for, except a solid wall to the bathroom (we'd been warned – choose another room if you value privacy).' Chef Jack Levine's cooking is 'modern English pubby via Italy'; a dish of lemon sole on the bone was 'well conceived, with bursts of salty cockles'. While St Mary's church clock chimes, breakfast on croissants, fruit compotes and thick yogurt, and 'skilfully cooked' hot dishes.

25% DISCOUNT VOUCHERS

High Street
Dedham
CO7 6DF

T: 01206 323351
E: office@thesuninndedham.com
W: www.thesuninndedham.com

BEDROOMS: 7. 2 across the terrace, approached by Elizabethan staircase.
OPEN: all year except 25/26 Dec.
FACILITIES: lounge, bar, dining rooms, free Wi-Fi, in-room TV (Freeview), 1-acre garden (covered terrace, children's play area, garden bar), unsuitable for disabled.
BACKGROUND MUSIC: all day in public areas.
LOCATION: village centre.
CHILDREN: all ages welcomed.
DOGS: allowed by arrangement.
CREDIT CARDS: Amex, MasterCard, Visa.
PRICES: [2017] per room B&B £145, D,B&B £200. À la carte £28.50.

DITTISHAM Devon

Map 1:D4

FINGALS

'In an utterly peaceful valley, Richard Johnston's quirky B&B is a cross between a 1930s rural escape and an eccentric aristocrat's home, with a bit of adventure at every turn, and lots to keep you entertained.' Guide inspectors were beguiled by this 'artistically extended', dog- and family-friendly 17th-century manor house close to the River Dart. 'The charm comes from Richard himself, the beautiful gardens, the sense of escapism, the intention behind it all. And children have a lovely time.' Casually run and maintained, it may not be everyone's cup of tea: 'Some rooms have a slightly haphazard grandeur to them, and a tidy-up would help, but details like mattresses and linens are second to none.' 'There's no such thing as a standard room' – one has a balcony overlooking a wild brook, another a four-poster bed so high you need to climb into it – so ring ahead to discuss options. Guests gather in the lounge and bar or around the greenhouse pool; about twice a week, the host cooks a three-course dinner using organic local ingredients. 'Old-fashioned in a lovely way; a very different experience.' (AN, and others)

Old Coombe Manor Farm
Dittisham
TQ6 0JA

T: 01803 722398
E: info@fingals.co.uk
W: www.fingals.co.uk

BEDROOMS: 4. 1 in separate building by stream, plus 8 self-catering rooms available as B&B off-season.
OPEN: Easter–New Year, self-catering only at Christmas, restaurant closed mid-week unless by arrangement.
FACILITIES: dining room, honesty bar, sitting room, games room, free Wi-Fi, in-room TV (Freeview), indoor swimming pool (8 by 4 metres), 2-acre garden, grass tennis court, unsuitable for disabled.
BACKGROUND MUSIC: classical in bar and breakfast room.
LOCATION: in hamlet, 7 miles N of Dartmouth.
CHILDREN: all ages welcomed.
DOGS: allowed in bedrooms, not in public rooms.
CREDIT CARDS: Amex, MasterCard, Visa.
PRICES: [2017] per room B&B £110–£210. Set dinner £36.

DODDISCOMBSLEIGH Devon

Map 1:C4

THE NOBODY INN

Previous César winner

Pile in for the jolly quiz night, or sample one of the whiskies from an astonishing collection at Sue Burdge's 17th-century dwelling house–turned–lively village pub-with-rooms. 'It seems like a film set from a period romp, but this is the real thing: low beams and parchment-stained plaster; a cornucopia of maps, prints and pictures of times past; welcome murmurings, chit-chat and laughter in the background.' In the characterful dining room, choose from the short menu of 'amazing-value' pub dishes, perhaps home-made steak-and-ale pie with 'a crackling crust'. Afterwards, pass through the log fire-warmed bar, and mount steep stairs to the 'well-appointed', oak-beamed bedrooms (some are small). 'Our delightful room had a supremely comfy mattress topper and crisp pillowcases, plus plenty of current magazines and a dear little decanter of amontillado.' In the morning, breakfast on 'masses' of home-smoked salmon and scrambled eggs; 'award-worthy' devilled kidneys. Sister outfit The Cridford Inn, Trusham (see entry), enters the Guide this year. (Evan Morgans, F and HN)

Doddiscombsleigh
EX6 7PS

T: 01647 252394
F: 01647 252978
E: info@nobodyinn.co.uk
W: www.nobodyinn.co.uk

BEDROOMS: 5.
OPEN: all year except 24/25 Dec, 31 Dec, 1 Jan, restaurant closed Sun, Mon.
FACILITIES: 2 bars, restaurant, free Wi-Fi (may be patchy), in-room TV (Freeview), garden, patio, parking, unsuitable for disabled.
BACKGROUND MUSIC: none.
LOCATION: in village 8 miles SW of Exeter.
CHILDREN: not under 5 for overnight stays, not under 14 in 1 bar.
DOGS: on lead, in bar.
CREDIT CARDS: MasterCard, Visa.
PRICES: [2017] per room B&B £79–£105, D,B&B £110–£135. À la carte £32.

DUNSTER Somerset

Map 1:B5

THE LUTTRELL ARMS HOTEL

In a medieval village in Lorna Doone country, this 'well-managed' 15th-century coaching inn overlooking National Trust parkland is owned by Anne and Nigel Way. The characterful pub, all mismatched seating and intriguing ornaments, has 'a good mix of people' (and dogs). Gather by the huge fireplace or copper-topped bar for local ales and ciders, and a snack or heartier dish off the varied menu – Luttrell Scotch egg, black pudding, maple and barbecue sauce, for instance. ('The lovely, fire-warmed sitting room is nice for those who prefer to be a little more highbrow.') In sunshine, take tea in the garden with views of Dunster Castle. Bedrooms, some with a terrace and garden access, are all different – choose one with a canopy bed and plaster friezes, or another with a vaulted ceiling, mullioned windows and a wood-burning stove. 'Ours, with a four-poster bed and a pretty view of the town, was lovely.' 'Nice dinners' in the smart restaurant focus on locally sourced ingredients in such dishes as roasted loin of venison, sea buckthorn, salt-baked celeriac. 'The bill was a pleasant surprise, too!' (RM-P)

32–36 High Street
Exmoor National Park
Dunster
TA24 6SG

T: 01643 821555
F: 01643 821567
E: enquiry@luttrellarms.co.uk
W: www.luttrellarms.co.uk

BEDROOMS: 28. Some on ground floor.
OPEN: all year.
FACILITIES: lounge, bar, restaurant, function rooms, free Wi-Fi, in-room TV, civil wedding licence, courtyard, garden (alfresco dining), only public areas suitable for disabled.
BACKGROUND MUSIC: none.
LOCATION: village centre, 3½ miles SE of Minehead.
CHILDREN: all ages welcomed.
DOGS: allowed in most bedrooms, bar, not in restaurant.
CREDIT CARDS: Amex, MasterCard, Visa.
PRICES: [2017] per room B&B from £150, D,B&B from £230. 2-night min. stay on weekends.

EAST CHISENBURY Wiltshire

Map 2:D2

THE RED LION FREEHOUSE

César award: inn of the year

'We loved the atmosphere, the amazing food and the beautiful bedrooms.' Watch the ducks whizz by on the river, as did recent guests, from the bedrooms of this popular gastropub-with-rooms. In the thatch-roofed pub, chef/patrons Guy and Brittany Manning win rave reviews for their informal modern British menu, which uses uber-local ingredients such as home-grown greens and eggs from home-reared hens. 'Their "Taste of Autumn" menu was a feast of flavours and textures, combined with some really interesting wines. All was explained by knowledgeable and friendly staff.' (Michelin inspectors come to the same, contented conclusion – the pub has had a star since 2013.) Across the road, each bedroom in the Troutbeck Guest House has a private deck and views of the River Avon and countryside. 'Our room had been decorated with enthusiasm and flair. In the bathroom: special toiletries in big jars, and a super shower over the bath.' The morning meal is worth waking for. 'Breakfast was beautifully presented, with some unusual ingredients and lovely home-made breads and jams.' (Jackie Tunstall-Pedoe, TS)

East Chisenbury
SN9 6AQ

T: 01980 671124
E: troutbeck@redlionfreehouse.com
W: www.redlionfreehouse.com

BEDROOMS: 5. On ground floor, in adjacent building; 1 suitable for disabled.
OPEN: all year.
FACILITIES: pub/restaurant, private dining room, free Wi-Fi, in-room TV (Freeview), 1-acre garden.
BACKGROUND MUSIC: in pub/restaurant.
LOCATION: in village, 6 miles S of Pewsey.
CHILDREN: all ages welcomed (under-2s free; children 2–10 £25 per night).
DOGS: allowed in pub, 1 bedroom (not unattended).
CREDIT CARDS: Amex, MasterCard, Visa.
PRICES: [2017] per room B&B from £180, D,B&B from £195. À la carte £42.

EAST GRINSTEAD Sussex

Map 2:D4

GRAVETYE MANOR

♀ Previous César winner

'Every comfort is anticipated' at this 'classy, tasteful' Elizabethan manor house, from the garden flowers in the public rooms to 'the most extensive cheese trolley we've ever seen'. 'It's like being in a private home,' says a Guide reader this year. 'In the morning, Andrew Thomason, the manager, greeted us; at evening turn-down, a hot-water bottle was left on our enormous bed, along with the Radio Times and the TV remote control.' The stone-built mansion is the former home of 'wild gardener' William Robinson; 'impeccably maintained', his gardens are 'colourful, stunning'. Inside, where 'huge log fires' burn in the sitting rooms, 'everything is generously sized: lounges, rooms, beds'. From May 2018, the hotel will reveal its new restaurant, in a garden-facing glass extension – a fitting backdrop for chef George Blogg's Michelin-starred, potager-to-plate cooking. Using produce from the orchards and 'the best kitchen garden ever', his dishes might include terrine of heritage beetroot, smoked cow's curd, puffed grains, wild sorrel – 'each plate a joy to look at'. (Nigel Barton, Zara Elliot, F and IW)

Vowels Lane
East Grinstead
RH19 4LJ

T: 01342 810567
F: 01342 810080
E: info@gravetyemanor.co.uk
W: www.gravetyemanor.co.uk

BEDROOMS: 17.
OPEN: all year.
FACILITIES: 2 lounges, bar, restaurant, 2 private dining rooms, free Wi-Fi, in-room TV (Sky), civil wedding licence, 1,000-acre grounds (woodland, ornamental and kitchen gardens, meadow, orchard, lake, croquet lawn, glasshouses), only restaurant suitable for disabled.
BACKGROUND MUSIC: none.
LOCATION: 4 miles SW of East Grinstead.
CHILDREN: not under 7.
DOGS: not allowed.
CREDIT CARDS: Amex, MasterCard, Visa.
PRICES: [2017] per room B&B £260–£550. Set dinner £30–£40, tasting menu £75–£85, à la carte £70. 1-night bookings sometimes refused at weekends.

EAST HOATHLY Sussex

Map 2:E4

OLD WHYLY

With a lily-scented terrace in the summer and a log fire in the winter, all is 'enchanting' at this 'elegant, comfortable' Georgian manor house. Sarah Burgoyne runs it with 'flair and efficiency'. 'Arriving at Old Whyly is a delight – there's always freshly baked cake and a cup of tea, served on delicate china,' says a Guide reader this year. Spacious bedrooms overlook the 'glorious gardens'; Irish linens and woollen blankets add to the country house style. Gather with fellow guests for aperitifs in the 'welcoming' drawing room filled with books and paintings; dinner is served in the candlelit dining room or, in balmy weather, under a vine-covered pergola. A Paris-trained cook, the hostess uses local and home-grown produce in her modern menus, perhaps including spinach-ricotta gnocchi, wild rocket; duck breast, red cabbage. At a 'hearty' communal breakfast, honey comes from bees in the orchard, eggs from the hens and ducks that wander the grounds. 'The marvellous home-made marmalade is a particular treat.' Book early for Glyndebourne (a ten-minute drive away), and for 'Sarah's practical, delicious tiffin-box picnics'. (Catrin Treadwell)

London Road
East Hoathly
BN8 6EL

T: 01825 840216
E: stay@oldwhyly.co.uk
W: www.oldwhyly.co.uk

BEDROOMS: 4.
OPEN: all year.
FACILITIES: drawing room, dining room, free Wi-Fi, in-room TV (Freeview), 4-acre garden, heated outdoor swimming pool (14 by 7 metres), tennis, unsuitable for disabled.
BACKGROUND MUSIC: none.
LOCATION: 1 mile N of village.
CHILDREN: all ages welcomed.
DOGS: allowed, not in dining room or unattended in bedrooms.
CREDIT CARDS: none.
PRICES: [2017] per room B&B £98–£145. Set dinner £38, Glyndebourne hamper £40 per person. 1-night bookings sometimes refused weekends in high season.

EASTBOURNE Sussex

Map 2:E4

BELLE TOUT LIGHTHOUSE

'Extraordinary light' surrounds this 'characterful B&B' in a decommissioned lighthouse. It stands remote on the cliffs overlooking the notorious lover's leap of Beachy Head. Owned by David and Barbara Shaw, it is run, with a 'generous spirit', by a team of three managers. 'On our visit, Paul – welcoming and likeable – was in charge and serenely on top of things.' Most bedrooms are in a squat extension: 'If you want to feel you're in a lighthouse, not just at one, book the Keeper's Loft, with brick walls and a ladder to climb into bed.' 'Our bright, adequately sized room overlooked the Downs, past the car park. Two armchairs sat at the foot of our soft, comfortable bed; the shower room had big towels on a heated rail.' Gather with fellow guests in the 'cosy' second-floor lounge for late-afternoon drinks – 'it brings people together in an atmosphere that could otherwise feel diffuse'. A takeaway supper from the nearby village may be eaten here, too. In the black of night, ascend to the lantern and marvel at the stars. Wake to a decent breakfast ('it's not a fresh-baked-bread, home-made-jam kind of outfit') of 'good coffee', 'very good fruit salad', hot dishes cooked to order.

Beachy Head Road
Eastbourne
BN20 0AE

T: 01323 423185
E: info@belletout.co.uk
W: www.belletout.co.uk

BEDROOMS: 6. 5 in house, 1 in lighthouse (bunk bed).
OPEN: all year except Christmas/New Year.
FACILITIES: 2 lounges, breakfast room, free Wi-Fi (in some rooms and some public areas), in-room TV (Freeview), terrace, garden, unsuitable for disabled.
BACKGROUND MUSIC: none.
LOCATION: 3 miles W of Eastbourne, 2 miles S of East Dean village (pub, deli).
CHILDREN: not under 15.
DOGS: not allowed.
CREDIT CARDS: MasterCard, Visa.
PRICES: [2017] per room B&B £160–£240. Min. 2-night stay, though 1-night bookings may be accepted 7–10 days in advance.

EASTBOURNE Sussex

Map 2:E4

THE GRAND HOTEL

A survivor from a more elegant age, this family-friendly Victorian hotel grandly stands on the seafront. Inside are 'beautiful, spacious public rooms, long corridors, lofty ceilings, arched windows – all very glamorous', said a Guide inspector this year. Glamour doesn't take the place of graciousness, however, as a visitor with a small baby discovered: 'It's not the small, family-run hotel we tend to prefer, but the staff behaved as if it were. From the moment we arrived, everyone was so helpful, friendly and kind.' Guests are greeted by porters, who whisk away their luggage; unburdened, head to one of the traditionally decorated bedrooms. The best have 'loads of room, and beautiful sea views from large windows' ('but an information pack would have been welcomed'). Food and drink are served all day – on the 'lovely terrace' in fine weather; once a month, the Palm Court Strings Orchestra accompanies the 'ceremony' of afternoon tea. At dinner in the Garden and 'very special' Mirabelle restaurants, smart casual dress is required ('but there were varying degrees of smartness among the guests'). 'We left feeling very well looked after.' (Valerie Rose Sheldon, CR)

King Edwards Parade
Eastbourne
BN21 4EQ

T: 01323 412345
F: 01323 412233
E: enquiries@grandeastbourne.com
W: www.grandeastbourne.com

BEDROOMS: 152. 1 suitable for disabled.
OPEN: all year, Mirabelle restaurant closed Sun, Mon, first 2 weeks Jan.
FACILITIES: 5 lounges, bar, 2 restaurants, function/meeting facilities, free Wi-Fi, in-room TV (Freeview), civil wedding licence, terrace, spa/health club (indoor and outdoor pools), 2-acre garden.
BACKGROUND MUSIC: in restaurants, live music at weekends.
LOCATION: seafront, 1 mile from town centre.
CHILDREN: all ages welcomed.
DOGS: allowed ('strictly controlled') in bedrooms, not in public rooms.
CREDIT CARDS: all major cards.
PRICES: [2017] per room B&B £190–£250, D,B&B £270–£330. Set dinners £43.50 (Mirabelle), £40 (Garden), à la carte £55.

ECKINGTON Worcestershire

ECKINGTON MANOR

Judy Gardner runs her rural restaurant-with-rooms and cookery school in an 'attractive conversion' of farm buildings, in a 'charming, peaceful' village on the edge of the Cotswolds. 'The restaurant is the centrepiece,' say Guide inspectors this year, who found 'every table taken' on a winter's evening. Husband-and-wife team Mark and Sue Stinchcombe are the chefs; their modern dishes (perhaps roasted venison, smoked beetroot and blackberry, potato gnocchi) use home-grown produce and beef from cows reared on surrounding farmland. 'It's the sort of place where the waiter or waitress explains each dish's ingredients – and there are lots of exotic ingredients, imaginatively used. The best bit, for us: an exquisite tangerine soufflé.' Bedrooms are spread over four converted outbuildings, each with a wealth of original features – wall timbering, oak beams, flagstones. 'Our room, with a big bed, a sofa and a wood-burning stove, had been made over in good taste, with quality materials; the shower room was small but well designed. Pity about the poor lighting.' In the morning, breakfast brings a small buffet, 'chunky toast' and 'plenty of cooked dishes', including an 'excellent kipper'.

Hammock Road
Eckington
WR10 3BJ

T: 01386 751600
F: 01386 751362
E: info@eckingtonmanor.co.uk
W: www.eckingtonmanor.co.uk

BEDROOMS: 17. All in courtyard annexes, 1 suitable for disabled.
OPEN: all year except 25/26 Dec, restaurant closed Sun evening, Mon, Tues.
FACILITIES: lift, 2 sitting rooms, restaurant, function rooms, free Wi-Fi, in-room TV (Freeview), civil wedding licence, cookery school, 260-acre grounds (lawns, herb garden, orchard, working farm).
BACKGROUND MUSIC: in garden bar and restaurant.
LOCATION: 4 miles SW of Pershore.
CHILDREN: not under 8.
DOGS: allowed in 2 bedrooms, not in public rooms.
CREDIT CARDS: Amex, MasterCard, Visa.
PRICES: [2017] per room B&B £139–£269. Set dinner £48.

EDENBRIDGE Kent

Map 2:D4

STARBOROUGH MANOR

'An ideal B&B', Lynn and Jonathan Mathias's Georgian manor house, much made over in Victorian times, is approached via a tree-lined drive through large grounds. 'It's definitely a place for people who like to chat and get to know their hosts,' say Guide inspectors in 2017. 'Lynn and Jonathan are extremely friendly, and were pleased to tell us the history of their house. In the morning, they gave us helpful suggestions for our day.' The house stands in large grounds, overlooking a lake with an island folly built on the ruins of medieval Starborough Castle; there are 'lovely views over the peaceful setting' from the 'fine, spacious' drawing room. Bedrooms, each different, are 'elegant and tasteful'. 'Our enormous bed had the most comfortable, deep duvet; soft towels and indulgent bath products in the bathroom. Our hosts provided us with crockery, cutlery and glasses to eat our picnic supper.' At breakfast in the roomy kitchen, 'Lynn was happy to adapt a very good cooked breakfast to my slightly fussy requirements'. On the side: 'a delicious array' of fruits, cereals, yogurts and jams. Historic Hever Castle and the National Trust's Standen House and garden are within a 20-minute drive.

Moor Lane
Marsh Green
Edenbridge
TN8 5QY

T: 01732 862152
E: lynn@starboroughmanor.co.uk
W: www.starboroughmanor.co.uk

BEDROOMS: 4.
OPEN: all year.
FACILITIES: 2 sitting rooms, dining room, kitchen/breakfast room, laundry for guests' use, function facilities, free Wi-Fi, in-room TV (Freeview), 4-acre gardens in 13-acre grounds (parkland, tennis, heated outdoor swimming pool in season), unsuitable for disabled.
BACKGROUND MUSIC: none.
LOCATION: 1½ miles W of Edenbridge.
CHILDREN: all ages welcomed.
DOGS: not allowed.
CREDIT CARDS: Amex, MasterCard, Visa.
PRICES: [2017] per room B&B £145, 1-night bookings usually refused weekends in summer.

SEE ALSO SHORTLIST

EGTON BRIDGE Yorkshire

Map 4:C5

BROOM HOUSE

NEW

Georgina and Michael Curnow's 'upmarket B&B' stands in garden and woodlands just beyond a 'pretty village' in the North York Moors national park. It receives an upgrade to a full entry thanks to a recommendation in 2017 from a regular Guide correspondent who had a 'delightful stay'. Outside are wide views of the Esk valley; within the stone-built Victorian farmhouse, garden posies brighten the lawn-facing sitting room. Garden- and valley-view bedrooms vary in size, from a cosy double on the top floor to a two-bedroom cottage suite with a separate sitting room and private patio. 'Modern, clean and well thought through, our spacious, newly finished cottage extension had comfortable beds in both bedrooms.' Pick a book from the neat bookshelf to read over a 'good breakfast' of local produce (dietary needs may be catered for); the 'short menu' includes fruit smoothies, home-made jams, Whitby kippers, 'particularly good scrambled eggs'. Coast and countryside are within easy reach; in the evening, 'a pleasant ten-minute walk takes you to a pub, with stepping stones over the river'. 'We would happily stay here again.' (DW, and others)

Broom House Lane
Egton Bridge
YO21 1XD

T: 07423 636783
E: mail@broom-house.co.uk
W: www.broom-house.co.uk

BEDROOMS: 9. 2 (1 on ground floor) in converted barn suite.
OPEN: Mar–Nov.
FACILITIES: lounge, breakfast room, free Wi-Fi, in-room TV (Freeview), 1-acre garden.
BACKGROUND MUSIC: in breakfast room.
LOCATION: ½ mile W of village.
CHILDREN: all ages welcomed, by arrangement.
DOGS: not allowed.
CREDIT CARDS: MasterCard, Visa.
PRICES: [2017] per room B&B £89–£200. 2-night min. bookings preferred.

EMSWORTH Hampshire

36 ON THE QUAY

🏆 Previous César winner

Coast and countryside flavour this restaurant-with-rooms between Chichester harbour and the South Downs national park – look out for shore-harvested sea buckthorn and foraged ceps and chanterelles on the modern menus. Karen and Ramon Farthing set up their modest enterprise in this fishing village more than 20 years ago; today, they run it with Gary and Martina Pearce, who are chef and manager. The simply furnished bedrooms in the 17th-century building are 'spotlessly clean', and supplied with good coffee, bottled water, biscuits and 'fluffy towels'. One spacious room has a window seat taking in quayside views, two are snugger. Still, this is 'a foodie destination', and the cooking is the main attraction. In the dining room overlooking the 'quaint harbour', the chef's short but imaginative menus might include sirloin of Welsh Wagyu beef, barbecued onions, braised shin, tartare with chives; poached chalk-stream trout, roasted scallop, peas, morels, asparagus velouté. (Even the amuse-bouche are praised.) Breakfast is continental: 'good toast and jams', croissants, pain au chocolat.

47 South Street
Emsworth
PO10 7EG

T: 01243 375592
E: info@36onthequay.co.uk
W: www.36onthequay.co.uk

BEDROOMS: 4.
OPEN: all year except 24–26 Dec, 2 weeks Jan, 1 week May, 1 week Nov, restaurant closed Sun/Mon.
FACILITIES: bar area, restaurant, free Wi-Fi, in-room TV (Freeview), small terrace, limited parking, only restaurant suitable for disabled.
BACKGROUND MUSIC: none.
LOCATION: on harbour.
CHILDREN: all ages welcomed.
DOGS: not allowed.
CREDIT CARDS: Amex, MasterCard, Visa.
PRICES: [2017] per room B&B single £75–£110, double £110–£200. À la carte £57.95, tasting menu £65.

ERMINGTON Devon

Map 1:D4

PLANTATION HOUSE

'No airs and graces here': guests enjoy the 'friendly informality', 'care and concern' and ready supply of leaf teas ('oh, joy!') at Richard Hendey's small hotel, in a restored Georgian rectory between Dartmoor and the Devon coast. 'Richard, a welcoming host, seemed to be everywhere.' Settle in with tea and cake upon arrival, or opt for a locally brewed beer from the bar; the lounge is a pleasing place to be in, with tropical plants and garden blooms, modern artwork and artefacts. There are 'lovely treats' in the countryside-view bedrooms: bottled water, fruit, home-baked cake and biscuits; a hot-water bottle at bedtime. 'Our beautifully furnished room at the front of the hotel had good views.' Dinner, using garden produce, wild ingredients and local meat and seafood, is 'very good'. With John Raines, Richard Hendey cooks 'first-class' multi-course meals with 'unusual, enjoyable combinations', perhaps slow-cooked Devon duckling, wild garlic dauphinoise, stir-fried greens, roast baby onions. Breakfast well on home-made bread and marmalade, 'excellent' fruit salads, tasty cooked options. 'Well located for exploring the South Hams.' (Mary Coles, and others)

Totnes Road
Ivybridge
Ermington
PL21 9NS

T: 01548 831100
E: info@plantationhousehotel.co.uk
W: www.plantationhousehotel.co.uk

BEDROOMS: 8.
OPEN: all year, restaurant closed midday, some Sun evenings.
FACILITIES: lounge/bar, 2 dining rooms, free Wi-Fi, in-room TV (Freeview), terrace, 1-acre garden, unsuitable for disabled.
BACKGROUND MUSIC: classical/easy jazz in public rooms, 'whenever required'.
LOCATION: 10 miles E of Plymouth.
CHILDREN: all ages welcomed.
DOGS: allowed in 1 bedroom, not in public rooms.
CREDIT CARDS: Amex, MasterCard, Visa.
PRICES: per room B&B £110–£230, D,B&B £190–£410. Set dinner £39.50. 1-night bookings sometimes refused.

EVERSHOT Dorset

Map 1:C6

THE ACORN INN   [NEW]

Tess of the d'Urbervilles skirted this stone-built 16th-century inn, named the Sow and Acorn in Thomas Hardy's novel, but locals and visitors today know better. 'It's a lovely spot in a charming village,' says a regular Guide correspondent in 2017. (The 'warm welcome' from 'attentive staff' extends to dogs, who are offered biscuits, a water bowl and towel.) Quiz nights, a skittle alley, a beech-shaded garden and a fine roster of local ales give the place a faithful village-pub feel. The restaurant strikes a smart note, with modern takes on country cooking. A typical dish: pan-seared duck breast, sweet potato fondant, confit duck leg, savoy cabbage. Colourful, elegant bedrooms are each given a name with Hardy resonance, and supplied with bottled water, home-made shortbread and top-end toiletries. Rooms vary in size and style; one of the best, lavish in toile de Jouy, has an antique carved-oak four-poster bed. 'My room had a large bed and a sofa; a snug bathroom with tons of hot water.' There's 'great choice' at breakfast, plus bread fresh from the village bakery a minute's walk down the street. 'The full English was the best I've had in a long while.' (Ian Dewey)

28 Fore Street
Evershot
DT2 0JW

T: 01935 83228
E: stay@acorn-inn.co.uk
W: www.acorn-inn.co.uk

BEDROOMS: 10.
OPEN: all year.
FACILITIES: 2 bars, restaurant, lounge, free Wi-Fi, in-room TV (Sky, Freeview), skittle alley, small beer garden, access to spa and gym at sister hotel opposite (£15 charge), unsuitable for disabled.
BACKGROUND MUSIC: in bar and restaurant.
LOCATION: in village, 10 miles S of Yeovil.
CHILDREN: all ages welcomed.
DOGS: allowed (£12 charge).
CREDIT CARDS: Amex, MasterCard, Visa.
PRICES: [2017] per room B&B from £99, D,B&B from £159. À la carte £30. 2-night min. stay at weekends during peak season.

FAVERSHAM Kent

Map 2:D5

READ'S

'Our stay was close to perfect. It was like spending a weekend at a country house where the hostess has impeccable taste and is a first-rate cook. All this at an outstandingly reasonable price, in an interesting and accessible corner of Kent.' Regular Guide readers in 2017 'strongly recommend' Rona and David Pitchford's restaurant-with-rooms, in a Georgian manor house surrounded by cedar and horse chestnut trees reaching skywards. In the restaurant, David Pitchford's seasonal offerings follow the whims of the walled kitchen garden, the aim of local gamekeepers and the daily catch hauled into nearby Whitstable and Hythe. Among the European classics: wild duck breast, blackberries, Granny Smith apples, creamed potato. 'We sampled a good cross-section of the menu; dishes ranged from good to very good indeed, and were served attentively and with care.' Retire to one of the traditionally, but 'unfussily', decorated bedrooms after dinner. 'Our room was capacious and furnished with style, with an eye to practical comfort as well as appearance.' In the morning, breakfast, 'served in a very comfortable room', is equally praised.

Macknade Manor
Canterbury Road
Faversham
ME13 8XE

T: 01795 535344
F: 01795 591200
E: enquiries@reads.com
W: www.reads.com

BEDROOMS: 6.
OPEN: all year except Christmas, 1st week Jan, 2 weeks Sept, restaurant closed Sun/Mon.
FACILITIES: sitting room/bar, 3 dining rooms, free Wi-Fi, in-room TV (Freeview), civil wedding licence, 4-acre garden (terrace, outdoor dining), only restaurant suitable for disabled.
BACKGROUND MUSIC: none.
LOCATION: ½ mile SE of Faversham.
CHILDREN: all ages welcomed.
DOGS: not allowed in public rooms.
CREDIT CARDS: all major cards.
PRICES: [2017] per room B&B single £140–£195, double £180–£210, D,B&B single £185–£250, double £290–£320. Set dinner £60, tasting menu £65.

FELIXKIRK Yorkshire

Map 4:C4

THE CARPENTERS ARMS

'A fashionable place that attracts far-flung customers', this updated pub-with-rooms stands in a small village overlooking the Vale of Mowbray, on the edge of the North York Moors. 'The outstanding rooms and welcoming staff make it a great place to stay.' The rustic pub looks the part: there are flagstones, low beams, wooden settles, a log fire in cool weather; local beers and hand-pulled ales. Here, in the 'tastefully decorated' restaurant, and on the tiered terrace in sunshine, tuck in to 'good cooking at reasonable prices'. Straightforward and hearty, county-showcasing dishes include roast rack and slow-braised shoulder croquette of Yorkshire lamb; 'a tasty medium-rare sirloin steak with a Yorkshire Blue sauce'. Most of the 'well-appointed bedrooms' are set around a courtyard garden (watch out for slippery steps after rain); two are in the main building. 'All the rooms are equally good.' 'My spacious garden room had a three-seater sofa and two easy chairs. A gas-fired imitation log fire made it all very cosy.' 'Tempting breakfasts' are 'promptly served'. Cleveland Tontine, Northallerton (see Shortlist entry), is part of the same Provenance Inns group. (Robert Gower, D and KW)

Felixkirk
YO7 2DP

T: 01845 537369
E: enquiries@
   thecarpentersarmsfelixkirk.com
W: www.
   thecarpentersarmsfelixkirk.com

BEDROOMS: 10. 8 in garden annexe, 1 suitable for disabled.
OPEN: all year.
FACILITIES: bar/sitting area, restaurant, private dining room, free Wi-Fi, in-room TV (Freeview), terrace (alfresco meals), garden.
BACKGROUND MUSIC: 'generally at mealtimes' in bar and garden room.
LOCATION: in village 3 miles NE of Thirsk.
CHILDREN: all ages welcomed.
DOGS: welcomed in garden bedrooms, bar and some dining areas.
CREDIT CARDS: Amex, MasterCard, Visa.
PRICES: [2017] per room B&B from £120, D,B&B from £180. À la carte £37.50.

FLEET Dorset

Map 1:D6

MOONFLEET MANOR

Just the ticket for 'young children and their exhausted parents', this Georgian manor house stands in 'beautiful, romantic' countryside. It has a 'friendly, relaxed' atmosphere that's 'really geared for kids'. 'I give it a million out of a million,' said a five-year-old guest. (A grandfather was glad that, after slots for children's tea and family dinner, evenings in the restaurant are exclusively for grown-ups.) The facilities for young guests are 'excellent': there are trampolines, a skittle alley, table tennis, cinema sessions, indoor pools, a mini-beast hunt through the grounds; at the Sunday-morning breakfast club, children are collected, fed and looked after by Ofsted-registered nannies 'until their grateful parents surface'. 'Comfortable, interestingly furnished' bedrooms in the main house and two annexes come in different sizes and with different sleeping arrangements; some rooms connect to accommodate a family group. For more privacy, book the two-bedroom, two-bathroom Coach House, with its own lounge. There are 'great' children's options at lunch and dinner; when night falls, adults have 'plenty of choice' on the Mediterranean-inspired British menu. (JB, and others)

Fleet Road
Fleet
DT3 4ED

T: 01305 786948
F: 01305 774395
E: info@moonfleetmanorhotel.co.uk
W: www.moonfleetmanorhotel.co.uk

BEDROOMS: 36. 3 in Coach House, 3 in villa, 3 on ground floor.
OPEN: all year.
FACILITIES: 2 lounges, family snug, restaurant, indoor playroom, crèche, cinema room, free Wi-Fi, in-room TV (Freeview), civil wedding licence, indoor swimming pools, terrace, 17-acre garden (play areas).
BACKGROUND MUSIC: contemporary in restaurant.
LOCATION: 7 miles W of Weymouth.
CHILDREN: all ages welcomed.
DOGS: allowed in bedrooms, not in public rooms.
CREDIT CARDS: Amex, MasterCard, Visa.
PRICES: [2017] per room B&B £120–£525, D,B&B £190–£595. À la carte £40. 1-night bookings sometimes refused.

FOWEY Cornwall

Map 1:D3

FOWEY HALL

⚜ Previous César winner

Close to heritage coast and sandy cove, this 'delightful old mansion', the Victorian pile that inspired Kenneth Grahame's Toad Hall, is packed with 'first-rate facilities' for young and old. It is part of the Luxury Family Hotels group, whose 'highly motivated staff want to make sure guests have a good time'. Children paint, splash, swing, tumble and squeal; grown-ups may book a spa treatment or soak in the hot tub looking towards the sea. There are 'bee hotels', and chickens to feed; Bramble, the house dog, willingly accompanies guests on a stroll or a scamper. 'Large, well-furnished' bedrooms in the main house and converted coach house across the courtyard are 'a proper retreat if it all gets too much in the public spaces'. 'Ours, warm and welcoming, had a delightful view across the garden to the harbour beyond.' At mealtimes, a flexible approach suits all ages, too. Opt for an informal family meal in the early evening, or feed the young ones at children's high tea, then turn on the in-room baby-listening service and come back for a candlelit dinner à deux. Before heading to the beach the next day, borrow fishing nets, buckets and spades. (AK-H)

Hanson Drive
Fowey
PL23 1ET

т: 01726 833866
е: info@foweyhallhotel.co.uk
w: www.foweyhallhotel.co.uk

BEDROOMS: 36. 8 in coach house, some on ground floor, 2 suitable for disabled.
OPEN: all year.
FACILITIES: 2 lounges, library/snug, 2 restaurants, free Wi-Fi, in-room TV (Freeview), crèche, games rooms, civil wedding licence, spa, 12-metre indoor swimming pool, 7-acre grounds (trampoline, zip wire).
BACKGROUND MUSIC: 'easy listening' in restaurants.
LOCATION: ½ mile from town centre.
CHILDREN: all ages welcomed.
DOGS: allowed in main house bedrooms (£15), not in restaurant.
CREDIT CARDS: Amex, MasterCard, Visa.
PRICES: [2017] per room B&B £190–£750. Set dinner £30–£40, à la carte £39. 1-night bookings refused at weekends.

SEE ALSO SHORTLIST

GITTISHAM Devon

Map 1:C5

THE PIG AT COMBE NEW

'There is much to like and laugh about' at this utterly transformed Elizabethan manor house, in a 'glorious setting' in the Otter valley. The newest of the litter, it shares a distinct ('friendly, boho-chic') family resemblance with Robin Hutson's other Pig hotels. Step straight into the 'busy, buzzing' wood-panelled bar; 'inviting sitting areas' and open fires are beyond. 'In good weather, outside is the place to be: the well-groomed gardens are a pleasure; there are beautiful views to soak in from the swings or benches.' 'Charming, quirky bedrooms' are spread across the property. Careful selection may be necessary: one guest thought a snug room in the main house 'compact'; a 'comfy, tastefully decorated' superior room in the otherwise 'brilliantly converted stables' had noise from rooms above. In the conservatory restaurant and restored garden folly, chef Daniel Gavriilidis cooks food with 'excellent pedigree' – perhaps crispy pig's cheek, piccalilli, wild chives. Breakfast is worthy of a pig-out ('but why is it charged extra?'). A buffet holds yogurt, fruit, pastries, 'an excellent apricot compote'; hot dishes are cooked to order. (Wendy Ashworth, and others)

Gittisham
EX14 3AD

T: 01404 540400
E: info@thepigatcombe.com
W: www.thepighotel.com

BEDROOMS: 30. 10 in stable yard, 3 in cottages, 2 suitable for disabled.
OPEN: all year.
FACILITIES: bar, 2 lounges, restaurant, Folly alfresco drinking/eating area, meeting/private dining rooms, free Wi-Fi, in-room TV (Freeview), civil wedding licence, spa treatment rooms, terrace, 3,500-acre grounds (3 walled gardens).
BACKGROUND MUSIC: all day in public areas.
LOCATION: on outskirts of village.
CHILDREN: all ages welcomed.
DOGS: not allowed.
CREDIT CARDS: Amex, MasterCard, Visa.
PRICES: [2017] room £155–£490. À la carte £35. 1-night bookings sometimes refused.

GRASMERE Cumbria

Map 4: inset C2

🏆 FOREST SIDE

César award: romantic hotel of the year

'A universe away from the village's tourist throng', this Gothic pile at the end of a winding driveway has been given a 'fabulous' modern-rustic makeover. 'Top of the market', it is the brainchild of Andrew Wildsmith, who also owns Hipping Hall, Cowan Bridge, and The Ryebeck, Bowness-on-Windermere (see full and Shortlist entries). 'Elegantly understated, it strikes the right balance between smartness and informality. And the views of the surrounding fells are delightful,' says a Guide reader in 2017. 'Almost every aspect of the place impresses', from the 'friendly, attentive staff' and the 'beautiful bedrooms' to chef Kevin Tickle's 'fantastic, accomplished' Michelin-starred cooking in the light-filled dining room. 'We were offered, to start, crunchy bread made with a six-year-old damson "mother", and a seaweed broth of marsh herbs and surf clams. More traditional mains included cod with charred onion shoots, and a good slab of shorthorn rib. Great puddings, too.' In the afternoon, explore the restored gardens, returning for a 'completely indulgent tea'. (Michael Williams, RN, Stephanie Thompson and Keith Sutton)

Keswick Road
Grasmere
LA22 9RN

T: 015394 35250
E: info@theforestside.com
W: www.theforestside.com

BEDROOMS: 20. 1 suitable for disabled.
OPEN: all year.
FACILITIES: lounges, bar, restaurant, function/private dining rooms, civil wedding licence, free Wi-Fi, in-room TV, terrace, garden (1-acre kitchen garden).
BACKGROUND MUSIC: in public areas.
LOCATION: outskirts of village.
CHILDREN: all ages welcomed.
DOGS: allowed in some bedrooms (max. 2 per room, £20 per dog, includes welcome pack).
CREDIT CARDS: MasterCard, Visa.
PRICES: [2017] per room B&B £209–£349. Set dinner £60–£95.

GRASMERE Cumbria

Map 4: inset C2

THE GRASMERE HOTEL

'Hands-on' owners Rob van der Palen and Anton Renac run their 'excellent hotel' with 'thoughtful attention', friendliness and more than a touch of Grasmere gingerbread. 'The welcoming staff guarantee a happy stay.' 'Comfy armchairs and sofas' are grouped around low tables and a fire in linked lounges; the conservatory restaurant gazes on to the neat lawn reaching towards the River Rothay. 'Pleasant bedrooms', each named after a Lake poet or a local luminary, are 'modern and spotless'; a ground-floor room opens on to the garden. 'Ours, spacious and well lit, was restful and quiet despite facing the busy road out front.' Anton Renac's four-course dinners are served almost every night of the week. (A mixed platter is taken in the lounge when the restaurant is closed.) Start with 'delicious' home-baked bread, then choose from an 'excellent menu' that includes a daily special. Among the 'splendid dishes': fricassée of woodland mushrooms in a filo pastry basket; slow-cooked lamb, pearl onions, lamb croquette. Walkers, ask for a packed lunch; the hosts have easy rambles and more challenging hikes to suggest. (MS, Jean Muir, J and DA)

Broadgate
Grasmere
LA22 9TA

T: 015394 35277
E: info@grasmerehotel.co.uk
W: www.grasmerehotel.co.uk

BEDROOMS: 11.
OPEN: all year except 31 Dec–end Jan, restaurant closed Tues.
FACILITIES: lounge, restaurant, free Wi-Fi, in-room TV (Freeview), ½-acre garden, unsuitable for disabled.
BACKGROUND MUSIC: in lounge and restaurant during mealtimes.
LOCATION: in village.
CHILDREN: not under 10.
DOGS: 1 small to medium dog allowed, by arrangement, in some bedrooms, not in public rooms.
CREDIT CARDS: MasterCard, Visa.
PRICES: per room B&B single £67–£97, double £122–£154, D,B&B single £92–£122, double £172–£204. Set dinner £29–£32. 2-night min. stay normally required (check for 1-night availability), Sat and bank holiday Sun night reservations must include dinner.

GRASMERE Cumbria

OAK BANK

'We know what to expect when we come: outstanding food, lovely staff, a restful stay,' writes a returning guest this year at Glynis and Simon Wood's family-run hotel in Cumbria's most popular village. 'The owners' raison d'être is to ensure that guests experience the best hospitality,' comments another. 'What more could you want?' Well, a little sharper service in the dining room, say some (otherwise satisfied) Guide readers. All praise the 'friendly welcome', the comforts of log fires, the pleasure of a beer in the garden. 'Really nice' bedrooms are supplied with still and sparkling water, bathrobes, good toiletries; the best have a double-ended bath or spa bath in the bathroom. In the dining room, Stephen Collier's 'superb, imaginative' modern dishes might include braised asparagus, Parmesan, duck egg, tomato essence; Herdwick lamb, pickled cabbage, seaweed, anchovy. 'The canapés are a bonus.' Wake to fruit smoothies on a 'fresh, varied' breakfast menu; fruit compotes, cereals and freshly baked croissants are accompanied by fish dishes, omelettes or Scotch pancakes with maple syrup. (Ann McEwan, Flora Marriott, Sandra Ashton, and others)

Broadgate
Grasmere
LA22 9TA

T: 015394 35217
F: 015394 35685
E: info@lakedistricthotel.co.uk
W: www.lakedistricthotel.co.uk

BEDROOMS: 13. 1 on ground floor.
OPEN: all year except 17–26 Dec, 2–18 Jan.
FACILITIES: lounge, bar, restaurant, conservatory dining room, free Wi-Fi, in-room TV (Freeview or FreeSat), ½-acre garden, unsuitable for disabled.
BACKGROUND MUSIC: classical at breakfast, 'easy listening'/R&B at dinner in dining areas.
LOCATION: just outside village centre.
CHILDREN: not under 10 in restaurant or public rooms after 6 pm.
DOGS: allowed in 3 bedrooms, front lounge.
CREDIT CARDS: MasterCard, Visa.
PRICES: per room B&B £80–£170, D,B&B £123–£235. Set dinner £45, tasting menu £65. 1-night bookings usually refused weekends.

HALNAKER Sussex

THE OLD STORE

In a pretty hamlet close to Goodwood, this former bakery and village store is run as a B&B by 'accommodating, thoughtful hosts' Heather and Patrick Birchenough. 'It might be a modest operation, but the things that really matter are there.' The treats that matter are in evidence, too: 'We arrived to the smell of baking, and were served a tasty chocolate cake and fruit bread; a little parcel of it was also left in our room.' Downstairs, the sitting room is 'snug, but clean and carefully maintained'; there are travel guides and 'a small, well-stocked library' to browse. Bedrooms have a 'nicely equipped' tea tray and 'a bible of local information'. 'Our bijou room had a gorgeously comfortable bed; a powerful shower, fat towels and lovely smellies in the bathroom.' Breakfast, with freshly baked bread and home-made jams, is in a 'bright, sun-filled' room with vintage milk bottles lining a beam – 'a sweet nod to the building's past'. Here, award-winning sausages, 'good, strong' coffee and 'possibly the nicest muesli in England' set you up for a hike on the South Downs. The Arundel wildfowl and wetland nature reserve and the market towns of Petworth and Midhurst are within a 20-minute drive.

Stane Street
Halnaker
PO18 0QL

T: 01243 531977
F: 01243 531977
E: theoldstore4@aol.com
W: www.theoldstoreguesthouse.
   co.uk

BEDROOMS: 7. 1 on ground floor.
OPEN: Mar–Dec.
FACILITIES: lounge, breakfast room, free Wi-Fi, in-room TV (Freeview), ¼-acre garden with seating.
BACKGROUND MUSIC: none.
LOCATION: 4 miles NE of Chichester.
CHILDREN: all ages welcomed.
DOGS: not allowed.
CREDIT CARDS: MasterCard, Visa.
PRICES: [2017] per person B&B £40–£60 (higher for Goodwood 'Festival of Speed' and 'Revival' meetings). 1-night bookings refused weekends, sometimes other nights in high season.

HAMBLETON Rutland

Map 2:B3

⚜ HAMBLETON HALL

César award: luxury hotel of the year

'Tim and Stefa Hart's country house hotel is consistently outstanding, with service I have yet to see bettered: courteous, attentive, unobtrusive. And Aaron Patterson's Michelin-starred cooking never fails.' Standing amid formal gardens, this 'classy, delightful hotel' inspires devotion among its guests. 'It does not disappoint,' a regular Guide reader sums up in 2017. Modern luxury mixes with period features in the 19th-century hunting lodge. Well-equipped bedrooms have thoughtful touches (fresh flowers, pre-stamped postcards, biscuits by the bedside) that add to the general feeling of being 'wonderfully spoilt'. 'Our room overlooked lovely Rutland Water under lowering skies on a winter Sunday.' Stroll round the 'beautiful gardens' or, if the weather turns, find a spot on one of the 'inviting sofas' in the 'ever-comfortable lounges' ('the lighting's a little low for reading, though'). Dinner is 'superb'; breakfast, with 'good, strong coffee and fresh hot cross buns', is 'exemplary'. 'Long may the current owners and chef remain.' Sister establishment Hart's Hotel is in Nottingham (see entry). (Robert Gower, Anthony Bradbury, Robert Sandham)

Oakham
Hambleton
LE15 8TH

T: 01572 756991
E: hotel@hambletonhall.com
W: www.hambletonhall.com

BEDROOMS: 17. 2-bedroomed suite in cottage.
OPEN: all year.
FACILITIES: lift, hall, drawing room/bar, restaurant, 2 private dining rooms, free Wi-Fi, in-room TV (Sky), civil wedding licence, 17-acre grounds (tennis, swimming pool (heated May–Sept), croquet, vegetable garden).
BACKGROUND MUSIC: none.
LOCATION: 3 miles SE of Oakham, Rutland.
CHILDREN: all ages welcomed, only children 'of a grown-up age' in restaurant in evening.
DOGS: allowed in bedrooms (not unattended), hall, not in public rooms.
CREDIT CARDS: all major cards.
PRICES: [2017] per room B&B from £280, D,B&B from £400. Set dinner £69. 1-night bookings normally refused weekends.

HAROME Yorkshire

Map 4:D4

THE PHEASANT   NEW

Wellies line the stone-flagged floor, a couple of stuffed pheasants take in the scene: an 'oasis of calm' overlooking the village duck pond, Jacquie Pern's chic, rustic hotel on the edge of the North Yorkshire Moors is a 'really nice place to stay'. Converted from a former village shop, smithy and barn, it re-enters the Guide this year thanks to readers who praise the 'friendly staff', 'first-class food', 'stylish bedrooms' and 'peaceful setting'. 'In a decade of visits, we have never been disappointed,' says a fan in 2017. 'Characterful bedrooms' in a modern country mix of plaids and florals are set around a courtyard of fruit trees; a stone cottage is in a secluded corner. All have 'nice touches': cafetière coffee, fresh milk, sloe gin. In the restaurant, and on the vine-hung patio on a sunny day, chef/co-owner Peter Neville's 'superb meals' are 'deftly cooked'. Foraged finds mix with local ingredients in dishes such as beef tartare, truffle mayonnaise, sourdough; wild sea bass, Jerusalem artichoke, Cumbrian pancetta. (Leave room for the 'wonderful desserts'.) 'Good choice' at breakfast, including honey from moorland heather. (Shirley B Gray, Peter Anderson)

Harome
YO62 5JG

T: 01439 771241
E: reservations@thepheasanthotel.com
W: www.thepheasanthotel.com

BEDROOMS: 16. 3 on ground floor, 1 in cottage.
OPEN: all year.
FACILITIES: bar, lounge, conservatory, restaurant, free Wi-Fi, in-room TV (Freeview), heated indoor swimming pool, terrace.
BACKGROUND MUSIC: in public areas.
LOCATION: village centre.
CHILDREN: all ages welcomed.
DOGS: allowed in some bedrooms, not in public rooms.
CREDIT CARDS: MasterCard, Visa.
PRICES: per room B&B single £95–£240, double £180–£270, D,B&B single £135–£280, double £260–£350. Tasting menu £75, à la carte £45.

HAROME Yorkshire

Map 4:D4

THE STAR INN

In its 'quiet village setting' on the edge of the North York Moors, this 14th-century thatch-roofed inn looks pure chocolate box; as with all the best chocolate boxes, there is deliciousness within. Chef/patron Andrew Pern took on the decrepit pub in 2002, revamped it and raised it to Michelin-star status. His 'superb cooking' draws on the kitchen garden, Yorkshire producers and the untamed countryside for such dishes as forager's broth of mushrooms, hedgerow roots, wild rabbit taco; rump of Yorkshire hogget, suet-braised beetroot, roast almonds. 'Spotlessly clean and comfortable' bedrooms are in former farm buildings, two minutes away. Each room is 'characterful, if slightly eccentric': one has an upright piano, another, a snooker table. Two rooms sharing a hallway would suit a family. 'The accommodation is entirely self-sufficient. On return from a Ryedale Festival event, the chance to have a drink and a platter of local cheeses and biscuits was more than welcome.' 'Outstanding breakfasts' are taken communally at a 'vast circular table – like something out of Camelot'. Look out for offers – 'the gourmet break is excellent value for money'. (Richard Osborne, and others)

High Street
Harome
YO62 5JE

T: 01439 770397
E: reservations@
thestarinnatharome.co.uk
W: www.thestaratharome.co.uk

BEDROOMS: 9. All in Cross House Lodge opposite, 3 on ground floor.
OPEN: all year, restaurant closed midday Mon.
FACILITIES: lounge, restaurant, The Wheelhouse private dining room, free Wi-Fi, in-room TV (Freeview), civil wedding licence, terrace, 2-acre garden, unsuitable for disabled.
BACKGROUND MUSIC: 'gentle jazz' in lounge and dining room.
LOCATION: village centre.
CHILDREN: all ages welcomed.
DOGS: not allowed.
CREDIT CARDS: MasterCard, Visa.
PRICES: per room B&B £150–£260. Market menus £20–£25, tasting menu £85, à la carte £48.

HARWICH Essex

Map 2:C5

THE PIER AT HARWICH

'A beacon of urbanity and flair on the quay',
Paul Milsom's hotel is praised for its 'obliging,
well-intentioned' staff. Refurbishment has
resulted in a slick ground-floor bar with 'a
serious gin and cocktail "library"', and a chic
first-floor restaurant and estuary-view terrace,
Guide inspectors discovered in 2017. Bedrooms
are 'generously stocked with good-quality
drinks and biscuits' ('chilled glasses in the fridge,
too – nice'). 'Our room overlooked the navy
yard and estuary – a pleasure at dusk, when
the ships and cargo cranes on the water light
up. The room lacked pizzazz, but was clean
and comfortable. We slept well.' By day, lunch
on 'satisfying bowls of chowder' in the bar; at
night, join the 'encouraging mix of locals and
visitors' in the split-level restaurant. ('Critiques
about uneven meals were handled with grace.')
At breakfast, 'a gleaming copper table holds a
neat buffet (shame about the packaged cereals)'.
'We were served by a lovely, good-humoured
woman – exactly who you want to see in the
morning.' Among the 'interesting variety' of
cooked dishes, 'I loved the perfectly ripe avocado
and expertly fried egg served on a thick slice of
rye bread'.

25% DISCOUNT VOUCHERS

The Quay
Harwich
CO12 3HH

T: 01255 241212
F: 01255 551922
E: pier@milsomhotels.com
W: www.milsomhotels.com

BEDROOMS: 14. 7 in annexe, 1 on
ground floor.
OPEN: all year.
FACILITIES: lift, bar, lounge (in
annexe), restaurant, private dining
room, free Wi-Fi, in-room TV (Sky,
Freeview), civil wedding licence,
balcony (alfresco meals), small front
terrace.
BACKGROUND MUSIC: none.
LOCATION: on quay, in old town.
CHILDREN: all ages welcomed.
DOGS: allowed in bedrooms, bar.
CREDIT CARDS: all major cards.
PRICES: [2017] per room B&B from
£130. À la carte £35.

HASTINGS Sussex

Map 2:E5

THE OLD RECTORY

Vintage furnishings mix with contemporary local art, trompe l'oeil touches surprise above stripped wooden floors… 'it's altogether delightful' at this 'friendly, beautifully kept' B&B 'in an excellent location for walking into the historic Old Town'. Lionel Copley, the owner, also co-owns Swan House (see next entry); manager Tracey-Anne Cook is 'gracious, professional, helpful'. Public spaces are stylish – outré, say some guests – while the bedrooms are highly individual: choose Tackleway for the garden views through a large picture window; in Crown, find the loo hidden behind a bookcase. In every room, teas, good coffee and a home-made sweet treat are provided; a carafe of water is set by 'the most comfortable bed'. (Some rooms overlook the road – it's 'completely quiet at night', but you might find yourself waving to the bus queue in the morning.) The 'impeccably maintained' walled garden is a fine place to sit. Five minutes' walk away, 'we loved the First In Last Out pub for dinner'. Breakfast is 'super': much is home made (from bread to sausages); most everything else is locally procured. (Diana Goodey, A and BB)

Harold Road
Hastings
TN35 5ND

T: 01424 422410
E: info@theoldrectoryhastings.co.uk
W: www.theoldrectoryhastings.co.uk

BEDROOMS: 8. One 2-bed, 2-bath suite.
OPEN: all year except 1 week Christmas, 2 weeks Jan.
FACILITIES: 2 lounges (honesty bar), breakfast room, free Wi-Fi, local telephone calls, in-room TV (Freeview), civil wedding licence, walled garden, unsuitable for disabled.
BACKGROUND MUSIC: in breakfast room and main lounge.
LOCATION: edge of Old Town (limited parking spaces, complimentary parking permits).
CHILDREN: not under 10.
DOGS: not allowed.
CREDIT CARDS: Amex, MasterCard, Visa.
PRICES: [2017] per room B&B £90–£175. 1-night bookings refused most weekends.

HASTINGS Sussex

Map 2:E5

SWAN HOUSE

Come in to 'a lovely, warm atmosphere and a good mood' at Lionel Copley and Brendan McDonagh's town-centre B&B, in a pretty cul-de-sac behind the High Street. Bedrooms have character in their old beams, hand-printed wallpapers, fresh flowers and well-picked vintage furnishings; a cosy ground-floor room leads to the patio garden. 'Our room on the first floor looked on to St Clement's church. There were fluffy rugs on the gently sloping floor; lovely, crisp linen on the large bed. A flask of water and a tumbler had been put on each side table; on the tea tray were boiled sweets and a couple of blueberry flapjacks. It was absolutely quiet at night.' An honesty bar ('thinly disguised as a bookcase') in the open-plan lounge quenches pre- and post-dinner thirst. In the morning, the breakfast tables are laid with linen napkins. 'Brendan brought us freshly squeezed orange juice, cafetière coffee and very good scrambled eggs. My Greek yogurt came in a glass bowl – so much nicer than a plastic tub.' The town's pubs and antique shops are a short walk away; Jerwood Gallery, overlooking the fishing boats in the water, is a five-minute stroll.

1 Hill Street
Hastings
TN34 3HU

T: 01424 430014
E: res@swanhousehastings.co.uk
W: www.swanhousehastings.co.uk

BEDROOMS: 4. 1 on ground floor.
OPEN: all year except 24–26 Dec.
FACILITIES: lounge/breakfast room, free Wi-Fi, in-room TV, patio garden, parking permits supplied.
BACKGROUND MUSIC: none.
LOCATION: in old town, near seafront.
CHILDREN: not under 5.
DOGS: not allowed.
CREDIT CARDS: all major cards.
PRICES: [2017] per room B&B £120–£150. 1-night bookings refused weekends.

HATCH BEAUCHAMP Somerset

Map 1:C6

FROG STREET FARMHOUSE

Somerset born and Somerset bred, Louise and David Farrance have run their B&B in this wisteria-hung 15th-century Somerset longhouse for nearly ten years. Their hospitality wins them fans. 'David and Louise now treat us like old friends,' report regular Guide readers in 2017, after their fifth stay. Other returning guests agree: 'It is just as good as before.' Tea and cake – taken in the 'lovingly tended' garden on fine days – mark the start of a visit. Downstairs, the lounge is all wooden beams, uneven stone floors and a log fire; upstairs, garden-fresh flowers appear in the characterful country-style bedrooms in summer months. 'While they no longer serve an evening meal, the Farrances directed us to a gastropub a mile away, where we had a really good dinner.' An alternative: guests are provided with plates, cutlery and glasses to eat a take-away meal in the sitting or dining room – 'which we did, enjoying the log-burner that had been lit for us'. Breakfast is substantial, with local bacon and sausages, home-made bread and preserves. 'An ideal stopover place for travellers to and from Cornwall.' (Mary and Rodney Milne-Day, Michael Gwinnell)

Hatch Beauchamp
TA3 6AF

T: 01823 481883
E: frogstreet@hotmail.com
W: www.frogstreet.co.uk

BEDROOMS: 4. 1 with private entrance.
OPEN: all year except Dec–Jan.
FACILITIES: lounge, dining room, free Wi-Fi, in-room TV (Sky), 150-acre grounds (½-acre garden, farmland), unsuitable for disabled.
BACKGROUND MUSIC: none.
LOCATION: 6 miles SE of Taunton.
CHILDREN: all ages welcomed in family suite.
DOGS: not allowed.
CREDIT CARDS: all major cards.
PRICES: [2017] per person B&B from £40.50. 1-night bookings refused weekends May–Sept.

HATHERSAGE Derbyshire

Map 3:A6

THE GEORGE HOTEL

'Delightful and characterful', this centuries-old former coaching inn is 'a happy ship', Guide readers say. Eric Marsh, the owner, is 'the perfect host, wonderful with everyone'; the 'good-natured staff' are consistently 'friendly and helpful'. The hotel, in the centre of a historic Peak District village, is an effective mix of ancient and modern – a private art collection ('which grows in leaps and bounds') sits well against original beams and bare stone walls. Smart bedrooms (some facing the busy road) are 'comfortable and well appointed', with ample storage and a good bathroom. Commendable housekeeping, too: 'Bottles of mineral water are regularly replenished, facecloths are changed daily.' 'Our ground-floor room did involve 37 steps up and down, owing to the age of the building, but staff helped with luggage.' At mealtimes, choose from chef Helen Prince's short, appealing menu, including, perhaps, lobster ravioli 'simply bursting with sweet lobster', or 'a generous portion of well-cooked monkfish tail, firm and full-flavoured', with cauliflower purée, cumin-spiced potatoes, charred lemon. 'It's all excellent, from breakfast to bar snacks to dinner.' (Joan Rudd, PH)

Main Road
Hathersage
S32 1BB

T: 01433 650436
F: 01433 650099
E: info@george-hotel.net
W: www.george-hotel.net

BEDROOMS: 24.
OPEN: all year.
FACILITIES: lounge/bar, restaurant, 2 function rooms, free Wi-Fi, in-room TV, civil wedding licence, courtyard, only restaurant suitable for disabled.
BACKGROUND MUSIC: light jazz in restaurant.
LOCATION: in village centre, parking.
CHILDREN: all ages welcomed.
DOGS: not allowed.
CREDIT CARDS: Amex, MasterCard, Visa.
PRICES: [2017] per room B&B £115–£184. Set dinner £33.50–£39.95 (plus 5% service charge on all goods and services, for distribution directly to staff). 1-night bookings sometimes refused.

HEREFORD Herefordshire

Map 3:D4

CASTLE HOUSE

In 'a pleasant location' close to the cathedral, David Watkins's family-run hotel has long pleased visitors who praise its 'quality and comfort', and its 'cheerful, intelligent, helpful' staff. 'The imposing Regency building stands in harmony with the architecture around it, in turn lending charm and the gentility of the early 19th century to the general setting,' a regular Guide correspondent said this year. Charm and gentility are in the bedrooms, too, in the main building and in Number 25, a Georgian town house down the street. Rooms vary in size and style (traditional in Castle House, more modern in the town house); two, in Number 25, have access to a private garden. 'Our large room was well furnished and equipped, with a nice sitting area.' In the restaurant, chef Claire Nicholls cooks modern dishes with produce and pedigree meat from the owner's Wye valley farm. More informal meals may be taken in the bistro; when the sun shines, 'a peaceful stretch of water – the old castle moat – behind the hotel provides a most agreeable backcloth to drinks and meals on the lawn'. (David Nicholls, PC)

25% DISCOUNT VOUCHERS

Castle Street
Hereford
HR1 2NW

T: 01432 356321
E: info@castlehse.co.uk
W: www.castlehse.co.uk

BEDROOMS: 24. 8 in town house (a short walk away), some on ground floor, 1 suitable for disabled.
OPEN: all year.
FACILITIES: lift, lounge, bar/bistro, restaurant, free Wi-Fi, in-room TV (Freeview), civil wedding licence, terrace, garden.
BACKGROUND MUSIC: occasionally in public areas.
LOCATION: central.
CHILDREN: all ages welcomed.
DOGS: not allowed.
CREDIT CARDS: Amex, MasterCard, Visa.
PRICES: [2017] per room B&B from £150, D,B&B from £195. À la carte £35.

HEXHAM Northumberland

Map 4:B3

BATTLESTEADS

◊ Previous César winner

'Surely one of the best places to stay in the north of England', Dee and Richard Slade's historic coaching inn is run as a 'characterful, modern' pub, hotel and restaurant, where some of the best views are to be found at night. It is in Europe's largest Dark Sky park; 'inspirational, enthusiastic' guided observatory tours of the stars come complete with a pair of binoculars. The Slades have impressive eco credentials ('though we thought the in-room eco notices a touch bossy'), including a sizeable organic garden. 'A morning tour of the fascinating grounds with Richard is a highlight.' Individually decorated bedrooms are in the main building and a row of 'wonderfully different' timber lodges, each with a spa bath and separate sitting area, in the grounds. In the restaurant, Edward Shilton's 'imaginative' dishes – perhaps home-made roasted pepper and goat's cheese ravioli, Brinkburn cheese, mustard butter – are 'beautifully cooked and presented, and satisfyingly portioned'. Drinks are taken seriously, too: 'If you haven't had a pint of Magus, you haven't lived!' (Colin Bradshaw, P and SG, and others)

Wark-on-Tyne
nr Hexham
NE48 3LS

T: 01434 230209
F: 01434 230039
E: info@battlesteads.com
W: www.battlesteads.com

BEDROOMS: 22. 4 on ground floor, 5 in lodge, 2 suitable for disabled.
OPEN: all year except 25 Dec.
FACILITIES: bar, dining room, function facilities, drying room, free Wi-Fi, in-room TV (Freeview), civil wedding licence, 2-acre grounds (walled garden, kitchen garden, dark sky observatory).
BACKGROUND MUSIC: none.
LOCATION: 12 miles N of Hexham.
CHILDREN: all ages welcomed.
DOGS: allowed in public rooms, some bedrooms (£10 per night).
CREDIT CARDS: Amex, MasterCard, Visa.
PRICES: [2017] per room B&B from £120, D,B&B from £165. À la carte £32.50.

SEE ALSO SHORTLIST

HOPE Derbyshire

Map 3:A6

UNDERLEIGH HOUSE

A green philosophy underpins this 'excellent-value' B&B, in a Derbyshire longhouse within the Peak District national park. 'Helpful and welcoming' owners Vivienne and Philip Taylor offer to greet guests arriving by train; once you've settled in over afternoon tea, the hosts have plenty of ideas for local car-free explorations, including bicycle rentals, and invigorating walks to take in the best views. Country-style bedrooms, three with a private lounge, each have their own character; all have views reaching across the garden to the hills beyond. To get close to nature, choose the garden suite: its patio leads to rose beds and views of the nuthatches, tits and woodpeckers who visit the nest boxes and feeders. In the morning, the beamed, flagstoned breakfast room, once part of a shippon that kept wintering livestock warm, hosts communal meals taken at a long refectory table. The award-winning breakfast is 'quite a ceremony': choose among Derbyshire oatcakes, Cheshire bacon, Cumbrian sausages and Aga-cooked porridge; Philip Taylor's preserves, using local blackcurrants or damsons, are ideal slathered on home-baked granary bread.

Lose Hill Lane
off Edale Road
Hope
S33 6AF

T: 01433 621372
F: 01433 621324
E: info@underleighhouse.co.uk
W: www.underleighhouse.co.uk

BEDROOMS: 4. 3 suites with a private lounge.
OPEN: all year except mid-Dec to mid-Feb.
FACILITIES: lounge, breakfast room, free Wi-Fi, in-room TV (Freeview), ¼-acre garden, unsuitable for disabled.
BACKGROUND MUSIC: none.
LOCATION: 1 mile N of Hope.
CHILDREN: not under 12.
DOGS: not allowed in public rooms, allowed in 1 suite by prior arrangement.
CREDIT CARDS: MasterCard, Visa (both 1.75% surcharge; no surcharge for debit cards).
PRICES: [2017] per room B&B £95–£125. 1-night bookings refused Fri/Sat, bank holidays.

HOUGH-ON-THE-HILL Lincolnshire

Map 2:A3

THE BROWNLOW ARMS

A 'micro-country house' in a peaceful Lincolnshire village, Paul and Lorraine Willoughby's 17th-century inn 'oozes character'. Guide readers enthuse about the 'little touches' the hosts provide (an electric blanket in cool weather, a tray for muddy shoes). 'All was lovely and warm on a bitterly cold night,' reports a Guide reader in 2017. Bedrooms have a 'plush, cosy, classic' feel, with 'tasteful fabrics', 'excellent lighting' and 'beautifully upholstered armchairs'. 'We enjoyed an epic night's sleep – it's very quiet, both inside the hotel and on the road outside.' There's no guest lounge, but the 'atmospheric, buzzy' bar has plenty of nooks and crannies to hide in. 'Lorraine and her staff serve with care and ripples of laughter' in the bar and the 'stunning' grey-panelled dining rooms. Here, chef Ruaraidh Bealby ('so inspiring, and full of great ideas') concocts 'imaginative, well-balanced' dishes such as twice-baked cheese soufflé, chestnut mushrooms, Parmesan cream; venison shepherd's pie, kale, broccoli with almonds. Breakfast has much choice, plus 'decent coffee' and 'the tastiest bacon'. (F and IW, Mary Milne-Day, and others)

High Road
Grantham
Hough-on-the-Hill
NG32 2AZ

T: 01400 250234
F: 01400 250234
E: armsinn@yahoo.co.uk
W: www.thebrownlowarms.com

BEDROOMS: 5. 1 on ground floor in barn conversion.
OPEN: all year except 25/26 Dec, 1 Jan, restaurant closed Sun evening, Mon, Tues midday.
FACILITIES: bar, 3 dining rooms, free Wi-Fi, in-room TV, unsuitable for disabled.
BACKGROUND MUSIC: in public areas.
LOCATION: rural, 2 miles E of town centre.
CHILDREN: not under 8.
DOGS: not allowed.
CREDIT CARDS: MasterCard, Visa.
PRICES: [2017] per room B&B single £70, double £110. À la carte £50.

HUNSTANTON Norfolk

Map 2:A5

NO. 33

NEW

Part of the new wave of 'boutique B&Bs', this refurbished Victorian villa stands on a 'quiet, attractive street', with a 'friendly welcome' and a platter of cream scones within. 'What a treat to have that delicious, and complimentary, afternoon tea.' Decorated in a 'bold, contemporary style', it is owned by Jeanne Whittome, who runs an upmarket café/deli in neighbouring Thornham. Sophisticated bedrooms – one with a bath in the room, the best with a private balcony – are supplied with Fairtrade coffee, tea and biscuits. 'Our immaculate, well-designed bedroom was a pleasure. The six-foot bed had good-quality linen; the wet room, stocked with soft towels, was a pleasant surprise.' In the quirky dining room (metallic walls; scuffed, orange-topped tables), 'generous breakfasts' are 'well cooked, with plenty of choice': freshly baked pastries, home-made granola, local meats. Lighter options (smoked salmon bagels, jammy croissants) may be taken in the room. The public areas may be snug, but the spread of the north Norfolk coast awaits – and B&B residents receive a discount on gourmet picnic hampers from the deli. (Stephen and Jane Marshall)

33 Northgate
Hunstanton
PE36 6AP

T: 01485 524352
E: reception@33hunstanton.co.uk
W: 33hunstanton.co.uk

BEDROOMS: 5. 1, suitable for disabled, on ground floor.
OPEN: all year.
FACILITIES: small sitting room, breakfast room, free Wi-Fi, in-room TV (Freeview), small garden.
BACKGROUND MUSIC: none.
LOCATION: town centre.
CHILDREN: all ages welcomed.
DOGS: allowed in bedrooms, not in dining room.
CREDIT CARDS: MasterCard, Visa.
PRICES: [2017] per room B&B £125–£185.

HUNTINGDON Cambridgeshire

Map 2:B4

THE OLD BRIDGE

'We had total faith that everything would be the best it could be during our stay.' Guide readers arriving at this ivy-swagged Georgian town house on the River Ouse found a popular local spot 'buzzing with guests enjoying the casual, cosy setting of the log fire-warmed lounge and bar areas'. John Hoskins is the 'warm, friendly' owner; the staff are 'helpful and pleasant'. 'The well-trained young team, under the discreet but watchful eye of the owner, gives the place a welcome dynamism. We never had to ask for anything twice; there wasn't anything that was overlooked or misunderstood.' Bedrooms are individually styled with 'a tasteful mixture' of traditional and bold contemporary furnishings – 'plush without a whiff of pretension'.

Those facing the busy road have triple-glazed windows. 'Our inviting river-view room was impeccably clean, quiet and comfortable, with a light, wonderfully spacious bathroom.' Chef Jack Woolner gives a modern spin to classic cooking in the 'atmospheric, intimate' Terrace restaurant; breakfast, with fresh fruit, home-made compotes and 'a good selection' of cooked dishes, is 'impressive'. 'Ten out of ten.' (A and BB, Peter Yaxley)

1 High Street
Huntingdon
PE29 3TQ

T: 01480 424300
F: 01480 411017
E: office@huntsbridge.co.uk
W: www.huntsbridge.com

BEDROOMS: 24. 2 on ground floor.
OPEN: all year.
FACILITIES: lounge, bar, restaurant, private dining room, wine shop, business centre, free Wi-Fi, in-room TV (Freeview), civil wedding licence, 1-acre grounds (riverside terrace, garden), fishing, jetty, boat trips, parking, unsuitable for disabled.
BACKGROUND MUSIC: none.
LOCATION: 500 yds from town centre, station 10 mins' walk.
CHILDREN: all ages welcomed.
DOGS: allowed in 2 bedrooms, lounge and bar, not in restaurant.
CREDIT CARDS: MasterCard, Visa.
PRICES: [2017] per room B&B single from £95, double from £148, D,B&B double from £210. À la carte £35.

ILMINGTON Warwickshire

Map 3:D6

THE HOWARD ARMS NEW

On the green of an 'idyllic' Cotswold village, this centuries-old inn is 'an attractive place to stay', with a 'relaxed, easy' ambience, say Guide inspectors in 2017. 'Low-ceilinged and dark-beamed, with naturally friendly staff, it's a lovely place in which to hunker down.' There are armchairs by the log fire; alcoves with tables and seating; country scenes and 'wonderful old photographs' – try to spot the Ilmington Morris Men before dinner. In the 'informally elegant' mezzanine dining area, an 'appealing' menu of pub classics and 'more ambitious' dishes might include 'a generous portion' of steak and ale stew or 'beautifully cooked' duck breast and Jerusalem artichokes. Bedrooms are divided between the main building and a modern extension. 'Our capacious garden room, in the well-soundproofed annexe, was supplied with ground coffee and buttery biscuits, plus a helpful guide to nearby villages. (Some slippers would have been appreciated for the cool bathroom floor, though.) We had an excellent night's sleep in the comfy bed.' Breakfast the morning after is 'low key': 'pleasant' porridge with Cotswold honey; 'nice' scrambled eggs.

Lower Green
Ilmington
CV36 4LT

T: 01608 682226
E: info@howardarms.com
W: www.howardarms.com

BEDROOMS: 8. 4 in extension, 1 on ground floor.
OPEN: all year.
FACILITIES: snug, bar, restaurant, free Wi-Fi, in-room TV (Freeview), terrace, garden (alfresco dining), only bar suitable for disabled.
BACKGROUND MUSIC: all day in public areas.
LOCATION: 8 miles S of Stratford-upon-Avon, 6 miles NE of Chipping Campden.
CHILDREN: all ages welcomed.
DOGS: allowed in bar only.
CREDIT CARDS: MasterCard, Visa.
PRICES: [2017] per room B&B £110–£150. À la carte £30. 1-night bookings sometimes refused.

IREBY Cumbria

Map 4: inset B2

OVERWATER HALL

♔ Previous César winner

There are open fires here, and views of
Skiddaw; the traditional chintz and prints
are 'part of the charm', says a devotee in
2017. Standing in 'lovely, quiet grounds' ideal
for spotting red squirrels, the 19th-century
battlemented house has been run as a dog-
friendly hotel for 25 years by Stephen Bore and
Angela and Adrian Hyde. 'Friendly, warm,
lived-in – it was the most peaceful, relaxed
holiday we've had.' Even the smallest bedroom
has a king-size bed and seating space; all rooms
are provided with fresh fruit, fresh milk and
flowers. 'Our spacious, high-ceilinged turret
room, with large, curved windows, was rather
grand: two armchairs and a four-poster bed with
high-quality bedlinen; modern fittings and fluffy
towels in the bathroom. A marble fireplace
held a collection of fir cones.' In the restaurant,
'favoured by local farmers and families for
special occasions', cooking is on the robust
side of fine dining. Local produce comes to the
fore, perhaps rack and liver of lamb, haggis,
dauphinoise potatoes, root vegetables. 'Breakfast
was memorable for the kippers – served whole,
not in fillets.' (ST, JB)

25% DISCOUNT VOUCHERS

Ireby
CA7 1HH

T: 017687 76566
F: 017687 76921
E: welcome@overwaterhall.co.uk
W: www.overwaterhall.co.uk

BEDROOMS: 11. 1 on ground floor.
OPEN: all year except first 2 weeks
Jan.
FACILITIES: drawing room, lounge,
bar area, restaurant, free Wi-Fi,
in-room TV (Freeview), civil
wedding licence, 18-acre grounds,
Overwater tarn 1 mile.
BACKGROUND MUSIC: in restaurant
in evening.
LOCATION: 2 miles NE of
Bassenthwaite Lake, 10 miles N of
Keswick.
CHILDREN: all ages welcomed, not
under 5 in restaurant (high tea at
5.30 pm).
DOGS: allowed except in main
lounge, restaurant.
CREDIT CARDS: MasterCard, Visa.
PRICES: [2017] per person B&B
£90–£130 (£50 single supplement).
Set dinner £50. 1-night bookings
refused Sat.

KELMSCOTT Oxfordshire

Map 3:E6

THE PLOUGH

'The wonderful setting alone – in a gorgeous village hidden on the banks of the Thames – makes this a desirable place to stay', but visitors to the 17th-century inn discover much more to like. The pub-with-rooms, owned by Sebastian and Lana Snow, has been refurbished in modern rustic style: arrive to a 'warm, informal' greeting and find out why locals (and their dogs) visit the beamed, flagstoned pub. Past the bar area, with its exposed-brick walls, mismatched tables and chairs, and blackboard menus of 'good wines and interesting craft beers', Matt Read's 'delicious cooking' in the restaurant might include kiln-smoked local trout, fennel, cucumber, blood orange, pomegranate; chicken Kiev, thyme and duck-fat roasties. Summer meals are taken under large parasols in the garden. Upstairs, 'shabby-chic' bedrooms each have their own character. (Some might have pub noise, too – sensitive sleepers should discuss rooms before booking.) 'Our room overlooking the front garden had a large, comfortable bed with good linen. In the bathroom: a freestanding double-ended bath.' Breakfast on Kelmscott sausages and crispy bacon, then head out on a riverside stroll, minutes away.

Kelmscott
GL7 3HG

T: 01367 253543
E: info@theploughinnkelmscott.com
W: www.theploughinnkelmscott.com

BEDROOMS: 8.
OPEN: all year except 25 Dec, restaurant closed Mon eve and Sun from 6.45 pm.
FACILITIES: bar, restaurant, private dining room in Hideaway bar, free Wi-Fi, in-room TV (Freeview), garden (alfresco drinks and meals), unsuitable for disabled.
BACKGROUND MUSIC: none.
LOCATION: 3 miles E of Lechlade.
CHILDREN: all ages welcomed.
DOGS: allowed in public rooms, not in bedrooms.
CREDIT CARDS: MasterCard, Visa.
PRICES: [2017] per room B&B single £70–£90, double £90–£130. Set dinner (6 pm–7 pm Mon–Fri) £24, à la carte £30.

KESWICK Cumbria

Map 4: inset C2

HAZEL BANK

♔ Previous César winner

Local couple Gary and Donna MacRae 'revel' in making their Borrowdale valley hotel 'welcoming, relaxed – so enjoyable'. 'It is in a magical setting, with lawns rolling down to a small river, and hills looming up into the mist. We approached the charming Victorian country house over a sweet little stone bridge, across a gurgling stream. When we arrived, we were given tea and ginger cake in the sitting room.' 'Well-equipped, comfortable' bedrooms, each with 'wonderful views', are supplied with fresh flowers, bottled water, truffles on the tea tray. The bathrooms have been refurbished this year. Graze on canapés in the log fire-warmed sitting room ('guests are encouraged to mingle') before sitting down to an 'excellent' candlelit four-course dinner, perhaps including Cumbrian smoked trout pâté, gooseberry sauce; seared fillet of Gressingham duck breast, dauphinoise celeriac. After a 'very good' breakfast – perhaps while watching the red squirrels in the garden – head outside. 'Walking the fells can be addictive', and the hotel, with 'truly superb' hikes starting from the door, is well placed for those who gladly succumb.

Borrowdale
Keswick
CA12 5XB

T: 017687 77248
F: 017687 77373
E: info@hazelbankhotel.co.uk
W: www.hazelbankhotel.co.uk

BEDROOMS: 7. 1 on ground floor.
OPEN: all year except 12 Dec–27 Jan.
FACILITIES: lounge, dining room, drying room, free Wi-Fi, in-room TV (Freeview), 4-acre grounds (croquet, woodland walks).
BACKGROUND MUSIC: none.
LOCATION: 6 miles S of Keswick on B5289 to Borrowdale.
CHILDREN: not under 15.
DOGS: not allowed.
CREDIT CARDS: MasterCard, Visa.
PRICES: [2017] per person B&B £75–£82, D,B&B £107–£117. Set dinner £34. 1-night bookings sometimes refused.

SEE ALSO SHORTLIST

KING'S LYNN Norfolk

Map 2:A4

BANK HOUSE

Overlooking the historic quayside, this popular spot, 'well used by locals', is 'just what one hopes for and expects from a hotel in a large town'. The owners, Anthony and Jeannette Goodrich, 'have done a lovely job' restoring the historic Georgian building, a former bank; the 'sympathetically updated' interiors are 'imaginative, without losing a sense of the building's character'. 'Helpful, friendly' staff set a 'relaxed atmosphere'. Settle into one of the 'comfortable' bedrooms (some are smaller than others), each well stocked with books, magazines and home-made biscuits; a 'memorable' bathroom might have a freestanding claw-footed bath. There's a choice of dining areas, inside and out; in all of them, chef Stuart Deuchars serves an 'excellent' modern brasserie menu that might include duck terrine, quince jelly, toasted sourdough; spatchcock poussin, vegetable couscous, crisp Parma ham. (Pub classics and wild-rice bowls cater to diners hungry for simpler fare.) On a fine evening, head for the riverside terrace, cocktail in hand, to watch the 'glorious sunset' over the Ouse. The Goodriches also own The Rose & Crown, Snettisham (see entry).

King's Staithe Square
King's Lynn
PE30 1RD

T: 01553 660492
E: info@thebankhouse.co.uk
W: www.thebankhouse.co.uk

BEDROOMS: 12.
OPEN: all year.
FACILITIES: bar, 3 dining rooms, meeting/function rooms, vaulted cellars for private parties, free Wi-Fi, in-room TV (Freeview), riverside terrace, courtyard, unsuitable for disabled.
BACKGROUND MUSIC: 'mellow jazz' in public areas ('but can be turned down or off').
LOCATION: central.
CHILDREN: all ages welcomed.
DOGS: allowed in bar and on terrace, not in bedrooms.
CREDIT CARDS: Amex, MasterCard, Visa.
PRICES: [2017] per room B&B single £85–£120, double £115–£220, D,B&B double £170–£275. Pre-theatre dinner £15–£20, à la carte £28.

KING'S LYNN Norfolk

Map 2:A4

CONGHAM HALL

Arrangements of garden flowers scent the public rooms at this 'lovely country hotel', where each of the 'pretty bedrooms' is named after a herb. In a pastoral setting close to the north Norfolk coast, the Georgian house is surrounded by greenery, from the gardens – including the acclaimed herb garden planted with 400 varieties of culinary and medicinal herbs – to horse-grazed parkland beyond. Nicholas Dickinson is the owner; 'cheerful staff' are 'friendly, efficient and helpful'. Most of the bedrooms in the main house have been refurbished in a fresh, modern style. Brighter bedrooms, each with a private patio, are grouped around the spa garden. All rooms have an espresso machine, fresh milk, home-made biscuits and bathrobes. 'Super food' in the restaurant 'may not be haute cuisine', but the cooking successfully exploits the bounty of the kitchen garden and orchard in such dishes as roast rump of local lamb, aubergine, courgette, vine tomato. Stroll in the herb garden at dusk to breathe in the heady aroma, or book a visit to the spa, where the massages and body treatments use seasonal herbs and fresh blossoming flowers. (RV, and others)

Lynn Road
Grimston
King's Lynn
PE32 1AH

T: 01485 600250
F: 01485 601191
E: info@conghamhallhotel.co.uk
W: www.conghamhallhotel.co.uk

BEDROOMS: 26. 11 garden rooms, 1 suitable for disabled.
OPEN: all year.
FACILITIES: sitting room, bar, library, restaurant, free Wi-Fi, in-room TV (Freeview), civil wedding licence, conference facilities, terrace, spa, 12-metre swimming pool, 30-acre grounds, herb garden.
BACKGROUND MUSIC: 'mellow' in bar and restaurant.
LOCATION: 6 miles E of King's Lynn.
CHILDREN: all ages welcomed.
DOGS: allowed in some bedrooms, bar.
CREDIT CARDS: MasterCard, Visa.
PRICES: [2017] per room D,B&B £219–£329, room only (Mon–Thurs) £135–£260. À la carte £35. 1-night bookings sometimes refused.

KIRKBY STEPHEN Cumbria

Map 4:C3

AUGILL CASTLE

🏵 Previous César winner

'It's a home away from home,' chorus fans in 2017 of the Bennett family's 'stunning, well-preserved' 19th-century pile striking a pose in rambling grounds in the Eden valley. Sure – if home has claw-footed baths, turrets for wardrobes, an honesty bar packed with local ales and spirits, and stained-glass windows with wide countryside views. 'A nice mix of castle and comfort', with a 'relaxed, welcoming atmosphere', this is 'no staid hotel': 'the down-to-earth owners make your stay very special'. Scattered with antiques, 'comfortable bedrooms' in the castle, former gatehouses and converted orangery are each 'very different' – book a room with a cast iron fireplace, or one with poetry on the ceiling. Weekend nights, 'glorious dinners' of local produce are served, house-party style, at shared tables (cold platters are available on other evenings). There are open fires, an Art Deco cinema (popcorn included), a library with games and dressing-up clothes for children. Outside, set off on wooded walks or take on the windswept fells beyond. 'Simply first class.' (Donna Harrison, Daniel McWilliams, Jan Hallam, Renee Cole, Debbie Dean)

Leacett Lane
Brough
Kirkby Stephen
CA17 4DE

T: 01768 341937
E: office@stayinacastle.com
W: www.stayinacastle.com

BEDROOMS: 15. 2 on ground floor, 7 in stableyard conversion.
OPEN: all year, dinner served Fri/Sat, cold platters on other nights, children's high tea every day.
FACILITIES: hall, drawing room, library (honesty bar), music (sitting) room, conservatory bar, dining room, cinema, free Wi-Fi, in-room TV (Freeview), civil wedding licence, 20-acre grounds (landscaped garden, tennis).
BACKGROUND MUSIC: none.
LOCATION: 3 miles NE of Kirkby Stephen.
CHILDREN: all ages welcomed.
DOGS: allowed in 2 bedrooms.
CREDIT CARDS: all major cards.
PRICES: [2017] per room B&B £180–£220. Set dinner £20–£25. 1-night bookings sometimes refused weekends.

LACOCK Wiltshire

Map 2:D1

SIGN OF THE ANGEL NEW

Guests in search of an 'authentic, olde-worlde atmosphere' find it in the flagstone passageways, huge fireplaces, wonky beams and creaky floorboards of this 15th-century coaching inn, in an 'exquisitely preserved' National Trust village. Guide inspectors in 2017 ducked through latched doorways to find 'pleasant staff', 'delightful bedrooms' and 'imaginative meals', 'artistically served'. Up 'narrow stairs', bedrooms have antiques and quirky features (perhaps a bathroom down 'tricky steps'). 'Through a hobbit-like doorway, our room was compact, with small windows, but comfortable: hotel-quality linen, a large bath, a Roberts radio, home-made treats.' Reserve a place for chef/director John Furby's sustainably sourced lunches and dinners, served on weathered wooden tables. 'After canapés of breaded veal bonbons, we had refined dishes of avocado panna cotta and king prawns; roasted spring lamb and smoked garlic.' Residents have a 'large, lovely' sitting room, but warm weather calls for a seat in the 'sweet orchard garden' reaching down to the stream. At a 'fine breakfast' on 'beautiful pottery': a 'nice buffet'; 'huge portions of excellent scrambled eggs'.

6 Church Street
Lacock, nr Chippenham
SN15 2LB

T: 01249 730230
F: 01249 730527
E: info@signoftheangel.co.uk
W: www.signoftheangel.co.uk

BEDROOMS: 5.
OPEN: all year except Mon.
FACILITIES: small bar, 3 dining rooms, residents' sitting room, private dining room, free Wi-Fi, no mobile phone signal, garden (alfresco drinking and eating), unsuitable for disabled.
BACKGROUND MUSIC: 'soft' in public areas.
LOCATION: 4 miles S of Chippenham.
CHILDREN: all ages welcomed.
DOGS: allowed.
CREDIT CARDS: Amex, MasterCard, Visa.
PRICES: [2017] per room B&B single £80–£110, double £110–£140. À la carte £36.

LANGAR Nottinghamshire

Map 2:A3

LANGAR HALL

Down an avenue of lime trees stands this characterful hotel in 'magical grounds', its apricot-washed facade a welcome sight to its legions of loyal fans. After the death of its spirited chatelaine, Imogen Skirving, Lila Arora, her granddaughter, now stands at the helm, supported by an 'enthusiastic team' of long-serving, 'well-trained' staff. 'With the obvious exception, everything is exactly as before,' says a Guide reader this year. 'It is, as it always has been, like staying with friends in the country.' Within the Georgian house, highly individual bedrooms and faintly eccentric public rooms (some with an air of England-by-way-of-India) are filled with fine paintings, antiques, 'a relaxed atmosphere'. 'Dinner continues to be reliable, from the Marmite popcorn onwards.' A typical dish: 'very good' roast Belvoir pheasant, potato terrine, bread sauce croquette. Most striking, perhaps, is the spirit of generosity and openness – a reflection of its founder. 'The first time money was mentioned during my stay was when I paid the bill the morning of my departure. What a refreshing change from those establishments that produce a chit to sign at every turn.' (Nick Patton, Peter Jowitt)

Church Lane
Langar
NG13 9HG

T: 01949 860559
F: 01949 861045
E: info@langarhall.co.uk
W: www.langarhall.com

BEDROOMS: 12. 1 on ground floor, 1 in garden chalet.
OPEN: all year.
FACILITIES: sitting room, study, library, bar, garden room, restaurant, free Wi-Fi, in-room TV (Freeview), civil wedding licence, 30-acre grounds (gardens, children's play area), unsuitable for disabled.
BACKGROUND MUSIC: none.
LOCATION: 12 miles SE of Nottingham.
CHILDREN: all ages welcomed, by arrangement.
DOGS: small dogs on a lead allowed by arrangement, not unaccompanied.
CREDIT CARDS: MasterCard, Visa.
PRICES: [2017] per room B&B £100–£225. Set dinner (Fri, Sat) £49.50, other nights £25–£30.

LANGHO Lancashire

Map 4:D3

NORTHCOTE

In the rural Ribble valley, this extended Victorian manor has basked in Michelin stardom under chef/co-owner Nigel Haworth for more than 20 years. Today, a 'convivial atmosphere' presides – the contentedness of the well fed and well rested. Stylish bedrooms in the contemporary country house are equipped with bathrobes, complimentary soft drinks and up-to-date technology; some have a private terrace. Lodge bedrooms, across the garden from the main house, share their own lounge and pantry kitchen. In the dining room, a chandelier dazzles over Nigel Haworth and Lisa Goodwin-Allen's modern cooking. The seasonal menus (including one for vegetarians) use plenty of organic produce from the kitchen garden in dishes such as juniper fern-cured fennel, wasabi, pickled radish, wild herbs; Herdwick lamb, sour onions, nasturtium, whey. Breakfast, accompanied by the day's newspapers, has the same gourmet touch: pick from a choice of omelettes, salmon smoked over juniper and beech, a melting Lancashire cheese soufflé. There's 'easy access' to this 'lesser-known but stunning area' and its riverside paths, ancient villages and medieval abbey.

Northcote Road
Langho
BB6 8BE

T: 01254 240555
F: 01254 246568
E: reception@northcote.com
W: www.northcote.com

BEDROOMS: 26. 8 in garden lodge, 8 on ground floor, 2 suitable for disabled.
OPEN: all year.
FACILITIES: lift, 2 lounges, cocktail bar, restaurant, private dining/meeting room, free Wi-Fi, in-room TV (Sky), civil wedding licence, 3-acre garden.
BACKGROUND MUSIC: in bar in evening.
LOCATION: 5½ miles N of Blackburn, on A59.
CHILDREN: all ages welcomed.
DOGS: not allowed.
CREDIT CARDS: Amex, MasterCard, Visa.
PRICES: [2017] per room B&B from £280, D,B&B from £375. À la carte £60, tasting menus £75–£95, vegetarian tasting menu £69.50.

LASTINGHAM Yorkshire

Map 4:C4

LASTINGHAM GRANGE

Birdsong fills the air around the Wood family's 'really lovely hotel', which stands in large, peaceful grounds on the edge of the North York Moors. The Grange started life as a 16th-century farmhouse and was made over in the country house manner in the '20s. Today, brothers Bertie and Tom Wood and their mother, Jane, 'make the place' with the warmth of their welcome. Some may find the setting old-fashioned – a grandfather clock stands in the hallway, a dark wood dresser holds a china collection, and floral bedspreads cover the beds in the 'comfortable bedrooms' – but fans come for the 'outstanding service' and staunchly traditional atmosphere, where 'everyone immediately knows your name'. Enjoy tea on the terrace or by the fire, with scones perhaps still warm from the oven. In the evening, sit down to a nightly-changing menu of straightforward but tasty dishes: poached halibut, Pernod hollandaise, say, or fillet steak, salpicon sauce. The chefs are happy to oblige, too: when recent guests especially loved a halibut dish one night, the kitchen cheerfully repeated it the following evening. 'Superb walking' starts right at the door.

High Street
Lastingham
YO62 6TH

T: 01751 417345
E: reservations@lastinghamgrange.com
W: www.lastinghamgrange.com

BEDROOMS: 11. Plus self-catering cottage in village.
OPEN: Mar–end Nov.
FACILITIES: hall, lounge, dining room, laundry facilities, free Wi-Fi, in-room TV (Freeview), 10-acre grounds (terrace, garden, orchard, croquet, boules), unsuitable for disabled.
BACKGROUND MUSIC: none.
LOCATION: 5 miles NE of Kirkbymoorside.
CHILDREN: all ages welcomed (adventure playground, special meals).
DOGS: not allowed in dining room or unattended in bedrooms.
CREDIT CARDS: all major cards.
PRICES: [2017] per room B&B single £150, double £210, D,B&B single £175, double £275. Set dinner £42.

LAVENHAM Suffolk

Map 2:C5

THE GREAT HOUSE

♻ Previous César winner

Martine and Régis Crépy's 'enjoyable, enormously comfortable' restaurant-with-rooms adds a dash of French flavour in a medieval wool village as English as they come. 'The atmosphere is excellent – formal yet friendly'; 'the dining experience is top-notch'. On the heated patio and in the handsome dining rooms (dark wood floors, tables laid with white linens and a posy), modern plates use fine ingredients in season. Characteristic dishes: deep-fried Colchester rock oysters, pickled carrot and cucumber, chilli lemon mayonnaise; saddle of local venison, parsnip and parsley root mash, juniper berries. Upstairs, bedrooms retain character with their Tudor beams and sloping ceilings, half-timbered walls or a Jacobean four-poster bed. Most are spacious, with a separate seating area, though one guest deemed an attic room under the eaves too snug. 'Our ample Grand Room had a good-sized bathroom with robes and slippers. A nice touch: complimentary sherry.' Wander round the town after breakfast: you're on the historic market square; shops, art galleries and charming crooked cottages are in every direction. (Patricia Jay, DG, and others)

Market Place
Lavenham
CO10 9QZ

T: 01787 247431
E: info@greathouse.co.uk
W: www.greathouse.co.uk

BEDROOMS: 5.
OPEN: Feb–Dec, except 2 weeks in summer, restaurant closed Sun night, Mon, Tues midday.
FACILITIES: lounge/bar, restaurant, free Wi-Fi, in-room TV (BT, Freeview), patio dining area, ½-acre garden, unsuitable for disabled.
BACKGROUND MUSIC: 'easy listening' in restaurant.
LOCATION: town centre (free public car park).
CHILDREN: all ages welcomed.
DOGS: not allowed.
CREDIT CARDS: Amex, MasterCard, Visa.
PRICES: [2017] per room B&B from £184, D,B&B from £257. Set dinner £36.50, à la carte £52 (Sat only). 1-night bookings sometimes refused Sat.

LEAMINGTON SPA Warwickshire

Map 2:B2

EIGHT CLARENDON CRESCENT

'Lively hosts' Christine and David Lawson 'delight in sharing their space', a 'peaceful' Regency villa near the town centre. 'It's homely in an elegant sort of way,' says a Guide reader this year. The 'remarkably good-value' B&B has period furnishings, paintings and prints; a grand piano in the drawing room for the budding Chopin. 'The secluded gardens and beautiful private dell at the back are particular delights on a sunny day.' Spacious bedrooms are up a wide staircase. 'My single room was warm and comfortably furnished, with an immaculate bathroom. Even with the window open, it was so quiet that it was difficult to believe I was close to the middle of a large town. I enjoyed a blissful, uninterrupted sleep.' Breakfast, ordered the night before off a limited menu, is served communally. 'The meal was superbly cooked and presented: coffee in a silver pot; fresh fruit and yogurt; freshly squeezed orange juice; home-baked bread; delicious bacon, sausage and egg.' 'You leave with a sense of pleasure in having experienced such excellent hospitality in a gracious private home.' (Trevor Lockwood, and others)

8 Clarendon Crescent
Leamington Spa
CV32 5NR

T: 01926 429840
F: 01926 424641
E: lawson@lawson71.fsnet.co.uk
W: www.eightclarendoncrescent.
   co.uk

BEDROOMS: 4.
OPEN: all year except national and bank holidays.
FACILITIES: drawing room, breakfast room, free Wi-Fi, in-room TV, ¾-acre garden (private dell), unsuitable for disabled.
BACKGROUND MUSIC: none.
LOCATION: 2 miles E of town centre.
CHILDREN: by arrangement.
DOGS: not allowed.
CREDIT CARDS: none.
PRICES: [2017] per room B&B single £50, double £85.

LEDBURY Herefordshire

THE FEATHERS

25% DISCOUNT VOUCHERS

A riot of Tudor black and white, with 17th- and 19th-century additions, David Elliston's ancient coaching inn–turned–spa hotel has been receiving guests since the reign of Elizabeth I. (Some won't leave – rumour has it a ghost or two linger.) It's a popular spot in town, with an 'excellent ambience': join the locals at tea by the fire in the lounge or, on a fine day, on the garden terrace. The interiors are a mix of styles: sleep in one of the characterful Coaching Rooms, with beamed ceiling and timber-frame walls, or in a high-ceilinged Dancing Room, in the former Victorian ballroom. All have bottled water, fluffy bathrobes, toiletries. At mealtimes, find a seat in Fuggles brasserie among the hops and horse brasses. Suzie Isaacs, the chef, serves appealing modern British dishes such as filo basket of oyster mushrooms, white truffle cream, pecorino; cod fillet, pink fir apple potatoes, curly kale, cucumber and lemon beurre blanc. Breakfast in Quills restaurant offers a good choice. Wander the streets of independent shops in this historic market town; the Malvern hills are a half-hour drive away. (Gwyn Morgan)

High Street
Ledbury
HR8 1DS

T: 01531 635266
F: 01531 638955
E: enquiries@feathers-ledbury.co.uk
W: www.feathers-ledbury.co.uk

BEDROOMS: 22. 1 suite in cottage, also self-catering apartments.
OPEN: all year.
FACILITIES: lounge, bar, brasserie, restaurant (for breakfast, private dining), free Wi-Fi, in-room TV (Sky, Freeview), function facilities, spa (heated 11-metre swimming pool, whirlpool, gym), civil wedding licence, terraced garden, car park, unsuitable for disabled.
BACKGROUND MUSIC: none.
LOCATION: town centre.
CHILDREN: all ages welcomed.
DOGS: allowed in bedrooms and bar, only guide dogs in restaurant and brasserie.
CREDIT CARDS: Amex, MasterCard, Visa.
PRICES: [2017] per room B&B £155–£240, D,B&B £185–£270. À la carte £30.

LETCOMBE REGIS Oxfordshire

Map 2:C2

THE GREYHOUND INN NEW

'The welcome is excellent' at this revitalised 18th-century free house, on a quiet road running through a 'peaceful Downland village full of birdsong' – just ask the locals coming in for tea or a high-stakes round at the 'jolly quiz night'. 'Village residents Martyn Reed and Catriona Galbraith have given this old inn a new lease of life,' say Guide inspectors in 2017. 'A local hub', it has a fine selection of real ales to match chef Phil Currie's 'accomplished cooking'; Lidia Dhorne, the manager, 'couldn't be more helpful'. Bedrooms are up 'steep stairs' (help is offered with luggage). Some are beamed, some have a sloping wood floor, all have a Roberts radio, natural toiletries and home-baked biscuits. 'Our room, Uffington, was smallish, but adequate for a couple of nights. The comfortable bed had blankets and sheets as we'd requested; the smart, well-lit bathroom had thick towels, and a monsoon shower above the bath.' Eat in the main bar or one of the dining areas leading off it; a blackboard menu lists daily specials: 'delicious local asparagus with a poached egg and crunchy bits', perhaps, and a 'perfect lemon posset'. The Berkshire Downs are to the south.

Main Street
Letcombe Regis
OX12 9JL

T: 01235 771969
E: info@thegreyhoundletcombe.co.uk
W: www.thegreyhoundletcombe.co.uk

BEDROOMS: 8.
OPEN: all year except 24/25 Dec.
FACILITIES: bar, snug, 3 dining rooms, function room, free Wi-Fi, in-room TV (Freeview), garden, only bar/restaurant suitable for disabled.
BACKGROUND MUSIC: occasionally in public rooms, 'but can be turned off on request'.
LOCATION: in village 2 miles SW of Wantage.
CHILDREN: all ages welcomed.
DOGS: allowed in 2 bedrooms, bar, garden.
CREDIT CARDS: MasterCard, Visa.
PRICES: [2017] per room B&B single £75–£120, double £90–£135. À la carte £30, 2-course Midweek Fix dinner (Wed) £12.

LEWDOWN Devon

Map 1:C3

LEWTRENCHARD MANOR

'It's up there with the top hotels we've stayed at,' writes a reader this year of Sue and James Murray's romantic rebuild of a Jacobean manor house, surrounded by parkland. Today a 'wonderful hotel', it contains a wealth of historic features imported by the Revd Sabine Baring-Gould (best known for penning the hymn 'Onward, Christian Soldiers'), who transformed 'Lew House' over 30 years from 1881 – look out for Renaissance woodwork, a Jacobean ceiling, a Rococo fireplace. The Murrays have filled the 'beautiful' public rooms with antiques, books and paintings; bedrooms are a mix of traditional and contemporary. 'All the rooms are attractive': St Gertrude has an ornate ceiling and mullioned windows; the four-poster bed in Melton once belonged to Charles I's wife Henrietta Maria. After fireside canapés, head into the dining room, where portraits look down from panelled walls over Matthew Peryer's 'delicious food'. Characteristic dishes: Brixham mackerel, garden beetroot, apple and horseradish salad; roasted Devon beef fillet, broccoli, girolles, watercress purée. Breakfast is generous and varied. 'It's family owned, which gives it a special feel.' (RB, and others)

Lewdown
EX20 4PN

T: 01566 783222
F: 01566 783332
E: info@lewtrenchard.co.uk
W: www.lewtrenchard.co.uk

BEDROOMS: 14. 1 in folly, 4 with separate entrance, 1 suitable for disabled.
OPEN: all year.
FACILITIES: front-hall lounge, bar, library, restaurant, function facilities, free Wi-Fi, in-room TV (Freeview), civil wedding licence, 12-acre gardens.
BACKGROUND MUSIC: none.
LOCATION: rural, 10 miles N of Tavistock.
CHILDREN: all ages welcomed, not under 8 at dinner.
DOGS: allowed in bedrooms (not unattended), not in restaurant or kitchen garden.
CREDIT CARDS: Amex, MasterCard, Visa.
PRICES: [2017] per room B&B £200–£280, D,B&B £290–£370. Set dinner £49.50, tasting menu £69, chef's table £79. 1-night bookings sometimes refused.

LICHFIELD Staffordshire

Map 2:A2

NETHERSTOWE HOUSE

A tree-lined driveway leads to the 'peace
and quiet' of Ben Heathcote's small hotel, in
another lifetime a Georgian mill house and
wool manufactory. The enterprise is family run;
staff are 'most accommodating'. Guide readers
write of a generous spirit (a surprise upgrade, a
waived cancellation fee). Choose a bedroom in
the main house or (more petite) in the adjacent
lodge, or spread out in a 'spacious, well-
equipped' contemporary courtyard apartment.
Each room is individually decorated; three
recall Lichfield's most famous sons. Garrick has
a deep sofa in front of the cast iron fireplace;
Darwin (Erasmus, not Charles) has an easy
chair by the picture window; Johnson (Samuel,
not Boris) has a roll-top bath with a waterproof
TV in the large bathroom. Eat in the bar or
the lounge, from a short menu of sandwiches,
salads and a stew of the week – or, if your room
is conducive to dining, have something sent up.
'Our room-service order arrived promptly. And
we appreciated that there wasn't a tray charge.'
Among the unusual cooked items at breakfast:
fried eggs and chorizo; sliced avocado on
sourdough toast. (Michael Gwinnell, SL)

25% DISCOUNT VOUCHERS

Netherstowe Lane
Lichfield
WS13 6AY

T: 01543 254270
F: 01543 419998
E: info@netherstowehouse.com
W: www.netherstowehouse.com

BEDROOMS: 16. 7 in adjacent lodge,
5 on ground floor, plus 8 serviced
apartments in annexe.
OPEN: all year.
FACILITIES: 2 lounges, bar, 2 dining
rooms, private dining room, free
Wi-Fi, in-room TV (Freeview),
gym, 1-acre grounds, unsuitable for
disabled.
BACKGROUND MUSIC: in restaurant
and lounges.
LOCATION: 1 mile N of city centre.
CHILDREN: not under 12 overnight
in hotel, but all ages welcomed in
serviced apartments.
DOGS: not allowed.
CREDIT CARDS: Amex, MasterCard,
Visa.
PRICES: [2017] per room B&B
£105–£195.

SEE ALSO SHORTLIST

LIFTON Devon

Map 1:C3

THE ARUNDELL ARMS

'As delightful as ever', reports a trusted Guide correspondent in 2017, of Adam Fox-Edwards's former coaching inn-turned-sporting hotel near Dartmoor. Justly popular with anglers, the hotel has fishing rights over 20 miles of the River Tamar, plus expert ghillies, and a tackle shop in an 18th-century cockfighting pit. It is also 'a wonderful place in which to relax': the residents' sitting room, 'charming and spacious', has log fires, 'marvellous oil paintings', 'lots of really comfy seating' and 'pretty (not old-fashioned!) chintz'; doors lead directly to the garden. 'All the glossies and several daily papers are here, too, for more indolent days.' Country-style bedrooms are 'cosy and comfortable' with antiques, home-made biscuits and 'lovely views over the pretty garden'. Hungry diners eat in either of the two bars or in the main dining room, where long-serving chef Steve Pidgeon's award-winning modern British dishes might include free-range chicken fillet, hay-smoked celeriac, creamed leeks, honey-glazed parsnips. 'Our group meal was a cut above the average event dinner, but the highlight was the fabulous full English the next morning.' (Abigail Kirby-Harris)

25% DISCOUNT VOUCHERS

Fore Street
Lifton
PL16 0AA

T: 01566 784666
E: reservations@arundellarms.com
W: www.arundellarms.com

BEDROOMS: 27. 4 on ground floor, 4 in adjacent Church Cottage.
OPEN: all year.
FACILITIES: lounge, bar, village pub, restaurant, brasserie, private dining rooms, conference rooms, free Wi-Fi, in-room TV (Freeview), skittle alley, civil wedding licence, 1-acre garden, lake, 20 miles fishing rights on River Tamar and tributaries, unsuitable for disabled.
BACKGROUND MUSIC: none.
LOCATION: 3 miles E of Launceston.
CHILDREN: all ages welcomed.
DOGS: allowed in bedrooms and some public rooms, not in restaurant.
CREDIT CARDS: Amex, MasterCard, Visa.
PRICES: [2017] per room B&B single from £120, double £160–£195, D,B&B single from £150, double £260–£295. Tasting menu £49.50, à la carte £35.

LIVERPOOL Merseyside

2 BLACKBURNE TERRACE

'The personal service, facilities and little extras put this upmarket B&B in a class above quite a few better-rated hotels we've stayed in.' Guests in 2017 were charmed by Sarah and Glenn Whitter's chic city hideaway on a hill in the Georgian quarter. 'The hosts are delightful, dedicated and keen.' (There's a four-legged friend to be made, too: 'Ask to meet Miles, the Rhodesian ridgeback.') In 'a quiet location' between the two cathedrals, the refurbished town house is 'perfect for exploring the city by foot'; theatres and restaurants are within walking distance. Step into one of the 'well-appointed', high-ceilinged bedrooms: there are cathedral or rooftop views from the large sash windows, and 'interesting paintings and antiques' – perhaps a Victorian sofa or a maple secretaire. Nice touches: macaroons and sloe gin, an antique tea service, 'a good coffee-maker'. The drawing room has a collection of books on art and local history; a secluded walled garden is fine on a balmy day. Breakfast is a near-festive affair. At a communal table set with crystal and silver cutlery, feast on 'a wide range' of cooked dishes; an 'enormous buffet'. (Kenneth Wilkins, DR, Anne Thornthwaite)

2 Blackburne Terrace
Liverpool
L8 7PJ

T: 0151 708 5474
E: info@2bbt.co.uk
W: www.2blackburneterrace.com

BEDROOMS: 4.
OPEN: all year.
FACILITIES: drawing room, dining room, free Wi-Fi, in-room smart TV, walled garden, unsuitable for disabled.
BACKGROUND MUSIC: none.
LOCATION: city centre.
CHILDREN: not under 10.
DOGS: not allowed.
CREDIT CARDS: Visa.
PRICES: [2017] per room B&B £130–£270.

SEE ALSO SHORTLIST

LODSWORTH Sussex

THE HALFWAY BRIDGE

'An agreeable, solidly comfortable base for exploring the area', Sam and Janet Bakose's updated 18th-century inn sits off the A272 in the South Downs national park. A plus: 'the remarkable kitchen turning out very good food indeed', say Guide inspectors this year. There are balls of fuzzy moss on the low roof tiles, and logs of wood piled up by the front door. Inside, 'it's a near-pitch-perfect "great British inn" experience, all exposed-brick walls and archival photographs of the local area; games and a pleasing Penguin collection of food writing; chairs with jauntily patterned cushions'. Motion-sensor lights illuminate the way across a country lane to bedrooms in converted stables, each supplied with magazines, ground coffee, 'nice teas', bottled water and biscuits. 'Our room was enormous, with a high, beamed ceiling; out the picture window, a view of green fields.' At lunch and dinner, the modern cooking ('with unusual gastropubby choices') is 'inventive yet approachable'; at breakfast, help yourself from a 'vast' buffet. 'We cleaned our plates of large portions of creamy scrambled eggs, good bacon, a generous serving of smoked salmon.'

Lodsworth
GU28 9BP

T: 01798 861281
E: enquiries@halfwaybridge.co.uk
W: www.halfwaybridge.co.uk

BEDROOMS: 7. In converted barns, 165 yds from main building.
OPEN: all year.
FACILITIES: bar, restaurant, free Wi-Fi, in-room TV (Freeview), small beer garden, unsuitable for disabled.
BACKGROUND MUSIC: 'quiet' in bar and restaurant.
LOCATION: 3 miles W of Petworth, on A272.
CHILDREN: all ages welcomed.
DOGS: allowed in bar, not in bedrooms.
CREDIT CARDS: Amex, MasterCard, Visa.
PRICES: per room B&B £145–£230. À la carte £32. 1-night bookings may be refused weekends.

LONG MELFORD Suffolk

Map 2:C5

LONG MELFORD SWAN

'A fantastic place to stay', this 'friendly, accommodating' restaurant-with-rooms stands on the main street of a 'lovely village' of antique stores, art galleries and independent shops. It is part of the family-run Stuart Inns group, which is 'totally committed to getting it right'. The 'informal, yet polished' restaurant is a 'buzzy' local destination, where diners come for 'creative, well-presented meals' – perhaps Suffolk asparagus mousse, crispy pheasant egg; Lavenham lamb, smoked aubergine, fried quinoa. Sleep in one of the 'boldly furnished, beautifully finished bedrooms' in the main house or in Melford House next door. (No staff remain overnight.) Rooms vary in size – a snug room has a claw-footed bathtub in the bathroom; a superior room has a deep armchair in the bay window – but all have a super-king-size bed, still and sparkling water, fruit and home-made brownies. Ideal for a family, a new suite has a large copper bath in the master bedroom, and a pull-out sofa bed in a separate sitting area. Sample the 'delightfully nutty granola' at breakfast before stocking up on treats and East Anglian food items at the Duck Deli next door. (Antony Wallace, and others)

Hall Street
Long Melford
CO10 9JQ

T: 01787 464545
E: info@longmelfordswan.co.uk
W: www.longmelfordswan.co.uk

BEDROOMS: 7. 4 in adjacent Melford House, 2 on ground floor.
OPEN: all year.
FACILITIES: bar, restaurant, deli, free Wi-Fi, in-room TV, garden.
BACKGROUND MUSIC: all day in public areas.
LOCATION: village centre.
CHILDREN: all ages welcomed.
DOGS: allowed in bar only.
CREDIT CARDS: Amex, MasterCard, Visa.
PRICES: [2017] per room B&B single £95–£120, double £155–£210, D,B&B double £246–£300. Tasting menu £75, à la carte £40.

LONG SUTTON Somerset

Map 1:C6

THE DEVONSHIRE ARMS

Contented guests praise the 'friendly, efficient staff', 'comfy beds' and 'good food' at Philip Mepham's inn on the village green. Past the assertive porch of the 19th-century hunting lodge, enter the open-plan bar and restaurant: there are timber and flagstone floors, comfortable contemporary styling, armchairs and banquettes, walls variously papered, painted, panelled and hung with prints. Modern bedrooms, in 'small', 'medium' and 'large', are decorated with restful colours; two are in a cottage behind the inn. 'Our good-sized room had a four-poster bed, and two armchairs next to the large window overlooking the green. Despite our being in the village centre, our room was quiet. We slept well.' When Cromwell passed this way in the Civil War, he found Long Sutton 'extremely wanting in provisions'. Things have looked up since chef Chris De Courcy Wheeler arrived at the inn: his 'excellent' country cooking might include home-cured salmon, cucumber and dill salad; Somerset pork belly cassoulet. Open fires warm in cool weather; on fine days, eat alfresco on the lawn, or get stuck into croquet, boules, a game of garden Jenga. (PA)

Long Sutton
TA10 9LP

T: 01458 241271
E: info@thedevonshirearms.com
W: www.thedevonshirearms.com

BEDROOMS: 9. 2, on ground floor, in annexe behind main building.
OPEN: all year except 25/26 Dec.
FACILITIES: open-plan bar and restaurant, private dining room, free Wi-Fi, in-room TV (Freeview), courtyard, garden (croquet lawn), only public areas suitable for disabled.
BACKGROUND MUSIC: in bar.
LOCATION: by the village green.
CHILDREN: all ages welcomed.
DOGS: allowed in bar only.
CREDIT CARDS: MasterCard, Visa.
PRICES: [2017] per room B&B from £100, D,B&B from £170. À la carte £29.50. 1-night booking sometimes refused weekends.

LONGHORSLEY Northumberland

Map 4:B3

THISTLEYHAUGH FARM

♦ Previous César winner

'Take time to admire the sheep', and much more besides, at this creeper-smothered Georgian farmhouse on an organic farm on the River Coquet. The farm dates from 1780, and the Nelless family have ploughed their furrow here for three generations; Enid Nelless and her daughter-in-law, Zoë, are today's 'sweet, sincere' hostesses. Come in to the comforts of a family home. Spacious bedrooms are traditionally furnished; there are antiques, artwork, fresh milk and home-baked biscuits. The B&B is a good base for exploring the area: head north to the hare-brained Hotspur's Alnwick Castle, or drive to the coast (perhaps to Craster, where the breakfast kippers come from). In the morning, choose from local sausages, home-cured bacon and organic eggs from free-range hens – or conjure up another order entirely. 'If there is something else you'd like and we haven't got it, we'll get it for you the following day,' the hostesses say. Bring a good map: the farmhouse is approached via winding back roads, giving it a remote, 'away from it all' feel. 'If we can find it again, we will return.' (EMA)

Longhorsley
NE65 8RG

T: 01665 570098
E: thistleyhaugh@hotmail.com
W: www.thistleyhaugh.co.uk

BEDROOMS: 4.
OPEN: Feb–Christmas.
FACILITIES: 2 lounges, garden room, dining room, free Wi-Fi, in-room TV (Freeview), ¼-acre garden (summer house), fishing, shooting, golf, riding nearby, unsuitable for disabled.
BACKGROUND MUSIC: none.
LOCATION: 10 miles N of Morpeth, W of A697.
CHILDREN: all ages welcomed.
DOGS: not allowed (kennels nearby).
CREDIT CARDS: MasterCard, Visa.
PRICES: per person B&B single £70–£90, double £50.

LOOE Cornwall

Map 1:D3

TRELASKE HOTEL & RESTAURANT

An 'enchanting, peaceful place' surrounded by wild flower meadows, trees and wildlife, Hazel Billington and Ross Lewin's 'friendly' hotel continues to charm Guide readers. 'Ross is a superb cook, while Hazel, dedicated and supremely organised, is a wizard at running the business. Both do everything with pleasure and grace.' Standing in 'lavish grounds' – 'our rabbit had a lovely time lounging in the sun on his own private terrace' – the house is 'very comfortable, with its many nooks and crannies'. The rooms have been designed to give 'total privacy'. Well-appointed bedrooms in the main house have a balcony; two rooms in the garden annexe suit a family. 'Our spacious garden room had wonderful views through the picture window of the lawns and fields beyond.' With the historic ports of Looe and Polperro close by, fish and shellfish (perhaps mackerel fillets, chorizo, braised leek, shallot crisps) figure large on the 'deliciously original' daily-changing dinner menu. In the morning, 'the generous breakfast is something to look forward to'. 'Twelve out of ten!' (Céline la Frenière, Mr and Mrs BJ Hillier, David Patrick Allen)

Polperro Road
Looe
PL13 2JS

T: 01503 262159
E: info@trelaske.co.uk
W: www.trelaske.co.uk

BEDROOMS: 7. 4 garden rooms, on ground floor, in adjacent building.
OPEN: Mar–Nov.
FACILITIES: 2 lounges, dining room, free Wi-Fi (in main house), in-room TV (Freeview), function facilities, terrace (summer barbecues), 4-acre grounds, unsuitable for disabled.
BACKGROUND MUSIC: in lounge bar and restaurant.
LOCATION: 2 miles W of Looe, 3 miles NE of Polperro.
CHILDREN: all ages welcomed (no under-4s in restaurant).
DOGS: allowed in 2 bedrooms (£7.50 per night), not in public rooms.
CREDIT CARDS: Amex, MasterCard, Visa.
PRICES: per room B&B £130, D,B&B £190. Set dinner £27.50–£33.50. 1-night bookings sometimes refused.

SEE ALSO SHORTLIST

LORTON Cumbria

NEW HOUSE FARM

'Peace and quiet' surround Hazel Thompson's Lake District B&B in the Vale of Lorton. The 'beautifully restored' Grade II listed farmhouse stands in acres of field and pasture, ponds and stream, with fell views all around. 'Everything about it gets five stars: the rooms, the breakfasts, the roaring log fire, the wonderful hot tub in the garden,' says a fan in 2017. The large, traditionally decorated bedrooms have glorious vistas, antiques, perhaps a slipper bath in a Victorian-style bathroom; each has its own character. Swinside, with an original fireplace, has a brass bed; the Old Dairy, at the end of the barn, has a solid-oak four-poster bed against a rustic stone wall, and a spacious, beamed bathroom. From spring to autumn, come in time for tea in the former byres, across the cobbled yard from the main house: there may be fairy cakes and cucumber sandwiches, or fruit scones with Cumberland rum butter. Light lunches (smoked duck; sandwiches; Solway shrimps on brown bread) are served here as well or, on a fine day, alfresco in the Old Midden, facing Low Fell and the surrounding fields. (John Thompson)

Lorton
CA13 9UU

T: 07841 159818
E: hazel@newhouse-farm.co.uk
W: www.newhouse-farm.com

BEDROOMS: 5. 1 in stable, 1 in Old Dairy.
OPEN: all year.
FACILITIES: entrance hall, 2 lounges, dining room, free Wi-Fi, civil wedding licence, 17-acre grounds (garden, hot tub, streams, woods, field, lake and river, safe bathing 2 miles), unsuitable for disabled.
BACKGROUND MUSIC: none.
LOCATION: on B5289, 2 miles S of Lorton.
CHILDREN: not under 6.
DOGS: 'clean and dry' dogs with own bed allowed in bedrooms (£20 charge per night), not in public rooms.
CREDIT CARDS: MasterCard, Visa.
PRICES: per room B&B from £120.

LOUTH Lincolnshire

THE OLD RECTORY AT STEWTON

'At the end of a country lane, yet close to the beautiful Georgian town', 'charming owners' Alan and Linda Palmer run their B&B in a Georgian-style former Victorian rectory. It keeps company in the hamlet with a Norman church rebuilt in the 19th century, amid 'the calm, deep peace' of the Wolds beloved of local lad Alfred Tennyson. Come into the garden, Maud, or sit in the conservatory, and you might spot fox or pheasant, even herons on the lawn amid the mature trees. Inside, 'the decor and furniture are wonderful throughout', with deep leather sofas, books and paintings; traditionally furnished bedrooms have 'lots of lovely touches'. A suite with a sofa bed and a private sitting room can accommodate a family. Early risers may breakfast at 6.30 am, slugabeds 'as late as you like – within reason'. Ingredients are local where possible – Lincolnshire sausages, free-range eggs, kippers, smoked haddock – with vegetarian options. The shops, pubs and restaurants of historic Louth are two miles away; the beaches and bird sanctuaries of the wild coastline a short drive.

Stewton
Louth
LN11 8SF

T: 01507 328063
E: alanjpalmer100@aol.com
W: www.louthbedandbreakfast.co.uk

BEDROOMS: 3.
OPEN: all year except Christmas–New Year.
FACILITIES: sitting room, breakfast room, conservatory, free Wi-Fi, in-room TV (Freeview), 3-acre garden, unsuitable for disabled.
BACKGROUND MUSIC: none.
LOCATION: in the countryside, 2½ miles SE of Louth.
CHILDREN: all ages welcomed.
DOGS: 'well-trained' dogs allowed (£10 charge, owners provide bedding and food).
CREDIT CARDS: MasterCard, Visa.
PRICES: [2017] per room B&B £75–£85.

LOWER BOCKHAMPTON Dorset

Map 1:D6

YALBURY COTTAGE

◑ Previous César winner

'High standards are upheld' at Ariane and Jamie Jones's 'lovely' small hotel deep in Thomas Hardy country, say returning guests in 2017. 'The staff are charming, always friendly; the meals are superb.' 'Our dogs were made very welcome, too.' The 18th-century shepherd's home, with a newly thatched roof, is run as a family affair: the Jones's son, Nikolas, has begun apprenticing in the kitchen. 'Warm, comfortable' bedrooms, each with 'lashings of hot water' in the bathroom, face the garden or green fields. 'Our spacious room had been upgraded since our last visit. The peaceful location and comfy king-size bed gave us a consistently good night's sleep. A bonus: home-made rosemary-lemon biscuits.' In the evening, the host's 'good-value' meals are 'inventive, flavourful, consistently outstanding'. 'The fish dishes – divine scallops! – were especially tasty and original.' Guests on a special diet needn't despair: 'They produced a separate gluten-free menu for me, with extensive choice.' 'Breakfast is good, too': home-made yogurt, plenty of fruit and cereals, 'a variety of freshly cooked dishes'. (Sara Price, Steve Hur, Simon Rodway)

25% DISCOUNT VOUCHERS

Lower Bockhampton
DT2 8PZ

T: 01305 262382
E: enquiries@yalburycottage.com
W: www.yalburycottage.com

BEDROOMS: 8. 6 on ground floor.
OPEN: all year except 23 Dec–18 Jan.
FACILITIES: lounge, restaurant, free Wi-Fi (in bedrooms), in-room TV (Freeview), garden with outdoor seating, unsuitable for disabled.
BACKGROUND MUSIC: 'easy listening' in lounge from 6 pm.
LOCATION: 2 miles E of Dorchester.
CHILDREN: all ages welcomed, no under-12s in restaurant after 8 pm.
DOGS: allowed in bedrooms, lounge, not in restaurant.
CREDIT CARDS: MasterCard, Visa.
PRICES: [2017] per room B&B single £75–£85, double £99–£125, D,B&B single £99–£115, double £160–£185. À la carte £39.50.

LUDLOW Shropshire

Map 3:C4

THE CLIVE

In a town that hosts a clutch of food and drink festivals every year, this 'excellent-value' restaurant-with-rooms is but a stroll from the popular Ludlow Food Centre. 'We've stayed a dozen times in as many years. The staff are efficient and friendly, and the food is very good,' says a regular Guide correspondent. The 18th-century farmhouse stands on the Earl of Plymouth's acres-wide estate, which supplies chef Peter Mills with prime ingredients for his modern dishes. 'We ate in all three nights we stayed. The menu seems to have shrunk, but salmon, fillet steak and wonderfully tender pork were highlights.' Contemporary bedrooms, including a family suite, are in the converted stables set around a courtyard. Some are jollier than others, but all are 'big, quiet and comfortable', and supplied with cafetière coffee and leaf tea. 'We never bother booking a superior room – there isn't any need.' Breakfast in the sister café brings Gloucester Old Spot bacon and sausages, home-made bread and jams. You're in a good position for the Shropshire hills area of outstanding natural beauty: tranquil villages, ancient woodland and historic inns are within reach. (Peter Anderson)

Bromfield
Ludlow
SY8 2JR

T: 01584 856565
E: reservations@theclive.co.uk
W: www.theclive.co.uk

BEDROOMS: 14. All in adjoining annexes, some on ground floor, 1 suitable for disabled.
OPEN: all year except 26 Dec.
FACILITIES: bar, café, restaurant, free Wi-Fi, in-room TV (Freeview), conference room, courtyard.
BACKGROUND MUSIC: in public areas.
LOCATION: 4 miles NW of Ludlow.
CHILDREN: all ages welcomed.
DOGS: allowed in 1 bedroom, bar, not in restaurant.
CREDIT CARDS: all major cards.
PRICES: [2017] per room B&B £115–£150, D,B&B £165–£225. À la carte £30.

SEE ALSO SHORTLIST

LUDLOW Shropshire

Map 3:C4

OLD DOWNTON LODGE

'Panoramic vistas peppered with sheep and lambs' surround Willem and Pippa Vlok's 'tranquil' restaurant-with-rooms. One-of-a-kind bedrooms in stone and brick outbuildings sprawl around a courtyard (low automatic lights show the way). 'Our rustic, well-designed room, up a short flight of stairs, had soaring rafters, a super-king-size bed and lots of quality fittings.' Consider discussing bedrooms before booking: a ground-floor room on the way to the restaurant was found lacking in privacy. Pre-dinner drinks may be taken alfresco, or in front of a log fire in a 'massive, stunning' converted barn. Across the 'delightfully laid-out' gardens, chef Karl Martin cooks 'wonderfully tasty' daily-changing tasting menus, 'ideal for one-off, very special occasions'. A typically succinctly described dish: venison, artichoke, walnuts, blue cheese, pear. 'Our seven-course menu was a master class, with top-quality locally sourced ingredients.' At breakfast, 'good portions of wholesome offerings' (smoked salmon, scrambled eggs, fresh fruit salad, home-made marmalade) are just right for country walks straight from the door. (JV, and others)

Downton on the Rock
Ludlow
SY8 2HU

T: 01568 771826
E: bookings@olddowntonlodge.com
W: www.olddowntonlodge.com

BEDROOMS: 10. In buildings around courtyard.
OPEN: all year, except Christmas, restaurant closed Sun, Mon.
FACILITIES: sitting room, dining room, museum/function room, free Wi-Fi, in-room TV (Freeview), civil wedding licence, 1-acre courtyard, unsuitable for disabled.
BACKGROUND MUSIC: soft classical in sitting room and dining room.
LOCATION: 6 miles W of Ludlow.
CHILDREN: not under 13.
DOGS: allowed in some bedrooms by prior arrangement.
CREDIT CARDS: Amex, MasterCard, Visa.
PRICES: [2017] per room B&B £135–£185, D,B&B £215–£268. Tasting menus £50–£70.

SEE ALSO SHORTLIST

LURGASHALL Sussex

THE BARN AT ROUNDHURST

An 'oasis of calm' in the South Downs national park, Moya and Richard Connell's rural B&B/restaurant-with-rooms centres on a 'stunningly restored' 17th-century threshing barn set on a working organic farm. The sitting area in the lofty, open-plan space, dramatic with huge oak beams, has modern artwork, vintage leather seating and rough-hewn wooden pieces; there's an honesty bar and a small library up the curving staircase. In the winter, a log-burning stove makes things cosy. Tables in the dining area are laid with white linens and candles four nights a week, for a four-course dinner using ingredients from the farm and surrounding woodland. A typical dish: organic beef, wild mushrooms, onion purée. Cold platters of meats, cheeses and salads may be prepared on other nights. Well-equipped bedrooms (with all the usual amenities, plus wine glasses, a corkscrew and a yoga mat) are in converted farm buildings set around a courtyard. 'Our room was spacious and comfortable, but with a dimly lit bathroom.' Farm produce appears on the breakfast table in the morning: newly laid eggs, freshly baked bread, home-made jams – 'no packaging to be seen'.

Lower Roundhurst Farm
Jobson's Lane
Lurgashall
GU27 3BY

T: 01428 642535
E: bookings@thebarnatroundhurst.com
W: thebarnatroundhurst.com

BEDROOMS: 6.
OPEN: all year, dining room closed Sun–Tues (cold platters available).
FACILITIES: open-plan lounge/dining area, library/bar, free Wi-Fi, in-room TV (Freeview), meeting/function facilities, small garden on 250-acre farm.
BACKGROUND MUSIC: mixed in lounge.
LOCATION: 2 miles S of Haslemere, Surrey.
CHILDREN: not under 12.
DOGS: not allowed.
CREDIT CARDS: all major cards.
PRICES: [2017] per room B&B £138–£240. Set menu £40.

LYMINGTON Hampshire

BRITANNIA HOUSE

Hats off to Tobias Feilke, owner of this
characterful B&B on the harbour of an old
port town at the mouth of the Solent. The fun
begins when you step inside to find a wall hung
with assorted headgear – from pith helmet to
homburg – and a suit of armour standing sentry.
'We cannot praise our stay highly enough,'
enthuse Guide readers this year. 'We were
made to feel very welcome.' It's a homely place,
where the first-floor sitting room, with views
over the marina, is comfy and cosy with squashy
sofas and books to borrow. Bedrooms, some
in a newer building opposite, are individually
decorated with antiques and prints – 'they're
certainly not bland or impersonal'. A ground-
floor suite overlooking the courtyard and
evergreen garden is a tranquil choice, but, for
more privacy, a two-storey apartment with its
own balcony and art-hung sitting room is just
the ticket. The host has advice to offer on local
restaurants; for guests open to striking out
further, Beaulieu, a 15-minute drive away, has
good options (see entries). Breakfast is a relaxed
affair, taken at a shared table in the open-plan
kitchen. 'Tobias cooked our breakfast just when
we wanted it, and it was exceptional.'

Station Street
Lymington
SO41 3BA

T: 01590 672091
E: enquiries@britannia-house.com
W: www.britannia-house.com

BEDROOMS: 5. 2 on ground floor, one
2-storey apartment.
OPEN: all year.
FACILITIES: lounge, kitchen/breakfast
room, free Wi-Fi, in-room TV
(Freeview), courtyard garden,
parking, unsuitable for disabled.
BACKGROUND MUSIC: none.
LOCATION: 2 mins' walk from High
Street/quayside, close to station.
CHILDREN: not under 8.
DOGS: not allowed.
CREDIT CARDS: MasterCard, Visa.
PRICES: [2017] per room B&B
£90–£119. 1-night bookings refused
weekends.

LYNDHURST Hampshire

Map 2:E2

LIME WOOD

Think of anything you might want from a luxury hotel – 'friendly, professional staff', 'well-appointed bedrooms', 'delightful' public spaces, a 'memorable' breakfast with peerless granola. Chances are, at this family-friendly country house hotel, it's already been thought of. There's the house: Regency, with a collection of lodges and cottages in extensive grounds. The situation: the peaceful heart of the New Forest. The style: 'stunning'. No wonder it's a favoured celebrity retreat, liked for its 'lack of airs and graces'. Bedrooms of every size have restful decor, fluffy bathrobes, a pantry of goodies and views into greenery; even the smallest room is well conceived, with a 'lovely' bathroom. In the restaurant, chefs Angela Hartnett and Luke Holder cook dishes with an Italian accent and bravura – perhaps hare lasagne; hake, Salcombe crab, sweet onion. (A grazing menu of good-for-you foods is available in the glass-encased Herb House Spa.) Loaf if you must, but there's plenty to do: forest foraging, yoga in the rooftop herb garden, a crash course in crustacea at the cookery school, bicycle rides down wooded paths. (JW)

Beaulieu Road
Lyndhurst
SO43 7FZ

T: 02380 287177
F: 02380 287199
E: info@limewood.co.uk
W: www.limewoodhotel.co.uk

BEDROOMS: 32. 5 on ground floor, 2 suitable for disabled, 16 in pavilions and cottages in the grounds.
OPEN: all year.
FACILITIES: lifts, 2 bars, 3 lounges, 2 restaurants, private dining rooms, free Wi-Fi, in-room TV (Freeview), civil wedding licence, spa (16-metre swimming pool), 14-acre gardens (outdoor hot pool), cookery school.
BACKGROUND MUSIC: all day in public areas.
LOCATION: in New Forest, 12 miles SW of Southampton.
CHILDREN: all ages welcomed.
DOGS: allowed in outside bedrooms, not in main house.
CREDIT CARDS: MasterCard, Visa.
PRICES: [2017] room from £330. Breakfast £16.50–£25, à la carte £65. 1-night bookings refused most weekends, bank holidays.

MARGATE Kent

SANDS HOTEL

Admire 'marvellous sea views' from Nick Conington's 'stylishly refurbished' Victorian hotel on the seafront of one of Kent's original resort towns. The place has been 'impeccably maintained'; the 'buzzy' bar and 'striking, contemporary' restaurant are 'furnished attractively and in good taste'. Bedrooms have an 'airy, peaceful' feel – even a smaller double room has 'ample space'. 'We had a good view of the sunset across the sands, from the balcony of our spacious sea-view room. There was no coffee table, which made it difficult to eat our room-service breakfast, but they brought a folding table when we asked.' Light sleepers, pack earplugs: guests in beachfront rooms have reported noise from the bar next door. At lunch and dinner, chef Ryan Tasker's modern menu might include 'very fresh, skilfully cooked' dishes such as wild turbot, artichoke, pancetta mussels, boulangère potatoes. (Leave room for a sweet treat from the ice cream parlour downstairs.) A special mention for the 'very friendly' staff, who 'show a genuine interest in guests', including successfully laundering a shirt stained by a rogue cafetière. (Michael Gwinnell, A and BB)

16 Marine Drive
Margate
CT9 1DH

T: 01843 228228
E: enquiries@sandshotelmargate.co.uk
W: www.sandshotelmargate.co.uk

BEDROOMS: 20. 1 suitable for disabled.
OPEN: all year.
FACILITIES: lift, bar, restaurant, free Wi-Fi, in-room TV (Freeview), civil wedding licence, roof terrace, ice cream parlour.
BACKGROUND MUSIC: varied, in public areas.
LOCATION: town centre.
CHILDREN: all ages welcomed (family rooms, children's menus).
DOGS: not allowed.
CREDIT CARDS: MasterCard, Visa.
PRICES: [2017] per room B&B £140–£200, D,B&B £200–£260. À la carte £32.

SEE ALSO SHORTLIST

MARKET DRAYTON Shropshire

Map 3:B5

GOLDSTONE HALL

All is peaceful at John and Sue Cushing's 18th-century manor house hotel, approached down a country lane embraced by green fields. 'Intimate and informal', the 'uniformly brilliant' family enterprise was begun by Mr Cushing's mother, Helen Ward, in 1983; today, the Cushings' daughter Victoria is a 'chatty and personable' presence front-of-house. Bedrooms are stocked with bathrobes and slippers, fresh milk, home-baked biscuits and 'lots of different teas'. 'Our cosy room was tastefully furnished, and had delightful views of the grounds. The bed was super comfy – we could have slept for days.' 'Inviting' lounges have plenty of space to breathe easy, but make time for a stroll down the great lawn and into the walled garden – the work of 'talented gardeners'. At dinner – there's an open fireplace in the Arts and Crafts-style dining room – chef Chris Weatherstone's 'beautifully presented' dishes, perhaps poussin, braised leeks, chervil root, make imaginative use of produce from the 'extraordinary' fruit and vegetable garden. Breakfast is roundly praised: freshly squeezed orange juice, home-baked bread, 'perfectly poached eggs', 'excellent veggie options'. (PI, and others)

Goldstone Road
Market Drayton
TF9 2NA

T: 01630 661202
F: 01630 661585
E: enquiries@goldstonehall.com
W: www.goldstonehall.com

BEDROOMS: 12.
OPEN: all year except Christmas.
FACILITIES: bar, lounge, drawing room, dining room, orangery, free Wi-Fi, in-room TV (Sky), function facilities, civil wedding licence, 5 acres of grounds (walled garden, kitchen garden), unsuitable for disabled.
BACKGROUND MUSIC: in bar and dining room.
LOCATION: 5 miles N of Newport, 5 miles S of Market Drayton.
CHILDREN: all ages welcomed (toys and dressing gowns provided).
DOGS: not allowed.
CREDIT CARDS: MasterCard, Visa.
PRICES: per room B&B single £95–£115, double £150–£180, D,B&B single £138–£158, double £246–£276. Set dinner £48.50.

MARTINHOE Devon

Map 1:B4

HEDDON'S GATE HOTEL

In a valley on the north Exmoor coast, Mark
and Pat Cowell's 'friendly, unpretentious' hotel
stands at the end of a long private drive 'close to
wonderful walks and fabulous scenery'. Guide
readers in 2017 praise the owners' generous
spirit and relaxed hospitality – 'they left us
totally spoiled!' 'Mark met us on arrival, helped
unload the car and took our bags upstairs.
One sunny evening, as we sat on the terrace
reading, they offered to set up a table for us
to have dinner alfresco.' Most bedrooms are
traditionally styled; three in a newer wing
are more contemporary. 'Our deluxe room,
furnished with a comfortable Victorian bed and
a couple of ornate chairs, had a great view over
the front garden.' At dinner, chef Justin Dunn
takes a flexible approach to his menu. 'He asked
what we'd like, and cooked special dishes for us,
as we were staying several days. One night, he
prepared a fillet steak with delicious peppercorn
sauce, another, a lovely risotto.' There's freshly
squeezed orange juice at breakfast, plus
lemon pancakes, 'first-class smoked salmon', a
'wonderful berry compote'. Outside, there's only
birdsong, and the rushing River Heddon below.
(Jill and Mike Bennett, Denis Owen)

25% DISCOUNT VOUCHERS

Martinhoe
EX31 4PZ

T: 01598 763481
E: stay@heddonsgatehotel.co.uk
W: www.heddonsgatehotel.co.uk

BEDROOMS: 11.
OPEN: 10 Feb–11 Nov, restaurant
closed Tues, group bookings over
Christmas and New Year.
FACILITIES: lounge, bar, TV room,
library, breakfast/dining room,
free Wi-Fi in public areas, in-room
TV (Freeview), no mobile phone
signal (guests may use landline free
of charge), sun terrace, 2½-acre
grounds, unsuitable for disabled.
BACKGROUND MUSIC: in dining room,
'but silence is also available on
request'.
LOCATION: 6 miles W of Lynton.
CHILDREN: all ages welcomed.
DOGS: allowed in bedrooms (not
unattended), not in dining room.
CREDIT CARDS: Amex, MasterCard,
Visa.
PRICES: per room B&B £110–£150,
D,B&B £140–£180. Set dinner £28.
1-night bookings sometimes refused
Sat, bank holidays.

MARTINHOE Devon

Map 1:B4

THE OLD RECTORY HOTEL

❦ Previous César winner

In 'what must be one of the most tranquil places in the country', Huw Rees and Sam Prosser run their 'splendid' hotel, a handsomely converted Georgian rectory in large, well-maintained grounds. 'It took some finding but was well worth the search.' Bedrooms in the main building and converted coach house are 'tastefully furnished and superbly appointed'; each is supplied with cafetière coffee, posh toiletries and spring water on tap. ('A grab rail in the shower would have been appreciated.') 'Our comfortable room overlooked the garden, with its waterfall and little stream – delights for eye and ear.' In the evening, mingle with fellow guests while skimming the menu over pre-dinner drinks. The 'excellent' meal that follows, cooked by Huw Rees, uses locally sourced ingredients including fish from day boats and produce from the garden. Typical dishes: wild garlic soup; Lundy turbot, Noilly Prat sauce. After breakfast (local apple juice; home-made preserves; various egg dishes), take a walk along the Exmoor coast – but hurry back for tea with home-made cakes. (Peter Govier, Gwyn Morgan, Roger Down)

Berry's Ground Lane
Martinhoe
EX31 4QT

T: 01598 763368
E: reception@oldrectoryhotel.co.uk
W: www.oldrectoryhotel.co.uk

BEDROOMS: 11. 2 on ground floor, 3 in coach house.
OPEN: Mar–end Oct.
FACILITIES: 2 lounges, orangery, dining room, free Wi-Fi, in-room TV (Freeview), 3-acre grounds.
BACKGROUND MUSIC: 'very quiet' in dining room.
LOCATION: 4 miles W of Lynton.
CHILDREN: not under 14.
DOGS: not allowed.
CREDIT CARDS: Amex, MasterCard, Visa.
PRICES: [2017] per room B&B £180–£260, D,B&B £220–£275. À la carte £30.

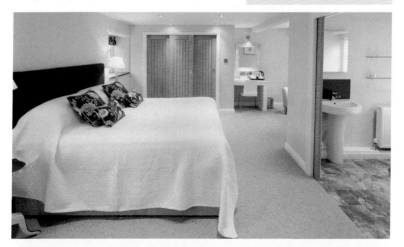

MAWGAN PORTH Cornwall

Map 1:D2

BEDRUTHAN HOTEL AND SPA

♀ Previous César winner

A short stroll from the beach, this 'top-of-the-class', 'exceptionally family-friendly' hotel is 'in a great cliff-top location' overlooking the sea. Among the numerous activities for young guests, there are children's clubs, games rooms, outdoor play areas, holiday programmes and a choice of swimming pools. Accompanying grown-ups might sign up their offspring for two hours of complimentary childcare, then avail themselves of the 'fantastic' spa and fitness facilities – a new sensory spa garden takes visitors from cedar wood sauna to seaweed-and-salt scrub – or one of the 'many restful spaces in which to relax'. ('Avoid the school holidays if you're after a really quiet break.') Bedrooms have a sunny Scandinavian air; picture windows in sea-view rooms give on to the breathtaking coast. Families may choose to eat at the casual Wild Café, with its small plates, soups and pizzas; its grown-up cousin, the Herring, is for sunset suppers over rare beef, pickled shimeji mushrooms, shisu cress, perhaps, or stone bass, spiced lentils, shrimp samosa. Adults-only The Scarlet, for 'a more sophisticated stay', is nearby (see next entry).

Mawgan Porth
TR8 4BU

T: 01637 860860
E: stay@bedruthan.com
W: www.bedruthan.com

BEDROOMS: 101. 1 suitable for disabled, apartment suites in separate block.
OPEN: all year except 3 weeks Jan.
FACILITIES: lift, 2 lounges, bar, restaurant, café, free Wi-Fi, in-room TV (Freeview), poolside snack bar, indoor and outdoor play areas, spa (indoor swimming pool), art gallery, civil wedding licence, 5-acre grounds (heated swimming pools, tennis, playing field).
BACKGROUND MUSIC: 'laid-back' in restaurant, café and bar.
LOCATION: 4 miles NE of Newquay.
CHILDREN: all ages welcomed.
DOGS: allowed in some bedrooms, some public areas.
CREDIT CARDS: MasterCard, Visa.
PRICES: [2017] per room B&B from £156, D,B&B from £202. Set dinner £24.50–£32.50.

MAWGAN PORTH Cornwall

Map 1:D2

THE SCARLET

Clean, contemporary design, eco credentials and 'wonderful views' attract guests to this voguish, adults-only hotel overlooking 'a classic Cornish bay'. 'A special mention, too, for the engaging staff who managed to find a charging device for my prehistoric phone,' says a Guide reader in 2017. With a private balcony or courtyard terrace, every one of the 'excellent bedrooms' – some small, others spacious enough to have a generous sitting area – has its own piece of the sky. Guests prone to bashfulness, be warned: in many rooms, a bathtub in the bedroom or a loo behind frosted glass 'offer little privacy'. Spend the day in 'well-maintained' swimming pools, or in the lantern-lit spa treatment rooms; further afield, the South West Coastal Path runs in both directions from the doorstep. In the restaurant overlooking the water, chef Tom Hunter's 'first-rate cooking' is distinctly Cornish, with vegetarian options (perhaps Jerusalem artichoke tarte Tatin, smoked Westcombe ricotta, white bean purée) to tempt the most ardent carnivore. Guests-to-be with children in tow should check out sister hotel Bedruthan Hotel and Spa (see previous entry). (Nick Patton, and others)

25% DISCOUNT VOUCHERS

Tredragon Road
Mawgan Porth
TR8 4DQ

T: 01637 861800
F: 01637 861801
E: stay@scarlethotel.co.uk
W: www.scarlethotel.co.uk

BEDROOMS: 37. 2 suitable for disabled.
OPEN: all year except 2 Jan–2 Feb.
FACILITIES: lift, 2 lounges, bar, library with pool table, restaurant, free Wi-Fi, in-room TV (Freeview), civil wedding licence, spa (indoor swimming pool, 4 by 15 metres, steam room, hammam, treatment room), natural outdoor swimming pool (40 sq metres), seaweed baths, terrace, meadow garden.
BACKGROUND MUSIC: all day in bar and restaurant.
LOCATION: 4 miles NE of Newquay.
CHILDREN: not under 16.
DOGS: allowed in selected bedrooms, some public areas.
CREDIT CARDS: MasterCard, Visa.
PRICES: per room B&B from £210, D,B&B from £280. Set dinner £45.50. 1-night bookings refused Fri/Sat.

MAWNAN SMITH Cornwall

Map 1:E2

BUDOCK VEAN

'The beautiful location, wonderful service and excellent food keep us coming back.' Guide readers who returned this year to Martin Barlow's hotel, in wooded acres on the Helford river, discovered that 'tasteful refurbishment' has created a 'fresh seaside feel'. Another plus: the 'amazing facilities for active people, right on the doorstep'. The 18th-century manor house has lounges aplenty (including one on the river foreshore), plus tennis courts, a golf course, a spa, a swimming pool, and wide swathes of garden and woodland to explore. Where to begin? Unpack in one of the well-equipped bedrooms – each is supplied with 'everything we needed', including bathrobes, slippers, bottled Cornish water. Newly revamped rooms are light and modern; others retain their traditional air. Dress smartly for dinner in the restaurant, where chef Darren Kelly's modern menus have 'plenty of fish', perhaps locally landed hake or wild Cornish turbot. Lighter meals and afternoon tea can be had in the cocktail bar or conservatory, or on the terrace. Find your sea legs: kayak tours go up Frenchman's Creek; a 'terrific' river cruise is 'a highlight'. (Mary Coles, SL, and others)

nr Helford Passage
Mawnan Smith
TR11 5LG

T: 01326 252100
F: 01326 250892
E: relax@budockvean.co.uk
W: www.budockvean.co.uk

BEDROOMS: 57. Plus 4 self-catering cottages.
OPEN: all year except 2–20 Jan.
FACILITIES: lift, 3 lounges, cocktail bar, conservatory, Golf bar (Sky Sports), restaurant, snooker room, free Wi-Fi, in-room TV (Freeview), civil wedding licence, 65-acre grounds (covered heated swimming pool, 15 by 7 metres), spa, 9-hole golf course, tennis.
BACKGROUND MUSIC: 'gentle' live piano or guitar music in evening in restaurant.
LOCATION: 6 miles SW of Falmouth.
CHILDREN: all ages welcomed (children's high tea, family dinners).
DOGS: allowed in most bedrooms, not in public rooms.
CREDIT CARDS: MasterCard, Visa
PRICES: [2017] per person B&B from £73, D,B&B from £94. Set dinner £42.

MELLS Somerset

THE TALBOT INN

♥ Previous César winner

Close to the fine church in an 'attractive' medieval wool village, this 'friendly, well-patronised' 15th-century coaching inn has 'the warm, buzzy feel of a country pub', say Guide readers in 2017. 'Attentive staff' serve local ales and sausage rolls in the 'rustic, homely' bar; in winter, mulled wine and cider are warmed in the fireplace. Join locals in the dining rooms for modern British dishes 'cooked to a very high standard'. (Weekends are for hearty meals of grilled meats or fish, perhaps locally caught trout, straight off the charcoal and wood fire.) 'We enjoyed delicious, lightly smoked monkfish; lamb cooked to perfection and served with an imaginative combination of vegetables. Even pub staples, such as fish and chips, were prepared with care and skill.' Hung with local artwork, 'comfortable' modern bedrooms (most up 'steep stairs') are pleasingly uncluttered; vintage Welsh blankets and all-natural bath products are a welcome touch. 'The finest ingredients' ('excellent croissants'; 'tasty pancetta') show up at breakfast. The Beckford Arms, Tisbury (see entry), is under the same ownership. (Joan and Robert Grimley)

Selwood Street
Mells
BA11 3PN

T: 01373 812254
E: info@talbotinn.com
W: www.talbotinn.com

BEDROOMS: 8. 1 on ground floor.
OPEN: all year except 25 Dec.
FACILITIES: sitting room, bar, restaurant, coach house grill room, free Wi-Fi, in-room smart TV, courtyard, garden.
BACKGROUND MUSIC: in public areas.
LOCATION: in village.
CHILDREN: all ages welcomed.
DOGS: allowed in 1 bedroom, dining areas.
CREDIT CARDS: MasterCard, Visa.
PRICES: [2017] per room B&B £100–£160 (family suite £200). À la carte £30.

MEVAGISSEY Cornwall

Map 1:D2

TREVALSA COURT

NEW

'There is something Enid Blytonish about this place, romantically set just above the Coastal Path on the way out of Mevagissey. A big house (rather than a hotel) in feel, it has an endearing mixture of eccentricity and solid good taste.' Susan and John Gladwin's small hotel earns a full entry thanks to a regular Guide reader this year, who returned to find it 'even better than before'. Take in 'fantastic views' along the Cornish coast from the house or sub-tropical gardens; within the Arts and Crafts home, there are books, board games, an intimate bar, crackling fires in cool weather. The staff are 'helpful and friendly in just the right way'. Most of the 'comfortable, spotless' bedrooms, simple and pretty in seaside colours, look on to the water. The village is a ten-minute downhill walk away, but stay in for dinner: chef Adam Cawood's modern meals (perhaps monkfish, hazelnuts, peas, wild garlic velouté, monk's beard) are 'excellent'. 'The highlight was a delicious strawberries-and-cream ice cream that was a magical combination of rich flavours.' Strap on your boots in the morning: 'The Coastal Path is simply glorious.' (Mike Craddock)

School Hill
Mevagissey
PL26 6TH

T: 01726 842468
E: stay@trevalsa-hotel.co.uk
W: www.trevalsa-hotel.co.uk

BEDROOMS: 15. 3, plus family suite, on ground floor.
OPEN: 10 Feb–20 Nov.
FACILITIES: lounge, bar, restaurant, free Wi-Fi, in-room TV (Freeview), 2-acre garden, summer house, unsuitable for disabled.
BACKGROUND MUSIC: all day in bar.
LOCATION: on cliff-top, at edge of village.
CHILDREN: all ages welcomed.
DOGS: allowed in bar, lounge, bedrooms (not unattended), not in restaurant.
CREDIT CARDS: Amex, MasterCard, Visa.
PRICES: [2017] per room B&B single £70–£120, double £125–£290, D,B&B (min. 2 nights) single £92.50–£147.50, double £180–£345. À la carte £38. 1-night bookings refused high season.

SEE ALSO SHORTLIST

MILTON ABBOT Devon

Map 1:D3

HOTEL ENDSLEIGH

◊ Previous César winner

Olga Polizzi's countryside retreat, at its origin a Regency fishing lodge created for the Duchess of Bedford, is today an 'unpretentious, wholly enjoyable' hotel 'decorated with charm and taste'. 'A few days here feeds the historical imagination,' say guests in 2017. 'Reading in the beautifully candlelit library in the evening, it's easy to imagine yourself as a guest of the duke and duchess in the early 19th century, down in Devon for a few days' hunting and fishing.' The cottage orné stands in a 'magical landscape' of Humphry Repton-designed flower-filled arbours and manicured gardens ('glorious even in the depths of January'); there are ancient trees, bridges over streams, and picnic spots to discover. Inside, every bedroom has its own personality: admire hand-painted wallpaper here, soak in a freestanding bath there. Two suites, handy for a family, are in converted stables. At lunch and dinner, chef Jose Graziosi's modern dishes look to Italy for inspiration. A typical dish: sea bream, Parmesan gnocchi, cavolo nero, crab bisque. 'Memorable in every way.' (Andrew and Hannah Butterworth, and others)

Milton Abbot
PL19 0PQ

T: 01822 870000
F: 01822 870578
E: mail@hotelendsleigh.com
W: www.hotelendsleigh.com

BEDROOMS: 18. 1 on ground floor, 2 in stables, 1 in lodge (1 mile from main house).
OPEN: all year.
FACILITIES: drawing room, library, card room, bar, 2 dining rooms, free Wi-Fi, in-room TV (Freeview), civil wedding licence, terraces, 108-acre estate (fishing, ghillie available).
BACKGROUND MUSIC: none.
LOCATION: 7 miles NW of Tavistock.
CHILDREN: all ages welcomed.
DOGS: allowed, not in restaurant, or in library during afternoon tea.
CREDIT CARDS: Amex, MasterCard, Visa.
PRICES: [2017] per room B&B £190–£425, D,B&B £255–£490. Set dinner £47. 1-night bookings refused weekends.

MORSTON Norfolk

Map 2:A5

MORSTON HALL

Previous César winner

'The Michelin star is well earned' at Tracy and Galton Blackiston's friendly restaurant-with-rooms close to the north Norfolk coast. In an elegant dining room whose picture windows look out on to neat lawns, Galton Blackiston and Greg Anderson's 'superb' modern menus list a daily-changing selection of 'excellent' dishes, perhaps North Sea Dover sole, Beaufort crust, salsify purée; Holkham Hall venison, salt-baked beetroot, cabbage, white pepper jus. With 'lovely, helpful' staff, 'the whole operation runs like clockwork': drinks and menu deliberations at 7.15 pm, dinner at 8 pm. After coffee and home-made chocolates, head to one of the bedrooms made country house comfortable with 'all the amenities you might expect'. Rooms in the garden pavilion have a separate sitting area and a private terrace; some bathrooms have a spa bath. At breakfast, croissants are home baked, marmalade is home made, haddock and kippers come straight from the on-site smokehouse. Take a muddy walk down to the quay for 'lovely views' of Blakeney Point – 'it'll give you a good appetite for your next meal'. (WS, SJ, Minda Alexander)

The Street
Morston
NR25 7AA

T: 01263 741041
F: 01263 740419
E: reception@morstonhall.com
W: www.morstonhall.com

BEDROOMS: 13. 6 on ground floor, 100 yds from house, in garden pavilion.
OPEN: all year except 24–26 Dec, Jan.
FACILITIES: lounge, 2 conservatories, restaurant, free Wi-Fi, in-room TV (Freeview), civil wedding licence, 3-acre garden (pond, croquet).
BACKGROUND MUSIC: none.
LOCATION: 2 miles W of Blakeney.
CHILDREN: all ages welcomed.
DOGS: allowed in bedrooms (£10 per night, free in kennels), not in public rooms.
CREDIT CARDS: Amex, MasterCard, Visa.
PRICES: [2017] per person D,B&B £175–£205. Set dinner £75, 4-course Sunday lunch £40.

MOUSEHOLE Cornwall

Map 1: E1

THE OLD COASTGUARD

The 'wonderful sea views' from this 'fantastic' hotel are but part of its charm: it is equally praised for its 'pleasant, helpful staff', 'most delicious food' and 'great atmosphere'. It is owned by brothers Charles and Edmund Inkin, whose Gurnard's Head, Zennor, and Felin Fach Griffin, Felin Fach (see entries), have the same carefree feel. ('It's a pleasure to recommend them all.') A 'youthful, buzzy' spot, the hotel has plenty of activities to suggest: yoga weekends, foraging walks, a sailing trip with a seafood lunch. Still, there's always room to simply gather in the bar, as did Guide readers, over evening games of bridge. Simple, cheering bedrooms are decorated with Cornish art. Each one is different: a room with a balcony taking in the panorama was deemed 'excellent'; a smaller one 'with no view to speak of' was less liked. At lunch and supper, dine on creative, seafood-heavy dishes, perhaps hake, pinto beans, monk's beard, nduja mayonnaise, while gazing over to St Clement's Isle. A good base for local exploration: 'We walked to Newlyn one morning to see the fishing boats; another day we took the bus to the Penlee gallery in Penzance.' (EO, BW, Michael Eldridge)

The Parade
Mousehole
TR19 6PR

T: 01736 731222
E: bookings@oldcoastguardhotel.co.uk
W: www.oldcoastguardhotel.co.uk

BEDROOMS: 14.
OPEN: all year except 24/25 Dec.
FACILITIES: bar, sun lounge, restaurant, free Wi-Fi, sea-facing garden with path to beach, unsuitable for disabled.
BACKGROUND MUSIC: Radio 4 at breakfast, selected music at other mealtimes.
LOCATION: 2-min. walk from village, 3 miles S of Newlyn.
CHILDREN: all ages welcomed.
DOGS: welcomed (treats, towels, dog bowls), not allowed in dining room.
CREDIT CARDS: MasterCard, Visa.
PRICES: [2017] per room B&B £140–£225, D,B&B £192.50–£277.50. Set dinner £19.50–£24.50, à la carte £24.50.

MULLION COVE Cornwall

Map 1:E2

MULLION COVE HOTEL

'A place where the guest comes first', the Grose family's 'lovely traditional hotel' is run by 'attentive staff who want to make your visit as enjoyable as possible'. 'I arrived to a smiling greeting and the feeling that I was going to be well looked after. And so it proved – my comfortable room had everything I required, and there was always a kindly acknowledgement in the restaurant, bar or reception,' writes a regular Guide correspondent in 2017. Four-legged friends aren't forgotten: 'This is one of the best places we've discovered for taking our dog – in fact, the special dog-friendly lounge seemed the social centre of the hotel while we were there.' On the cliff-top, with 'fabulous views' over Mounts Bay and down to Mullion Cove, the hotel has many bedrooms facing the sea. ('The vista was spectacular even from my partial-sea-view room.') In the Atlantic View restaurant, chef Paul Stephens's 'excellent' daily-changing menus include locally landed fish and seafood, perhaps pan-roasted sea bass, Serrano crushed new potatoes, chard, dill and tomato velouté. 'Delightful – and breakfast was first rate, too.' (Peter Govier, and others)

25% DISCOUNT VOUCHERS

Cliff Road
Mullion Cove
TR12 7EP

T: 01326 240328
F: 01326 240998
E: enquiries@mullion-cove.co.uk
W: www.mullion-cove.co.uk

BEDROOMS: 30. Some on ground floor.
OPEN: all year.
FACILITIES: lift, 3 lounges, bar, restaurant, free Wi-Fi, in-room TV (Freeview), 1-acre garden, 10-metre heated outdoor swimming pool, unsuitable for disabled.
BACKGROUND MUSIC: none.
LOCATION: on edge of village.
CHILDREN: all ages welcomed, no under-7s in restaurant in evening.
DOGS: allowed in some bedrooms, 1 lounge.
CREDIT CARDS: Amex, MasterCard, Visa.
PRICES: [2017] per room B&B £115–£310, D,B&B from £146. Set dinner £39.95, à la carte £33.

NEAR SAWREY Cumbria

Map 4: inset C2

EES WYKE COUNTRY HOUSE

In a 'stunning' Lake District location overlooking Esthwaite Water, Richard Lee's 'admirable' country hotel is liked for its 'comfortable bedrooms', 'first-class food', 'fabulous views' and all-round 'lovely ambience'. It was once the holiday home of Beatrix Potter, who checked printer's proofs for her nascent Tale of Peter Rabbit during her stay; guests today may expect a more restful sojourn. Settle in to one of the traditional, country-style bedrooms before taking a sunset pre-dinner stroll by the lake; in winter months, hole up with a book by the window in one of the fire-warmed lounges. 'Staying in for dinner is a winning decision.' Served on white table linen, the host's 'superb' daily-changing, three-course menu focuses on produce from local suppliers, perhaps pan-fried noisettes of local lamb, wine jus. 'Every course was beautifully presented; the flavours were wonderful.' Rise to home-baked bread, local sausages and bacon, and a varied buffet at an 'excellent' breakfast. 'There was even a small jug of whisky next to the porridge – and appreciative noises from those who tried it.' (Jenny and Ian Sherman, KS, Allan Campbell)

Near Sawrey
LA22 0JZ

T: 015394 36393
E: mail@eeswyke.co.uk
W: www.eeswyke.co.uk

BEDROOMS: 8. 1 on ground floor.
OPEN: all year, except Christmas.
FACILITIES: 2 lounges, restaurant, free Wi-Fi, in-room TV (Freeview), veranda, ½-acre garden, unsuitable for disabled.
BACKGROUND MUSIC: none.
LOCATION: edge of village 2½ miles SE of Hawkshead on B5285.
CHILDREN: not under 12.
DOGS: not allowed.
CREDIT CARDS: MasterCard, Visa.
PRICES: per room B&B £90–£155, D,B&B £150–£215. Set dinner £29.95. 1-night bookings sometimes refused at weekends, bank holidays.

NETHER WESTCOTE Oxfordshire

Map 3:D6

THE FEATHERED NEST

🏆 Previous César winner

'However you look at it, it's truly a delight.'
Guide readers find nothing to ruffle their
feathers at Tony and Amanda Timmer's
'delightful' restaurant-with-rooms. The
rustic 300-year-old Cotswold malthouse sets
a high standard, with a warm welcome and
'Michelin-quality food'. In the 'attractive' dining
room looking out across the Evenlode valley,
Raymond Blanc protégé Kuba Winkowski
creates 'stand-out dishes that could be works of
art'. Among his 'stunning', minimalist plates:
scallop, langoustine, pork belly, sea urchin;
fallow deer, beetroot, salsify, miso, cocoa bean.
On a fine day, ask to eat on the garden terrace,
under the old sycamore tree. Wind down with
a nightcap by the fire in the bar, then head
upstairs to one of the 'spacious, comfortable'
bedrooms. Decorated in a modern rustic style,
and with views of rolling countryside, each is
'thoughtfully equipped' with fresh flowers,
books, magazines; an 'efficient' walk-in shower
(most have a separate bathtub as well). Wake to
a 'delicious' breakfast, then head out on a ramble
through wild flower meadows filled with 'all
manner of butterflies'. (JH, and others)

Chipping Norton
Nether Westcote
OX7 6SD

T: 01993 833030
F: 01993 833031
E: info@thefeatherednestinn.co.uk
W: www.thefeatherednestinn.co.uk

BEDROOMS: 4.
OPEN: all year except 25 Dec,
restaurant closed Mon except bank
holidays.
FACILITIES: 2 bars, small lounge,
dining room, free Wi-Fi, in-room
TV (Freeview), civil wedding
licence, 45-acre grounds, unsuitable
for disabled.
BACKGROUND MUSIC: in bar all day.
LOCATION: in hamlet, 5 miles S of
Stow-on-the-Wold.
CHILDREN: not under 16 overnight.
DOGS: allowed in bar, not in
bedrooms.
CREDIT CARDS: Amex, MasterCard,
Visa.
PRICES: [2017] per room B&B
£245–£295, D,B&B £360–£410.
À la carte £68. 1-night bookings
refused weekends.

NETLEY MARSH Hampshire

Map 2:E2

HOTEL TERRAVINA

🏆 Previous César winner

A hotel that 'lifts the spirits' – with regular wine tastings and cellar tours to raise them even higher – the Bassets' Victorian villa on the edge of the New Forest is an oenophile's delight. Gérard Basset is an award-winning sommelier, Nina Basset, a former hotel inspector; their combined talents are evident in the attention to detail at this 'consistently excellent' enterprise. 'This is a friendly place, where we're always made to feel totally welcome by the owners and their team,' says a regular returnee in 2017. Well-equipped with an espresso machine, organic toiletries and 'bedside lights you can actually read by', 'the immaculately presented bedrooms are very special'. Three have a patio garden, three a roof terrace. 'And the outdoor pool is perfect, in summer, for the children.' From the dining room designed to evoke Californian wine country (the host's passion), watch chef Gavin Barnes at work in the open kitchen. An example of his 'fantastic', unfussy cooking: roast New Forest venison, garlic kale, pommes Anna, chestnuts. 'It certainly pays to ask Gérard to recommend a wine to go with the meal.' (Claire Clark)

174 Woodlands Road
Woodlands
Netley Marsh
SO40 7GL

T: 02380 293784
E: info@hotelterravina.co.uk
W: www.hotelterravina.co.uk

BEDROOMS: 11. 3 on ground floor, 1 suitable for disabled.
OPEN: all year.
FACILITIES: bar, lounge, restaurant, private dining/meeting room, free Wi-Fi, in-room TV (Sky, Freeview), civil wedding licence, 1½-acre grounds (terraces, small heated outdoor swimming pool).
BACKGROUND MUSIC: none.
LOCATION: 8 miles W of Southampton, 4 miles N of Lyndhurst.
CHILDREN: all ages welcomed.
DOGS: not allowed.
CREDIT CARDS: Amex, MasterCard, Visa.
PRICES: [2017] per room B&B £165–£265, D,B&B £215–£255. À la carte £45. 2-night bookings preferred at weekends.

NEW MILTON Hampshire

Map 2:E2

CHEWTON GLEN

'Superb', 'excellent', 'impressive', 'delightful' – on the edge of the New Forest, this model of a country house hotel and spa is on top form, having celebrated its golden anniversary. 'Friendly, attentive staff' extend 'the warmest welcome' at the 18th-century manor house and throughout the massive estate; there are indoor and outdoor swimming pools, cooking classes, a children's club, a woodland stream to follow to the beach. Choose one of the many 'beautiful, oh-so-comfortable' bedrooms and suites, or aim even higher: tree-house suites in a leafy setting have a mini-kitchen, a wood-burning stove, a spa bath, and a breakfast hamper in the morning. Simon Addison is now chef in the conservatory dining room, where produce from the kitchen garden informs the 'divine' modern menu (perhaps including Quantock duck breast, sweet potato, sprouting broccoli, heritage carrots). Informal meals (superfood salads; wood-fired pizzas) are served in the 'brilliant' new Kitchen restaurant, part of the sleek, purpose-built cookery school, complete with its own lounge and terrace. 'We can't speak highly enough of the place.' (Chris Turner, Jenny Russell, and others)

Christchurch Road
New Milton
BH25 6QS

T: 01425 275341
E: reservations@chewtonglen.com
W: www.chewtonglen.com

BEDROOMS: 70. 14 on ground floor, 12 tree-house suites in grounds, 1 suitable for disabled.
OPEN: all year.
FACILITIES: 3 lounges, bar, 2 restaurants, function rooms, free Wi-Fi, in-room TV (Sky), civil wedding licence, cookery school, spa, indoor 17-metre swimming pool, 130-acre grounds (outdoor 15-metre heated swimming pool, tennis centre, par-3 golf course).
BACKGROUND MUSIC: 'subtle' in public areas.
LOCATION: on S edge of New Forest.
CHILDREN: all ages welcomed.
DOGS: allowed in tree-house suites, not in public rooms.
CREDIT CARDS: Amex, MasterCard, Visa.
PRICES: [2017] room £325–£1,425. Breakfast £26.50, à la carte £60, tasting menu £70. 1-night bookings refused weekends.

NEW ROMNEY Kent

Map 2:E5

ROMNEY BAY HOUSE

🏆 Previous César winner

'Comfortable all over and pleasantly relaxed', Clinton and Lisa Lovell's small hotel continues to win rave reviews from guests, who say 'it's like staying with good friends'. 'We were made to feel as if we were being welcomed into the family home,' say returning guests this year. More praise: 'The owners were friendly but discreet, looking after us well but allowing us privacy at the same time.' The 1920s mansion, across a quiet road from the coastline, has homey, restful bedrooms, each 'immaculate'. 'And the attention to detail is striking, down to the binoculars provided in a thick leather case on the window sill of our sea-view room.' The 'stunning' surroundings beg to be explored: 'We set out on our bikes along the six-mile sea wall, cycling into the wind, then sailed home.' Return to the host's 'beautifully presented' four-course set menu, 'served with care by Lisa and her staff'. 'Our evening meals were as good as it gets, including the best cheeseboard we'd ever seen.' 'We left feeling as if we should write them a thank-you letter.' (Charles Medawar, and others)

Coast Road
Littlestone
New Romney
TN28 8QY

T: 01797 364747
E: romneybayhouse@aol.co.uk
W: www.romneybayhousehotel.
   co.uk

BEDROOMS: 10.
OPEN: all year except 2 weeks Christmas, dining room closed midday, Sun/Mon/Thurs evenings.
FACILITIES: 2 lounges, bar, conservatory, dining room, free Wi-Fi, in-room TV (Freeview), small function facilities, 1-acre garden, unsuitable for disabled.
BACKGROUND MUSIC: none.
LOCATION: 1½ miles from New Romney.
CHILDREN: not under 14.
DOGS: not allowed.
CREDIT CARDS: Amex, MasterCard, Visa.
PRICES: per room B&B £95–£164. Set dinner £47.50. 1-night advance bookings refused weekends.

NEWBIGGIN-ON-LUNE Cumbria

Map 4:C3

BROWNBER HALL

'Enthusiastically and admirably run' by its 'hard-working young owners', this Victorian house between the Lake District and the Yorkshire Dales stands on a wooded hillside with 'magnificent views' over green fields and grazing sheep to the fells beyond. Amanda Walker and Peter Jaques have done 'a grand job' since taking over the B&B in 2016, say Guide inspectors this year. Come in to a 'warm welcome' – a sideboard of 'tempting cakes' is just beyond. Modern photographs and older watercolours make an 'eye-catching contrast'; the book-filled sitting room hosts a vintage corner bar. 'Well-designed bedrooms' are up the curving staircase. 'Our good-sized, well-lit room at the front had a comfortable bed; an avocado-hued shower room with fluffy towels, a powerful shower and plenty of hot water. We woke to that wonderful view stretching to the North Pennines.' A 'praiseworthy breakfast' is served on 'proper tablecloths, with linen napkins', in the 'light, bright dining room': 'buttery croissants, delicious home-baked sourdough, creamy scrambled eggs'. Pick up a walking stick at the front door, afterwards, and stride straight onto the Dales High Way.

25% DISCOUNT VOUCHERS

Newbiggin-on-Lune
CA17 4NX

T: 01539 623208
E: enquiries@brownberhall.co.uk
W: www.brownberhall.co.uk

BEDROOMS: 8.
OPEN: all year except Christmas and New Year.
FACILITIES: 2 lounges (log fire, honesty bar), dining room, free Wi-Fi, in-room TV (Freeview), 1-acre garden, bicycle storage, unsuitable for disabled.
BACKGROUND MUSIC: in public rooms.
LOCATION: 6¼ miles SW of Kirkby Stephen – 'follow the hosts' clear directions, not sat nav'.
CHILDREN: all ages welcomed.
DOGS: allowed in 2 bedrooms, public rooms.
CREDIT CARDS: MasterCard, Visa.
PRICES: [2017] per room B&B single £55–£60, double £90–£140. 1-night bookings refused on busy weekends.

NEWCASTLE UPON TYNE Tyne and Wear Map 4:B4

JESMOND DENE HOUSE

♥ Previous César winner

In 'an oasis of calm', Peter Candler's 'impressive, imposing' hotel stands in 'an attractive wooded dell, with paths leading into woodland for exploration'. 'Customer care is a priority here,' says a Guide inspector in 2017 who was 'warmly greeted' by name. 'Spacious' wood-panelled lounges have prints and pictures; there are 'grand fireplaces'; 'a variety of comfortable seating is arranged for small groups'. Pick one of the modern, uncluttered bedrooms in the main building or adjacent New House: each is supplied with ground coffee, biscuits and fresh milk on the tea tray, good toiletries in the bathroom. 'Up a narrow back staircase, my upper-floor room had a balcony with seating; a dimly lit bathroom. Housekeeping was efficient.' In the restaurant, chef Michael Penaluna's short, seasonally-changing menu lists inventive dishes ('served in designer-style portions'), perhaps 'perfectly cooked Northumberland venison saddle with wafer-thin, crisp, smoky bacon'. At breakfast: 'an extensive cold buffet; good-quality toast and scrambled eggs; wonderful fresh orange juice, chilled and inspiringly tart – just right to wake one up'.

Jesmond Dene Road
Newcastle upon Tyne
NE2 2EY

T: 0191 212 3000
F: 0191 212 3001
E: info@jesmonddenehouse.co.uk
W: www.jesmonddenehouse.co.uk

BEDROOMS: 40. 8 in adjacent New House, 2 suitable for disabled.
OPEN: all year.
FACILITIES: lift, lounge, cocktail bar, billiard room, restaurant, conference/function facilities, terrace, free Wi-Fi, in-room TV (Sky), civil wedding licence, parking, 2-acre garden.
BACKGROUND MUSIC: 'easy listening' in public areas and restaurant.
LOCATION: 2 miles from city centre.
CHILDREN: all ages welcomed.
DOGS: allowed in one New House bedroom.
CREDIT CARDS: Amex, MasterCard, Visa.
PRICES: [2017] per room B&B from £140, D,B&B from £200. Set dinner £20.50–£24.50, tasting menu £55, à la carte £45.

NEWMARKET Suffolk

Map 2:B4

THE PACKHORSE INN

Here is Tom Pearce's old grey mare crossed with Arkle – a Victorian taproom given the 'terrific' thoroughbred treatment by Philip Turner's Chestnut Inns. Its situation is pleasing, beside a medieval packhorse bridge in an attractive village close to Newmarket Racecourse, stables and gallops. 'It has been decorated very well' and serves 'excellent food', Guide readers report. Antique paintings of jockeys flank the entrance; inside, there are leather armchairs on scuffed wooden floors, and a smart, rustic look throughout. Individually styled bedrooms are in the main building and the coach house at the rear, each furnished with a large bed made inviting with quality linen, a goose-down duvet and a mohair throw. Pick one to suit: two look over the village green; one has a claw-footed bath in the room. Coach house rooms open on to a terrace – useful for dog owners. At dinner, the modern European choices on the menu are 'unusual – but not annoyingly so'. Typical dishes: confit chicken wing, cauliflower, toasted yeast; Denham estate venison, truffle potato, salsify, shiitake and pine emulsion. Bar food is simpler: salmon fishcakes, grilled steaks, a house burger with mooli slaw.

Bridge Street
Moulton
Newmarket
CB8 8SP

T: 01638 751818
E: info@thepackhorseinn.com
W: www.thepackhorseinn.com

BEDROOMS: 8. 4 on ground floor in coach house suitable for disabled.
OPEN: all year.
FACILITIES: bar/restaurant, function room, free Wi-Fi, in-room TV, courtyard.
BACKGROUND MUSIC: in public rooms.
LOCATION: opposite green in Moulton village, 3 miles from Newmarket.
CHILDREN: all ages welcomed.
DOGS: allowed in courtyard rooms (£10 a night).
CREDIT CARDS: Amex, MasterCard, Visa.
PRICES: [2017] per room B&B £100–£195. À la carte £36.

SEE ALSO SHORTLIST

NEWTON ABBOT Devon

Map 1:D4

THE ROCK INN

Rock-solid traditional values win praise for the Graves family's late Georgian village inn, at the centre of a terrace of cottages on the edge of Dartmoor. A reader who has known it for three decades this year awards it '11 out of ten for cosiness'. 'The people are lovely and the food is top class.' Hearty pub favourites and local real ales draw locals and passers-by at lunchtime; at dinner in the snug bar and series of dining rooms, the cooking 'clearly has a reputation'. Locally grown produce and locally sourced meat and game feature in such dishes as duck Scotch egg, chilli jam; pan-fried rib-eye steak, mushroom and truffle purée, fine beans, chunky chips. Bedrooms, balconied, beamed or creaky-floored, are individually decorated, and have views of moors or garden. 'Our room was rather small, but warm and cosy, with everything we needed, including a teapot on the tray.' In the morning, there are 'great poached eggs' and exemplary kippers at breakfast. Fuel up: Becky Falls is easily reached; the top of Haytor Rock, with commanding views across south Devon, is a 25-minute hike away. (Diana Goodey, and others)

Haytor Vale
Newton Abbot
TQ13 9XP

T: 01364 661305
F: 01364 661242
E: info@rock-inn.co.uk
W: www.rock-inn.co.uk

BEDROOMS: 9.
OPEN: all year except 25/26 Dec.
FACILITIES: bar, 4 dining rooms, free Wi-Fi, in-room TV (Freeview), ¼-acre garden, unsuitable for disabled.
BACKGROUND MUSIC: none.
LOCATION: 3 miles W of Bovey Tracey.
CHILDREN: all ages welcomed, not under 14 in main bar area.
DOGS: allowed in some bedrooms, bar, 1 dining room.
CREDIT CARDS: Diners, MasterCard, Visa.
PRICES: [2017] per room B&B £100–£160, D,B&B £160–£220. Set dinner £19.95–£24.95, à la carte £32. 1-night bookings sometimes refused.

NORTH WALSHAM Norfolk

Map 2:A6

BEECHWOOD HOTEL

'Everything is provided for guests' comfort' at this 'relaxed, friendly hotel', in a market town close to the north Norfolk coast. It is owned and run with a personal touch by Emma and Hugh Asher, who are 'most welcoming, and much in evidence', says a Guide reader this year. The red brick Georgian building is traditionally decorated inside, with dark wood furnishings and leather club chairs in the small bar. Browse the novels, magazines, newspapers and local guides in the lounge; in summer, French windows open to the garden, its rose walk and fishpond. Bedrooms, too, carry on the traditional theme, with swagged curtains or an original fireplace, perhaps a quilted bedspread on a carved-wood four-poster bed. Flannels are provided in the 'well-equipped bathrooms'; at turn-down, chocolates are placed on pillows. Among the better bedrooms, three garden rooms have direct access to an outdoor seating area. In the large restaurant – 'a popular place to dine' – 'chef Steven Norgate's food continues to attract a loyal following'. Among his 'tasty, filling dishes': pan-seared Tavern Tasty pork fillet, parsnip purée, kale, crackling. 'Good choice at breakfast, too.' (Mary Coles)

20 Cromer Road
North Walsham
NR28 0HD

T: 01692 403231
F: 01692 407284
E: info@beechwood-hotel.co.uk
W: www.beechwood-hotel.co.uk

BEDROOMS: 18. 4 on ground floor, 1 suitable for disabled.
OPEN: all year except Christmas, restaurant closed midday Mon and Tues.
FACILITIES: 2 lounges, bar, restaurant, free Wi-Fi, in-room TV (Freeview), 100-metre garden (croquet).
BACKGROUND MUSIC: all day in public rooms.
LOCATION: near town centre.
CHILDREN: all ages welcomed.
DOGS: allowed, not in restaurant.
CREDIT CARDS: all major cards.
PRICES: [2017] per room B&B single £70–£90, double £100–£175. Set dinner £40. 2-night min. stay Fri or Sat.

NORWICH Norfolk

Map 2:B5

THE ASSEMBLY HOUSE

'Ideally situated' in a quiet pocket of the city, this ornate building has hosted entertainment for more than 260 years, from genteel balls and concerts to waxwork exhibitions and a cinema. More recently, a cookery school was added to 'luxurious, comfortable' accommodation. The 'impressive restoration' of the Regency mansion resulted in 'fine interiors' and a 'gentle clash' of patterns and styles, creating the feel of a contemporary country house in the city. Head down a modern extension to a whitewashed older house where 'fruit, biscuits and umbrellas are freely available'. Bedrooms here are 'tastefully put together', each different as can be; some have a private garden with a parasol over patio seating. 'My room was appealingly decorated: bold colours, woven mats, countryside prints, a collection of polished brass cooking moulds. All the mod cons were there (espresso machine, adjustable reading lamp, chilled milk); the bathroom was spotlessly clean.' A short dinner menu is served till 8.30 pm. Breakfast on freshly squeezed juice, leaf tea, 'very fine' coffee by the cup; cooked dishes include an Arnold Bennett omelette ('naughtily creamy, with first-rate smoked haddock').

Theatre Street
Norwich
NR2 1RQ

T: 01603 626402
E: admin@assemblyhousenorwich.co.uk
W: www.assemblyhousenorwich.co.uk

BEDROOMS: 11. All in St Mary's House extension, 6 with private garden, 2 suitable for disabled.
OPEN: all year.
FACILITIES: entrance hall, dining room, private dining and function rooms, civil wedding licence, free Wi-Fi, in-room TV (Sky, Freeview), 1-acre grounds.
BACKGROUND MUSIC: none.
LOCATION: central, car park permits for pay-and-display.
CHILDREN: all ages welcomed.
DOGS: not allowed.
CREDIT CARDS: Amex, MasterCard, Visa.
PRICES: [2017] per room B&B £170–£270. À la carte £28.

SEE ALSO SHORTLIST

NORWICH Norfolk

Map 2:B5

THE OLD RECTORY

'One of the nicest small hotels', Sally and Chris Entwistle's Georgian rectory close to the centre affords guests 'a cosseted, home-away-from-home experience'. 'They're kind, helpful hosts, who have plenty of information about Norwich and the countryside to share.' Arrive to 'a welcome that's all you'd expect from a good hotelier', then settle in to one of the traditionally furnished bedrooms in the main house or converted coach house – most have garden views. Each room is supplied with bottled water, bathrobes and books; 'housekeeping is immaculate'. 'Our lovely, large room at the top of the house gave us the peace we required. We had a comfortable, supportive bed; double-glazing kept traffic noise to an acceptable level.' 'Food is an important feature', with chef James Perry using the best local ingredients for such dishes as 'melt-in-the-mouth' medallions of Attleborough beef, potato and celeriac purée, buttered spring greens. 'I was tempted to photograph my meal!' (The owners have good local eateries to recommend, for nights the dining room is closed.) Mornings, 'well-presented' breakfasts are cooked to order. 'It won't be our last visit.' (S and JJ, and others)

25% DISCOUNT VOUCHERS

103 Yarmouth Road
Thorpe St Andrew
Norwich
NR7 0HF

T: 01603 700772
F: 01603 300772
E: enquiries@oldrectorynorwich.com
W: www.oldrectorynorwich.com

BEDROOMS: 8. 3 in coach house.
OPEN: all year except Christmas/New Year, restaurant closed Sun and Mon.
FACILITIES: drawing room, conservatory, dining room, free Wi-Fi, in-room TV (Freeview), 1-acre garden, unheated swimming pool, unsuitable for disabled.
BACKGROUND MUSIC: classical/jazz at dinner.
LOCATION: 2 miles E of Norwich.
CHILDREN: all ages welcomed.
DOGS: only assistance dogs allowed.
CREDIT CARDS: all major cards.
PRICES: [2017] per room B&B £100–£185, D,B&B (min. 2 nights) £125–£235. Set dinner £35.

SEE ALSO SHORTLIST

NORWICH Norfolk

Map 2:B5

38 ST GILES

Father-and-son team Dennis and George Bacon run their upmarket modern B&B in a 'convenient central location' within walking distance of the Theatre Royal and the hum and hustle of the central marketplace. Beyond the 'sweet, neat sitting room', there are fresh flowers and high-end toiletries in the uncluttered bedrooms and suites. Tea and 'really good home baking' are offered as a sweet greeting. 'Our first-floor suite had panelled walls and original stripped-and-stained wood floors; a lounge area with a chesterfield sofa bed. The bathroom, though small, was very good; the loo and extra washbasin were separate.' (A two-bedroom apartment and Georgian town house nearby can also be booked for a family or travelling group.) In the morning, home-baked bread and home-made jams and marmalade make breakfast special. The tables in the 'elegant dining room' are 'beautifully laid' with bone china; cooked to order, breakfast dishes include pancakes, labneh, maple syrup, berries; scrambled eggs, whisky-smoked Scottish salmon; a full English. In fine weather, ask to eat in the courtyard garden. Private parking, 'slightly awkward to find', is nearby.

38 St Giles Street
Norwich
NR2 1LL

T: 01603 662944
E: booking@38stgiles.co.uk
W: www.38stgiles.co.uk

BEDROOMS: 8. 1 on ground floor, plus 2-bed serviced apartment.
OPEN: all year except Christmas.
FACILITIES: breakfast room, free Wi-Fi, in-room TV (Freeview), courtyard garden.
BACKGROUND MUSIC: Radio 3 at breakfast.
LOCATION: central, limited private parking (advance booking, £15 per day).
CHILDREN: all ages welcomed.
DOGS: not allowed.
CREDIT CARDS: MasterCard, Visa.
PRICES: [2017] per room B&B £120–£245.

SEE ALSO SHORTLIST

NOTTINGHAM Nottinghamshire

Map 2:A3

HART'S HOTEL

In 'an attractive, central setting', with 'a commanding vista' over the city, Tim Hart's hotel is 'a clear choice for business travellers and parents visiting offspring at university,' say Guide inspectors this year. Past 'a personable greeting', public spaces are contemporary and uncluttered. Light bites are served all day in the bar; 'a well-tended balcony garden is set high on the hillside'. (Some bedrooms have direct access to the secluded garden – 'a pleasing spot' for an alfresco breakfast.) 'Our room was smallish, and some of the furnishings looked their age. But there was a large bed, and the bathroom, though snug, was clean.' Chef Daniel Burridge's daily-changing modern menu is served in the 'well-decorated' restaurant, next door. 'We enjoyed plump, meaty pheasant breast and lentils; a dish of smoked haddock and poached egg was well presented. Bread, from the owner's Hambleton Bakery, remains first class. The cheese platter could have been more generous, however.' In the morning, 'good' hot and cold options at breakfast include 'pleasantly sloppy scrambled eggs'. Hambleton Hall, Hambleton (see entry), is under the same ownership.

25% DISCOUNT VOUCHERS

Standard Hill
Park Row
Nottingham
NG1 6GN

T: 0115 988 1900
F: 0115 947 7600
E: reception@hartshotel.co.uk
W: www.hartsnottingham.co.uk

BEDROOMS: 32. 2 suitable for disabled.
OPEN: all year, restaurant closed 1 Jan.
FACILITIES: lift, reception/lobby with seating, bar, restaurant (30 yds), free Wi-Fi, in-room TV (Sky, Freeview), conference/banqueting facilities, small exercise room, civil wedding licence, courtyard, private garden, secure car park (£9.50).
BACKGROUND MUSIC: 'light' in bar.
LOCATION: city centre.
CHILDREN: all ages welcomed.
DOGS: not allowed in public rooms, or unattended in bedrooms.
CREDIT CARDS: Amex, MasterCard, Visa.
PRICES: [2017] room from £134. Set dinner £22–£28, à la carte £37.50.

OLD HUNSTANTON Norfolk

Map 2:A5

THE NEPTUNE

The creeper-covered, red brick building appears modest from the outside, but there are 'excellent dinners' within: Kevin and Jacki Mangoelles's restaurant-with-rooms has a 'well-deserved' Michelin star. Minutes from sandy Old Hunstanton beach, the 18th-century coaching inn has been updated with an unpretentious coastal air: there are Lloyd Loom chairs on varnished floorboards; a seascape painting above an open fire. Sit down to dinner at a table laid with 'modern, elegant china and glass' – the chef/patron's menus are short and appealing ('no lengthy dissertations on ingredients'). Characteristic dishes: sake-poached salmon, oyster mayonnaise, apple, rocket; dry-aged Dexter beef sirloin, spinach, spaetzle, carrot and ginger purée. The hostess is 'also a wine buff' – ask for drink recommendations. The bedrooms aren't huge, but they're 'spotless, with plenty of storage'; extra touches include an espresso machine, 'delicious' home-made biscuits, fresh milk. Don't roost in your room, anyway – after a breakfast of home-baked croissants and good cooked dishes, head to Victorian 'Sunny Hunny' Hunstanton, or admire classical statuary at Palladian Holkham Hall.

85 Old Hunstanton Road
Old Hunstanton
PE36 6HZ

T: 01485 532122
E: reservations@theneptune.co.uk
W: www.theneptune.co.uk

BEDROOMS: 4. Plus self-catering cottage.
OPEN: all year, except 26 Dec, 3 weeks Jan, 1 week May, 1 week Nov, Mon.
FACILITIES: 2 bar areas, restaurant, free Wi-Fi, in-room TV (Freeview), unsuitable for disabled.
BACKGROUND MUSIC: in restaurant in evening.
LOCATION: village centre, on A149.
CHILDREN: not under 10.
DOGS: not allowed.
CREDIT CARDS: Amex, MasterCard, Visa.
PRICES: per room B&B £155–£180, D,B&B £260–£295. Set menus £60–£78. 1-night bookings sometimes refused weekends.

OLDSTEAD Yorkshire

Map 4:D4

THE BLACK SWAN AT OLDSTEAD

♕ Previous César winner

In 2006, an ancient inn in a small village in the North York Moors national park was set to close, when local farmers Tom and Ann Banks stepped in to save it. Today, their 'rustic but sophisticated' Michelin-starred restaurant-with-rooms is a family-run enterprise, with elder son James as manager, and his brother, Tommy, working wonders in the kitchen with produce grown and foraged on the doorstep. Come inside the candlelit bar, with its flagstone floor and shelves of books. Take a seat in a bay window, accept the cocktail that's pressed upon you, and peruse the modern menu. 'The food ranks among the most memorable I've tasted': rhubarb-cured scallops; monkfish and hen-of-the-woods; ewe's milk with a Douglas fir lollipop. The staff, too, are 'second to none'. 'The waiters and waitresses are knowledgeable and passionate, and indeed have often picked some of the produce.' 'Cosy', stylish bedrooms in a separate wing and a Georgian house opposite are just the place to lay your head, afterwards. Breakfast is everything it should be. (Flora Marriott)

Oldstead
YO61 4BL

T: 01347 868387
E: reception@blackswanoldstead.co.uk
w: www.blackswanoldstead.co.uk

BEDROOMS: 9. 4, on ground floor, in annexe; 5 in Ashberry House, 50 yds away.
OPEN: all year except Christmas.
FACILITIES: bar, restaurant, private dining room, free Wi-Fi, in-room TV (Freeview), garden, 2-acre kitchen garden and orchard.
BACKGROUND MUSIC: in restaurant.
LOCATION: in village 7 miles E of Thirsk.
CHILDREN: not under 10 in restaurant, only over-18s to stay overnight.
DOGS: not allowed.
CREDIT CARDS: MasterCard, Visa.
PRICES: [2017] per room D,B&B £230–£480. Tasting menu £95.

ORFORD Suffolk

Map 2:C6

THE CROWN AND CASTLE

Previous César winner

'The attention to detail, excellent service and quality of cooking at this brilliant restaurant-with-rooms have set the standard by which other hotels will be judged.' Guide readers this year continue to endorse this 'great' enterprise, owned by Ruth and David Watson and Tim Sunderland, in a pretty town on the River Ore. 'To find somewhere that gets it all right without a single false note is a joy.' Some guests may be rattled by the house rules that accompany each booking (gadgets discouraged at dinner, etc), but others find them 'clear, helpful and very welcome – a major delight'. In the much-praised restaurant, dine on 'an interesting, Italian-influenced mix' of 'knock-out food' – perhaps Orford-landed cod, sautéed salsify, girolles, potato gnocchi – accompanied by a 'fun, eclectic' wine list. ('A request for gluten-free options was acknowledged with no fuss.') Spend the night, afterwards, in one of the 'tastefully styled' bedrooms. 'Our immaculate suite had a good-sized sitting area, a splendid modern bathroom, even a little balcony. Best of all: a big, really comfortable bed.' (Gwyn Morgan, Iseult Beatty, Tony and Ginny Ayers, and others)

Market Hill
Orford
IP12 2LJ

T: 01394 450205
E: info@crownandcastle.co.uk
W: www.crownandcastle.co.uk

BEDROOMS: 21. 10 (all on ground floor) in garden, 2 (on ground floor) in terrace, 1 in courtyard, 1 suite in stable block.
OPEN: all year except 4–8 Dec 2017 'for essential maintenance'.
FACILITIES: lounge/bar, restaurant, private dining room, free Wi-Fi, in-room TV (Freeview), limited on-site parking, ¼-acre garden.
BACKGROUND MUSIC: none.
LOCATION: market square, about 100 yds from the castle.
CHILDREN: not under 8 in restaurant in evening or overnight in hotel; all ages welcomed at lunch.
DOGS: allowed in 5 garden rooms, at 'doggie table' in restaurant, limited number in bar.
CREDIT CARDS: MasterCard, Visa.
PRICES: [2017] per room B&B from £140, D,B&B from £200. À la carte £38. 1-night bookings refused Fri/Sat.

OSWESTRY Shropshire

Map 3:B4

PEN-Y-DYFFRYN

'We can't wait to go again,' say guests this year, of Miles and Audrey Hunter's small hotel on the Welsh border. Many returning visitors agree: 'A constant repetition of "excellent" seems unnecessary, but we must report we always look forward to our visit.' 'A lovely place', the Hunters' stone rectory is run with 'sensitivity and generosity'; thoughtful touches, such as welcome tea and scones, and a morning newsletter with suggested activities, are much appreciated. Each bedroom is different – some have a private patio, others a spa bath – so ring ahead to discuss room choices: guests this year praised the 'wonderfully large' bed in their garden room, but wished for more space overall. In the dining room, chef Richard Jones's 'imaginative, varied' menus use locally sourced ingredients, perhaps haunch of venison, blueberry and Herefordshire cassis jus. Breakfast, always good, has got better: 'Among new dishes this time was bruschetta, avocado, smoked salmon and perfect poached eggs.' Borrow walk notes and a map, and head for the hills – sandwiches are readily provided. (Deborah Cross and Bob Steel, Helen Anthony, MH, and others)

25% DISCOUNT VOUCHERS

Rhydycroesau
Oswestry
SY10 7JD

T: 01691 653700
E: milesjmhunter@gmail.com
W: www.peny.co.uk

BEDROOMS: 12. 4, each with patio, in coach house, 1 on ground floor.
OPEN: all year except Christmas.
FACILITIES: 2 lounges, bar, restaurant, free Wi-Fi, in-room TV (Freeview), 5-acre grounds (summer house, dog-walking area, fly-fishing pool), unsuitable for disabled.
BACKGROUND MUSIC: in evening in bar and restaurant.
LOCATION: 3 miles W of Oswestry.
CHILDREN: not under 3.
DOGS: allowed in some bedrooms, not in public rooms after 6 pm.
CREDIT CARDS: MasterCard, Visa.
PRICES: [2017] per person B&B from £69, D,B&B from £97. Set dinner £41. 1-night bookings refused Sat.

OXFORD Oxfordshire

Map 2:C2

OLD BANK

♔ Previous César winner

Town and gown gather at the smart restaurant and buzzy bar of Jeremy Mogford's sleek, 'perfectly positioned' hotel between All Souls and Oriel colleges. (Gown and town, too, debate the merits of the modern art that adorns the public spaces.) The 'obliging staff' and 'well-appointed bedrooms' make this an 'excellent hotel', Guide readers say. 'It may not be cheap, but I wouldn't stay anywhere else in Oxford,' one correspondent comments. Recently refurbished, the stylish bedrooms have luxury fabrics and more striking artwork. Discuss room choices before booking: some rooms may be 'compact but serviceable'; others, quiet, peer on to a side alleyway; others yet have a 'delightful view of the High'. All have a 'comfy bed', a 'well-stocked minibar' and fluffy bathrobes. A 'commendable breakfast' includes porridge with a quince compote, or salmon fishcakes and spinach; at lunch and dinner, the food – perhaps warm octopus, chickpeas, paprika; confit duck, salsify, gem lettuce – is 'generally good'. Eat on the garden terrace in balmy weather. 'The car park, though tight, is a bonus.' (E and JG, and others)

92–94 High Street
Oxford
OX1 4BJ

T: 01865 799599
E: reception@oldbank-hotel.co.uk
W: www.oldbank-hotel.co.uk

BEDROOMS: 42. 1 suitable for disabled.
OPEN: all year.
FACILITIES: lift, residents' library/bar, bar, dining terrace, 2 meeting/private dining rooms, free Wi-Fi, in-room TV, small garden.
BACKGROUND MUSIC: none.
LOCATION: central, car park.
CHILDREN: all ages welcomed.
DOGS: not allowed.
CREDIT CARDS: Amex, MasterCard, Visa.
PRICES: [2017] room from £194. Breakfast (full English) £15, à la carte £40 (plus 12½% discretionary service charge).

SEE ALSO SHORTLIST

OXFORD Oxfordshire

Map 2:C2

OLD PARSONAGE

An open fire in the entrance hall sets the tone at Jeremy Mogford's clubby, upmarket hotel, a much-extended 17th-century building where visitors give in to the charms of bookish Oxford. The owner's fine collection of paintings and artwork hangs in the public spaces; guests are encouraged to explore the town on the hotel's wicker-basketed bicycles; a private library, well stocked with tomes on art, literature, culture, politics and local history, is 'a particular joy'. Bedrooms are modern, with a marble bathroom; some have their own terrace overlooking the garden. 'My well-equipped room was nicely furnished and blissfully quiet.' Among the 'special touches': fresh flowers, and a bedside booklet of short stories by winners of the annual Mogford Prize for Food and Drink Writing. Make time for afternoon tea with home-baked scones. Bistro-style lunches and dinners – perhaps roasted beetroot, goat's curd and watercress salad; fillet steak tartare, chips – are 'pleasantly served' in the restaurant. 'We thought the dining room charming, with its informal seating, and charcoal-grey walls hung with portraits.' Breakfast languidly, till late. (CR, VM, PJ)

1 Banbury Road
Oxford
OX2 6NN

T: 01865 310210
E: info@oldparsonage-hotel.co.uk
W: www.oldparsonage-hotel.co.uk

BEDROOMS: 35. 10 on ground floor, 2 suitable for disabled.
OPEN: all year.
FACILITIES: lounge, library, bar/restaurant, free Wi-Fi, in-room TV (Freeview), civil wedding licence, terrace, rear garden with summerhouse.
BACKGROUND MUSIC: 'very light' in restaurant and bar.
LOCATION: NE end of St Giles, small car park.
CHILDREN: all ages welcomed.
DOGS: not allowed.
CREDIT CARDS: Amex, MasterCard, Visa.
PRICES: [2017] per room B&B from £225, D,B&B from £299. Set dinner £37.50, à la carte £35 (plus 12½% discretionary service charge). 1-night bookings sometimes refused.

SEE ALSO SHORTLIST

PADSTOW Cornwall

Map 1:D2

PADSTOW TOWNHOUSE

With a champagne- and cake-filled pantry to plunder, plus boozy hot chocolate before bed, this glamorous operation turns traditional notions of a B&B on their head. It is owned by Michelin-starred chef Paul Ainsworth and his wife, Emma, who also run No. 6, the acclaimed modern restaurant, down the hill. Within the Georgian town house, each spacious suite, furnished with a mix of vintage and contemporary pieces and decorated with modern artwork, has its own personality. The largest each have a two-person oak and copper bath, but all the rooms are 'luxurious and cocooning', with thoughtful technology (good speakers, an internet-connected TV, movies on demand), a coffee machine and a 'well-stocked minibar', and herb-scented, locally made toiletries. In the honesty pantry, cheeses, chic juices and freshly baked pastries are among the treats on hand. Breakfast is served in the room, or in sister restaurant Rojano's in the Square, a five-minute walk (or swift, chauffeur-driven electric-car ride) away. Overindulged? Borrow a vintage-style bicycle or a pair of walking boots – the staff can advise on cycle trails and coastal walks, and provide a picnic to match.

16–18 High Street
Padstow
PL28 8BB

T: 01841 550950
E: stay@padstowtownhouse.co.uk
W: www.padstowtownhouse.co.uk

BEDROOMS: 6. 2 on ground floor.
OPEN: all year.
FACILITIES: honesty pantry, free Wi-Fi, in-room smart TV, electric car for guest transport, unsuitable for disabled.
BACKGROUND MUSIC: none.
LOCATION: in old town, 5 mins' walk from harbour.
CHILDREN: not under 16.
DOGS: not allowed.
CREDIT CARDS: MasterCard, Visa.
PRICES: [2017] per suite B&B from £280.

PADSTOW Cornwall

Map 1:D2

THE SEAFOOD RESTAURANT

A stroll from the town centre, Rick and Jill Stein's restaurant-with-rooms – 'a foodie destination' – opened as a modest bistro in 1975. 'The changes since have been dramatic,' writes a Guide inspector who knew it in the early days of red-checked tablecloths. It is today the flagship of the Stein empire, where chef Stephane Delourme continues the tradition of creating classic dishes with fresh fish and seafood often landed within sight. In the 'spectacular' restaurant, diners watch as chefs assemble platters of fruits de mer at a central zinc bar; the menu is 'extensive and exemplary', ranging from cod and chips to Goan hake curry to a 'light, delicious' lobster thermidor. Above the restaurant, modern bedrooms of varying sizes are supplied with proper coffee and teas, biscuits, novels and cookbooks. For sea views, book one of the rooms overlooking the estuary – the best has a private roof terrace. 'Our room looked over neighbouring rooftops, with a nesting seagull, right up to the sandy shore of Rock across the water.' Seafood dishes at breakfast include 'fat and juicy kippers'; a 'copious' crab omelette.

Riverside
Padstow
PL28 8BY

T: 01841 532700
E: reservations@rickstein.com
W: www.rickstein.
    com/stay/the-seafood-restaurant/

BEDROOMS: 16.
OPEN: all year except Christmas.
FACILITIES: wheelchair-accessible lift, lounge, reading room, restaurant, free Wi-Fi, in-room TV (Freeview).
BACKGROUND MUSIC: in restaurant.
LOCATION: town centre.
CHILDREN: all ages welcomed, not under 3 in restaurant.
DOGS: welcomed in some bedrooms.
CREDIT CARDS: Diners, MasterCard, Visa.
PRICES: [2017] per room B&B £165–£286, D,B&B from £250. À la carte £55. 1-night bookings refused Sat.

PAINSWICK Gloucestershire

Map 3:D5

THE PAINSWICK

'Stylish but informal, fun and relaxing – a grand job overall.' In a south Cotswold village that spills down a hillside in the Slad valley, this altered and extended late-Palladian mansion has found 'a new lease of life' within the Calcot Hotels group. 'It's a splendid place that will appeal to all ages,' Guide inspectors said. 'Tasteful and contemporary', it has 'lovely sitting rooms' with log fires and magazines, a 'stunning bar' (with a 'charismatic barman'), and a 'small, beautiful garden with pleasant terraces'. 'Luxurious bedrooms' are 'cleverly designed', and have a 'well-equipped bathroom'. 'We loved our semi-circular room, which had four windows giving village and valley views. A sitting area had armchairs, a coffee table and up-to-date glossy magazines – a good touch.' Dine in the 'low-key yet sophisticated restaurant', or alfresco in the loggia – inside or out, chef Michael Bedford's cooking is 'fabulous'. Among his 'imaginative dishes', perhaps: Wye valley asparagus, Parmesan shortbread, bacon-and-egg ice cream. In the morning, choose from an 'excellent buffet' and a 'wide-ranging cooked menu' (kippers, omelettes, 'the Full Elvis').
(P and JT, Jonathan Gerber)

Kemps Lane
Painswick
GL6 6YB

T: 01452 813688
E: enquiries@thepainswick.co.uk
W: www.thepainswick.co.uk

BEDROOMS: 16. 7 in garden wing, 4 in chapel wing.
OPEN: all year.
FACILITIES: bar, lounge, restaurant, games room, private dining room, free Wi-Fi, in-room TV (Sky, Freeview), civil wedding licence, terrace, beauty treatment rooms, ¾-acre garden, unsuitable for disabled.
BACKGROUND MUSIC: all day in public areas.
LOCATION: in village 5 miles NE of Stroud.
CHILDREN: all ages welcomed.
DOGS: allowed in some garden rooms, on terrace, in lounge (£15 per night).
CREDIT CARDS: Amex, MasterCard, Visa.
PRICES: [2017] room from £129. Continental breakfast £6, cooked dishes £6–£12, à la carte dinner £40. 1-night bookings refused weekends.

PENRITH Cumbria

ASKHAM HALL

'We felt we were staying at a grand house rather than a hotel,' say regular Guide correspondents this year of Charles and Juno Lowther's Grade I listed ancestral home, built around a medieval pele tower and brimming with the owners' personality. A return visit found it 'as good as ever'. There's a 'shabby-chic feel' in the public rooms: allow for 'the odd frayed carpet or torn lampshade', and relax by the log fire with a drink from the honesty bar. Every one of the 'comfortable' country house-style bedrooms is different: choose one with a four-poster bed and an antique bath, or something more modern. The largest rooms, in the tower, have views over garden, river and fells. In the conservatory dining room, Richard Swale cooks with produce from gardens, farm and forest, plus game in season. A typical dish: Rough Fell lamb, barbecue offal kebab, ewe's curd, wild garlic risotto. 'The food is excellent, and the staff are friendly and attentive.' The Grade II listed gardens, with terraces, topiary, ponds and woodland, and the Kitchen Garden Café are open to the public. Follow a trail to watch rare breed pigs, boer goats, chickens and ducks go about their day. (Kay and John Patterson)

Askham
Penrith
CA10 2PF

T: 01931 712350
E: enquiries@askhamhall.co.uk
W: www.askhamhall.co.uk

BEDROOMS: 15.
OPEN: all year except Christmas, early Jan to mid-Feb, restaurant closed Sun.
FACILITIES: drawing room, library, billiard room, 3 dining rooms, free Wi-Fi, in-room TV (Freeview), civil wedding licence, 12-acre grounds, spa, 10 by 5 metre heated outdoor swimming pool (Apr–Oct), only restaurant suitable for disabled.
BACKGROUND MUSIC: in reception rooms in evening.
LOCATION: 10 mins from Penrith and junction 40 on M6.
CHILDREN: all ages welcomed.
DOGS: allowed in bedrooms and public rooms, not in restaurant.
CREDIT CARDS: all major cards.
PRICES: [2017] per room B&B £150–£290. Set dinner £50, tasting menu £65.

PENRITH Cumbria

Map 4: inset C2

TEBAY SERVICES HOTEL

'There's a feeling of complete well-being about the place,' write Guide readers in 2017 of the Dunning family's hotel and upmarket farm shop just off the M6. 'It has a special character, no doubt thanks to the owners and friendly, efficient staff. Looking out over the fells, it's hard to believe that a busy motorway is only a stone's throw away.' The modern, Alpine-style building has an informal lounge and bar area where food is served all day, plus 'lots of good details': books, board games for all ages, a shoe-shining kit at the top of the stairs. Bedrooms are 'nothing fancy, but they're well designed'. 'Ours had an especially comfortable bed; two chairs and a coffee table by the window; a modern bathroom. Flagons of water and home-made biscuits were supplied with the tea tray.' 'Meals at both ends of the day are excellent': 'a splendid breakfast buffet'; 'perfect' new-season lamb from the Dunnings' farm at dinner. 'Highly recommended' for visitors stopping over between England and Scotland, but also 'ideal as a base for exploring the area' – 'you can get into the Lakes, Dales and Eden valley within minutes'. (Simon and Mithra Tonking, Desmond and Jenny Balmer)

nr Orton
Penrith
CA10 3SB

T: 01539 624351
E: reservations@tebayserviceshotel.
   com
W: www.tebayserviceshotel.com

BEDROOMS: 51. 1 suitable for disabled.
OPEN: all year except Christmas.
FACILITIES: lounge with log fire, bar, mezzanine, restaurant, free Wi-Fi, in-room TV, function/conference facilities, farm shop.
BACKGROUND MUSIC: none.
LOCATION: 2½ miles SW of Orton.
CHILDREN: all ages welcomed.
DOGS: allowed in some bedrooms (£10 per dog, max 2 dogs), not in public rooms.
CREDIT CARDS: Amex, MasterCard, Visa.
PRICES: [2017] per room B&B from £104. À la carte £30.

PENSFORD Somerset

Map 2:D1

THE PIG NEAR BATH

'The shabby-chic style suits the relaxed atmosphere' at this 'fresh, appealing' candidate, one of Robin Hutson's sty of Pig hotels. At this Georgian manor in the Mendips, the young staff are 'attentive and friendly', and the ambience is informal and fun, say regular Guide correspondents this year. Deep sofas roost on stripped wooden floors, walls are hung with gilt-framed paintings, open fires crackle in cool weather. In the 'stylish but casual' conservatory dining room, chef Kamil Oseka makes use of the 'high quality and variety of fruit and vegetables' from the Victorian greenhouses and walled kitchen garden. His 'straightforward and wholesome' dishes might include potted Madgett's Farm duck, rhubarb chutney; purple mizuna, garden pickles, chargrilled chicken. Bedrooms in the main house, coach house and garden cottages are equipped with a larder of snacks and an espresso machine. 'Our room was spacious and comfortable, with a far-from-shabby bathroom.' In the morning, garden-fresh feasting continues. 'The breakfast buffet, with much home-grown produce on offer, was one of the best we've experienced.' (John and Kay Patterson, and others)

Hunstrete House
Pensford
BS39 4NS

T: 01761 490490
E: info@thepignearbath.com
W: www.thepighotel.com

BEDROOMS: 29. 5 in gardens, some on ground floor, 1 suitable for disabled.
OPEN: all year.
FACILITIES: 2 lounges, bar, restaurant, snug, private dining room, free Wi-Fi, in-room TV (Freeview), civil wedding licence, treatment room, kitchen garden, wild flower meadow, deer park.
BACKGROUND MUSIC: all day in public areas.
LOCATION: 7 miles SW of Bath.
CHILDREN: all ages welcomed.
DOGS: not allowed.
CREDIT CARDS: Amex, MasterCard, Visa.
PRICES: [2017] room £155–£315. Breakfast £10–£15, à la carte £35. 1-night bookings refused weekends, Christmas/New Year.

PENZANCE Cornwall

Map 1:E1

CHAPEL HOUSE

'An inviting building in a lovely location', this 18th-century admiral's town house-turned-chic B&B has undergone a sea change in the hands of 'caring, hands-on' owner Susan Stuart. Mount the stone steps to enter the 'beautifully decorated' house: all is 'immaculate'. Against a palette of soft marine greys, greens and blues, the walls are hung with a revolving gallery of works curated by the Newlyn School of Art. There are fresh flowers in the spacious hallway; the 'chic, relaxing' drawing room has 'comfy sofas and fine sea views'. 'Stylish, uncluttered' bedrooms look on to the water, too – some have views stretching over the harbour and Mount's Bay all the way to Lizard Point. Graze on tea, coffee and cake in the afternoons; on Friday and Saturday evenings, the hostess cooks a simple seasonal menu using plenty of local produce – Cornish asparagus with fresh hollandaise, perhaps, or pan-fried brill and samphire. (Ask to eat in the garden on a fine day.) There are smoothies and freshly baked breads at breakfast, plus a west Cornwall speciality: sizzled cod roe, smoked bacon, samphire and a poached egg. Sunday brunch, open to the public, is a feast.

Chapel Street
Penzance
TR18 4AQ

T: 01736 362024
E: hello@chapelhousepz.co.uk
W: www.chapelhousepz.co.uk

BEDROOMS: 6.
OPEN: all year, closed Sun evening.
FACILITIES: drawing room, open-plan kitchen/dining area, free Wi-Fi, in-room TV (Freeview), function facilities, terrace, garden, unsuitable for disabled.
BACKGROUND MUSIC: none.
LOCATION: town centre.
CHILDREN: all ages welcomed.
DOGS: 'well-behaved dogs' allowed, not on beds or furniture.
CREDIT CARDS: MasterCard, Visa.
PRICES: [2017] per room B&B £150–£190. Set dinner £22.

SEE ALSO SHORTLIST

PENZANCE Cornwall

Map 1:E1

TREREIFE

NEW

The Le Grice clan's 'fantastic family home' stands in parterre gardens and horse-grazed parkland, with lashings of home-made medlar jelly within. 'Lovely people', the hosts are the sixth and seventh generation of Le Grices to occupy the Elizabethan farmhouse-turned-Queen Anne manor house since the 18th century. The grand old house is filled with family heirlooms – ornate mirrors, oil paintings, antiques, a Herbert Ward sculpture or two (the artist–adventurer was an ancestor). Good-value B&B accommodation is in traditionally furnished bedrooms. Two rooms have direct access to the courtyard, but better rooms upstairs are huge, and have 'stunning views' over the grounds. 'There are no fancy touches, but everything you need is provided': tea- and coffee-making facilities, a flat-screen TV, a pocket-sprung bed. A 'great breakfast' brings home-baked bread, and hot dishes cooked to order; a buffet includes cereals, yogurts, fruit salad – and that jelly, from the medlar trees in the orchard. A good base for west Cornwall and the Isles of Scilly; Newlyn's eating places and contemporary art gallery are five minutes' drive away. (Michael Eldridge)

Penzance
TR20 8TJ

T: 01736 362750
E: trereifepark@btconnect.com
W: trereifepark.co.uk

BEDROOMS: 4. 2 on ground floor. Plus 2 self-catering apartments, and bell tent for glamping.
OPEN: Mar–Christmas, self-catering all year.
FACILITIES: sitting room (honesty bar), dining room, civil wedding licence, 10-acre grounds (parterres, walled garden, woodland), parking.
BACKGROUND MUSIC: none.
LOCATION: 1¼ miles SW of Penzance.
CHILDREN: all ages welcomed.
DOGS: allowed in ground-floor bedrooms, not in public rooms.
CREDIT CARDS: MasterCard, Visa.
PRICES: [2017] per room B&B £75–£150. 2-night min. stay for self-catering.

SEE ALSO SHORTLIST

PETERSFIELD Hampshire

Map 2:E3

JSW

The low, whitewashed building, a 17th-century coaching inn, sits on a modest street, but within this 'seriously impressive' restaurant-with-rooms, the modern dishes are 'exquisitely executed – very much deserving of the Michelin star'. In the beamed dining room ('we liked the generous table spacing'), John Saul Watkins, the chef/patron, focuses on 'top-quality' seasonal produce – fish from the Solent, fruit and vegetables from Hampshire, meat from Cumbria – with a prodigious wine list for accompaniment. Characteristic among his 'imaginative' dishes: wild local sea bass, crab and potato risotto, sea herbs; sucking pig belly, pickled pear, dandelion. Vegetarians have their own menu, perhaps including root vegetables, cavolo nero, thyme and roasted garlic gel. 'Really comfortable, immaculately maintained' bedrooms are on the first floor. 'Ours was bright, quiet and peaceful.' (Light sleepers may want to bring earplugs – some guests have commented on street noise – or book the courtyard-facing room.) A 'straightforward' continental breakfast has French pastries; home-made lemon curd and home-baked bread; fresh fruit and juice. (A and BB, B and MB)

20 Dragon Street
Petersfield
GU31 4JJ

T: 01730 262030
E: jsw.restaurant@btconnect.com
W: www.jswrestaurant.com

BEDROOMS: 4.
OPEN: all year except New Year, 2 weeks Jan, 2 weeks Apr, 2 weeks Sept, restaurant closed Sun evening–Wed lunch.
FACILITIES: restaurant, function room, free Wi-Fi, in-room TV (Freeview), courtyard with outside seating, unsuitable for disabled.
BACKGROUND MUSIC: none.
LOCATION: town centre.
CHILDREN: all ages welcomed but 'good behaviour a requirement'.
DOGS: not allowed.
CREDIT CARDS: MasterCard, Visa.
PRICES: [2017] per room D,B&B £195–£360. Set dinner £45–£55, tasting menus £65–£90. 1-night bookings sometimes refused.

PETWORTH Sussex

Map 2:E3

THE OLD RAILWAY STATION

Pull into this converted train station and take up residence in one of the refurbished Pullman carriages on the disused tracks: 'quirky and charming', this is a B&B with a difference. It is owned by Gudmund Olafsson and Catherine Stormont, and run with 'warm and welcoming' staff. Check in at the old parcels office in the restored Victorian station building before heading to one of the 'comfortable, well-furnished' bedrooms. Each has been redecorated with colonial flair: two in the main building (one reached via a cast iron spiral staircase) have plantation shutters and a brass bedstead; those in the well-thought-out train carriages have Edwardian fittings and a 'surprisingly spacious' bathroom. The former waiting room is today a 'wonderful space' with leather armchairs, train memorabilia and black-and-white photographs of the railway's heyday. Sit here for a cream tea or, in fine weather, take it under a parasol on the old platform overlooking lush greenery. The pubs and restaurants of Petworth village are a five-minute drive away; alternatively, a lively pub is just across the river and up the lane – a wind-up torch is provided for the stroll. (BN)

Station Road
Petworth
GU28 0JF

T: 01798 342346
F: 01798 343033
E: info@old-station.co.uk
W: www.old-station.co.uk

BEDROOMS: 10. 8 in Pullman carriages.
OPEN: all year except 22–26 Dec.
FACILITIES: lounge/bar/breakfast room, free Wi-Fi, in-room TV (Freeview), platform/terrace, 2-acre garden, unsuitable for disabled.
BACKGROUND MUSIC: 'soft '20s, '30s, '40s music' at breakfast.
LOCATION: 1½ miles S of Petworth.
CHILDREN: not under 10.
DOGS: not allowed.
CREDIT CARDS: Amex, MasterCard, Visa.
PRICES: per room B&B (Station House) £110–£158, (Pullman carriages) £130–£240.

PICKERING Yorkshire

THE WHITE SWAN

Once a stopover for the York-to-Whitby stagecoach, this 16th-century coaching inn is today a 'lovely, friendly' spot, its window boxes abloom in season. It has been owned by the Buchanan family for 35 years. The cosy, traditional bar (old beams, tartan carpet, local ales, mismatched wooden chairs) is a popular watering hole; in the restaurant, chef Darren Clemmit's 'short and simple' menus please. Served in the smart dining room, Yorkshire produce features in 'honest dishes' such as grilled Lowna goat's cheese, beetroot relish, Cheddar biscuit; 'beautifully cooked rabbit with pistachio and pickled raspberries'. Stay the night in a bedroom supplied with tea, coffee, home-made biscuits and the bathrobes to enjoy them in. Rooms in the main house are more traditionally styled; those in the converted stables are 'a delight: airy, spacious, well appointed'. Board games and books await by the log-burner in the beamed Bothy lounge. The inn stands in the midst of the action in this 'delightful market town', so plug in the electric car (there are three charging units) and explore on foot; two minutes down the street, hop aboard the heritage steam train to the coast.

Market Place
Pickering
YO18 7AA

T: 01751 472288
E: welcome@white-swan.co.uk
W: www.white-swan.co.uk

BEDROOMS: 21. 9 in annexe.
OPEN: all year.
FACILITIES: lounge, bar, restaurant, private dining room, Bothy residents' lounge/event room, free Wi-Fi, in-room TV (Freeview), small terrace (alfresco meals), secure bicycle storage, 1½-acre grounds, unsuitable for disabled.
BACKGROUND MUSIC: none.
LOCATION: central.
CHILDREN: all ages welcomed.
DOGS: allowed in bedrooms (not unattended), not in restaurant (owners may dine with dogs in snug).
CREDIT CARDS: Amex, MasterCard, Visa.
PRICES: [2017] per room B&B single £129–£169, double £159–£199, D,B&B single £159–£199, double £219–£259. À la carte £38. 1-night bookings sometimes refused.

PICKHILL Yorkshire

Map 4:C4

THE NAGS HEAD

Janet and Edward Boynton's 19th-century coaching inn between moors and dales is roundly endorsed by Guide readers, who praise its 'hospitable, interesting owners', 'enjoyable dinners', 'relaxing atmosphere' and 'excellent value'. 'It's the "go-to" local hostelry: on a Sunday evening, the bar was buzzing and the restaurant was full.' There are 'horse pictures everywhere' in the 'welcoming pub' (Thirsk is nearby); a blackboard menu lists 'absolutely wonderful comfort food, served in vast portions'. Particularly enjoyed in 2017: 'Delicious chicken-liver parfait and salad, followed by steak pie.' Also pleasing: 'A wine list that might be the envy of grander establishments.' 'Comfortable bedrooms', including a 'spacious' family room, are up narrow stairs. 'My first-floor room was compact and warm, if just functional, with plenty of towels in the spotless, well-lit bathroom.' Breakfast includes 'a tempting home-made berry smoothie, delicious scrambled eggs, tasty black pudding'. 'An unbeatable stop' for motorists travelling between England and Scotland. (Henry and Priscilla McDougall, David and Wendy Millar, Robert Gower, Michael Green)

25% DISCOUNT VOUCHERS

Pickhill
YO7 4JG

T: 01845 567391
F: 01845 567212
E: enquiries@nagsheadpickhill.
co.uk
W: www.nagsheadpickhill.co.uk

BEDROOMS: 7.
OPEN: all year except 24/25 Dec (open for food 24 Dec).
FACILITIES: tap room, lounge bar, dining/breakfast room, free Wi-Fi, in-room TV (Freeview), unsuitable for disabled.
BACKGROUND MUSIC: in bars and dining room.
LOCATION: 5 miles SE of Leeming.
CHILDREN: all ages welcomed.
DOGS: allowed in 2 bedrooms (not unattended), not in public areas.
CREDIT CARDS: Amex, MasterCard, Visa.
PRICES: [2017] per room B&B single from £60, double from £80. À la carte £25.

PORLOCK Somerset

Map 1:B5

THE OAKS

'Clearly cherished by its owners, this small, serene hotel oozes good taste without a hint of affectation,' say Guide inspectors in 2017 of Tim and Anne Riley's Edwardian house on a steep hillside. 'There's a domestic ambience, with statuary, distinctive porcelain, a ginger jar collection and gently chiming clocks. It's traditional but not in the least old-fashioned or faded.' Spacious bedrooms have views of the sea, the village or the hills. 'Everything we might have needed had been provided in our pleasant, airy room: a mini-clock, a Roberts radio by the bed, a hospitality tray with real cafetière coffee and lovely Portmeirion china. At turn-down, chocolate hearts were placed on each bedside table.' While Tim Riley is the 'consummate friendly host', Anne Riley's home cooking, accompanied by an 'impressive wine list', is 'just great'. 'Local magret de canard was perfectly pink and tender; a light rhubarb cake with vermouth ice cream was perfectly judged.' A bonus: 'Every guest in the restaurant has a breathtaking view of the sunset over the hills above Porlock, followed at dusk by the magic of lights coming on in the village below.' At breakfast, tuck into 'everything you could want'.

Porlock
TA24 8ES

T: 01643 862265
F: 01643 863131
E: info@oakshotel.co.uk
W: www.oakshotel.co.uk

BEDROOMS: 7.
OPEN: Easter–end Oct.
FACILITIES: 2 lounges, bar, restaurant, free Wi-Fi, in-room TV (Freeview), 1-acre garden, patio, pebble beach 1 mile, unsuitable for disabled.
BACKGROUND MUSIC: none.
LOCATION: edge of village.
CHILDREN: not under 8.
DOGS: not allowed.
CREDIT CARDS: MasterCard, Visa.
PRICES: [2017] per room D,B&B £240.

PORTSCATHO Cornwall

Map 1:E2

DRIFTWOOD HOTEL

⚜ Previous César winner

'A charming place in a charming situation', Fiona and Paul Robinson's 'stylish, informal' New England-inspired hotel soaks in the spread of Gerrans Bay. There's no flash or ostentation, Guide readers say, just 'attentive, amiable staff', a family-friendly, seasidey feel and an 'abundance of calm'. The 'beautifully landscaped' garden is dotted with Adirondack chairs; in the evening, hurricane lamps are set out for alfresco drinks and nibbles. Comfortable contemporary rooms (some with a private terrace; all but one with a coastal view) are decorated in a palette of sand and sea. In the airy restaurant – dine early so you can eat in the glow of the evening light through the large windows – chef Chris Eden has a Michelin star for his 'delicious, flavourful', flower- and herb-strewn dishes. Among his 'very special' plates: asparagus, fresh verbena curd, truffle, confit egg yolk; John Dory, mussels, pickled cucumber, samphire, morels. Have a 'plentiful breakfast' before making your way across the lawn and down the woodland path to the peaceful private beach – a picnic hamper can be packed on request. (JP, and others)

Rosevine
Portscatho
TR2 5EW

T: 01872 580644
E: info@driftwoodhotel.co.uk
W: www.driftwoodhotel.co.uk

BEDROOMS: 15. 4 accessed via courtyard, 2 in cabin (2 mins' walk).
OPEN: 2 Feb–10 Dec.
FACILITIES: bar, restaurant, drawing room, snug, children's games room, free Wi-Fi, in-room TV (Freeview), 7-acre grounds (terraced gardens, private beach, safe bathing), unsuitable for disabled.
BACKGROUND MUSIC: all day in restaurant and bar.
LOCATION: 1½ miles N of Portscatho.
CHILDREN: all ages welcomed, no under-7s in restaurant in evening (early supper provided).
DOGS: not allowed.
CREDIT CARDS: Amex, MasterCard, Visa.
PRICES: [2017] per room B&B from £185, D,B&B from £240. Tasting menus £75–£95, à la carte £65. 1-night bookings refused weekends.

PURTON Wiltshire

Map 3:E5

THE PEAR TREE AT PURTON

♥ Previous César winner

'The epitome of a perfect British, family-run country hotel,' writes a Guide reader this year, about Anne Young's restored 16th-century vicarage. Alix Baldwin, the owner's daughter, is the manager; 'friendly staff are always on hand to help'. The attention to detail is praised: 'We celebrated a wedding anniversary ten years after our last fête at the hotel, and were amazed at how Anne and her team dug up records of each guest's accommodation, so they could be offered the same room again.' These bedrooms, each 'delightfully named after a local figure', are 'well equipped' with bathrobes, mineral water, fresh fruit and home-made shortbread; some have garden views, too. In the conservatory restaurant, chef Adam Conduit's 'imaginative' modern cooking is thought 'outstanding'. His seasonal menus – perhaps accompanied by the 'enjoyable' Cuvée Alix from the vineyard – may include Creedy Carver duck, chilli-and-thyme potato rösti, griottine cherry, kale. Try the honey at breakfast, then stroll through the 'extensive, well-kept' grounds, past flower meadows and wetlands, in search of the hotel's beehives. (Jeanette and David Leibling, AW, and others)

Church End
Purton
SN5 4ED

T: 01793 772100
F: 01793 772369
E: stay@peartreepurton.co.uk
W: www.peartreepurton.co.uk

BEDROOMS: 17. 6 on ground floor.
OPEN: all year except 25/26 Dec, restaurant closed Mon.
FACILITIES: lounge/bar, library, conservatory restaurant, free Wi-Fi, in-room TV (Freeview), function/conference facilities, civil wedding licence, 7½-acre grounds (croquet, pond, vineyards, wildflower meadow, jogging route).
BACKGROUND MUSIC: none.
LOCATION: village outskirts, 5 miles NW of Swindon.
CHILDREN: all ages welcomed, not under 12 in restaurant after 8.30 pm.
DOGS: allowed, not unattended in bedrooms, not in restaurant.
CREDIT CARDS: Amex, MasterCard, Visa.
PRICES: [2017] per room B&B £110–£151, D,B&B £165–£220. À la carte £38.

RADNAGE Buckinghamshire

Map 2:C3

🦌 THE MASH INN NEW

César award: newcomer of the year
'The distinctive cooking brings the customers'
to this 'greatly enjoyable' restaurant-with-rooms
in a village in the wooded Chiltern hills. Owner
Nick Mash has given the 18th-century inn a
'sparkling new look'. Beyond the flagstoned bar,
the semi-open kitchen/dining room is 'bright
and airy'; garden doors give on to a 'beguiling
view'. Chef Jon Parry forages and hand-picks
produce for his modern dishes – 'one of the
best meals we've eaten,' say Guide inspectors in
2017. 'Asparagus came with rich cows' curd and
black garlic; the smoothest chicken liver parfait,
with pickled celeriac. Maple syrup and soy-
marinated cod was full of flavour.' 'Simplicity is
the order of the day' in the 'clean, contemporary
bedrooms'. 'Ours had Anglepoise lights by
the king-size bed; a Roberts radio instead of a
TV; no wardrobe, just hangers on a hook. A
welcome surprise: the dinnertime turn-down.'
A 'fine breakfast' is brought to the room
('though it's a bit silly when you have just one
chair'): dark granola and buttermilk; turmeric
ginger beer; freshly cut orange slices; home-
made croissants and marmalade; leaf tea.

Horseshoe Road
Bennett End
Radnage
HP14 4EB

T: 01494 482440
E: hello@themashinn.com
W: themashinn.com

BEDROOMS: 4.
OPEN: all year, closed Sun eve, Mon,
Tues.
FACILITIES: bar, semi-open-plan
kitchen/dining room, free Wi-Fi,
2½-acre garden, unsuitable for
disabled.
BACKGROUND MUSIC: in public areas.
LOCATION: in hamlet 7 miles NW of
High Wycombe.
CHILDREN: not under 16.
DOGS: not allowed.
CREDIT CARDS: Amex, MasterCard,
Visa.
PRICES: [2017] per room B&B
£100–£130. Tasting menu £55,
à la carte £34.

RAMSGILL-IN-NIDDERDALE Yorkshire   Map 4:D3

THE YORKE ARMS

'Frances Atkins, the chef/patron, is lovely, and the food is divine' at this creeper-covered 18th-century coaching inn run by the Michelin-starred chef and her husband, Bill. In an 'unsurpassed setting' overlooking the green in a Dales village, the restaurant-with-rooms wins many returnees, who praise the 'first-class hospitality'. Kick off an evening with 'delicious canapés' by the log fire in the lounge. 'Excellent daily-changing menus' showcase produce from the large kitchen garden, along with wild foods, and locally sourced meat and fish. Characteristic offerings: blanquette of Nidderdale lamb, courgette, pickled gooseberry; truffled brill, shrimp butter, lemon balm. Rest, afterwards, in a room at the inn (some 'bijou but well equipped') or in one of the 'super' two-storey courtyard suites, 'faultlessly styled' and stocked with 'everything you'd expect from a luxury hotel – magazines, delicious biscuits, first-class toiletries'. In the morning, breakfast on home-made breads and preserves; 'excellent smoked haddock'. 'Not cheap, but it's worth every penny.' (William Wood, David and Lorna Hellard, F and IW, and others)

Ramsgill-in-Nidderdale
HG3 5RL

T: 01423 755243
E: enquiries@yorke-arms.co.uk
W: www.yorke-arms.co.uk

BEDROOMS: 15. 4 in courtyard, 1 suitable for disabled.
OPEN: all year except 25 Dec, closed Sun and Mon.
FACILITIES: lounge, bar, 2 dining rooms, free Wi-Fi, in-room TV (Freeview), function facilities, 2-acre grounds.
BACKGROUND MUSIC: classical in dining rooms.
LOCATION: centre of village.
CHILDREN: not under 12.
DOGS: allowed in 1 bedroom, bar.
CREDIT CARDS: Amex, MasterCard, Visa.
PRICES: [2017] per room D,B&B £345–£430. Tasting menu £85, à la carte £65.

RAVENSTONEDALE Cumbria

Map 4:C3

THE BLACK SWAN

♔ Previous César winner

'Warm and friendly', and 'good value' to boot, Louise Dinnes's Victorian pub-with-rooms stands in a conservation village surrounded by national parkland of windswept fells. The popular eating and drinking areas – with panelled walls, tartan carpeting, nature prints, a stag's head, and hops hanging – enjoy 'brisk trade'. 'And rightly so!' Besides the real ales and Cumbrian spirits behind the bar, chef Scott Fairweather's food is 'outstanding', say guests in 2017. 'We enjoyed a starter of goat's cheese and beetroot, with gingerbread, raspberries and balsamic cubes; scallops with butternut risotto; fish pie topped with creamy potato, enfolding a poached egg.' 'Well-maintained' bedrooms (some, with external access, suitable for guests travelling with their dogs) vary in size and style; each is supplied with welcome touches such as extra-large towels and organic toiletries. The Yorkshire Dales call for a hearty expedition: staff can advise on local rambles; there are bicycles and helmets for hire. For those visitors keen on a sit-down, the riverside garden, with its resident red squirrels, is a fine spot on a sunny day. (TL, SW, Robert Gower)

25% DISCOUNT VOUCHERS

Ravenstonedale
CA17 4NG

T: 015396 23204
F: 015396 23204
E: enquiries@blackswanhotel.com
W: www.blackswanhotel.com

BEDROOMS: 16. 6 in annexe, 4 on ground floor suitable for disabled. Plus 3 'glamping' tents.
OPEN: all year.
FACILITIES: 2 bars, lounge, 2 dining rooms, free Wi-Fi, in-room TV (Freeview), beer garden in wooded grounds, tennis and golf in village.
BACKGROUND MUSIC: in public areas all day, but optional.
LOCATION: in village 5 miles SW of Kirkby Stephen.
CHILDREN: all ages welcomed.
DOGS: allowed in 4 ground-floor bedrooms, not in restaurant.
CREDIT CARDS: all major cards.
PRICES: per room B&B single from £85, double from £100. À la carte £30. 1-night bookings sometimes refused.

REEPHAM Norfolk

THE DIAL HOUSE

'I count only the sunny hours,' reads the Latin inscription on the sundial set in the wall above the entrance to this 'eclectically decorated' Georgian house. It's just one of many curious and 'inspiring' features in Iain Wilson's hotel, restaurant and interiors shop on the marketplace of an 'appealing' small town. Guide inspectors found the building 'tastefully bedecked with interesting furniture and curios, all stylishly displayed – and almost all for sale'. 'Even the afternoon tea was beautifully presented – china cups and saucers, a lovely teapot, large slices of delicious cake.' Bedrooms, with a 'spacious' marble bathroom, have been conceived with 'faultless taste'. Each takes as inspiration an element of a 21st-century Grand Tour: China is done in blue and white to 'astonishing effect'; 'we could have been in Italy, in our Italian Palace room.' 'Uncomplicated food' is informally served from early to late – perhaps white wine and mustard-braised rabbit, spring greens, mash. An 'inviting breakfast buffet' has home-made jams, 'huge scones', yogurts and fruit; cooked options come with home-baked bread. 'Even the Marmite jars looked charming!' (Yvonne Walsh, and others)

Market Place
Reepham
NR10 4JJ

T: 01603 879900
E: info@thedialhouse.org.uk
W: www.thedialhouse.org.uk

BEDROOMS: 8.
OPEN: all year.
FACILITIES: lounge, restaurant, private dining rooms, free Wi-Fi, in-room TV (Sky), terrace, unsuitable for disabled.
BACKGROUND MUSIC: jazz at dinner.
LOCATION: on main square.
CHILDREN: all ages welcomed.
DOGS: allowed on terrace only.
CREDIT CARDS: all major cards.
PRICES: [2017] per room B&B £130–£190, D,B&B £170–£230. À la carte £30.

RICHMOND Yorkshire

Map 4:C3

THE COACH HOUSE AT MIDDLETON LODGE

♔ Previous César winner

Horses and coaches once trundled up the tree-lined avenue to this former stables in Yorkshire countryside; today, James Allison's 'low-key, relaxing' hotel attracts a rather smarter set. 'The place has been refurbished with a view to preserving all that is interesting and unusual from the past, but its interiors have been carefully designed for modern hospitality.' The result is 'thoroughly enjoyable': 'chic, unshabby' bedrooms; 'charming, enthusiastic' staff; a restaurant 'buzzing with happy customers'. 'Altogether excellent' bedrooms are in the Georgian coach house and farmhouse; garden rooms have a small private terrace with outdoor seating. In the dining room, chef Gareth Rayner takes an estate-to-plate approach to his 'fine, interesting' menus, using wild sorrel, say, and garden plums. (A two-and-a-half-acre kitchen garden was well into development as the Guide went to press.) A typical dish: Yorkshire chicken, roast onion risotto, mushrooms. Plan a visit around cultural events in the summer: the hotel hosts open-air film and theatre events when the weather turns warm. (P and JT)

Kneeton Lane
Middleton Tyas
Richmond
DL10 6NJ

T: 01325 377 977
F: 01325 377 065
E: info@middletonlodge.co.uk
W: www.middletonlodge.co.uk

BEDROOMS: 15. 6 in farmhouse (a short walk away), 5 on ground floor, 1 suitable for disabled.
OPEN: all year except 24–26 Dec, 1 Jan.
FACILITIES: lounge, bar, snug, restaurant, free Wi-Fi, in-room TV (Sky), civil wedding licence, treatment rooms, courtyard, garden in 200-acre grounds.
BACKGROUND MUSIC: in public areas.
LOCATION: 1 mile N of village, E of Scotch Corner.
CHILDREN: all ages welcomed.
DOGS: allowed in 1 bedroom, most public spaces, not in restaurant.
CREDIT CARDS: Amex, MasterCard, Visa.
PRICES: [2017] per room B&B from £160, D,B&B from £210. À la carte £35.

SEE ALSO SHORTLIST

RICHMOND Yorkshire

Map 4:C3

MILLGATE HOUSE

♔ Previous César winner

It's hard to pinpoint what Guide readers like best at Tim Culkin and Austin Lynch's 'lovely', characterful B&B, for we hear praise of the 'warm welcome'; the 'stylish, comfortable' rooms; the 'outstanding' breakfasts; the 'beautiful', award-winning garden. 'The hosts have a passion for Georgian interiors', and it shows: just off the cobbled square, their 'nicely designed' town house is filled with 'gorgeous' antique furniture, silver, paintings and objets d'art – 'such a collection!' From curios to prints and pictures, there's plenty to admire in the handsome bedrooms, where even the bathrooms have flair: in one, huge candles flank a Botticelli-like shell; in another, a Turkish rug lies between an Edwardian bath and a cast iron fireplace. The garden, tumbling towards the River Swale, is 'inspiring', with fine masses of snowdrops, ferns, hostas and old roses. In the morning, 'the best breakfast' includes an 'outstanding array' of local produce, fresh fruit, 'a wide range of interesting cereals'; coffee is taken seriously. 'A good base for exploring the Yorkshire Dales'; Easby Abbey is a ten-minute drive away. (L and RM, and others)

Richmond
DL10 4JN

т: 01748 823571
е: Millgate1@me.com
w: www.millgatehouse.com

BEDROOMS: 4.
OPEN: all year.
FACILITIES: hall, drawing room, dining room, free Wi-Fi, in-room digital TV, ⅓-acre garden, unsuitable for disabled.
BACKGROUND MUSIC: none.
LOCATION: town centre.
CHILDREN: all ages welcomed.
DOGS: not in public rooms, or unattended in bedrooms.
CREDIT CARDS: none.
PRICES: per room B&B £125–£165.

SEE ALSO SHORTLIST

RICHMOND-UPON-THAMES Surrey

Map 2:D3

BINGHAM

'Sumptuous' inside and out, Ruth and Samantha Trinder's refined hotel on the River Thames is in a 'tranquil spot' that belies its easy connection to the scramble and dash of London. 'We felt we were in a luxury version of home, rather than in a fancy hotel.' Past the unassuming Georgian facade, terraces and lawns at the rear reach down to the river towpath; on sunny days, parasols appear on the green to shade alfresco eaters. Newly refurbished bedrooms, now Scandinavian-stylish in sustainable natural materials, are individually furnished with restored mid-century pieces. The best, and most spacious, have an in-room copper bath and riverside views, but even the most compact double rooms are kitted out with modern amenities including a high-tech audio system with a pre-programmed music library. Join well-heeled locals in the smart restaurant for modern dishes such as cured trout, white asparagus, lovage pesto; in the 'magnificent bar', clink cocktail glasses over sweet and savoury snacks and taster plates. At the weekend, borrow one of the hotel's Pashley bicycles for a turn around nearby Richmond Park, then return for a sophisticated Sunday lunch, served till late.

61–63 Petersham Road
Richmond-upon-Thames
TW10 6UT

T: 020 8940 0902
E: info@thebingham.co.uk
W: www.thebingham.co.uk

BEDROOMS: 15.
OPEN: all year, restaurant closed Sun evening.
FACILITIES: bar, restaurant, function room, free Wi-Fi, in-room TV, civil wedding licence, terrace, garden, unsuitable for disabled.
BACKGROUND MUSIC: in lounge/bar and restaurant.
LOCATION: ½ mile S of centre.
CHILDREN: all ages welcomed.
DOGS: not allowed.
CREDIT CARDS: all major cards.
PRICES: [2017] room from £190. Tasting menu £60, à la carte £45, continental breakfast buffet £12.50 (plus 12½% discretionary service charge).

ROMALDKIRK Co. Durham

Map 4:C3

THE ROSE AND CROWN

Pull a Windsor chair over to the log fire at Cheryl and Thomas Robinson's creeper-covered 18th-century inn, in a picture-postcard village in the North Pennines. This is a 'most welcoming' place, with a 'comfortable, relaxed atmosphere' hanging about the copper pans, age-polished benches and rural prints, say Guide readers in 2017. (Dogs feel the same way, too, particularly after they've been given one of the locally small-batch-baked doggy treats.) 'The inn may be small in size, but it is professionally run, with eager-to-please staff – a large part of its appeal.' Each of the bedrooms has its own character – one has a stone fireplace, another has dark beams, others yet have a window seat. All are in 'tip-top order': 'housekeeping is excellent'. There are 'great walks' from the door; follow a route down to the river and back along the old railway line, returning in time for dinner. Chef Dave McBride's 'delicious, beautifully presented' modern British dishes, perhaps lamb loin, belly and ragout, kale, fondant potato, are 'the star of the show'. Headlam Hall, Darlington (see Shortlist), is under the same ownership. (Alwyn Ellis, Kevin Johnson, Adam Gibson)

25% DISCOUNT VOUCHERS

Romaldkirk
Barnard Castle
DL12 9EB

T: 01833 650213
E: hotel@rose-and-crown.co.uk
W: www.rose-and-crown.co.uk

BEDROOMS: 14. 2 in Monk's Cottage, 5 in rear courtyard, some on ground floor.
OPEN: all year except 23–28 Dec.
FACILITIES: 2 lounges, bar, Crown Room (bar meals), restaurant, free Wi-Fi, in-room TV (Freeview), boot room; fishing, grouse shooting, birdwatching nearby.
BACKGROUND MUSIC: all day in restaurant.
LOCATION: village centre, 6 miles W of Barnard Castle.
CHILDREN: all ages welcomed.
DOGS: allowed.
CREDIT CARDS: Amex, MasterCard, Visa.
PRICES: [2017] per room B&B £115–£200, D,B&B £185–£270. À la carte £40.

ROSS-ON-WYE Herefordshire

Map 3:D5

WILTON COURT

In a 'charming setting' by the River Wye, this 'good-value' restaurant-with-rooms occupies a 'lovely old building' a 15-minute walk, over the bridge, from town. It is owned by Helen and Roger Wynn. Guide readers who visited in the springtime were greeted by 'the perfume of Mexican orange blossoms by the entrance gate, and a positive welcome at the door'. A former Magistrates' Court, the Elizabethan building is 'steeped in history': the library, once part of the courtroom, stands above a cellar passage that led to a neighbouring jail. Elsewhere, there are mullioned windows, ancient wooden beams and an original fireplace or two. Each of the bright bedrooms is provided with bottled water, kimonos and fluffy towels. 'Our beamed room on the upper floor, while compact, had all the comforts we expect, plus glorious river views.' There's 'good choice' in the conservatory restaurant at mealtimes – perhaps crispy Ragstone salad, tomato and chilli salsa; sea bass, olive, chive crust. In good weather, the patio and 'pretty garden' are a 'wonderful place to relax' – find a shady spot and watch wildfowl drift past the riverbank. (Bob and Jean Henry, PA)

25% DISCOUNT VOUCHERS

Wilton Lane
Ross-on-Wye
HR9 6AQ

T: 01989 562569
F: 01989 768460
E: info@wiltoncourthotel.com
W: wiltoncourthotel.com

BEDROOMS: 11. 1 on ground floor.
OPEN: all year except first 2 weeks Jan.
FACILITIES: library, bar, restaurant, private dining room, free Wi-Fi, in-room TV (Freeview), ½-acre grounds, only restaurant suitable for disabled.
BACKGROUND MUSIC: in restaurant at mealtimes.
LOCATION: ½ mile from centre.
CHILDREN: all ages welcomed.
DOGS: allowed, not in restaurant.
CREDIT CARDS: Amex, MasterCard, Visa.
PRICES: [2017] per room B&B single £110–£160, double £135–£195, D,B&B (min. 2 nights) single £125–£175, double £175–£235. Set dinner £32.50, à la carte £45. 1-night bookings refused weekends Apr–Oct.

ROWSLEY Derbyshire

Map 3:A6

THE PEACOCK AT ROWSLEY

The 'efficient, friendly staff', 'comfortable bedrooms' and 'first-class food' make this 17th-century manor house on the edge of the Peak District national park a 'brilliant hotel', Guide readers say. It is owned by Lord and Lady Manners of medieval Haddon Hall, nearby; Laura Ball is the manager. Smart, modern decor coexists with mullioned windows, gilt-framed artwork and an antique piece or two. The cosy bar is characterful with beams, stone walls and an open log fire. Chic bedrooms have prints and paintings, and a marble bathroom stocked with top-end toiletries. (Rooms facing the busy road have double-glazed windows.) 'Our room, lovely and quiet, overlooked the garden.' In the restaurant, after amuse-bouche, sample chef Dan Smith's modern cooking, perhaps wild garlic and nettle velouté, goat's curd; Derbyshire beef fillet, glazed brisket, smoked mashed potatoes. For something less formal, 'excellent' bar classics include a fish of the day and rib-eye steak with chips. On a sunny day, traipse down the garden to the River Derwent – the staff can recommend local walks. Fisherfolk are well catered for: seven miles of fly fishing on the River Wye are 'a real bonus'.

Bakewell Road
Rowsley
DE4 2EB

T: 01629 733518
F: 01629 732671
E: reception@thepeacockatrowsley.com
w: www.thepeacockatrowsley.co.uk

BEDROOMS: 15.
OPEN: all year except 2 weeks Jan.
FACILITIES: lounge, bar, 2 dining rooms, free Wi-Fi, in-room TV (Freeview, Apple TV), civil wedding licence, ½-acre garden on the river, fishing rights on rivers Wye and Derwent, unsuitable for disabled.
BACKGROUND MUSIC: none.
LOCATION: village centre.
CHILDREN: not under 10 at weekends.
DOGS: allowed in bedrooms only (food and water bowls provided).
CREDIT CARDS: MasterCard, Visa.
PRICES: [2017] per room B&B £205–£310, D,B&B £285–£425. À la carte £45. 1-night bookings sometimes refused.

RUSHLAKE GREEN Sussex

Map 2:E4

STONE HOUSE

Grandeur and charm come in equal measure at the Dunn family's ancestral home, a Tudor manor house standing in extensive, 'well-maintained grounds' that are 'a pleasure to explore' in any season. (Shooting parties come to bag pheasants in the late autumn.) Guide inspectors this year were impressed by the 'handsome building' – its ancient portraits, 'roaring fires' and 'luxurious reception rooms' – and the 'friendly, accommodating staff'. Peter Dunn, the 'personable, impeccably dressed patriarch', died in 2016, but Jane Dunn remains in charge 'and still does all the cooking'. Traditional bedrooms are each 'delightfully different'. 'Our high-ceilinged, opulently furnished room had a comfy four-poster bed, gloriously draped but requiring some dexterity to clamber in. Down a short flight of steep steps, the spacious, marbled bathroom (cool during a winter frost) had an enormous bath.' At dinner, the hostess, a Master Chef, uses garden and estate produce in her 'well-balanced menu'. A typical dish: grilled saddle of wild rabbit, thyme and three-mustard cream sauce. Breakfast, 'hearty' and cooked to order, is accompanied by 'delicious juice' from apples in the orchard.

Rushlake Green
TN21 9QJ

T: 01435 830553
F: 01435 830726
E: stonehousehotel@aol.co.uk
W: www.stonehousesussex.co.uk

BEDROOMS: 7.
OPEN: all year except 16 Dec–2 Jan,
16 Feb–7 Mar.
FACILITIES: drawing room, library,
dining room, billiard room, free
Wi-Fi, in-room TV (Freeview),
6½-acre garden on 850-acre estate
(farm, woodland, croquet, pheasant/
clay-pigeon shooting, 2 lakes,
rowing, fishing), unsuitable for
disabled.
BACKGROUND MUSIC: none.
LOCATION: 4 miles SE of Heathfield,
by village green.
CHILDREN: not under 9.
DOGS: allowed in bedrooms, not in
public rooms.
CREDIT CARDS: MasterCard, Visa.
PRICES: [2017] per room B&B
£160–£310. À la carte £36.50.
1-night bookings refused weekends
16 May–1 Sept.

RYE Sussex

Map 2:E5

THE GEORGE IN RYE   `NEW`

In a 'prime High Street spot', this 'thoroughly enjoyable' hotel has 'the perfect mix of historic charm and up-to-date style and decor'. The centuries-old coaching inn has been a landmark since it entertained, in succession, the first three King Georges; today, 'fashionable, quirky and fun', it remains a hotspot for locals, passers-by and regular Guide correspondents who report being 'well looked after'. The 'cosy bar' draws the crowds with its cocktails, local ales and English wines; in the all-day restaurant ('a tasteful melange of appealing patterns'), sample a modern European menu packed with Rye Bay seafood. Bedrooms have 'all the comforts of a good hotel', plus whimsical touches – a collection of Penguin Classics, perhaps – and 'lots of nice products' in the bathroom. Some rooms are well suited for a family. Ground-floor courtyard rooms open on to a 'pretty, sunny' alfresco eating and drinking area – ask for a room in the main building for more privacy, Guide readers suggest. Inside or out, breakfast is 'delicious': 'tasty sausages; excellent eggs Florentine; a perfectly poached egg'. 'They happily tailored the cooked options to our desires.' (AW, ANR, David Berry)

98 High Street
Rye
TN31 7JT

T: 01797 222114
F: 01797 224065
E: reception@thegeorgeinrye.com
W: www.thegeorgeinrye.com

BEDROOMS: 34. 17 in annexe, some with private entrance.
OPEN: all year.
FACILITIES: lounge, bar, restaurant, function rooms, free Wi-Fi, in-room TV (Freeview), civil wedding licence, decked courtyard garden, unsuitable for disabled.
BACKGROUND MUSIC: in bar and restaurant.
LOCATION: town centre.
CHILDREN: all ages welcomed.
DOGS: not allowed.
CREDIT CARDS: MasterCard, Visa.
PRICES: [2017] per room B&B £125–£325. À la carte £45.

SEE ALSO SHORTLIST

RYE Sussex

Map 2:E5

JEAKE'S HOUSE

'Just as welcoming, beautiful, comfortable and relaxing as ever.' A Guide reader returning this year to Jenny Hadfield's B&B, on a cobbled street in this ancient town, found high standards being upheld. The 17th-century building, a former wool storehouse, combines with the adjoining men's club and Elders House to create an atmospheric whole. Past the creeper-smothered exterior, there are beamed ceilings, roaring fires, dark wood panelling, steep stairs; a 'dramatic and glamorous bar'. The walls are hung with prints and oil paintings, the rooms filled with antiques, clocks, lamps and ornaments. Similarly characterful bedrooms have views over rooftops and the wild expanse of Romney Marshes. 'My room was charmingly higgledy-piggledy, old-fashioned but not tired. There was ample comfortable seating and a spacious, well-equipped bathroom.' In a 'handsome', galleried room, breakfast is 'exquisite': choose from local sausages, oak-smoked haddock, wild Scottish salmon. Richard Martin, the chef, is a dab hand outside of the kitchen, too: 'He was so helpful about Rye's attractions.' 'We felt at home and were loath to leave.' (Mary Ellin Osmond, Richard Osborne)

Mermaid Street
Rye
TN31 7ET

T: 01797 222828
E: stay@jeakeshouse.com
W: www.jeakeshouse.com

BEDROOMS: 11.
OPEN: all year.
FACILITIES: parlour, bar/library, breakfast room, free Wi-Fi, in-room TV (Freeview), unsuitable for disabled.
BACKGROUND MUSIC: chamber music in breakfast room.
LOCATION: central, private car park, 6 mins' walk away (charge for parking permit, advance booking).
CHILDREN: not under 8.
DOGS: allowed on leads and 'always supervised'.
CREDIT CARDS: Diners, MasterCard, Visa.
PRICES: [2017] per room B&B £95–£150. 1-night bookings sometimes refused.

SEE ALSO SHORTLIST

ST IVES Cornwall

Map 1:D1

BOSKERRIS HOTEL

On a hill above the beach at Carbis Bay, Marianne and Jonathan Bassett's 'well-situated' 1930s hotel is a stylish, bright and breezy retreat with 'stunning sea views' across the water to Godrevy lighthouse. The staff are bright and breezy, too, Guide readers report this year: 'They were friendly and helpful throughout, and took a real interest in our plans each day.' Sunshine streams through glass doors on to stripped floorboards; the decor is in fresh, seascape-inspired shades. The bedrooms vary in size, but all are supplied with cafetière coffee (fresh milk on request), good toiletries, bathrobes, slippers and magazines. ('One niggle: we thought the light a little dim for reading.') Choose a room facing the sea: the best in the house has a panoramic view of St Ives Bay. Walk the South West Coastal Path or catch one of the frequent trains into the buzzy town; return for an alfresco cream tea or, most nights, a simple but 'very good' supper – maybe a beetroot and feta salad, or fish soup with rouille. Plenty of choice at breakfast: local farm sausages and dry-cured bacon, French toast, oak-smoked salmon, Burford Brown eggs, ricotta hotcakes. (Geoffrey and Sue Bignell)

Boskerris Road
Carbis Bay
St Ives
TR26 2NQ

T: 01736 795295
E: reservations@boskerrishotel.co.uk
W: www.boskerrishotel.co.uk

BEDROOMS: 15. 1 on ground floor.
OPEN: mid-Mar to mid-Nov, restaurant closed Sun, Mon.
FACILITIES: lounge, bar, breakfast room, supper room, free Wi-Fi, in-room TV (Freeview), decked terrace, massage and reflexology treatment room, 1½-acre garden, parking.
BACKGROUND MUSIC: all day in public rooms.
LOCATION: 1½ miles from centre (20 mins' walk), close to station.
CHILDREN: not under 10.
DOGS: not allowed.
CREDIT CARDS: MasterCard, Visa.
PRICES: [2017] per room B&B £155–£290. À la carte £27. 1-night bookings sometimes refused in high season.

SEE ALSO SHORTLIST

ST LEONARDS-ON-SEA Sussex

Map 2:E4

ZANZIBAR INTERNATIONAL HOTEL

🏵 Previous César winner

'Splendidly quirky', Max O'Rourke's characterful seafront hotel is filled with a 'relaxed, utterly unpretentious' atmosphere, and an 'interesting collection' of ornaments and objects from far-flung lands. Highly individual accommodation is set over several floors, but sip a welcome drink while 'efficient staff' bring your suitcases up to the room. 'Bedrooms vary hugely', so get in touch to discuss before booking. Each room – perhaps with 'wonderful sea views' – is decorated with a different city, country or continent in mind: split-level Morocco has kilim rugs, jewel-toned cushions and a bedroom up a spiral staircase; a New York-style penthouse loft has a jukebox and an aquarium coffee table (don't forget to feed the fish). 'The road in front is noisy by day, but quiet at night.' Take aperitifs in the courtyard or in the beachy bar overlooking the Channel; a menu of comfort food (potted pork and caper toast; moules marinière and chips) is served in the restaurant. Breakfast comes with the morning newspaper, plus a suggestion for the day's outing. More reports, please.

9 Eversfield Place
St Leonards-on-Sea
TN37 6BY

T: 01424 460109
E: info@zanzibarhotel.co.uk
W: www.zanzibarhotel.co.uk

BEDROOMS: 8. 1 on ground floor.
OPEN: all year.
FACILITIES: bar, restaurant, free Wi-Fi, in-room TV (Freeview), garden, beach across road, unsuitable for disabled.
BACKGROUND MUSIC: 'easy listening' in bar and restaurant.
LOCATION: seafront, 650 yds W of Hastings pier, free parking.
CHILDREN: not under 5.
DOGS: allowed in bedrooms (cleaning fee), not in public rooms.
CREDIT CARDS: Amex, MasterCard, Visa.
PRICES: [2017] per room B&B from £115. À la carte £35.

ST MARY'S Isles of Scilly

Map 1: inset C1

STAR CASTLE

♀ Previous César winner

'Everything you'd expect from a really good hotel is here,' writes a trusted Guide correspondent in 2017, fresh from celebrating the holidays at the Francis family's characterful hotel above Hugh Town. ('These chaps know how to run a good party!') 'It's a super place: comfy bedrooms with everything you could want; stupendous food at all mealtimes; friendly but professional staff.' Within star-shaped fortress walls, the hotel occupies a 16th-century castle; 'fine bedrooms' are in the main building and ramparts, and in chalet-style buildings (some with a veranda overlooking the sea) in the grounds. There are a tennis court and a new sun deck for good weather; for rainy days, or 'to simply relax in great comfort', there are 'well-stocked bookshelves' and plenty of board games. (Plenty of real ale, too, in the Dungeon bar.) In the original officers' mess and the vine-hung conservatory, Billy Littlejohn's cooking includes lots of seafood, perhaps crab and lobster from St Mary's harbour. Come morning, boatman Tim helps plan a day of island-hopping, or a tour of shipwrecks, seals and seabirds. (Abigail Kirby-Harris)

25% DISCOUNT VOUCHERS

The Garrison
St Mary's
TR21 0JA

T: 01720 422317
E: info@star-castle.co.uk
W: www.star-castle.co.uk

BEDROOMS: 38. 27 in 2 garden wings.
OPEN: all year, B&B only Nov–mid-Feb except New Year, closed Christmas.
FACILITIES: lounge, bar, 2 restaurants, free Wi-Fi, in-room TV (Freeview), civil wedding licence, sun deck, 2-acre gardens, covered swimming pool (12 by 4 metres), tennis, beach nearby, horse riding, golf, unsuitable for disabled.
BACKGROUND MUSIC: none.
LOCATION: ¼ mile from town centre, boat (2¾ hours)/helicopter.
CHILDREN: welcomed, no under-5s in restaurants in evening (children's dinner at 5.30 pm).
DOGS: allowed in garden rooms, not in restaurants or lounge.
CREDIT CARDS: Amex, MasterCard, Visa.
PRICES: [2017] per person B&B (Nov–mid-Feb) from £85, D,B&B from £95. À la carte £42.

ST MAWES Cornwall

Map 1:E2

IDLE ROCKS

In a 'wonderful position right by the water', this 'beautifully decorated' hotel is 'superbly run', by 'great staff', in a 'hospitable spirit'. Owned by Karen and David Richards, it is a modish place, in a pretty village 'well accustomed to well-heeled yachties and other sea-loving holidaymakers'. 'On a Sunday afternoon in the off season, the place was buzzing with people dropping in for lunch,' a Guide correspondent reports in 2017. 'Despite a full-scale gale blowing outside, the hotel was comfortably warm.' Smart bedrooms facing village or harbour vary in size; some suit a family. 'Our room had a supremely comfortable bed and crisp bedlinen; a huge walk-in shower that would easily have taken two. Small improvements would be welcomed, however: a full-length mirror, better bedside lighting, more power points.' Order a cocktail, then join the crowds in the restaurant or on the sun-bathed terrace raving about chef Guy Owen's 'high-quality cooking': his Cornish produce-packed menus might include wild bream, squid ink gnocchi, salsa verde, saffron. 'Breakfasts are excellent, the full Cornish and eggs Benedict particularly good.' (Oliver Thomas, AK-H, and others)

Harbourside
St Mawes
TR2 5AN

T: 01326 270270
E: reservations@idlerocks.com
W: www.idlerocks.com

BEDROOMS: 19. 4 in adjacent annexe, 1 suitable for disabled.
OPEN: all year.
FACILITIES: lounge, restaurant, kids' room, boot room, free Wi-Fi, in-room TV (Sky), terrace.
BACKGROUND MUSIC: all day in public areas.
LOCATION: central, on the harbour.
CHILDREN: all ages welcomed, not under 12 in restaurant after 8.30 pm.
DOGS: allowed in 2 bedrooms, not in public rooms.
CREDIT CARDS: all major cards.
PRICES: [2017] per room B&B £240–£395. À la carte £55, 5-course tasting menu £75. 1-night bookings sometimes refused at weekends.

SEE ALSO SHORTLIST

ST MAWES Cornwall

TRESANTON

🏆 Previous César winner

There's no escaping the sweep of the sea at this 'really super hotel' above Falmouth Bay: a wraparound deck catches the sun; French doors in the restaurant open on to terraces; nearly all the bedrooms look across the water towards St Anthony's lighthouse. The whole is 'wonderful, in sun and storm'. It is owned by Olga Polizzi, whose designer's eye is evident in the breezy, 'relaxed bedrooms' (all Cornish art, antiques and coastal stripes), and public spaces filled with 'interesting and original' artwork and objects. At mealtimes, the sea is inspiration, too: Paul Wadham's modern menu includes a catch of the day, perhaps brill on the bone, champ mash, cavolo nero. Meandering steps lead up through the lush gardens for excellent viewing points; children have their own grassy spot to enjoy. A Mediterranean-style beach club was in the works on the hotel's foreshore as the Guide went to press. Ask the 'helpful' staff about coastal strolls; some days, guided walks take in secluded bays, secret creeks, seabirds and seals. 'Hiring the hotel's skippered yacht for a day is a wonderful experience.' Country cousin Hotel Endsleigh is in Milton Abbot (see entry).

27 Lower Castle Road
St Mawes
TR2 5DR

T: 01326 270055
F: 01326 270053
E: manager@tresanton.com
W: www.tresanton.com

BEDROOMS: 30. In 5 houses.
OPEN: all year.
FACILITIES: 2 lounges, bar, restaurant, cinema, playroom, conference facilities, free Wi-Fi, in-room TV (Freeview), civil wedding licence, terrace, ¼-acre garden, 25-foot yacht, unsuitable for disabled.
BACKGROUND MUSIC: none.
LOCATION: on seafront, valet parking (car park up hill).
CHILDREN: all ages welcomed, no under-6s in restaurant in evening.
DOGS: allowed in some bedrooms and in dogs' bar.
CREDIT CARDS: Amex, MasterCard, Visa.
PRICES: [2017] per room B&B from £260. À la carte £44. 1-night bookings refused weekends in high season.

SEE ALSO SHORTLIST

SEAHAM Co. Durham

Map 4:B4

SEAHAM HALL

Overlooking Durham's heritage coast, this Georgian mansion, all sea views and sofas for sinking into, is 'a wonderful place, combining luxury and style with a friendly, relaxed approach'. Styling throughout is contemporary – bold going on audacious. Spacious bedrooms, each equipped with bathrobes, slippers and an espresso machine, are individually styled; some have French windows that open onto a private terrace and garden. 'Our large suite had a huge bed with a wonderfully soft duvet – utter luxury.' Pick among a choice of eating places. Ozone restaurant serves light meals of pan-Asian fare; in Byron's restaurant – where the rich colours are inspired by a portrait of the mad, bad poet, who entered into an ill-fated marriage here – chef Ross Stovold's daily-changing menu places the emphasis on locally sourced ingredients. A typical dish: aged beef sirloin, celeriac, mushroom tapioca, fondant potato. Beaches and rugged cliffs await, with walking and cycling routes along the coast (and bicycles to borrow), but choose to dilly-dally: an atmospheric walkway leads to the Serenity Spa and its swimming pool, 'lovely just for relaxing in'. (P and SG)

25% DISCOUNT VOUCHERS

Lord Byron's Walk
Seaham
SR7 7AG

T: 0191 5161400
E: hotel@seaham-hall.com
W: www.seaham-hall.com

BEDROOMS: 20. 1 suitable for disabled.
OPEN: all year.
FACILITIES: lift, 2 lounges, bar, 2 restaurants, private dining room, conference facilities, free Wi-Fi, in-room TV (Sky), civil wedding licence, spa (treatment rooms, outdoor hot tubs, sun terrace, fitness suite, 20-metre heated swimming pool), 37-acre grounds (terraces, putting green).
BACKGROUND MUSIC: all day in public areas.
LOCATION: 5 miles S of Sunderland.
CHILDREN: all ages welcomed.
DOGS: not allowed.
CREDIT CARDS: Amex, MasterCard, Visa.
PRICES: [2017] per room B&B from £195, D,B&B from £255. Market menu £30, à la carte £50. 1-night bookings sometimes refused weekends.

SEAHOUSES Northumberland

Map 4:A4

🏆 ST CUTHBERT'S HOUSE

César award: B&B of the year

Jeff and Jill Sutheran's 'superb' B&B, in a coastal village on Lowgos Bay, 'fully deserves' its praise, say Guide readers this year, who were made to feel 'very much at home'. 'We had a great stay.' The B&B occupies a 'delightfully converted' Presbyterian church; the former sanctuary today serves as an 'elegant' open-plan lounge and breakfast room, with books, DVDs, travel guides and a well-stocked honesty bar. 'Spacious, comfortable' bedrooms have a 'stylish' bathroom and 'lots of great touches', such as dressing gowns, slippers, high-end toiletries, a capsule coffee machine, perhaps a fur rug by the bed. Breakfast is a generous, varied celebration of local produce: there's Northumbrian bacon from the local butcher, bread from the village bakery, kippers smoked in the smokehouse not a mile away. For a punchy start to the day, ask for a jug of monastery mead, brewed on Holy Island, to accompany the morning porridge. 'Jeff acted like our personal travel adviser, even checking the weather before booking our boat to the Farne Islands. His restaurant recommendations were spot on, too.' (Michael Green, and others)

192 Main Street
Seahouses
NE68 7UB

T: 01665 720456
E: stay@stcuthbertshouse.com
W: www.stcuthbertshouse.com

BEDROOMS: 6. 2 on ground floor, 1 suitable for disabled.
OPEN: all year except 'holiday periods in winter'.
FACILITIES: lounge, breakfast room, free Wi-Fi, in-room TV (Freeview), small garden.
BACKGROUND MUSIC: none.
LOCATION: under 1 mile from harbour and village centre.
CHILDREN: not under 12.
DOGS: not allowed.
CREDIT CARDS: MasterCard, Visa.
PRICES: [2017] per room B&B £110–£125. 1-night bookings sometimes refused.

SHAFTESBURY Dorset

Map 2:D1

LA FLEUR DE LYS

'The very friendly people are a key feature' of this 'excellent, expectation-exceeding' restaurant-with-rooms, a short walk from the centre of historic Shaftesbury. Very much a local presence, 'it appears to do or need little by way of direct advertising, relying on word of mouth' for publicity. Inside the ivy-clad former girls' boarding school, front-of-house maven Mary Griffin-Shepherd is well liked by visitors, who laud her 'helpfulness and hands-on attitude'. David Shepherd and Marc Preston's 'top-class grub' is served in the 'lovely' restaurant. Local farmers and suppliers provide seasonal ingredients for dishes such as guineafowl, smoked ham and mushroom terrine, blackcurrant, fig and apple chutney; grilled fillet of local sole, fresh asparagus, lemon-infused herb butter. 'Clean, comfortable' bedrooms, each named after a variety of grape, are simply decorated and 'well equipped' with fresh milk and home-made biscuits. Consider discussing room choices before booking – they vary in size from a standard single to a 'snug, one-night-only' double to a family room for three. Breakfast is 'a real treat'. (JB, CB, and others)

25% DISCOUNT VOUCHERS

Bleke Street
Shaftesbury
SP7 8AW

T: 01747 853717
E: info@lafleurdelys.co.uk
W: www.lafleurdelys.co.uk

BEDROOMS: 8. 1 on ground floor.
OPEN: all year.
FACILITIES: lounge, bar, dining room, conference room, free Wi-Fi, in-room TV (Freeview), small courtyard garden.
BACKGROUND MUSIC: none, occasional live music nights.
LOCATION: N edge of historic town centre.
CHILDREN: all ages welcomed.
DOGS: not allowed.
CREDIT CARDS: Amex, MasterCard, Visa.
PRICES: [2017] per room B&B from £100, D,B&B from £175. Set meals £30–£37, à la carte £40. 1-night bookings sometimes refused.

SHEFFIELD Yorkshire

Map 4:E4

BROCCO ON THE PARK

🌣 Previous César winner

'There's a vibrant atmosphere' at Tiina Carr's 'stylish, Scandi-chic' hotel, in a 'buzzy neighbourhood' that's 'worth a visit on its own'. Choose among modern bedrooms varying in size, from the snug Pigeon's Loft in the eaves to the spread-your-wings Dovecote, which has a Juliet balcony overlooking city and park. Every room has cotton robes, lambswool blankets, an espresso machine and a wicker-hamper tea tray. 'Traffic noise from the road didn't stop me from sleeping soundly in my comfortable, good-sized bed. From my spacious room, Chiffchaff's Post, the noise I did hear was a delightful dawn chorus of birdsong from the adjacent park.' The café/restaurant, 'aptly called a neighbourhood kitchen', is popular early to late. Here, and on the terrace in fine weather, 'smartly dressed and well-trained' staff serve chef Leslie Buddington's 'excellent, interesting' menu of 'Nordic tapas', picnic platters, small and big plates. Among vegan and gluten-free options, try, perhaps, an 'impressive' beetroot and lentil pie with a sweet-potato topping. At breakfast: waffles, smoothies, 'beautifully grilled' bacon. (Robert Sandham, and others)

92 Brocco Bank
Sheffield
S11 8RS

T: 0114 266 1233
E: hello@brocco.co.uk
W: www.brocco.co.uk

BEDROOMS: 8. 1 suitable for disabled.
OPEN: all year, restaurant closed Sun 6 pm.
FACILITIES: reception area with sofas, 2 restaurants (1 with bar), free Wi-Fi, in-room smart TV, terrace (barbecue, seating), bicycle hire.
BACKGROUND MUSIC: in restaurant, plus Sunday jazz afternoons.
LOCATION: 1½ miles W of city centre.
CHILDREN: all ages welcomed.
DOGS: not allowed.
CREDIT CARDS: Amex, MasterCard, Visa.
PRICES: [2017] room £90–£230. Cooked breakfast from £7, à la carte £40.

SIDLESHAM Sussex

Map 2:E3

THE CRAB & LOBSTER

NEW

'Excellently located' on the edge of Pagham Harbour nature reserve, this whitewashed restaurant-with-rooms is 'a wonderfully tranquil, timeless, tucked-away sort of place'. Outside, take in the 'wide sweep of marshland, with the sound of curlews under big skies'; step into the smartly refurbished centuries-old inn to find 'charming, friendly' staff and a bar and restaurant that are popular for the 'delicious', seafood-strong menu. It is owned by Sam and Janet Bakose, who also run The Halfway Bridge, Lodsworth (see entry). 'Comfortable, with a fine modern bathroom', bedrooms are chic in muted colours. Choose one with views over fields and sea – binoculars are supplied. At lunch and dinner, and on the sunny terrace in summer, Clyde Hollett's English and Mediterranean dishes use plenty of fish and seafood from Selsey. Among the 'fabulous flavours': pan-fried fillet of stone bass, seaweed dauphine potato, steamed clams, sea vegetables. 'We booked in for one night but ended up eating there two evenings.' Breakfast has 'a good fruit selection and some interesting cooked options'. 'Lots of different walks in the area.' (Peter Anderson, Diana Goodey, Danielle Hommel)

Mill Lane
Sidlesham
PO20 7NB

T: 01243 641233
E: enquiries@crab-lobster.co.uk
W: www.crab-lobster.co.uk

BEDROOMS: 4. 2 in self-catering Crab Cottage.
OPEN: all year.
FACILITIES: bar/restaurant, free Wi-Fi, in-room TV (Freeview), terrace, small beer garden, unsuitable for disabled.
BACKGROUND MUSIC: 'quiet' in restaurant and bar.
LOCATION: 6 miles S of Chichester.
CHILDREN: all ages welcomed.
DOGS: allowed in garden area.
CREDIT CARDS: Amex, MasterCard, Visa.
PRICES: [2017] per room B&B £175–£205. À la carte £37.50. 2-night min. stay at weekends.

SIDMOUTH Devon

Map 1:C5

HOTEL RIVIERA

Old-school service and attention to detail come to the fore at this 'splendid place' overlooking Lyme Bay. The proudly traditional hotel, in a Regency terrace where 'everything is of the highest quality', is owned by 'pleasant, charming' Peter Wharton; his staff 'do their best to ensure an enjoyable stay', say Guide readers in 2017. While some guests think the interiors 'old-fashioned', fans revel in the 'sumptuous decor bearing some resemblance to the displays at Fortnum & Mason'. 'The bar with the grand piano is very showbiz – that's not a complaint!' Bedrooms varying in size and style may need careful selection, but all are 'spotless', visitors agree. 'Housekeeping is excellent, and supplies (water, tea, wonderfully light shortbread biscuits) were generously topped up.' In the 'timeless' dining room, chef Martin Osedo serves 'a five-course banquet' of 'quite adventurous options'. 'The portions are well considered, and each dish is well executed – my battered monkfish was sublime – but we'd appreciate some simpler fare as well.' An 'extensive choice' of breakfast ('an even greater delight') is served at the table. (Mary Woods, Trevor Lockwood, Peter Govier, and others)

The Esplanade
Sidmouth
EX10 8AY

T: 01395 515201
F: 01395 577775
E: enquiries@hotelriviera.co.uk
W: www.hotelriviera.co.uk

BEDROOMS: 26. Some suitable for disabled.
OPEN: all year.
FACILITIES: lift, lounge, bar, restaurant, function facilities, free Wi-Fi, in-room TV (Freeview), terrace, opposite pebble/sand beach (safe bathing).
BACKGROUND MUSIC: in bar and restaurant, occasional live piano music in bar.
LOCATION: central, on the esplanade.
CHILDREN: all ages welcomed.
DOGS: small dogs allowed in some bedrooms, not in public rooms except foyer.
CREDIT CARDS: all major cards.
PRICES: [2017] per person B&B £112–£225, D,B&B £133–£246. Set dinner £40–£44, à la carte £44.

SEE ALSO SHORTLIST

SNETTISHAM Norfolk

Map 2:A4

THE ROSE & CROWN   NEW

Down the road from the village church, Jeannette and Anthony Goodrich's 'delightful, enjoyable', family-friendly inn gains a full entry this year thanks to a recommendation from a regular Guide correspondent. (A 'well-prepared' dish of pan-fried calf's liver and bacon, with Chantenay carrots, can't have hurt, either.) A country cousin to the Goodriches' Bank House in King's Lynn (see entry), the 14th-century pub, the village local, looks the part: whitewashed, with rambling roses outside; beams, low doorways and open fires inside; a jolly walled garden, with parasols and picnic tables, out back. Chef Jamie Clarke's 'very good' menu of pub classics and more exotic fare highlights produce sourced from within a 20-mile radius: mussels, lobster and crab from Brancaster and Thornham; salads from village allotments; meat from the local butcher. Stay the night in one of the simply decorated bedrooms stocked with books, magazines and fine toiletries. 'Our room at the rear, reached by a steep, narrow staircase, was comfortable, with fluffy towels in the excellent bathroom. Fresh milk in the room, too – always a bonus.' (Sara Price)

Old Church Road
Snettisham
PE31 7LX

T: 01485 541382
E: info@roseandcrownsnettisham.co.uk
W: www.roseandcrownsnettisham.co.uk

BEDROOMS: 16. 2 on ground floor, 1 suitable for disabled.
OPEN: all year.
FACILITIES: 3 bar areas, 3 dining areas, free Wi-Fi, in-room TV (Freeview), large walled garden (children's play area).
BACKGROUND MUSIC: 'laid-back and low-key' in dining areas.
LOCATION: in village centre, 5 miles S of Hunstanton.
CHILDREN: all ages welcomed.
DOGS: 'well-behaved dogs' allowed in bedrooms, bars, not in dining areas.
CREDIT CARDS: all major cards.
PRICES: [2017] per room B&B single £100–£120, double £120–£140. À la carte £28. 2-night min. over bank holiday weekends.

SOAR MILL COVE Devon

Map 1:E4

SOAR MILL COVE HOTEL

César award: seaside hotel of the year

From dolphin-spotting to table tennis, there is plenty to enjoy at Keith Makepeace's family-friendly hotel, which stands in expansive countryside, with views towards the sea. Fortify yourself with a clotted cream scone on the terrace (or 'divine' Pavlova, once made for Audrey Hepburn), then take a turn about the 'immaculate lawns and flowerbeds'. Adventurers, set off on the South West Coastal Path (maps are provided), or head straight for the craggy rocks on the beach in the valley below – it's 'a nice walk, under the gaze of cows in nearby fields'. For exercise on cold days, there is an indoor saltwater swimming pool. At dinner, chef Ian MacDonald's market-style menus highlight seaside-fresh produce, perhaps 'delicious fish cakes; genuine chowder with mussels and shrimps in their shells'. No need to shut it all away when night falls: every bedroom, whether cosy for couples or grand for a group, has French windows that open on to a private garden-facing patio. In the morning, there's much choice at breakfast: freshly squeezed orange juice, home-made conserves, local sausages, Salcombe smokies. (CE)

Soar Mill Cove
TQ7 3DS

T: 01548 561566
E: info@soarmillcove.co.uk
W: www.soarmillcove.co.uk

BEDROOMS: 22. All on ground floor.
OPEN: all year, except New Year, Jan.
FACILITIES: lounge, 2 bars, restaurant, coffee shop, free Wi-Fi in reception, in-room TV (Freeview), indoor swimming pool (15 by 10 metres), spa (sauna, treatments), gym, civil wedding licence, 10-acre grounds (tennis, play area), sandy beach.
BACKGROUND MUSIC: none.
LOCATION: 3 miles SW of Salcombe.
CHILDREN: all ages welcomed (children's tea, baby-listening service, games room, children's entertainment in summer).
DOGS: allowed in bedrooms, bar, coffee shop.
CREDIT CARDS: Amex, MasterCard, Visa.
PRICES: [2017] per room B&B £199–£329, D,B&B £269–£409. À la carte £35. 1-night bookings refused holiday weekends.

SOMERTON Somerset

Map 1:C6

THE LYNCH COUNTRY HOUSE

Black swans glide on the lake in the 'lovely' garden; sun pours in through Venetian windows. Here, perched on a lynch, or ridge, above the Cary river valley, is a Georgian country house run as a 'very good' B&B with 'a touch of class'. It is owned by jazz musician Roy Copeland; Lynne Vincent is the 'delightful, helpful' manager. Traditionally decorated bedrooms in the main house and converted coach house are 'comfortable, clean and well presented'. They share a country feel in their use of pretty floral fabrics, but each is different, and they vary in size. A room in the eaves, with a private bathroom across the landing, is ideal for a family. 'Our room in the main house had lots of character, plus old-fashioned-looking bathroom fixtures, which all worked!' On a fine day, climb up to the belvedere: the view stretches across Somerton and the surrounding countryside. At dinnertime, head for the centre of the medieval market town – the White Hart (see Shortlist) is a popular choice. A 'superb breakfast' in the orangery includes French yogurts and freshly squeezed orange juice; the full cooked breakfast is a feast. (Mary and Rodney Milne-Day)

4 Behind Berry
Somerton
TA11 7PD

T: 01458 272316
F: 01458 272590
E: enquiries@
thelynchcountryhouse.co.uk
W: www.thelynchcountryhouse.
co.uk

BEDROOMS: 9. 4, in coach house, on ground floor.
OPEN: all year, only coach house rooms at Christmas and New Year, no breakfast 25 Dec/1 Jan.
FACILITIES: breakfast room, small sitting area, free Wi-Fi, in-room TV (Freeview), ¾-acre grounds (lake), unsuitable for disabled.
BACKGROUND MUSIC: none.
LOCATION: edge of town.
CHILDREN: all ages welcomed.
DOGS: allowed (not unattended) in 1 coach house room, not in public rooms.
CREDIT CARDS: Amex, MasterCard, Visa.
PRICES: [2017] per room B&B single £70–£95, double £80–£125.

SEE ALSO SHORTLIST

SOUTH DALTON Yorkshire

Map 4:D5

THE PIPE AND GLASS INN   NEW

Look out for the 'stunning spire' of St Mary's church on the approach to this 'enchanting village'. It's a divine landmark that leads believers to the 'very best hospitality' and 'outstanding food' at James and Kate Mackenzie's pub-with-rooms, report Guide inspectors in 2017. Past the 'modest country pub exterior', there's a 'warm, friendly' welcome, and the Michelin-starred cooking that has people 'chafing at the bit to get in'. The traditional bar, with its dark beams, open fire, and copper pots hanging, is just the spot for sandwiches and hand-pulled ales; in the restaurant, the chef/patron's daily specials might include pea and mint ravioli, Yorkshire Fine Fettle cheese, pea shoots, nettle; 'a perfectly grilled steak'. 'Well-appointed' bedrooms, each with a patio, are set around a 'beautifully maintained' herb garden. 'Our super-king-size bed was adorned with a luxurious wool throw; there was an efficient shower in the sizeable bathroom. Smart touches included a modern chandelier and a striking sunray mirror.' Mornings, the pre-ordered breakfast 'wins universal plaudits': chilled juices, yogurt and fruits; 'golden eggs and salty bacon on home-baked bread'.

West End
South Dalton
HU17 7PN

T: 01430 810246
E: email@pipeandglass.co.uk
W: www.pipeandglass.co.uk

BEDROOMS: 5. All on ground floor in garden, suitable for disabled.
OPEN: all year, no room reservations Sun, closed Mon except bank holidays.
FACILITIES: bar, restaurant, private dining rooms, free Wi-Fi, in-room TV (Freeview), patio (alfresco dining), garden.
BACKGROUND MUSIC: in bar and restaurant.
LOCATION: 7 miles NW of Beverley.
CHILDREN: all ages welcomed.
DOGS: not allowed.
CREDIT CARDS: Amex, MasterCard, Visa.
PRICES: [2017] per room B&B £190–£225. À la carte £100.

SOUTHAMPTON Hampshire

Map 2:E2

THE PIG IN THE WALL

A Pig with pedigree, the second of Robin
Hutson's sounder of swine, this Georgian
house set into the medieval town wall has been
given the hotel group's signature shabby-chic
treatment by designer Judy Hutson. Enter to
find 'characterful' spaces with bare floorboards,
exposed brick walls, mismatched furnishings,
vintage china, a gilt-framed portrait or three.
'We had a good stay,' says a Guide reader
this year. 'And we loved the pubby lounge
downstairs.' Here, pots of herbs are peppered
about; salads, sandwiches and 'piggy bits' are
available all day from the deli counter. In the
evening, a simple supper might bring a pie of
the day or a veggie stew; alternatively, pile into
a Land Rover and be ferried to the mother Pig
at Brockenhurst (see entry) for the full spread.
From snug to spacious, bedrooms are all kitted
out with an espresso machine and a larder of
snacks, and a monsoon shower in the bathroom.
Breakfast on smoked salmon and ciabatta or
a ham and cheese croissant. 'Walk the walls,'
urges a sign on the street outside: do just that,
armed with a takeaway lunch, perhaps, of a
New Forest goat's cheese and pickled beetroot
sandwich. (Lucy Rose)

8 Western Esplanade
Southampton
SO14 2AZ

T: 02380 636900
E: reception@thepiginthewall.com
W: www.thepighotel.com

BEDROOMS: 12. 2 on ground floor.
OPEN: all year.
FACILITIES: open-plan lounge/bar/
deli counter, free Wi-Fi, in-room
TV (Freeview), unsuitable for
disabled.
BACKGROUND MUSIC: in public areas.
LOCATION: on the outskirts of the
city.
CHILDREN: all ages welcomed.
DOGS: not allowed.
CREDIT CARDS: Amex, MasterCard,
Visa.
PRICES: [2017] room £135–£190.
Breakfast £10.

SEE ALSO SHORTLIST

STAMFORD Lincolnshire

Map 2:B3

THE GEORGE

A hostelry of some sort has stood on this spot for a millennium, gradually sweeping up a church, motley outbuildings and a hospital to create this traditionally run hotel that remains 'very much a part of the town'. No wonder: with log fires and deep sofas, a panelled bar, and a courtyard for alfresco entertaining, 'the place heaves from morning coffee to afternoon tea'. Arrive to 'a friendly welcome' – the staff are 'pleasant, attentive, efficient'. Bedrooms are variously sized and shaped, with different outlooks. 'Our mini-suite, actually a comfortable, large double room, had a sunken bath and lots of storage space in the bathroom. The room overlooked the courtyard; there was some noise in the early evening, but all was quiet at night.' Join the revellers for a 'faultless' informal dinner in the Garden Room ('our lobster spaghetti and summer pudding made one of the best meals of the year'), or an 'excellent' traditional meal in the Oak restaurant. In the morning, alongside good cooked dishes, the 'impressive fruit selection' might include a 'perfect exotic fruit salad'. (JM, PA, and others)

71 St Martins
Stamford
PE9 2LB

T: 01780 750750
F: 01780 750701
E: reservations@
   georgehotelofstamford.com
W: www.georgehotelofstamford.com

BEDROOMS: 45.
OPEN: all year.
FACILITIES: 2 lounges, 2 bars, 2 restaurants, 4 private dining rooms, business centre, free Wi-Fi, in-room TV (Sky, Freeview), civil wedding licence, 2-acre grounds (courtyard, gardens), only public areas suitable for disabled.
BACKGROUND MUSIC: none.
LOCATION: ¼ mile from centre.
CHILDREN: all ages welcomed.
DOGS: allowed, not unattended in bedrooms, only guide dogs in restaurants.
CREDIT CARDS: all major cards.
PRICES: [2017] per room B&B single from £125, double £150–£275. À la carte £50.

SEE ALSO SHORTLIST

STANTON WICK Somerset

Map 1:B6

THE CARPENTER'S ARMS

In a 'very quiet' Chew valley hamlet criss-crossed by public footpaths ideal for a ramble, this 'most appealing' inn is 'a good base and a real bargain', say Guide readers this year. In summer, the flowerbeds and hanging baskets fronting the row of former miners' cottages come abloom; parasols open over alfresco food and drinks. When winter creeps in, a fire blazes in the low-beamed bar, its books, sofas and log piles a 'thoroughly attractive' backdrop to dinner. Bedrooms are modern, with 'good furniture, fittings and lighting'. 'Our room was nice – on the small side, but fine for a night's stay. I liked the efficient shower in the bathroom.' Join locals over pints of Butcombe in the evening, then order from Chris Dando's menu of honest fare: fish from Cornwall, local game in season, 'plenty of veg', a much-appreciated passion fruit and mango roulade. ('Roasts dominated on a Sunday evening, with a fine Yorkshire pudding.') 'There's no danger of going hungry – the portions are generous.' In the morning, 'the fresh fruit platter was particularly enjoyed'. (Peter Anderson, and others)

Wick Lane
Stanton Wick
BS39 4BX

T: 01761 490202
F: 01761 490763
E: carpenters@buccaneer.co.uk
W: www.the-carpenters-arms.co.uk

BEDROOMS: 13.
OPEN: all year except evenings 25/26 Dec, 1 Jan.
FACILITIES: bar, snug, lounge, 2 restaurants, function room, free Wi-Fi, in-room TV (Freeview), patio, secure parking, only public areas suitable for disabled.
BACKGROUND MUSIC: none.
LOCATION: 8 miles S of Bristol, 8 miles W of Bath.
CHILDREN: all ages welcomed.
DOGS: allowed in bar and outside areas.
CREDIT CARDS: Amex, MasterCard, Visa.
PRICES: [2017] per room B&B single from £80, double from £120, D,B&B single from £102.50, double from £165. À la carte £36.50.

STUDLAND Dorset

Map 2:E2

THE PIG ON THE BEACH

♔ Previous César winner

The fourth of Robin Hutson's informal, coolly rustic hotels, this little Pig went to the beach, settling in a 'wonderful location' – a rambling manor house in gardens facing Studland Bay. 'Beautifully designed bedrooms' range from 'cheap and cheerful' to rather more generous, via a couple of cottages and two quirky shepherds' huts with sea views. 'We were upgraded to the Bothy, a wonderful thatched solus room within the bountiful walled kitchen garden. It's eclectic and shabby-chic, which is fun, but more importantly, it works. Everything in the room is there both for a purpose and to make it special, without any sense of bling.' Plus: 'It's got the best-stocked minibar I've ever encountered.' The kitchen garden dictates the dishes served in the conservatory dining room. 'The 25-mile menu was difficult to choose from, because we wanted to try so many things. Everything we did choose hit the spot – we're still raving about the juicy, tender partridge.' (When weekend drop-in diners threaten to overwhelm, a separate residents' area is 'a welcome retreat'.) 'We loved breakfast.' (Danielle Hommel, James Waghorn)

Manor House
Manor Road
Studland
BH19 3AU

T: 01929 450288
E: info@thepighotel.com
W: www.thepighotel.com

BEDROOMS: 23. Some on the ground floor, 2 Dovecot hideaways, Harry's Hut and Pig Hut in grounds.
OPEN: all year.
FACILITIES: bar, lounge, snug, restaurant, private dining room, free Wi-Fi, in-room TV (Freeview), 2 treatment cabins, garden, unsuitable for disabled.
BACKGROUND MUSIC: all day in public areas.
LOCATION: cliff-top above Studland beach.
CHILDREN: all ages welcomed.
DOGS: not allowed.
CREDIT CARDS: Amex, MasterCard, Visa.
PRICES: [2017] room £155–£330. Breakfast £10–£15, à la carte £35. 1-night bookings refused at weekends, Christmas, New Year.

STURMINSTER NEWTON Dorset

Map 2:E1

PLUMBER MANOR

Richard and Brian Prideaux-Brune, with
Richard's wife, Alison, run their Jacobean
ancestral home as a characterful – some say
eccentric – hotel where guests are 'cosseted and
cared for' by 'charming staff'. In a 'timeless
setting' of log fires, gilt-framed portraits and
antique sofas, the hosts, and their Labradors,
extend a warm welcome. Some guests find the
large old house showing its age ('like the rest
of us'), but fans come for the good humour,
the hearty food, the sense of 'true escape' – the
authentic country house experience. Bedrooms
are comfortable, if dated, with liberal use of
floral fabrics, and 'lovely views' of the 'well-
cared-for gardens' and surrounding countryside.
Each is provided with home-made shortbread
and (the height of modernity!) 'colour
television'. Ten, in a converted stone barn, have
views of the river and topiary courtyard. All
is 'wonderfully quiet'. Front-of-house man
Richard Prideaux-Brune mixes a mean Bloody
Mary; his brother, Brian, cooks 'excellent
dinners' ('though we would have liked more
variety') and Sunday lunches – perhaps roast
pork, apricot, rosemary jus; halibut gratinée
with chorizo. (H and FN, and others)

Sturminster Newton
DT10 2AF

T: 01258 472507
F: 01258 473370
E: book@plumbermanor.com
W: www.plumbermanor.com

BEDROOMS: 16. 10 on ground floor in
courtyard, 2 suitable for disabled.
OPEN: all year except Feb.
FACILITIES: snug, bar, dining room,
gallery, free Wi-Fi, in-room TV
(Freeview), 1-acre grounds (garden,
tennis, croquet, stream).
BACKGROUND MUSIC: none.
LOCATION: 2½ miles SW of
Sturminster Newton.
CHILDREN: all ages welcomed.
DOGS: allowed in 4 bedrooms, not in
public rooms.
CREDIT CARDS: all major cards.
PRICES: [2017] per room B&B
£160–£240. Set dinner £30–£38.

SWAFFHAM Norfolk

Map 2:B5

STRATTONS

Down 'a blink-and-you'll-miss-it lane' in the middle of town, Les and Vanessa Scott's bohemian, family-friendly hotel is 'an enjoyable place' for guests in search of 'a comfortable bedroom and excellent food'. 'Up the stone steps of the Palladian-style house, we were greeted by two preening cats. In the sitting area: a wonderfully mad Tim Burton-esque chandelier; arresting, eclectic pieces of art,' trusted readers said in 2017. Hannah and Dominic Hughes, the Scotts' daughter and her husband, manage 'cordial, welcoming' staff. Bedrooms in the main house and converted outbuildings have 'quirky, imaginative' features, such as a Moroccan-style tented ceiling or a mermaid mosaic. 'Our ground-floor suite had an attractive bedroom and lounge, but the bathroom had a deep bathtub ill advised for people of our age.' In the award-winning basement restaurant, Jules Hetherton's modern British dinners celebrate local, foraged fare, perhaps pork and rabbit pithivier, parsnip purée, crispy kale. For midday sustenance, pop in to 'tiny, bustling' CoCoes deli, for 'rightly famous fishcakes with an exceptional fennel slaw'. (MAS, and others)

4 Ash Close
Swaffham
PE37 7NH

T: 01760 723845
E: enquiries@strattonshotel.com
W: www.strattonshotel.com

BEDROOMS: 14. 6 in annexes, 1 on ground floor.
OPEN: all year except 1 week at Christmas.
FACILITIES: drawing room, reading room, restaurant, free Wi-Fi, in-room TV (Freeview), terrace, café/deli, 1-acre garden, unsuitable for disabled.
BACKGROUND MUSIC: all day in public areas.
LOCATION: central, parking.
CHILDREN: all ages welcomed.
DOGS: allowed in some bedrooms (£10 per day), lounges, not in restaurant.
CREDIT CARDS: Amex, MasterCard, Visa.
PRICES: [2017] per room B&B from £99, D,B&B from £159. À la carte £30. 1-night bookings refused weekends, 3-night min. bank holidays.

SWALLOWCLIFFE Wiltshire

Map 2:D1

THE ROYAL OAK

❦ Previous César winner

A Sleeping Beauty in a wooded valley, this thatch-roofed inn had lain dormant for years when, in 2015, it was given the kiss of life by a village consortium. Today 'charming, warm' and 'completely, magnificently refurbished', it is 'easily the most elegant and comfortable pub we've visited in many years of travel', one visitor wrote. Guests consistently single out Wiltshire designer Matthew Burt for the 'attractive, highly original custom furnishings' – 'they add the wow factor'. Find a spot to sit in the 'succession of superbly lit drinking and dining areas' – 'everything has been decorated with flair', down to the 'arrangements of twigs, flowers and plants'. Danny Durose is the new chef, whose 'interesting menu' of superior pub dishes (chorizo, orecchiette and raw courgette salad; venison casserole) relies on produce from local farmers and suppliers. The pub's cool, contemporary look continues in the bedrooms, where plenty of tea, proper coffee and fluffy towels are supplied. 'Everything was immaculate in our large room; the state-of-the-art shower was highly effective.' Breakfast is 'copious'. (Josie Mayers, and others)

Swallowcliffe
SP3 5PA

T: 01747 870211
E: hello@royaloakswallowcliffe.com
W: www.royaloakswallowcliffe.com

BEDROOMS: 6. 1 suitable for disabled.
OPEN: all year.
FACILITIES: lift, bar, dining room, Oak Room, free Wi-Fi, in-room TV (Freeview), garden with outdoor seating.
BACKGROUND MUSIC: none.
LOCATION: 2 miles SE of Tisbury.
CHILDREN: all ages welcomed.
DOGS: 'friendly, well-behaved' dogs allowed in 1 room, public rooms (treats, towels provided).
CREDIT CARDS: Amex, MasterCard, Visa.
PRICES: [2017] per room B&B £100–£150. À la carte £29.

SWINBROOK Oxfordshire

Map 3:D6

THE SWAN INN

In 'splendid Cotswold countryside', this 'informal inn' by the sprightly River Windrush charms guests with its 'heavenly setting'. Wisteria blooms hang over the doorway of the old pub in springtime; there's space inside and out to soak in the rustic atmosphere. Decorated in modern country-cottage style, bedrooms are in converted stables by the orchard and a riverside cottage across the way. 'Our cottage room had plenty of storage space, two upholstered chairs and a large, comfortable bed that was a treat to sleep in. A creaky barn door led to the well-laid-out bathroom. The cleaners do a good job, but we thought some redecoration wouldn't go amiss.' Amid folksy touches and black-and-white photographs of the Mitford clan (the late Dowager Duchess of Devonshire spent her childhood in the village), tuck in to 'sophisticated' dishes such as roast Cotswold lamb, wild garlic and Parmesan croquette. On a summer evening, sit in the 'lovely garden' (its chickens freely ranging) from dusk till the fairy lights come on in the trees. Landlords Archie and Nicola Orr-Ewing also own The King's Head Inn, Bledington (see entry). (Richard Osborne, and others)

25% DISCOUNT VOUCHERS

Swinbrook
OX18 4DY

T: 01993 823339
E: info@theswanswinbrook.co.uk
W: www.theswanswinbrook.co.uk

BEDROOMS: 11. 7 on ground floor, 5 in riverside cottage.
OPEN: all year except Christmas/ New Year.
FACILITIES: bar, restaurant, free Wi-Fi, in-room TV (Freeview), garden, orchard, unsuitable for disabled.
BACKGROUND MUSIC: in bar and restaurant.
LOCATION: 2 miles E of Burford.
CHILDREN: all ages welcomed.
DOGS: not allowed.
CREDIT CARDS: Diners, MasterCard, Visa.
PRICES: [2017] per room B&B from £125, D,B&B from £185. À la carte £30. 1-night bookings sometimes refused.

TALLAND-BY-LOOE Cornwall

Map 1:D3

TALLAND BAY HOTEL

A spirit of fun flits about Teresa and Kevin O'Sullivan's cliff-top hotel, from the sub-tropical sculpture garden full of surprises ('you feel like Alice walking into Wonderland') to the 'delightfully humorous artwork scattered throughout'. The atmosphere is welcoming; the staff are 'smiley and friendly from start to finish'. Pick a spot to relax in – there are panelled lounging areas and 'lots of space outside to sit and admire the view'. Not all the bedrooms face the sea, but each has its own charm – perhaps a four-poster bed, a terrace or an original fireplace – and ornaments (model boats, toy pandas) to raise a smile. On cool days, a log fire burns in the bright, seaward restaurant; all year round, chef Nick Hawke's 'wonderful' modern menus have 'lots of fish'. A typical dish: Looe turbot, brown shrimp, tarragon gnocchi, girolles. The brasserie serves simpler fare (burgers, fish and chips, Fowey River mussels in white wine and cream). 'Generous portions' of 'everything you could possibly expect' are served at breakfast. Bring Rover – a nightly charge includes a blanket, bowl and doggie treat. The South West Coastal Path skirts the bottom of the hill.

Porthallow
Talland-by-Looe
PL13 2JB

T: 01503 272667
F: 01503 272940
E: info@tallandbayhotel.co.uk
W: www.tallandbayhotel.co.uk

BEDROOMS: 23. 4 in cottages, 6 on ground floor.
OPEN: all year.
FACILITIES: lounge, bar, restaurant, brasserie, free Wi-Fi, in-room TV (Freeview), civil wedding licence, terrace, outside seating, 2-acre garden.
BACKGROUND MUSIC: in bar and restaurant.
LOCATION: 2½ miles SW of Looe.
CHILDREN: all ages welcomed.
DOGS: allowed in bedrooms and brasserie, not in restaurant.
CREDIT CARDS: all major cards.
PRICES: [2017] per room B&B £140–£330, D,B&B £215–£405. Set menus £38–£46, à la carte (brasserie) £32. 1-night bookings refused weekends in peak season.

TAPLOW Berkshire

Map 2:D3

CLIVEDEN HOUSE

For 'exceptional service', a scandalous history, and rich views of the Thames, you'd be hard pressed to better this extensively restored Italianate mansion. The 'beautiful grounds', 'stunning bedrooms', 'exquisite cuisine' and 'attentive, personable staff' win praise from guests, who consider the experience 'worth every penny'. The many bedrooms – 'some opulent, some austere, all different' – have been 'stunningly refurbished' in a pleasing mix of modern and classic styles. Even some of the smallest have a private terrace with a hot tub and courtyard views. 'Our suite was eccentric and fabulous at the same time, with a lovely, old-fashioned bathroom.' Gather in the informal Astor Grill for classic American and British dishes, or nab a table by a window in the 'flawless' restaurant to gaze over the 19th-century parterre while dining on chef André Garrett's 'excellent' modern meals. On a fine day, the river beckons: hire one of the hotel's vintage launches for a champagne cruise or picnic lunch on the water. Under the same private ownership as Chewton Glen, New Milton (see entry).

Bourne End Road
Taplow
SL6 0JF

T: 01628 668561
F: 01628 661837
E: reservations@clivedenhouse.co.uk
W: www.clivedenhouse.co.uk

BEDROOMS: 48. Some on ground floor, plus 3-bed cottage in grounds.
OPEN: all year.
FACILITIES: Great Hall, library, 2 restaurants, private dining rooms, free Wi-Fi, in-room TV (Freeview), civil wedding licence, spa, swimming pools, terrace, tennis, 376-acre National Trust gardens.
BACKGROUND MUSIC: all day in public spaces.
LOCATION: 20 mins from Heathrow, 40 mins Central London.
CHILDREN: all ages welcomed.
DOGS: not allowed in restaurants, spa or parts of garden.
CREDIT CARDS: all major cards.
PRICES: [2017] per room B&B £495–£2,175, D,B&B £615–£2,295. Tasting menu £97.50, à la carte £72.50. 1-night bookings occasionally refused.

TAVISTOCK Devon

THE HORN OF PLENTY

'The amiable staff at this charming country hotel make you feel like a guest in a good friend's house.' Praise this year from contented visitors, after a return trip to Julie Leivers and Damien Pease's 'splendid' 19th-century stone manor, where the views over the wooded Tamar valley are 'spectacular'. The well-tended gardens are just the spot for an alfresco drink in good weather; when cool winds blow in, a fire is lit in the lounge. Most bedrooms are in the converted coach house, a minute's walk from the main building. Some rooms tend to the traditional, while others are more contemporary, but 'all are well equipped, stylish and very comfortable'. 'Ours was faultless, with French windows looking over the valley.' In the restaurant, new chef Ashley Wright's modern dishes – 'perfectly cooked scallops; best-ever venison' – are 'a delight'. Mealtimes feed the spirit, too: 'The vista from the dining room enhances the good food experience.' Fill up on a 'good-quality breakfast' of local produce before striking out for the day. 'There are plenty of opportunities for walking and sightseeing'; Cotehele and the Garden House are easily reached. (Mr and Mrs R Bradley, Peter Anderson)

Gulworthy
Tavistock
PL19 8JD

T: 01822 832528
F: 01822 834390
E: enquiries@thehornofplenty.
co.uk
W: www.thehornofplenty.co.uk

BEDROOMS: 16. 12 in coach house (20 yds), 7 on ground floor, 1 suitable for disabled.
OPEN: all year.
FACILITIES: lounge/bar, library, drawing room, restaurant, free Wi-Fi, in-room TV (Freeview), civil wedding licence, 5-acre grounds.
BACKGROUND MUSIC: in restaurant and lounge/bar 'when it's quiet'.
LOCATION: 3 miles SW of Tavistock.
CHILDREN: all ages welcomed.
DOGS: allowed in some rooms and library, not in restaurant or drawing room.
CREDIT CARDS: MasterCard, Visa.
PRICES: [2017] per room B&B from £120, D,B&B from £200. Set dinner £49.50, tasting menu £65.

SEE ALSO SHORTLIST

TEFFONT EVIAS Wiltshire

Map 2:D1

HOWARD'S HOUSE

Previous César winner

'Comfort and homeliness' draw guests to this 17th-century mellow-stone house in a tranquil, 'totally unspoilt' village in the valley of the River Nadder. The staff are 'warmly welcoming', the service is 'excellent without being overdone', Guide readers say. Freshly cut garden blooms brighten the public spaces; in cool weather, an open fire burns in the lounge – just right for mid-afternoon tea and toast (dominoes are optional). Pleasing country-style bedrooms overlook garden, courtyard or countryside. An attic room is charming with its sloping ceiling, but guests looking for more space should book a large second-floor room, done up with a sofa and two armchairs. Gourmands, come hungry: 'The food is a great attraction.' Besides sampling the daily-changing menus of locally sourced, seasonal produce (perhaps including Creedy Carver duck breast, butternut squash purée, kale, spiced duck jus), sign up for a foraging walk and workshop led by chef and co-owner Nick Wentworth. Before heading out on a day of country walks, ask for a picnic hamper or 'hiker's knapsack' of salads, charcuterie, cheeses, fruit, cakes and home-baked bread.

25% DISCOUNT VOUCHERS

Teffont Evias
SP3 5RJ

T: 01722 716392
E: enq@howardshousehotel.co.uk
W: www.howardshousehotel.co.uk

BEDROOMS: 9.
OPEN: all year except 23–27 Dec.
FACILITIES: lounge, snug, restaurant, function facilities in coach house, free Wi-Fi, in-room TV, 2-acre grounds (garden terrace, croquet), river, fishing nearby, only restaurant suitable for disabled.
BACKGROUND MUSIC: in dining room.
LOCATION: 10 miles W of Salisbury.
CHILDREN: all ages welcomed.
DOGS: allowed (£15 charge) in bedrooms, not in public rooms.
CREDIT CARDS: Amex, MasterCard, Visa.
PRICES: [2017] per room B&B single £120, double from £190. Tasting menu £65, à la carte £45.

TEMPLE SOWERBY Cumbria

Map 4: inset C3

TEMPLE SOWERBY HOUSE

In a Knights Templar village in the Eden valley, Julie and Paul Evans's personable small hotel 'goes from strength to strength', reports a Guide reader in 2017. 'The owners are warm and enthusiastic, and every member of staff is genuinely interested, friendly and helpful.' Traditionally styled bedrooms in the Georgian mansion and converted coach house 'may not all be large, but they're comfortable, and guests who prefer good, old-fashioned sheets and blankets have only to ask'. 'Our very nice room was big, with a dressing area and a roomy bathroom with a spa bath and separate shower. It was quiet, despite facing the road.' There's 'plenty of room' in the bar and lounges for 'tempting canapés'. In the conservatory restaurant ('overlooking the garden and its engaging ducks'), new chef Jack Bradley's seasonal modern menus are 'a real treat'. Among the 'interesting, excellent' dishes: pork loin and cheek, rye salt-baked carrot, foraged salsa verde, freekeh. 'One gets to the end of the meal feeling thoroughly satisfied and at peace with the world.' The countryside calls: walkers, bring your boots; anglers, your rods. (Simon Tonking, Peter Anderson, A and EW)

25% DISCOUNT VOUCHERS

Temple Sowerby
CA10 1RZ

T: 017683 61578
F: 017683 61958
E: stay@templesowerby.com
W: www.templesowerby.com

BEDROOMS: 12. 2 on ground floor, 4 in coach house (20 yds).
OPEN: all year except Christmas.
FACILITIES: 2 lounges, bar, restaurant, conference/function facilities, free Wi-Fi, in-room TV (Freeview), civil wedding licence, 1½-acre garden (croquet); unsuitable for disabled.
BACKGROUND MUSIC: 'carefully chosen' music in restaurant in the evening.
LOCATION: village centre.
CHILDREN: not under 12.
DOGS: allowed in Coach House rooms (not unattended), not in public rooms or gardens.
CREDIT CARDS: MasterCard, Visa.
PRICES: [2017] per room B&B single £110–£120, double £150–£170, D,B&B single £150–£165, double £220–£250. Set dinner £35–£45. 1-night bookings occasionally refused.

TETBURY Gloucestershire

Map 3:E5

CALCOT MANOR

'You can hear the sounds of birds all around' this converted 14th-century farmhouse. It stands in 'lovely, manicured grounds' looking out over Gloucestershire hills. 'Light, bright and informal, classy without being posh, this is a cheerful, family-friendly spot with commendable, happy-making facilities and an easy atmosphere,' say Guide inspectors in 2017, dipping their hand into the 'huge jar of sweets' at reception. Modern rustic bedrooms are 'beautifully furnished, with plenty of lovely touches – a jug of water by the bed; good teas; excellent, bendy night lights'. (Choose wisely – an otherwise comfortable room overlooking the car park wasn't completely pleasing.) 'The super-comfy parental bed in our family suite afforded a brilliant night's sleep, but younger children might have better luck than my 14-year-old – his feet hung off the end of his bed.' At mealtimes, young and old are well catered for in the conservatory restaurant, where the goose-fat chips are 'a must'. There are 'peaceful lounges' and 'newspapers galore', but tuck in to a 'very good breakfast' then head out to explore – perhaps borrowing a bicycle for a countryside ride.

Tetbury
GL8 8YJ

T: 01666 890391
E: receptionists@calcot.co
W: www.calcot.co

BEDROOMS: 35. 10 (for families) in cottage, 13 around courtyard, on ground floor, some suitable for disabled.
OPEN: all year.
FACILITIES: lounge, 2 bars, 2 restaurants, crèche, free Wi-Fi, in-room TV (Sky, Freeview), civil wedding licence, 220-acre grounds (tennis, heated outdoor 8-metre swimming pool, play area, spa with 16-metre swimming pool).
BACKGROUND MUSIC: in restaurants.
LOCATION: 3 miles W of Tetbury.
CHILDREN: all ages welcomed.
DOGS: allowed in courtyard bedrooms, not in public rooms.
CREDIT CARDS: Amex, MasterCard, Visa.
PRICES: [2017] per room B&B from £209, D,B&B from £289. À la carte £40. 1-night bookings refused weekends.

SEE ALSO SHORTLIST

TISBURY Wiltshire

Map 2:D1

THE BECKFORD ARMS

Dan Brod and Charlie Luxton's 'attractive old stone-built pub' on the edge of the Fonthill Estate has an 'airy, modern vibe' amid traditional elements. A log fire burns in the 'cosy, beamed bar'; there are 'comfy sofas' in the 'pretty, wood-floored sitting room'. French doors in the restaurant open to a 'charming terrace' and the pub garden – this is where locals come for the inspired-by-the-seasons menu of 'interesting, beautifully presented' food. Typical dishes: goat's curd gnocchi, smoked beetroot purée, pickled walnuts; pork Tomahawk steak, celeriac, Puy lentils, crispy kale. (On Fridays and Saturdays, come for the wood-fired pizzas, and meats off the charcoal barbecue.) Above the pub, and in two lodges 15 minutes' stroll away, 'elegantly decorated bedrooms' are supplied with a 'large, comfortable bed' made up with 'lovely, fresh linens', and 'superior toiletries' in the bathroom. 'Full marks for the fresh coffee and cafetière!' Some rooms are small, others 'spacious and light' – choose wisely. Stonehenge and stately homes are within easy reach; an estate walk leads to a ridge with 'magnificent views'. The owners' Talbot Inn is in Mells (see entry). (RG, S and JJ)

Fonthill Gifford
Tisbury
SP3 6PX

T: 01747 870385
E: info@beckfordarms.com
W: www.beckfordarms.com

BEDROOMS: 10. 2 in lodges on Fonthill Estate.
OPEN: all year except 25 Dec.
FACILITIES: sitting room (sometimes Sunday classic-movie nights), bar, restaurant, private dining room, free Wi-Fi, in-room TV (Freeview), function facilities, 1-acre garden.
BACKGROUND MUSIC: in public areas all day.
LOCATION: in village, 1 mile N of Tisbury.
CHILDREN: all ages welcomed.
DOGS: allowed in 1 bedroom, public areas.
CREDIT CARDS: MasterCard, Visa.
PRICES: [2017] per room B&B £95–£130. À la carte £30–£35. 1-night bookings sometimes refused.

SEE ALSO SHORTLIST

TITCHWELL Norfolk

Map 2:A5

BRIARFIELDS

Birdwatchers are in their element at this low-key, dog- and family-friendly hotel occupying a series of brick-and-stone farm buildings close to the RSPB Titchwell Marsh nature reserve. The landscape is pure north Norfolk – salt marshes under wide skies; a distant view of the sea at Brancaster Bay. Contemporary bedrooms are around a courtyard set back from the A road. They range in size; there are three family suites. Careful selection is advised: some guests this year liked their 'massive, beautifully furnished room'; others found their small double room 'basic, and in need of updating'. Take tea by the open fire in the beamed snug or on the decked terrace in sunshine. On a warm afternoon, sit by the fishpond in the peaceful suntrap courtyard. At lunch and dinner, crowd-pleasing menus include tapas and Indian snacks alongside more classic British dishes cooked with local seafood and meat from nearby farms. Typical offerings: pan-fried sea bass fillet, Norfolk Peer potatoes, Titchwell samphire; 17-hour sous-vide pork belly, roasted cauliflower. Pull on your wellies in the morning: marsh paths lead to the beach.

Main Road
Titchwell
PE31 8BB

T: 01485 210742
F: 01485 210933
E: info@briarfieldshotelnorfolk.
   co.uk
W: www.briarfieldshotelnorfolk.
   co.uk

BEDROOMS: 23. 20 around the courtyard, 1 suitable for disabled.
OPEN: all year.
FACILITIES: bar, dining room, snug, TV lounge (Sky), free Wi-Fi in public areas, in-room TV, meeting and wedding facilities, 5-acre garden (play area).
BACKGROUND MUSIC: all day in bar and restaurant.
LOCATION: off A149 between Burnham Market and Hunstanton.
CHILDREN: all ages welcomed.
DOGS: allowed in some bedrooms, bar.
CREDIT CARDS: MasterCard, Visa.
PRICES: per room B&B single £80–£125, double £115–£180, D,B&B single £105–£150, double £160–£230. À la carte £30.

TITCHWELL Norfolk

TITCHWELL MANOR

A 'cheering spot' with 'affable staff', Margaret
and Ian Snaith's Victorian farmhouse-turned-
jaunty hotel stands before a vista of 'green
fields and warm, golden marshes', within
easy reach of the sandy beach at Brancaster.
Enter the 'cosy, mood-lifting' foyer lounge
(mermaid-print wallpaper, a log fire, 'a
comically long chesterfield sofa', hand-drawn
maps for walkers); beyond are a smart bar, a
well-regarded conservatory restaurant, comfy
bedrooms and a small garden filled with
birdsong in the morning. 'The heroic selection
of breakfast granolas are a sterling addition, too,'
Guide inspectors in 2017 point out. Bedrooms
range from restrained to richly coloured. 'We
thought our room, in the handsome herb-garden
annexe, rather plain, but it was comfortable,
nicely warm and utterly quiet.' At dinner, Eric
Snaith, the owners' son, and Chris Mann cook
modern dishes with some surprises. 'We loved
an intriguing soup of mushrooms raw, pickled
and fermented; well-cooked plaice came with
shavings of raw cauliflower and never-before-
seen powdered butter.' (A simpler menu has
more straightforward options – Brancaster
oysters; fish pie.) 'Great twitching nearby.'

Titchwell
PE31 8BB

T: 01485 210221
E: info@titchwellmanor.com
W: www.titchwellmanor.com

BEDROOMS: 27. 12 in herb garden,
4 in converted farm building, 1
in Potting Shed, 2 suitable for
disabled.
OPEN: all year.
FACILITIES: lounge, bar, conservatory
restaurant, free Wi-Fi, in-room TV
(Freeview), civil wedding licence,
in-room treatments, ¼-acre walled
garden.
BACKGROUND MUSIC: in public rooms.
LOCATION: off A149 between
Burnham Market and Hunstanton.
CHILDREN: all ages welcomed.
DOGS: allowed in some rooms, public
rooms.
CREDIT CARDS: Amex, MasterCard,
Visa.
PRICES: [2017] per room B&B
£125–£235. Set menus £32–£38,
à la carte £30. 2-night min. stay
at weekends.

TITLEY Herefordshire

Map 3:C4

THE STAGG INN

♥ Previous César winner

'A warm welcome and excellent food' add up to a 'thoroughly enjoyable' stay at Nicola and Steve Reynolds's pub-with rooms, say Guide readers this year. The 'lovely old inn', hops hanging from its beamed ceiling, is a relaxed, unpretentious outfit, with 'friendly, professional' staff. There are real ales and local gins, and characterful 'nooks and crannies' in which to drink them. (Watch out for 'unexpected steps to trap the unwary'.) Steve Reynolds cooks 'a wonderful dinner', perhaps of artichoke soup ('the best I've tasted') or scallops with 'the tastiest pickled cauliflower'; but 'leave room for pudding!' Afterward, bed down in a quiet room at the back of the inn, or in the antique-packed Georgian vicarage down the country road (the hosts offer to drive the distance). 'Our spacious, well-appointed bedroom in the Old Vicarage had a large, very comfortable bed, and super toiletries in the bathroom. A minor grouse: poor bedside lighting. But we felt so well looked after, we didn't mind.' In the morning, scoop generous spoons of home-made marmalade at 'one of the best breakfasts ever'. (Kate MacMaster, RMP, MH)

25% DISCOUNT VOUCHERS

Titley
HR5 3RL

T: 01544 230221
E: reservations@thestagg.co.uk
W: www.thestagg.co.uk

BEDROOMS: 6. 3 at Old Vicarage (300 yds).
OPEN: all year except 24–26 Dec, 1 Jan, 1 week in Jan/Feb, first 2 weeks Nov, restaurant closed Mon, Tues.
FACILITIES: sitting room (Old Vicarage), bar, dining room, small outside seating area (pub), free Wi-Fi, in-room TV (Freeview), 1½-acre garden (Old Vicarage), unsuitable for disabled.
BACKGROUND MUSIC: none.
LOCATION: on B4355 between Kington and Presteigne.
CHILDREN: all ages welcomed.
DOGS: allowed in pub, some pub bedrooms.
CREDIT CARDS: Amex, MasterCard, Visa.
PRICES: [2017] per room B&B £70–£140. À la carte £35. 1-night bookings occasionally refused at bank holiday weekends.

TRUSHAM Devon

Map 1:D4

THE CRIDFORD INN   NEW

'Such a relaxed, friendly place', Sue Burdge's thatch-roofed pub-with-rooms, in an 'attractive village', is believed to be the oldest inn in the county, with a medieval mural and mullioned window to show for it. Guests today may find more interest, however, in the 'excellent selection of tempting gins' lined up in the bar. Come down single-track lanes to find the characterful Devon longhouse, its whitewashed cob walls, ancient beams and inglenook fireplaces. 'All our family were warmly welcomed. We can't praise the staff highly enough,' a Guide reader said in 2017. Bedrooms may not be the latest in style, but they're 'warm, comfortable and spotlessly clean'. Two cottages with a lounge and a kitchen are ideal for a family. One evening, sample Bill Keera's 'delicious meals', perhaps crispy pressed pork belly, black pudding mash, honey-roasted apple, cider sauce; another, dine at sister establishment The Nobody Inn, Doddiscombsleigh (see entry), an easy drive away. Despite the inn's proximity to Exeter, all is country quiet here; Dartmoor national park is across the River Teign. 'We awoke to birdsong and the calling of sheep and lambs.' (Elizabeth Thomas)

Trusham
TQ13 0NR

T: 01626 853694
E: reservations@thecridfordinn.co.uk
W: www.thecridfordinn.co.uk

BEDROOMS: 8. 4 in two 2-bed cottages.
OPEN: all year.
FACILITIES: bar, 2 dining areas, free Wi-Fi, in-room TV (Freeview), terrace, unsuitable for disabled.
BACKGROUND MUSIC: 'very light' in bar.
LOCATION: 12 miles SW of Exeter.
CHILDREN: not under 8.
DOGS: allowed in 1 bedroom, public rooms.
CREDIT CARDS: MasterCard, Visa.
PRICES: [2017] per room B&B £99–£105. À la carte £29.

TUDDENHAM Suffolk

Map 2:B5

TUDDENHAM MILL

'A graceful spot in Suffolk countryside, this modern make-over of a 243-year-old mill surprises with its boutiquey bedrooms and ambitious dinners,' say Guide inspectors in 2017. The beamed dining room is in the main mill building, whose 19th-century chimney cuts 'a striking silhouette'. After 'lots of complimentary nibbles', what follows, in 'countryside portions', might be 'an inspired combination of seaweed pommes Anna, roasted sprout heart, clapshot bridie and a painterly tangle of sea cabbage'; 'lamb rump cooked beautifully pink'. Dietary requirements are handled with 'generosity and graciousness'. Among the stylish bedrooms, five new 'nooks' have sprouted up in the meadow. 'Our large, well-thought-out room, in a good-looking clapboard building, was impressive, down to the pulpy, freshly squeezed orange juice in the mini-fridge. (We would have liked an option of twin beds, however.) Through glass terrace doors, the view towards the mill stream beyond the trees was simply dreamy.' Ask for a window seat in the morning, for breakfast (perhaps 'a picture-perfect plate of French toast' or a bowl of 'well-balanced' Bircher muesli) overlooking the resident swans on the water.

25% DISCOUNT VOUCHERS

High Street
Tuddenham
IP28 6SQ

T: 01638 713552
E: info@tuddenhammill.co.uk
W: www.tuddenhammill.co.uk

BEDROOMS: 20. 12 in 2 separate buildings, 8 on ground floor, 5 in 'nooks' in meadow, 1 suitable for disabled.
OPEN: all year.
FACILITIES: bar, restaurant, function rooms, free Wi-Fi, in-room TV (Freeview), civil wedding licence, 12-acre meadow.
BACKGROUND MUSIC: in bar and restaurant.
LOCATION: in village, 8 miles NE of Newmarket.
CHILDREN: all ages welcomed.
DOGS: welcomed in some bedrooms (£15 a night).
CREDIT CARDS: Amex, MasterCard, Visa.
PRICES: [2017] per room B&B £185–£345, D,B&B £235–£395. À la carte £39, early dining (Sun–Fri 6.30–7.30 pm) £19.50, tasting menu £55. 2-night min. stay at weekends.

TWO BRIDGES Devon

Map 1:D4

PRINCE HALL

'We will return,' vowed regular Guide correspondents after a stay at Chris Daly's 18th-century manor at the heart of Dartmoor – and so they have, to find it, in 2017, as 'friendly and laid-back' as ever. Nuthatches, starlings and skylarks may be seen in the large grounds. Inside the house, log fires burn in the lounges. 'Sitting in the dining room is an enjoyable experience: Chris's huge photographs of Dartmoor ponies and laughing Tamworth pigs, along with hand-thrown pottery plates on the distressed painted tables, add to the aura of the place.' A monthly-changing menu lists 'everything from snacks to the full Monty', including, perhaps, 'particularly enjoyable rabbit terrine; squash and Cornish Yarg tart; Barnsley chop with seasonal veg'. Individually decorated bedrooms, each named after a local tor, are supplied with home-baked biscuits. 'Our first-floor room was large, with two armchairs, plenty of storage space, a modern bathroom, and a pleasant view across the moor – very Hound of the Baskervilles, when the thick mist swirled about.' 'Plenty of high-quality options' at breakfast, including home-baked bread. (GC)

Two Bridges
PL20 6SA

T: 01822 890403
E: info@princehall.co.uk
W: www.princehall.co.uk

BEDROOMS: 9. Plus Shepherd's Hut in grounds.
OPEN: all year.
FACILITIES: lobby, bar, lounge, dining room, free Wi-Fi in bar/lounge, in-room TV (Freeview), terrace, 5-acre grounds, only ground floor suitable for disabled.
BACKGROUND MUSIC: none.
LOCATION: 3 miles E of Princetown.
CHILDREN: all ages welcomed.
DOGS: 'very much' allowed (treats; facilities for food storage and dog washing; pet-friendly garden and grounds), not in restaurant.
CREDIT CARDS: MasterCard, Visa.
PRICES: [2017] per room B&B single (with open en suite) £100, double £160–£190. À la carte £35.

ULLSWATER Cumbria

Map 4: inset C2

HOWTOWN HOTEL

For more than a century, the Baldry family's ancient farmhouse has stood in this remote, 'very special setting', where the 'fantastic views' reach over the garden and the sheep-dotted fields to the fells beyond. For more than a century, too, the family has greeted guests with 'a welcoming fire in one of the lounges, and an even more welcoming pot of tea'. 'Unashamedly old-fashioned', it is not to all tastes – some visitors rue the inflexible mealtimes and 'historic bedrooms' – but loyal supporters champion the traditional atmosphere and the nostalgia that infuses it all. 'Thoroughly cosseting, it's like staying at one's granny's house as a child,' a Guide inspector says. 'It certainly is a time warp, from the fringed lampshades and collection of glass bowls to the selection of dishes at dinner. But there's not a trace of dowdiness – everything is displayed and done with care and pride.' Morning tea is brought to the bedroom before the gong announcing the buffet breakfast; in the evening, a gong again heralds the single dinner sitting ('the food is acceptable but the service is slow'). In between, there are rural walks, steamer cruises and good, old-fashioned chats over a fireside scone or two.

Ullswater
CA10 2ND

T: 01768 486514
W: www.howtown-hotel.com

BEDROOMS: 15. 4 in annexe, plus 4 self-catering cottages.
OPEN: Mar–early Nov.
FACILITIES: 3 lounges, TV room, 2 bars, dining room, tea room, Wi-Fi in cottages only, 2-acre grounds, 200 yds from lake (private foreshore, fishing), walking, sailing, climbing, riding, golf nearby, unsuitable for disabled.
BACKGROUND MUSIC: occasionally in lounge.
LOCATION: 4 miles S of Pooley Bridge, bus from Penrith station 9 miles.
CHILDREN: all ages welcomed (no special facilities).
DOGS: allowed in some bedrooms (£4 per night charge), not in public rooms.
CREDIT CARDS: none.
PRICES: [2017] per person D,B&B £104. 1-night bookings sometimes refused.

UPPER SLAUGHTER Gloucestershire   Map 3:D6

LORDS OF THE MANOR

❦ Previous César winner

'Croquet on the lawn is a must' at this honey-stone former rectory surrounded by 'beautiful, magical' gardens – but that's not all of it. There are 'scrumptious' cakes to be had at a fireside tea, and drinks and 'excellent canapés' in the panelled bar; in the 'elegant' Michelin-starred restaurant, Charles Smith, the new chef, cooks 'accomplished' modern dishes using the best locally sourced produce (his go-to cheesemaker is just down the lane, for instance). Typical options on the seasonal menu: braised chicken wing, glazed veal sweetbread, pickled trompette mushroom; roasted loin of rabbit, watercress salsa, truffle potato croquette. Pick one of the individually decorated, country-style bedrooms to suit: some are thought 'fairly small', others, more spacious, are praised for their 'splendid views' over garden, village or surrounding hills. No matter the size, every bedroom is supplied with good toiletries and a decanter of organic cordial. In balmy weather, borrow a pair of wellies for a short walk into Lower Slaughter; the 'very pleasant' staff have recommendations aplenty for exploration further afield. (F and IW, and others)

Upper Slaughter
GL54 2JD

T: 01451 820243
F: 01451 820696
E: reservations@lordsofthemanor.com
W: www.lordsofthemanor.com

BEDROOMS: 26. 16 in converted granary and stables, 1 on ground floor.
OPEN: all year.
FACILITIES: drawing room, lounge bar, restaurant, library, games room, free Wi-Fi, in-room TV (Freeview), civil wedding licence, terrace, 8-acre grounds, unsuitable for disabled.
BACKGROUND MUSIC: none.
LOCATION: in village, 2 miles N of Bourton-on-the-Water.
CHILDREN: all ages welcomed, no under-15s in restaurant in evening (high teas/separate dining options).
DOGS: allowed in some bedrooms, not in restaurant.
CREDIT CARDS: Amex, MasterCard, Visa.
PRICES: [2017] per room B&B £150–£510, D,B&B £325–£640. Set menu £72.50, tasting menu £90.

UPPINGHAM Rutland

Map 2:B3

LAKE ISLE HOTEL & RESTAURANT

Arise and go now, and go to Uppingham, to find this 'delightful hotel in a delightful town', its poetic name recalling WB Yeats's yearning for the peace of Innisfree. Instead of the poet's clay-and-wattle cabin, Janine and Richard Burton's hotel and popular restaurant ('it has the locals piling in') occupies an 18th-century building on the High Street. Here, Stuart Mead's modern fusion cooking (perhaps molasses-cured rump of lamb, heritage carrots, whipped feta, couscous) may make poets of us all. 'We've never had a less-than-perfect meal here. And the puddings are to die for,' writes a Guide reader who has known the place for years. Plus, 'the food is some of the best at the price in the country'. Some bedrooms may be petite – guests wanting to spread out should book a cottage room with a sitting area – but 'they're plenty big enough, and right for the price'. 'Ours had a small bathroom; all was scrupulously clean.' In the morning, find 'proper choices and a proper feast' at breakfast. Drive now, and drive to Rutland Water, to hear lake water lapping by the shore. (KJ Salway, CLH, AD and J Lloyd)

16 High Street East
Uppingham
LE15 9PZ

T: 01572 822951
F: 01572 824400
E: info@lakeisle.co.uk
W: www.lakeisle.co.uk

BEDROOMS: 12. 2 in cottages.
OPEN: all year, restaurant closed Sun night, Mon lunch, bank holidays.
FACILITIES: bar, restaurant, free Wi-Fi, in-room TV (Freeview), small car park, unsuitable for disabled.
BACKGROUND MUSIC: in restaurant.
LOCATION: town centre.
CHILDREN: all ages welcomed.
DOGS: allowed in cottage rooms, not in public areas.
CREDIT CARDS: MasterCard, Visa.
PRICES: [2017] per room B&B single £70–£90, double £90–£120, D,B&B single £103–£123, double £156–£186. À la carte £35.

VENTNOR Isle of Wight

Map 2:E2

HILLSIDE

The mellow stone exterior and thatched roof belie the 'light-filled, airy', Scandinavian interiors of this Georgian villa high above Ventnor. Abstract paintings hang on white walls; Hans Wegner wishbone chairs sit on pale wooden floors. 'Everything carries conviction' – not least Gert Bach, the owner, who runs the place with 'friendly, helpful' staff. Most of the contemporary bedrooms, all with bold artwork and vintage Welsh blankets, have sea views. 'Ours was delightful, with fine linen on a comfortable bed. We were untroubled by what little traffic passed by on the road outside.' No coffee or tea is allowed in the bedroom ('what a shame'); instead, nurse a drink in one of the lounges – there's plenty of space to sit, read, relax. In the evening, choose between an 'excellent, if largely unchanging' set dinner in the dining room, and a 'slightly spicier' menu in sister restaurant The Bistro, in town. (Sure feet and strong legs are recommended for the hike back up the slope afterwards.) 'It's lovely to have fresh produce from the garden at breakfast' – worthy partners for the home-made conserves, yogurt and bread. (Lucy Rose, T and SM)

25% DISCOUNT VOUCHERS

151 Mitchell Avenue
Ventnor
PO38 1DR

T: 01983 852271
E: mail@hillsideventnor.co.uk
W: www.hillsideventnor.co.uk

BEDROOMS: 12. Plus self-catering apartment.
OPEN: all year, restaurant closed Sun dinner.
FACILITIES: restaurant, 2 lounges, conservatory, free Wi-Fi, in-room TV, terrace, 5-acre garden (vegetable garden, beehives), unsuitable for disabled.
BACKGROUND MUSIC: in restaurant in evening.
LOCATION: above village centre.
CHILDREN: not under 12.
DOGS: not allowed.
CREDIT CARDS: MasterCard, Visa.
PRICES: [2017] per person B&B £73–£93, D,B&B £97–£117. À la carte £28. Min. 2-night bookings preferred.

VENTNOR Isle of Wight

Map 2:E2

THE ROYAL HOTEL   **NEW**

'Splendid afternoon teas' are part of the 'olde-worlde charm' at this 'absolutely wonderful hotel' overlooking the esplanade and the English Channel. It is owned by William Bailey, a son of Isle of Wight hoteliers. A grande dame of traditional seaside hotels, in a 'perfect location for exploring the island', it earns a full entry this year thanks to regular Guide readers who praise its 'high standards', 'kind, efficient staff' and 'scrumptious orange soufflé'. Outside are a geranium-festooned veranda and sea-view picnic spots in an expanse of sub-tropical gardens; in the smart brasserie, 'beautiful conservatory' and chandelier-hung dining room, chef Steven Harris's cooking is 'superb in every way'. 'Of note: delicious Isle of Wight Gallybagger cheese soufflé; excellent Ventnor Bay crab; sirloin steak with plenty of good veg; a fruity meringue dessert.' The classy bedrooms – some within sound of the sea – are elegant without being old-fashioned; the best, and most spacious, have garden views and extra seating space. Cliff-top walks are minutes away; lunches on a skippered boat may be arranged. 'Steephill Cove, near the botanic garden, is not to be missed.' (Mary Woods, Mary Coles)

Belgrave Road
Ventnor
PO38 1JJ

T: 01983 852186
E: enquiries@royalhoteliow.co.uk
W: www.royalhoteliow.co.uk

BEDROOMS: 52. 1 suitable for disabled.
OPEN: all year.
FACILITIES: lift, lounge, bar, 2 restaurants, conservatory, function rooms, free Wi-Fi, in-room TV, civil wedding licence, spa treatment rooms, Riviera Terrace (summer only), 2-acre grounds, outdoor heated swimming pool (May–Sept), rigid inflatable boat for charter.
BACKGROUND MUSIC: in public areas, pianist on peak-season weekends.
LOCATION: short walk from town centre.
CHILDREN: all ages welcomed.
DOGS: allowed in some bedrooms, not in public areas where food is served.
CREDIT CARDS: all major cards.
PRICES: [2017] per room B&B £190–£290, D,B&B £260–£360. Set dinners £31–£40, à la carte £33. 2-night min. stay at peak weekends.

VERYAN-IN-ROSELAND Cornwall
Map 1:D2

THE NARE

'In lush, beautifully tended gardens, this
wonderful cliff-top hotel offers a sense of
timeless peace and isolation.' Guide readers this
year continue to be drawn to Toby Ashworth's
family-friendly hotel and spa, founded 29 years
ago by his grandmother. 'The warm hospitality
makes the train journey worthwhile. Even
among strangers, here, there's a feeling of
old friends reunited.' Traditionally decorated
bedrooms, many sea-facing, have a 'sumptuous
bed' and 'excellent reading lights', but it's the
old-fashioned touches that make them special:
a valet to unpack your bags, a hot-water bottle,
a laundry service. 'It is, in many ways, a time
warp, but that's what makes it enjoyable.' Dress
up to dine from a nightly-changing table d'hôte
menu in the silver-service restaurant (perhaps
including 'superlative pork in Calvados from
the flambé trolley'), or eat more informally in
the Quarterdeck. There may be a faint hint
of change in the air – wasabi paste in a roast-
beef sandwich! – but the 'varied breakfast
spread' and 'delicious afternoon tea' remain key
moments in the day. 'Fellow guests said it's the
best hotel they've stayed in. I can only agree.'
(Matthew Caminer, Stanley Salmon)

Carne Beach
Veryan-in-Roseland
TR2 5PF

T: 01872 501111
F: 01872 501856
E: stay@narehotel.co.uk
W: www.narehotel.co.uk

BEDROOMS: 37. Some on ground
floor, 1 in adjacent cottage,
5 suitable for disabled.
OPEN: all year.
FACILITIES: lift, lounge, drawing
room, sun lounge, gallery, study,
bar, library, light lunch/supper
room, 2 restaurants, conservatory,
free Wi-Fi, in-room TV (Freeview),
gym, indoor and outdoor swimming
pools, 2-acre grounds, tennis, sandy
beach.
BACKGROUND MUSIC: none.
LOCATION: S of Veryan.
CHILDREN: all ages welcomed, no
under-7s in restaurant in evening.
DOGS: allowed in bedrooms, not in
public areas (except assistance dogs).
CREDIT CARDS: Amex, MasterCard,
Visa.
PRICES: [2017] per room B&B
£290–£440, D,B&B £480–£586. Set
dinner £50, à la carte £50.

WAREHAM Dorset

Map 2:E1

THE PRIORY

'The setting, ambience and gardens are possibly the most attractive of any hotel we've stayed in, anywhere,' writes a Guide reader this year of the Turner family's country hotel, in a 16th-century priory on the River Frome. Its fans, who praise the 'delightful riverside gardens', 'admirable staff' and timeless charm, agree. 'It must be 30 years since we last stayed, but it hasn't changed a bit – and I mean that as a compliment.' Guests have a choice of 'well-equipped' accommodation in the main house and a converted boathouse. Individually styled, each room is supplied with fresh fruit, a minibar, books, magazines; robes and high-end toiletries in the bathroom. Boathouse suites on the river have a balcony or veranda: while away the hours watching life on the water. The 'attractive' drawing room, where French doors open to the river terrace, is a winning place for afternoon tea; at sundown ask for a drink, over canapés, in the cosy Cloisters bar. In the oak-beamed Abbots Cellar and the newly refurbished Garden Room restaurant, Stephan Guinebault's modern dishes take inspiration from French and English traditions. (Robert Cooper)

25% DISCOUNT VOUCHERS

Church Green
Wareham
BH20 4ND

T: 01929 551666
F: 01929 554519
E: admin@theprioryhotel.co.uk
W: www.theprioryhotel.co.uk

BEDROOMS: 17. Some on ground floor (in courtyard), 4 suites in Boathouse.
OPEN: all year.
FACILITIES: sitting room, drawing room, snug bar, 2 dining rooms, free Wi-Fi, in-room TV (Freeview), 4½-acre gardens (croquet, river frontage, moorings, fishing), unsuitable for disabled.
BACKGROUND MUSIC: pianist in drawing room Sat evenings 'and special occasions'.
LOCATION: town centre.
CHILDREN: not under 12.
DOGS: not allowed.
CREDIT CARDS: Amex, MasterCard, Visa.
PRICES: [2017] per room B&B £220–£380, D,B&B £265–£430. Set dinner £49.50.

WELLS Somerset

Map 2:D1

STOBERRY HOUSE

'An eartly paradise in warm sunshine.'
Approached by a drive through parkland, Tim
and Frances Meeres Young's upmarket B&B,
in an 18th-century coach house, is surrounded
by gardens 'tended with love and skill'. 'The
glory of the house is the superb panoramic
view' from the orangery breakfast room, taking
in the cathedral, and Glastonbury Tor on the
horizon. Arrive to a 'warm welcome': 'Frances
is an attentive, unfailingly friendly hostess.'
The many sitting rooms hold magazines, books
and board games; a help-yourself pantry is a
nice addition. 'Tastefully appointed' bedrooms,
including a studio suite with its own outdoor
sitting area, are all supplied with fruit, flowers,
robes and slippers. For guests too ensconced to
head into town (Wells is a five-minute drive
or 20-minute downhill walk away), simple
evening meals or 'silver-service' group dinners
may be served by arrangement. In the morning,
the 'amazing breakfast' has 'a splendid range'
of breads, pastries and home-made preserves;
charcuterie, smoked fish and cheeses. Plus: 'You
can't help but feel good looking at that view.'
(Robert Gower, Robert and Joan Grimley,
Elizabeth Laczynska, PR)

Stoberry Park
Wells
BA5 3LD

T: 01749 672906
E: stay@stoberry-park.co.uk
W: www.stoberryhouse.co.uk

BEDROOMS: 5. 1 in studio cottage.
OPEN: all year except 2 weeks over
Christmas and New Year.
FACILITIES: 3 sitting rooms (1 with
pantry), breakfast room, orangery,
free Wi-Fi, in-room TV (Freeview),
6½-acre garden in 25 acres of
parkland, unsuitable for disabled.
BACKGROUND MUSIC: none.
LOCATION: outskirts of Wells.
CHILDREN: all ages welcomed (in
studio suite only).
DOGS: not allowed.
CREDIT CARDS: Amex, MasterCard,
Visa.
PRICES: [2017] per room B&B
(continental) single £85, double
£95–£155. Cooked breakfast £5.50.

WEST END Surrey

Map 2:D3

THE INN AT WEST END

'A standard to judge other places by.' A 'genuinely friendly' spot, Gerry and Ann Price's 'well-run' pub/restaurant-with-rooms is popular with locals, who drop by morning and evening for coffee and a chat. Stay for more: in the wood-floored bar and 'attractive' restaurant (thumbs up for the 'well-spaced tables'), 'the food is excellent'. Try beetroot-cured salmon, citrus crème fraîche, radish salad, treacle soda bread; slow-braised ox cheek, bone marrow crumb, buttered greens, mash. A 'serious' wine list accompanies. 'Well set back' on a courtyard garden (all the better to keep a distance from the busy road), 'well-designed, practical' bedrooms are 'bright and modern without being trendy'. 'Our spacious room had a large, comfortable bed and two armchairs; a smart wet room with an excellent shower. A feature wall behind the bed was covered in a charming paper of trees.' Breakfast is served till an unhurried 11 am on the weekend. Pick from 'a large choice' of cooked dishes – the kedgeree is praised. A good base for varied interests: Ascot and the RHS garden at Wisley are within easy reach; Bisley shooting ground is in the next village. (JS, CR)

25% DISCOUNT VOUCHERS

42 Guildford Road
West End
GU24 9PW

T: 01276 485842
E: gerryprice@btconnect.com
W: www.the-inn.co.uk

BEDROOMS: 12. 1 suitable for disabled.
OPEN: all year.
FACILITIES: pub/restaurant, wine shop, free Wi-Fi, in-room TV (Freeview), patio, courtyard garden.
BACKGROUND MUSIC: none.
LOCATION: 6 miles W of Woking.
CHILDREN: welcomed, if old enough to take their own room.
DOGS: allowed in 2 rooms.
CREDIT CARDS: all major cards.
PRICES: [2017] per room B&B from £130, D,B&B from £175 ('but ask for offers'). À la carte £35.

WEST HOATHLY Sussex

Map 2:E4

THE CAT INN

♀ Previous César winner

'What makes this 16th-century freehouse so
special is the atmosphere: informal and friendly,
yet 100% professional.' Visitors are greeted
with 'big smiles and a warm welcome' at this
well-liked inn, in a hilltop village in Sussex
countryside. 'Andrew Russell, the owner, has
the ability to make a total newcomer feel like
a favoured regular guest,' say Guide readers
this year. 'There's usually a fire burning in the
grate'; in the popular oak-beamed pub and
restaurant, chef Alex Jacquemin's 'superb food'
includes classic pub grub and more modern
fare, perhaps seared sea trout, Poole Bay clams,
spring vegetables. A drinks list spanning local
and cask beers and English wines makes good
accompaniment. No matter the menu, 'attentive
service' from 'knowledgeable staff' is the order
of the day. The 'clean, comfortable' rooms above
the inn, now redecorated, are praised for the
many 'little touches': a capsule coffee machine,
fresh milk, 'decent toiletries', reading material.
'Room 1, our favourite, is spacious yet cosy,
with a view onto the village church.' 'It was all
we could have hoped for.' (William Webster,
AD, and others)

25% DISCOUNT VOUCHERS

North Lane
West Hoathly
RH19 4PP

T: 01342 810369
E: thecatinn@googlemail.com
W: www.catinn.co.uk

BEDROOMS: 4.
OPEN: all year except Christmas.
FACILITIES: bar, 3 dining areas, free
Wi-Fi, in-room TV (Freeview),
terrace (alfresco meals), unsuitable
for disabled.
BACKGROUND MUSIC: none.
LOCATION: in village.
CHILDREN: not under 7.
DOGS: allowed in bedrooms, bar,
specific dining area.
CREDIT CARDS: MasterCard, Visa.
PRICES: per room B&B single
from £100, double from £130.
À la carte £28.

WESTONBIRT Gloucestershire

Map 3:E5

THE HARE AND HOUNDS   `NEW`

Up the tree- and hedgerow-lined road from the National Arboretum, this Cotswold-stone country hotel stands in gardens and woodland. It enters the Guide at the urging of regular readers in 2017. 'Standards are consistently high, and the staff are always attentive and obliging,' says a repeat guest. 'It's good value, too, for the area.' 'Well-furnished, log fire-warmed sitting rooms' in the Victorian building (part of Cotswold Inns & Hotels) have paintings of not a few hares and handsome hounds; there are books, board games, wide armchairs and a relaxed, dog-friendly bar. Choose one of the individually decorated bedrooms in the main house or garden annexes – some are traditional, others are more modern, others yet open on to a terrace. (Light sleepers might discuss accommodation before booking – rooms above the bar may have some noise.) In the lawn-facing restaurant, 'skilfully prepared dishes' include, perhaps, beef fillet, hay-smoked shin, girolles, truffle terrine. Simpler plates and sharing platters are served in the bar. Ask for a map, when it's time for walkies – Fido has woodland paths and country lanes to sniff out. (Mary Coles, ME Olorenshaw)

Westonbirt
GL8 8QL

T: 01666 881000
F: 01666 880241
E: reception@hareandhoundshotel.com
W: www.cotswold-inns-hotels.co.uk

BEDROOMS: 42. 2 suitable for disabled, 3 in coach house, 5 in garden cottage, 12 in Silkwood Court, 1 Game Keeper's Cottage.
OPEN: all year.
FACILITIES: drawing room, lounge, library, bar, restaurant, private dining room, free Wi-Fi, in-room TV (Freeview), civil wedding licence, meeting/function facilities, gardens, woodland.
BACKGROUND MUSIC: in lounge and bar.
LOCATION: 3 miles SW of Tetbury.
CHILDREN: all ages welcomed.
DOGS: allowed in some bedrooms, bar, garden, not in restaurant.
CREDIT CARDS: all major cards.
PRICES: [2017] per room B&B £99–£380, D,B&B £184–£465. Set menus £35.50–£42.50, tasting menu £60.

WHASHTON Yorkshire

Map 4:C3

THE HACK & SPADE

A few miles from busy Scotch Corner, up a single-track lane, lies an 'utterly peaceful' village with two important amenities – a postbox, and Jane Ratcliffe's 'enjoyable' pub-with-rooms. The refurbished and extended stone-built Georgian alehouse peers down rolling countryside into the valley; inside, there's a wood-burning stove and a 'warm greeting'. Bedrooms are up an oak staircase. Individually styled in pleasing heritage shades, they are 'uncluttered, cool and contemporary', with views of countryside or village green. Each has a king- or super-king-size bed ('ours should have been called emperor-size'), cafetière coffee and Fairtrade teas, bathrobes and essential-oil bath products. Come down for dinner in the candlelit dining room, where the tables are laid with crisp white linens and a posy or two. Here, the hostess's seasonal, local fare might include 'very good' twice-baked cheese soufflé; chicken breast, Yorkshire blue cheese, pine nuts. 'This being Yorkshire, we were also served a large dish of tasty vegetables – cauliflower, carrots, new potatoes and broccoli.' 'We were very well looked after.' The Yorkshire Dales national park is within easy reach. More reports, please.

25% DISCOUNT VOUCHERS

Whashton
DL11 7JL

T: 01748 823721
E: reservations@hackandspade.com
W: www.hackandspade.com

BEDROOMS: 5.
OPEN: all year except Christmas/New Year, last 2 weeks Jan, restaurant closed Sun–Wed.
FACILITIES: bar, small lounge, restaurant, free Wi-Fi, in-room TV (Freeview), garden, only restaurant suitable for disabled.
BACKGROUND MUSIC: 'soft' in restaurant in evening.
LOCATION: 4 miles NW of Richmond.
CHILDREN: not under 7.
DOGS: not allowed.
CREDIT CARDS: MasterCard, Visa.
PRICES: [2017] per room B&B £120–£140. À la carte £25.

WHITEWELL Lancashire

Map 4:D3

THE INN AT WHITEWELL

'The valley in which this inn sits seems to me one of the loveliest places on earth; from the back of the inn, the views of fells, river and parkland landscape are just about perfect. And the stillness at night is magical.' A Guide reader on a repeat visit this year was again charmed by Charles Bowman's characterful inn in the Forest of Bowland. The 'bustling' bar and restaurant have 'a good atmosphere and, in winter, plenty of open fires to keep it cosy'. Habitués come for Jamie Cadman's 'superb cooking', which uses 'abundant' local produce – roast rack of Burholme Lonk lamb, perhaps. A separate menu is served in the bar: 'The famous fish pie is as delicious as ever,' says one reader (though another found a portion short on fish – the one that got away!). The 'eccentric, individual' bedrooms, many with an open fire, are 'a treat'. Take your pick: they're 'studded with antique furniture' such as a vast four-poster bed or a Victorian cabinet bath 'nearly big enough to swim in'. 'Breakfast, with jugs of freshly squeezed orange juice, is almost impossible to fault' ('but we wish they'd serve it till later'). (Mike Craddock, Lynn Wildgoose)

nr Clitheroe
Whitewell
BB7 3AT

T: 01200 448222
F: 01200 448298
E: reception@innatwhitewell.com
W: www.innatwhitewell.com

BEDROOMS: 23. 4 (2 on ground floor) in coach house, 150 yds.
OPEN: all year.
FACILITIES: 3 bars, restaurant, boardroom, private dining room, in-house vintners, free Wi-Fi, in-room TV (Freeview), civil wedding licence, 5-acre grounds (wild flower meadow, large river terrace with tables), 7 miles fishing (ghillie available), unsuitable for disabled.
BACKGROUND MUSIC: none.
LOCATION: 6 miles NW of Clitheroe.
CHILDREN: all ages welcomed.
DOGS: allowed, not in dining room.
CREDIT CARDS: MasterCard, Visa.
PRICES: [2017] per room B&B single £97–£185, double £150–£237. À la carte £40.

WHITSTABLE Kent

Map 2:D5

THE CRESCENT TURNER HOTEL

NEW

From this hillside position above the town, take in the 'glorious vista' that stretches over the oyster beds and out to sea, with the Isle of Sheppey beyond. It's the kind of painterly seascape that enticed JMW Turner, after whom this 'stylish hotel' is named, to return to the Kentish coast. Step inside: the welcome, from a 'helpful, friendly team', is 'first class'. Guests whose visit coincided with a wedding party this year were impressed by especial attention from the staff: 'Rather than feeling neglected, we were looked after really well.' There are deep sofas by the wood-burning stove in the lounge, and 'plenty of space to sit and read on the lawn'. Up 'steep stairs' ('our cases were carried up for us'), bedrooms have plenty of glitzy touches: feature wallpaper, ornate mirrors, glamorous bedside tables. Many rooms have views of the sea. 'Superbly cooked, well-presented' classic British dishes, including local oysters, are served in the restaurant. 'My starter of scallops, bacon and pea-and-mint purée was so delicious I had it both evenings. We didn't need puddings, but enjoyed a lovely lemon posset all the same.' (Sara Price, and others)

Wraik Hill
Whitstable
CT5 3BY

T: 01227 263506
F: 01227 263506
E: info@crescentturner.co.uk
W: crescentturner.co.uk

BEDROOMS: 18. 5 on ground floor, 4 suitable for disabled.
OPEN: all year.
FACILITIES: bar/lounge, restaurant, function room, free Wi-Fi, in-room TV (Freeview), civil wedding licence, terrace, 2¼-acre garden.
BACKGROUND MUSIC: in public areas.
LOCATION: 2 miles SW of town centre.
CHILDREN: all ages welcomed.
DOGS: not allowed.
CREDIT CARDS: MasterCard, Visa.
PRICES: [2017] per room £110–£145. À la carte £35.

WILMINGTON Sussex

Map 2:E4

CROSSWAYS HOTEL

25% DISCOUNT VOUCHERS

The accolades continue as Clive James and David Stott celebrate their 30th year at their well-liked restaurant-with-rooms – 'a very special place' – at the foot of the South Downs national park. 'All the things we liked were still there,' says a returning guest this year. 'The gardens are in good shape, and the gazebos are enticing.' In this 'cheerful, meticulously informal' place, 'eating in the restaurant is a treat'. Served in the intimate dining room, David Stott's 'excellent dinners' make good use of local meat and game, plus a 'catch of the day' from Hastings. A typical dish: roast rack of lamb, port and redcurrant sauce. 'Comfortable and sparkling clean' bedrooms, each with a newly upgraded shower or bathroom, are individually decorated, with 'well-judged details': fresh milk in the fridge; earplugs ('though we never needed them') to counter the 'discreet hum' from the road close by. Guests heading to nearby Glyndebourne are well taken care of: 'Clive and David have a finely tuned awareness of the timetable of an evening at the opera, and prepared a cold bag for us at short notice.' (CM, Richard Parish)

Lewes Road
Wilmington
BN26 5SG

T: 01323 482455
F: 01323 487811
E: stay@crosswayshotel.co.uk
W: www.crosswayshotel.co.uk

BEDROOMS: 7. Plus self-catering cottage and apartment.
OPEN: all year except 21 Dec–late Jan, restaurant closed Sun/Mon.
FACILITIES: breakfast room, restaurant, free Wi-Fi, in-room TV (Freeview), 2-acre grounds (duck pond), unsuitable for disabled.
BACKGROUND MUSIC: occasionally, in dining areas.
LOCATION: 2 miles W of Polegate on A27.
CHILDREN: not under 12.
DOGS: not allowed.
CREDIT CARDS: Amex, MasterCard, Visa.
PRICES: [2017] per room B&B single £85, double £150–£175, D,B&B from £220. Set dinner £43.

WINCHESTER Hampshire

Map 2:D2

THE OLD VINE   NEW

'Beautifully situated' on the edge of the
cathedral close, this 'very pleasant' Grade II
listed 18th-century inn has guests singing its
praises. It is owned by Ashton Gray, and run
with 'enthusiastic, friendly and knowledgeable
young staff'. Outside, creepers wind their
way up the red brick building; inside, the
beamed pub and restaurant come complete
with Hampshire real ales and a log fire.
The bedrooms, including a top-floor suite
overlooking the cathedral, are 'furnished with
flair'. 'Our room, Zoffany, was beautiful and
had everything one could wish for: lovely
furniture and decor; a wonderfully comfortable
bed; peace and quiet – and a very reasonable
price.' In the kitchen, long-serving chefs turn
out light lunches, pub classics and 'extremely
good dinners from an imaginative menu',
perhaps shredded duck pâté, pear and walnut
chutney; baked miso salmon, wilted spinach,
bonito jus. In the summer, take a seat in the
flower-filled patio for alfresco meals and drinks.
Freshly baked bread and local preserves are a
hymn to breakfast. 'We walked across the green
to the cathedral to listen to evensong – magic.'
(Sir Franklin Berman, Diana Goodey)

8 Great Minster Street
Winchester
SO23 9HA

T: 01962 854616
E: reservations@oldvinewinchester.
   com
W: www.oldvinewinchester.com

BEDROOMS: 6. Self-contained 2-bed
apartment, with garage, in annexe.
OPEN: all year except Christmas Day.
FACILITIES: bar, restaurant, free
Wi-Fi, in-room TV (Freeview),
only public areas suitable for
disabled.
BACKGROUND MUSIC: none.
LOCATION: town centre, permits
supplied for on-street parking.
CHILDREN: all ages welcomed, not
under 6 in restaurant and bar.
DOGS: only in bar.
CREDIT CARDS: MasterCard, Visa.
PRICES: [2017] per room B&B
£150–£200. À la carte £30.

SEE ALSO SHORTLIST

WINDERMERE Cumbria

Map 4: inset C2

CEDAR MANOR

'From the excellent service, decor and food to the exceptional attention to detail, they've certainly got it right.' There's a chorus of praise this year for this 'impressive' small hotel. A former Victorian country retreat, it is a five-minute walk from the lake shore, and a stroll from town. Caroline and Jonathan Kaye are the owners – nay, 'the stand-out feature of the place'. 'Caroline is helpful and charming; Jonathan, a wealth of local information, exuberantly answered all our questions about the area.' Further admiration: 'We arrived at 9 pm, hungry and tired, and they provided us with cheese trays that included a variety of local products.' The 'superbly appointed' bedrooms are each different – choose one with a canopy bed or a four-poster, perhaps one with a view of the eponymous ancient cedar. Sandwiches and light meals are served all day in the lounge; in the evening, chef Roger Pergl-Wilson's 'first-class' modern menus, which might include hake in dry sherry sauce, caramelised fennel, sea vegetables, make a 'wonderful dining experience'. (Jane Brown, Beth Caplan, the Brass family, Rick Fairclough)

Ambleside Road
Windermere
LA23 1AX

T: 01539 443192
E: stay@cedarmanor.co.uk
W: www.cedarmanor.co.uk

BEDROOMS: 10. 1 split-level suite in coach house.
OPEN: all year except 18–26 Dec, 3–19 Jan.
FACILITIES: 2 lounges, restaurant, free Wi-Fi, in-room TV (Freeview), patio, ¼-acre garden, unsuitable for disabled.
BACKGROUND MUSIC: 'very quietly', at mealtimes, in lounge and restaurant.
LOCATION: 5-min. walk from town centre.
CHILDREN: all ages welcomed.
DOGS: not allowed.
CREDIT CARDS: MasterCard, Visa.
PRICES: [2017] per room B&B £145–£425, D,B&B £231–£511. Set dinner £32.95–£42.95. 2-night min. stay at weekends preferred.

WINDERMERE Cumbria

GILPIN HOTEL AND LAKE HOUSE

'Nothing compares to this special place,' says a Guide reader in 2017 after a return visit to the Cunliffe family's glamorous country house hotel. 'They reinvent themselves constantly, and the staff couldn't be nicer.' Among the choice of accommodation 'to appeal to all guests': 'well-equipped' bedrooms in the Edwardian house; modern spa lodges in the grounds, with an outdoor hot tub and views of the Lake District moors; open-plan suites in the secluded Lake House that look over the water into peaceful woodland. In the Michelin-starred restaurant, chef Hrishikesh Desai cooks contemporary British-with-a-twist dishes (perhaps chilli-glazed lobster, claw fritters, confit lime and grapefruit). A new, informal dining room serves plates pepped up with Asian spices (tikka masala-marinated grilled whole fish, say). The cooking is thought 'superb', though a guest this year wished for larger portions. Bowness is a ten-minute drive away, but there's plenty in the 'lovely grounds' to fill the day, including strolls through the Victorian flower gardens and a peek at the llama paddock. (Joan Campbell, and others)

Crook Road
Windermere
LA23 3NE

T: 015394 88818
E: hotel@thegilpin.co.uk
W: www.thegilpin.co.uk

BEDROOMS: 31. 6 in orchard wing, 5 in spa lodges in grounds, 6 in Lake House (½ mile from main house).
OPEN: all year.
FACILITIES: Gilpin Hotel: bar, lounge, 2 restaurants, terraces, gardens, 22-acre grounds (llama paddock); Lake House: lounge, conservatory, spa (hot tubs, 20-metre heated swimming pool), 100-acre grounds; free Wi-Fi, in-room TV (Sky), civil wedding licence, unsuitable for disabled.
BACKGROUND MUSIC: in restaurants.
LOCATION: on B5284, 2 miles SE of Windermere.
CHILDREN: not under 7.
DOGS: allowed in 2 bedrooms, not in public rooms.
CREDIT CARDS: all major cards.
PRICES: [2017] per room B&B from £265, D,B&B from £334. Set dinner £65. 1-night bookings refused weekends and bank holidays.

WINDERMERE Cumbria

Map 4: inset C2

HOLBECK GHYLL

The views are 'stunning' from this privately owned, ivy-clad Victorian hunting lodge standing in large grounds above Lake Windermere, the panorama of fells stretching wide. Among the individually decorated bedrooms at the 'lovely hotel' – each supplied with a welcoming tot of damson gin – those with a lake view are the most sought after; some also have a balcony or direct access to a garden area. Interconnecting suites suit a family. 'Our room at the back of the main house had a captivating view, and we appreciated being able to let the dogs out first thing in the morning and last thing at night.' In the oak-panelled dining room, young chef Jake Jones is making a name for himself (be sure to book in for dinner). On his very modern menus, perhaps: Isle of Mull scallop, rhubarb, sea kale, caramelised celeriac; shorthorn beef aged in its own fat, salsify, monk's beard, miso butter. A gripe this year: neglectful service from restaurant staff. ('What a pity!') Breakfast sets you up for a day of walking the fells – or simply gazing at them: air-dried Cumbrian ham, Cumberland sausages, kippers, freshly baked breads and pastries. All best enjoyed at a window table, of course.

Holbeck Lane
Windermere
LA23 1LU

T: 015394 32375
E: stay@holbeckghyll.com
W: www.holbeckghyll.com

BEDROOMS: 29. 1 suitable for disabled, 13 outside the main house, plus 2-bed and 4-bed cottages.
OPEN: all year except first 2 weeks Jan.
FACILITIES: 2 lounges, bar, restaurant, private dining rooms, conference facilities, free Wi-Fi, in-room TV, civil wedding licence, small spa, 17-acre grounds (tennis, putting, croquet, jogging track).
BACKGROUND MUSIC: piano in lounge and restaurant in evening.
LOCATION: 4 miles N of Windermere.
CHILDREN: all ages welcomed, not under 8 in restaurant.
DOGS: allowed in lodge rooms (£25 per stay, VIP package £50).
CREDIT CARDS: Amex, MasterCard, Visa (charge for credit card use).
PRICES: [2017] per room B&B from £320, D,B&B from £400. Set dinner £68, tasting menu £88. 1-night bookings sometimes refused Sat.

WOLD NEWTON Yorkshire

Map 4:D5

THE WOLD COTTAGE

'The homely ambience and first-rate hospitality make this friendly place exceptionally attractive.' A cottage in name only, Katrina and Derek Gray's Georgian manor house in the Yorkshire Wolds stands amid landscaped gardens, farmland, and grounds shared, improbably, with a caravan club. Guide inspectors in 2017 stepped into a 'gracious entrance hall' to receive a 'warm welcome'. 'Personable and easy with conversation – as is her husband, who farms the lambs – Katrina offered help with the suitcase, and a cup of tea.' There are fresh flowers, original art and a pair of Staffordshire china dogs in the public rooms; 'excellent-value accommodation' is upstairs in the main house and in a converted barn across the paved yard. 'Our spacious, elegant suite had a huge bed and a spotlessly clean bathroom. Thick curtains – and a bottle of sloe gin – ensured that we were always cosy.' For guests too cosy to head out in the evening, Katrina Gray cooks a communal dinner by arrangement. 'We enjoyed a fresh prawn and avocado starter, chicken casserole with vegetables and rice, and decent wine by the glass – with a free top-up.' Breakfast, with home-made jams and bread, is praised.

Wold Newton
YO25 3HL

T: 01262 470696
F: 01262 470696
E: katrina@woldcottage.com
W: www.woldcottage.com

BEDROOMS: 6. 2 in converted barn, 1 on ground floor, 2 self-catering cottages.
OPEN: all year.
FACILITIES: lounge, dining room, free Wi-Fi, in-room TV (Freeview), 3-acre gardens (croquet) in 240-acre grounds (farmland, woodland).
BACKGROUND MUSIC: at breakfast in dining room.
LOCATION: just outside village.
CHILDREN: all ages welcomed.
DOGS: not allowed.
CREDIT CARDS: MasterCard, Visa.
PRICES: [2017] per room B&B £110–£180, family room £135–£200. 1-night bookings refused at weekends.

WOLTERTON Norfolk

Map 2:A5

THE SARACEN'S HEAD

Wide Norfolk countryside stretches out on either side of this 'very special' place. Ivy-covered and Tuscan-inspired, the Georgian inn is owned and run by Janie and Tim Elwes in a 'beautifully rural setting'. ('We're in the middle of nowhere,' the owners proudly admit. 'Turn on the satnav,' guests advise.) Parasols open over tables in the courtyard on sunny days; when the weather turns cold, a fire is lit in the large open fireplace. Inside and out, 'the staff are friendly and efficient'; a 'lovely, relaxed atmosphere' reigns. Simple, homely bedrooms are 'quiet and spacious', and supplied with ground coffee for the cafetière, plus handmade Norfolk toiletries in the bathroom. A family room sleeps four. In the kitchen, chef Mark Sayers uses produce as local as it gets: meat from nearby Aylsham; fish freshly caught just up the coast; eggs from free-range hens in the next village. Typical offerings on the blackboard menu: Cromer crab, pink grapefruit salad, Parmesan crisp; roast wild duck breast, braised red cabbage, apples. The coast and the Broads are easily reached; National Trust houses and gardens at Blickling and Felbrigg are within a 20-minute drive. (J and JA)

Wall Road
Wolterton
NR11 7LZ

T: 01263 768909
F: 01263 768993
E: info@saracenshead-norfolk.
   co.uk
W: www.saracenshead-norfolk.
   co.uk

BEDROOMS: 6.
OPEN: all year except 24–27 Dec, 2 weeks late Feb/early Mar, restaurant closed Sun evening, Mon in Nov–Apr.
FACILITIES: lounge, bar, restaurant, free Wi-Fi, in-room TV (Freeview), courtyard, 1-acre garden, unsuitable for disabled.
BACKGROUND MUSIC: in bar and dining rooms.
LOCATION: 5 miles N of Aylsham.
CHILDREN: all ages welcomed.
DOGS: allowed in bedrooms, back bar, not in restaurant.
CREDIT CARDS: MasterCard, Visa.
PRICES: [2017] per room B&B £110, D,B&B £175. À la carte £36.

WOOTTON COURTENAY Somerset

Map 1:B5

DUNKERY BEACON COUNTRY HOUSE

'A close approximation to perfection.' Long-time fans praise John and Jane Bradley's 'peaceful, hugely enjoyable' Edwardian hunting lodge, with 'beautiful views' towards the summit of Dunkery Beacon. 'There have been small but significant changes since our last visit: improvements to the car park, upgraded bedroom heating systems, new raised beds for growing vegetables in the garden.' Walkers particularly appreciate the daily supply of apples in the lounge. 'Clean, comfortable' bedrooms have their own character; all have fresh milk, locally ground coffee, chilled spring water. John Bradley is a keen forager; wild foods complement his 'creative cooking'. A characteristic dish: pan-fried Holnicote venison, fondant potato, sautéed kale, parsnip purée, blackberries. Jane Bradley's 'well-chosen, comprehensive wine list' is fine accompaniment. Nights, take advantage of Exmoor's Dark Sky designation (a telescope is set up to maximise stargazing opportunities); in daytime, there's 'wonderful walking, with maps and guides provided, straight from the hotel'. (Andrew Butterworth, Bob and Jean Henry)

25% DISCOUNT VOUCHERS

Wootton Courtenay
TA24 8RH

T: 01643 841241
E: info@dunkerybeacon
   accommodation.co.uk
W: www.dunkerybeacon
   accommodation.co.uk

BEDROOMS: 8. 1 on ground floor.
OPEN: mid-Feb–27 Dec, restaurant closed Sun/Mon/Tues.
FACILITIES: lounge, restaurant, breakfast room, free Wi-Fi in public areas and some bedrooms, in-room TV (Freeview), limited mobile phone reception, ¾-acre garden (alfresco meals), unsuitable for disabled.
BACKGROUND MUSIC: in restaurant in evening.
LOCATION: 4 miles SW of Dunster.
CHILDREN: not under 10.
DOGS: allowed in 2 bedrooms (£5 per night), not in public rooms.
CREDIT CARDS: MasterCard, Visa.
PRICES: [2017] per room £85–£170, D,B&B £147–£232. À la carte £31. 1-night bookings refused Fri/Sat.

WROXTON Oxfordshire

Map 2:C2

WROXTON HOUSE HOTEL   NEW

'The little things really matter' at this 'friendly' hotel, in a row of cottages opposite the thatched church in a village of honey-stone houses. A Best Western member, it is owned by John and Gill Smith, under whose stewardship Guide readers have been urging an upgrade to a full entry. 'They really deserve promotion!' writes a regular correspondent in 2017. 'We were so impressed by the professional staff and the spotless rooms, even by the quality toiletries, and the perfectly spreadable room-temperature butter at breakfast.' Bedrooms of various sizes may lack verve, but they're 'very comfortable'; superior rooms are particularly well equipped with fresh fruit and juice, robes and slippers. In the oak-beamed restaurant, or on the terrace on a warm day, the food is 'delicious'. 'My scallop starter was first class; all the fish dishes were excellent. Smallish portions, though.' In the morning, there's 'great choice' at a 'superb breakfast'. The hotel is popular with functions and weddings ('it's understandably the go-to place in the area'), 'but we weren't neglected despite the celebrations going on during our stay'. (Elizabeth Thomas, Mary Milne-Day)

Silver Street
Wroxton
OX15 6QB

T: 01295 730777
F: 01295 730800
E: reservations@
  wroxtonhousehotel.com
W: www.wroxtonhousehotel.com

BEDROOMS: 32. 7 on ground floor, 3 in adjoining cottage.
OPEN: all year except Christmas, restaurant closed for lunch Mon–Sat.
FACILITIES: 2 lounges, bar, restaurant, private function rooms, free Wi-Fi, in-room TV (Sky, Freeview), civil wedding licence, terrace, unsuitable for disabled.
BACKGROUND MUSIC: in public areas.
LOCATION: 3 miles NW of Banbury.
CHILDREN: all ages welcomed.
DOGS: not allowed.
CREDIT CARDS: Amex, MasterCard, Visa.
PRICES: [2017] per room B&B from £128, D,B&B from £184. À la carte £33. 2-night min. stay at weekends.

YARM Yorkshire

Map 4:C4

♔ JUDGES

César award: country house hotel of the year
'It's the little touches' that make the Downs
family's Victorian country house a 'lovely,
charming place', confirm Guide readers in 2017.
'And the staff are exceptional – friendly from
our first contact, by telephone from Sydney,
and relaxed and professional throughout our
stay. On a return visit, we were pleased to be
welcomed by name by several staff members.'
Standing in 'fine grounds' on the edge of the
North Yorkshire moors, the hotel has 'gorgeous
bedrooms' (traditionally styled with swagged
curtains, wingback chairs, perhaps a generous
spread of toile de Jouy) stocked with treats.
'We appreciated the free sherry and fruit in our
large, comfortable rooms, as well as the jug of
fresh milk for morning tea.' In the evening,
sit by the fire in the lounge for drinks and
'delicious canapés', then sample an 'excellent'
nightly-changing menu that might include king
scallops, Yorkshire chorizo, pickled leek salad;
locally farmed beef fillet, Wye valley asparagus,
poached quail's egg. A 'good breakfast' has
kippers and smoked haddock, plus a classic
bacon and eggs. (Christopher and Veronica
Clair, Mr and Mrs Wright, and others)

25% DISCOUNT VOUCHERS

Kirklevington Hall
Kirklevington
Yarm
TS15 9LW

T: 01642 789000
F: 01642 782878
E: reception@judgeshotel.co.uk
W: www.judgeshotel.co.uk

BEDROOMS: 21. Some on ground
floor.
OPEN: all year.
FACILITIES: lounge, bar, restaurant,
private dining room, free Wi-Fi,
in-room TV (Freeview), function
facilities, business centre, civil
wedding licence, 36-acre grounds
(paths, running routes), access to
local spa and sports club, unsuitable
for disabled.
BACKGROUND MUSIC: none.
LOCATION: 1½ miles S of centre.
CHILDREN: all ages welcomed.
DOGS: not allowed.
CREDIT CARDS: all major cards.
PRICES: [2017] per room B&B
£145–£225, D,B&B £220–£300. Set
menu £25, à la carte £35.

YARMOUTH Isle of Wight

Map 2:E2

THE GEORGE

NEW

In a busy harbour town on the Isle of Wight, this 'very welcoming' hotel is in a 'great waterfront position' between the castle and the old wooden pier. Come into the 'charming old building' (the multi-million-pound refurbishment retained ancient panelling, uneven floors and stone flags) and head to the rear: the wide terrace spills on to the parasol-dotted garden towards the shingle beach, the yachts on the Solent beyond. Some of the 'lovely bedrooms' are country cosy, while others are cool and contemporary, but all have 'pretty touches' – a seascape painting, a mirror framed in driftwood. Ask for a room with sea views, and wake to the sound of the waves washing on the shore. Sophisticated menus are served in the elegant restaurant; in the brasserie, the style is informal and unfussy – lobster macaroni cheese; rosemary and Isle of Wight garlic gnocchi, sautéed spring greens. Try to keep your eyes on the 'tasty breakfast' in the morning: the fruit smoothies, freshly baked pastries, home-made granola, whisky-glazed porridge and local cheeses are more than a match for the uninterrupted view of life waking up on the water. (Josie and Guy Mayers)

Quay Street
Yarmouth
PO41 0PE

T: 01983 760331
E: info@thegeorge.co.uk
W: www.thegeorge.co.uk

BEDROOMS: 17. 1, on ground floor, suitable for disabled.
OPEN: all year, Isla's restaurant closed Sun–Tues.
FACILITIES: bar, lounge, 2 restaurants, private dining room, free Wi-Fi, in-room TV (Freeview), civil wedding licence, meeting/function facilities, terrace, garden.
BACKGROUND MUSIC: in bar and restaurant, occasional live guitar music in lounge.
LOCATION: town centre, 'leave your car on the mainland and use the island's good bus service'.
CHILDREN: all ages welcomed.
DOGS: 'well-behaved dogs' allowed in some bedrooms, in garden on lead, not in public rooms.
CREDIT CARDS: Amex, MasterCard, Visa.
PRICES: per room B&B £140–£380. Tasting menu (Isla's) £45, à la carte (Conservatory) £35.

YORK Yorkshire

Map 4:D4

MIDDLETHORPE HALL & SPA

'A cheerful, likeable hotel', this 'stunning' William and Mary mansion stands in Italianate parkland, with easy access to the city centre. Built in 1699 with an eye on Wren's Hampton Court, it was rescued and restored by the National Trust in the 1980s. An oak staircase sweeps upwards from the entrance hall; the 'grand public rooms' ('seriously comfortable for pre- and post-dinner gin-and-tonics') are filled with antiques and fine pictures. Bedrooms, fittingly, are traditional – 'old-fashioned', some say – and decorated with not a few frilly valances. 'I felt, at first, as if I were visiting a rich grandmother at her country pile. But I came to appreciate my high-ceilinged room, whose well-coordinated decor suited the hotel's ethos.' There's a spa in a 'lovely brick cottage' ('where some rejuvenation wouldn't go amiss'), but wander in the 'well-cared-for gardens' instead – 'there are lots of corners to explore'. Dinner is 'nice, without being cordon bleu' – perhaps lamb loin, ricotta, wild garlic – 'and the chefs offer to rustle up an alternative if you fancy something different'. 'Breakfast provides all the choice you need.' The A64 rumbles close by. (Anthony Bradbury, Michael Gwinnell, and others)

Bishopthorpe Road
York
YO23 2GB

T: 01904 641241
F: 01904 620176
E: info@middlethorpe.com
W: www.middlethorpe.com

BEDROOMS: 29. 17 in courtyard, 2 in cottage, some suitable for disabled.
OPEN: all year.
FACILITIES: drawing room, sitting rooms, library, bar, restaurant, 2 private dining rooms, free Wi-Fi, in-room TV (Freeview), civil wedding licence, 20-acre grounds, spa (10 by 6 metre indoor swimming pool).
BACKGROUND MUSIC: none.
LOCATION: 1½ miles S of centre.
CHILDREN: not under 6.
DOGS: allowed in garden suites and cottage, not in main house.
CREDIT CARDS: Amex, MasterCard, Visa.
PRICES: per room B&B from £143, D,B&B from £218. Set gourmet dinner £75, seasonal menu £45, à la carte £59. 1-night bookings refused summer weekends.

SEE ALSO SHORTLIST

ZENNOR Cornwall

Map 1:D1

THE GURNARD'S HEAD

♀ Previous César winner

'Our favourite pub-with-rooms, it truly lives up to its motto of "simple things done well",' say regular Guide correspondents in 2017 of the Inkin brothers' 'excellent', family-friendly spot in rugged west Cornwall, minutes from the cliff edge. 'There's a great atmosphere', encouraged by 'friendly staff who clearly enjoy their work'; with manager Chris Curnow, 'they create a relaxing place in which to chill out'. 'Splendid' bedrooms look out to sea or sheep-grazed moors. They're simple but full of character, with fresh flowers, local art, a Roberts radio, Welsh blankets and all-natural toiletries. No TV – instead, a library of paperbacks to flip through. In the popular bar and restaurant, join the locals choosing from the 'marvellous range' of drinks and 'fantastic food'. 'Our lunch and dinner menus had a good choice of meat, fish and vegetarian dishes. A plate of pheasant came with a parsnip tagliatelle to die for; we also enjoyed tasty, succulent monkfish.' Plan guided foraging walks or simply head out, into the wind, on the Coastal Path. 'Tremendous-value' package offers are worth checking out. (Chris Savory, Michael Eldridge)

Treen
Zennor
TR26 3DE

T: 01736 796928
E: enquiries@gurnardshead.co.uk
W: www.gurnardshead.co.uk

BEDROOMS: 7.
OPEN: all year except 24/25 Dec.
FACILITIES: bar, restaurant, lounge area, free Wi-Fi, 3-acre garden (alfresco dining), unsuitable for disabled.
BACKGROUND MUSIC: Radio 4 at breakfast, selected music at other times, in bar and restaurant.
LOCATION: 7 miles SW of St Ives, on B3306.
CHILDREN: all ages welcomed.
DOGS: allowed, not in dining room.
CREDIT CARDS: MasterCard, Visa.
PRICES: [2017] per room B&B £120–£185, D,B&B £170–£235. Set menus £21–£26.50, à la carte £26.50.

SCOTLAND

Urquhart Castle and Loch Ness, Scottish Highlands

ARDUAINE Argyll and Bute

Map 5:D1

LOCH MELFORT HOTEL

Overlooking a bay on the Argyll coast, Calum and Rachel Ross's 'friendly, good-value' country house, next door to the exotic Arduaine Garden, is in 'the most stunning spot'. 'There's something magical about the light, at all times and in all weathers.' In the bedrooms, the sea views are the main feature. 'Our annexe room was clean and well kept, warm and comfortable (the decor could have done with some updating, though). There was plenty of storage space; the bathroom, small but adequate, had soft towels and plenty of hot water.' Watch the light fade around the islands over home-made canapés and pre-dinner drinks (perhaps 'really good' Crinan gin or Loch Fyne beer). At dinner, chef Michael Knowles's 'tasty and beautifully presented' dishes might include guineafowl with a 'delicious' risotto; 'masses of local cheeses'; a lemon dessert, 'light and perfect for the end of the meal'. 'Breakfast was well cooked and efficiently served. I had the "wee breakfast" – what I'd call a "full Scottish"!' Fido's not forgotten: there are dog-friendly ground-floor rooms; the coast is nearby.

Arduaine
PA34 4XG

T: 01852 200233
F: 01852 200214
E: reception@lochmelfort.co.uk
W: www.lochmelfort.co.uk

BEDROOMS: 25. 20 in Cedar Wing annexe, 10 on ground floor, 1 suitable for disabled.
OPEN: all year except Mon–Wed Nov–Mar, 3 weeks Dec/Jan, open Christmas/New Year.
FACILITIES: sitting room, library, bar/bistro, restaurant, free Wi-Fi, in-room TV, wedding facilities, 17-acre grounds (including National Trust for Scotland's Arduaine Garden).
BACKGROUND MUSIC: in restaurant and bistro.
LOCATION: 19 miles S of Oban.
CHILDREN: all ages welcomed (under-2s free).
DOGS: allowed in 6 bedrooms (£9 per night), not in public rooms.
CREDIT CARDS: MasterCard, Visa.
PRICES: [2017] per person B&B £81–£147, D,B&B £117–£168, £30 single supplement. Set menu £42.

AUCHENCAIRN Dumfries and Galloway

Map 5:E2

BALCARY BAY HOTEL

'Happily, as good as ever,' writes a Guide reader this year, revisiting Graeme Lamb's 'well-run' hotel on the Solway Firth, where the views stretch across the bay towards the hills of Cumbria. 'The setting, beside the sea, is wonderful. We woke early one morning to a stunning sunrise.' Allegedly linked to the 17th-century smuggling trade, the whitewashed hotel is these days entirely respectable, with an old-fashioned charm. 'Its guests, like us, mostly retired, return year after year.' Choose a bedroom with an outlook on the water, within sound of the waves; fritter away the day in the mature gardens or in one of the sea-view lounges. In the restaurant ('well spoken of throughout Galloway'), chef Craig McWilliam's daily-changing menu is 'efficiently served'. Typical dishes: shrimps, home-made bread, herb butter; beef fillet, celeriac purée, rösti, spinach. 'Good lunches may be taken in the bar'; breakfast is 'especially good – a wide choice of lovely fish dishes'. Bring binoculars for birdwatching; gardens and golf clubs are within a half-hour's drive. (Mabel Tannahill, Elspeth and John Gibbon)

Shore Road
Auchencairn
DG7 1QZ

T: 01556 640217
F: 01556 640272
E: reservations@balcary-bay-hotel.
co.uk
W: www.balcary-bay-hotel.co.uk

BEDROOMS: 20. 3 on ground floor.
OPEN: 2 Feb–2 Dec.
FACILITIES: 2 lounges, cocktail bar, conservatory, restaurant, free Wi-Fi in lounge, in-room TV (Freeview), 3-acre grounds.
BACKGROUND MUSIC: none.
LOCATION: 2 miles SW of village.
CHILDREN: all ages welcomed.
DOGS: allowed in bedrooms, not in public rooms.
CREDIT CARDS: MasterCard, Visa.
PRICES: per person B&B £80–£96, D,B&B £90–£127 (min. 2 nights). 1-night bookings usually refused weekends.

SEE ALSO SHORTLIST

AULDEARN Highland

Map 5:C2

BOATH HOUSE

♔ Previous César winner

There are whisky and castle trails to strike out on, but begin, perhaps, with a stroll around the Matheson family's 'lovely' mansion – 'the grounds are wonderful,' say Guide inspectors in 2017. 'They can be quite wild in places, but mown paths lead to the lake, where we came close to a heron one morning.' The organic walled garden, as well, is 'so interesting'. Scottish artwork hangs in the Regency house; bedrooms retain their period character. 'As we were travelling with our dog, the garden room, French doors opening on to a small conservatory, was perfect for us. The comfortable bedroom had a well-dressed bed, an armchair, lots of storage; an efficient bathroom. Home-made biscuits and a bowl of apples, too.' Chef Charlie Lockley's modern set menu – 'a real treat' – is served at 7.30 pm. 'Beautifully cooked West Coast halibut; a perfect chocolate fondant. It's obvious why the chef has a Michelin star.' (A garden café was in planning as the Guide went to press.) At breakfast, everything is brought to the table: 'plenty of toast and home-made jams; a pleasant smoothie; good cooked dishes'.

Auldearn
IV12 5TE

T: 01667 454896
F: 01667 455469
E: info@boath-house.com
W: www.boath-house.com

BEDROOMS: 9. 2 in cottages (50 yds), suitable for disabled.
OPEN: all year.
FACILITIES: 2 lounges, whisky bar/library, restaurant, private dining room, free Wi-Fi, in-room TV (Freeview), wedding facilities, 22-acre grounds (woods, gardens, meadow, streams, trout lake).
BACKGROUND MUSIC: none.
LOCATION: 2 miles E of Nairn.
CHILDREN: all ages welcomed, not under 8 at main dinner service.
DOGS: allowed in some bedrooms, not in public rooms.
CREDIT CARDS: Amex, MasterCard, Visa.
PRICES: [2017] per room B&B from £295, D,B&B from £380. Set dinner £45–£70.

BALLANTRAE Ayrshire

Map 5:E1

GLENAPP CASTLE

NEW

25% DISCOUNT VOUCHERS

Enter through the 'splendid' wrought iron gates and continue up a 'beautifully wooded' drive: in 'meticulously tended' grounds stands this 'impressive' 19th-century Scottish baronial castle. It is now owned by Paul and Poppy Szkiler; John Orr, the manager, is 'calm, kind, perceptive – very much a people person'. Within oak-panelled halls, all is 'refined', from the 'magnificent' staircases and Corinthian columns to a 'delightful flight of carved ivory elephants'. 'The spacious, immaculate lounge, with its deep, high-backed sofas, has the feeling of a grand entrance hall.' Traditionally decorated bedrooms have views of garden and woodland, or the wild Ayrshire coast. 'Our gracious room looked over lush gardens towards Ailsa Craig rising majestically in the sea. In the large period bathroom: soft towels and bathrobes. Housekeeping was excellent.' In the restaurant, 'high-quality' French–Scottish dishes (perhaps roast chicken, pommes purée, baby vegetables, black pudding bonbon) use produce from the Victorian greenhouse and the kitchen garden. Breakfast, 'served promptly', continues the feast: home-made muesli and yogurt; 'a wide selection of tempting hot dishes'. (Robert Gower)

Ballantrae
KA26 0NZ

T: 01465 831212
F: 01465 831000
E: info@glenappcastle.com
W: www.glenappcastle.com

BEDROOMS: 17. 7 on ground floor, some suitable for disabled.
OPEN: all year.
FACILITIES: lift, drawing room, library, 2 dining rooms, wedding facilities, free Wi-Fi, in-room TV (Freeview), 36-acre grounds (walled gardens, woodland, lake, tennis, croquet), boat for charter, access to local spa.
BACKGROUND MUSIC: none.
LOCATION: 2 miles S of Ballantrae.
CHILDREN: all ages welcomed.
DOGS: allowed in 2 bedrooms, not in public rooms.
CREDIT CARDS: Amex, MasterCard, Visa.
PRICES: [2017] per room B&B from £350, D,B&B from £450. 1-night bookings sometimes refused.

BLAIRGOWRIE Perth and Kinross

Map 5:D2

KINLOCH HOUSE

'Guests' comfort is prioritised' at the Allen family's Victorian country house hotel, which stands in parkland, gazing over Highland cattle and gently rolling hills. 'The feeling is that of a Scottish baronial home,' say Guide inspectors in 2017. 'A magnificent bear guards the front hall; antlers and sheep horns hang from the panelled walls; an aromatic log fire entices visitors in.' Paul Knott, the manager, is 'warm and friendly'; Mrs Allen, the 'impeccably turned-out' proprietress, is 'perceptive, redoubtable – a true professional'. Choose among traditional bedrooms furnished with antiques; many have countryside views. 'Our south-facing suite was surely the best room in the house. It had a large bedroom and smaller sitting room; a table and chairs in the oriel window; much reading material. Tasteful lamps lent an atmosphere of intimacy.' In the dining room, chef Steve MacCallum uses Scottish meat, fish and game, with produce from the garden, in his 'enjoyable' dishes, perhaps 'guineafowl and rare steaks cooked to perfection'; 'a mouth-watering salted caramel dessert'. 'It may not be cheap, but it offers value for money – and satisfied customers, like our fellow guests, regularly return.'

Dunkeld Road
Blairgowrie
PH10 6SG

T: 01250 884237
E: reception@kinlochhouse.com
W: www.kinlochhouse.com

BEDROOMS: 15. 4 on ground floor.
OPEN: all year except 2 weeks late Dec, open for New Year.
FACILITIES: bar, lounge, drawing room, conservatory, dining room, private dining room, free Wi-Fi, in-room TV (Freeview), civil wedding licence, 28-acre grounds.
BACKGROUND MUSIC: none.
LOCATION: 3 miles W of Blairgowrie, on A923.
CHILDREN: all ages welcomed, not under 6 in dining room at night.
DOGS: not allowed.
CREDIT CARDS: Amex, Mastercard, Visa.
PRICES: [2017] per room B&B from £200. Set dinner £53. 1-night bookings refused at busy periods.

CALLANDER Perth and Kinross

POPPIES HOTEL AND RESTAURANT

On the edge of Loch Lomond and the Trossachs, John and Susan Martin's small hotel – 'a haven of tranquillity and good food' – is liked for its 'ideal location' and 'friendly, efficient' staff. 'John is a particularly affable host,' say Guide readers in 2017. After 13 years juggling home and hearth, the Martins have handed over management of the restaurant to a local restaurateur couple, Veronica and Csaba Brunner. (The Martins, and their collection of more than 120 malt whiskies, will still stick around.) Some of the 'tastefully decorated' bedrooms have views across the main road to meadows and river, and the hills beyond; 'double glazing provides efficient sound insulation'. 'Our spacious superior room had a super-king-size bed and a small sitting area with a sofa.' At dinner, Csaba Brunner's menu, accompanied by a 'reasonably priced' wine list, has 'some unusual combinations'. 'We especially liked the seared duck fillet with a parsnip purée.' 'It's good value, with the bonus of easy access to some of the best Highland scenery – even for those, like us, without a car.' (Philip Bright, Alan and Edwina Williams, John and Theresa Stewart, John and Elspeth Gibbon)

25% DISCOUNT VOUCHERS

Leny Road
Callander
FK17 8AL

T: 01877 330329
F: 01877 332679
E: info@poppieshotel.com
W: www.poppieshotel.com

BEDROOMS: 9. 1 on ground floor.
OPEN: Feb–23 Dec.
FACILITIES: bar, restaurant, free Wi-Fi, in-room TV (Freeview), small front garden, unsuitable for disabled.
BACKGROUND MUSIC: in bar and restaurant.
LOCATION: on A84, ½ mile from town centre.
CHILDREN: all ages welcomed.
DOGS: allowed in 2 bedrooms, not in public rooms.
CREDIT CARDS: Amex, MasterCard, Visa.
PRICES: [2017] per room B&B single £65–£85, double £105–£115, D,B&B rates available. À la carte £35.

CHIRNSIDE Scottish Borders

CHIRNSIDE HALL

In mature grounds a short drive from the coast stands this 19th-century gentleman's country mansion. There is plenty of good cheer within: Guide readers on a return visit to the Tudor-gabled hotel were 'enthusiastically welcomed back' by owners Tessa and Christian Korsten. 'We stayed during a quiet time midweek, but the fires were lit especially for us in the lounge and dining room, and they gave us the best window table at dinner.' There are hunting trophies on the walls (the hotel is popular with shooting parties), and a 'grand lounge' is 'full of settees and piles of The Field magazine'. On the upper floors, bedrooms have individual character in their traditional furnishings. Each is different: a large room with space for a sofa has been praised; another, with a small bathroom, was thought to need sprucing up. All rooms are well equipped with bathrobes and good toiletries; some have 'far-reaching views towards the distant Cheviot hills'. In the evening, sit down to 'wholesome, well-prepared dinners' ('not fancy, but enjoyable') using game from the estate. Next day, 'excellent kippers' are among the 'heaps of choices' at breakfast.

Chirnside
TD11 3LD

T: 01890 818219
F: 01890 818231
E: reception@chirnsidehallhotel.com
W: www.chirnsidehallhotel.com

BEDROOMS: 10.
OPEN: all year except Mar.
FACILITIES: 2 lounges, dining room, private dining room, free Wi-Fi, in-room TV (Freeview), billiard room, fitness room, library/conference rooms, wedding facilities, 5-acre grounds, unsuitable for disabled.
BACKGROUND MUSIC: none.
LOCATION: 1½ miles E of Chirnside, NE of Duns.
CHILDREN: all ages welcomed.
DOGS: allowed in bedrooms (not unattended), not in public rooms.
CREDIT CARDS: Amex, MasterCard, Visa.
PRICES: [2017] per room B&B single £100, double £180, D,B&B single £135, double £240. À la carte £40.

COLINTRAIVE Argyll and Bute

Map 5:D1

COLINTRAIVE HOTEL **NEW**

Patricia Watt's rural hotel on the Cowal peninsula faces green fields close to the shoreline where cattle once crossed the water to the Isle of Bute. 'It's a fantastic setting,' says a Guide reader this year, who discovered a 'friendly' operation with a 'great bar', 'comfortable bedrooms' and 'terrific hosts'. 'The only pub in the area, it is the focal point of what goes on in the village.' A log fire and 'excellent Loch Fyne beer' create a homely atmosphere in the bar. In the dining room, take in views across the Kyles of Bute while enjoying much local produce: langoustines from the bay; local scallops; Bute lamb and beef. 'The food is very good, especially if you stick to the basics. A seafood salad with Isle of Bute hot smoked salmon and crayfish tails was commendable; a plain prawn cocktail much appreciated.' Upstairs, bedrooms (with 'luxury bedlinen') overlook coast or countryside. In the morning, take the ferry to Bute, keeping an eye out for seals and basking sharks; the hostess, a keen cyclist, can suggest the best walking and cycling routes. For sailors, there are six moorings on the bay for hotel guests. (Chris Elliott)

Kyles of Bute
Colintraive
PA22 3AS

T: 01700 841207
F: 01700 841207
E: enquiries@colintraivehotel.com
W: www.colintraivehotel.com

BEDROOMS: 4.
OPEN: all year.
FACILITIES: lounge, bar, restaurant, free Wi-Fi in reception, in-room TV (Freeview), wedding facilities, small beer garden, yacht moorings, unsuitable for disabled.
BACKGROUND MUSIC: in public areas.
LOCATION: in village, 20 miles W of Dunoon.
CHILDREN: all ages welcomed.
DOGS: allowed in bedrooms, not in restaurant or lounge.
CREDIT CARDS: Diners, MasterCard, Visa.
PRICES: [2017] per room B&B from £99, D,B&B (2 nights) from £298. À la carte £35.

COLONSAY Argyll and Bute

Map 5:D1

THE COLONSAY

Alight from the ferry on this unspoilt island, and chances are that Ivan Lisovyy, the 'can-do' manager of Jane and Alex Howard's unpretentious 18th-century inn, will be there to greet you. He is a fine representation of the 'relaxed hotel', which is 'the hub of village life, buzzy with locals and visitors having a good time'. 'A hands-on character, he answered all our requests with an obliging "Of course!",' report trusted Guide correspondents this year. The building is in 'pristine order' (though a guest this year thought better housekeeping was called for in her bedroom); public areas have 'a seaside feel', plus books and board games in the lounge. In the restaurant – try to get a table in 'a prime windowside position' – the slightly daily-changing menu is big on local seafood, perhaps Colonsay oysters or 'excellent sea bass'. Eat in the bar if you fancy ('Of course!'), or ask to have drinks alfresco ('Of course – the best place to have them'). Afterwards, spend the night in one of the modest bedrooms. Some may be snug, but they're comfortably, if simply, furnished, and many look across the water, to the seals and otters who call this place home. (Desmond Balmer, and others)

Colonsay
PA61 7YP

T: 01951 200316
F: 01951 200353
E: jane@colonsayestate.co.uk
W: www.colonsayholidays.co.uk

BEDROOMS: 9.
OPEN: mid-Mar–1 Nov, Christmas, New Year, check-in days Fri, Sat, Sun, Wed, Thurs.
FACILITIES: conservatory, lounge, log room, bar, restaurant, free Wi-Fi on ground floor, accommodation unsuitable for disabled.
BACKGROUND MUSIC: sometimes in restaurant, occasional live music in bar.
LOCATION: 400 yds W of harbour.
CHILDREN: all ages welcomed.
DOGS: allowed in 2 bedrooms, public rooms except restaurant.
CREDIT CARDS: MasterCard, Visa.
PRICES: [2017] per room B&B single £75–£80, double £95–£155. Set menus £13.50–£15.95, à la carte £30.

CONTIN Highland

Map 5:C2

COUL HOUSE

Steeped in stories of baronets and scandalous affairs, Susannah and Stuart Macpherson's 'beautiful Georgian house' is today a 'simply lovely hotel' standing in extensive gardens 'magnificent with mature trees'. ('A special "fairy trail" through the rhododendrons is worth a visit whatever your age.') 'There's a real feeling of warmth and invitation. They even made a tremendous fuss of our cockerpoo,' say Guide inspectors in 2017. Investigate the public rooms hung with hunting scenes and 'interesting paintings' before settling into one of the traditionally decorated bedrooms. 'Our fine, restful room looked towards a backdrop of hills. There were crisp sheets on the large bed; the small bathroom (a little old-fashioned) was stocked with fluffy towels and good-quality bath products. Among the local information were Stuart's fascinating accounts of the ups and downs of hotel-keeping.' Chef Garry Kenley's 'imaginative, well-cooked' dinners are served in the chandelier-lit dining room. 'We enjoyed venison and well-seasoned chicken.' In the morning, the 'colourfully described' breakfast menu is a pleasing start to the day. 'Promptly served, our Gardener's Breakfast was excellent.'

Contin
IV14 9ES

T: 01997 421487
F: 01997 421945
E: stay@coulhouse.com
W: www.coulhousehotel.com

BEDROOMS: 21. 4 on ground floor, 1 suitable for disabled.
OPEN: all year except 24–26 Dec.
FACILITIES: lounge bar, drawing room, front hall, restaurant, free Wi-Fi, in-room smart TV, conference/wedding facilities, 8-acre grounds (children's play area, 9-hole pitch and putt).
BACKGROUND MUSIC: 'mixed' in bar, classical in restaurant.
LOCATION: 17 miles NW of Inverness.
CHILDREN: all ages welcomed.
DOGS: allowed in some bedrooms, all public rooms except restaurant.
CREDIT CARDS: all major cards.
PRICES: [2017] per room B&B single £75–£110, double £95–£325. À la carte £32.

DUNVEGAN Highland

Map 5:C1

THE THREE CHIMNEYS AND THE HOUSE OVER-BY

'We needed a break from our busy day-to-day life, and we got it.' Guide readers had 'a wonderful stay' this year at Shirley and Eddie Spear's Isle of Skye restaurant-with-rooms overlooking Loch Dunvegan. 'It's at the back of beyond, which is, of course, part of its charm'; 'the whole experience is well worth the distance covered'. 'All is relaxed' at the well-regarded restaurant, where chef Scott Davies creates Nordic-inspired menus with produce from Skye farmers, fisherfolk, growers and foragers. Characteristic dishes: gin-cured salmon, Dunvegan crab, wasabi and apple sorbet; Soay lamb and ewe, braised cabbage, roasted parsnip purée. 'The service was excellent; the food and wine were delicious. The sommelier was particularly well informed.' In The House Over-By, across the courtyard, bedrooms are 'very civilised'. Each is supplied with bathrobes and slippers, fruit and home-made shortbread; patio doors lead to the garden. Make room for breakfast, where 'a wide choice' might include whisky and heather-honey porridge, almond and lemon beignets, smoked haddock omelettes with Isle of Mull Cheddar. (SW, and others)

Colbost
Dunvegan
IV55 8ZT

T: 01470 511258
E: eatandstay@threechimneys.co.uk
W: www.threechimneys.co.uk

BEDROOMS: 6. All on ground floor (5 split-level) in separate building, 1 suitable for disabled.
OPEN: all year except 11 Dec–18 Jan.
FACILITIES: lounge/breakfast room (House Over-By), restaurant, free Wi-Fi, in-room TV (Freeview), garden on loch.
BACKGROUND MUSIC: in lounge and restaurant, 'for different moods and times of day'.
LOCATION: 5 miles W of Dunvegan.
CHILDREN: all ages welcomed.
DOGS: not allowed.
CREDIT CARDS: Amex, MasterCard, Visa.
PRICES: [2017] per room B&B £345. Tasting menu £90, à la carte £65.

EDINBURGH

Map 5:D2

THE BONHAM

Three bay-fronted Victorian terrace town houses come together as one 'civilised, very satisfactory' hotel within walking distance of Princes Street and the National Gallery. Part of the privately owned Principal Hotels group, the one-time private clinic is appreciated by Guide readers. Public spaces are sleekly brooding and masculine, with chequerboard flooring, carved fireplaces, and modern art on wood-panelled walls. 'Comfortable bedrooms', some with 'splendid views' over the city's rooftops, have contemporary decor and furnishings. Rooms vary in size; the best, a spacious suite, has bay windows overlooking Drumsheugh Gardens. Order cocktails and cream teas in the Consulting Room bar; in the dining room (where an imposing chandelier strikes a feminine note), chef Marco Nobrega cooks a short menu of modern Scottish dishes 'with a European twist'. Typical choices: Scrabster hake, fennel croquettes, shellfish sauce; 35-day dry-aged sirloin steak from the Borders. Breakfast, served till 10.30 am at the weekend, has plenty of choice: porridge, Orkney kippers, Linlithgow-smoked salmon, the full Scottish with tattie scones. (CE)

35 Drumsheugh Gardens
Edinburgh
EH3 7RN

T: 0131 226 6050
E: bonhamreservations@
thebonham.com
W: www.thebonham.com

BEDROOMS: 49. 6 on ground floor, 1 suitable for disabled.
OPEN: all year.
FACILITIES: lift, reception lounge, bar, restaurant, free Wi-Fi, in-room TV (Freeview), conference/wedding facilities, secure car park (£15).
BACKGROUND MUSIC: jazz and classical in public areas.
LOCATION: West End.
CHILDREN: all ages welcomed.
DOGS: allowed in bedrooms, not in public rooms.
CREDIT CARDS: Amex, MasterCard, Visa.
PRICES: [2017] per room B&B from £90. À la carte £35. 1-night bookings sometimes refused.

SEE ALSO SHORTLIST

EDINBURGH

Map 5:D2

PRESTONFIELD NEW

The peacocks in the 'fantastic grounds' are but
a hint of the exotic style of local restaurateur
James Thomson's characterful hotel next to
Royal Holyrood Park. Inside the 17th-century
mansion, all is opulent, lavish, theatrical.
From lush flower arrangements to the gilded
furnishings, leather-panelled walls and armfuls
of swags and brocades, the place is 'an orgy
for the senses'. Individually decorated with
art and antiques, the bedrooms, including five
distinctive suites, are 'wonderful'. There may be
velvet-lined walls or a tapestry-hung tester bed;
in a bathroom lined in Venetian glass mosaic
and marble, find bathrobes, slippers and fluffy
towels. All rooms have views over gardens and
parkland. Take afternoon tea by a log fire, in
rose-filled gardens or in a Gothic tea house.
Come evening, dine on classic dishes (perhaps
roast roe deer loin, haunch pie, salt-baked
beetroot, confit potato, semi-dried cherries) by
candlelight in the glamorous restaurant. 'Every
member of staff is welcoming, helpful and
charming.' 'I had a great stay.' The Witchery
by the Castle (see Shortlist entry), in Edinburgh
Old Town, is under the same ownership. (Jean
Porter, and others)

Priestfield Road
Edinburgh
EH16 5UT

T: 0131 225 7800
F: 0131 220 4392
E: reservations@prestonfield.com
W: www.prestonfield.com

BEDROOMS: 23. 1 suitable for disabled.
OPEN: all year.
FACILITIES: lift, 2 drawing rooms, sitting room, library, whisky bar, restaurant, private dining rooms, free Wi-Fi, in-room TV, civil wedding licence, terraces, tea house, 20-acre grounds (gardens, croquet, putting, secure dog run, paddocks, woodland walk).
BACKGROUND MUSIC: 'when suitable' in public areas.
LOCATION: next to Royal Holyrood Park.
CHILDREN: all ages welcomed.
DOGS: allowed.
CREDIT CARDS: all major cards.
PRICES: [2017] per room B&B from £335. Set dinner £36, à la carte £50.

SEE ALSO SHORTLIST

EDINBURGH

Map 5:D2

24 ROYAL TERRACE

NEW

A 20-minute walk from the Royal Scottish Academy, modern art – and art lovers – find a home at this privately owned boutique hotel in a peaceful row of Georgian town houses facing leafy gardens. The former merchant's home, refurbished with some flamboyant touches, is hung with contemporary Scottish and Australian aboriginal artwork: at an 'excellent breakfast', consume a potato scone under the gaze of one of Peter Howson's hardmen. Most of the stylish bedrooms are up the red-carpeted stairs (the listed building has no lift); all have views over the garden or towards the Firth of Forth. 'Nicely furnished and very comfortable', each room is well equipped with fine teas, ground cafetière coffee, a lambswool throw, and robes and slippers. Tech-obsessed guests, rejoice: smart TVs stream movies on demand; USB charging points are exactly where you need them. Stay in for afternoon tea with champagne in the snug bar, or knock back a cocktail or two before stepping out into the city. Platters of ham, cheeses and smoked fish may be ordered till late, but many of the city's restaurants are easily reached on foot – Michelin-starred 21212 (see Shortlist entry) is a three-minute walk away.

24 Royal Terrace
Edinburgh
EH7 5AH

T: 0131 297 2424
E: reservations@24royalterrace.com
W: www.24royalterrace.co.uk

BEDROOMS: 16. 1 on ground floor.
OPEN: all year.
FACILITIES: bar, free Wi-Fi, in-room smart TV, terrace, garden, unsuitable for disabled.
BACKGROUND MUSIC: in public areas.
LOCATION: east of city centre.
CHILDREN: all ages welcomed.
DOGS: allowed in 1 room, garden, only assistance dogs allowed in bar.
CREDIT CARDS: Amex, MasterCard, Visa.
PRICES: [2017] room £120–£300. Continental breakfast £7, cooked breakfast £14.

SEE ALSO SHORTLIST

GAIRLOCH Highland

Map 5:B1

SHIELDAIG LODGE   NEW

The 'splendid aroma of peat, whisky and leather' defines this 'impressive' Victorian hunting lodge in a 'glorious setting' on Loch Gairloch. Guide inspectors in 2017 swooned into the scent, against an oak-panelled backdrop of crackling fires, deep sofas and uncountable bottles of whiskies and gins. 'The exceptional service, oh-so-cosy bedrooms and richly comfortable styling make this a special, wholly Scottish place. Enchanting, too: the views of cavorting seals.' Up tartan-carpeted stairs, individually decorated bedrooms look on to loch or garden. 'We entered our room to a stunning view over the water. There were glorious pillows on the beds; tweed-covered armchairs in the window alcove; shortbread on the hospitality tray; Scottish toiletries and enormous towels in the handsome, panelled bathroom.' Ask for a seat by the 'huge picture window' at dinner – the vista is a fine partner for the daily-changing menus that use home-grown vegetables, and lobster and scallops caught in front of the hotel. 'Breakfast hit the spot: rich coffee; creamy porridge with maple syrup; beautifully cooked bacon and succulent mushrooms; a perfect potato scone.'

Badachro
Gairloch
IV21 2AN

T: 01445 741333
E: reservations@shieldaiglodge.com
W: www.shieldaiglodge.com

BEDROOMS: 12.
OPEN: all year.
FACILITIES: lounge, library, bar, restaurant, snooker room, free Wi-Fi, in-room TV (Freeview), wedding facilities, garden, 26,000-acre estate (tennis, fishing, red deer stalking, falconry centre, Targa 44 motor boat for charter).
BACKGROUND MUSIC: in lounge, bar and restaurant.
LOCATION: 4¼ miles S of Gairloch.
CHILDREN: all ages welcomed.
DOGS: not allowed.
CREDIT CARDS: MasterCard, Visa.
PRICES: [2017] per room B&B £120–£350. Set dinner £34.50.

GLASGOW

Map 5:D2

GRASSHOPPERS

A sprightly hop, skip and jump from Central Station, this good-value, design-led hotel is 'an excellent choice' in the busy centre. 'It hasn't got all the frills and fancies of a large hotel but, at this price and quality, it is brilliant.' Step through the classical portal of Caledonian Chambers, between bland shopfronts, and take the lift to the penthouse to discover Scandinavian-influenced urban cool, and a welcome with tea, coffee and treats (perhaps cupcakes today, ice cream tomorrow). Neatly styled bedrooms (some snug) have a wooden floor and cheery colours; a power shower in a bathroom 'pod'. Well-thought-through details, such as blackout curtains, bespoke desks and feather-and-down duvets, make them better than basic. 'Our room was quiet, despite overlooking the dramatic glass roof of the train station.' The city's eating places are all within easy reach, but guests wishing to stay in may appreciate the simple suppers, sourced from local delis, served four days a week. There's 'a wide choice' at breakfast: fresh fruit, yogurt and freshly baked bread; cheeses and cold meats; eggs cooked to order. (ADL, JL)

6th floor Caledonian Chambers
87 Union Street
Glasgow
G1 3TA

T: 0141 222 2666
F: 0141 248 3641
E: info@grasshoppersglasgow.com
W: www.grasshoppersglasgow.com

BEDROOMS: 29.
OPEN: all year except 4 days Christmas, supper Mon–Thurs.
FACILITIES: breakfast/supper room, sitting room, free Wi-Fi, in-room TV (Sky), unsuitable for disabled.
BACKGROUND MUSIC: none.
LOCATION: by Central Station.
CHILDREN: all ages welcomed.
DOGS: allowed.
CREDIT CARDS: Amex, MasterCard, Visa.
PRICES: per room B&B £85–£125, D,B&B £100–£140. À la carte £17.

SEE ALSO SHORTLIST

GLENELG Highland

Map 5:C1

THE GLENELG INN NEW

Soak in the 'great, cosy, country-pub atmosphere'
at this log fire-warmed waterside inn, where
even the resident whippet is an 'affable
character'. Run by 'friendly, welcoming owner'
Sheila Condie, the pub-with-rooms re-enters
the Guide thanks to a regular correspondent
who praised the 'excellent staff', 'wonderful
dinners' and 'amazing views' across the
Kylerhea narrows to the Isle of Skye. Maritime
knick-knacks and old photographs decorate
the jovial pub; a blackboard menu lets Verity
Hurding, the 'creative, enthusiastic chef', make
quick changes should a fisherman show up with
freshly trapped langoustines. After a dinner of
squat lobsters on fresh pasta, say, stay the night
in one of the simple, homely bedrooms (but
ask about the regular live music events before
booking the room above the bar). 'Our room,
past the beer barrels down the side of the inn,
opened on to the sea-facing garden dotted with
tables for alfresco drinking and eating. The
comfortable bed had nice linen; a bathroom
alcove – no door, just a moveable screen – had
modern fittings and a walk-in shower.' In the
morning, take the heritage car ferry to Skye, or
head for tranquil Sandaig bay, down the coast.

Glenelg
IV40 8JR

T: 01599 522273
F: 01599 522283
E: info@glenelg-inn.com
W: www.glenelg-inn.com

BEDROOMS: 7. 2 on ground floor,
suitable for disabled.
OPEN: all year but 'contact us to
check Oct–early Mar'.
FACILITIES: bar, restaurant, free
Wi-Fi, garden.
BACKGROUND MUSIC: in public areas,
regular live music events.
LOCATION: 10 miles W of Shiel
Bridge over the Mam Rattigan.
CHILDREN: all ages welcomed.
DOGS: allowed in some bedrooms,
public rooms.
CREDIT CARDS: MasterCard, Visa.
PRICES: [2017] per room B&B single
£85, double £110–£130.

THE GOOD HOTEL GUIDE 2018

Use this voucher to claim a 25% discount off the normal price for bed and breakfast at hotels with a 25% DISCOUNT VOUCHERS sign at the end of the entry. **You must request a voucher discount at the time of booking and present this voucher on arrival. Further details and conditions overleaf.** Valid to 9th October 2018.

THE GOOD HOTEL GUIDE 2018

Use this voucher to claim a 25% discount off the normal price for bed and breakfast at hotels with a 25% DISCOUNT VOUCHERS sign at the end of the entry. **You must request a voucher discount at the time of booking and present this voucher on arrival. Further details and conditions overleaf.** Valid to 9th October 2018.

THE GOOD HOTEL GUIDE 2018

Use this voucher to claim a 25% discount off the normal price for bed and breakfast at hotels with a 25% DISCOUNT VOUCHERS sign at the end of the entry. **You must request a voucher discount at the time of booking and present this voucher on arrival. Further details and conditions overleaf.** Valid to 9th October 2018.

THE GOOD HOTEL GUIDE 2018

Use this voucher to claim a 25% discount off the normal price for bed and breakfast at hotels with a 25% DISCOUNT VOUCHERS sign at the end of the entry. **You must request a voucher discount at the time of booking and present this voucher on arrival. Further details and conditions overleaf.** Valid to 9th October 2018.

THE GOOD HOTEL GUIDE 2018

Use this voucher to claim a 25% discount off the normal price for bed and breakfast at hotels with a 25% DISCOUNT VOUCHERS sign at the end of the entry. **You must request a voucher discount at the time of booking and present this voucher on arrival. Further details and conditions overleaf.** Valid to 9th October 2018.

THE GOOD HOTEL GUIDE 2018

Use this voucher to claim a 25% discount off the normal price for bed and breakfast at hotels with a 25% DISCOUNT VOUCHERS sign at the end of the entry. **You must request a voucher discount at the time of booking and present this voucher on arrival. Further details and conditions overleaf.** Valid to 9th October 2018.

CONDITIONS

1. Hotels with a **25% DISCOUNT VOUCHERS** sign have agreed to give readers a discount of 25% off their normal bed-and-breakfast rate.
2. One voucher is good for the first night's stay only, at the discounted rate for yourself alone or for you and a partner sharing a double room.
3. Hotels may decline to accept a voucher reservation if they expect to be fully booked at the full room price.

CONDITIONS

1. Hotels with a **25% DISCOUNT VOUCHERS** sign have agreed to give readers a discount of 25% off their normal bed-and-breakfast rate.
2. One voucher is good for the first night's stay only, at the discounted rate for yourself alone or for you and a partner sharing a double room.
3. Hotels may decline to accept a voucher reservation if they expect to be fully booked at the full room price.

CONDITIONS

1. Hotels with a **25% DISCOUNT VOUCHERS** sign have agreed to give readers a discount of 25% off their normal bed-and-breakfast rate.
2. One voucher is good for the first night's stay only, at the discounted rate for yourself alone or for you and a partner sharing a double room.
3. Hotels may decline to accept a voucher reservation if they expect to be fully booked at the full room price.

CONDITIONS

1. Hotels with a **25% DISCOUNT VOUCHERS** sign have agreed to give readers a discount of 25% off their normal bed-and-breakfast rate.
2. One voucher is good for the first night's stay only, at the discounted rate for yourself alone or for you and a partner sharing a double room.
3. Hotels may decline to accept a voucher reservation if they expect to be fully booked at the full room price.

CONDITIONS

1. Hotels with a **25% DISCOUNT VOUCHERS** sign have agreed to give readers a discount of 25% off their normal bed-and-breakfast rate.
2. One voucher is good for the first night's stay only, at the discounted rate for yourself alone or for you and a partner sharing a double room.
3. Hotels may decline to accept a voucher reservation if they expect to be fully booked at the full room price.

CONDITIONS

1. Hotels with a **25% DISCOUNT VOUCHERS** sign have agreed to give readers a discount of 25% off their normal bed-and-breakfast rate.
2. One voucher is good for the first night's stay only, at the discounted rate for yourself alone or for you and a partner sharing a double room.
3. Hotels may decline to accept a voucher reservation if they expect to be fully booked at the full room price.

GLENFINNAN Highland

Map 5:C1

GLENFINNAN HOUSE HOTEL

A Victorian remodelling of an 18th-century inn, this stone mansion stands tall in a 'beautiful situation', with views of Ben Nevis and lawns stretching to the shore of Loch Shiel. It is owned by Jane MacFarlane; Manja and Duncan Gibson have been resident managers for the better part of two decades. Come in to Jacobite-themed paintings on pine-panelled walls; 'in all the public rooms, roaring log fires, even at the end of May, add to the warmth and comfort of the place'. 'Comfortably furnished' loch- or garden-view bedrooms are made welcoming with fresh flowers and a fruit bowl. No room key is offered ('though there was no hesitation providing one when we asked for it') – imagine you're staying with friends. 'Our Jacobean Suite had a high four-poster bed; in the bathroom, a separate shower and bath, all nicely finished.' In the restaurant, Duncan Gibson cooks 'superb' Scottish recipes with French flair – perhaps roast Lochaber lamb, potato gratin, young leeks. Another day, pull up at the bar, where the menu has 'good choices – some plain, some fancy, all excellent'. A fine base for the western Highlands; spot golden eagles and red deer from a cruise on the loch. (LW, A and EW)

Glenfinnan
PH37 4LT

T: 01397 722235
F: 01397 722344
E: availability@glenfinnanhouse.com
W: www.glenfinnanhouse.com

BEDROOMS: 14.
OPEN: 23 Mar–4 Nov.
FACILITIES: drawing room, bar/lounge, playroom, restaurant, wedding facilities, free Wi-Fi, 1-acre grounds (play area), unsuitable for disabled.
BACKGROUND MUSIC: Scottish in bar and restaurant.
LOCATION: 15 miles NW of Fort William.
CHILDREN: all ages welcomed.
DOGS: allowed, not in restaurant or drawing room.
CREDIT CARDS: Amex, MasterCard, Visa.
PRICES: [2017] per room B&B £120–£240. À la carte £30.

GLENFINNAN Highland

Map 5:C1

THE PRINCE'S HOUSE

Follow the fabled Road to the Isles and pass the head of Loch Shiel to reach Ina and Kieron Kelly's 17th-century coaching inn, today a friendly family-run hotel with 'comfortable bedrooms' and 'outstanding meals'. 'The owners' son, who was home for the summer, looked after us, and was delightful,' says a Guide reader this year. Bedrooms vary in size and style; the best, and most spacious, has a Jacobean four-poster bed and lots of extras: Scottish toiletries, fresh flowers, chocolates, a decanter of Whisky Mac. The beamed restaurant occupies the original part of the old inn. Here, Kieron Kelly's 'delicious' four-course dinners use locally sourced ingredients: venison from the surrounding hills, fish and shellfish from the boats at Mallaig, vegetables and fruit from a small-scale grower, lamb from a coastal farm nearby. Typical dishes: wild mushroom ravioli, asparagus; roast best end of lamb, Madeira and thyme jus. Simpler dishes (perhaps breaded Mallaig haddock) may be taken in the bistro. Next day, after a 'good' breakfast, take a short walk to the station and board the Jacobite steam train. (Richard Bright)

Glenfinnan
PH37 4LT

T: 01397 722246
E: princeshouse@glenfinnan.co.uk
W: www.glenfinnan.co.uk

BEDROOMS: 9.
OPEN: mid-Mar–end Oct, 27 Dec–2 Jan, restaurant open Easter–end Sept, New Year.
FACILITIES: restaurant, bistro/bar, free Wi-Fi, in-room TV (Freeview), small front lawn, only bar suitable for disabled.
BACKGROUND MUSIC: in restaurant and bar.
LOCATION: 17 miles NW of Fort William, 330 yards from Glenfinnan station.
CHILDREN: all ages welcomed.
DOGS: allowed in bar.
CREDIT CARDS: Amex, MasterCard, Visa.
PRICES: [2017] per room B&B single £75–£90, double £130–£200. Set menu (in restaurant) £45, à la carte (in bistro) £28.

GRANTOWN-ON-SPEY Highland

Map 5:C2

CULDEARN HOUSE

There's plenty of good walking around this converted Speyside villa – and plenty of whisky to warm the cockles at the end of a long day. This 'well-run operation' comes 'strongly recommended' by Guide readers: 'attentive, genuinely caring' owners William and Sonia Marshall 'take enormous pride in their labour of love'. 'It's as good as ever,' says a visitor returning after a three-year break. 'And Sonia's fillet steak is still the best I've eaten.' Amid traditional decor, many original period features, including a marble fireplace, have been retained; the bedrooms are furnished with a mix of antique and more modern pieces. 'Our spacious, beautifully appointed bedroom had a splendid view over gardens and local woodland.' In the 'well-decorated' sitting room, pre-dinner drinks, with 'a nice little amuse-bouche', are 'a pleasant opportunity to chat' with fellow guests. Afterwards, take a place at a table for the hostess's 'beautifully cooked and presented' daily-changing traditional Scottish menus. 'William's extensive wine list is fine accompaniment, but naught compared with the number of malt whiskies on offer!' (Mike Bennett, Kevin Sykes).

Woodlands Terrace
Grantown-on-Spey
PH26 3JU

T: 01479 872106
F: 01479 873641
E: enquiries@culdearn.com
W: www.culdearn.com

BEDROOMS: 6. 1 on ground floor.
OPEN: all year.
FACILITIES: drawing room, dining room, free Wi-Fi, in-room TV (Freeview), ¾-acre garden, unsuitable for disabled.
BACKGROUND MUSIC: none.
LOCATION: edge of town (within walking distance).
CHILDREN: not under 10.
DOGS: not allowed.
CREDIT CARDS: MasterCard, Visa.
PRICES: [2017] per person B&B single £65–£75, double £75–£85, D,B&B single £90–£110, double £100–£150. À la carte £45.

SEE ALSO SHORTLIST

INVERKEILOR Angus

GORDON'S

'Nothing disappoints' at this 'well-presented' restaurant-with-rooms in a village close to the North Sea coast, say Guide readers in 2017. The family-run enterprise, in a 'tastefully made-over' Victorian terrace house, was opened by Gordon and Maria Watson 30 years ago, and has been 'warmly welcoming' guests since. The former host died last year, but Maria Watson carries the torch; Garry, the Watsons' son, is the award-winning chef. In the 'warm, elegant' dining room (where a wood-burning stove 'adds to the character'), 'they've clearly got their sights on a Michelin star'. Among the modern dishes 'cooked with flair': double-baked soufflé, Isle of Mull Tobermory Cheddar; Angus beef fillet, artichoke and truffle ravioli, bacon jam, hay-baked celeriac. A 'comprehensive' wine list complements the 'top-quality produce'. Dine well, then sleep in one of the 'luxurious' bedrooms supplied with 'everything one might need'. 'Our large, comfortable bedroom had been done up in modern Scottish decor and had a well-appointed bathroom.' Breakfast is 'excellent' with home-baked bread and 'the best scrambled eggs'. Walk it off on the beach at Lunan Bay. (Bill Wood, JG)

Main Street
Inverkeilor
DD11 5RN

T: 01241 830364
E: gordonsrest@aol.com
W: www.gordonsrestaurant.co.uk

BEDROOMS: 5. 1 on ground floor in courtyard annexe.
OPEN: all year except Jan.
FACILITIES: lounge, restaurant, free Wi-Fi in reception, in-room TV, small garden and patio, unsuitable for disabled.
BACKGROUND MUSIC: none.
LOCATION: in hamlet, 6 miles NE of Arbroath.
CHILDREN: not under 12.
DOGS: not allowed.
CREDIT CARDS: MasterCard, Visa.
PRICES: [2017] per room B&B £110–£160. Set dinner £65.

IONA Argyll and Bute

ARGYLL HOTEL

An 'informal, warmly welcoming' place, this low-key small hotel is just the ticket for visitors in search of 'peace and quiet to experience the magic of this lovely, remote island'. In a 'fabulous position' overlooking the Sound of Iona, it is owned by Wendy and Rob MacManaway and Katy and Dafydd Russon – 'charming people'. 'It's not some luxury resort with all the mod cons, so some allowances have to be made – that, for us, is the lure of the place,' fans say. Simply decorated bedrooms in the row of former crofters' cottages vary in size and shape: there are single rooms, family rooms, rooms with a sloping ceiling, rooms overlooking the garden. The best room, newly refurbished, has a wood-burning stove and views towards the water. At dinner, chef Richard Shwe uses vegetables from local suppliers and the organic kitchen garden, sustainably landed fish, and meat from local crofters. Among the 'creative, imaginative' dishes on his menu of 'great food', perhaps Mull scallops, Jerusalem artichoke purée, pickled red chillies; roast loin of Iona lamb, rhubarb mustard seed jus, citrus labneh. Breakfast on organic fruit and eggs, Iona hogget, griddled bacon.

25% DISCOUNT VOUCHERS

Isle of Iona
PA76 6SJ

T: 01681 700334
E: reception@argyllhoteliona.co.uk
W: www.argyllhoteliona.co.uk

BEDROOMS: 17. 7 in linked extension.
OPEN: 1 Apr–26 Oct.
FACILITIES: 3 lounges (1 with TV), conservatory, dining room, free Wi-Fi in some public areas, wedding facilities, seafront lawn with benches, organic vegetable garden, unsuitable for disabled.
BACKGROUND MUSIC: contemporary Scottish, 'gentle' jazz or country music 'appropriate to the time of day' in dining room.
LOCATION: village centre.
CHILDREN: all ages welcomed.
DOGS: up to 2 allowed, not in dining room or sun lounge.
CREDIT CARDS: MasterCard, Visa.
PRICES: [2017] B&B per room £71–£195. À la carte £35. 1-night bookings sometimes refused.

KILBERRY Argyll and Bute

Map 5:D1

KILBERRY INN

♔ Previous César winner

On a single-track road that traces the wild coast of the Knapdale peninsula, Clare Johnson and David Wilson's unassuming cottage houses a 'thoroughly enjoyable' restaurant-with-rooms – 'our favourite', say regular Guide correspondents this year. Stone walls are hung with work by local artists; a log-burning stove adds to the cosy atmosphere. 'Brilliant at front-of-house', David Wilson has 'a pleasant, easy manner, and readily provides help and information to those new to the area'. Clare Johnson's 'very good' modern menus follow the seasons, with liberal use of West Coast ingredients. 'We enjoyed langoustine; cod with chorizo, tomato and haricot beans; a tasty treacle tart.' 'Simple yet comfortable' accommodation is in mini-cottages set around a courtyard, each provided with books, fresh milk, home-made shortbread and local information. 'David and Clare are constantly upgrading the rooms. Ours, Gigha, had had a very smart make-over, with a modern walk-in shower.' Breakfast is a treat: tattie scones, Isle of Ewe smoked salmon, 'excellent' porridge with honey and cream. (GC, John and Elspeth Gibbon)

Kilberry
PA29 6YD

T: 01880 770223
E: relax@kilberryinn.com
W: www.kilberryinn.com

BEDROOMS: 5. All on ground floor.
OPEN: Tues–Sun, mid-Mar–end Oct; Fri–Sun, Nov–Dec.
FACILITIES: restaurant, snug (wood-burning stove), variable Wi-Fi (Kilberry is a Wi-Fi 'not-spot'), in-room TV (Freeview), small garden, unsuitable for disabled.
BACKGROUND MUSIC: in restaurant at lunch and dinner.
LOCATION: 16 miles NW of Tarbert, on B8024.
CHILDREN: not under 12.
DOGS: allowed by arrangement in 1 bedroom, not in public rooms.
CREDIT CARDS: MasterCard, Visa.
PRICES: [2017] per room D,B&B £230. À la carte £40. 1-night bookings sometimes refused.

KILCHRENAN Argyll and Bute

Map 5:D1

ARDANAISEIG

Swing round a winding, single-track road to this turreted, Jacobean-style baronial mansion 'beautifully situated' on the shores of Loch Awe. It has been owned since 1995 by antiques dealer Bennie Gray, who has filled it with a dazzling and eccentric collection of artwork, statuary and 'quirky objects'. There are golden, throne-like chairs and a fine Bechstein piano; china elephants, and oversized still lifes rendered in oil. Outside is as dramatic as in: take a seat in the oriental-rugged, marble-pillared drawing room and soak up the 'superb romantic views' over gardens, loch and woodland all the way to the distant peak of Ben Lui. 'Beautifully furnished bedrooms' were styled by an opera-set designer. With views on to loch or garden, all rooms are large (some, in fact, are huge, and have a four-poster bed, fireplace or roll-top bath), and supplied with biscuits, Scottish toiletries and fresh flowers. New romantics, check out the cool, contemporary honeymoon suite in a converted boatshed right on the water. As evening draws in, pull up a seat in the painting-hung dining room for a four-course menu of Inverawe salmon, perhaps, local venison or 'perfectly tender' beef.

25% DISCOUNT VOUCHERS

Kilchrenan
PA35 1HE

T: 01866 833333
F: 01866 833222
E: hello@ardanaiseig.com
W: www.ardanaiseig.com

BEDROOMS: 19. Some on ground floor, 1 in Boatshed, 1 self-catering cottage.
OPEN: Easter–New Year.
FACILITIES: drawing room, library/bar, restaurant, free Wi-Fi, in-room TV (Freeview), wedding facilities, 120-acre lochside grounds (walled garden, crannog, woodlands), unsuitable for disabled.
BACKGROUND MUSIC: none.
LOCATION: 4 miles E of Kilchrenan.
CHILDREN: all ages welcomed.
DOGS: allowed.
CREDIT CARDS: all major cards.
PRICES: [2017] per room B&B from £218, D,B&B from £300. À la carte £50.

KILLIECRANKIE Perth and Kinross

Map 5:D2

KILLIECRANKIE HOTEL

♺ Previous César winner

'A treat of a hotel.' 'It has never failed us,' say regular guests of this 'exceptionally pleasant' 1840s dower house by the beautiful, wooded Pass of Killiecrankie. Assisted by 'cheerful yet professional' staff in tartan skirts and trews, the owner, Henrietta Fergusson, is roundly praised. 'From the clean, comfortable bedrooms and excellent food to the close attention paid to every detail, she delivers superbly on all counts.' Individually styled bedrooms may be modestly decorated – 'they might not have a "wow" factor, but we like them,' say reporters this year – but each is 'well furnished', thoughtfully equipped (down to the radio with an integral phone charger), and made cheery with fresh flowers. Visitors might want to discuss room choices before booking: recent guests thought their accommodation 'rather snug'. In summer, gorge on cream tea in the 'nicely tended', rhododendron-filled garden; in winter, settle before the open fire in the lounge. In all seasons, come hungry: chef Mark Easton's daily-changing menu is 'cooked to a high standard'. (Pauline and Stephen Glover, A and EW)

25% DISCOUNT VOUCHERS

Killiecrankie
PH16 5LG

T: 01796 473220
F: 01796 472451
E: enquiries@killiecrankiehotel.co.uk
W: www.killiecrankiehotel.co.uk

BEDROOMS: 10. 2 on ground floor.
OPEN: 24 Mar–3 Jan.
FACILITIES: sitting room, bar with conservatory, dining room, breakfast conservatory, free Wi-Fi, in-room TV (Freeview), 4½-acre grounds (gardens, woodland), unsuitable for disabled.
BACKGROUND MUSIC: none.
LOCATION: hamlet 3 miles W of Pitlochry.
CHILDREN: all ages welcomed.
DOGS: allowed in bar and some bedrooms (not unattended), not in sitting or dining rooms.
CREDIT CARDS: Amex, MasterCard, Visa.
PRICES: [2017] per room B&B single £115–£125, double £200–£240, D,B&B single £150–£160, double £270–£330. Set dinner £42. 1-night bookings sometimes refused weekends.

KINCLAVEN Perth and Kinross

Map 5:D2

BALLATHIE HOUSE

Watch for roaming deer as you follow the 'long, attractive drive' to the Milligan family's Victorian country house on the banks of the River Tay. It's a sporting place with beats for anglers, clay-pigeon shoots, lovely walks, and golf nearby. Inside the grand old house – built in the 1880s for an army general – paintings hang in gilt frames; trophy cases display the salmon that didn't get away. A staircase sweeps up from a hall with a log fire; there's a wood-panelled bar packed with malt whiskies, and everywhere 'plenty of space to sit'. Bedrooms in the main house have period features and traditional furnishings; those in a riverside building reached via a lit pathway through the garden have their own patio or balcony. Cheaper rooms in the Sportsman's Lodge in the grounds – ideal for muddy-booted walking and fishing parties – are 'plainly furnished but large and warm'. Casual lunches (club sandwiches, Caesar salads) may be taken in the bar; in the dining room, chef Scott Scorer gives a modern twist to the classics, using local beef and venison ('the best we've ever tasted'), and trout and salmon fresh from the river. 'Each dish is a work of art.' (RW, and others)

Kinclaven
PH1 4QN

T: 01250 883268
E: email@ballathiehousehotel.com
W: www.ballathiehousehotel.com

BEDROOMS: 50. 16 in riverside building, 12 in Sportsman's Lodge, some on ground floor, 1 suitable for disabled.
OPEN: all year.
FACILITIES: drawing room, bar, restaurant, private dining rooms, free Wi-Fi, in-room TV (Freeview), wedding/function facilities, 900-acre estate (golf, fishing, shooting).
BACKGROUND MUSIC: none.
LOCATION: 1½ miles SW of Kinclaven.
CHILDREN: all ages welcomed, no young children in restaurant in evening.
DOGS: allowed in some bedrooms (not unattended), not in public rooms.
CREDIT CARDS: MasterCard, Visa.
PRICES: [2017] per person B&B from £120, D,B&B from £160; in Sportsman's Lodge, per person B&B from £70, D,B&B from £115. Set dinner £55.

KINGUSSIE Highland

Map 5:C2

THE CROSS AT KINGUSSIE

⚜ Previous César winner

Long praised for the generous hospitality of its hosts, Derek and Celia Kitchingman, this 'very quiet' 19th-century tweed mill-turned-restaurant-with-rooms on the banks of the River Gynack is gaining attention, too, for its food. In the award-winning restaurant, chef David Skiggs's 'beautifully presented, high-quality' cooking 'keeps getting better', Guide readers say. On the three-course dinner menu and six-course tasting menu, seasonal Scottish produce is given top billing. Characteristic dishes: wild sea bass, butternut squash purée, cep dumpling, truffle jus; loin of local lamb, cannelloni of shoulder, violet artichokes. In the bedrooms, stone walls and rustic colours (inspired by the surrounding hills) are given a contemporary feel. 'Our large, airy room had plenty of storage and a modern bathroom; a small balcony overlooked the burn.' Find books, games and a log fire in the lounges (one for residents only); step outside into gardens and woodland to spot red squirrels and roe deer. Guests arriving on the sleeper train can look forward to a hearty breakfast buffet and 'a good choice' of cooked dishes. (MB, GC)

Tweed Mill Brae
Ardbroilach Road
Kingussie
PH21 1LB

T: 01540 661166
E: relax@thecross.co.uk
W: www.thecross.co.uk

BEDROOMS: 8.
OPEN: closed Christmas and Jan, except Hogmanay.
FACILITIES: 2 lounges (wood-burning stove), restaurant, free Wi-Fi, in-room TV (Freeview), 4-acre grounds (terraced garden, woodland), only restaurant suitable for disabled.
BACKGROUND MUSIC: none.
LOCATION: 440 yds from village centre.
CHILDREN: all ages welcomed.
DOGS: not allowed.
CREDIT CARDS: Amex, MasterCard, Visa.
PRICES: [2017] per room B&B £100–£190, D,B&B £200–£280. Set dinner £55, tasting menu £65.

KIRKBEAN Dumfries and Galloway

Map 5:E2

CAVENS

'A winning example of the small "hands-on" country house genre', the Fordyce family's 18th-century manor house on the Solway coast is 'charmingly run' with old-fashioned joie de vivre. Angus Fordyce, the 'hospitable host', is 'an all-round good egg', Guide readers say. Fans like the 'peaceful location', 'restful atmosphere', 'good food' and 'friendly, smiling' staff. (The traditionally decorated sitting rooms, with paintings, log fires, a grand piano, and books to browse, are also liked.) Overlooking the gardens and countryside, 'immaculate, comfortable' bedrooms are individually styled. 'My large room had space to sit and enjoy the view. In the bathroom: a bath for a giant.' Angus Fordyce's frequently changing market menu is praised at dinnertime. Resident guests choose any three courses from the menu, perhaps pan-fried scallops, lime, vermouth; venison haunch steak, redcurrants. Oenophiles, take note: the host is happy to conduct a tour of the small private wine cellar. Wake up to a 'particularly good' breakfast, with 'plenty of choice and well-presented cooked dishes', then roam the extensive grounds. Further afield, coastal walks are steps away. (DP, Brian Knox)

25% DISCOUNT VOUCHERS

Kirkbean
DG2 8AA

T: 01387 880234
F: 01387 880467
E: enquiries@cavens.com
W: www.cavens.com

BEDROOMS: 6. 1 on ground floor.
OPEN: Mar–Nov, exclusive use by groups at New Year.
FACILITIES: 2 sitting rooms, dining room, meeting facilities, free Wi-Fi, in-room TV (Freeview), 10-acre grounds, unsuitable for disabled.
BACKGROUND MUSIC: light classical all day in 1 sitting room, dining room.
LOCATION: in village.
CHILDREN: all ages welcomed (cots provided).
DOGS: allowed by arrangement, not in public rooms or unattended in bedrooms.
CREDIT CARDS: MasterCard, Visa.
PRICES: [2017] per room D,B&B £200–£300. 1-night bookings refused Easter, bank holidays.

KIRKCUDBRIGHT Dumfries and Galloway   Map 5:E2

GLENHOLME COUNTRY HOUSE

There's an array of panama hats in the wide, panelled hall, and a neat stack of antique steamer trunks; there are Victorian club chairs and framed photographs from the days of the Raj. Here is a guest house as 'idiosyncratic and characterful' as its owners, Laurence Bristow-Smith, an author and retired diplomat, and his artist wife, Jennifer. Guests receive a 'warm greeting' before being shown to one of four rooms, each named after a political figure. Balfour has an antique four-poster bed and a chandelier. Curzon, with 'spectacular views' of gardens and water meadows, is decked out in vintage fabrics and an eclectic mix of period furniture. There is no TV in the rooms, but the house has a fine library with 'a fascinating collection of well-thumbed books' – and there's always conversation to be had. At dinner, the host's cooking owes much to the kitchen garden and sojourns abroad, from China to Milan via Morocco. Try feta-stuffed peppers or Chinese dumplings one evening; monkfish, squid-ink risotto, asparagus spears another. All is 'very comfortable and relaxed'. Reach the town, a small fishing port, via a walk along the banks of the River Dee. More reports, please.

Tongland Road
Kirkcudbright
DG6 4UU

T: 01557 339422
E: info@glenholmecountryhouse.com
W: www.glenholmecountryhouse.com

BEDROOMS: 4.
OPEN: all year except Christmas, New Year.
FACILITIES: library, lounge, dining room, free Wi-Fi, 2-acre garden (formal gardens, vegetable plot, orchard), unsuitable for disabled.
BACKGROUND MUSIC: none.
LOCATION: 1 mile N of town, an easy walk along the river.
CHILDREN: not under 12.
DOGS: not allowed.
CREDIT CARDS: MasterCard, Visa (4% surcharge on credit-card payments).
PRICES: per room B&B single £95–£110, double £115–£135. Set dinner £38. 1-night bookings only on DB&B rates.

KYLESKU Highland

Map 5:B2

KYLESKU HOTEL

♕ Previous César winner

In 'one of the wildest and most beautiful locations', Tanja Lister and Sonia Virechauveix run their small hotel with 'informal warmth'. The 17th-century coaching inn stands by the former ferry slipway on the shores of Loch Glendhu: it's a 'superb setting', where grey seals loll on the rocks outside, and wild stags nose around the garden. (Dogs are 'welcome everywhere', too.) Inside, find bleached woods and muted shades; wood burners keep things warm. Bedrooms are in the main building and a purpose-built extension facing the loch. 'We took in stupendous views from our first-floor room in "Willie's Hoose". The room is compact and modern, with nice linen on the double bed, and glass sliding doors opening on to the balcony. There was a full set of good toiletries in the smart bathroom, but we would have liked some bathrobes, too.' At a 'casual, gastropubby' dinner ('no tablecloths or place settings'), super-local seafood is a speciality. Try to get a seat by the window: 'Even when darkness falls, there's a special atmosphere out across the loch.' (CA, J and DA, and others)

Kylesku
IV27 4HW

T: 01971 502231
E: info@kyleskuhotel.co.uk
W: www.kyleskuhotel.co.uk

BEDROOMS: 11. 4 in annexe, 1 suitable for disabled.
OPEN: mid-Feb–end Nov.
FACILITIES: lounge, bar, restaurant, free Wi-Fi in bar and lounge, in-room TV (Freeview), small garden (tables for outside eating).
BACKGROUND MUSIC: in afternoon and evenings, in bar and half the dining area.
LOCATION: 10 miles S of Scourie.
CHILDREN: all ages welcomed.
DOGS: allowed (£10 a night), but not unattended in bedrooms.
CREDIT CARDS: MasterCard, Visa.
PRICES: [2017] per room B&B £110–£170. À la carte £45.

LOCHEPORT Western Isles

LANGASS LODGE

A 'cosy spot' in a remote position overlooking Langass sea loch, Amanda and Niall Leveson Gower's family-friendly former sporting lodge is ideal for guests in search of fresh air and 'magnificent scenery'. This corner of North Uist, in the Outer Hebrides, is 'a paradise for wildlife'; the 'friendly hosts' are helpful with suggesting walks and providing maps. Ask for a tumbler of Harris gin in the traditional-feel bar (a wood-burning stove is lit here in cool weather); from the 'light, comfy, conservatory-like sitting room', take in the panorama across the water to the peak of Ben Eaval. In the main building and a modern extension reached via a covered walkway, 'lovely' bedrooms are made homely with smart tartan cushions, rugs on wooden floors, and 'extra-fancy throws' on the bed. (Two spacious rooms accommodate a family.) Dinner brings a 'fabulous' menu rich in local game, fish and shellfish, accompanied by vegetables and herbs from the garden. 'The local hand-dived scallops are particularly good.' There's plenty of diversion for active sorts: fishing, cycling, kayaking; otter walks to the edge of the loch. (Philip Bright, and others)

Locheport
HS6 5HA

T: 01876 580285
F: 01876 580385
E: langasslodge@btconnect.com
W: www.langasslodge.co.uk

BEDROOMS: 11. Some in extension, 1 suitable for disabled.
OPEN: May–end Oct.
FACILITIES: lounge, bar, restaurant, free Wi-Fi, in-room TV (Freeview), 11-acre garden in 200-acre grounds.
BACKGROUND MUSIC: in public rooms.
LOCATION: 7½ miles SW of Lochmaddy.
CHILDREN: all ages welcomed.
DOGS: not in restaurant.
CREDIT CARDS: Amex, MasterCard, Visa.
PRICES: [2017] per room B&B single £80–£115, double £95–£155, family room £120–£175. À la carte £38, bar meals £12.

LOCHINVER Highland

Map 5:B1

THE ALBANNACH

Between mountains and sea loch, Lesley Crosfield and Colin Craig's restaurant-with-rooms is the UK's most northerly Michelin-starred outpost, an accolade held by the self-taught chefs since 2009. 'It's as good as ever,' reports a Guide reader this year. The 200-year-old building has individually styled bedrooms and suites (two with an extra sofa bed); for a special occasion, book the Byre, which comes with a hot tub on a private terrace, 'great for drinking champagne in – and there were no midges!' In the evening, the hosts' modern Scottish cooking is the star attraction. Unfussy dishes let seasonal ingredients shine: fruit and vegetables harvested from the croft, fish and shellfish caught and landed in Ullapool and Lochinver, eggs from local crofters, honey from the hives. On the set five-course menu, perhaps: mousseline of wild halibut, lobster; roast saddle of wild roe deer, candy beetroot, truffled squash, potato galette. (When the restaurant is closed, nip down to sister pub The Caberfeidh, in the village, for a crab sandwich.) The surrounding area, remote and wild, calls for a meander; there are coastal paths, hilly hikes, even boat trips to nearby islands. (Richard Bright)

Baddidarroch
Lochinver
IV27 4LP

T: 01571 844407
E: info@thealbannach.co.uk
W: www.thealbannach.co.uk

BEDROOMS: 5. 1 suite in byre.
OPEN: 10 Feb–20 Nov, 16 Dec–4 Jan, closed Mon, Mon–Wed in winter.
FACILITIES: snug, conservatory, dining room, free Wi-Fi, in-room TV (Freeview), ¾-acre garden in 4 acres of grounds.
BACKGROUND MUSIC: none.
LOCATION: ½ mile from village.
CHILDREN: not under 12.
DOGS: not allowed.
CREDIT CARDS: Diners, MasterCard, Visa.
PRICES: [2017] per room B&B (Tues, Wed) £170–£250, D,B&B (Thurs–Sun) £320–£400. 1-night bookings generally refused Sat.

MELROSE Scottish Borders

Map 5:E3

THE TOWNHOUSE [NEW]

'A genuine delight to stay in.' The Henderson family's 'hard-to-fault' town-centre hotel receives an upgrade to a full entry this year thanks to regular Guide correspondents who praised the 'well-appointed bedrooms', and 'unfailingly charming and helpful staff, who go out of their way to provide good service'. It is 'well situated' for the historic Borders town – still lively today with its butcher, baker and candlestick purveyor – as well as for exploration further afield: 'there's good walking nearby, and lots of places of interest'. Individually styled bedrooms have modern wallcoverings and contemporary fittings; bathrooms are supplied with Scottish-made toiletries. Large superior rooms have a comfortable seating area. 'Our light, spacious room was beautifully decorated and spotlessly clean.' At lunch and dinner, the informal brasserie's the place to be: chef Johnny Millar's 'excellent, good-value' dishes are accompanied by an 'imaginative' wine list. (Save space for the sticky toffee pudding 'to die for'.) Breakfast, with Scottish stalwarts porridge and kippers, is 'excellent every day'. Sister hotel Burts is across the street (see Shortlist entry). (Andrew Warren, and others)

Market Square
Melrose
TD6 9PQ

T: 01896 822645
F: 01896 823474
E: enquiries@
thetownhousemelrose.co.uk
W: www.thetownhousemelrose.
co.uk

BEDROOMS: 11. 1 on ground floor.
OPEN: all year except Christmas Day, Boxing Day.
FACILITIES: bar/brasserie, restaurant, free Wi-Fi, in-room TV (Freeview), wedding/function facilities, decked patio, parking.
BACKGROUND MUSIC: in brasserie and restaurant.
LOCATION: town centre.
CHILDREN: all ages welcomed.
DOGS: not allowed.
CREDIT CARDS: Amex, MasterCard, Visa.
PRICES: per room B&B single from £100, double from £136, D,B&B (2-night min. stay) single from £125, double from £190. À la carte £30, 'early bird' menu £16.95–£20.95.

SEE ALSO SHORTLIST

MUIR OF ORD Highland

Map 5:C2

THE DOWER HOUSE

♕ Previous César winner

'We were thoroughly spoiled.' Mena and Robyn Aitchison are much appreciated by Guide readers for the 'wonderful hospitality' at their 'well-located' Georgian stone cottage orné outside Inverness. Everywhere is something to catch the eye. Outside, find a miniature orchard, a large goldfish pond, woodland paths and a riot of colour in the 'beautiful' gardens; inside, 'their house is a treasure chest' where 'interesting objects' abound (antiques, Persian rugs, Chinese vases, potted plants, well-stocked bookshelves). The result is the 'pleasant, peaceful' atmosphere of a 'home away from home'. Lounge about in a 'cosy', garden-view bedroom thoughtfully equipped with fresh flowers and dressing gowns; pour yourself a glass from one of the range of malts in the drinks cupboard; play a board game in front of a wood-burning stove in the lounge. In sunshine, sit on one of the garden benches and simply enjoy the wild flower-dotted surroundings. Dinner is no longer on the menu, but a 'first-rate' breakfast includes proper porridge, and eggs from the house's free-range hens. (CE, HA, and others)

Highfield
Muir of Ord
IV6 7XN

T: 01463 870090
F: 01463 870090
E: info@thedowerhouse.co.uk
W: www.thedowerhouse.co.uk

BEDROOMS: 3. All on ground floor, plus small self-contained 2-bed flat.
OPEN: Apr–Oct.
FACILITIES: lounge, dining room, snug/TV room, free Wi-Fi, in-room TV (Freeview), wedding facilities, 5-acre grounds, unsuitable for disabled.
BACKGROUND MUSIC: none.
LOCATION: 14 miles NW of Inverness.
CHILDREN: all ages welcomed.
DOGS: allowed in bedrooms (not on bed or furniture), not in public rooms.
CREDIT CARDS: MasterCard, Visa.
PRICES: [2017] per room B&B £145–£165.

MUTHILL Perth and Kinross

Map 5:D2

BARLEY BREE

'The restaurant, the room and, in particular, the hospitality exceeded our expectations,' say returning visitors this year. Alison and Fabrice Bouteloup's restaurant-with-rooms occupies a red-stone former coaching inn, in a pretty conservation village. Hands-on hosts, the owners are 'attentive but informal'; their staff are 'efficient and friendly'. A grandson of farmers, the French-born chef/patron is praised for his 'tasty local flavours'. In the dining room ('attractively decorated to reflect the rural surroundings'), cuisine grand-mère meets modern European cooking in his daily-changing menus. A typical dish: saddle of lamb, shoulder croquette, Puy lentils, honeyed parsnips. Alison Bouteloup, who has a background in the wine trade, discusses grape varieties and vintages with aplomb. And so to bed, in one of the 'spotlessly clean and inviting' bedrooms. These vary in size and aspect, but all have a miniature bottle of the restaurant's own-label whisky on the tea tray. At breakfast, there's 'plenty of toast' – Fabrice Bouteloup's bread is so good it's sold in the village shop – with home-made jam and marmalade; 'delicious' cooked dishes.

6 Willoughby Street
Muthill
PH5 2AB

T: 01764 681451
F: 01764 910055
E: info@barleybree.com
W: www.barleybree.com

BEDROOMS: 6.
OPEN: all year except Christmas, 1 week July, restaurant closed Mon, Tues.
FACILITIES: lounge bar, restaurant, free Wi-Fi, in-room TV (Freeview), small terrace and lawn, drying facilities, unsuitable for disabled.
BACKGROUND MUSIC: in lounge bar and restaurant.
LOCATION: village centre.
CHILDREN: all ages welcomed (family room, children's menu).
DOGS: not allowed.
CREDIT CARDS: MasterCard, Visa.
PRICES: [2017] per room B&B from £95. À la carte £42.

OBAN Argyll and Bute

Map 5:D1

THE MANOR HOUSE

Sit on the terrace of Leslie and Margaret Crane's 'relaxed, friendly' Georgian stone mansion overlooking Oban bay, and watch the ferries slip out of the harbour, bound for the Isles. A former ducal dower house, the traditional hotel has 'lovely, cosy Scottish decor'– winged armchairs, gilt-framed pictures, a grandfather clock. The 'well-appointed bedrooms' (some small) are made welcoming with fruit, biscuits and flowers; five, overlooking the harbour, contain a pair of binoculars. The food is highly rated, Guide readers report, 'from the hearty Scottish breakfasts to well-balanced dinners' that make use of local produce. Informal lunches (West Highland fish soup; veggie risotto) may be taken in Nelson's bar. In the dining room, chef Shaun Squire's daily-changing menu, preceded by 'delicious canapés', might include West Coast scallop ceviche, chilli and mango salsa, cucumber gin granita; apple and apricot-stuffed pork, truffle mash, Stornoway black pudding. The harbour and ferry terminal are within easy walking distance: book a ride on the early ferry to spend a day on the Isle of Mull – the 'helpful staff' have plenty of local knowledge and are happy to advise.

Gallanach Road
Oban
PA34 4LS

T: 01631 562087
F: 01631 563053
E: info@manorhouseoban.com
W: www.manorhouseoban.com

BEDROOMS: 11. 1 on ground floor.
OPEN: all year except 25/26 Dec.
FACILITIES: 2 lounges, bar, restaurant, free Wi-Fi, in-room TV (Freeview), wedding facilities, 1½-acre grounds, access to nearby gym and golf, unsuitable for disabled.
BACKGROUND MUSIC: traditional in bar and dining room.
LOCATION: ½ mile from centre.
CHILDREN: not under 12.
DOGS: allowed by arrangement, not in public rooms.
CREDIT CARDS: all major cards.
PRICES: [2017] per room B&B £125–£260, D,B&B £205–£340. Set dinner £44, all dishes available à la carte.

SEE ALSO SHORTLIST

PEAT INN Fife

Map 5:D3

THE PEAT INN

Chef/patron Geoffrey Smeddle and his wife, Katherine, run their 'luxurious, very special' restaurant-with-rooms in an 18th-century coaching inn close to St Andrews and the Fife coast. A 'warm welcome' includes a decanter of sherry in the bedrooms – 'which we were urged to help ourselves to'. Past the 'blazing log fire' in the reception lounge, sit down, in one of three dining rooms, to the sort of 'outstanding' modern cooking that earned the restaurant a Michelin star. 'I had a beetroot starter, veal sweetbreads and an apricot soufflé – all outstanding.' Diners opting for the tasting menu may need to clear the evening: 'The cooking was superb, but we thought three hours for six courses was too long.' Alternatively, eat off the à la carte menu or, like other Guide readers, settle in and enjoy the 'unhurried feel'. In the separate residence, 'nice, modern' suites have a large lounge area stocked with chess, draughts and magazines; a 'beautifully tended garden' is 'lovely both to look out upon, and to sit in'. A continental breakfast is brought to the room at a pre-arranged time: smoked haddock, soft-boiled eggs, pastries and home-made preserves. (J and HT-P, Anthony Bradbury)

Peat Inn
KY15 5LH

T: 01334 840206
F: 01334 840530
E: stay@thepeatinn.co.uk
W: www.thepeatinn.co.uk

BEDROOMS: 8. All suites, on ground floor in annexe, 7 split-level.
OPEN: all year except 1 week Christmas, 1 week Jan, open from 27 Dec for Hogmanay, restaurant closed Sun/Mon.
FACILITIES: lounge (log fire) in restaurant, free Wi-Fi, in-room TV, ½-acre garden.
BACKGROUND MUSIC: in restaurant.
LOCATION: 6 miles SW of St Andrews.
CHILDREN: all ages welcomed, not under 7 in restaurant at dinner.
DOGS: not allowed.
CREDIT CARDS: Amex, MasterCard, Visa.
PRICES: [2017] per room B&B from £195, D,B&B (including tasting menu) from £325. Set dinner £50, tasting menu £70, à la carte £58.

PITLOCHRY Perth and Kinross

Map 5:D2

CRAIGATIN HOUSE AND COURTYARD

In a former surgeon's home built in the early 1800s, Andrea and Martin Anderson offer guests a 'warm welcome', 'great local advice' and, at a 'superb breakfast', a 'divine' Arnold Bennett omelette – perhaps just what the doctor ordered. The bucolic exterior belies the B&B's contemporary interior: expect handsome, high-end wallpapers and Farrow & Ball colours. Split between the main house and converted stables, individually decorated rooms (three updated in 2017) are well equipped with coffee, teas and locally made biscuits. 'Our delightful, spotlessly clean courtyard suite was well appointed, with comfortable chairs in a light, bright sitting area. Although the room is nearest to the road, we weren't disturbed by traffic noise.' Take in the morning over breakfast in the double-height, light-filled cedarwood extension overlooking 'beautifully kept' gardens. The morning meal is a superlative one, guests say. Porridge comes with a choice of toppings (whisky, cream and sugar; Perthshire honey; summer berry compote); apple pancakes with grilled bacon are made, in season, with garden fruit. 'The best breakfast of our Scottish tour!' (DC)

25% DISCOUNT VOUCHERS

165 Atholl Road
Pitlochry
PH16 5QL

T: 01796 472478
E: enquiries@craigatinhouse.co.uk
W: www.craigatinhouse.co.uk

BEDROOMS: 14. 7 in courtyard, 2 on ground floor, 1 suitable for disabled.
OPEN: Mar–Dec, closed Christmas, open New Year.
FACILITIES: lounge, 2 breakfast rooms, free Wi-Fi, in-room TV (Freeview), 2-acre garden.
BACKGROUND MUSIC: at breakfast.
LOCATION: central.
CHILDREN: not under 13.
DOGS: not allowed.
CREDIT CARDS: MasterCard, Visa.
PRICES: per room B&B £107–£134. 1-night bookings refused Sat.

SEE ALSO SHORTLIST

PITLOCHRY Perth and Kinross

DALSHIAN HOUSE

Vibrant Victorian Pitlochry offers many diversions, but to escape the bustle, head for Martin and Heather Walls's guest house, a 'beautiful' Georgian house on the outskirts of town. Approached by a private drive, it stands in an acre of woodland and mature gardens teeming with wildlife – watch out for the red squirrels, rabbits and robins. Come for the 'friendly, family welcome', and the 'warm, comfortable' log fire-warmed lounge stocked with nibbles and magazines. In the 'fantastic' bedrooms, where traditional furnishings mix with bold modern touches, you might find shortbread on the hospitality tray. The generous, locally sourced breakfast, 'a great start to the day', includes local honey, perhaps spiced plums or gingered rhubarb, plus tattie scones, Dunkeld smoked salmon, and porridge with or without a nip of Edradour whisky. (The Wallses cater for special diets, too.) 'Warm and welcoming', the hosts are pleased to advise guests on how to spend the day. Blair Castle is a short drive away; historic Dunkeld and Birnam are nearby; packed lunches can be provided for a forest ramble. Eating places abound in the town. (SM)

25% DISCOUNT VOUCHERS

Old Perth Road
Pitlochry
PH16 5TD

T: 01796 472173
E: dalshian@btconnect.com
W: www.dalshian.co.uk

BEDROOMS: 7.
OPEN: all year except Christmas.
FACILITIES: lounge, dining room, free Wi-Fi, in-room TV (Freeview), 1-acre garden, unsuitable for disabled.
BACKGROUND MUSIC: none.
LOCATION: 1 mile S of centre.
CHILDREN: all ages welcomed.
DOGS: allowed by arrangement, not in public rooms.
CREDIT CARDS: MasterCard, Visa.
PRICES: [2017] per person B&B £37.50–£45.

SEE ALSO SHORTLIST

PITLOCHRY Perth and Kinross

Map 5:D2

THE GREEN PARK

♔ Previous César winner

On the banks of Loch Faskally, two generations of the McMenemie family run this much-liked Victorian hotel with 'cheerful efficiency' and an 'informal, personable' air. 'We loved the all-day spread of coffees, teas and home-made cakes, and later sherry, in the splendid lounges full of comfortable chairs.' Idle with binoculars and a book of Scottish birds in one of the seating areas; pick up a map to the hotel's many Scottish artworks: a lesson in art history awaits. Bedrooms are in the main house and several sympathetic extensions. 'We were so pleased with our large room overlooking the immaculate front lawn and, just beyond, lovely Loch Faskally.' At dinner, chef Chris Tamblin's daily-changing Franco-Scottish menu is served 'in substantial portions, with lashings of potatoes and vegetables'. (Earlier mealtimes, just as enthusiastically attended, are available for guests heading to the Pitlochry Festival Theatre.) In the morning, help yourself from three breakfast buffet tables carrying 'the greatest range of choices we have ever seen'; an 'ample variety' of cooked dishes is served at the table. (AB)

25% DISCOUNT VOUCHERS

Clunie Bridge Road
Pitlochry
PH16 5JY

T: 01796 473248
F: 01796 473520
E: bookings@thegreenpark.co.uk
W: www.thegreenpark.co.uk

BEDROOMS: 51. 13 on ground floor, 1 suitable for disabled.
OPEN: all year except Christmas.
FACILITIES: 2 lifts, 3 lounges, library, bar, restaurant, free Wi-Fi, in-room TV (Freeview), 3-acre garden.
BACKGROUND MUSIC: none.
LOCATION: ½ mile N of town centre.
CHILDREN: all ages welcomed.
DOGS: allowed, not in public rooms.
CREDIT CARDS: MasterCard, Visa.
PRICES: [2017] per person B&B £83–£93, D,B&B £94–£118. Set menus £25–£29.

SEE ALSO SHORTLIST

PITLOCHRY Perth and Kinross

KNOCKENDARROCH HOTEL & RESTAURANT

'Bright flowers around the house add to the charm' on a spring day at Struan and Louise Lothian's Victorian stone mansion, in sloping gardens on a quiet street. A 'well-established hotel', it is in and of the town, though the views, across the Tummel valley towards the surrounding hills, might suggest a more rural setting. With modern country house flair, newly updated bedrooms, varying in size and style, are 'fresh and tasteful'; some have a small balcony, and binoculars to match. Two spacious, well-equipped suites were added in 2017, each decorated in uplifting colours, and with chairs and a table by the window for a scenic in-room breakfast. Downstairs in the 'large, comfortable', log fire-warmed lounges, there are books, wide armchairs, whiskies galore in a cabinet. Light lunches, drinks and pre-dinner canapés are taken here. In the evening, Graeme Stewart's daily-changing modern menu might include braised feather blade of Scottish beef, horseradish mash, carrot purée, purple sprouting broccoli, shallot jam. 'Delicious – we were spoilt for choice.'

25% DISCOUNT VOUCHERS

Higher Oakfield
Pitlochry
PH16 5HT

T: 01796 473473
E: bookings@knockendarroch.
co.uk
W: www.knockendarroch.co.uk

BEDROOMS: 14. 2 on ground floor.
OPEN: Feb–20 Dec.
FACILITIES: 2 lounges, restaurant, free Wi-Fi, in-room TV (Freeview), 2-acre woodland garden, bicycle storage, unsuitable for disabled.
BACKGROUND MUSIC: in restaurant in evening.
LOCATION: central.
CHILDREN: not under 10.
DOGS: not allowed.
CREDIT CARDS: Amex, MasterCard, Visa.
PRICES: [2017] per room B&B £145–£280, D,B&B £175–£330. Set dinner £42. 1-night bookings sometimes refused on Sat.

SEE ALSO SHORTLIST

POOLEWE Highland

POOL HOUSE

'Old-fashioned in the best way', the Harrison family's 'lovely, eclectic guest house' on the shores of Loch Ewe is run by 'friendly, informative hosts who make a real effort to ensure every guest is taken care of'. 'Sisters Elizabeth and Mhairi are welcoming and obliging; their father, Peter, is full of interesting stories,' say Guide inspectors in 2017, who were plied with leaf tea and cake by the drawing room fire. The 18th-century fishing lodge has 'an extraordinary history'; 'family photographs nearly a century old' sit well with a dining room decorated to a maritime theme. Each singular suite has views across the water. 'The walls and curtains in our suite had stars trailing up them and on to the ceiling. The fire had been lit in our sitting room; seats, and binoculars, in the bay window took in great views of the loch. The four-poster bed was enormous; the bathroom, an Edwardian masterpiece.' After canapés, a 'well-curated set dinner' might include 'beautifully presented chicken with Parma ham' and an 'utterly delicious' Granny Smith sorbet. ('They impressively catered for a host of dietary restrictions, too.') At breakfast: 'tasty mushrooms on toast'; 'a perfect sausage'.

by Inverewe Garden
Poolewe
IV22 2LD

T: 01445 781272
E: stay@pool-house.co.uk
W: www.pool-house.co.uk

BEDROOMS: 4 suites.
OPEN: Easter–early Nov, 23 Dec–2 Jan, closed Mon except bank hols, dining room closed Sun (soup and sandwiches available).
FACILITIES: reception room, drawing room/library, dining room, private dining room, billiard/whisky room, free Wi-Fi in public areas, in-room TV (Freeview), ½-acre garden, unsuitable for disabled.
BACKGROUND MUSIC: none.
LOCATION: in village 6 miles NE of Gairloch.
CHILDREN: not under 14.
DOGS: not allowed.
CREDIT CARDS: Amex, MasterCard, Visa.
PRICES: [2017] per room B&B £225–£375. Set menu £48. 1-night bookings refused at weekends.

PORT APPIN Argyll and Bute

Map 5:D1

THE AIRDS HOTEL

'The views are stunning' from Shaun and Jenny McKivragan's 'wonderful' small hotel, in a dramatic setting above Loch Linnhe, with the Morvern mountains beyond. Within the former ferry inn, there's more that pleases: 'comfortable bedrooms', 'excellent dinners' and 'attentive, but not overpowering, service'. 'We like the personal feel; it was great to see the owners engaging with the guests.' Traditionally decorated public rooms are hung with original artwork; there are fresh flowers, log fires, tartan armchairs, books to borrow. The bedrooms vary in style, from country house to more contemporary, but each has 'everything you might need' – robes and slippers, iced water in silver jugs, a decanter of Whisky Mac. 'Ours was delightful, with views over the loch and mountains.' In the candlelit restaurant, chef Chris Stanley's 'top-notch cooking' is served on crisp table linen. Local produce, including 'the freshest of fish and shellfish', features in modern dishes such as crab ravioli, shellfish sauce, wild garlic. On a clear day, request a packed lunch and help with bicycle hire, and take the ferry to Lismore – the lucky might spot dolphins or golden eagles along the way. (Susan Sutton, and others)

Port Appin
PA38 4DF

T: 01631 730236
F: 01631 730535
E: airds@airds-hotel.com
W: www.airds-hotel.com

BEDROOMS: 11. 2 on ground floor, plus 2 self-catering cottages.
OPEN: all year, restaurant closed Mon/Tue Nov–end Jan (open Christmas and New Year).
FACILITIES: 2 lounges, conservatory, whisky bar, restaurant, civil wedding licence, free Wi-Fi, in-room TV (Freeview), spa treatments, ½-acre garden (croquet, putting), mountain bike hire, unsuitable for disabled.
BACKGROUND MUSIC: none.
LOCATION: 20 miles N of Oban.
CHILDREN: all ages welcomed, no under-8s in dining room in evening (children's high tea).
DOGS: allowed in bedrooms (not unattended), not in public rooms.
CREDIT CARDS: MasterCard, Visa.
PRICES: [2017] per room DB&B £305–£485.

PORT APPIN Argyll and Bute

Map 5:D1

THE PIERHOUSE

NEW

Nick and Nikki Horne run their 'top-class hotel' in a 'fantastic location' on the shores of Loch Linnhe, where the 'spectacular vista' stretches across the water to the islands and beyond. Turn your view inside, if you can bear to: 'Nick and Nikki are superb hosts'; their staff are 'exceptionally friendly and professional'. Steps from the beach, the 'cosy' 19th-century piermaster's house has a wood stove–warmed bar popular for its seafood platters, Scottish gins and malt whiskies. In the restaurant – come in time for a sunset supper – chef Laura Milne's 'very nice, reasonably priced' menu specialises in 'delicious' local fish and shellfish. (Look out for lobsters and crabs in creels at the end of the pier.) 'Well-appointed' bedrooms are supplied with Scottish toiletries, shortbread, still and sparkling water; some rooms suit a family. 'Try to get a sea-view room' (for 'peace, quiet and the gentle lap of waves'), but even cliff-facing bedrooms have outdoor entertainment in the form of the chaffinches, siskins and wrens who visit the bird tables nearby. Breakfast has freshly baked croissants and home-made jams. Afterwards, the ferry to Lismore awaits. (Brian Irving, Chris Elliott)

Port Appin
PA38 4DE

T: 01631 730302
F: 01631 730509
E: reservations@pierhousehotel.co.uk
W: www.pierhousehotel.co.uk

BEDROOMS: 12.
OPEN: all year except 24–26 Dec.
FACILITIES: residents' snug, lounge, bar, restaurant, private dining room, free Wi-Fi, in-room TV (Freeview), civil wedding licence, sauna (treatments available), terrace, yacht moorings, unsuitable for disabled.
BACKGROUND MUSIC: in bar and restaurant.
LOCATION: in village, 20 miles N of Oban.
CHILDREN: all ages welcomed.
DOGS: 'well-behaved, quiet and house-trained dogs' allowed in 3 bedrooms (not unattended), not in public rooms.
CREDIT CARDS: Amex, MasterCard, Visa.
PRICES: [2017] per room B&B £90–£255. À la carte £35–£40.

PORTPATRICK Dumfries and Galloway

KNOCKINAAM LODGE

On a sheltered cove on the wildly scenic Galloway coast, Sian and David Ibbotson's stone hunting lodge is liked for its 'tranquil setting', its 'professional, friendly, caring' staff, and its fine collection of single malts. Inside the traditionally decorated 19th-century building, there are log fires, fresh flowers, deep armchairs on oriental carpets, and 'cosy, comfortable' lounges ideal for afternoon tea. No surprise, perhaps, that some guests come for special occasions: 'It's our go-to for celebrating anniversaries.' Stay in the Churchill suite, where the former PM once stayed: the king-size sleigh bed and walk-in shower may be new, but the 100-year-old enamelled bath in which he soaked is still there. Other bedrooms – varying in size, all different – look out across the sea, with views to Northern Ireland. At dinner, chef Tony Pierce's modern Scottish cuisine, perhaps including roast Speyside beef, Knockinaam new potatoes, garlic beignet, is 'superb'. Breakfast well before heading off on one of the many walks from the door, or simply traipse through the landscaped gardens to reach a private sandy beach. (HH, and others)

25% DISCOUNT VOUCHERS

Portpatrick
DG9 9AD

T: 01776 810471
F: 01776 810435
E: reservations@knockinaamlodge.com
W: www.knockinaamlodge.com

BEDROOMS: 10.
OPEN: all year.
FACILITIES: 2 lounges, bar, restaurant, free Wi-Fi, in-room TV (Freeview), wedding facilities, 20-acre grounds, only restaurant suitable for disabled.
BACKGROUND MUSIC: 'easy listening'/classical in restaurant in evening.
LOCATION: 3 miles S of Portpatrick.
CHILDREN: all ages welcomed, no under-12s in dining room in evening (high tea at 6 pm).
DOGS: allowed in some bedrooms, not in public rooms.
CREDIT CARDS: Amex, MasterCard, Visa.
PRICES: [2017] per person D,B&B £145–£220. 1-night bookings sometimes refused.

PORTREE Highland

VIEWFIELD HOUSE

Unstuffy, informal, perhaps a touch eccentric, the Macdonald family's 'fabulous' Victorian country house stands in large wooded grounds with far-reaching views of Portree Bay. Hugh Macdonald, the laid-back, affable host, continues to live at the ancestral home, but his daughter, Iona, has now stepped up to the helm, continuing the welcoming tradition her great-grandmother began. Fans like the homely interior, busy with antiques and curios, china collections and oriental carpets, stags' antlers and colonial memorabilia, though one guest this year found it 'rather too much "home" and not enough "hotel"'. Traditional bedrooms are individually decorated with vintage furnishings ('mine had a Victorian washstand with a bowl and jug'). Some are country cosy with floral prints or a cast iron bedstead; others might have a window seat overlooking the lawn. There's no TV in the room, but gather with fellow guests by the fire in the lounge (maybe over cream scones or pre-dinner cocktails), or head outside for a round of croquet or a stroll into the town – umbrellas and wellies stand by the entrance. Dinners are straightforward; breakfast brings 'very nice home-made marmalade'.

Viewfield Road
Portree
IV51 9EU

T: 01478 612217
F: 01478 613517
E: info@viewfieldhouse.com
W: www.viewfieldhouse.com

BEDROOMS: 11. 1, on ground floor, suitable for disabled.
OPEN: Apr–Oct.
FACILITIES: drawing room, morning/TV room, dining room, free Wi-Fi, 20-acre grounds (croquet, swings).
BACKGROUND MUSIC: none.
LOCATION: S side of Portree.
CHILDREN: all ages welcomed.
DOGS: allowed in bedrooms, not in public rooms.
CREDIT CARDS: MasterCard, Visa.
PRICES: [2017] per person B&B £68–£85, D,B&B £93–£115. Set dinner £25 (if booked in advance). 1-night bookings sometimes refused.

RANNOCH STATION Perth and Kinross   Map 5:D2

MOOR OF RANNOCH HOTEL

✿ Previous César winner

'Talk about off the beaten track!' Scott Meikle and Stephanie Graham's 'little jewel of a hotel' stands at the end of the road, amid a vast moorland wilderness of lochs and lochans. Sixteen miles from the nearest settlement, it is beyond the reach of mobile phone and Wi-Fi signals. The result: a 'relaxing, chilled-out atmosphere' its fans swoon into. Arrive by sleeper train in time for a 'hearty breakfast' of free-range eggs or porridge with Drambuie and cream, then unpack in one of the 'well-equipped' bedrooms – they're 'just big enough, with a good bed'. Most attractive, perhaps, is the 'captivating wild scenery' seen from the bedroom window – look out for red deer and stags. At dinnertime, eat in (you can hardly do otherwise!) and enjoy the hostess's daily-changing menus. Typical dishes: Aga-cooked ox cheek, neep and tattie gratin; pan-fried halibut, roast tomato sauce, lemon and herb couscous, griddled aubergine. 'Dinner was good value, with generous portions.' There are bikes to hire, and forest tracks for all abilities; so take it slow, order a packed lunch and simply start walking. (DS, JM)

Rannoch Station
PH17 2QA

T: 01882 633238
E: info@moorofrannoch.co.uk
W: www.moorofrannoch.co.uk

BEDROOMS: 5.
OPEN: 8 Feb–end Oct.
FACILITIES: lounge, bar, conservatory dining room, no Wi-Fi or TV, unsuitable for disabled.
BACKGROUND MUSIC: none.
LOCATION: on a single-track, dead-end road, 40 miles W of Pitlochry.
CHILDREN: all ages welcomed.
DOGS: 'welcomed in all areas of the hotel'.
CREDIT CARDS: all major cards.
PRICES: per room B&B single £125, double £180. Set meals £28–£35.

RATHO Midlothian

Map 5:D2

THE BRIDGE INN AT RATHO

Run with 'an easy, informal air', Graham and Rachel Bucknall's 'bright, lively' inn on the historic Union Canal has 'all the character you could hope for'. Jackie Fergus manages a 'cheerful team'. Bright fires warm the 'smartly decorated' guest parlour and popular pub; an admirable range of Scottish ales and whiskies warms the hearts of locals and visitors. Upstairs, smart, rustic bedrooms overlooking the canal are given modern touches (a flat-screen TV, good Wi-Fi, tea- and coffee-making facilities). Each is different from the others: duck-egg-blue Bonnington has a mahogany four-poster bed and an antique chandelier; pretty Baird, with a freestanding slipper bath in the bathroom, has space for an extra bed. In the 'light-filled' restaurant, chef Ben Watson's 'delicious' fare uses plenty of freshly picked produce from the 'huge, interesting' walled garden, a stroll up the canal. A typical dish, made with pork from the owners' rare-breed pigs: caramelised onion and black pepper sausage, mashed potato, crackling, Ramsay's black pudding. Breakfast is 'enormous' and 'very good', with haggis, tattie scones and eggs from the ducks up the way.

27 Baird Road
Ratho
EH28 8RU

T: 0131 333 1320
E: info@bridgeinn.com
W: www.bridgeinn.com

BEDROOMS: 4.
OPEN: all year except Christmas.
FACILITIES: 2 bars, restaurant, free Wi-Fi, in-room TV (Freeview), wedding facilities, terrace (beer garden, boat shed), only bar and restaurant suitable for disabled.
BACKGROUND MUSIC: 'relaxed' all day, monthly live music nights.
LOCATION: in village, 7 miles W of Edinburgh.
CHILDREN: all ages welcomed.
DOGS: allowed in main bar only.
CREDIT CARDS: MasterCard, Visa.
PRICES: [2017] per room B&B £100–£130. À la carte £30.

ST OLA Orkney Islands

Map 5:A3

THE FOVERAN

'What a delightful place!' write regular Guide correspondents this year, of the Doull family's restaurant-with-rooms. Overlooking Scapa Flow and the southern Orkney isles, it is 'welcoming and comfortable', with 'helpful local staff'. It's a showcase of all things Orcadian, from the art and craft pieces on display to the bere bunno (a traditional flatbread) baked daily. Showing off, too, the scrumptious strengths of the islands, Paul Doull and Roddy Belford's short seasonal menus depend on local suppliers for the vegetables, cheese, meat and seafood served in the popular, newly extended restaurant. 'Our Blue Badge guide told us she's never been able to eat there as it's always booked up. And rightly so – the food is delicious, especially the Orkney scallops and the North Ronaldsay mutton.' Well fed, consider a nightcap by the pellet stove in the lounge (whiskies from local distilleries, of course) before heading to one of the simply furnished bedrooms. Rest well – in the morning, breakfast, with local black pudding and sausages, home-made preserves and traditional Scottish bannocks, is 'delightful', too. (Mary and Rodney Milne-Day)

St Ola
KW15 1SF

T: 01856 872389
F: 01856 876430
E: info@thefoveran.com
W: www.thefoveran.com

BEDROOMS: 8. All on ground floor, 1 single room with bathroom across the hall.
OPEN: Apr–early Oct, by arrangement at other times, restaurant closed variable times in Apr, Oct.
FACILITIES: lounge, restaurant, free Wi-Fi, in-room TV, 12-acre grounds (private rock beach), unsuitable for disabled.
BACKGROUND MUSIC: local/Scottish traditional in restaurant.
LOCATION: 3 miles SW of Kirkwall.
CHILDREN: all ages welcomed.
DOGS: not allowed.
CREDIT CARDS: MasterCard, Visa.
PRICES: [2017] per room B&B single from £80, double from £120, D,B&B single from £105, double from £170. À la carte £35.

SCARISTA Western Isles

SCARISTA HOUSE

☺Previous César winner

'It's a spectacular drive' to this whitewashed manse in an 'extraordinary setting' on the west coast of Harris. Owned by Neil King and Patricia and Tim Martin, this is 'a splendid small establishment', say Guide inspectors in 2017. 'Patricia greeted us in cheffing togs with a friendly smile; after we'd settled in, we were given a decadent tea – fresh home-baking, home-made jam.' The house has a 'lived-in feel', with 'squashy sofas and stuffed bookcases'; bedrooms are in the main building and Glebe House, across the rear garden. 'We would have preferred to be in the main house, but our large room in the converted outbuilding was comfy enough. We had a soft bed and a good hospitality tray (despite the instant coffee); a glorious, high-ceilinged bathroom; a delightful anteroom for soaking in the sunset.' Evenings, the hostess cooks a no-choice menu (dietary needs are 'imaginatively accommodated' with advance notice). 'Dinner was a winner: we started with beautiful canapés; a flavourful soufflé followed, then Stornoway cod with a delicious pea, fennel and coriander purée.' 'Tasty breakfasts, too.'

Scarista
HS3 3HX

T: 01859 550238
E: bookings@scaristahouse.com
W: www.scaristahouse.com

BEDROOMS: 6. 3 in annexe.
OPEN: Mar–mid-Dec.
FACILITIES: drawing room, library, 2 dining rooms, free Wi-Fi in most bedrooms and all public areas, wedding facilities, 1-acre garden, unsuitable for disabled.
BACKGROUND MUSIC: none.
LOCATION: 15 miles SW of Tarbert.
CHILDREN: all ages welcomed (early supper provided for young children).
DOGS: allowed by arrangement.
CREDIT CARDS: Amex, MasterCard, Visa.
PRICES: [2017] per room B&B single £153–£165, double £218–£233. Set dinner £45–£52.

SKEABOST BRIDGE Highland

Map 5:C1

SKEABOST HOUSE HOTEL NEW

Catch sight of this 'impressive' Victorian hunting lodge through the trees as you approach; closer up, discover the 'manicured grounds' running down to Loch Snizort. (Golfers will be pleased to discover the shoreline golf course, too.) 'Ultra-modern, with an air of "boutique city hotel"', it has been revamped by Anne Gracie and Ken Gunn, who also own two Skye hotels on Sleat (see main and Shortlist entries). 'Despite the size of the place, it maintains a feeling of intimacy – you really feel you're being looked after by the lovely, accommodating staff,' say Guide inspectors in 2017. Bedrooms are sleekly contemporary. 'Our room was well equipped with waffle bathrobes, a coffee machine, good teas, fresh milk and shortbread; a magnificent monsoon shower in the bathroom. From our private patio, the view stretched over the lawn to the loch beyond.' Let the fresh loch air whip up an appetite: James Dixon's cooking, in two restaurants, is praised. 'Off the short, appealing menu in the casual West Pier: tasty gin-and-thyme smoked salmon; unusual, delicious chicken with haggis.' Leave room for desserts – they're 'divine' – then wake to 'faultless buttermilk pancakes' at breakfast.

Skeabost Bridge
IV51 9NP

T: 01470 532202
E: info@skeabosthotel.com
W: www.skeabosthotel.com

BEDROOMS: 18. 4 in garden annexe.
OPEN: all year, 57°27' restaurant open in summer months.
FACILITIES: bar, drawing room, morning room, 2 restaurants, private dining room, free Wi-Fi, in-room TV (Freeview), wedding facilities, 23-acre grounds, 9-hole golf course, fishing (ghillie available), 50-foot yacht for charter, unsuitable for disabled.
BACKGROUND MUSIC: none.
LOCATION: 6½ miles NW of Portree.
CHILDREN: all ages welcomed.
DOGS: not allowed.
CREDIT CARDS: MasterCard, Visa.
PRICES: [2017] per person B&B £84–£179, D,B&B £129–£224.

SLEAT Highland

Map 5:C1

TORAVAIG HOUSE

Ten minutes' drive from the ferry, Anne Gracie and Ken Gunn's whitewashed hotel has 'fine views' across the Sound of Sleat. Fine, too, is the contemporary update the 1930s house has been given: a 'lovely little drawing room', with baby grand piano and marble fireplace, is 'stylishly furnished'; in the 'smartly decorated restaurant', tables are laid with white linens for dinner. (Sister Skye hotels in Skeabost Bridge and further up along the Sleat peninsula – see main and Shortlist entries – share the same 'boutique hotel' predilection.) 'Comfy modern bedrooms', each named after a Scottish island, look on to the hillside or across the water; one of the best, 'generously sized', has a bay window for taking in the sea views. At mealtimes, the menus reflect the abundance of island produce from land and sea, including herbs and edible flowers from the hotel's garden and polytunnels. Typical offerings: line-caught sea bass, samphire, braised fennel; pork loin, Stornoway black pudding, golden beetroot purée, purple carrots. Spend a day sailing aboard the 50-foot yacht skippered by Ken Gunn; return for a malt whisky by the log fire. More reports, please.

Knock Bay
Sleat
IV44 8RE

T: 01471 820200
F: 01471 833404
E: info@skyehotel.co.uk
W: www.toravaig.com

BEDROOMS: 9.
OPEN: Mar–Nov.
FACILITIES: lounge, dining room, free Wi-Fi, in-room TV (Freeview), wedding facilities, 2-acre grounds, 50-foot yacht for charter, unsuitable for disabled.
BACKGROUND MUSIC: none.
LOCATION: 7 miles S of Broadford.
CHILDREN: not under 12.
DOGS: not allowed.
CREDIT CARDS: MasterCard, Visa.
PRICES: [2017] per person B&B £94–£144, D,B&B £144–£194. Set dinner £49, à la carte £40.

SEE ALSO SHORTLIST

STRACHUR Argyll and Bute

Map 5:D1

THE CREGGANS INN NEW

Friendly, folksy, 'comfy and unpretentious', Gill and Archie MacLellan's 'terrific inn' stands in 'a glorious location' on the shores of Loch Fyne. A log fire, 'two chummy dogs' and a wide range of malt whiskies are within. (Look out, too, for trophies won by the local shinty team, whose players have adopted the bar as their unofficial clubhouse.) Guide readers praise the 'affable staff' and 'all-round positive experience'. 'We went on a dreich – as they say in Scotland – winter afternoon, and the welcome couldn't have been warmer: tea and cake were instantly produced, at no charge.' Many of the bedrooms (some a touch old-fashioned) have 'stunning views' over the water. Choose wisely: 'My comfortable loch-view room also came with noise from the busy road out front.' The residents' lounge on the first floor is a 'very nice retreat', with a view that's 'especially fine at sunset'. In the informal bistro, the cooking is, 'on the whole, very good'. 'I had an excellent meal: Loch Fyne scallops with black pudding; sea bass fillet and garlicky potatoes; a seriously good Pouilly-Fumé.' Breakfast is a more straightforward affair, accompanied by a 'strong coffee'. (GC, Gordon Mursell, Chris Elliott)

Strachur
PA27 8BX

T: 01369 860279
F: 01369 860637
E: info@creggans-inn.co.uk
W: www.creggans-inn.co.uk

BEDROOMS: 14.
OPEN: all year, except Christmas.
FACILITIES: 2 lounges, bar, bistro, free Wi-Fi, in-room TV (Freeview), function facilities, 2-acre grounds, moorings for guests arriving by boat, unsuitable for disabled.
BACKGROUND MUSIC: all day in bar.
LOCATION: in village.
CHILDREN: all ages welcomed.
DOGS: allowed in bar, bedrooms (not unattended).
CREDIT CARDS: Amex, MasterCard, Visa.
PRICES: [2017] per room B&B £130–£190. À la carte £32.

STRATHTAY Perth and Kinross

Map 5:D2

RIVERWOOD

The River Tay flows by wooded grounds awash with bluebells in springtime, at Ann and Alf Berry's modern B&B, in a pretty conservation village. Kick off your shoes on arrival and step into the slippers provided. 'Comfortable, spacious' bedrooms are light and airy in pale shades, and have views of the garden stretching down to the water. They vary in size – a ground-floor suite has a separate lounge and dressing room, while another has a private deck – but even the smaller rooms have seating space and are well supplied with a mini-fridge, a capsule coffee machine and Scottish toiletries. 'Book dinner if you can': on selected nights, guests may bring wine and sit down to a candlelit three-course meal cooked by the hostess. (The Berrys are helpful with reservations at local restaurants on other evenings.) In the morning, a 'wonderful' breakfast is best enjoyed alfresco, while watching red squirrels cavorting. Among the many choices on the menu: Dunkeld smoked salmon, potato rösti, griddled pancakes and French toast with crispy bacon. At tee-time, head for the Strathtay Golf Club, minutes away (B&B guests have complimentary access). (RD)

Strathtay
PH9 0PG

T: 01887 840751
E: info@riverwoodstrathtay.com
W: www.riverwoodstrathtay.com

BEDROOMS: 7. 4 suites on ground floor.
OPEN: 6 Feb–20 Dec, 28 Dec–New Year.
FACILITIES: lounge/dining room, library, free Wi-Fi, in-room TV (Freeview), 4½-acre grounds (lawns, woodland, fishing), access to nearby golf course.
BACKGROUND MUSIC: 'easy listening' in dining room at mealtimes.
LOCATION: in village, 9½ miles SW of Pitlochry.
CHILDREN: not under 12.
DOGS: not allowed.
CREDIT CARDS: Diners, MasterCard, Visa.
PRICES: per room B&B £110–£160, D,B&B (on selected nights) £170–£220. 1-night bookings sometimes refused.

STRATHTUMMEL Perth and Kinross

Map 5:D2

THE INN AT LOCH TUMMEL   NEW

'The warmth of the welcome is striking' at this 'carefully refurbished' 19th-century coaching inn with 'superb views' over Loch Tummel. Owned by Alice and Jade Calliva, it enters the Guide thanks to the urging of a regular reader, who stepped into the rustic, stone-built building to find hosts who 'couldn't have been friendlier'. A mini-library has deep velvet sofas and shelves of books; a residents' lounge ('with the fire lit – welcome even in August') sees clear across the loch to Schiehallion. The scenery matches Craig Rushton's 'outstanding cooking'. Using produce from the kitchen garden, seasonal menus served in the smart, wood-floored bar might include pea and nettle soup; 'tender local venison in a rich gravy'. Bed down in one of the 'comfortable, well-appointed' bedrooms (some up a 'steep staircase'); decorated in a modern country style, each is supplied with peaty whisky and home-baked biscuits. Come morning, try to sit by the huge picture window for an 'excellent breakfast' of home-made jams, compotes and granola; porridge oats from a local farm shop; eggs from the inn's own hens. (Gordon Mursell)

Queens View
Strathtummel
PH16 5RP

T: 01882 634317
E: info@theinnatlochtummel.com
W: www.theinnatlochtummel.com

BEDROOMS: 6. 1 on ground floor.
OPEN: all year except Christmas, Jan/Feb, restaurant closed Sun eve, Mon.
FACILITIES: snug, library, bar, dining room, free Wi-Fi, patio (alfresco meals and drinks).
BACKGROUND MUSIC: in bar/restaurant.
LOCATION: 10 miles W of Pitlochry.
CHILDREN: not under 5.
DOGS: allowed.
CREDIT CARDS: MasterCard, Visa.
PRICES: [2017] per room B&B £105–£145. À la carte £27.

STRATHYRE Perth and Kinross

Map 5:D2

CREAGAN HOUSE

'Cherry and Gordon Gunn clearly know their stuff', having run their 'lovely place to stay' for more than 30 years. 'It's always a pleasure, with Cherry's superb hospitality and Gordon's excellent cooking,' say returning visitors, trusted Guide correspondents, this year. The extended 17th-century farmhouse stands in the romantic Walter Scott countryside of the Trossachs: 'Birdlife is prolific, and red squirrels come in the morning.' Inside, the style is 'neo-baronial' (the vaulted dining room, with a stone fireplace, half-imagines it's a great hall). B&B accommodation is in bedrooms traditionally decorated with antique furnishings ('in keeping with the rest of the house'); one has a canopy bed, another a four-poster. Each room is supplied with bottled water, fresh milk and high-end toiletries. In the morning, the host cooks 'very good' full Scottish breakfasts with 'creamy scrambled eggs', 'lovely bacon' and local black pudding. Climb a woodland path, along a stream, to an 'idyllic little seating area', or strike out farther afield, perhaps on the Rob Roy trail: Loch Lomond and The Trossachs national park is all around. (Bill Wood, A and EW)

25% DISCOUNT VOUCHERS

Strathyre
FK18 8ND

T: 01877 384638
E: eatandstay@creaganhouse.co.uk
W: www.creaganhouse.co.uk

BEDROOMS: 5. 1 on ground floor.
OPEN: 23 Mar–22 Oct, closed Mon–Thurs.
FACILITIES: lounge bar, writing room, restaurant, free Wi-Fi, in-room TV (Freeview), ¾-acre grounds.
BACKGROUND MUSIC: none.
LOCATION: just N of village.
CHILDREN: all ages welcomed.
DOGS: not allowed in public rooms.
CREDIT CARDS: MasterCard, Visa.
PRICES: [2017] per room B&B single £90–£100, double £135–£155, discounts if booked directly with hotel.

STRONTIAN Highland

KILCAMB LODGE

'Everything is presented with care and style' at Sally and David Ruthven-Fox's small hotel on the 'peaceful shores' of Loch Sunart. In a 'beautiful situation' on the Ardnamurchan peninsula – 'remote but accessible' – the old stone house stands in 'gorgeous countryside', against a backdrop of hills; take in 'glorious views' all around. Inside, 'welcoming staff' are 'keen to make you feel at home'. There are flowers, 'comfy sofas', walls hung with pictures and maps. The best of the traditionally decorated bedrooms ('smart and well furnished') looks towards the loch and mountains. 'A jar of home-made shortbread and a jug of iced water had been set out in our good-sized room; after dinner, they brought a Thermos flask of fresh milk, ready for the morning.' In the evening, sit in the lounge over drinks and canapés before sampling chef Gary Phillips's 'quite fancy food' (perhaps quail ballotine, apricot mousse, celeriac slaw) in the restaurant. Alternatively, dine more informally on easy classics (steaks; fish and chips) or a blackboard menu of seafood specials in the brasserie. Next day, ask about boat trips or bicycle hires, or simply stroll to the shoreline in search of otters and oyster catchers.

Strontian
PH36 4HY

T: 01967 402257
F: 01967 402041
E: enquiries@kilcamblodge.co.uk
W: www.kilcamblodge.co.uk

BEDROOMS: 11.
OPEN: all year except Jan.
FACILITIES: drawing room, lounge, bar, restaurant, brasserie, free Wi-Fi, in-room TV (Sky), wedding facilities, 22-acre grounds, unsuitable for disabled.
BACKGROUND MUSIC: in restaurant and brasserie in evening.
LOCATION: edge of village.
CHILDREN: all ages welcomed.
DOGS: allowed in 4 bedrooms, not in public rooms (£12 per night).
CREDIT CARDS: MasterCard, Visa.
PRICES: [2017] per room B&B £160–£260, D,B&B £220–£435. Tasting menu £69, à la carte £35.

TARLAND Aberdeenshire

Map 5:C3

DOUNESIDE HOUSE NEW

25% DISCOUNT VOUCHERS

Find a spot for quiet contemplation, as did Guide readers this year, in the expertly maintained gardens or graceful public rooms of this 'lovely place' on the edge of the Cairngorms national park. The MacRobert family home has been 'extensively and beautifully refurbished': there are portraits on panelled walls, low armchairs by a grand piano, a library with an open fire. On a balmy evening, take drinks on the front terrace facing 'sweeping views' of the Grampian mountains. Genteel bedrooms in the main house look over the grounds and Aberdeenshire countryside. Architect-designed apartments and cottages on the estate, most with a kitchenette, suit a family or a group of friends. 'We had a good room at the back of the hotel. The view of the glorious morning sun spreading its golden rays through the cloud and on to the frosted ground was a sight to remember.' At lunch and dinner, chef David Butters cooks 'excellent, inventive' Scottish menus using organic vegetables and fruit from the walled garden. 'We enjoyed a pumpkin panna cotta starter and a wonderful Jerusalem artichoke velouté; excellent venison; an elegant cheese plate.' (David Birnie)

Tarland
nr Aboyne
AB34 4UL

T: 013398 81230
E: manager@dounesidehouse.co.uk
W: www.dounesidehouse.co.uk

BEDROOMS: 23. 9 in cottages, plus 4 apartments in Casa Memoria.
OPEN: all year, reserved for military personnel mid-July–end Aug, Christmas.
FACILITIES: bar, parlour, library, bistro/restaurant, conservatory, free Wi-Fi, in-room smart TV (Freeview), wedding facilities, health centre (heated indoor pool, spa, steam room, gym, games room), 17-acre grounds (walled garden, arboretum, stream, tennis, croquet lawn, putting green).
BACKGROUND MUSIC: in bar and restaurant.
LOCATION: 7 miles NW of Aboyne.
CHILDREN: all ages welcomed.
DOGS: allowed in cottages, not in public rooms.
CREDIT CARDS: MasterCard, Visa.
PRICES: [2017] room from £150. Breakfast £17, set dinner £35, tasting menu £60.

THORNHILL Dumfries and Galloway

Map 5:E2

TRIGONY HOUSE

Atop a tree-lined drive, arrive to a 'cheerful welcome' at Jan and Adam Moore's 'excellent' hotel, in an 18th-century hunting and fishing lodge. With 'friendly, unobtrusive' staff, the Moores have created a comfortably dog-friendly spot, where well-travelled pooches are allowed 'everywhere but the dining room'. Ring ahead to discuss room choices, as bedrooms vary in size. Spacious or snug, however, all are 'spotless and well cared for', with views of the 'very pretty' garden ('spring bulbs everywhere when we visited'). 'My large room was well appointed, with tremendously thick curtains. The only sound I heard came from the sociable rooks outside,' said a guest this year. Adam Moore's 'beautifully cooked, well-presented' rustic menu takes an inventive approach to local and home-grown produce, including an 'outstanding' smoked grouse starter. In the morning, wake to 'delicious' home-made granola and 'perfectly cooked' hot dishes, including local whole kippers. There are walks to be had nearby – a guide of local routes is in the room – but guests looking for more languid activity may prefer booking into the new garden spa.

25% DISCOUNT VOUCHERS

Closeburn
Thornhill
DG3 5EZ

T: 01848 331211
F: 01848 331303
E: info@trigonyhotel.co.uk
W: www.trigonyhotel.co.uk

BEDROOMS: 9. 1 on ground floor.
OPEN: all year except 25–27 and 31 Dec.
FACILITIES: lounge, bar, dining room, free Wi-Fi, in-room TV (Freeview), spa treatment room in private garden (outdoor wood-fired hot tub), wedding facilities, 4-acre grounds, unsuitable for disabled.
BACKGROUND MUSIC: in bar in evening.
LOCATION: 1 mile S of Thornhill.
CHILDREN: all ages welcomed.
DOGS: 'well-behaved' dogs welcomed.
CREDIT CARDS: all major cards.
PRICES: [2017] per room B&B £120–£165, D,B&B £190–£235. À la carte £35. 1-night bookings sometimes refused Sat.

THURSO Highland

Map 5:B2

FORSS HOUSE

Wooded grounds and the meandering River Forss set a tranquil scene for this Georgian hotel with strong fishing links. 'We were warmly greeted by the manager, Anne Mackenzie (what a lovely character); all the staff were naturally welcoming.' The bedrooms are well equipped, and individually decorated in traditional style; two of the best, 'large and airy', have fresh fruit, and river views from tall Georgian windows. Whisky aficionados, grab a glass: a 'stunning range of serious whiskies' lines the bar, 'each served with a teardrop of water to release the aroma'. At dinnertime, the pleasure is in chef Andrew Manson's 'interesting' weekly-changing menus, which offer 'unusual combinations' of seasonal and locally sourced ingredients. Characteristic dishes: Mey beef, Strathdon Blue cheese butter, truffled green beans, braised oxtail; goat's cheese ravioli, tomato fondue, pickled onions. (The chef ably rises to the occasion for vegetarians, says a Guide reader who liked her 'very pretty veggie meal'.) Try the 'perfect' Finnan haddock at breakfast in the sunny conservatory, then let the manageress reel you in with bits of fishing lore. (GC, DB)

Forss
Thurso
KW14 7XY

T: 01847 861201
F: 01847 861301
E: anne@forsshousehotel.co.uk
W: www.forsshousehotel.co.uk

BEDROOMS: 14. 3 in main house on ground floor, 4 in River House, 2 in Sportsmen's Lodge.
OPEN: all year except 23 Dec–4 Jan.
FACILITIES: dining room, breakfast room, lounge, bar, free Wi-Fi, in-room TV (Freeview), meeting room, wedding facilities, 19-acre grounds with river and waterfall.
BACKGROUND MUSIC: in public areas in morning and evening.
LOCATION: 5 miles W of Thurso.
CHILDREN: all ages welcomed (under-5s free).
DOGS: allowed in Sportsmen's Lodge only.
CREDIT CARDS: all major cards.
PRICES: [2017] per room B&B single £99–£135, double £135–£185, D,B&B single £137–£170, double £205–£260. À la carte £35.

TIRORAN Argyll and Bute

Map 5:D1

TIRORAN HOUSE

Arrive to tea, flapjacks and a spread of incredible nature at Katie and Laurence Mackay's Victorian hunting lodge on the Isle of Mull. The extensive estate encompasses waterfalls, an old Victorian trout pond, a private beach and woodland walks beside a tumbling burn; the 'wonderful garden' is ideal for 'relaxing in, and admiring the eagles'. 'We were welcomed with grace and enthusiasm,' say regular returnees this year. 'Laurence and Katie are continually updating the place – there are improvements every time we visit.' In the 19th-century house and its annexes, traditionally furnished bedrooms look on to garden, loch, orchard or hills. Each room is supplied with biscuits, bathrobes and smart toiletries. Gather with fellow guests for pre-dinner drinks (perhaps a glass of in-house Whitetail gin), then sit down to dinner in the atmosphere of a house party. Chef Michael Scotford's 'imaginative' nightly menus use local Scottish produce in dishes such as island game terrine, fresh berry chutney; Loch Awe sea trout, seared kale. Leave on a wildlife trip or sea safari in the morning; the hosts can point you in the direction of the best beaches and otter-sighting spots. (Dr Gillian Todd)

Tiroran
PA69 6ES

T: 01681 705232
F: 01681 705232
E: info@tiroran.com
W: www.tiroran.com

BEDROOMS: 10. 2 on ground floor, 4 in annexes, plus 2 self-catering cottages.
OPEN: all year except Nov–Feb, open New Year.
FACILITIES: 2 sitting rooms, dining room, conservatory, free Wi-Fi, in-room TV (Freeview), 17½-acre gardens in 56-acre grounds, beach with mooring, wedding facilities, licensed tearoom, unsuitable for disabled.
BACKGROUND MUSIC: none.
LOCATION: N side of Loch Scridain.
CHILDREN: all ages welcomed.
DOGS: allowed (not unattended) in some bedrooms and tearoom.
CREDIT CARDS: MasterCard, Visa.
PRICES: [2017] per room B&B £175–£245. À la carte £35–£45.

ULLAPOOL Highland

Map 5:B1

THE CEILIDH PLACE

'Everything is done with a smile and a bit of banter' at Jean Urquhart's 'warm and welcoming' bookshop-with-rooms, formed from a clutch of whitewashed cottages in this old fishing village. Effie MacKenzie manages 'friendly local staff' with 'charm and experience'. 'The place feeds your soul in every way possible. If you want to lose yourself in a book, you won't be disturbed, but if you're after a nice chat, you're in the right place, too.' By day, the dining room ('spacious yet cosy, with a log burner blazing brightly') is run as a café; in the evening, it turns into a 'very popular' restaurant. Join those in the know: Scott Morrison's 'seriously tasty', 'deliciously fresh' dishes go well with the 'great selection' of wines and beers. Stay on a shoestring in the clubhouse with its bunk beds, or choose one of the simply furnished bedrooms, each filled with rustic charm and 'lots of books'. 'Our room, smallish but comfortable, faced Loch Broom. A bonus: the relaxing guest lounge/pantry/honesty bar, with a balcony overlooking the village.' 'Discovering the well-stocked bookshop, with its excellent supply of works by Scottish authors and publishers, was the icing on the cake.' (Emma Grundy Haigh, EB)

12–14 West Argyle Street
Ullapool
IV26 2TY

T: 01854 612103
E: stay@theceilidhplace.com
W: www.theceilidhplace.com

BEDROOMS: 13. 10 with facilities en suite, plus 11 in Bunkhouse across road.
OPEN: all year except two weeks from 5 Jan.
FACILITIES: bar, parlour, coffee shop, restaurant, bookshop, conference/function facilities, free Wi-Fi, civil wedding licence, 2-acre garden, only public areas suitable for disabled.
BACKGROUND MUSIC: 'eclectic' in public areas.
LOCATION: village centre (large car park).
CHILDREN: all ages welcomed.
DOGS: allowed, not unattended in bedrooms.
CREDIT CARDS: MasterCard, Visa.
PRICES: per room B&B £132–£180 (rooms in Bunkhouse from £24 per person). À la carte £26.

SEE ALSO SHORTLIST

WALLS Shetland

🏨 BURRASTOW HOUSE

César award: Scottish hotel of the year

'It's like being a guest at a country house in an extraordinarily beautiful location,' say Guide readers this year: Pierre Dupont's 18th-century dwelling stands on a bay overlooking the Sound of Vaila. In this 'informal, laid-back' place, 'Pierre is a charming, unobtrusive host'. Take shelter from the Shetland chill in one of the individually styled bedrooms. 'Our splendid, spacious Laird's Room had stunning views on two sides. The bathroom plumbing sounded eccentric, but worked perfectly well.' There's neither turn-down nor fancy toiletries, but downstairs find a drinks cabinet, a 'remarkably well-stocked library' and 'a cosy lounge' with 'an enormous wood-burning stove' and 'a well-worn feel'. 'A call at the kitchen door produces coffee on demand.' In the evening, the host cooks 'straightforward, uncomplicated fare'. 'The fish, naturally, was particularly good.' 'The most memorable features of our dinners were the conversations that arose between the tables in the intimate dining room.' Make breakfast memorable, too, with 'irresistible kippers – the best I've ever tasted.' (Andrew and Hannah Butterworth, DB)

Walls
ZE2 9PD

T: 01595 809307
E: info@burrastowhouse.co.uk
W: www.burrastowhouse.co.uk

BEDROOMS: 7. 3 in extension, 2 on ground floor.
OPEN: Apr–Oct.
FACILITIES: sitting room, library, dining room, free Wi-Fi in reception, in-room TV (Freeview), 'weak mobile phone signal', wedding facilities, unsuitable for disabled.
BACKGROUND MUSIC: none.
LOCATION: 2 miles from Walls, 27 miles NW of Lerwick.
CHILDREN: all ages welcomed (under-13s half price).
DOGS: not allowed.
CREDIT CARDS: MasterCard, Visa.
PRICES: per person B&B £60, D,B&B £95.

WALES

River Conwy at Llanrwst, North Wales

ABERAERON Ceredigion

Map 3:C2

HARBOURMASTER HOTEL

The harbour wall in front of Glyn and Menna Heulyn's 'popular, personally managed' hotel on the Georgian quayside has been dubbed 'the longest bar in Europe' – join the locals soaking in the view, then spend the night in one of the 'comfortable, colourful' bedrooms. Harbour-facing rooms in the original harbourmaster's building are reached via a winding staircase; rooms in the converted warehouse next door (two with a terrace overlooking Cardigan Bay) are particularly spacious. 'Well equipped and smartly styled', all rooms have posh toiletries, Welsh blankets, a Roberts radio. The bar, where 'happy, motivated' staff 'truly look after' visitors, is where the 'real buzz' is. Welsh and English are spoken; 'you get the sense that the Harbourmaster is a part of this pretty fishing port, rather than just being located here'. In the maritime-cool restaurant, chef Ludo Dieumegard's dishes, perhaps Cardigan Bay crab and parsley salad, chilled pea soup, brown crab fritter, give a taste of the place. Work it all off the next day – the Wales Coast Path goes right by the front door. 'The team at this hotel could teach many in the hospitality business just how it's done.' (LW)

Pen Cei
Aberaeron
SA46 0BT

T: 01545 570755
F: 01545 570762
E: info@harbour-master.com
W: www.harbour-master.com

BEDROOMS: 13. 2 in cottage, 1 suitable for disabled.
OPEN: all year except 24 (evening)–26 Dec, drinks only on Boxing Day.
FACILITIES: lift, bar, restaurant, free Wi-Fi, in-room TV (Freeview), small terrace, pebble beach (safe bathing nearby).
BACKGROUND MUSIC: all day in bar.
LOCATION: central, on the harbour.
CHILDREN: not under 5 to stay, must have own room.
DOGS: not allowed.
CREDIT CARDS: all major cards.
PRICES: [2017] per room B&B single from £75, double from £120, D,B&B double from £180. Set dinner £27.50–£35, à la carte £35. 1-night bookings refused weekends in high season, min. 2-night stay for D,B&B rate.

ABERDYFI Gwynedd

Map 3:C3

TREFEDDIAN HOTEL

'The sun doesn't have to shine before you get a warm welcome,' writes a reader in 2017, of this much-loved hotel overlooking Cardigan Bay. 'It's everything the doctor ordered, including the ability to chill out wherever you choose.' The games room, library, seaward lounges and indoor pool offer plenty of diversion, whatever the weather; in sunshine, the golf course and miles of sandy beach come into their own. The Cave family has owned and run the child-friendly, dog-friendly hotel since 1907; devotees praise the sense of tradition. 'I first went with two small daughters and now have grandchildren of 20. The hotel has kept its standards.' 'Immaculately clean' bedrooms, some large, are filled with light. 'Those with a balcony are ideal in the summer.' Flexible eating options include bar snacks, packed lunches, a children's supper; grown-ups might kick off sandshoes and shorts and dress up for a five-course dinner. A typical dish: steamed Dover sole, prawn mousse, Cardinal sauce. After a 'generous breakfast', pick up a leaflet on nearby walks and drives, then head out to explore. (Susan Hanslow, and many others)

Tywyn Road
Aberdyfi
LL35 0SB

T: 01654 767213
F: 01654 767777
E: info@trefwales.com
W: www.trefwales.com

BEDROOMS: 59. 1 suitable for disabled.
OPEN: all year except 10 Dec–14 Jan.
FACILITIES: lift, lounge bar, study, family lounge, adult lounge, restaurant, games room (snooker, table tennis, air hockey), free Wi-Fi, in-room TV (Freeview), indoor swimming pool (6 by 12 metres), beauty salon, 15-acre grounds (lawns, sun terrace, tennis, putting green).
BACKGROUND MUSIC: none.
LOCATION: ¼ mile N of Aberdyfi.
CHILDREN: all ages welcomed.
DOGS: allowed in 1 lounge, some bedrooms.
CREDIT CARDS: MasterCard, Visa.
PRICES: [2017] per person B&B from £70, D,B&B from £100. Set dinner £29.50. 2-night min. stay preferred (but check for 1-night availability).

ABERGAVENNY Monmouthshire

Map 3:D4

THE ANGEL HOTEL

Take your lead from the locals beating a path to the door of this 'handsomely refurbished' 19th-century coaching inn: there are 'very good scones, elegantly served on pretty china' at the renowned afternoon tea, say trusted reporters this year. There's much more besides. William Griffiths's 'fine family-run hotel', on the main street of a 'busy, almost gentrified' market town, is 'a classy place' where staff are 'professional yet friendly'. Charlotte Griffiths, William's wife, is the manager; Pauline, his mother, who runs a local art gallery, has hung the public spaces with original works. Her artist's eye is evident, too, in the 'cheerful, wonderfully comfortable' bedrooms. In the Oak Room restaurant, chef Wesley Hammond wins praise for his modern British dishes. 'We had braised beef with a fancy bubble and squeak; pecan pie good enough for Louisiana. Everything looked good, and tasted as good as it looked.' The breakfast menu, complete with breakfast cocktails, 'would satisfy a Welsh XV prop forward'. Take a piece of it with you – the hotel's new bakery, next door, sells sandwiches and all manner of baked goods.

15 Cross Street
Abergavenny
NP7 5EN

T: 01873 857121
F: 01873 858059
E: info@angelabergavenny.com
W: www.angelabergavenny.com

BEDROOMS: 34. 2 in adjacent mews, plus three 2-bedroom cottages.
OPEN: all year except 24–27 Dec.
FACILITIES: lift, lounge, bar, tea room, restaurant, private function rooms, bakery, free Wi-Fi, in-room TV (Freeview), civil wedding licence, courtyard.
BACKGROUND MUSIC: in restaurant and tea room.
LOCATION: town centre.
CHILDREN: all ages welcomed (cots free of charge, Z-beds for under-12s £26).
DOGS: allowed in some bedrooms (£25 charge), not in restaurant or tea room.
CREDIT CARDS: Amex, MasterCard, Visa.
PRICES: [2017] per room B&B from £99, D,B&B from £155. Set dinner £28, à la carte £35. 1-night bookings sometimes refused.

ABERGAVENNY Monmouthshire

Map 3:D4

THE HARDWICK

🍷 Previous César winner

'The buzz of contented diners fills the air' at this 'enjoyable, excellent' restaurant-with-rooms in an 'attractive rural setting' outside the market town. Here, chef/patron Stephen Terry and his wife, Joanna, have transformed a former roadside pub into a 'popular local destination' that's 'well worth the detour'. The bar and trio of dining rooms are 'unpretentious yet stylish': there are rafters and old beams; candles and linen napkins on mismatched wooden tables; copper pans hanging by the wood stove. 'Provenance is everything' on the long menu – 'and the many interesting dishes make decisions difficult'. Try, perhaps, hot and cold Severn and Wye valley smoked salmon, pickled cucumber; crispy shoulder and ragout of Brecon lamb. 'Nothing disappoints.' 'Comfortable modern bedrooms' are in a Scandinavian-style courtyard annexe to the rear. 'Ours had smart fittings and furnishings and ample storage. Kilner jars with coffee and lots of different teas were supplied; there were design books and magazines as well. Adjustable shutters allowed plenty of light from the floor-to-ceiling windows.' Breakfast, a sit-down affair, is prepared to order.

Old Raglan Road
Abergavenny
NP7 9AA

T: 01873 854220
E: info@thehardwick.co.uk
W: www.thehardwick.co.uk

BEDROOMS: 8. 5 on ground floor, 1 suitable for disabled.
OPEN: all year.
FACILITIES: bar, restaurant, private dining facilities, free Wi-Fi, in-room TV, courtyard, small garden.
BACKGROUND MUSIC: 'unintrusive' in public areas.
LOCATION: 2¾ miles S of Abergavenny.
CHILDREN: all ages welcomed.
DOGS: not allowed.
CREDIT CARDS: MasterCard, Visa.
PRICES: [2017] per room B&B single (Mon–Thurs) £115, double £135–£150. À la carte £30.

ABERSOCH Gwynedd

PORTH TOCYN HOTEL

'Relaxed and comfortable', this 'lovely, wacky' hotel overlooking Cardigan Bay is 'ideal for rest, fresh air, beach and coastal walks'. It has been owned by the Fletcher-Brewer family for 70 years. 'There's a home-away-from-home feel, with books and magazines, a playroom, coffee in the hall to help ourselves to, vases of irises and lilies in the lounges.' The soul of the place, Nick Fletcher-Brewer, is 'a character: jolly, jokey, casual and quirky'. 'Simple, unfussy' bedrooms have antique pieces and paintings, perhaps a distant sea view. Dinner, which might include 'melt-in-the-mouth pork belly with superb crispy crackling', is cooked by Louise Fletcher-Brewer and Darren Shenton-Morris. 'Our three-course meal included nibbles, amuse-bouche, delicious breads and home-made petits fours with coffee.' (A light supper menu appeals to those who may have overindulged.) At breakfast, 'tasty sausages, proper toast, home-made marmalade and delicious local yogurts' set you up for a day's wanderings: walk along the Wales Coastal Path, swim in the pool, or take a dip in the sea, a five-minute walk away. (C and GJ)

Bwlchtocyn
Abersoch
LL53 7BU

T: 01758 713303
F: 01758 713538
E: bookings@porthtocynhotel.co.uk
W: www.porthtocynhotel.co.uk

BEDROOMS: 17. 3 on ground floor.
OPEN: week before Easter–early Nov.
FACILITIES: sitting rooms, children's snug, small bar, dining room, free Wi-Fi, in-room TV (Freeview), 20-acre grounds (swimming pool, 10 by 6 metres, heated May–end Sept, tennis), call to discuss disabled access.
BACKGROUND MUSIC: none.
LOCATION: 2 miles outside village.
CHILDREN: all ages welcomed (high tea for under-5s; no babies or young children at dinner).
DOGS: not allowed in public rooms.
CREDIT CARDS: MasterCard, Visa.
PRICES: [2017] per room B&B single £82.50–£95, double £115–£195. Set dinner £47 (£23.50 for 6–14s). 1-night bookings occasionally refused.

ABERYSTWYTH Ceredigion

Map 3:C3

GWESTY CYMRU

Huw and Beth Roberts bid croeso to guests arriving at their smart hotel, in a 'great seafront position' in this university town. Enter the Grade II listed Victorian terrace house to find modern interiors imbued with real character and a strong sense of place: locally handcrafted furniture inlaid with Welsh slate; Welsh poetry on display; emphatic oil paintings inspired by the surrounding landscape, created by a local artist. The bedrooms are individually and 'excellently' decorated, says a regular Guide reader in 2017, who praised his 'fantastic' top-floor room under sturdy oak beams. 'The rooms overlooking the sea are very good, with chairs in the bay window so you can enjoy the passing scene.' In the modern-rustic dining room, chef William Ainsworth's cooking is 'highly recommended'. There are small plates, large plates, tasting platters and a 'magic' Welsh rarebit at lunch; at dinner, characteristic dishes include mushroom, tarragon and Perl Wen cheese arancini; fillet of cod, herb mash, buttered savoy cabbage. The resort town has plenty of diversion – down to the winter starlings roosting under the pier. (Michael Eldridge, and others)

19 Marine Terrace
Aberystwyth
SY23 2AZ

T: 01970 612252
F: 01970 623348
E: info@gwestycymru.co.uk
W: www.gwestycymru.co.uk

BEDROOMS: 8. 2 on ground floor.
OPEN: all year except 22 Dec–2 Jan, restaurant closed for lunch Tues.
FACILITIES: small bar area, restaurant, seafront terrace, free Wi-Fi, in-room TV (Freeview), secure parking (book in advance), unsuitable for disabled.
BACKGROUND MUSIC: 'easy listening' in reception and restaurant.
LOCATION: central, on seafront.
CHILDREN: all ages welcomed at lunch, no under-5s to stay or in restaurant in evenings.
DOGS: not allowed.
CREDIT CARDS: MasterCard, Visa.
PRICES: [2017] per room B&B single from £70, double £90–£150. À la carte £35.

BALA Gwynedd

BRYNIAU GOLAU

◊ Previous César winner

Landscaped grounds lead down to Bala Lake from Katrina Le Saux and Peter Cottee's Victorian house in Snowdonia national park, with a vista of mountains in the blue distance. The views come inside, too – B&B accommodation is in comfortable, traditionally styled bedrooms, all with an outlook on the lake. Each room has its own character: Berwyn and Arenig have an antique four-poster bed; in Aran, steep in a freestanding bath by the window. Thoughtful touches are everywhere: fresh flowers and home-baked biscuits; books and glossy magazines; an electric blanket on the bed; underfloor heating in the bathroom. When the sun shines, bask on the terrace; in the cooler months, a log fire burns in the sitting room – good accompaniment for a glass of something from the honesty bar. In the morning, a hearty breakfast on fine china includes home-made bread and preserves, and honey from the hosts' bees. There are 'lovely walks in the area' (and drying facilities on site), but make it back in time to watch the sun set over the Arenig mountain.

Llangower
Bala
LL23 7BT

T: 01678 521782
E: katrinalesaux@hotmail.co.uk
W: www.bryniau-golau.co.uk

BEDROOMS: 3.
OPEN: Mar–Dec (not Christmas).
FACILITIES: sitting room, dining room, free Wi-Fi, in-room TV (Freeview), ½-acre garden (terrace), drying facilities, canoe/bicycle storage, unsuitable for disabled.
BACKGROUND MUSIC: none.
LOCATION: 2 miles SE of Bala.
CHILDREN: babes in arms, and over-10s welcomed.
DOGS: not allowed.
CREDIT CARDS: MasterCard, Visa.
PRICES: [2017] per room B&B single £90–£100, double £110–£120. 1-night bookings may be refused weekends.

SEE ALSO SHORTLIST

BARMOUTH Gwynedd

Map 3:B3

COES FAEN

NEW

Gazing over the Mawddach estuary from the foot of a tree-covered hillside, this 'stunning, ultra-modern B&B' is owned by Sara and Richard Parry-Jones. Local stone and natural rock sit easily with precision-cut glass in the sustainably redesigned 19th-century house: all is 'fabulous, and extremely comfortable'. 'A brilliant project, run by hospitable hosts,' say Guide inspectors in 2017. Each of the coastal-view bedrooms has a spa feature – a cedar and Welsh slate steam room, for instance, or a spa bath on the terrace. 'Up the glass staircase, our strikingly designed room had a high, comfy bed, a cinema-worthy TV screen, a bathroom of white marble. Particularly inspiring: the evening light over the river and the mountains beyond. Though the road ran below us, we slept well with the window open, to the restful sound of waves.' Twice a week, a Tuscan-inspired dinner is served in the stone-walled dining room. 'From the short, interesting selection, we enjoyed crab ravioli, seared turbot with spring vegetables and an excellent chocolate tart, elegantly served.' Breakfast too is delicious: 'wonderfully buttery scrambled eggs; the best fresh orange juice we've had in ages'.

Barmouth
LL42 1TE

T: 01341 281632
E: croeso@coesfaen.co.uk
W: coesfaen.co.uk

BEDROOMS: 6. 1, on ground floor, suitable for disabled.
OPEN: all year except Christmas, Jan, restaurant open Fri and Sat evenings.
FACILITIES: entrance hall, snug with honesty bar, dining room, free Wi-Fi, in-room TV (Freeview), in-room spa treatments, 15-acre grounds (woodland garden), stable for visiting dogs and horses.
BACKGROUND MUSIC: in public areas.
LOCATION: 1 mile E of town centre.
CHILDREN: not under 18.
DOGS: 'clean, well-behaved, indoor-trained dogs (no puppies)' allowed in 1 bedroom, not in public rooms.
CREDIT CARDS: all major cards.
PRICES: [2017] per room B&B £165–£240, D,B&B £225–£320. Set menus £30–£40, à la carte £35.

BARMOUTH Gwynedd

Map 3:B3

LLWYNDU FARMHOUSE

Rustic and folksy, Paula and Peter Thompson's 'quirky' 16th-century farmhouse at the base of the Rhinog mountains is a 'friendly, welcoming' spot and a fine base for exploring a 'lovely part of the country'. There's old-world charm in the log fires, ancient oak beams and spiral stone staircase; fans come for the homespun ambience. 'A wood-burner lit in the afternoon made the lounge a cosy place in the evening.' Unpretentious bedrooms (some with a newly updated bathroom) are in the main building and a converted 18th-century granary. Ring to discuss room choices before booking: every one is different. In the oak-beamed hall lit with lamps and candles, 'dinner is the highlight'. Peter Thompson's 'commendable' daily-changing menu puts the emphasis on local seafood and meats in dishes such as Rhydlewis smoked salmon, lemon and horseradish mayonnaise; Welsh Black beef rib-eye steak, red onion and crab apple marmalade. An 'interesting' wine list provides liquid accompaniment. Step outside before dusk: 'Most enchanting of all, the views across Cardigan Bay gave a sunset that would compare with anywhere else in the world.'

Llanaber
Barmouth
LL42 1RR

T: 01341 280144
F: 01341 281236
E: intouch@llwyndu-farmhouse.co.uk
W: www.llwyndu-farmhouse.co.uk

BEDROOMS: 6. 3 in granary, 1 on ground floor.
OPEN: all year except Christmas, restaurant closed Sun and Wed.
FACILITIES: lounge, restaurant, free Wi-Fi, in-room TV (Freeview), ¼-acre garden in 4-acre grounds, unsuitable for disabled.
BACKGROUND MUSIC: 'occasionally and on demand' in dining room.
LOCATION: 2 miles N of Barmouth.
CHILDREN: all ages welcomed.
DOGS: not allowed.
CREDIT CARDS: MasterCard, Visa.
PRICES: [2017] per room B&B £110–£135, D,B&B £165–£195. Set dinner £25–£40. 1-night bookings sometimes refused weekends and in peak season.

BEAUMARIS Isle of Anglesey

THE BULL

Behind a Georgian facade, this 17th-century
inn in the seaside town is today a 'well-run
hotel' with 'excellent accommodation'. Spread
between the characterful main building and
the contemporary Townhouse, bedrooms are a
mix of traditional and modern, though all the
amenities are bang up to date: biscuits, fresh
milk, a capsule coffee machine, Beaumaris-
made toiletries. 'Our spacious, ultra-modern
Townhouse room had top-quality furniture
and linen, and a pleasant bay window seating
area where we could sit and watch life in the
main street below. One niggle: the buzzing air
conditioner.' Rub shoulders with locals over a
seasonal cocktail or hand-drawn ale in the cosy
bar hung with artefacts and oddities, then stay
for dinner. In the 'bright and cheerful' brasserie
('where a log fire roars, even at breakfast'), tuck
into informal meals, perhaps a platter of local
seafood or 'particularly imaginative, flavourful'
small plates. Four nights a week in the
restaurant, chef Andy Tabberner cooks a short
menu using local, seasonal ingredients. Among
his 'interesting dishes': Anglesey lamb shoulder,
wild garlic; shallot tart, Moelyci cheese, leek,
kale. (Alan and Edwina Williams, and others)

Castle Street
Beaumaris
LL58 8AP

T: 01248 810329
F: 01248 811294
E: info@bullsheadinn.co.uk
W: www.bullsheadinn.co.uk

BEDROOMS: 25. 2 on ground floor, 1 in
courtyard, 13 in The Townhouse
adjacent, 1 suitable for disabled.
OPEN: all year, but limited opening
in Christmas period, Loft restaurant
closed lunch, Sun–Tues nights.
FACILITIES: lift (in The Townhouse),
lounge, bar, brasserie, restaurant,
free Wi-Fi, in-room TV (Freeview),
courtyard, charging station for
electric cars.
BACKGROUND MUSIC: 'upbeat,
contemporary' in brasserie.
LOCATION: central.
CHILDREN: all ages welcomed, no
under-7s in restaurant.
DOGS: allowed in some bedrooms,
bar and lounge.
CREDIT CARDS: MasterCard, Visa.
PRICES: [2017] per room B&B from
£115, D,B&B from £155. Set dinner
(restaurant) £35–£50, à la carte
(brasserie) £28.

BRECHFA Carmarthenshire

Map 3:D2

TY MAWR

🔱 Previous César winner

Thick stone walls, beamed ceilings, works by local artists, an inglenook fire and 'friendly, hospitable hosts' give this 16th-century country house-turned-hotel heaps of rustic charm. A bonus: in clement weather, 'drinks on the manicured lawn, before dinner in the pretty dining room, are divine'. Annabel and Stephen Thomas, the owners, are 'great fun'; the atmosphere is 'relaxed and informal'. Bedrooms, some surprisingly large, are simple in style, but 'immaculately maintained' and well stocked with 'all the amenities you'd expect in a five-star hotel'. In the restaurant, choose from Stephen Thomas's local produce-packed, daily-changing menu, perhaps including smoked Cardigan Bay mackerel and horseradish pâté, Ty Mawr apple and mustard seed chutney; organic Welsh Black beef fillet, braised oxtail. At breakfast, 'leisurely and very civilised', there are pork-and-leek sausages, eggs Royale with Severn and Wye valley smoked salmon, sometimes even juice from the garden apples. Country lanes stretch out, afterwards, and walks in the Brechfa forest – all moss, thick ferns, ancient trees and busy birdlife – await. More reports, please.

25% DISCOUNT VOUCHERS

Brechfa
SA32 7RA

T: 01267 202332
E: info@wales-country-hotel.co.uk
W: www.wales-country-hotel.co.uk

BEDROOMS: 6. 2 on ground floor, 1 with private access.
OPEN: all year.
FACILITIES: sitting room, bar, breakfast room, restaurant, free Wi-Fi, in-room TV (Freeview), 1-acre grounds, unsuitable for disabled.
BACKGROUND MUSIC: classical in restaurant during dinner.
LOCATION: village centre.
CHILDREN: not under 10.
DOGS: not allowed in breakfast room, restaurant.
CREDIT CARDS: Amex, MasterCard, Visa.
PRICES: [2017] per room B&B £115–£130, D,B&B £160–£175. Set dinner £25–£30. 1-night bookings occasionally refused on Sat in summer.

CARDIGAN Ceredigion

Map 3:D2

CAEMORGAN MANSION

Readers are unequivocal in their praise for Beverley and David Harrison-Wood's 'startlingly good guest house', in a 19th-century mansion refurbished to eco-friendly standards. 'We liked this very friendly, well-presented place.' Bedrooms on the first and second floors (some with beams and a sloping ceiling) have a large bed and plenty of extras: robes and slippers, a capsule coffee/hot chocolate machine, fresh milk and home-baked biscuits, books and DVDs to borrow. In the evening, stay in for 'a really special dining experience'. Large windows, a striking central log burner and deep red walls give the dining room a 'tranquil, elegant' feel. Chefs Abbie Jenkins and David Harrison-Wood's modern European cooking is 'particularly good'. (A steak menu, from a locally bred herd, is particularly pleasing to meat eaters.) Characteristic dishes: pan-seared duck, passion fruit reduction; sea bass, coriander and vanilla velouté, deep-fried spinach. 'And then there is breakfast – another delight.' Fill up on a full Welsh, then head into the day: the Coastal Path is minutes away, for walkers and cyclists; the hosts can help arrange dolphin-spotting trips. (PW, BS)

Caemorgan Road
Cardigan
SA43 1QU

T: 01239 613297
F: 01239 393070
E: guest@caemorgan.com
W: www.caemorgan.com

BEDROOMS: 5.
OPEN: all year except Christmas.
FACILITIES: bar, restaurant, free Wi-Fi, in-room TV (Freeview), function facilities, 2-acre gardens, unsuitable for disabled.
BACKGROUND MUSIC: none.
LOCATION: ½ mile N of town centre.
CHILDREN: not under 16.
DOGS: not allowed.
CREDIT CARDS: MasterCard, Visa.
PRICES: [2017] per room B&B from £95. À la carte £30. 1-night bookings often refused peak weekends.

CRICKHOWELL Powys

Map 3:D4

GLIFFAES

♔ Previous César winner

'Timeless standards of comfort' keep guests coming back to this Italianate mansion 'in a wonderful position' on the River Usk. The sporting hotel, 'a fine house', has been owned by three generations of the same family for 72 years; today, Susie and James Suter and Peta Brabner are at the helm. Past the foyer wallpapered in fishing prints, bedrooms are decorated in period country house style – a spread of toile de Jouy here, a hand-embroidered canopy over a four-poster bed there. Downstairs, dusky-rose walls are hung with paintings in the book- and flower-filled drawing room – a popular spot for afternoon tea. Come evening, chef Karl Cheetham uses seasonal, local and home-grown produce in his 'flavourful, inventive' modern dishes, perhaps roast lamb, crisp sweetbread and faggot, swede mash, rosemary tuile. 'It's first-class value for money,' say regular Guide readers this year. 'And we appreciate that the chef responds to special requests if he is able.' In sunshine, laze on the terrace, or follow an 'impressive' walk among 'magnificent' specimen trees. (M and PB, and others)

25% DISCOUNT VOUCHERS

Gliffaes Road
Crickhowell
NP8 1RH

T: 01874 730371
F: 01874 730463
E: calls@gliffaeshotel.com
W: www.gliffaeshotel.com

BEDROOMS: 23. 4 in cottage, 1 on ground floor suitable for disabled.
OPEN: all year except Jan.
FACILITIES: 2 sitting rooms, conservatory, bar, dining room, free Wi-Fi, in-room TV, civil wedding licence, 33-acre garden (tennis, croquet, private stretch of the River Usk for fly-fishing).
BACKGROUND MUSIC: in bar in evening.
LOCATION: 3 miles W of Crickhowell.
CHILDREN: all ages welcomed.
DOGS: not allowed indoors (kennels available).
CREDIT CARDS: all major cards.
PRICES: [2017] per room B&B £139–£298, D,B&B £217–£376. À la carte £40. 1-night bookings refused high-season weekends.

DOLFOR Powys

Map 3:C4

THE OLD VICARAGE

In a rural setting close to the medieval market town of Newtown, Helen and Tim Withers fill their eco-friendly country guest house with 'an atmosphere of heart-warming hospitality'. The red brick Victorian vicarage stands in large gardens, with mature trees, a potager and a wildlife pond. Inside, 'all the important things' are there. Pretty bedrooms are decorated in traditional rustic style, each different: cosy Mule has a sloping ceiling and a fetching toile de Jouy wallcovering; two-bedroomed Severn suits a family. An evening meal is served at 7 pm, by arrangement. Sip an aperitif in the lounge, then sit down to Tim Withers's limited-choice menu (guests' likes and dislikes are discussed when booking). 'It's simple, no-nonsense cookery that does not bow to fashion', perhaps hot-smoked salmon, beetroot and apple salad; chicken basquaise, sweet potato wedges, purple sprouting broccoli. In the morning, help yourself to cereals, yogurt, fruit and dollops of home-made preserves; interesting cooked options include organic sausages, traditionally cured kippers, and omelettes made with Welsh Cheddar or laver bread. (JVdB, and others)

Dolfor
SY16 4BN

T: 01686 629051
F: 01686 207629
E: tim@theoldvicaragedolfor.co.uk
W: www.theoldvicaragedolfor.co.uk

BEDROOMS: 4.
OPEN: all year except last 3 weeks Dec, dining room closed Sun.
FACILITIES: drawing room, dining room, free Wi-Fi, in-room TV (Freeview), 1½-acre garden, unsuitable for disabled.
BACKGROUND MUSIC: none.
LOCATION: 3 miles S of Newtown.
CHILDREN: all ages welcomed.
DOGS: not allowed.
CREDIT CARDS: all major cards.
PRICES: [2017] per person B&B £37.50–£90, D,B&B £62.50–£115. Set dinner £25–£30. 1-night bookings sometimes refused.

DOLGELLAU Gwynedd

Map 3:B3

FFYNNON
NEW

In walkers' country, within the Snowdonia national park, this handsome Victorian rectory stands in a market town at the foot of Cadair Idris. Up a 'testing, narrow lane', the contemporary guest house has books to borrow, and a piano in the lounge; the honesty bar stocks local beers and snacks. Former managers Angela and Bernhard Lanz, an 'impressive couple', took over ownership in 2017. 'The Lanzes are all-rounders: they manned the office, showed us to our room, cooked and served the food. And they couldn't have been friendlier or more obliging.' 'Imaginatively decorated' bedrooms, including two huge top-floor suites, have views over town and valley, or landscaped gardens. 'Entering our Eastern-themed room was like walking on to a stage set for "The Mikado". There was a comfortable super-king-size bed, excellent lighting, and easy chairs that were a joy to loll in. We slept well, in silence.' Five nights a week, sample the daily-changing menu of 'excellent' modern Welsh dishes. 'We had a crisp salad with pink duck breast and orange vinaigrette; an artistic leek and spinach roulade with Perl Las and tomato sauce. Outstanding.' (Sarah and Tony Thomas)

Love Lane
Dolgellau
LL40 1RR

T: 01341 421774
F: 01341 421779
E: info@ffynnontownhouse.com
W: www.ffynnontownhouse.com

BEDROOMS: 6.
OPEN: all year except Christmas.
FACILITIES: sitting room, dining room, study/hall, butler's pantry, free Wi-Fi, in-room TV (Freeview), 'reasonably sized' garden (secluded outdoor hot tub), parking, unsuitable for disabled.
BACKGROUND MUSIC: all day in sitting room and dining room.
LOCATION: town centre.
CHILDREN: all ages welcomed.
DOGS: not allowed.
CREDIT CARDS: Amex, MasterCard, Visa.
PRICES: [2017] per room B&B £150–£210. Set dinner £27.95–£34.95. 2-night min. stay at weekends.

DOLYDD Gwynedd

Y GOEDEN EIRIN

๕ Previous César winner

'More than a B&B, this is a home that welcomes you for bed and breakfast.' Trusted Guide correspondents in 2017 heartily endorse this characterful place, a converted cowshed infused with the personality of its owner, Eluned Rowlands, and her late husband, John. 'The hostess is enthusiastic about Welsh paintings and painters', and the house is filled with artwork by the late Kyffin Williams, alongside many 'interesting objects'. Bedrooms are rustic ('rugged, not twee'). 'Our room was practically a bedsit, with an alcove dressing room between bedroom and bathroom. We watched the stars through the skylight window above the bed before pulling down the blind. I slept like a hedgehog.' Dine in Caernarfon, a ten-minute drive away; in the morning, wake to an Aga-cooked breakfast at the chunky oak table in the spacious dining/living room – perhaps a 'plump, juicy kipper' or local bacon and sausages off the 'extensive' breakfast menu. Tregarth-born, Eluned Rowlands has much knowledge to share on public footpaths and nearby places of interest – and will happily advise in Welsh, if you prefer. (Sarah and Tony Thomas)

Y Goeden Eirin
Dolydd
LL54 7EF

T: 01286 830942
E: eluned.rowlands@tiscali.co.uk
W: www.ygoedeneirin.co.uk

BEDROOMS: 3. 2 in annexe 3 yds from house.
OPEN: all year except Christmas/New Year.
FACILITIES: breakfast room, lounge, free Wi-Fi, in-room TV (Freeview), 20-acre pastureland, electric car charging point, unsuitable for disabled.
BACKGROUND MUSIC: none.
LOCATION: 3 miles S of Caernarfon.
CHILDREN: not under 12.
DOGS: may be allowed by prior arrangement – ring to discuss.
CREDIT CARDS: none, cash or cheque payment requested on arrival.
PRICES: per room B&B single £65, double £90–£100.

EGLWYSWRW Pembrokeshire

Map 3:D2

AEL Y BRYN

♛ Previous César winner

'Consummate hosts' Robert Smith and Arwel Hughes run their peaceful B&B against the 'superb backdrop' of the Preseli mountains. 'High standards are completely normal for Robert and Arwel, as is the cheerful care we always receive,' say returning guests this year. Another Guide reader, who uses a wheelchair, agrees: 'It's sheer perfection.' Come in to tea and tiered platters of home-baked cakes – 'a great icebreaker to meet fellow travellers arriving the same day' – then unpack in one of the spacious bedrooms, each 'wanting for nothing' (not even 'mouth-watering shortbread'). 'Our room looked towards the pond, and the woodpeckers and jays on the bird table.' A two-course dinner of 'refined comfort food' (perhaps creamy leek tart; lamb shanks, home-made cranberry sauce) may be served, by arrangement. 'We stayed for a week, and there was a different menu – a feast! – each day. The potatoes were dug from the garden at 6 pm and cooked for 7 pm – you couldn't get fresher than that.' Next morning, breakfast is 'top of the class'. (Jacqui and Karl Parr, Lois and John Nightingale, Sabrina Dey, Susan Raymond, and many others)

25% DISCOUNT VOUCHERS

Eglwyswrw
SA41 3UL

T: 01239 891411
E: stay@aelybrynpembrokeshire.co.uk
W: www.aelybrynpembrokeshire.co.uk

BEDROOMS: 4. All on ground floor.
OPEN: all year except Christmas/New Year.
FACILITIES: library, music room, dining room, conservatory (telescope), free Wi-Fi, in-room TV (Freeview), courtyard, 2½-acre garden (wildlife pond, stream, bowls court).
BACKGROUND MUSIC: occasionally in music room in evening.
LOCATION: ½ mile N of Eglwyswrw.
CHILDREN: not under 14.
DOGS: not allowed.
CREDIT CARDS: all major cards.
PRICES: [2017] per room B&B £105–£140. Set dinner £25–£29.

FELIN FACH Powys

THE FELIN FACH GRIFFIN

⚜ Previous César winner

'A wonderful place', the Inkin brothers' dining pub-with-rooms combines a 'relaxed, happy-making atmosphere' with 'decently sized, nicely furnished bedrooms'. In a hamlet between the Brecon Beacons and the Black mountains, the 'charming spot' – family-friendly and dog-friendly to boot – shares the carefree-yet-professional approach of sister ventures in Zennor and Mousehole (see entries). Mismatched armchairs sit by the fire in the pub (a gathering place for locals). In the 'appealing, shabby-chic' dining room, short daily menus of 'amazing' food draw on the best local ingredients, including vegetables and soft fruit from the kitchen garden. Typical among the 'inventive, creatively presented' dishes: mackerel fillet, harissa; Welsh beef sirloin, watercress, bone marrow. Some of the smart, country-style bedrooms may be snug, but all the key elements are there: filter coffee, leaf tea, fresh milk, shortbread; magazines and a Roberts radio; 'a lovely shower'. After breakfast – the apple juice is local – strike out on a hike, or simply browse the bookshops in Hay-on-Wye, a 20-minute drive away. 'I'd happily stay here again.'

Felin Fach
LD3 0UB

T: 01874 620111
E: enquiries@felinfachgriffin.co.uk
W: www.felinfachgriffin.co.uk

BEDROOMS: 7.
OPEN: all year except 24/25 Dec.
FACILITIES: bar area, dining room, breakfast room, private dining room, free Wi-Fi, limited mobile phone signal, 3-acre garden (stream, kitchen garden, alfresco dining), only bar/dining room suitable for disabled.
BACKGROUND MUSIC: Radio 4 at breakfast, 'easy listening' at other times, in bar and restaurant.
LOCATION: 4 miles NE of Brecon, in village on A470.
CHILDREN: all ages welcomed.
DOGS: allowed in bedrooms, not in restaurant.
CREDIT CARDS: MasterCard, Visa.
PRICES: [2017] per room B&B £135–£175, D,B&B £190–£230. À la carte £33.

FISHGUARD Pembrokeshire

Map 3:D1

THE MANOR TOWN HOUSE

The powder-blue facade of Helen and Chris
Sheldon's Georgian town house, with its smart
portico, gives a hint of chic B&B accommodation
within. The revelation is the view from the
rear terrace, where guests take tea while gazing
across Cardigan Bay and down upon the
harbour. (A well-stocked honesty bar provides
a stronger tipple.) The lounges are welcoming,
with fresh flowers, books and DVDs, bright
throws on pale sofas, and log fires in winter; on
the walls hang local photography and paintings
by Welsh artists. Most of the bedrooms have sea
views; the best have a sofa and bed positioned
for watching the sunrise and sunset across
Fishguard Bay. All rooms are smartly styled,
and made comfortable with bottled water,
dressing gowns and good toiletries. At breakfast,
elegantly served, choose from a menu of
waffles, award-winning sausages, freshly baked
pastries, a cooked daily special. Afterwards,
wander down to the picture-postcard Lower
Town, or ask for a packed lunch and walk
the Pembrokeshire Coastal Path, which runs
through the wooded valley below the garden.
More reports, please.

11 Main Street
Fishguard
SA65 9HG

T: 01348 873260
E: info@manortownhouse.com
W: www.manortownhouse.com

BEDROOMS: 6.
OPEN: all year except 23–28 Dec.
FACILITIES: 2 lounges, breakfast
room, free Wi-Fi, in-room TV
(Freeview), small walled garden,
unsuitable for disabled.
BACKGROUND MUSIC: classical at
breakfast.
LOCATION: town centre.
CHILDREN: all ages welcomed.
DOGS: not allowed.
CREDIT CARDS: MasterCard, Visa.
PRICES: [2017] per room B&B £85–
£125. 1-night bookings sometimes
refused peak weekends.

GLYNARTHEN Ceredigion

Map 3:D2

PENBONTBREN

♗ Previous César winner

'A cross between a hotel, a B&B and a holiday cottage, with the advantages of each, this is a very special place,' say regular Guide readers this year. 'Generous, caring and enthusiastic' hosts Richard Morgan-Price and Huw Thomas own this 'first-rate' conversion of a 19th-century livestock farm set in 'beautiful grounds'. Accommodation is in 'magnificently equipped' suites in former farm outbuildings. 'Our well-lit suite, with a private, garden-facing patio, had masses of storage space and a large, warm bathroom. Magazines and novels had been provided, along with extra lamps for reading by. Fresh Welsh cakes appeared daily; a splendid farm shop at the end of the lane supplied a good supper, eaten in the comfort of our sizeable sitting room – a new and satisfying venture for us. The well-stocked kitchen had everything we needed, and housekeeping staff did the washing-up next morning. We were quite happy to forgo hotel dinners!' A varied breakfast is 'of the highest quality' – 'no mugs, but beautiful tea cups and saucers'. (Janet Allom, Hilary Cameron, Tony Fisher, and others)

25% DISCOUNT VOUCHERS

Glynarthen
SA44 6PE

T: 01239 810248
F: 01239 811129
E: contact@penbontbren.com
W: www.penbontbren.com

BEDROOMS: 6. 5 in annexe, 1 in garden, 3 on ground floor, 1 family suite, 1 suitable for disabled.
OPEN: all year except Christmas.
FACILITIES: breakfast room, free Wi-Fi, in-room TV (Freeview), 7-acre grounds.
BACKGROUND MUSIC: none.
LOCATION: 5 miles N of Newcastle Emlyn.
CHILDREN: all ages welcomed.
DOGS: allowed in some bedrooms, not in breakfast room.
CREDIT CARDS: MasterCard, Visa.
PRICES: [2017] per room B&B £99–£125. 1-night bookings sometimes refused weekends.

HARLECH Gwynedd

Map 3:B3

CASTLE COTTAGE

What first smites the eye is the town's medieval castle, formidable on its cliff-top. Steps behind it, this restaurant-with-rooms – in two adjoining 16th-century buildings restored and refurbished with contemporary flair – is no less of a surprise. Chef/patron Glyn Roberts and his wife, Jacqueline, have run their 'impressive' enterprise for nearly 30 years; today, it continues to attract guests who come for the 'excellent accommodation' and 'delicious cooking'. The dining room is hung with Welsh art, its oak tables laid with crisp linen. Here, the menu changes with the seasons, each time drawing on fine Welsh produce – crab and fish from Aberdaron; lobster from Shell Island; pork and beef from Bala. Typical dishes: grilled asparagus, Carmarthen ham, roasted tomatoes; rack of local lamb, rosemary and garlic potatoes, buttered carrots. In the main building and characterful annexe (a former inn), some of the dark-beamed modern bedrooms have 'wonderful' views over mountains and sea. There's freshly squeezed orange or grapefruit juice at breakfast, with more local flavours (laver bread and Llyn peninsula bacon, for example) on the menu. More reports, please.

25% DISCOUNT VOUCHERS

Y Llech
Harlech
LL46 2YL

T: 01766 780479
E: glyn@castlecottageharlech.co.uk
W: www.castlecottageharlech.co.uk

BEDROOMS: 7. 4 in annexe, 2 on ground floor.
OPEN: all year except Christmas and 3 weeks Nov, restaurant closed Sun–Wed in winter months.
FACILITIES: bar, lounge, restaurant, free Wi-Fi, in-room TV (Freeview), unsuitable for disabled.
BACKGROUND MUSIC: in bar and restaurant at mealtimes.
LOCATION: town centre.
CHILDREN: all ages welcomed.
DOGS: not allowed.
CREDIT CARDS: MasterCard, Visa.
PRICES: [2017] per room B&B £130–£175. Set menus £35–£40, tasting menu £45.

LAMPETER Ceredigion

Map 3:D3

THE FALCONDALE

At the end of a mile-long drive through 'lovely surroundings' of rolling pastureland, Chris and Lisa Hutton lay on an 'absolutely perfect' welcome at their 'striking Victorian pile' in 'handsome' landscaped gardens. The greeting sets tails wagging, too: pooches receive a blanket, a water bowl and treats. 'Spacious, pleasant' public rooms are decorated with 'interesting pictures' and 'good traditional taste'; from the veranda, there are 'magnificent views' down the Teifi valley. The great green vista continues through the bedrooms, too: all of them look out on to garden, valley or woodland. The best, and largest, rooms have a Juliet balcony, but even the smaller of the 'classically styled' bedrooms have 'their own character, with a special ornament or two'. (The lift doesn't access all rooms; guests with special requirements should ring to discuss the best options.) At lunch and dinner, chef Alex Rees cooks 'enjoyable' dishes using local produce and garden-grown herbs, perhaps Welsh pork belly, cheek and loin, celeriac, pommes Anna. Spend the day strolling the grounds ('our dogs appreciated the lovely walks off the lead'); in fine weather, a stone terrace captures all the sunshine. (GE, AW, and others)

25% DISCOUNT VOUCHERS

Falcondale Drive
Lampeter
SA48 7RX

T: 01570 422910
E: info@thefalcondale.co.uk
W: www.thefalcondale.co.uk

BEDROOMS: 18.
OPEN: all year.
FACILITIES: lift, bar, 3 lounges, conservatory, restaurant, free Wi-Fi, in-room TV (Freeview), civil wedding licence, beauty treatment room, terrace, 14-acre grounds (lawns, woodland), unsuitable for disabled.
BACKGROUND MUSIC: in restaurant and lounges.
LOCATION: 1 mile N of Lampeter.
CHILDREN: all ages welcomed.
DOGS: allowed, not in main dining room.
CREDIT CARDS: MasterCard, Visa.
PRICES: [2017] per room B&B £125–£195, D,B&B (min. 2 nights) £185–£255. À la carte £40.

LLANDRILLO Denbighshire

Map 3:B4

TYDDYN LLAN

In this thickly rural corner of north Wales, Susan and Bryan Webb run their much-admired, 'friendly, relaxed' restaurant-with-rooms. 'It's the benchmark by which we judge other hotels,' write regular guests, trusted Guide correspondents, this year. 'Bryan is the best cook in Wales; Susan, a treasure, runs the place with good-humoured efficiency.' Bedrooms in the mellow-stone Georgian shooting lodge are done in country style (a brass bedstead here, a tartan armchair or vintage chest of drawers there), and have 'lovely views' over the garden. The rooms vary in size, but all are 'absolutely fine – quiet, with a comfy bed and a modern bathroom'. In the pretty, light-filled dining room, it's Bryan Webb's Michelin-starred cooking that sets the place apart: 'No surprise that the restaurant was full, midweek.' 'We ate in all four nights, and everything was wonderful. The new-season grouse was sublime; a starter of half a lobster with ginger, garlic and coriander butter left my wife struggling to finish her main course. She still managed a pudding, though!' (Peter Anderson, Gwyn Morgan)

25% DISCOUNT VOUCHERS

Llandrillo
LL21 0ST

T: 01490 440264
F: 01490 440414
E: info@tyddynllan.co.uk
W: www.tyddynllan.co.uk

BEDROOMS: 13. 3 with separate entrance, 1, on ground floor, suitable for disabled.
OPEN: all year except last 2 weeks Aug, restaurant closed Mon and Tues.
FACILITIES: 2 lounges, bar, 2 dining rooms, free Wi-Fi, in-room TV (Freeview), civil wedding licence, 3-acre garden.
BACKGROUND MUSIC: none.
LOCATION: 5 miles SW of Corwen.
CHILDREN: all ages welcomed.
DOGS: allowed in some bedrooms (£10 per night), not in public rooms.
CREDIT CARDS: Amex, MasterCard, Visa.
PRICES: per room B&B £190–£320, D,B&B £310–£420. Set dinner £65, tasting menus £75–£90 (plus optional 10% service on food and drink charges).

LLANDUDNO Conwy

Map 3:A3

BODYSGALLEN HALL & SPA

'A lovely old house', this historic mansion on the slopes of Pydew mountain has glorious views of Snowdonia. 'The staff are very friendly, the fire is always lit, and early morning tea brought to our room was a treat,' says a Guide reader this year. 'It's a real special-occasion place.' In the care of the National Trust, the Grade I listed house ('with creaky floors, and quirky corners everywhere') stands within acres of lush parkland, in 'beautiful, well-kept gardens that are worth a visit in themselves'. The panelled drawing room, with two fireplaces, is furnished with antiques and paintings. In the main house and cottages in the grounds, traditionally decorated bedrooms are 'immaculate'. 'Our spacious room had uninterrupted views towards Conwy Castle.' Dress smartly for dinner in the Main Hall dining room, where chef John Williams's 'delicious modern cooking' might include game ravioli, creamed lentils, smoked pigeon 'tea'; slow-cooked Welsh lamb, fennel pollen, smoked red-pepper purée. Next day, lose yourself on a woodland walk or pick your way through the garden straight to the farmhouse spa – a secluded sunbathing terrace is just right for a summer's day. (RM-P, and others)

The Royal Welsh Way
Llandudno
LL30 1RS

T: 01492 584466
E: info@bodysgallen.com
W: www.bodysgallen.com

BEDROOMS: 31. 16 in cottages, 1 suitable for disabled.
OPEN: all year, restaurant closed Mon lunch.
FACILITIES: hall, drawing room, library, bar, dining room, free Wi-Fi, in-room TV (Sky, Freeview), civil wedding licence, 220-acre park (gardens, tennis, croquet), spa (16-metre swimming pool).
BACKGROUND MUSIC: none.
LOCATION: 2 miles S of Llandudno and Conwy.
CHILDREN: no under-6s in hotel, under-8s in spa (set swimming times).
DOGS: not allowed.
CREDIT CARDS: Amex, MasterCard, Visa.
PRICES: [2017] per room B&B £165–£395. À la carte £55. 1-night bookings sometimes refused.

SEE ALSO SHORTLIST

LLANDUDNO Conwy

Map 3:A3

OSBORNE HOUSE

Steps from the Victorian pier, Elyse and Michael Waddy's 19th-century house takes in the 'elegant sweep' of the promenade at this popular seaside resort. The third generation of a local hotelier family, the Waddys have run their small hotel since 2001 (big-sister property the Empire is around the corner, with spa facilities to share). The former gentleman's residence is ornately decorated with a wealth of original features, antique furnishings, drapes, paintings, 'table lamps everywhere' – 'it's all very atmospheric'. Upstairs, the 'beautifully furnished bedrooms' – spacious suites, really, with a separate sitting room – are suitably grand. Each has fine art and motley antiques, oriental rugs on bare floorboards, an original marble fireplace, perhaps a draped canopy bed or two. Second-floor rooms have the 'best views of the beautiful bay and the cliffs in all their glory'. The all-day bistro has high-flown decor (chandeliers, fluted pillars, grand portraits), but the food is down-to-earth – sample a slow-roasted lamb shank, say, or curried monkfish and king prawns. Continental breakfasts are served here; alternatively, visit the Empire for a hot dish. More reports, please.

17 North Parade
Llandudno
LL30 2LP

T: 01492 860330
F: 01492 860791
E: sales@osbornehouse.com
W: www.osbornehouse.co.uk

BEDROOMS: 6.
OPEN: all year, except 10 days Christmas, open New Year.
FACILITIES: sitting room, bar, café/bistro, free Wi-Fi, unsuitable for disabled.
BACKGROUND MUSIC: in public rooms.
LOCATION: on promenade.
CHILDREN: not under 14.
DOGS: not allowed.
CREDIT CARDS: all major cards.
PRICES: [2017] per room B&B £125–£175, D,B&B £155–£205. À la carte £27. 1-night bookings sometimes refused.

SEE ALSO SHORTLIST

LLANGAMMARCH WELLS Powys

Map 3:D3

THE LAKE

Approached via quiet lanes bordered by hedgerows and dark-limbed trees, Jean-Pierre Mifsud's Victorian hunting lodge-turned-country house hotel stands in extensive grounds stretching to a lake on the River Irfon. Outside is a mix of mock-Tudor timbering, French windows and verandas; within, the lounges have chandeliers and polished oak, antiques and objets d'art, paintings and portraits. A fire burns in the snug library on cool days; when the sun's out, afternoon tea may be served on the patio, under the spreading chestnut tree. (No surprise, perhaps, that some Guide readers choose to make this 'a regular haunt'.) Bedrooms have individual character – traditional in the main house, modern in the lodge. Tables are laid with white linen in the 'first-class' dining room, where new chef Josh Donachie serves contemporary Welsh dishes, perhaps duck breast, apricot chutney, beetroot, roast cauliflower. After breakfast ('we thought the portions could have been more generous'), head out into lush countryside – a riverbank stroll leads to the village. Northcote Manor, Burrington, England (see entry), is under the same ownership. (RM-P, and others)

25% DISCOUNT VOUCHERS

Llangammarch Wells
LD4 4BS

T: 01591 620202
F: 01591 620457
E: info@lakecountryhouse.co.uk
W: www.lakecountryhouse.co.uk

BEDROOMS: 32. 12 suites in adjacent lodge, 7 on ground floor, 1 suitable for disabled.
OPEN: all year.
FACILITIES: lounge, bar, restaurant, breakfast room, free Wi-Fi, in-room TV (Freeview), spa (15-metre swimming pool, restricted hours for under-16s), civil wedding licence, 50-acre grounds (tennis, trout lake, 9-hole, par-3 golf course).
BACKGROUND MUSIC: none.
LOCATION: 8 miles SW of Builth Wells.
CHILDREN: all ages welcomed, no under-8s in spa, or in dining room at night.
DOGS: allowed (£10 charge), not in main lounge or dining room.
CREDIT CARDS: Amex, MasterCard, Visa.
PRICES: per room B&B £195–£260, D,B&B (min. 2 nights) £245–£320. Set dinner £45.

LLANTHONY Monmouthshire

LLANTHONY PRIORY HOTEL NEW

'The setting in the Welsh Borders could hardly be more romantic.' In a wild and secluded valley where the Black mountains rise up all round, this characterful hotel is tucked in next to the timeworn remains of a 12th-century Augustinian priory. It enters the Guide thanks to a recommendation from a trusted reporter in 2017. Modest accommodation is up a medieval tower embraced by ivy (reached via a steep spiral staircase, with aid from 'helpful, friendly' staff), or in a Grade I listed prior's lodging adjoining atmospheric abbey ruins. 'Years ago, the rooms looked like a country auction. After a sympathetic refurbishment, the bedrooms are tasteful, restful, minimal yet appropriate for the ancient building. My room had a comfortable bed with fine bedding, a chair, a dressing table, good bedside lights and not much else.' There's neither TV nor Wi-Fi, nor even a mobile phone signal, but the 'beautiful landscape' is yours for the adventuring; a track behind the ruins leads to Offa's Dyke Path. Return at dusk for Welsh ales and pub dinners, perhaps an abbot's beef casserole, in the vaulted crypt. (Anne Thackray)

Llanthony
NP7 7NN

T: 01873 890487
E: llanthonypriory@btconnect.com
W: www.llanthonyprioryhotel.co.uk

BEDROOMS: 7. All with shared shower/bathrooms.
OPEN: Fri–Sun, Nov–Mar, Tues–Sun, Apr–Oct, closed Mon except bank holidays.
FACILITIES: lounge, bar, dining room, no Wi-Fi, extensive grounds (including priory ruins), unsuitable for disabled.
BACKGROUND MUSIC: none.
LOCATION: 10 miles N of Abergavenny.
CHILDREN: not under 10.
DOGS: not allowed.
CREDIT CARDS: none.
PRICES: [2017] per room B&B single £70–£75, double £90–£97.50.

LLYSWEN Powys

Map 3:D4

LLANGOED HALL

Deep in the Wye valley, this privately owned 17th-century manor house stands in 'a great atmosphere of peace', overlooking green meadows leading to the river. After a spell as an Edwardian country house, it was opened as a hotel by Sir Bernard Ashley; his 'fabulous collection' of art and antiques still sits among Laura Ashley's characteristic prints. All is 'pleasant and comfortable' – an atmosphere encouraged by 'impeccable staff'. There are fresh flowers and open fires; afternoon tea is served on gold-leaf china; in the organic kitchen garden, chickens and ducks peck and rustle. 'Lovely bedrooms' are 'faultlessly decorated' ('like a bedroom in a luxurious country house') and supplied with fresh fruit, bottled waters and a decanter of sherry. Hot drinks and a newspaper are brought to the room in the morning. Try the 'delicious scones' at teatime, but save room for dinner. 'The food is elaborate and expensive, but superb.' Chef Nick Brodie's tasting menus (including one for vegetarians) showcase Welsh produce in modern dishes such as turbot, seaweed, mussel butter, romanesco; venison, barley, cabbage, cauliflower. Stroll to the river in the morning: 'Birdsong fills the air.'

Llyswen
LD3 0YP

T: 01874 754525
F: 01874 754545
E: enquiries@llangoedhall.com
W: www.llangoedhall.com

BEDROOMS: 23.
OPEN: all year.
FACILITIES: great hall, morning room, library, bar/lounge, restaurant, billiard room, function rooms, free Wi-Fi, in-room TV (Freeview), civil wedding licence, 23-acre gardens and parkland, unsuitable for disabled.
BACKGROUND MUSIC: none.
LOCATION: 12 miles NE of Brecon.
CHILDREN: all ages welcomed, only 'well-behaved children' in dining room (babysitting can be arranged).
DOGS: allowed in bedrooms with £120 professional allergy clean, heated kennels available.
CREDIT CARDS: Amex, MasterCard, Visa.
PRICES: [2017] per room B&B £175–£650. Four-course table d'hôte menu £75, tasting menus £75–£95.

NARBERTH Pembrokeshire

Map 3:D2

THE GROVE

♦ Previous César winner

In 'flourishing gardens' near the coast, Neil and Zoë Kedward's 'beautifully quiet' hotel is 'a real haven – particularly when you arrive in the dark after a long drive'. Encouraged by 'young, charming and helpful' staff, Guide readers in 2017 willingly sank into the comfort of this stylishly refurbished 18th-century mansion. There are squishy sofas and cheering fires; candles and cocktails; a 'library of good books' to browse. In the main house and three cottages, 'luxurious bedrooms' are stocked with home-made biscotti and fine bath products. 'It's not cheap', but Allister Barsby's 'commendable cooking', perhaps a 'chicken and foie gras terrine to die for', is 'well worth the money'. 'We had the seven-course tasting menu one night with the recommended flight of wines – a well-considered and unusual selection.' For the less hungry, a short room-service menu's the ticket. 'I took supper, a light and savoury Welsh rarebit, on a velvet sofa by a delicious crackling log fire, in a pleasing wood-panelled sitting room. (It was awkward to eat from a coffee table, however.)' 'A sterling centre' for touring Pembrokeshire. (Tessa Stuart, Peter Jacobsen)

25% DISCOUNT VOUCHERS

Molleston
Narberth
SA67 8BX

T: 01834 860915
E: reservations@grovenarberth.co.uk
W: www.thegrove-narberth.co.uk

BEDROOMS: 26. 12 in cottages in the grounds, some on ground floor.
OPEN: all year.
FACILITIES: 3 lounges, bar, 3 restaurant rooms, free Wi-Fi, in-room TV (Sky), civil wedding licence, 26-acre grounds.
BACKGROUND MUSIC: in public areas.
LOCATION: 1 mile S of Narberth.
CHILDREN: all ages welcomed, not under 10 in restaurant after 7 pm.
DOGS: allowed in some bedrooms, not in main building.
CREDIT CARDS: Amex, MasterCard, Visa.
PRICES: [2017] per room B&B from £210, D,B&B from £328. Tasting menu £94, à la carte £64.

SEE ALSO SHORTLIST

NEWPORT Pembrokeshire

Map 3:D1

CNAPAN

In a 'fantastic area to explore', between the Preseli hills and Pembrokeshire national park, this 'exceptionally friendly and welcoming' guest house was first listed in the Guide more than 30 years ago. Today, third-generation owners Michael and Judith Cooper run their personable B&B with the help of 'well-informed staff, several of whom are family'. The early 19th-century building stands just back from the road, close to shops and galleries, beach and Coastal Path. Bedrooms are contemporary and uncluttered, with pictures by local artists on the walls. Each has a super-king-size bed (made with sheets and a Welsh wool blanket if you prefer) and views of garden, mountain, church or Norman castle. A family room sleeps three. Sit in the quiet rear garden with a book over afternoon tea, or clink glasses of Prosecco at sundown. Dinner is no longer served except for large groups or exclusive-use residents, but there are several good options within strolling distance; the excellent Llys Meddyg is just up the road (see next entry). Spread your toast with home-made marmalade and local jams at breakfast; hot dishes are cooked to order. (JL)

East Street
Newport
SA42 0SY

T: 01239 820575
F: 01239 820878
E: enquiry@cnapan.co.uk
W: www.cnapan.co.uk

BEDROOMS: 5. Plus self-catering cottage.
OPEN: Mar–mid-Dec.
FACILITIES: sitting room, bar, restaurant (for parties of 20 or more), free Wi-Fi, in-room TV, small garden, only restaurant suitable for disabled.
BACKGROUND MUSIC: none.
LOCATION: town centre.
CHILDREN: all ages welcomed.
DOGS: not allowed.
CREDIT CARDS: MasterCard, Visa.
PRICES: [2017] per room B&B £95, 1-night bookings sometimes refused at peak times.

NEWPORT Pembrokeshire

⚜LLYS MEDDYG

César award: Welsh restaurant-with-rooms of the year

Edward and Louise Sykes's 'personable, wholly likeable' restaurant-with-rooms occupies a Georgian house on the main street of an 'appealing village', minutes from the Pembrokeshire Coastal Path. 'There's an affable air to the place. One afternoon, Ed returned from foraging razor clams and sank into a chair by the fire in the lounge to chat. Lou, and Ed's mother, Cecilia, popped in, offering hot drinks. The house is infused with their personality – warm, open, genuinely interested in people.' In the 'pretty, rustic' restaurant and popular cellar bar, and in the 'congenial' garden dining room in the summer, Stuart Wills's 'sophisticated, well-assembled' modern dishes highlight Welsh produce from land and sea. Typical dishes: Solva crab, green apple, fennel; lamb, pearl barley, wild garlic, granola. Bedrooms are 'chic and unfussy'. 'Ours was compact but well organised. Sweet touches: a plate of biscuits; chocolate bars and fresh milk in the fridge.' Breakfast on 'fine fruit crêpes with thick yogurt'; eggs and home-smoked salmon. 'We would return anytime.' (A and LH, and others)

25% DISCOUNT VOUCHERS

East Street
Newport
SA42 0SY

T: 01239 820008
E: info@llysmeddyg.com
W: www.llysmeddyg.com

BEDROOMS: 8. 1 on ground floor, 3 in mews annexe, plus a cottage.
OPEN: all year.
FACILITIES: bar, lounge, restaurant, kitchen garden dining area (open in summer holidays), free Wi-Fi, in-room TV (Freeview), civil wedding licence, garden, unsuitable for disabled.
BACKGROUND MUSIC: in bar and dining room.
LOCATION: central.
CHILDREN: all ages welcomed.
DOGS: allowed in 3 annexe bedrooms, bar.
CREDIT CARDS: MasterCard, Visa.
PRICES: [2017] per room B&B £100–£120, D,B&B £200–£220. À la carte £33. 1-night bookings sometimes refused.

PENALLY Pembrokeshire

Map 3:E2

PENALLY ABBEY

Overlooking the Pembrokeshire coast, Melanie and Lucas Boissevain's chic hotel is 'clearly on the up', say Guide readers this year. 'It's a happy place, and well run, too, with willing staff. One of the owners carried our luggage when we arrived, and was pleased to chat whenever we met during our stay.' While away the hours in the book- and magazine-filled drawing room ('they readily lit a fire in the afternoon, when I asked'); on a balmy day, take tea on the 'lovely terrace' with 'attractive views towards the sea'. Bedrooms are individually styled; those in the coach house open directly on to the garden. 'Up steepish stairs, our spacious, high-ceilinged room, nicely renovated, had sash windows that opened easily for air. Our bed, rather high, was large and comfortable. The room was probably the quietest I've ever experienced in a hotel, resulting in a good night's sleep.' Chef Paul Barnes's 'excellently prepared' candlelit dinners are 'very good in every sense'. In the morning, breakfast ('conventional, but expertly cooked, with quality ingredients') brings home-baked bread, local butcher's sausages, eggs from free-range hens. (Peter and Kay Rogers, and others)

Penally
SA70 7PY

T: 01834 843033
F: 01834 844714
E: info@penally-abbey.com
W: www.penally-abbey.com

BEDROOMS: 11. 4 in coach house (100 yds), 2 on ground floor.
OPEN: all year except Jan.
FACILITIES: drawing room, snug bar, sun room, restaurant, The Courtyard private function room, free Wi-Fi, in-room TV (Freeview), civil wedding licence, in-room massages and beauty treatments, terrace, 1-acre lawns.
BACKGROUND MUSIC: in bar and restaurant.
LOCATION: 1½ miles SW of Tenby.
CHILDREN: all ages welcomed.
DOGS: allowed in bar, sun room, coach house bedrooms (not unattended), not in restaurant.
CREDIT CARDS: MasterCard, Visa.
PRICES: [2017] per room B&B from £140, D,B&B from £220. À la carte £40.

PENARTH Vale of Glamorgan

Map 3:E4

RESTAURANT JAMES SOMMERIN

NEW

A glamorous addition on the esplanade of this quiet seaside town, this contemporary restaurant-with-rooms remains, at its heart, a family affair: James Sommerin is the acclaimed head chef; his wife, Louise, holds court as front-of-house; his daughter, Georgia, dons her whites as chef de partie. The whole outfit, says a regular Guide correspondent in 2017, is 'excellent'. Clink cocktail glasses in the small bar before sitting down to keenly modern dishes on the à la carte and custom-created tasting menus. 'From lobster to guineafowl, the food, impeccably served, lives up to the Michelin star. Lovely puddings, too. A welcome touch: the chefs regularly leave the kitchen to present their dish to the customers.' Among the cheery bedrooms – each stocked with Welsh-made toiletries – choose one of the sea-facing five with floor-to-ceiling windows, all the better to take in the views. 'Our large room, with a comfy bed and a modern bathroom, overlooked the pier and the Severn estuary.' There's home-made granola, yogurt and strong coffee at breakfast; 'eggs any way you like'. 'We can't speak too highly of the place.' (Peter Anderson)

The Esplanade
Penarth
CF64 3AU

T: 02920 706559
E: info@jamessommerinrestaurant.co.uk
W: www.jamessommerinrestaurant.co.uk

BEDROOMS: 9. 1 suitable for disabled.
OPEN: all year except Mon.
FACILITIES: bar, restaurant, private dining room, free Wi-Fi, in-room smart TV.
BACKGROUND MUSIC: in bar and restaurant.
LOCATION: on the esplanade.
CHILDREN: all ages welcomed.
DOGS: not allowed.
CREDIT CARDS: MasterCard, Visa.
PRICES: [2017] per room B&B £150–£170, D,B&B (Sun, Tues–Thurs) £240–£260. Tasting menu £70–£90, à la carte (Sun, Tues–Thurs) £40.

PWLLHELI Gwynedd

Map 3:B2

THE OLD RECTORY

Guests praise the 'outstanding attention to detail' at Gary and Lindsay Ashcroft's B&B, in an 18th-century rectory at the end of a leafy drive. 'They've thought of everything when it comes to visitors' comfort, including special treats in the bedrooms.' The 'charming, welcoming' hosts greet visitors with offers of tea in the sitting room, where, in cold weather, a log fire burns in front of deep leather sofas. Up the stairs, homely garden-view bedrooms come equipped with sherry and chocolates; massages and beauty treatments can also be arranged. An evening meal is not served, 'but the Ashcrofts sent us an extensive list of restaurants before we arrived'. In the morning, a communal breakfast is taken in the dining room overlooking the garden. Cereals and fresh fruits are 'in abundance'; generous portions of cooked dishes use local meat, and eggs from free-range hens. 'Friendly and helpful', the Ashcrofts are pleased to advise on local towns to visit, and the wealth of activities nearby: golf, boat trips, heritage railway rides and more. Ask, too, for a packed lunch – ye shall receive. (AR, and others)

25% DISCOUNT VOUCHERS

Boduan
Pwllheli
LL53 6DT

T: 01758 721519
E: theashcrofts@theoldrectory.net
W: www.theoldrectory.net

BEDROOMS: 4. Plus a self-catering cottage and lodge.
OPEN: all year except Christmas.
FACILITIES: drawing room, dining room, free Wi-Fi, in-room TV (Freeview), 3-acre grounds, beach hut in season, unsuitable for disabled.
BACKGROUND MUSIC: none.
LOCATION: 4 miles NW of Pwllheli.
CHILDREN: all ages welcomed.
DOGS: only assistance dogs allowed in house (kennel and run available).
CREDIT CARDS: MasterCard, Visa.
PRICES: [2017] per room B&B £75–£115. 1-night bookings refused some weekends, high season and bank holidays.

PWLLHELI Gwynedd

Map 3:B2

PLAS BODEGROES

'There's much to enjoy here: good food, a relaxed atmosphere and well-maintained gardens in an area of outstanding natural beauty.' Chris and Gunna Chown's restaurant-with-rooms, in a Georgian country house on the remote Lleyn peninsula, enchants visitors old and new. 'On our third stay, it was just as good as ever,' said Guide readers this year. New fans report: 'Some 30 years after they first opened, we were pleasantly surprised that the standards were still high.' Each of the 'lovely, cleverly lit' bedrooms has a garden view. 'A short, covered walk from the breakfast room, our large, well-furnished courtyard room had two armchairs and a super-king-size bed. In the autumn, fat rosehips wound round the cast iron pillars of the courtyard: stunning.' After a hiatus, chef Hugh Bracegirdle is back in the kitchen, cooking 'original, delicious' meals using garden-grown produce. 'We especially liked our well-presented starters, with their unusual ingredients – pickled mushrooms, a scattering of onion seeds.' In the morning, 'friendly breakfast ladies' ply guests with 'nicely cooked hot dishes', leaf teas, home-made jams and 'as much toast as you can eat'. (Mary Coles, GC)

Nefyn Road
Efailnewydd
Pwllheli
LL53 5TH

T: 01758 612363
F: 01758 701247
E: info@bodegroes.co.uk
W: www.bodegroes.co.uk

BEDROOMS: 10. 2 in courtyard cottage.
OPEN: all year except 3 Jan–6 Feb. Restaurant closed Sun and Mon nights.
FACILITIES: lounge, bar, breakfast room, restaurant, free Wi-Fi, in-room TV (Freeview), 5-acre grounds (courtyard garden), unsuitable for disabled.
BACKGROUND MUSIC: none.
LOCATION: 1 mile W of Pwllheli.
CHILDREN: all ages welcomed.
DOGS: allowed in some bedrooms, not in public rooms.
CREDIT CARDS: MasterCard, Visa.
PRICES: [2017] per room B&B £110–£150, D,B&B £180–£220. Set dinner £45. 1-night bookings sometimes refused bank holidays.

SAUNDERSFOOT Pembrokeshire

Map 3:D2

ST BRIDES SPA HOTEL   **NEW**

'The sea views, over Saundersfoot Bay, are exceptional' at this family-friendly hotel, perched above a village in the Pembrokeshire Coast national park. 'This old hotel has been rebuilt with the ambition, vision and impressive style one might more readily associate with California or Australia,' say trusted Guide correspondents this year. Lindsey and Andrew Evans are the owners; 'plenty of efficient staff' add to the 'low-key ambience'. 'They were very welcoming to our children and grandchildren, who were staying nearby.' Among 'Good', 'Better' and 'Best' bedrooms, choose one with a balcony to take in the coastal panorama. 'Our sea-view room, one of the smaller ones available, was stylish and very pleasant (but we'd go for a larger room next time). Dressing gowns and slippers were provided; there was fresh milk in the fridge.' Dine well in the newly refurbished restaurant, perhaps on 'wonderful scallops' accompanied by a 'particularly good' wine list; next day, feed the soul with dramatic landscapes from the Coastal Path passing by the front door. (Pauline and Stephen Glover, A and AG)

St Brides Hill
Saundersfoot
SA69 9NH

T: 01834 812304
E: reservations@stbridesspahotel.com
W: www.stbridesspahotel.com

BEDROOMS: 34. 1 suitable for disabled. Plus six 2-bed apartments in grounds, and self-catering apartments in village.
OPEN: all year.
FACILITIES: lift, lounge, bar, restaurant, Gallery dining area, meeting/function rooms, free Wi-Fi, in-room TV (Sky, Freeview), civil wedding licence, terraces, art gallery, spa (treatment room, infinity hydro pool).
BACKGROUND MUSIC: all day in public spaces.
LOCATION: hillside, 3 mins' walk to village.
CHILDREN: all ages welcomed.
DOGS: allowed in some apartments.
CREDIT CARDS: Amex, MasterCard, Visa.
PRICES: [2017] per room B&B £170–£310, D,B&B from £200 (at limited times of the year). À la carte £35.

SKENFRITH Monmouthshire

Map 3:D4

THE BELL AT SKENFRITH

'A congenial atmosphere and a happy buzz' greeted Guide inspectors arriving at Richard Ireton and Sarah Hudson's refurbished 17th-century coaching inn, in a 'postcard-worthy rural setting' by the stone bridge over the River Monnow. Walkers and their dogs receive a 'friendly welcome' (and a dog biscuit or two) in the 'cosy nook of a bar'. In the 'smart, rustic restaurant' (flagstones, 'hefty tables', countryside pictures and prints), chef Joseph Colman's 'refined pub grub' is 'very good and very satisfying'. Typical dishes: 'light, refreshing' Cornish crab tian; a 'generous portion' of roast rack of pork, ham hock croquette, buttery mash, sautéed cabbage. 'Handsome contemporary bedrooms' are upstairs. 'Ours was under the eaves. Small bedside windows looked into the trees; a larger window offered a brilliant view of the bridge over the quick-running river. Guides and good local information had been provided; a container of shortbread biscuits sat next to a good selection of teas, coffee and hot chocolate mix.' Breakfast on fruit salad, local yogurt, 'exemplary croissants', 'thick country slices of delicious home-baked bread'; 'copious servings' of hot dishes are brought to the table.

25% DISCOUNT VOUCHERS

Skenfrith
NP7 8UH

T: 01600 750235
F: 01600 750525
E: enquiries@skenfrith.co.uk
W: thebellatskenfrith.co.uk

BEDROOMS: 11.
OPEN: all year.
FACILITIES: sitting room, bar, restaurant, function facilities, free Wi-Fi, in-room TV (BT, Freeview), 2-acre grounds (terrace, garden), unsuitable for disabled.
BACKGROUND MUSIC: 'intermittently' in bar and restaurant.
LOCATION: 9 miles W of Ross-on-Wye.
CHILDREN: all ages welcomed, no under-8s in restaurant after 7 pm.
DOGS: 'well-behaved dogs' allowed in bedrooms and bar.
CREDIT CARDS: MasterCard, Visa.
PRICES: [2017] per room B&B from £150, D,B&B from £190. À la carte £28.

TYWYN Gwynedd

DOLFFANOG FAWR

In the Tal-y-llyn valley, with Cadair Idris for a backdrop, Alex Yorke and Lorraine Hinkins are the 'dedicated hosts' at this 18th-century farmhouse-turned-'exceptional guest house'. Bedrooms are made inviting with a Welsh wool blanket and local artwork; tea- and coffee-making facilities and good toiletries are supplied. Each room has a window framing a countryside vista, but book one of the three with a window seat to better take in the views of lake, mountain and hills. In the lounge, borrow a volume from the crammed shelves of the glass-fronted bookcase, then settle into a sofa by the log-burning stove. Another day, step into the garden and scan the skies for red kites. Dinner, cooked by the hostess four nights a week, is 'simple but seriously good' – perhaps twice-baked Welsh cheese soufflé; rack of salt marsh lamb ('the best we've eaten anywhere in Britain or Ireland'). An 'extremely generous' breakfast is just what's needed before exploring southern Snowdonia: a historic steam railway leaves Tywyn Wharf for a waterfall trail in Nant Gwernol; the fantastic Precipice Walk around the peak of Moel Cynwch is within reach. More reports, please.

Tal-y-llyn
Tywyn
LL36 9AJ

T: 01654 761247
E: info@dolffanogfawr.co.uk
W: www.dolffanogfawr.co.uk

BEDROOMS: 4.
OPEN: Mar–Oct, dinner served Wed–Sat.
FACILITIES: lounge, dining room, free Wi-Fi, in-room TV (Freeview), 1-acre garden (hot tub), unsuitable for disabled.
BACKGROUND MUSIC: none.
LOCATION: by lake 10 miles E of Tywyn.
CHILDREN: not under 10.
DOGS: allowed in bedrooms, and lounge 'if other guests don't mind'.
CREDIT CARDS: MasterCard, Visa.
PRICES: [2017] per room B&B £100–£120, D,B&B £156–£176. À la carte £28. 1-night bookings sometimes refused.

WHITEBROOK Monmouthshire

Map 3:D4

THE WHITEBROOK

Amid stone walls and wooded lanes deep in the Wye valley, Chris and Kirsty Harrod's Michelin-starred restaurant-with-rooms is liked for its 'relaxing atmosphere', 'excellent, professional staff' and 'unpretentious, really super food'. 'The unspoilt woods and countryside are an ideal position for chef/patron Chris to pursue his love of foraging for wild and unusual ingredients' – and the results, including a sophisticated vegetarian menu, 'surprise and delight'. Unusual herb combinations and garden flowers share culinary glory with locally grown produce in 'fresh, modern, attractive' dishes, perhaps roast Jerusalem artichokes, goat's curd, forest findings, rosemary; organic Rhug Estate venison, smoked beets, celeriac. 'Restful, well-decorated' bedrooms, some recently refurbished, are the cherry on top. Choose well – a first-floor room was found to be 'a good size', while one on the second floor was called 'small, but comfortable'. All, however, have a 'comfy bed', 'good toiletries' and 'plenty of towels'. Breakfast brings 'very freshly squeezed' orange juice; an 'interesting list' of cooked dishes. 'Absolutely spot-on.' (P and JT, T and GA)

Whitebrook
NP25 4TX

T: 01600 860254
E: info@thewhitebrook.co.uk
W: www.thewhitebrook.co.uk

BEDROOMS: 8.
OPEN: all year except 24–26 Dec, restaurant closed Mon.
FACILITIES: lounge/bar, restaurant, business facilities, free Wi-Fi, in-room TV (Freeview), terrace, 3-acre garden, River Wye 2 miles (fishing), only restaurant suitable for disabled.
BACKGROUND MUSIC: 'chill-out music' in restaurant and lounge.
LOCATION: 6 miles S of Monmouth.
CHILDREN: not under 12.
DOGS: only guide dogs allowed.
CREDIT CARDS: Amex, MasterCard, Visa.
PRICES: [2017] per room D,B&B £223–£363. Tasting menu £74, set dinner £59.

CHANNEL ISLANDS

La Coupée isthmus, Sark

HERM

Map 1: inset D6

THE WHITE HOUSE

'We love it,' write regular Guide readers this year, after their fifth holiday at the best, and only, hotel on this tiny, car-free island. Alight at the harbour and stroll to the former country house surrounded by palm trees, while a tractor brings your baggage – 'it's all part of the enjoyment'. Bedrooms have no TV, no telephone, not even a clock ('good Wi-Fi, though'), but many rooms, including well-thought-out family accommodation, have a balcony and 'wonderful' sea views. Take tea by the pool, play croquet on the lawn, head to 'stunning' beaches, or 'just enjoy sitting in the garden'; a coastal path winds round the island. Take your pick of eating places: casual meals in the Mermaid Tavern and refurbished Ship Inn brasserie; sunset dinners in the Conservatory restaurant. 'The food this year was probably the best we've had here – the sea trout was particularly enjoyable.' Island life appeals to the youngest visitors. 'It's a great place for kids, with bunk beds, a children's high tea, and the freedom to visit the village shop on their own.' (Jane Thornton, ML)

Herm
GY1 3HR

T: 01481 750075
F: 01481 710066
E: hotel@herm.com
W: www.herm.com

BEDROOMS: 40. 18 in cottages, some on ground floor.
OPEN: late Mar–early Oct.
FACILITIES: 3 lounges, 2 bars, 2 restaurants, conference room, free Wi-Fi, 1-acre garden (tennis, croquet, 7-metre solar-heated swimming pool) 'plus the entirety of Herm', beach 200 yds, Herm unsuitable for disabled.
BACKGROUND MUSIC: none.
LOCATION: by harbour, air/sea to Guernsey, then ferry from Guernsey (20 mins).
CHILDREN: all ages welcomed.
DOGS: allowed in 2 bedrooms (£20 per dog per night), reception lounge, garden bar.
CREDIT CARDS: MasterCard, Visa.
PRICES: [2017] per person B&B from £85, D,B&B from £107. Set dinner £34. 1-night bookings refused Sat.

ST BRELADE Jersey

Map 1: inset E6

THE ATLANTIC HOTEL

'Nothing has changed. All is great,' say guests on a return visit to Patrick Burke's luxury hotel, whose well-tended grounds overlook St Ouen's Bay. In truth, a great deal has been modified since the owner's father, Henry, opened the hotel in 1970; an annual programme of refurbishment keeps things shipshape. 'We've not seen such a well-maintained hotel anywhere else.' Unpack in one of the 'well-appointed', contemporary bedrooms (each has fancy toiletries in a marble bathroom), then take in the views: upper-floor rooms have full-height windows and a balcony overlooking the ocean or adjoining golf course; ground-floor rooms have a private terrace with direct access to the hotel gardens. Pack the day with tennis, swimming, coastal walks, visits to the spa; in the evening, find out why Mark Jordan, the chef, has a Michelin star for his 'lovely food'. In the Ocean restaurant, there are 'lots of local dishes' on the menu, perhaps grilled Jersey sole, brown shrimp and caper butter, spring onion purée. Guests hungering for simpler, bistro-style fare might take a 15-minute drive to sister restaurant, Mark Jordan at the Beach. (P and AD)

Le Mont de la Pulente
St Brelade
JE3 8HE

T: 01534 744101
E: patrick@theatlantichotel.com
W: www.theatlantichotel.com

BEDROOMS: 50. Some on ground floor.
OPEN: 3 Feb–2 Jan.
FACILITIES: lift, lounge, library, cocktail bar, restaurant, private dining room, fitness centre (swimming pool, sauna, mini-gym), free Wi-Fi, in-room TV (Sky), civil wedding licence, 6-acre garden (tennis, indoor and outdoor heated swimming pools, 10 by 5 metres), unsuitable for disabled.
BACKGROUND MUSIC: in restaurant, lounge and cocktail bar in evenings.
LOCATION: 5 miles W of St Helier.
CHILDREN: all ages welcomed.
DOGS: not allowed.
CREDIT CARDS: all major cards.
PRICES: [2017] per room B&B £150–£310, D,B&B £250–£410. Set dinner £55, tasting menu £85, à la carte £65.

SEE ALSO SHORTLIST

ST PETER Jersey

Map 1: inset E6

GREENHILLS

Approach this 'elegant, attractive hotel' by way of country roads – flanked by flower-filled planters, mature shrubs and trees, it's in a 'lovely, quiet location'. It is owned by the local Seymour family; long-serving resident managers Carmelita Fernandes and Joe Godinho are 'much in evidence'. The oldest part of the building dates from 1674, but much has been brought up to date: the newly refurbished bedrooms are 'first class'. Decorated in country house style with a mix of contemporary and traditional furnishings and 'high-quality fittings', they look on to the lawn or have direct garden access. All rooms are supplied with tea, coffee and home-made biscuits; bathrobes and smart toiletries. At lunch and dinner, the restaurant's tables are laid with white linens for chef Lukasz Pietrasz's seasonal menus, which draw on the wealth of local produce (the start of Jersey Royal potato season is something to celebrate). A typical dish: lemon sole, seafood ragout, pancetta, caper berries. At other times, take afternoon tea or snack on light bites in the lounge or bar; when the sun shines, as it often does on this southerly island, go alfresco on the pool terrace. 'Faultless.' (A and HM)

Mont de L'École
St Peter
JE3 7EL

T: 01534 481042
E: reservations@greenhillshotel.com
W: www.greenhillshotel.com

BEDROOMS: 31. 10, on ground floor, suitable for disabled.
OPEN: all year except last Sun before Christmas–mid-Feb.
FACILITIES: 2 lounges, bar, restaurant, garden, terrace (alfresco meals), free Wi-Fi, in-room TV (Sky, Freeview), outdoor heated swimming pool, complimentary access to leisure club at sister hotel, The Merton.
BACKGROUND MUSIC: in public areas.
LOCATION: 8 miles NW of St Helier.
CHILDREN: all ages welcomed.
DOGS: allowed in some bedrooms.
CREDIT CARDS: Diners, MasterCard, Visa.
PRICES: [2017] per room B&B from £150. À la carte £42.

ST PETER PORT Guernsey

Map 1: inset E5

LA FRÉGATE

'The views are fantastic' from this clifftop 18th-century manor house overlooking town, harbour and the smattering of neighbouring islands. Overnight stays are 'enjoyable and memorable', too, say guests in 2017. Smartly designed sea-view bedrooms are divided between the main house and a modern extension. 'Our spacious room had a comfortable, supportive bed, and great views from large windows. At turn-down, the cups on the tea tray were washed, and the supply of biscuits was topped up. Delayed flights resulted in our extending our stay; helpful staff gave us another bay-view room that was just as good.' The terrace is ideal for lunch on fine days; at dinner, chef Neil Maginnis's menus use much freshly caught fish and seafood. 'We worked our way through the set, à la carte and vegetarian menus. Interesting breads accompanied; there was plenty of variety. Especially delicious: the baked goat's cheese crottin with caramelised pecans.' At breakfast, fresh fruit (but 'boring cereal') accompanies 'a large range' of cooked dishes. 'Well worth the trek from town – but take a taxi!' (JR, Jill and Mike Bennett)

Beauregard Lane
Les Cotils
St Peter Port
GY1 1UT

T: 01481 724624
F: 01481 720443
E: enquiries@lafregatehotel.com
W: www.lafregatehotel.com

BEDROOMS: 22.
OPEN: all year.
FACILITIES: lounge/bar, restaurant, private dining/function rooms, free Wi-Fi, in-room TV (Freeview), patio (alfresco dining), ½-acre terraced garden, unsuitable for disabled.
BACKGROUND MUSIC: in bar.
LOCATION: hilltop, 5 mins' walk from centre.
CHILDREN: all ages welcomed.
DOGS: not allowed.
CREDIT CARDS: Amex, MasterCard, Visa.
PRICES: [2017] per room B&B single £99.50, double £199.50–£230. Set dinner £37.50, à la carte £50.

SEE ALSO SHORTLIST

ST SAVIOUR Jersey

Map 1: inset E6

LONGUEVILLE MANOR

There are 'plenty of smiles' at the Lewis family's centuries-old manor house standing in extensive grounds – and not just from the 'professional, attentive' staff. 'The whole place is spectacular and sumptuous, but with a personal touch.' The luxury hotel and spa is in the hands of third-generation owners Malcolm and Patricia Lewis; the fourth generation is already hard at work – son David is the kitchen gardener. Sunny daytimes are spent on woodland walks, tennis and croquet on manicured lawns, a dip in the outdoor swimming pool; in cooler weather, head for the mini-spa and log fire-warmed lounges. Even the youngest guests are well taken care of, with plentiful school-holiday activities and a 'little needs' service for babies. From small to spacious, each of the elegant bedrooms is supplied with thoughtful surprises: Scrabble for a lazy afternoon; lavender sleep spray in the evening. In the Garden Room and oak-panelled restaurant, chef Andrew Baird uses produce from the Victorian kitchen garden in his modern menus. A characteristic dish: monkfish and langoustine ragout, vegetable spaghetti, Asian broth. 'Imaginative, and very tasty.'
(YP, and others)

Longueville Road
St Saviour
JE2 7WF

T: 01534 725501
F: 01534 731613
E: info@longuevillemanor.com
W: www.longuevillemanor.com

BEDROOMS: 30. 8 on ground floor, 2 in cottage.
OPEN: all year except 3–31 Jan.
FACILITIES: lift, 2 lounges, cocktail bar, 2 dining rooms, free Wi-Fi, in-room TV (Sky), function/conference/wedding facilities, spa (treatments, mini-gym, spa pool, terrace), 18-acre grounds (croquet, tennis, outdoor heated swimming pool, woodland), unsuitable for disabled.
BACKGROUND MUSIC: in bar and restaurant.
LOCATION: 1½ miles E of St Helier.
CHILDREN: all ages welcomed.
DOGS: allowed, not in public rooms.
CREDIT CARDS: all major cards.
PRICES: per room B&B from £195, D,B&B from £285. Set dinner £45, 'discovery' menu £80, à la carte £60. 1-night bookings sometimes refused.

SARK

LA SABLONNERIE

'The distilled essence of Sark – relaxed, laid-back and tranquil – this remains a most charming place.' Guide readers this year gave in willingly to the allure of this whitewashed 16th-century farmhouse, approached via horse-drawn carriage on the rugged, car-free island. Elizabeth Perrée, the owner, is the soul of the place. Perrée père and mère opened their small guest house in 1948 with just three rooms; today, guests find rustic accommodation in the rose-swagged main building and a collection of nearby cottages. 'For those who are unconcerned about the absence of TV, radio and Wi-Fi', it is, in a word, 'paradise'. Take a dip in the rock pools of Venus and Adonis, sunbathe or snorkel; alternatively, like some Guide correspondents, simply 'sit and read, and enjoy wonderful sea views'. 'We took a boat ride around the island on a calm day, and the boatman kindly took my wife up and down the harbour hill in the bucket of his tractor. Such larks!' Return with an appetite for Colin Day's 'superb cooking' – perhaps lobster thermidor or spring lamb and vegetables from the family farm. On warm nights, eat outdoors; on chillier days, gather by the fire in the beamed lounge. (Robert Cooper, JB)

Little Sark
Sark, via Guernsey
GY10 1SD

T: 01481 832061
F: 01481 832408
E: reservations@sablonneriesark.com
W: www.sablonneriesark.com

BEDROOMS: 22. Some in nearby cottages.
OPEN: mid-Apr–Oct.
FACILITIES: 3 lounges, 2 bars, restaurant, Wi-Fi by arrangement, wedding facilities, 1-acre garden (tea garden/bar, croquet), Sark unsuitable for disabled.
BACKGROUND MUSIC: classical/piano in bar.
LOCATION: Little Sark, via boat from Guernsey (guests will be met at the harbour on arrival).
CHILDREN: all ages welcomed.
DOGS: allowed at hotel's discretion, but not in public rooms.
CREDIT CARDS: MasterCard, Visa.
PRICES: per person B&B £50–£115.50, D,B&B £100–£195. Set menus £29.50. À la carte £49.50.

IRELAND

Doonagore Castle, nr Doolin, Co. Clare

BAGENALSTOWN Co. Carlow
Map 6:C6

LORUM OLD RECTORY

🏵 Previous César winner

Built of granite cut from the surrounding Blackstairs mountains, Bobbie Smith's 19th-century rectory is 'cosy, comfortable and spotless', report contented Guide readers this year. 'It is a beautiful house, but what really makes the difference is how welcoming Bobbie is.' A turf fire burns in the lounge; tea and home-made biscuits await guests in ample bedrooms. With views on to Mount Leinster or the Kilkenny countryside, each room has antique furniture, perhaps even a stove or fireplace. Meals are a communal affair. Taken at the long mahogany table (all the better to showcase the 'beautiful silver collection' and local pottery), the dinner experience is 'like eating in your own intimate restaurant'. The hostess, a Euro-Toques chef, uses local, organic produce where possible; like the fresh flowers throughout the house, some ingredients come straight from the garden. 'Dinner was so delicious that we ended up eating in both nights we stayed.' Breakfast is 'a four-course meal' with home-made bread and jams. Tuck in, then head out on a stroll or cycle along the Barrow Canal towpath. (Anne McEneaney, SR)

Kilgreaney
Bagenalstown

T: 00 353 59 977 5282
E: bobbie@lorum.com
W: www.lorum.com

BEDROOMS: 4.
OPEN: Feb–Nov.
FACILITIES: drawing room, study, dining room, snug, free Wi-Fi, 1-acre garden (croquet) in 18-acre grounds, unsuitable for disabled.
BACKGROUND MUSIC: none.
LOCATION: 4 miles S of Bagenalstown on R705 to Borris.
CHILDREN: by arrangement.
DOGS: by arrangement, not in public rooms.
CREDIT CARDS: MasterCard, Visa.
PRICES: per room B&B €160, D,B&B €260.

BALLINGARRY Co. Limerick

Map 6:D5

THE MUSTARD SEED AT ECHO LODGE

'The Mustard Seed, with its great tradition of Irish hospitality, is in safe hands,' says a Guide reader this year of a return visit to John Edward Joyce's 'lovely, charming' restaurant-with-rooms. 'Under new ownership, it remains an oasis of peace and calm, where it always seems to be summer.' The 'delightful gardens' are 'full of colour' in season; all year round, 'the spacious public rooms exude tranquillity'. Some of the individually decorated bedrooms have views of the vine-hung courtyard garden, others of the orchard and the countryside beyond. 'Little touches make each visit special: coffee and buttery home-made biscuits as a lovely greeting; a vase of roses in our sitting room; handmade soaps and gorgeous Irish toiletries in the bathroom.' In the evening, chef Angel Pirev's 'well-presented' four-course dinners use plenty of local produce in season. Typical dishes: poached egg, artichoke and broccoli purée, oyster mushrooms; Ballinwillin suckling pig, white pudding gnocchi, hedgehog mushrooms. Try the smoked salmon at breakfast – 'it's delicious' – then explore the pretty village and its rural surrounds. (Helena Shaw)

Ballingarry

T: 00 353 69 68508
F: 00 353 69 68511
E: mustard@indigo.ie
W: www.mustardseed.ie

BEDROOMS: 16. 1, on ground floor, suitable for disabled.
OPEN: all year except 24–26 Dec.
FACILITIES: 3 public rooms, library, entrance hall, sun room, free Wi-Fi (in public areas, some bedrooms), in-room TV (Freeview), wedding facilities, 12-acre grounds.
BACKGROUND MUSIC: piano on occasion in restaurant.
LOCATION: in village, 18 miles SW of Limerick.
CHILDREN: all ages welcomed.
DOGS: allowed in 1 bedroom, not in public rooms.
CREDIT CARDS: Amex, MasterCard, Visa.
PRICES: [2017] per person B&B from €90, D,B&B from €129. Set menus €47–€60.

BALLYCASTLE Co. Mayo

Map 6:B4

STELLA MARIS

'It is dramatically beautiful here, and totally tranquil.' On the Wild Atlantic Way, this 19th-century former coastguard headquarters and sometime convent is a place of escape and relaxation. 'It's a very cosy place to holiday alone, if that's what you prefer. While everyone is on a first-name basis, there's no pressure to be convivial.' Owner Frances Kelly-McSweeney presides, assisted by young local staff. On the seaward side of the building runs a long conservatory, ideal for coffee, aperitifs, 'or just sitting' – flip through one of the many books lying around, borrow binoculars to watch for dolphins, take in the changing light over Bunatrahir Bay. Most of the 'very comfortable' bedrooms (traditional, with a restrained elegance) have a sea view. At dinner, the hostess's 'small, daily-changing menu' is served in one of a series of dining rooms. Typical dishes: grilled prawns; curried parsnip soup; smoked chicken, tagliatelle, garlic cream. 'Everything is local and freshly prepared – ditto for breakfast.' The surrounds are remote, with walking trails tracing the cliffs; windswept Downpatrick Head is along the coast. At low tide, join the locals looking for mussels on Ballycastle beach. (RP)

Ballycastle

T: 00 353 96 43322
F: 00 353 96 43965
E: info@stellamarisireland.com
W: www.stellamarisireland.com

BEDROOMS: 11. 1, on ground floor, suitable for disabled.
OPEN: late Apr–early Oct.
FACILITIES: lounge, bar, restaurant, conservatory, free Wi-Fi ('most dependable in public areas'), in-room TV (Freeview), wedding facilities, 2-acre grounds.
BACKGROUND MUSIC: none.
LOCATION: 1½ miles W of Ballycastle.
CHILDREN: not under 5.
DOGS: not allowed.
CREDIT CARDS: MasterCard, Visa.
PRICES: [2017] per room B&B €150–€190. À la carte €35.

BALLYMOTE Co. Sligo

Map 6:B5

TEMPLE HOUSE

History hangs about Roderick and Helena Perceval's Georgian mansion, approached via a drive through sheep-grazed parkland. History, yes – there have been Percevals on this land since 1665 – but, on a given day, there may be the scent of freshly baked honey almond biscuits as well. On a sweeping estate including ancient woods and a lakeside Knights Templar castle, the ancestral home has antiques, gilt-framed portraits, 'plenty of country and nature scenes', 'a lived-in feel'. B&B accommodation is in large, high-ceilinged bedrooms decorated in period style (some were refurbished this year). Gather with fellow guests in the 'cosy' drawing room, its French windows overlooking the croquet lawn and terraced gardens; on chilly days, a log fire blazes here. In the evening, a set menu of 'quality country house cuisine', served communally, might include lamb from the estate and 'generous portions' of home-grown vegetables. Sleep well – 'heavy curtains on the bedroom windows mean it's completely dark if that's how you like it' – then wake to home-made muesli, local sausages, 'delicious fruit compotes' made with fruit from the walled garden.

Ballinacarrow
Ballymote
F56 NN50

T: 00 353 87 997 6045
E: stay@templehouse.ie
W: www.templehouse.ie

BEDROOMS: 6.
OPEN: Apr–mid-Nov.
FACILITIES: drawing room, dining room, table tennis room, free Wi-Fi, wedding facilities, 1½-acre garden on 1,000-acre estate, water sports on site, unsuitable for disabled.
BACKGROUND MUSIC: none.
LOCATION: 12 miles S of Sligo.
CHILDREN: all ages welcomed.
DOGS: not allowed.
CREDIT CARDS: all major credit cards.
PRICES: per room B&B €150–€210. Set dinner €49.

BALLYVAUGHAN Co. Clare

GREGANS CASTLE HOTEL

In the otherworldly limestone landscape of the Burren, with distant views across valley and mountain to Galway Bay, husband-and-wife team Simon Haden and Frederieke McMurray run their 18th-century manor house as an 'absolutely top-rate hotel'. The staff are 'unfailingly friendly and helpful', and the atmosphere is 'soothing', but most outstanding, says a Guide reader this year, is 'the sheer ambition of the cooking'. Tables are 'beautifully set' in the dining room for chef David Hurley's 'creative modern dishes'. 'The amuse-bouche were exquisite – tiny savoury meringues, and smoked potato-filled Parmesan crisps. From foie gras with apricots to cod with lobster mousse and artichoke, the intensity of flavours and visual impact were stunning.' After dinner, retire to one of the 'voguish bedrooms', each individually decorated in contemporary country house style with antiques and modern artwork. Books, bathrobes and chic toiletries are supplied; tea and coffee can be provided, on request. At breakfast, choose among home-made jams, breads and pastries; egg dishes, pancakes with apple syrup, or a grilled fresh fish of the day are brought to the table. (Richard Parish)

Gragan East
Ballyvaughan
H91 CF60

T: 00 353 65 707 7005
E: stay@gregans.ie
W: www.gregans.ie

BEDROOMS: 21. 7 on ground floor, 1 suitable for disabled.
OPEN: Feb–Nov, restaurant closed Wed, Sun (except bank holiday weekends).
FACILITIES: drawing room, bar, dining room, free Wi-Fi, 15-acre grounds (ornamental pool, croquet), wedding facilities, safe sandy beach 4½ miles, golf, riding, hill walking nearby.
BACKGROUND MUSIC: all day in bar, during meals in dining room.
LOCATION: 3½ miles SW of Ballyvaughan.
CHILDREN: all ages welcomed, no under-7s in dining room at night.
DOGS: allowed in bedrooms with garden access, not in public rooms.
CREDIT CARDS: all major cards.
PRICES: [2017] per room B&B from €235, D,B&B from €345. Set menu €72. 1-night bookings sometimes refused.

BANGOR Co. Down

Map 6:B6

CAIRN BAY LODGE

'Chris and Jenny Mullen's commitment to guests' comfort and enjoyment is hard to match' at this personable, family-friendly B&B on the Mourne Coastal Route. Facing Ballyholme Bay, the Edwardian villa is 'beautifully appointed' with an eclectic mix of knick-knacks, vintage furnishings and flea market finds that give the place a 'comfy, cosy' feel. From a snug single room to a spacious sea-view double to a two-bedroom, two-bathroom family suite, bedrooms are 'bright' and individually styled: find a collection of antique mirrors in one, an old trunk serving as a tea hamper in another. Every room is supplied with treats: crisps, chocolate, organic Irish seaweed toiletries. Nab a table on the terrace at the Starfish café to make the most of the vista, as the locals do; brunch (potato cakes, bacon, home-made plum chutney; local crab and eggs on wheaten bread; a traditional Ulster fry) is popular. The house is well placed for coastal walks or bicycle rides, or for a stroll to the busy marina and the town; Belfast is a train ride away. Still, there's no shame in staying in – the beauty salon has organic and holistic treatments for face and body. More reports, please.

278 Seacliff Road
Ballyholme
Bangor
BT20 5HS

T: 028 9146 7636
F: 028 9145 7728
E: info@cairnbaylodge.com
W: www.cairnbaylodge.com

BEDROOMS: 8.
OPEN: all year, café closed Sun, Mon.
FACILITIES: lounge, breakfast room, café, free Wi-Fi, in-room TV (Freeview), beauty salon, ¼-acre garden, unsuitable for disabled.
BACKGROUND MUSIC: 9 am–4 pm in café.
LOCATION: ¼ mile E of town centre.
CHILDREN: all ages welcomed.
DOGS: not allowed.
CREDIT CARDS: Amex, MasterCard, Visa.
PRICES: [2017] per person B&B £40–£50. 1-night bookings refused weekends June–Sept.

CASTLEHILL Co. Mayo

Map 6:B4

ENNISCOE HOUSE

From the Georgian steps of pale-pink Enniscoe House, take in the 'enchanting view of Lough Conn shimmering through a break in the woods'. Susan Kellett and her son, DJ, are the 'genuinely kind, accommodating' hosts at this 230-year-old family house filled with curios, antiques, paintings, period furnishings and 'an otherworldly air of genteel shabbiness'. Up a grand elliptical staircase (peer at the 'wonderful skylight' on your way), bedrooms are as different as can be. 'Ours, high-ceilinged and full of natural light, had two great windows with splendid views to Mount Nephin in the distance. We slept well in the fabulously comfortable beds.' At dinner, the hostess's traditional cooking is 'a delight', with vegetables foraged or home-grown, and much else from local farms and fisheries. (Special diets are imaginatively catered for.) In the morning, a 'marvellous' breakfast might include 'the best mushrooms I've ever eaten'. Step out to explore the restored Victorian garden and woodland path (extended in 2017); return to tea, in the 'decidedly aristocratic' sitting room, with home-made soda bread and jam before a blazing fire.

25% DISCOUNT VOUCHERS

Castlehill
F26 EA34

T: 00 353 96 31112
F: 00 353 96 31773
E: mail@enniscoe.com
W: www.enniscoe.com

BEDROOMS: 6. Plus self-catering units behind house.
OPEN: Apr–end Oct, New Year.
FACILITIES: 2 sitting rooms, dining room, free Wi-Fi (in public rooms, some bedrooms), wedding facilities, 160-acre estate (3-acre garden, tea room, farm, heritage centre, conference centre, forge, fishing, woodland walks), unsuitable for disabled.
BACKGROUND MUSIC: occasionally.
LOCATION: 2 miles S of Crossmolina, 12 miles SW of Ballina.
CHILDREN: all ages welcomed.
DOGS: allowed in bedrooms, not in public rooms.
CREDIT CARDS: MasterCard, Visa.
PRICES: per person B&B €85–€125, D,B&B €130–€170. Set menus €45–€50.

CASTLELYONS Co. Cork

Map 6:D5

BALLYVOLANE HOUSE

♨ Previous César winner

Approached up a long drive, this 'beautifully maintained' 18th-century country house stands in extensive grounds – 'a delight to the eye'. The Georgian dwelling, thick with legend, has been home to the Green family since 1953; today, Justin and Jenny Green run it as a family-friendly spot with a house-party atmosphere. 'We were greeted with great charm,' Guide inspectors say. The public rooms are 'magnificent', stuffed with antiques, art and the marks of 'warm domesticity'. Individually styled bedrooms are supplied with home-made fruit cordial, freshly baked cookies and an espresso machine. 'Our spacious room had a marble fireplace with an eclectic selection of (mostly Irish) books.' There's no television in the room, but plenty to see and do outdoors: a walled garden and bluebell woods to explore; tractor rides for the children; a visit to the distillery in a converted cattle shed. (The house gin, Bertha's Revenge, is 'wonderfully fragrant'.) The traditional Irish country house dinner is 'immaculately but informally served' (guests may choose to eat communally); in the morning, breakfast is 'splendid'.

Castlelyons
P61 FP70

T: 00 353 25 36349
F: 00 353 25 36781
E: info@ballyvolanehouse.ie
W: www.ballyvolanehouse.ie

BEDROOMS: 6. Plus 'glamping' tents May–Sept.
OPEN: all year except Christmas, New Year (self-catering only).
FACILITIES: hall, drawing room, honesty bar, dining room, free Wi-Fi, wedding facilities, 80-acre grounds (15-acre garden, croquet, 3 trout lakes, woodland, fields), unsuitable for disabled.
BACKGROUND MUSIC: none.
LOCATION: 22 miles NE of Cork.
CHILDREN: all ages welcomed (tree house, farm animals, games, high tea).
DOGS: allowed, but kept on lead during shooting season July–Jan.
CREDIT CARDS: MasterCard, Visa.
PRICES: [2017] per room B&B from €198, D,B&B from €258. Set dinner €60.

CLIFDEN Co. Galway

Map 6:C4

THE QUAY HOUSE

'Delightful hosts' Julia and Paddy Foyle run their harbourside B&B with 'generosity of spirit and a genuine interest in seeing guests happy', Guide inspectors say. 'We arrived to a very nice welcome tea and ready advice on touring the area.' The B&B occupies four linked houses, including the 19th-century harbourmaster's house. Everywhere, there's a 'plethora of auction finds' to catch one's eye. 'The main sitting room is a great, airy space filled with vases of fresh flowers, mismatched furnishings and lamps, curio upon curio, plus rugs on the wooden floors, and stacks of magazines and books.' Each of the individually styled bedrooms has a terrace or balcony. 'Our spacious room had splendid views over the ever-changing harbour. There was a squashy sofa and a plump armchair by the electric fireplace; a neat table and chairs by the Juliet balcony.' In the morning, breakfast ('good muesli, excellent coffee, even two breakfast cakes') is served in a 'lovely, bright conservatory'. 'Toby, the Foyles' son, is an innovative cook. A well-rounded dish of eggs Benedict with a spinach–mushroom mix was properly indulgent.'

Beach Road
Clifden
H71 XF76

T: 00 353 95 21369
F: 00 353 95 21608
E: thequay@iol.ie
W: www.thequayhouse.com

BEDROOMS: 16. 3 on ground floor, 1 suitable for disabled, 7 studios (6 with kitchenette) in annexe.
OPEN: end Mar–end Oct.
FACILITIES: 2 sitting rooms, breakfast conservatory, free Wi-Fi, in-room TV (Freeview), small garden, fishing, sailing, golf, riding nearby.
BACKGROUND MUSIC: none.
LOCATION: harbour, 8 mins' walk from centre.
CHILDREN: all ages welcomed.
DOGS: not allowed.
CREDIT CARDS: MasterCard, Visa.
PRICES: per room B&B €160.

SEE ALSO SHORTLIST

CLIFDEN Co. Galway

Map 6:C4

SEA MIST HOUSE

There's a 'relaxed atmosphere' and 'a sense of lightness and warmth' at Sheila Griffin's 'characterful' B&B, in a heritage town between the Atlantic and the Twelve Bens. A cherry-red front door marks the spot; to the rear of the 'attractive' Georgian house, the 'well-cared-for' garden – 'a rush of colour' – slopes upwards. 'Spacious' sitting rooms full of books have 'very comfortable' sofas to sink into, and a 'lovely' peat fire in the evening. 'There's a family feel, with framed old pictures of the town, the house, and the family as it has grown over the years.' Upstairs, the bedrooms are traditionally styled. 'Our room had comfortable twin beds and excellent bedside lighting; a well-equipped tray with teas, instant coffee and biscuits, topped up daily. The narrow walk-in shower had lots of hot water.' At a 'marvellous' breakfast, ingredients range from the local to the very local – much comes from the garden, its beehives and hens. (Special dietary requests are particularly well met, with advance notice.) Go beyond the full Irish for Connemara smoked salmon, home-baked brown bread and spiced fruit compote, then wash it all down with 'the best coffee I've had in Ireland'.

Seaview
Clifden
H71 NV63

T: 00 353 95 21441
E: sheila@seamisthouse.com
W: www.seamisthouse.com

BEDROOMS: 4.
OPEN: mid-Mar–end Oct.
FACILITIES: 2 sitting rooms, conservatory dining room, mini-library, free Wi-Fi, ¾-acre garden, unsuitable for disabled.
BACKGROUND MUSIC: none.
LOCATION: just down from the main square, on the edge of town.
CHILDREN: not under 4.
DOGS: not allowed.
CREDIT CARDS: Amex, MasterCard, Visa.
PRICES: per person B&B €40–€60.

SEE ALSO SHORTLIST

CLONES Co. Monaghan

Map 6:B6

HILTON PARK

At the end of a mile-long drive through 'an estate of great tranquillity and beauty' stands Fred and Joanna Madden's Italianate mansion. 'The gracious 18th-century house is characterised by tasteful flower arrangements, historic heirlooms and stacks of books reflecting a considerable diversity of interest,' say Guide inspectors in 2017, 'though domesticity is ensured by two affectionate, stumpy Jack Russell terriers. And Joanna is a warm, friendly hostess, whose commitment and enthusiasm are quite infectious.' Antique-filled bedrooms with sweeping views of the estate have much to appreciate. 'On the second floor, our room had an abundance of period furniture and reading material; a comfortable, super-king-size bed; a view of lush greenery.' Candlelit dinners take their inspiration from bang-on-season produce from the huge walled garden, and meat and fish from the estate. 'Our excellent meal brought tuna carpaccio with home-made pickles and delicious soda bread; a perfect fillet steak. Piped muzak was the only downside.' Breakfast 'gets the day off to a superb start': home-baked bread, strawberry and lavender marmalade, 'molten scrambled eggs'.

Clones

T: 00 353 47 56007
E: mail@hiltonpark.ie
W: www.hiltonpark.ie

BEDROOMS: 6.
OPEN: Mar–end Nov; groups only at Christmas/New Year.
FACILITIES: 3 drawing rooms, study, breakfast room, dining room, games room, free Wi-Fi (in public areas), wedding facilities, 600-acre grounds (3 lakes for fishing and wild swimming, golf course, croquet), unsuitable for disabled.
BACKGROUND MUSIC: occasionally in dining room.
LOCATION: 4 miles S of Clones.
CHILDREN: all ages welcomed.
DOGS: not allowed.
CREDIT CARDS: all major cards.
PRICES: [2017] per person B&B from €95, D,B&B from €150. Set dinner €60.

DONEGAL TOWN Co. Donegal

Map 6:B5

ARD NA BREATHA

Cosy, unpretentious and welcoming, Theresa and Albert Morrow's traditional guest house is on the working family farm between Lough Esk and the town. 'Some may think it old-fashioned, but we were very comfortable. Theresa does a good job as front-of-house, and Albert, who really does farm, cooked us breakfast.' Good-value bedrooms overlooking sheep-dotted farmland are in a converted barn, reached via a covered walkway from reception. They're straightforward, with the expected amenities: a TV, a tea tray. A residents' lounge with an honesty bar is further made homely with card games and an open fire. In the bright, beamed dining room, 'pleasant, knowledgeable staff' serve 'satisfactory dinners' with lamb and vegetables from the farm. 'Our three-course menu was supplemented by a mushroom amuse-bouche and a sorbet; the wine list was long enough to give a good choice.' 'There's not a pre-pack in sight' at breakfast: a buffet holds fresh fruit, yogurt, cheeses, cereals and home-baked bread; French toast, say, or smoked salmon and scrambled eggs are cooked to order. The Bluestack mountains are easily reached; Donegal Town is a 15-minute stroll away. (EC)

Drumrooske Middle
Donegal Town

T: 00 353 74 972 2288
F: 00 353 74 974 0720
E: info@ardnabreatha.com
W: www.ardnabreatha.com

BEDROOMS: 6. All in converted barn.
OPEN: mid-Feb–end Oct.
FACILITIES: bar, lounge, restaurant, free Wi-Fi, in-room TV (Freeview), 1-acre grounds, unsuitable for disabled.
BACKGROUND MUSIC: in bar and restaurant during breakfast and dinner.
LOCATION: 1¼ miles NE of town centre.
CHILDREN: all ages welcomed.
DOGS: allowed in bedrooms (not unattended), not in public rooms.
CREDIT CARDS: MasterCard, Visa.
PRICES: [2017] per room B&B €62–€134. Set dinner €39, à la carte €40.

SEE ALSO SHORTLIST

DRINAGH Co. Wexford

Map 6:D6

KILLIANE CASTLE NEW

Drive through green countryside to come to this peaceful, family-run B&B steeped in centuries-old history. On a working dairy farm, John and Kathleen Mernagh's 17th-century house adjoins the remains of a 15th-century Norman castle. Inside, rooms are 'attractively decorated' in period style: vintage furnishings, gilt-framed mirrors, a grandfather clock. 'We were graciously welcomed by Kathleen. The fire had been lit in the lounge; tea and coffee were offered in a snug, along with Kathleen's home-made biscuits.' Up the wide staircase, bedrooms (two suitable for a family) look over the lawns and surrounding fields. 'Our beautiful room had a comfortable super-king-size bed with good linen; lovely amenities and a bathtub in the tastefully decorated bathroom.' In the spring and summer months, the hosts prepare a limited-choice home-cooked dinner using garden salads, and meat from the farm. Come morning, a 'fresh, tasty' breakfast, with home-baked bread and home-made yogurt, is 'a highlight' – fine fuel for climbing to the top of the castle tower, the best spot to get the lay of the land. (Rebecca Fishwell, Simon Simmons)

Drinagh
Y35 YPH6

T: 00 353 53 915 8885
E: info@killianecastle.com
W: www.killianecastle.com

BEDROOMS: 8.
OPEN: mid-Feb–end Dec.
FACILITIES: reception, lounge (honesty bar), coffee room, dining room, free Wi-Fi, in-room TV (Freeview), garden, large grounds (nature trail, tennis, croquet, pitch and putt, 300-metre driving range) on 230-acre dairy farm, unsuitable for disabled.
BACKGROUND MUSIC: in reception area and dining room.
LOCATION: 4 miles S of Wexford.
CHILDREN: all ages welcomed.
DOGS: not allowed.
CREDIT CARDS: Diners, MasterCard, Visa.
PRICES: [2017] per room B&B from €52, D,B&B (spring and summer months) from €78.

GLASLOUGH Co. Monaghan

Map 6:B6

CASTLE LESLIE

'Positively flourishing', the Leslie family's sprawling estate has remained in the hands of its founding family for nearly three and a half centuries. 'The whole place is well run, with polite and attentive staff.' Bedrooms are in the castle – each wildly different, each with a tale to tell – and in the stone-built lodge, a 'splendidly labyrinthine Victorian pile'. 'Our very smart, very comfortable Lodge room was well designed, with a good bathroom.' Fill the waking hours: traipse into ancient woodland with a picnic lunch; try for monster pike in the lough; discover the 19th-century walled garden; take afternoon tea in the castle's high-ceilinged drawing room; borrow a pair of wellies and head off on a stomp through the integrated wetlands. In the evening, choose an informal country-style dinner at Conor's bar, or dine on more modern dishes (perhaps baked pork fillet, braised rib, pork tail rillettes, spiced baby apple) in Snaffles restaurant. Have a right royal time at breakfast, too, with home-baked breads and home-made preserves, leaf teas, 'butter served in a proper dish'. (EC)

Glaslough

T: 00 353 47 88100
F: 00 353 47 88256
E: info@castleleslie.com
W: www.castleleslie.com

BEDROOMS: 49 bedrooms. 29 in Lodge (some suitable for disabled).
OPEN: all year except 23–27 Dec.
FACILITIES: drawing rooms, bar, breakfast room, restaurant, conservatory, billiard room, library, cinema, free Wi-Fi, in-room TV, wedding/conference facilities, spa, 14-acre gardens in 1,000-acre grounds (equestrian centre, tennis, walking trails, wildlife, lakes, boating, fishing).
BACKGROUND MUSIC: all day in public areas of Lodge.
LOCATION: 7 miles NE of Monaghan.
CHILDREN: all ages welcomed.
DOGS: allowed on estate, not in rooms (overnight in stables in equestrian centre).
CREDIT CARDS: Amex, MasterCard, Visa.
PRICES: [2017] per room B&B from €130, D,B&B from €230. 1-night bookings sometimes refused.

GOREY Co. Wexford

MARLFIELD HOUSE

The Bowe family has been providing 'prompt and attentive service' in their 'beautiful' Regency-style mansion, which stands in woodland and extensive formal gardens, for more than 35 years. Guide inspectors found 'a guest-centred, ambitious hotel' whose 'inviting public rooms' are filled with 'interesting artwork, and fittings to fascinate the eye'. Bedrooms are traditionally styled with antiques and paintings. 'Our pleasant garden-view room had three easy chairs and a large Victorian wardrobe, a well-lit marble bathroom, and a super-king-size bed for a most restful sleep.' In the frescoed Conservatory restaurant, Ruadhan Furlong's 'Division 1' cooking might include such modern dishes as roasted Irish veal sirloin, apple and potato purée, charcoal oil, turnips. 'We could happily have eaten our way through the menu over successive nights.' More casual options (perhaps smoked chicken breast, warm Puy lentils, chorizo) are taken in the airy Duck restaurant, in converted fieldstone stables by the vegetable and rose garden. At an 'excellent breakfast', feast anew on home-made preserves, leaf teas, local yogurt, 'sumptuous' smoked salmon and scrambled eggs. 'Atmospheric' wooded walks await.

25% DISCOUNT VOUCHERS

Courtown Road R742
Gorey

T: 00 353 53 942 1124
E: info@marlfieldhouse.ie
W: www.marlfieldhouse.com

BEDROOMS: 19. 8 on ground floor.
OPEN: Feb–New Year, Conservatory restaurant closed Mon/Tues, Wed night/Sun night from Feb–mid-May, Oct–Dec, Duck restaurant closed Mon/Tues Jan–Apr, Oct–Dec.
FACILITIES: reception hall, drawing room, library/bar, 2 restaurants, free Wi-Fi, in-room TV (Freeview), wedding facilities, 36-acre grounds (gardens, tennis, croquet, wildfowl reserve, lake), unsuitable for disabled.
BACKGROUND MUSIC: all day in library/bar.
LOCATION: 1 mile E of Gorey.
CHILDREN: all ages welcomed, no under-8s at dinner (high tea, babysitting).
DOGS: allowed ('always on a lead') by prior arrangement, not in public rooms.
CREDIT CARDS: all major cards.
PRICES: per room B&B from €230, D,B&B from €350. Set dinner €66.

KENMARE Co. Kerry

Map 6:D4

BROOK LANE HOTEL

'Stylish, comfortable and attractively priced',
Una and Dermot Brennan's family-run
boutique hotel puts the emphasis on a 'warm,
friendly' Kerry welcome. Public rooms are
hung with 'good modern art', much of it local;
leather sofas set in alcoves 'allow a degree of
privacy'. Bedrooms in varying sizes are stocked
with robes and slippers and a yoga mat; freshly
brewed tea and coffee are brought to the room
on request, with home-made chocolate chip
cookies. 'Our good-sized ground-floor room had
two comfy armchairs, a super-king-size bed,
a work table with an Anglepoise lamp. In the
spotless bathroom: modern fittings, wonderful
underfloor heating.' The informal bar/
restaurant serves food all day, from lunchtime
club sandwiches to traditional-with-a-twist
mains such as Dermot's rare-breed pork belly
duo, confit cabbage, hazelnuts. (A 15-minute
walk away, sister restaurant No. 35 has more
modern dishes, perhaps salted hake, smoked
bacon and mixed bean stew, burnt onion purée,
seaweed butter.) A good base for scenic tours of
the Beara peninsula, the Ring of Kerry and the
Wild Atlantic Way; the hotel's local walking
guide has ideas closer to home. (RG)

Sneem Road
Kenmare

T: 00 353 64 664 2077
E: info@brooklanehotel.com
W: www.brooklanehotel.com

BEDROOMS: 22. 9 on ground floor,
1 suitable for disabled.
OPEN: all year except 24–26 Dec.
FACILITIES: lift, bar/restaurant,
library, free Wi-Fi, in-room TV,
wedding facilities.
BACKGROUND MUSIC: all day in public
areas.
LOCATION: 5-min. walk from town
centre.
CHILDREN: all ages welcomed.
DOGS: not allowed.
CREDIT CARDS: Diners, MasterCard,
Visa.
PRICES: [2017] per room B&B from
€99, D,B&B from €134. Set menus
from €35, à la carte €28.

SEE ALSO SHORTLIST

KINSALE Co. Cork

Map 6:D5

THE OLD PRESBYTERY NEW

Jolly flower baskets flank the bright red front door of this personable B&B on a quiet street in the centre of a historic port and fishing town. 'We arrived to a warm welcome. Noreen and Philip McEvoy, the owners, are a likeable couple who enjoy chatting with their guests,' said Guide readers this year. Once the residence of the parish priests, the nearly 270-year-old house is 'charming, quirky and filled with family memorabilia'. Each of the traditionally decorated bedrooms (up a 'steep, narrow' staircase in the main house) is different: one has a roof garden with views over the town; a 'generously sized' penthouse suite is ideal for a family. For those in need of a mid-afternoon pick-me-up, cheese, wine, coffee and tea are served between 4.30 pm and 6 pm – 'a novel and much appreciated touch'. In the morning, help yourself to fresh fruit and home-made granola, part of an 'excellent' breakfast of organic and Fairtrade produce; Philip McEvoy, a professional chef, cooks a seafood special of the day. 'It may not be cheap by B&B standards, but you get good value for money.' (Esler Crawford)

43 Cork Street
Kinsale

T: 00 353 21 477 2027
E: info@oldpres.com
W: www.oldpres.com

BEDROOMS: 9. 3 in adjacent annexe.
OPEN: Mar–Oct.
FACILITIES: sitting room, dining room, free Wi-Fi, in-room TV (Freeview), patio with seating, secure parking, unsuitable for disabled.
BACKGROUND MUSIC: in dining room at breakfast.
LOCATION: town centre.
CHILDREN: all ages welcomed.
DOGS: not allowed.
CREDIT CARDS: MasterCard, Visa.
PRICES: per room B&B €95–€190. 1-night bookings sometimes refused.

LETTERFRACK Co. Galway

Map 6:C4

ROSLEAGUE MANOR

☙ Previous César winner

'Supremely comfortable in that unique Irish
country house way', this pink-washed Regency
manor house on the shores of Ballinakill Bay
continues to please, say Guide readers this
year. Mark Foyle, a 'sympathetic, hands-on'
owner, is the third generation of the family
to run the show; his 'energy and seemingly
endless enthusiasm help make Rosleague a very
special place'. Past the open log fires, historical
paintings and home-baked teatime scones,
bedrooms have antique furnishings and outlooks
on forest or sea. 'Our room overlooked the herb
garden, giving us a good view of a member of
the kitchen staff picking the herbs for dinner.'
The evening meal is a traditional affair: in
the dining room, 'a fine place to eat', chef
Emmanuel Neu's menu focuses on local produce
such as Killary lobster and Connemara lamb.
'Vegetarians are catered for, though perhaps
not as well as meat- and fish-eaters.' There's
a goodly spread at breakfast: home-baked
bread, freshly squeezed juice, fresh and
stewed fruit, devilled kidneys and fresh fish
alongside more conventional cooked dishes.
(Esler Crawford, AW)

Letterfrack

T: 00 353 95 41101
F: 00 353 95 41168
E: info@rosleague.com
W: www.rosleague.com

BEDROOMS: 21. 2 on ground floor.
OPEN: mid-Mar–mid-Nov.
FACILITIES: 2 drawing rooms,
conservatory/bar, dining room, free
Wi-Fi, in-room TV (Freeview),
wedding facilities, 25-acre grounds
(tennis), unsuitable for disabled.
BACKGROUND MUSIC: none.
LOCATION: 7 miles NE of Clifden.
CHILDREN: all ages welcomed.
DOGS: 'well-behaved dogs' allowed.
CREDIT CARDS: MasterCard, Visa.
PRICES: [2017] per person B&B
€75–€115, D,B&B €95–€145. Set
dinner €36–€50. 1-night bookings
sometimes refused.

LIMERICK Co. Limerick

Map 6:D5

NO. 1 PERY SQUARE

Patricia Roberts's stylish town house hotel sits in a row of Georgian terraces in the centre, nearly within paint-splattering distance of the art gallery. The Grade I listed building has been 'attractively restored': there's an open fire in the bar; books and candles sit on window sills; exposed brick and original stonework bring atmosphere to the vaulted basement spa. 'From the very pleasant first-floor restaurant, we enjoyed watching the world pass by.' Bedrooms vary in size and style. Smaller Club Rooms with contemporary decor overlook the courtyard or the neighbouring red brick houses, but opt for one of the 'elegant, spacious' period-style rooms reached via the house's original staircase. These have large sash windows, perhaps a roll-top bath or handmade brass-and-gilt bed. In the handsome bistro restaurant, chef Tim Harris puts a 'tasty' modern French twist on traditional Irish dishes, perhaps Burren oak-smoked salmon, beetroot, capers; braised pork cheek, fennel compote, apple purée, chicory. At breakfast, choose among sweet and savoury crêpes, egg dishes on potato farl, organic Irish porridge oats 'served as you like'.

Georgian Quarter
1 Pery Square
Limerick

T: 00 353 61 402402
F: 00 353 61 313060
E: info@oneperysquare.com
W: www.oneperysquare.com

BEDROOMS: 20. 2 suitable for disabled.
OPEN: all year except 24–27 Dec.
FACILITIES: lift, lounge, drawing room, restaurant, private dining room, free Wi-Fi, in-room TV (Freeview), wedding facilities, small kitchen garden, terrace, basement spa, deli/wine shop.
BACKGROUND MUSIC: in restaurant and lounge.
LOCATION: central.
CHILDREN: all ages welcomed.
DOGS: not allowed.
CREDIT CARDS: Amex, MasterCard, Visa.
PRICES: [2017] per room B&B from €195, D,B&B from €295. Set dinner €25–€35, à la carte €45.

LISDOONVARNA Co. Clare

Map 6:C4

SHEEDY'S

Come back to Martina and John Sheedy's small hotel, after a windswept walk in 'wonderful' Burren countryside, to enjoy a quiet drink by the fire or in the sunroom overlooking the rose garden – it's the small touches that make the place. The hotel has been in the family for four generations; today, 'the combination of Martina's warm welcome and John's cooking is formidable'. Large, traditionally furnished bedrooms in the 18th-century country house are supplied with fine toiletries, up-to-date magazines and home-made cookies. For extra space, book a junior suite with a generous sitting area. No newcomer to sustainable food, the chef/patron has been using local suppliers in his kitchen for more than 30 years. Among his Irish dishes grounded in classical French techniques: pork belly, cauliflower purée, apple coulis; seared scallops, lentils. At a buffet-free breakfast, 'the hosts offer something a little different (although if you want a traditional Irish fried breakfast, you won't find a better one)'. There are pancakes, bagels with St Tola goat's cheese, organic porridge with Baileys; jams, marmalade and breads are all home made. More reports, please.

Lisdoonvarna

T: 00 353 65 707 4026
F: 00 353 65 707 4555
E: info@sheedys.com
W: www.sheedys.com

BEDROOMS: 11. Some on ground floor, 1 suitable for disabled.
OPEN: Easter–Sept, closed Mon/Tues in Apr, restaurant closed Sun evening July–Sept.
FACILITIES: sitting room/library, sun lounge, bar, restaurant, free Wi-Fi, in-room TV (Freeview), ½-acre garden (rose garden).
BACKGROUND MUSIC: 'easy listening' at breakfast, light jazz at dinner.
LOCATION: 20 miles SW of Galway.
CHILDREN: not under 12.
DOGS: not allowed.
CREDIT CARDS: MasterCard, Visa.
PRICES: [2017] per room B&B €120–€180, D,B&B €220–€280. À la carte €48. 1-night bookings refused weekends in Sept.

LONGFORD Co. Longford

Map 6:C5

🏨 VIEWMOUNT HOUSE

César award: Irish hotel of the year

In 'cleverly designed, well-maintained gardens' on the outskirts of town, Beryl and James Kearney's elegant Georgian mansion has 'uninterrupted views' of the surrounding land, and a 'cheerful ambience' within. 'Beryl, warm and friendly, is a dynamo; James's relaxed Irish geniality radiates a sense of confidence in an arriving guest,' says a Guide inspector in 2017. There are log fires in the sitting rooms, and paintings and ornaments throughout. Bedrooms, individually furnished with period pieces, have contemporary flair. 'On two levels, my tastefully decorated room had rugs on wood flooring; a metal-and-marble fireplace; an immaculate bathroom with underfloor heating. A pine staircase led to a small, galleried sitting area.' In the old stables, chef Gary O'Hanlon's modern cooking (perhaps salt-fried sirloin steak, Crozier Bleu gratin) is thought 'superb'. 'As the restaurant was closed on a Sunday evening, we had a late lunch at 4 pm. Tasty fishcakes were followed by aged blade of beef and horseradish potatoes; rhubarb crumble rounded off the fine meal.' Breakfast, with freshly squeezed clementine juice, is 'delicious'.

Dublin Road
Longford
N39 N2X6

T: 00 353 43 334 1919
E: viewmt@iol.ie
W: www.viewmounthouse.com

BEDROOMS: 12. 7 in modern extension, some on ground floor, 1 suitable for disabled.
OPEN: all year except 28 Oct–7 Nov, restaurant closed Mon, Tues, 25–27 Dec.
FACILITIES: reception room, library, sitting room, breakfast room, restaurant, free Wi-Fi, in-room TV, wedding facilities, 4-acre grounds (pond, orchard, herb garden, Japanese garden).
BACKGROUND MUSIC: none.
LOCATION: 1 mile E of town centre.
CHILDREN: all ages welcomed.
DOGS: not allowed.
CREDIT CARDS: Amex, MasterCard, Visa.
PRICES: per person B&B from €75, D,B&B from €135. Set dinner €65 (early bird €37.50).

MAGHERALIN Co. Armagh

Map 6:B6

NEWFORGE HOUSE

♧ Previous César winner

In a swaddle of green grounds unravelling towards the River Lagan, John and Louise Mathers are the 'personable, totally customer-centred' hosts of this 'remarkable' guest house. Come into the 'gracious' entrance hall of the restored Georgian house: paintings of Irish scenes hang on the walls; the lounge is an 'intimate, comfortable room', with seating arranged around the fireplace. Elegant bedrooms are furnished with family antiques. 'My third-floor room overlooked the front lawn. Everything had been tastefully put together: a chaise longue, a slender wardrobe, a chest of drawers with polished brass handles. A helpful information folder included a comprehensive list of local activities.' Flowers decorate the lawn-facing dining room, where the host cooks a three-course dinner five days a week, with much food locally sourced. (Light suppers are available the rest of the week.) 'Home-baked soda bread accompanied a delicious pea and mint soup. A rib-eye steak was perfectly cooked; an elderflower panna cotta exquisite.' In the morning, perhaps after Henry, the resident cockerel, sounds the call, breakfast is 'simply superb'. (RG)

58 Newforge Road
Magheralin
BT67 0QL

T: 028 9261 1255
E: enquiries@newforgehouse.com
W: www.newforgehouse.com

BEDROOMS: 6.
OPEN: Feb–Dec.
FACILITIES: drawing room, dining room, free Wi-Fi, in-room TV (Freeview), wedding facilities, 2-acre gardens (vegetable garden, wild flower meadow, orchard, woodland) in 50 acres of pastureland, unsuitable for disabled.
BACKGROUND MUSIC: in dining room.
LOCATION: edge of village, 20 miles SW of Belfast.
CHILDREN: under-1s and over-10s welcomed.
DOGS: not allowed.
CREDIT CARDS: Diners, MasterCard, Visa.
PRICES: [2017] per room B&B £125–£195, D,B&B from £210. À la carte £44.

MULTYFARNHAM Co. Westmeath

Map 6:C5

MORNINGTON HOUSE

The O'Hara family seat since 1858, this 18th-century house in 'rolling countryside' is run with 'indomitable spirit' by Warwick and Anne O'Hara. 'A stay at their home is a unique experience,' say Guide inspectors in 2017. 'Anne radiates a sense of calm and scholarship; Warwick is a most remarkable gentleman. At breakfast he cut a striking figure, immaculate as ever in his red-striped apron.' Guests are welcomed with tea and 'a delicious variety of cake' by the fire in the drawing room (original wallpaper, 'pretty flower arrangements', family photos on the grand piano); in the evening, sherry and gin are set out for pre-dinner drinks. Traditionally furnished bedrooms look out over the 'well-designed garden' and grounds. 'Our elegant room had an ornate wardrobe and dressing table; a smallish, brass-framed double bed.' Join fellow guests in the fire-warmed dining room ('candlelight lends an intimate atmosphere') for communal home-cooked dinners using produce from the large walled garden and greenhouse. Typical offerings: deep-fried Brie, redcurrant sauce; 'braised beef with plenty of vegetables' – 'all served by Warwick, with obvious love for his work.'

25% DISCOUNT VOUCHERS

Multyfarnham
N91 NX92

T: 00 353 44 937 2191
F: 00 353 44 937 2338
E: stay@mornington.ie
W: www.mornington.ie

BEDROOMS: 4.
OPEN: Apr–end Oct.
FACILITIES: drawing room, dining room, free Wi-Fi in reception, wedding facilities, 50-acre grounds (¾-acre garden, croquet, bicycle hire), unsuitable for disabled.
BACKGROUND MUSIC: none.
LOCATION: 9 miles NW of Mullingar.
CHILDREN: all ages welcomed.
DOGS: not allowed.
CREDIT CARDS: all major cards.
PRICES: [2017] per room B&B single €95, double €150. Set dinner €45.

OUGHTERARD Co. Galway

Map 6:C4

CURRAREVAGH HOUSE

'The wonderful views of Lough Corrib, combined with warm, easy-going hospitality, make this a place in which we could stay for ages.' Built in 1842 by an enterprising forebear, the Hodgson family's manor house standing in parkland draws guests back year after year. 'Henry Hodgson and his mother, June, make a perfect front-of-house team: she greets visitors and oversees afternoon tea; he manages the enterprise. Henry organised an afternoon's fishing with a local ghillie, then arranged to cook the brown trout my husband caught so all the guests could enjoy it at breakfast.' A 'true country house atmosphere' reigns: there's no TV in the spacious, traditionally decorated bedrooms, but there's a croquet set at the ready, 'plenty of books to borrow', and 'walks to enjoy – plus rain gear in the hall'. Listen for the gong summoning guests to dinner at 8 pm. In the 'inviting dining room', Lucy Hodgson's daily-changing, no-choice menus (perhaps including Black Angus beef sirloin, horseradish romesco, kale) are 'delicious'. 'And "seconds" are always offered – excellent.' 'Generous breakfasts' bring freshly baked soda bread and 'exceptional Seville marmalade'. (Patricia Higgins, Richard Parish)

25% DISCOUNT VOUCHERS

Oughterard

T: 00 353 91 552312
F: 00 353 91 552731
E: mail@currarevagh.com
W: www.currarevagh.com

BEDROOMS: 12.
OPEN: 15 Mar–31 Oct.
FACILITIES: sitting room/hall, drawing room, library/bar with TV, dining room, free Wi-Fi, 180-acre grounds (lake, fishing, ghillies available, boating, swimming, tennis, croquet), golf, riding nearby, unsuitable for disabled.
BACKGROUND MUSIC: none.
LOCATION: 4 miles NW of Oughterard.
CHILDREN: all ages welcomed (50% discount for under-16s).
DOGS: allowed in 1 bedroom, not in public rooms.
CREDIT CARDS: all major cards.
PRICES: per person B&B €75–€90, D,B&B €110–€135. Set dinner €50.

RATHMULLAN Co. Donegal

Map 6:B5

RATHMULLAN HOUSE

On the shores of Lough Swilly, give in to the 'old-fashioned demeanour' of the Wheeler family's hotel, as did guests this year, who found it – and its collection of lough-facing sitting rooms – 'endearing'. 'The Georgian holiday home is filled with antiques, but there's an unstuffy, totally relaxed feel to the place. Family photographs share wall space with botanical prints and oil portraits of the house's previous owners.' Large bedrooms in the main building and the Regency-style wing are decorated with a mix of vintage pieces. 'Our huge superior room had views down to the lough. There were contemporary touches in all the right places, down to the wool blankets on the bed.' In the 'lovely' restaurant, a daily-changing dinner under the starry, tented ceiling may include pan-seared fillet of Greencastle-landed hake, potato and Parmesan gnocchi, garden spinach, wild mushrooms. Informal pizza feasts may be taken in the cellar Tap Room, with slugs of locally brewed craft beer. At breakfast, 'a scrumptious buffet had delicious surprises from the kitchen garden'. (Lesley and Peter Sevitt, and others)

Rathmullan

T: 00 353 74 915 8188
F: 00 353 74 915 8200
E: info@rathmullanhouse.com
W: www.rathmullanhouse.com

BEDROOMS: 34. Some on ground floor, 1 suitable for disabled.
OPEN: Feb–Dec, 28 Dec–3 Jan.
FACILITIES: 4 sitting rooms, library, TV room, cellar bar/pizza parlour, restaurant, free Wi-Fi, in-room TV (Freeview), wedding facilities, 15-metre indoor swimming pool, 7-acre grounds (tennis, croquet).
BACKGROUND MUSIC: none.
LOCATION: ½ mile N of village.
CHILDREN: all ages welcomed.
DOGS: allowed in 1 bedroom, not in public rooms.
CREDIT CARDS: Amex, MasterCard, Visa.
PRICES: [2017] per person B&B €95–€140. À la carte €50. 1-night bookings sometimes refused.

RIVERSTOWN Co. Sligo

Map 6:B5

COOPERSHILL

Peace and quiet surround the O'Hara family's Georgian mansion, which stands in great expanses of woodland and pasture for sheep and red deer. Now in the hands of Simon and Christina O'Hara, the seventh generation of the family, 'the small stately home has the easy grandeur and graciousness of more than 200 years of continuous occupation – no hotel furnisher could simulate that'. In a dining room hung with 18th-century family portraits, sit for dinner at a table set with Irish crystal and silver. The limited four-course menu uses garden fruit and vegetables in season, and venison from the estate. 'We ate too well.' Retire, afterwards, to one of the large, antique-filled bedrooms, each furnished in period style. In the bathroom: robes and slippers, luxury toiletries and a roll-top bath or walk-in shower; the taps produce natural spring water. There's no TV or radio in the room, but newspapers and a selection of novels make good company. Wake to views of the River Unshin or Keashcorran mountain, then tuck in to breakfast (with home-baked bread and home-made yogurt) before heading out into Yeats country. 'A special place.' (CG, and others)

25% DISCOUNT VOUCHERS

Riverstown

T: 00 353 71 916 5108
E: reservations@coopershill.com
W: www.coopershill.com

BEDROOMS: 7.
OPEN: Apr–Oct, off-season house parties by arrangement.
FACILITIES: front hall, drawing room, dining room, snooker room, free Wi-Fi, wedding facilities, 500-acre estate (garden, tennis, croquet, woods, farmland, river with trout fishing), unsuitable for disabled.
BACKGROUND MUSIC: none.
LOCATION: 11 miles SE of Sligo.
CHILDREN: not under 12.
DOGS: not allowed in the house.
CREDIT CARDS: MasterCard, Visa.
PRICES: [2017] per room B&B from €112, D,B&B from €168. Set dinner €56.

SHANAGARRY Co. Cork

Map 6:D5

BALLYMALOE HOUSE

'Excellent all round.' It is more than 50 years since farmer's wife Myrtle Allen launched the modest restaurant that would burgeon into hotel, shop, café, cookery school and event space. Still, traditional values endure. 'It maintains the personal touch and intimacy of a country house,' say Guide readers this year. The family enterprise is centred on a Georgian house grafted onto the remains of a Norman castle keep. 'We enjoyed walking the grounds, visiting the chickens and piglets, and strolling in the well-maintained walled garden and cookery school potager.' Bedrooms are pretty and traditional, and made cheery with garden blooms. 'Our large room opened on to a small patio near the swimming pool. We had plenty of storage space; a beautifully appointed bathroom with fluffy towels, a bathtub and an excellent shower.' Dinner, including multiple courses of chef Jason Fahey's 'very good food', is 'an elaborate affair that pleases the foodies'. Here, home-grown produce stars in country dishes such as poached monkfish, tomato and basil sauce, green beans. Sample more garden glories at breakfast, with dollops of home-made jams and compotes. (Patricia Higgins, and others)

Shanagarry
P25 Y070

T: 00 353 21 465 2531
E: res@ballymaloe.ie
W: www.ballymaloe.ie

BEDROOMS: 29. 9 in adjacent building, 4 on ground floor, 5 self-catering cottages suitable for disabled.
OPEN: all year, except 24–26 Dec, 7 Jan–3 Feb.
FACILITIES: drawing room, 2 small sitting rooms, conservatory, 7 dining rooms, free Wi-Fi, wedding/event/conference facilities, 6-acre gardens, 300-acre farm, tennis, outdoor swimming pool (10 by 4 metres), cookery school nearby, café/kitchen shop.
BACKGROUND MUSIC: none.
LOCATION: 20 miles E of Cork.
CHILDREN: all ages welcomed.
DOGS: allowed in 3 rooms, not in public rooms.
CREDIT CARDS: Amex, MasterCard, Visa.
PRICES: per room B&B from €215, D,B&B from €350. Set dinner €65.

THURLES Co. Tipperary

Map 6:C5

INCH HOUSE

'Warm and charming in its small-scale grandeur', the Egan family's Georgian mansion sits amid a cereals farm in Tipperary countryside. 'The character of the building has been lovingly maintained, even if it is gently shabby in spots; there are remarkable antique furnishings and quality textiles throughout,' report Guide inspectors in 2017. Each bedroom is 'distinctive', with 'stunning countryside views'. 'Our dual-aspect room had an ample four-poster bed. In the spotless bathroom, a roll-top bath took pride of place in front of the massive sash window.' There are 'cosy nooks' and a 'small, well-stocked bar' in the drawing room, ideal for a pre-dinner cocktail; in the 'stunning dining room', 'the menu may cater to more traditional palates, but the food is, without exception, perfectly cooked'. ('Shame about the cheesy muzak.') Wake to breakfast with 'the sun streaming through the windows'. A buffet is laid out on a 'covetable collection' of Nicholas Mosse pottery; the 'short, simple selection' of hot dishes includes 'perfect smoked salmon with eggs'. Get your boots: 'The Inch Loop walk made the stay for us, giving the house historical context, and showing off the Irish countryside.'

Bouladuff
Nenagh Road
Thurles

T: 00 353 504 51348
E: info@inchhouse.ie
W: www.inchhouse.ie

BEDROOMS: 5.
OPEN: all year except Christmas, New Year and Easter, dining room closed Sun and Mon night.
FACILITIES: drawing room, restaurant, free Wi-Fi, in-room TV (Freeview), wedding facilities, 4-acre garden in 250-acre farm, walking trail, unsuitable for disabled.
BACKGROUND MUSIC: Irish in evening in dining room.
LOCATION: 4 miles NW of Thurles on R498 to Nenagh.
CHILDREN: all ages welcomed.
DOGS: not allowed.
CREDIT CARDS: MasterCard, Visa.
PRICES: [2017] per room B&B €120–€140, D,B&B €170–€240. À la carte €45, set menu (Tues–Fri) €40.

SHORTLIST

The Shortlist complements our main section by including potential but untested new entries and appropriate places in areas where we have limited choice. It also has some hotels that have had a full entry in the Guide, but have not attracted feedback from our readers.

Artist Residence Oxfordshire, South Leigh

LONDON

Map 2:D4

THE ALMA, 499 Old York Road, Wandsworth, SW18 1TF. Tel 020 8870 2537, www.almawandsworth.com. Off the tourist trail, this brick-and-tile Victorian pub (Young & Co's Brewery) is popular with south Londoners. Beyond the hubbub of the bar, spacious accommodation is found in a quiet coaching-house courtyard. The stylish rooms have hand-printed wallpaper, bespoke furnishings, a capsule coffee machine; some rooms can accommodate a fold-out bed for a child. Among the more spacious, a garden suite has a private terrace and outdoor seating. Sip local brews in the buzzy bar and sup on gastropub dishes in the light, modern dining room. Weekends have a leisurely start: breakfast is served until 11 am. (Opposite Wandsworth Town railway station; 15 mins to Waterloo) BEDROOMS 23. 2 on ground floor suitable for disabled. FACILITIES Bar, restaurant (Sunday roasts), function room, free Wi-Fi, in-room TV (Sky, Freeview), civil wedding licence, complimentary use of Virgin spa and gym nearby. BACKGROUND MUSIC In bar and restaurant. CHILDREN All ages welcomed (extra bed £15 per night). PRICES Per room B&B from £129. À la carte £35.

THE AMPERSAND, 10 Harrington Road, South Kensington, SW7 3ER. Tel 020 7589 5895, www.ampersandhotel.com. Reap the riches of South Kensington from this eclectic hotel: the wealth of the neighbourhood's museums are minutes away. These local landmarks infuse the hotel's contemporary design, too. Choose a bedroom according to theme: the high-ceilinged rooms and suites (some small; 16 allow smoking) were inspired by the fields of astronomy, botany, geometry, music and ornithology; each has velvet fabrics, bold colours, a stylish tiled bathroom, and free soft drinks in the minibar. Enjoy cocktails and modern Mediterranean cuisine in the basement restaurant Apero, under the cellar arches; light meals and afternoon tea are taken in the drawing room. (Underground: South Kensington) BEDROOMS 111. Some suitable for disabled. FACILITIES Lifts, bar, restaurant, private dining room, drawing rooms, business centre, games room (table tennis), gym, free Wi-Fi, in-room TV, public parking nearby (reservation required). BACKGROUND MUSIC Contemporary in public areas. CHILDREN All ages welcomed. DOGS Allowed. PRICES Room from £192. Buffet breakfast £16, à la carte £32.

THE ARCH LONDON, 50 Great Cumberland Place, Marble Arch, W1H 7FD. Tel 020 7724 4700, www. thearchlondon.com. There's an intimate feel at the Bejerano family's sprawling, characterful hotel, which occupies seven Georgian town houses and two mews homes close to Hyde Park. 'Well-thought-through details' and 'unfailingly helpful staff' make guests feel looked after. An art history lesson awaits in the corridors, which are lined with the work of emerging British artists. The 'comprehensively equipped bedrooms' have a stylish blend of original features, cutting-edge technology and boldly coloured furnishings. 'Splendid' modern British dishes (perhaps salt beef croquettes, horseradish mayonnaise) are served in the 'excellent' brasserie. Cocktails appear at the push of a button in the elegant martini 'library'; opt for afternoon tea, with a glass of bubbly, in the champagne lounge. (Underground: Marble Arch) BEDROOMS 82. 2 suitable for disabled. FACILITIES 2 bars, brasserie, library, gym, free Wi-Fi, in-room TV (Sky), valet parking. BACKGROUND MUSIC In public spaces. CHILDREN All ages welcomed (toy box, books, bedtime milk and cookies). DOGS Allowed. PRICES Room from £264. Set menus £35–£45.

BATTY LANGLEY'S, 12 Folgate Street, Spitalfields, E1 6BX. Tel 020 7377 4390, www.battylangleys.com. Behind the sedate exterior of this plush Spitalfields spot is a host of Georgian eccentricities. Opulent yet playful, Peter McKay and Douglas Blain's hotel occupies two 18th-century buildings. In its characterful singularity, it recalls the owners' other London hotels (see The Rookery and Hazlitt's, main entries). Comfy sofas and a well-stocked honesty bar in the cosy sitting rooms (all polished antiques, old portraits and wood panelling) provide an alternative to the throng of Brick Lane and the City outside. Bedrooms have discreet modern comforts amid crushed velvet bedspreads and goose-down-filled pillows; decadent bathrooms may have a cast-iron roll-top bath or a 'bathing machine'. A breakfast of yogurt, fruit, granola, fresh pastries and bagels is delivered to the room. (Underground: Liverpool Street; Overground: Shoreditch High Street) BEDROOMS 29. 1 suitable for disabled. OPEN All year. FACILITIES Lift, library, parlour, Tapestry room, meeting rooms, free Wi-Fi, in-room TV, small courtyard. BACKGROUND MUSIC None.

CHILDREN All ages welcomed. PRICES Room from £294. Breakfast £11.95.

BERMONDSEY SQUARE HOTEL, 9 Bermondsey Square, Tower Bridge Road, Bermondsey, SE1 3UN. Tel 020 7378 2450, www. bermondseysquarehotel.co.uk. In buzzy Bermondsey, this youthful, privately owned hotel has good-value accommodation near art galleries, the Fashion and Textile Museum and an arthouse cinema. The modern bedrooms vary in size, but each has a 'comfortable bed with plenty of pillows and cushions'; some rooms have access to a shared terrace. Head to the top: spacious loft suites have panoramic views from Big Ben to the Shard. British dishes are served all day in the open-plan lounge/restaurant; in fine weather, dine on the patio on the lively square. (No alcohol is served, but glasses are provided for guests who bring their own drinks to have in the room.) Interesting options at breakfast, including smoothies and a breakfast burrito. (Underground: Bermondsey, Tower Hill) BEDROOMS 90. 4 suitable for disabled. OPEN All year. FACILITIES Lift, open-plan lounge/restaurant/co-working space, free Wi-Fi, in-room TV, meeting rooms, yoga classes, terrace. BACKGROUND MUSIC In public spaces. CHILDREN All ages welcomed. DOGS Allowed (boutique dog beds). PRICES Per room B&B from £159.

THE BULL & THE HIDE, 4 Devonshire Row, Bishopsgate, EC2M 4RH. Tel 020 7655 4805, www.thebullandthehide.com. A tavern since the 1680s, this stylish Square Mile inn is still the place to go for a hearty pint or a snifter of locally made gin. It is now part of the Cunning

Plan Pub Company. Check-in is at the copper-fronted bar; snappily designed bedrooms (interesting textures, good lighting, high-end toiletries, underfloor heating in the bathroom) are upstairs. Guests in superior rooms have anytime access to a shared pantry. There's a choice of eating options: a seasonal modern menu is served in the Hide restaurant; the bar has sophisticated twists on classic pub grub (octopus, paprika mayonnaise; bacon steak, fried duck egg, fries) throughout the day. Breakfast in the bar includes light bites and butties. Some early-morning street noise can be expected as the City comes awake. (Underground: Liverpool Street) BEDROOMS 7. OPEN All year except Christmas. FACILITIES Bar, restaurant (closed Sat lunch, Sun), private dining room, honesty bar, pantry, free Wi-Fi and local telephone calls, in-room TV (Sky). CHILDREN All ages welcomed. PRICES Room from £125. Breakfast £7.95, à la carte £38.

CHARLOTTE STREET HOTEL, 15–17 Charlotte Street, Bloomsbury, W1T 1RJ. Tel 020 7806 2000, www.firmdalehotels. com. A flurry of colour and fine art define this cheerfully decorated hotel within sauntering distance of Soho and the West End theatres. It is part of Tim and Kit Kemp's Firmdale group; Jennifer McCabe is the manager. Original art by Vanessa Bell, Duncan Grant and Roger Fry decorate the public spaces (the Bloomsbury set was an inspiration for the hotel's design); there are log-burning fires and an honesty bar in the drawing room and library. Bright, boldly styled bedrooms vary in size; some can be connected to accommodate a larger group. A bounty

awaits younger guests: a welcome gift, a mini-bathrobe, milk and cookies at bedtime, books and board games to borrow. Feast on modern British classics all day in the buzzy restaurant. (Underground: Goodge Street, Tottenham Court Road) BEDROOMS 52. Some suitable for disabled. FACILITIES Bar, restaurant, drawing room, library, private dining/meeting rooms, free Wi-Fi, in-room TV, civil wedding licence, in-room beauty treatments, 75-seat private cinema, gym. BACKGROUND MUSIC None. CHILDREN All ages welcomed. PRICES Per room B&B from £278. Set menu £22.50–£25, à la carte £45.

CITIZENM BANKSIDE, 20 Lavington Street, Southwark, SE1 0NZ. Tel 020 3519 1680, www.citizenm.com. 'Budget' is far from 'boring' at this style-led, 'excellent-value' hotel within easy access of the city's financial and cultural quarters. Part of an international chain aimed at 'mobile citizens', the 'impressive hotel' has a cool, contemporary atmosphere. There's a DIY feel to the place – guests check themselves in and take themselves to their room – but 'friendly and helpful staff' are on hand whenever needed. The vast lobby and open-plan bar and canteen are accessible all day and night. Bright modular bedrooms have a huge bed, blackout blinds and high-tech details (a touch-screen tablet controls lighting, room temperature, window blinds and on-demand TV); a fridge holds free lemonades and chocolate bars. At breakfast: 'divine' freshly squeezed clementine juice; 'truly excellent' coffee. (Underground: London Bridge, Southwark) BEDROOMS 192. 12 suitable for disabled. FACILITIES Lift, open-plan lobby/bar/deli, work stations, meeting rooms, free Wi-Fi, in-room TV. CHILDREN All ages welcomed. PRICES Room from £112. Breakfast from £13.95. Registered 'Citizens' receive the best available rate and a complimentary drink on arrival.

CITIZENM TOWER OF LONDON, 40 Trinity Square, City of London, EC 3N 4DJ. Tel 020 3519 4830, www. citizenm.com. Jolly and jaunty inside, this modern hotel is part of a global group that provides budget-friendly accommodation with bundles of style. The large 'living room lobby' has contemporary designer furniture, iMac-adorned work stations and a library of design, fashion and travel books. The open-kitchen canteen serves breakfasts, light lunches and simple dinners before transforming into a cocktail bar later in the evening. Check yourself in (multilingual staff are on hand to help if required), then zip upstairs to a snug, state-of-the-art bedroom: there's a large bed; a free minibar; an iPad to control lighting, temperature and the TV; and, if you choose well, picture-window views straight on to the Tower of London. On the top floor, a residents-only bar gazes over London old and new. (Underground: Tower Hill) BEDROOMS 370. Some suitable for disabled. FACILITIES Lift, residents' bar, open-plan lobby/canteen/workspace, meeting rooms, free Wi-Fi, in-room TV. CHILDREN All ages welcomed. PRICES Room from £130. Registered 'Citizens' receive the best available rate and a complimentary drink on arrival.

THE CONNAUGHT, Carlos Place, Mayfair, W1K 2AL. Tel 020 7499 7070,

www.the-connaught.co.uk. In a quiet corner of Mayfair, this luxury hotel (part of the Maybourne group) 'far surpasses expectations'. Butlers attend to every request, and even the youngest guests are liberally treated: they have home-made snacks, a personalised bathrobe and, on request, a concierge-planned itinerary of family-friendly hotspots. Beyond the plushly buzzy lobby, period features, antique pieces and bespoke modern furniture blend well throughout the handsome building. Every bedroom has lavish touches such as a cashmere blanket, a marble bathroom, state-of-the-art technology. Take afternoon tea in the conservatory, or a cocktail or two in the intimate bar, but save room for chef Hélène Darroze's Michelin-starred French cooking in the wood-panelled restaurant (excellent vegetarian options). (Underground: Bond Street) BEDROOMS 119. 30 in new wing, some suitable for disabled. FACILITIES 2 bars, 2 restaurants, Art Deco-style ballroom, spa (swimming pool, treatment rooms, fitness centre), Moon Garden. BACKGROUND MUSIC In public areas. CHILDREN All ages welcomed (babysitting by arrangement). PRICES Room from £480. Breakfast £26.

COUNTY HALL PREMIER INN, Belvedere Road, Southbank, SE1 7PB. Tel 0871 527 8648, www.premierinn.com. Close to some of London's most-visited landmarks, this historic Portland stone-built former county hall now provides good-value accommodation as part of the Premier Inn hotel chain. What it may lack in individual character, it makes up for in its splendid riverside position. Check in at a self-service booth before heading to one of the straightforward, simply furnished bedrooms. Each has a desk and a hospitality tray, plus double-glazed windows to minimise street noise. Breakfast can be a crowded affair – skirt the hungry hordes with an early start. The Sea Life London Aquarium and the London Dungeon are within the same building; the Royal Festival Hall and Hayward Gallery are five minutes' walk away. Look up – the London Eye towers above. (Underground: Waterloo) BEDROOMS 314. Some suitable for disabled. FACILITIES Lift, lobby, bar, restaurant, free Wi-Fi, in-room TV (Freeview), conference facilities. BACKGROUND MUSIC In public areas. CHILDREN All ages welcomed. PRICES Room from £134. Meal deal (dinner and breakfast) £24.99.

COVENT GARDEN HOTEL, 10 Monmouth Street, Covent Garden, WC2H 9HB. Tel 020 7806 1000, www.firmdalehotels. com. A flair for the dramatic is evident at this smart hotel, a high-step and a shuffle away from London's longest-running theatre shows and West End debuts. Part of the sophisticated Firmdale group, it is liked for its 'superb comfort and fantastic service'. The wood-panelled drawing room and characterful, individually decorated bedrooms are given co-owner Kit Kemp's distinctive touch – find bold wallpapers, vintage prints and pleasingly mismatched furnishings. Most of the bedrooms have views across the city; some have a deep bathtub in a granite-and-oak bathroom. Families and groups should ask for connecting rooms. Sample the modern menu in Brasserie Max's, or ask room service to bring you a dish; a varied breakfast (charged extra) includes vegan and vegetarian options. (Underground: Covent Garden, Leicester Square) BEDROOMS 58. FACILITIES Drawing room, library (honesty bar), restaurant, free Wi-Fi, in-room TV, private dining/meeting room, screening room, spa treatment room, gym. BACKGROUND MUSIC None. CHILDREN All ages welcomed (amenities, treats, activities). DOGS Small dogs allowed by arrangement. PRICES Room from £330. Breakfast £15.50–£28.50. À la carte £42.

DORSET SQUARE HOTEL, 39–40 Dorset Square, Marylebone, NW1 6QN. Tel 020 7723 7874, www.firmdalehotels. com. On a garden square near the Sherlock Holmes Museum and Regent's Park, this discreet town house hotel shares the well-considered design of its siblings in the Firmdale Hotels group. The high-ceilinged drawing room, with honesty bar and open fire, is a fine mix of patterns and prints; there are imaginative nods to the square's past as the original site of Thomas Lord's cricket ground. Upstairs in the Regency building, many of the individually styled bedrooms (some small) have leafy views. Special toiletries and age-appropriate entertainment make children welcome. At lunch and dinner, pull up a seat in the Potting Shed restaurant for Mediterranean-inspired English brasserie dishes. When younger guests begin to flag in the afternoon, book them in for a children's tea – they can get creative with icing and toppings before tucking in. (Underground: Marylebone) BEDROOMS 38. 1 suitable for disabled. FACILITIES Lift, drawing room, bar, restaurant, free Wi-Fi, in-room TV, room service. BACKGROUND

MUSIC Live guitar evenings in bar and restaurant Tues and Thurs. CHILDREN All ages welcomed. DOGS Allowed by arrangement. PRICES Room from £240. Continental breakfast buffet £12.50, set menu £23.50, à la carte £33.

ECCLESTON SQUARE HOTEL, 37 Eccleston Square, Belgravia, SW1V 1PB. Tel 020 3503 0691, www.ecclestonsquarehotel. com. 'Domesticated heaven' meets high technology at Olivia Byrne's stylish Pimlico hotel. Within the Georgian building, 'comfortable bedrooms' are kitted out with many tech-focused features: a 'digital concierge' on an iPad; a smartphone with free mobile internet; shower walls that mist up at the touch of a button; an adjustable bed with massage settings. ('Super-friendly' staff are ready to guide less tech-savvy guests through it all.) There's a capsule coffee machine in the room, too, but tea may be brought up on request, in good, old-fashioned manner. Ask for room recommendations before booking: some rooms are small, others have a private balcony or patio. Plenty of restaurants and cafés are within walking distance; alternatively, the cocktail lounge has a short menu of snacks and simple dishes. (Underground: Victoria) BEDROOMS 39. FACILITIES Drawing room, cocktail lounge (oversized 3D TV), free Wi-Fi, in-room TV (Sky), parking discounts. BACKGROUND MUSIC In public areas. CHILDREN Not under 13. PRICES Per room B&B from £220.
25% DISCOUNT VOUCHERS

THE FIELDING, 4 Broad Court, off Bow Street, Covent Garden, WC2B 5QZ. Tel 020 7836 8305, www. thefieldinghotel.co.uk. For all the bustle of surrounding Covent Garden, this 'simple, well-located' small hotel down the lane from the Royal Opera House is 'remarkably quiet'. It is named after Henry Fielding, the novelist and one-time local magistrate who worked at the former courts next door. Down narrow corridors, recently refurbished bedrooms are smart but modest, with 'all the necessities': a comfortable bed and a clean, well-designed bathroom; 'excellent lighting'; bottled water, and tea- and coffee-making facilities. Slippers and an eye mask are nice touches. Breakfast isn't served, but many reliable options are nearby – the 'helpful staff' have recommendations to offer. 'Good value for its position.' (Underground: Covent Garden) BEDROOMS 25. FACILITIES Free Wi-Fi, in-room TV (Freeview), free access to nearby spa and fitness centre. BACKGROUND MUSIC None. CHILDREN All ages welcomed (travel cots). PRICES Single room from £90, double room from £140.

41, 41 Buckingham Palace Road, Victoria, SW1W 0PS. Tel 020 7300 0041, www.41hotel.com. Overlooking Buckingham Palace from the fifth floor of a historic building, this discreet luxury hotel (Red Carnation group) has an air of decadent exclusivity. Mahogany panelling, a personal butler and a generous invitation to 'plunder the pantry' create a clubby atmosphere. Guests fill in a questionnaire before their arrival to ensure that their personal specifications (preferred pillows, desire for a humidifier or a yoga mat) are met in the distinctive, black-and-white bedrooms. Asked for or not, rooms have plenty of thoughtful extras –

home-made treats and season-specific bathrobes among them. At lunch or dinner, visit sister hotel The Rubens at the Palace, which shares the building. Sleep in on Sunday: breakfast, served until 1 pm, will wait. Apples, rusks and bottles of water send guests on their way again. (Underground: Victoria) BEDROOMS 30. FACILITIES Lounge, honesty bar, pantry, free Wi-Fi, in-room TV (Freeview), room service, butler and chauffeur service, free access to nearby spa and fitness centre. BACKGROUND MUSIC In public areas. CHILDREN All ages welcomed. DOGS Allowed (concierge, welcome hamper, bed). PRICES Per room B&B from £407.

GOOD HOTEL, Royal Victoria Dock, Western Gateway, London Docklands, E16 1FA. Tel 020 3637 7401, www.goodhotellondon.com. The blocky exterior of this floating hotel at Royal Victoria Docks may not be entirely inspiring, but the ideas behind it more than make up for that. A social business, the hotel reinvests all profits into charitable causes, including on-the-job training for long-term-unemployed local people. Work, meet and eat in the open-plan lounging/dining space (pared-down industrial decor, communal tables, locally brewed beers, neighbourhood freelancers); in fine weather, move the action to the Astroturfed rooftop garden and terrace. Breakfast, salads, sharing platters and tapas dishes are served throughout the day. Bedrooms are boxy and minimalist, but the essentials are there: a desk area, a safe, tea-making facilities and bathrobes. Book a room with a river view and wake to the sight of the city across the water. Handy for ExCeL London.

(DLR: Royal Victoria) BEDROOMS 148. FACILITIES Lift, bar, lounge, library, restaurant, meeting rooms, free Wi-Fi, terrace, 24-hour concierge service, bicycle hire. BACKGROUND MUSIC In public areas. CHILDREN Not under 12. PRICES Per room B&B from £90.

GREAT NORTHERN HOTEL, Pancras Road, King's Cross, N1C 4TB. Tel 020 3388 0800, www.gnhlondon.com. Make good connections at this revamped Victorian railway stopover. Opening on to the western concourse of King's Cross station, the north London landmark-turned-luxury hotel, designed by Lewis Cubitt in 1851, stands within yards of the St Pancras International terminus – perfect for travellers en route to the Continent. Inspired by sleeper carriages of yore, well-thought-out bedrooms of varying sizes are sleek, with smart fittings and a sophisticated decor. A welcome element: a help-yourself pantry on each floor, stocked with teas and good coffee, biscuits or cakes, a jar of sweets and a fruit bowl. 'Excellent' modern dishes from the buzzy Plum + Spilt Milk restaurant may be delivered to the room. 'The charming staff were particularly accommodating of my two young children.' (Underground: King's Cross St Pancras, Euston) BEDROOMS 91. Some suitable for disabled. FACILITIES Lift, 3 bars, restaurant, Kiosk food stall, free Wi-Fi, in-room TV (Sky), room service. BACKGROUND MUSIC In bars and restaurant. PRICES Per room B&B from £219. À la carte £45.

HAM YARD HOTEL, One Ham Yard, Soho, W1D 7DT. Tel 020 3642 2000, www.firmdalehotels.com. Convenient for Soho and the bright lights of

Theatreland, this modern, purpose-built hotel bursts with artful joie de vivre. The large building – the splashiest of the Firmdale bunch – horseshoes around a tree-filled courtyard, where a towering bronze Tony Cragg sculpture greets guests. Inside, the public spaces have much to look at: vivid fabrics, quirky furniture and contemporary works by an international roster of artists. Chic bedrooms have floor-to-ceiling windows with city or courtyard views; a handsome granite-and-oak bathroom. Peruse the well-stocked library; follow the neon diver to the basement bar; slip on to a banquette in the vast restaurant for lunch or dinner. On a balmy day, head up to the rooftop terrace to peer at the beehives, then soak in the buzz of the city from high above. (Underground: Piccadilly Circus) BEDROOMS 91. 6 suitable for disabled. FACILITIES Lift, bar, restaurant (pre- and post-theatre menus), drawing room, library, private dining/meeting rooms, bowling-alley events space, cinema, spa, gym, free Wi-Fi, in-room TV, civil wedding licence, rooftop terrace and garden, valet parking (charge). BACKGROUND MUSIC None. CHILDREN All ages welcomed (amenities, treats, entertainment). PRICES Room from £318. Breakfast from £13.

HAYMARKET HOTEL, 1 Suffolk Place, West End, SW1Y 4HX. Tel 020 7470 4000, www.haymarkethotel.com. With vintage furnishings and bold works of art, this voguish Firmdale hotel is staged with a zest reminiscent of nearby Theatreland. Sarah Pinchbeck manages 'the most helpful staff'. Both the vividly designed library and the airy conservatory are ideal backdrops

for afternoon tea or evening drinks; poolside cocktails make a splash at the 'stunning' heated indoor pool's pewter bar. Bedrooms are decorated with co-owner Kit Kemp's signature modern English style. Choose from a bistro menu in Brumus restaurant (eat alfresco on the terrace when the weather's fine); come morning, sample huevos rancheros or waffles with Canadian maple syrup off the interesting breakfast menu. (Underground: Green Park, Piccadilly) BEDROOMS 50. Plus 5-bed town house. FACILITIES Lift, lobby, library, conservatory, bar, restaurant (post-theatre platters), indoor swimming pool, gym, free Wi-Fi, in-room TV, civil wedding licence. BACKGROUND MUSIC None. CHILDREN All ages welcomed (amenities, treats, entertainment). DOGS Allowed by arrangement. PRICES Room from £378. Breakfast from £14.

THE HOXTON HOLBORN, 199–206 High Holborn, WC1V 7BD. Tel 020 7661 3000, thehoxton.com. Consciously cool, this youthful hotel occupies a one-time office block, all traces of day-to-day drudgery erased. The capacious lobby doubles as casual meeting space, with communal tables, conveniently placed sockets and complimentary newspapers. Good-value bedrooms (Shoebox, Snug, Cosy, Roomy) are well designed with clever features (underbed storage, a flip-lid desk); each has thoughtful extras – blackout curtains, Penguin Classics, maps of nearby hotspots. There's a choice of eating options: Brooklyn-style Hubbard & Bell serves food all day plus weekend brunches; Holborn Grind has coffees, cocktails, salads and sandwiches; there are spit-roasted birds in the basement Chicken Shop. Hang a breakfast bag on your door handle before turning in; wake to find it filled with a granola pot, a banana and a bottle of orange juice. (Underground: Holborn) BEDROOMS 174. Some suitable for disabled. FACILITIES Lift, open-plan lobby/lounge/co-working space, café/bar, 2 restaurants, free Wi-Fi, free hour's worth of local and international phone calls, nail bar, meeting/function rooms. BACKGROUND MUSIC Live DJ nights. CHILDREN All ages welcomed. PRICES Per room B&B from £119.

THE HOXTON SHOREDITCH, 81 Great Eastern Street, Shoreditch, EC2A 3HU. Tel 020 7550 1000, thehoxton.com. The energy of trendy Shoreditch permeates this 'intensely stylish', good-value hotel in buzzy east London. The large lobby/lounge has a modern industrial look, with its exposed brick walls, scuffed wood flooring, factory shelving and vintage metal lampshades. Smartly designed bedrooms (choose between Cosy and Roomy) have a powerful shower in the 'splendid' bathroom. Helpful extras – a neighbourhood guide; an hour of free international calls – are standard for all guests. At lunch, dinner or whenever hunger strikes, sit down in a leather booth in the popular Hoxton Grill restaurant for a dish from the American-style menu: salt-beef hash, generous salads, a full grill selection. In the morning, a breakfast bag delivered to the door includes a granola pot, a fruit and a bottle of orange juice. (Underground: Old Street) BEDROOMS 210. 11 suitable for disabled. FACILITIES Lift, lounge, shop, free Wi-Fi, courtyard (with retractable roof), meeting rooms. BACKGROUND MUSIC In public areas.

CHILDREN All ages welcomed. PRICES Per room B&B from £99.

H10 LONDON WATERLOO, 284–302 Waterloo Road, Waterloo, SE1 8RQ. Tel 020 7928 4062, www.hotelh10londonwaterloo.com. Guests are welcomed with a complimentary glass of cava at this good-value hotel, part of a Spanish chain, within walking distance of the National Theatre and the South Bank. Understated modern bedrooms (some small) have floor-to-ceiling windows with 'good double-glazing'; the best rooms have panoramic views of London landmarks. Superior rooms have added extras – bathrobes, slippers, a capsule coffee machine. There are newspapers and magazines to read in the lounge, but head straight to the eighth-floor Waterloo Sky bar to gaze at the city from above – cocktails optional. 'Excellent cooked dishes' and a 'considerable breakfast buffet' are a good way to start the day. (Underground: Waterloo) BEDROOMS 177. FACILITIES Lift, lounge, 2 bars, restaurant, free Wi-Fi, in-room TV, meeting rooms, leisure centre (gym, sauna, massages). PRICES Per room B&B from £148. À la carte £30.

INDIGO, 16 London Street, Paddington, W2 1HL. Tel 020 7706 4444, www.ihg.com/hotelindigo. Occupying a row of nine Georgian town houses within easy reach of Paddington station and express trains to Heathrow, this contemporary hotel (InterContinental Hotels group) is ideally located for guests travelling onward. Take the great glass staircase and follow brightly decorated corridors to the well-equipped bedrooms. Each, with double-glazed windows, is decorated with a photographic mural of nearby neighbourhoods. Some rooms may be compact, but the key amenities are there: a desk, bathrobes, tea- and coffee-making facilities. A morning newspaper is delivered to the room. European-inspired dishes are served in the London Street brasserie; in the morning, breakfast with views over leafy Norfolk Square. Hyde Park is a ten-minute walk away. (Underground: Paddington) BEDROOMS 64. 2 suitable for disabled. FACILITIES Lounge/lobby, bar, brasserie, fitness studio, free Wi-Fi, in-room TV, terrace. BACKGROUND MUSIC In public areas. CHILDREN All ages welcomed. DOGS Assistance dogs allowed. PRICES Per room B&B from £181.

THE KENSINGTON, 109–113 Queen's Gate, Kensington, SW7 5LR. Tel 020 7589 6300, www.doylecollection.com/hotels/the-kensington-hotel. 'Elegant yet hip and fun', this 'conveniently located' hotel (part of the Doyle Collection) is minutes from the museums of South Kensington. The staff make it a place to return to, a Guide reader says in 2017: 'they're so pleasant, helpful and accommodating.' 'Well-equipped bedrooms' in the graciously decorated Victorian town house are 'clean and cosy'. They vary in size, but even the smallest has a marble bathroom with underfloor heating, aromatherapy-based bath products and a capsule coffee machine. The 'uncluttered drawing rooms' are an ideal place for afternoon tea (gluten-free options available), custom smoothies and juices. In the 'lovely restaurant' or the wood-panelled bar, chef Steve Gibbs's menu includes seasonal modern dishes, and meat and seafood cooked on the Josper grill. (Underground: South Kensington) BEDROOMS 150. FACILITIES 3 drawing rooms, bar, restaurant, free Wi-Fi, in-room TV, meeting rooms. BACKGROUND MUSIC None. PRICES Room from £278. Continental breakfast £17.

KNIGHTSBRIDGE HOTEL, 10 Beaufort Gardens, Knightsbridge, SW3 1PT. Tel 020 7584 6300, www.firmdalehotels.com. Hyde Park is minutes from this handsome 1860s town house hotel – assuming you don't dally at the many designer boutiques along the way, that is. Part of the Firmdale group, the hotel assumes co-owner Kit Kemp's characterful stance on contemporary design. Natural materials and earthy tones mix with statement pieces and antique prints in the cosy sitting rooms; original artworks add interest. Each bedroom is highly individual (though good bedside lighting and a powerful shower are a given); those at the front overlook leafy Beaufort Gardens. There is no restaurant, but a short room-service menu of classic dishes (pan-fried sea bass with seasonal greens; a superfood salad) staves off the hunger pangs. Pause for tea mid-afternoon – a Princes and Princesses option with jellies and milkshakes is a treat for younger guests. (Underground: Knightsbridge) BEDROOMS 44. FACILITIES Drawing room, library, bar, free Wi-Fi, in-room TV, civil wedding licence, room service, in-room body and beauty treatments by arrangement. BACKGROUND MUSIC None. CHILDREN All ages welcomed (books, board games, DVDs, treats). DOGS Small dogs allowed by arrangement. PRICES Room from £294. À la carte breakfast £3.50–£14.50.

THE LASLETT, 8 Pembridge Gardens, Notting Hill, W2 4DU. Tel 020 7792 6688, www.living-rooms.co.uk. Penguin classics, original artwork and vintage curios add character to the smart bedrooms at this modish hotel, which occupies a row of five cream cake-coloured Victorian town houses close to Portobello market. Creative London provides the inspiration for the place: the hotel (part of Tracy Lowy's Living Rooms collection) is named after Rhaune Laslett, a community activist who co-founded the Notting Hill Carnival; local architects, designers and makers contributed to the home-away-from-home feel of the place. Chic bedrooms vary from small 'spare rooms' to spacious, high-ceilinged suites; all are air conditioned, and well equipped with bathrobes and high-end toiletries. Brunch is served till 4 pm in the Henderson bar/café; small plates, large plates, sweets and nibbles are available all day. (Underground: Notting Hill Gate) BEDROOMS 51. 5 suitable for disabled. FACILITIES Lobby library, bar/coffee shop (a showcase for local designers, artists and craftsmen), terrace for alfresco eating, free Wi-Fi, in-room TV (Sky), room service, in-room spa treatments, complimentary passes to local gym, discounts at local shops and restaurants. BACKGROUND MUSIC All day in public areas. CHILDREN All ages welcomed. PRICES Room from £199. Breakfast £22.

LIME TREE HOTEL, 135–137 Ebury Street, Belgravia, SW1W 9RA. Tel 020 7730 8191, limetreehotel.co.uk. Surprisingly affordable in upmarket Belgravia, this smart, family-owned B&B occupies two Georgian town houses filled with uncluttered modern rooms and plenty of good cheer. It is owned by Charlotte and Matt Goodsall, who have retained the buildings' high ceilings, original cornicing and fireplaces while giving the place a fresh, contemporary feel. A small sitting room has guide books and glossy magazines; the neat rear garden is scented with roses in the summer. Simply styled bedrooms vary in size (those in the eaves are smallest), but all have the necessary basics – tea- and coffee-making facilities, good toiletries, a safe and a wide-screen TV. (Underground: Victoria; rail and bus station) BEDROOMS 25. FACILITIES Sitting room (computer for guests' use), breakfast room, free Wi-Fi, in-room TV (Freeview), meeting facilities, garden. BACKGROUND MUSIC None. CHILDREN All ages welcomed. PRICES Per room B&B single from £125, double from £185. 2-night min. stay at weekends.

THE MAIN HOUSE, 6 Colville Road, Notting Hill, W11 2BP. Tel 020 7221 9691, www.themainhouse.co.uk. Live like a local at this discreet home away from home. Conceived with the 'independent traveller' in mind, Caroline Main's quirky guest house in villagey Notting Hill makes an elegant base for city exploration. Each of the spacious, high-ceilinged suites (white walls, wood floors, Edwardian prints, a vintage commode or wardrobe) occupies an entire floor of the Victorian town house; all are well supplied with books, guides and maps, purified water, a fridge and motley other travellers' essentials (umbrellas, adaptor plugs, etc). Morning tea or coffee, with the day's newspaper, may be taken in the room or on the balcony overlooking the quiet street. Breakfast at one of the many delis or artisan bakeries nearby (guests receive discounts); keep up a gym routine at the local BodyWorksWest health club, where special day rates are available. (Underground: Notting Hill Gate) BEDROOMS 4. FACILITIES Free Wi-Fi, in-room TV (Sky, Virgin), roof terrace, airport chauffeur service (reasonable rates), DVD library. BACKGROUND MUSIC None. CHILDREN Well-behaved children of all ages welcomed. DOGS Not allowed. PRICES Room £110–£150 (3-night min. stay).

THE MONTAGUE ON THE GARDENS,

15 Montague Street, Bloomsbury, WC1B 5BJ. Tel 020 7637 1001, www. montaguehotel.com. The well-curated collection of antiques and curios in this Bloomsbury town house puts it in good stead with its venerable neighbour, the British Museum. It is part of the Red Carnation Hotels group; Dirk Crokaert is the long-serving manager. Genteel public spaces are filled with chandeliers, original artwork and richly patterned fabrics; plush, individually decorated bedrooms blend traditional (gilded mirrors, hand-crafted furniture) and high-tech (on-demand films, independently controlled air conditioning). Rooms at the back overlook the private garden. Among the thoughtful treats for all ages: games, DVDs, a mini-bathrobe and slippers for children; complimentary evening canapés for guests in the spacious junior suites. Eat in the relaxed Blue Door bistro or alfresco on the garden terrace. (Underground: Russell Square) BEDROOMS 100. 1 suitable for disabled. FACILITIES Lounge, bar, bistro, 2

conservatories, free Wi-Fi, in-room TV (Sky), civil wedding licence, meeting/ function rooms, garden terrace, cigar terrace. BACKGROUND MUSIC Classic/ contemporary in public areas, live jazz in bar in evening except Sun. CHILDREN All ages welcomed. DOGS Allowed. PRICES Per room B&B single from £243, double from £264.

THE NADLER KENSINGTON, 25

Courtfield Gardens, Kensington, SW5 0PG. Tel 020 7244 2255, www. thenadler.com. Style- and budget-conscious travellers like this modern hotel, part of the Nadler Hotels group, for its approach to 'affordable luxury'. (A sister hotel is in Liverpool – see Shortlist entry.) The pared-down bedrooms (some compact) may seem plain, but even the standard amenities are premium: a choice of pillows from a pillow menu; Fairtrade teas and a capsule coffee machine; a mini-kitchen kitted out with a microwave, a fridge and cutlery; individually controlled heating and air conditioning. Pick a size to suit: there are single rooms, snug doubles, family rooms that sleep four. There's no restaurant, but guests have their choice of local hotspots, and resident discounts at many of them. A continental breakfast (£8.50) may be delivered to the room. South Kensington's museums are a 20-minute walk or easy bus ride away. (Underground: Earl's Court, Gloucester Road) BEDROOMS 65. Some with bunk bed, 1 suitable for disabled. FACILITIES Lobby, free Wi-Fi, in-room TV, music library, games, access to local Fitness First gym, bicycle hire. BACKGROUND MUSIC In public areas. CHILDREN All ages welcomed. PRICES Room from £119.

THE PILOT, 68 River Way, Greenwich, SE10 0BE. Tel 020 8858 5910, pilotgreenwich.co.uk. One of the oldest surviving buildings on the Greenwich peninsula, this quirky historical inn has been updated in lively style with maps, nautical objects and unusual fittings. Seasonal pub food, sharing platters and daily specials (perhaps Serrano ham croquettes, roasted red pepper salsa; ricotta dumplings, chilli, sage, parmesan) are served in the popular dining areas; a menu of real ales, bottled beers, premium spirits and wines makes a fine partner. Accommodation is in compact but cheerful bedrooms individually decorated with vintage furnishings and quirky collections (record covers, clocks, sunglasses, etc). Good details, too: a capsule coffee machine, a Kilner jar of teas, herbal-extract bath products. Convenient for the O2 arena. Staying guests may park for free. (Underground: North Greenwich) BEDROOMS 10. FACILITIES Bar, restaurant, free Wi-Fi, in-room TV (Freeview), function facilities, garden, roof terrace, parking. BACKGROUND MUSIC In public areas. CHILDREN All ages welcomed. DOGS Assistance and guide dogs allowed. PRICES Per room B&B from £160.

QBIC HOTEL, 42 Adler Street, Whitechapel, E1 1EE. Tel 020 3021 3300, london.qbichotels.com. Close to Brick Lane, there's a fun, buzzy atmosphere at this modern hotel, a budget-friendly beacon for the young and the young-at-heart. Complimentary tea and coffee are available all day in the vast, wood-floored lobby (bright rugs, mismatched furniture); locals and hotel guests find a spot here to socialise,

work or simply soak up the scene. In the bedrooms, a futuristic, pre-fabricated unit combines comfortable bed and compact shower room. Clever touches: mood lighting, a Skype-ready television, free digital newspapers and magazines. With some of London's best street food, curry houses and bagelries on the doorstep, guests will barely notice the lack of restaurant. (Surprisingly well-stocked vending machines cater to those who insist on staying in.) Breakfast 'grab bags' contain juice, fruit and a cereal bar. (Underground: Aldgate East, Whitechapel) BEDROOMS 171. Some suitable for disabled. FACILITIES Lift, lounge, bar, free Wi-Fi, in-room TV. BACKGROUND MUSIC In public spaces. CHILDREN All ages welcomed. PRICES Room from £62. Breakfast buffet £8.

THE ROYAL PARK HOTEL, 3 Westbourne Terrace, Paddington, W2 3UL. Tel 020 7479 6600, www.theroyalpark. com. 'Extremely nice staff' create a 'comfortable, homely atmosphere' at this elegant town house hotel between Paddington station and Hyde Park. Public spaces are decorated with period furnishings and oil paintings; traditionally styled bedrooms look on to the tree-lined street or a private mews. The rooms vary in size – a four-poster suite has its own sitting room – but all have an antique desk, an easy chair, and a limestone shower or bathroom well supplied with bathrobes, slippers and high-end toiletries. Stay in for cocktails and sophisticated small plates (maybe scallops and boudin noir, sweetcorn purée, crispy sage; smoked venison saddle, blackberry and gin, cocoa oil) in the bar. Breakfast may be taken in the room. (Underground: Paddington, Lancaster Gate) BEDROOMS 48. FACILITIES Lift, bar, restaurant, free Wi-Fi, in-room TV, business/function facilities, garden, terrace, room service, limousine service, parking. CHILDREN All ages welcomed. PRICES Per room B&B (including welcome drink) from £173.

ST JAMES'S HOTEL AND CLUB, 7–8 Park Place, St James's, SW1A 1LS. Tel 020 7316 1600, www.stjameshotelandclub. com. At the end of a quiet street, there's a country-retreat ambience at this lavish Mayfair hotel, its sumptuous interiors and Michelin-starred kitchen giving the Victorian house contemporary flair. Plush bedrooms have handmade wallpaper, a Murano glass chandelier, high-end toiletries; two have a private terrace. A helpful touch: all guests have use of a smart phone with free calls to various countries. Sit down to a pre- or post-theatre supper in William's Bar & Bistro, or settle in to sample chef William Drabble's fine modern French cooking in the acclaimed Seven Park Place restaurant. More nostalgic indulgences are found at afternoon tea, devised in collaboration with Hamleys toy store, with treats (domino biscuits, snakes-and-ladders petits fours) based on popular parlour games. (Underground: Green Park) BEDROOMS 60. 2 on ground floor. FACILITIES Lounge, bar, bistro, restaurant (closed Sun, Mon), 4 private dining rooms, free Wi-Fi, in-room TV, civil wedding licence, in-room spa and beauty treatments, function rooms. BACKGROUND MUSIC None. CHILDREN All ages welcomed (dedicated kids' concierge). PRICES Per room B&B from £335, D,B&B from £449.

ST PAUL'S HOTEL, 153 Hammersmith Road, Hammersmith, W14 0QL. Tel 020 8846 9119, www.stpaulhotel.co.uk. From the chalk dust of a venerable former boys' school rises this smartly converted hotel close to the Olympia conference centre. It was built in 1884 by Alfred Waterhouse, the architect responsible for the Natural History Museum; well-maintained architectural details (Romanesque style, impressive arches, terracotta brickwork) here rival those of the more famous building. Period features appear in the uncluttered modern bedrooms, too – some rooms have an original fireplace. Put down your books and pick up a champagne flute at afternoon tea; dine on straightforward European dishes (home-smoked Cornish mackerel, quinoa, avocado, quail eggs; steaks off the grill) in the light-filled restaurant. (Underground: Hammersmith, Kensington Olympia, Barons Court) BEDROOMS 35. 1 suitable for disabled. FACILITIES Lift, bar, restaurant, free Wi-Fi, in-room TV, wedding/business facilities, room service, garden, limited parking (reservation necessary). BACKGROUND MUSIC In public areas. CHILDREN All ages welcomed. PRICES Room from £196. Continental breakfast £12.50, à la carte £35.

SLOANE SQUARE HOTEL, 7–12 Sloane Square, Chelsea, SW1W 8EG. Tel 020 7896 9988, www.sloanesquarehotel. co.uk. 'The wonderfully efficient staff look after everything' at this 'ideally located hotel' close to the Royal Court Theatre. Fans like the buzzy atmosphere and the hotel's ties to the 'charming neighbourhood' (it was a Beatles hang-out back in the day).

Bed down in one of the 'comfortable, well-designed' bedrooms, each supplied with a capsule coffee machine, blackout curtains and a well-stocked minibar. Choose sides: front rooms overlooking the 'lively square' allow for good people-watching; rear rooms looking on to an Art Deco church may be quieter. Families may be accommodated in interconnecting rooms. For dinner, visit the 'bustling' Côte brasserie next door, or ask for a dish to be 'promptly delivered' to the room. 'Good cooked options' at breakfast. (Underground: Sloane Square) BEDROOMS 102. FACILITIES Lift, bar, meeting rooms, free Wi-Fi, local and national phone calls, in-room TV, room service, parking (extra charge). BACKGROUND MUSIC In public areas. CHILDREN All ages welcomed. PRICES Room from £118. Cooked breakfast £9.95.

SOFITEL LONDON ST JAMES, 6 Waterloo Place, St James's, SW1Y 4AN . Tel 020 7747 2200, sofitelstjames.com. 'Wonderfully located' off Pall Mall, within a saunter of the National Gallery, this refined neoclassical hotel (part of the French hotel chain) is liked for its 'exceptionally comfortable bedrooms' and 'excellent meals'. Bedrooms of various sizes are restrained and modern (black-and-white photographs of London set the tone); each has a minibar, a capsule coffee machine, bathrobes, slippers and chic toiletries. Sweep down a spiral staircase into the elegant Balcon brasserie, where classic French dishes (perhaps sautéed snails; Bibb lettuce, golden beetroot, roquefort, walnut, pear) are served all day. The cosseting lounge, where a harpist plays, is the place for afternoon tea and old-world cocktails. The breakfast buffet is 'delicious'. (Underground: Charing Cross, Piccadilly Circus) BEDROOMS 183. 1 suitable for disabled. FACILITIES Lounge, bar, restaurant, spa, gym, free Wi-Fi, in-room TV, business facilities, room service, valet parking. BACKGROUND MUSIC In public areas. CHILDREN All ages welcomed (babysitting on request). PRICES Room from £292. Breakfast £25.

THE SOHO HOTEL, 4 Richmond Mews, off Dean Street, Soho, W1D 3DH. Tel 020 7559 3000, www.firmdalehotels. com. Designer and co-owner Kit Kemp insists on wit in a hotel. That explains the ten-foot Botero sculpture of a bronze feline, tongue gently poking out in greeting, in the lobby of this lively Firmdale property. Modern art, fresh flowers and peppy colour schemes dominate; huge windows let in plenty of natural light. Each bedroom is delightful and different, with a sleek, modern bath- or shower room. Bring the family: several rooms can be interconnected, and younger guests are spoiled with books, board games, a monthly film club, a mini-bathrobe, bedtime milk and cookies. A varied menu in the Refuel restaurant includes good vegetarian and vegan options. (Underground: Leicester Square) BEDROOMS 96. 4 suitable for disabled, plus 4 apartments. FACILITIES Lift, drawing room (honesty bar), library, bar, restaurant, 4 private dining rooms, free Wi-Fi, in-room TV, civil wedding licence, gym, beauty treatment rooms, 2 screening rooms, DVD library. BACKGROUND MUSIC In public spaces. CHILDREN All ages welcomed. DOGS Small dogs allowed by arrangement.

PRICES Room from £330. Breakfast £26 (à la carte selection also available), set dinner £23–£25, à la carte £36.

SOUTH PLACE HOTEL, 3 South Place, Bishopsgate, EC2M 2AF. Tel 020 3503 0000, www.southplacehotel.com. Guide readers '100% recommend' this modern luxury hotel in the midst of City buzz. Designed by Terence Conran, it's liked for its 'distinctly cool, European feel'. 'Our beautiful, quiet room had original artwork, bespoke furniture, state-of-the-art lighting and a dreamy bathroom.' Soft drinks, tea and coffee and a morning paper are included in the room rate. There's choice for every appetite: cocktails and snacks on the rooftop terrace; updated British classics in the Chop House; sophisticated seafood dishes in the Michelin-starred Angler restaurant (closed Sat lunch and Sun; Christmas). Come morning, 'friendly staff' may deliver pastries, fruit compote and cooked dishes to the room. (Underground: Liverpool Street, Moorgate) BEDROOMS 80. 4 suitable for disabled. FACILITIES Lift, 4 bars, 2 restaurants, Le Chiffre residents' lounge and games room, gym, steam, sauna, treatment room, free Wi-Fi, in-room TV, civil wedding licence, 5 private dining/meeting rooms, 'secret' garden. BACKGROUND MUSIC In public areas, live DJ Fri and Sat nights in bars. CHILDREN All ages welcomed. DOGS Small/medium-size dogs allowed. PRICES Per room B&B from £200. Tasting menus (Angler restaurant) £60–£90, set dinner (Chop House) £22.50–£27.50.

THE STAFFORD, 16–18 St James's Place, St James's, SW1A 1NJ. Tel 020 7493 0111, thestaffordhotel.co.uk. A favourite with Americans since at least the Second World War, when it hosted Allied officers and acted as a bomb shelter, this quintessential English town house hotel has a long and intriguing history. (Today, the 380-year-old cellars make an atmospheric setting for private wine tastings, though the underground passages to St James's Palace are off limits.) Rooms in the main house – the former London residence of Lord and Lady Lyttelton – retain a period feel; those in the Mews and Carriage House have more contemporary comforts. Head to the characterful American Bar for a cocktail amid Stateside ephemera, celebrity photographs and baseball memorabilia. For more than liquid sustenance, chef James Durrant's modern dishes are served in the new Game Bird restaurant. (Underground: Green Park) BEDROOMS 104. 11 in Carriage House, 26 in Mews, 1 suitable for disabled. FACILITIES Lift, lounge, bar, restaurant, free Wi-Fi, in-room TV, civil wedding licence, function facilities, courtyard, parking (charge). BACKGROUND MUSIC None. CHILDREN All ages welcomed. PRICES Per room B&B from £372.

TEN MANCHESTER STREET, 10 Manchester Street, Marylebone, W1U 4DG. Tel 020 7317 5900, www.tenmanchesterstreethotel.com. Ten minutes' walk from Regent's Park, this handsome Edwardian hotel is in a well-to-do neighbourhood of terraced houses and high-end boutiques. A haven for cigar aficionados, it is also home to an award-winning cigar lounge with a tasting room, a dedicated smoking terrace and an impressive selection of hand-rolled Havana cigars. Comfortable bedrooms decorated in neutral tones are well equipped with robes and slippers, bottled water, a minibar and a smart phone with free calls to selected countries. Some rooms may be small, but book a courtyard room for extra space – it opens on to a private terrace with seating, music and heaters. Modern Italian cuisine is served all day in the restaurant. (Underground: Baker Street, Bond Street, Marylebone) BEDROOMS 44. FACILITIES Bar, cigar lounge and terrace, free Wi-Fi, in-room TV (Sky), room service, chauffeur service, in-room spa and beauty treatments. BACKGROUND MUSIC None. CHILDREN All ages welcomed. PRICES Per room B&B £165–£375.

TOWN HALL HOTEL & APARTMENTS, Patriot Square, Bethnal Green, E2 9NF. Tel 020 7871 0460, www. townhallhotel.com. Architectural splendour and contemporary comforts are the big draws at this impeccably restored Edwardian former town hall in up-and-coming Bethnal Green. Spacious bedrooms range from double rooms to studio apartment suites with a fully fitted kitchen, each chic and inviting with one-off vintage pieces, a sheepskin rug by the bed and a barista-quality coffee machine. Bright, young things from the neighbourhood head to the Corner Room for casual lunches and dinners; in the Typing Room restaurant (closed Sun, Mon), chef Lee Westcott's modern cooking (perhaps Dorset char, white asparagus, celeriac, wild garlic) is much praised. Breakfast is a generous buffet. Free shuttle bus services to the City each weekday morning. (Underground:

Bethnal Green) BEDROOMS 98. 4 suitable for disabled. FACILITIES Lift, cocktail bar, 2 restaurants, indoor swimming pool, gym, free Wi-Fi, civil wedding licence, function facilities, limited street parking. BACKGROUND MUSIC In public areas. CHILDREN All ages welcomed. PRICES Room from £159. Breakfast from £15.

THE VICTORIA INN, 77–79 Choumert Road, Peckham, SE15 4AR. Tel 020 7639 5052, victoriainnpeckham.com. Part of the local landscape since 1878, this Victorian public house, newly restored and revamped, is today a smart, welcoming spot, with well-designed rooms, a modern, gastropubby restaurant and a fine selection of cask ales. It is managed by Joe Sheasgreen. Locals and residents congregate over biodynamic wines and locally sourced beers in the handsomely restored bar (wood flooring, dark leather banquettes, mismatched tables and chairs); in the dining room, imaginative seasonal dishes might include flat-iron Suffolk chicken, broccoli and spinach slaw, skin-on fries. Upstairs, bedrooms have a large bed and a mid-century-modern aesthetic; a capsule coffee machine and useful technology (air conditioning, Bluetooth sound system) come as standard. Light bites and big plates at breakfast. The city centre is easily reached. (Rail station: Peckham Rye) BEDROOMS 15. FACILITIES Bar, dining room, private function room, free Wi-Fi, in-room TV (Freeview), small beer garden. BACKGROUND MUSIC In public areas. CHILDREN All ages welcomed. DOGS Allowed. PRICES Per room B&B from £110. À la carte £35.

ENGLAND

ALFRISTON Sussex
Map 2:E4

DEANS PLACE, Seaford Road, BN26 5TW. Tel 01323 870248, www. deansplacehotel.co.uk. In 'well-maintained ornamental gardens', this 'handsome hotel' occupies an 'extensively enlarged' old farmhouse on the outskirts of a 'delightful' medieval village. It is run by 'friendly, attentive staff'. The bedrooms are 'clean and comfortable', but spend your day in the 'splendid outdoor spaces' in fine weather: a brook meanders through the garden; there are terraces with 'plenty of tables and seating', a croquet lawn and putting area. 'Inside and out, there are many secluded areas to enjoy some privacy.' 'High-quality' modern British dishes from a 'small but well-balanced menu' are served at lunch and dinner. Leave room for pudding: a dark chocolate fondant with banana ice cream was thought 'perfection on a plate'. 'Enormous portions' at breakfast. BEDROOMS 36. 1 suitable for disabled. OPEN All year. FACILITIES Bar, restaurant, function rooms, free Wi-Fi, in-room TV (Freeview), civil wedding licence, terrace, 4-acre garden, outdoor swimming pool (May–Sept). BACKGROUND MUSIC In dining room, occasional live jazz at Sunday lunch. CHILDREN All ages welcomed. DOGS Allowed in some bedrooms. PRICES Per room B&B from £100, D,B&B from £170. Set dinner £32–£38.
25% DISCOUNT VOUCHERS

WINGROVE HOUSE, High Street, BN26 5TD. Tel 01323 870276, www. wingrovehousealfriston.com. The colonial-style veranda that wraps around Nick Denyer's elegant 19th-century restaurant-with-rooms, on the High Street of this pretty village, sets a languid pace for arriving guests. Inside, friendly staff – and an 'immediately relaxing' open fire, in cool weather – encourage the cosseting atmosphere. Most of the stylish bedrooms have views of the village green and surrounding countryside; two have a heated balcony. In the candlelit restaurant, sample produce from local growers in chef Matthew Comben's 'top-quality' modern European dishes. Recent offerings off the two- and three-course menus: goat's cheese mousse, Sussex asparagus, raspberry; local cider-braised rabbit, savoy cabbage. Breakfast has 'lots of good choice'. All-weather terraces (one has heat lamps) have tables and seating. 20 mins' drive from Glyndebourne. BEDROOMS 7. FACILITIES Lounge/bar (extensive gin menu), restaurant (closed Mon–Wed lunch, special diets catered for), free Wi-Fi, in-room TV (Freeview), terrace, walled garden. BACKGROUND MUSIC In public areas. CHILDREN All ages welcomed. PRICES Per room B&B £125–£195. Set dinner £29–£35.

ALKHAM Kent
Map 2:D5

THE MARQUIS AT ALKHAM, Alkham Valley Road, CT15 7DF. Tel 01304 873410, www.themarquisatalkham. co.uk. Modern, Kent-inspired cuisine draws guests to this smart restaurant-with-rooms, in a little village between Dover and Folkestone. In the stylishly made-over 200-year-old former pub (Bespoke Hotels), chef/manager Stephen Piddock prepares his à la carte and tasting menus using locally sourced produce in season. Typical dishes: seared Rye Bay scallops, dry-cured ham, peas, parsley; Romney Marsh lamb rump and cannelloni of shoulder, fennel, sloe gin. Vegetarians have their own menu. Upstairs, and in nearby cottages, modern bedrooms have a large bed, underfloor heating, and views over the valley and the village cricket pitch. Light sleepers, ask for a room at the back. Extensive breakfasts; afternoon tea; Sunday lunch. On a busy road 4 miles W of Dover. BEDROOMS 10. 1 suitable for disabled, 3 rooms in 2 cottages, 3 mins' drive away. FACILITIES Lounge/bar, restaurant (closed Mon lunch), free Wi-Fi, in-room TV (Freeview), civil wedding licence, small garden. BACKGROUND MUSIC In restaurant. CHILDREN All ages welcomed, no under-8s in restaurant in evening. PRICES Per room B&B from £99, D,B&B from £189. Tasting menu £35–£65, à la carte £36.

APPLEDORE Devon
Map 1:B4

THE SEAGATE, The Quay, EX39 1QS. Tel 01237 472589, www.theseagate. co.uk. Pack the wellies and be ready to go off-road: this inviting quayside hotel welcomes dogs and muddy boots coming off the South West Coast Path. The white-painted 17th-century inn overlooking the Torridge estuary has a relaxed atmosphere and uncluttered, modern bedrooms – plus bunk beds in the family room for younger travellers. Tea- and coffee-making facilities and a flat-screen TV come as standard. Estuary-caught seafood features on the restaurant menu (keep watch on the daily fish specials board); in the

summer, the terrace is the place to eat it. Breakfast on local yogurts, fresh fruit, a good selection of cooked dishes. 2 miles from Bideford. BEDROOMS 10. FACILITIES Open-plan restaurant/bar (local ales and ciders), free Wi-Fi, in-room TV, 2 terraces, walled garden. BACKGROUND MUSIC In public areas. CHILDREN All ages welcomed. DOGS Allowed. PRICES Per room B&B single £70, double from £99. À la carte £24. 2-night min. stay at weekends preferred.

ARMSCOTE Warwickshire
Map 3:D6

THE FUZZY DUCK, Ilmington Road, CV37 8DD. Tel 01608 682635, www. fuzzyduckarmscote.com. Country comfort informs sister-and-brother team Tania and Adrian Slater's voguishly refurbished 18th-century coaching inn, in a tranquil village 8 miles from Stratford-upon-Avon. Locals and visitors come for the real ales and house cocktails, plus the modern twists on pub favourites: ham hock mac 'n' cheese, truffled cheese sauce, say, or chicken, leek and pancetta pie, champ mash. (The private dining area behind the double-aspect fireplace is a cosy spot for a special occasion.) There's room at the inn: four, in fact, each supplied with luxury linens, a woollen throw and complimentary goodies (the Slater siblings are behind beauty products company Baylis & Harding). Two rooms, ideal for a family, have a loft bed. Borrow a guide book and a pair of wellies, and head out on a ramble – the staff are happy to advise on the Fuzzy Duck Waddle. BEDROOMS 4. FACILITIES Bar, restaurant (closed Sun eve and Mon), free Wi-Fi, in-room smart TV, 1-acre garden. BACKGROUND MUSIC

In public areas. CHILDREN All ages welcomed (dress-up box). DOGS Allowed (welcome pack, home-made dog biscuits and snacks in the bar). PRICES Per room B&B from £110. À la carte £33.

ARNSIDE Cumbria
Map 4: inset C2
NUMBER 43, The Promenade, LA5 0AA. Tel 01524 762761, www.no43.org.uk. Lesley Hornsby's modern B&B on the promenade takes in uninterrupted views across the Kent estuary. Find a spot on the front terrace in sunshine; another day, lounge by the large bay window in the local art-hung sitting room, with a hot drink and a slice of home-baked cake. Understated bedrooms have plenty of thoughtful touches: biscuits, posh teas and freshly ground coffee; a jug of fresh milk in the silent mini fridge; chic toiletries; additional pillows and cushions. Two suites have binoculars for wildlife spotting. Breakfast is a hearty affair: thick yogurt, home-made compotes, home-roasted maple syrup granola, locally caught and smoked haddock. Light supper platters of smoked fish, local cheese and pâtés are available. BEDROOMS 6. OPEN All year. FACILITIES Lounge, dining room, free Wi-Fi, in-room TV (Freeview), honesty bar, patio. BACKGROUND MUSIC At breakfast. CHILDREN Not under 5. PRICES Per room B&B £125–£185.

ASTHALL Oxfordshire
Map 2:C2
THE MAYTIME INN, nr Burford, OX18 4HW. Tel 01993 822068, www.themaytime.com. In leather and tweed, burnished wood and rustic plaid, Dominic Wood's 'lovely old pub' is a 'delightful, friendly place'.

'It's extraordinarily good value, too,' adds a Guide reader this year. Popular with locals and visitors, who come for the buzzy Sunday lunches and week-round range of local ales and ciders, the 17th-century mellow stone coaching inn stands near a meandering stream off the River Windrush. Country-style bedrooms are in the main building and around the courtyard. 'Our comfortable, beautifully converted courtyard room afforded us a peaceful night.' Pub classics and more sophisticated plates (perhaps pan-fried hake, curly kale, truffle mash) populate the menu; breakfasts are 'top notch and imaginative'. Asthall Manor, the Mitford sisters' childhood home, is down the lane. 2 miles from Burford. BEDROOMS 6. All on ground floor. OPEN All year. FACILITIES Bar, restaurant, free Wi-Fi, in-room TV (Freeview), large terrace and garden (alfresco meals and drinks), outdoor bar, boules pitch. BACKGROUND MUSIC In bar and restaurant areas. CHILDREN All ages welcomed. DOGS Allowed in public areas, not in bedrooms. PRICES B&B per room £95–£160, D,B&B (off-peak times only) £135–£200. À la carte £30.

AYSGARTH Yorkshire
Map 4:C3
STOW HOUSE, Leyburn, DL8 3SR. Tel 01969 663635, www.stowhouse.co.uk. Solidly Victorian on the outside, cheerfully modern on the inside, this old rectory standing in open countryside has been filled by owners Phil and Sarah Bucknall with period pieces and pleasingly playful touches. Sip one of the hostess's made-to-order cocktails and contemplate the contemporary art in the sitting room, or pluck a book

from the shelf and sink into a bright-hued sofa before the wood-burner. Bedrooms have been styled with verve (a sky-blue velvet chaise longue here, a claw-footed bath under a papier mâché badger there), though the most arresting feature, arguably, is the view stretching over the dales. Breakfasts are packed with local produce, including the family butcher's home-made sausages. Dinner may be provided for groups of six or more. 7 miles W of Leyburn. BEDROOMS 7. 1 on ground floor. OPEN All year except 23–28 Dec. FACILITIES Sitting room (honesty bar), snug, dining room, free Wi-Fi, in-room TV (Freeview). BACKGROUND MUSIC None. CHILDREN All ages welcomed. DOGS Well-behaved dogs allowed in 5 bedrooms. PRICES Per room B&B £100–£175.

BAINBRIDGE Yorkshire
Map 4:C3
YOREBRIDGE HOUSE, Leyburn, DL8 3EE. Tel 01969 652060, www. yorebridgehouse.co.uk. In a Dales village on the River Ure, Charlotte and David Reilly have revamped this former Victorian school and headmaster's house with panache. Each of the spacious, lofty-ceilinged bedrooms, some with a private terrace, is stylish and characterful in its own way: ornate chandeliers hang from the rafters in one room; an antique Moroccan window serves as a bedhead in another; in a lofty bathroom, twin bathtubs allow for a side-by-side soak. Visit the Master's Room for afternoon tea, or take it in the large garden in fine weather. Candlelit dinners, preceded by canapés, are modern and locally inspired: perhaps Wensleydale beef, ox cheek, salsify, kale. BEDROOMS 12. Some

on ground floor suitable for disabled, 4 in schoolhouse, plus The Barn suite in village, 5 mins' walk. OPEN All year. FACILITIES Lounge, bar, garden room, restaurant, free Wi-Fi in public areas, in-room TV (Sky), civil wedding licence, 2-acre grounds. BACKGROUND MUSIC All day in public areas. CHILDREN All ages welcomed. DOGS Allowed in 2 rooms, by arrangement. PRICES Per room B&B £200–£295, D,B&B £310–£395. Set menu £60.

BAINTON Yorkshire
Map 4:D5
WOLDS VILLAGE, Manor Farm, YO25 9EF. Tel 01377 217698, www. woldsvillage.co.uk. Go on a bear hunt in the deepest Yorkshire Wolds. Sally and Chris Brealey, with Sally's mother, Maureen Holmes, have created a whimsical woodland art trail (including a sleuth of bear sculptures) that carves a path around their unusual enterprise. The Georgian farmstead includes a restaurant, tea shop, gift shop and art gallery; accommodation is in a sympathetically designed barn newly built using reclaimed materials. Each of the comfortable, soundproofed bedrooms is decorated with a nod to a different historic period – Tudor, Victorian, Edwardian, Art Deco; tea- and coffee-making facilities are provided. A wide-ranging menu of straightforward dishes (pies, traditional roasts, a soup of the day) is served in the restaurant all day. 6 miles W of Driffield. BEDROOMS 7. 3 on ground floor, some suitable for disabled. OPEN All year except 2 weeks from 28 Dec. FACILITIES Lounge, bar, restaurant (closed Sun eve), free Wi-Fi, in-room TV (Freeview), visitor information

centre, tea room, craft and gift shop, art gallery, 6-acre grounds. BACKGROUND MUSIC In restaurant. CHILDREN All ages welcomed. PRICES Per room B&B single £70, double £100. À la carte £25.

BARNSLEY Gloucestershire
Map 3:E6
THE VILLAGE PUB, GL7 5EF. Tel 01285 740421, www.thevillagepub.co.uk. Village gossip, quaffable ciders and country-chic accommodation combine at this popular stone-built restaurant-with-rooms (Calcot Hotels) in a pretty Cotswold village. Comfortable bedrooms (accessed via a separate entrance from the pub) have soft hues, old beams, a deep roll-top bath or four-poster bed. Light sleepers, ask for a room away from the road. Build up an appetite with a ramble around Rosemary Verey's acclaimed gardens at sister hotel Barnsley House (see main entry), a saunter down the road: pub residents have complimentary access. On your return, hearty classics-with-a-twist from the season-specific menu might include pork steak, parsley mash, kale, apple sauce. English farmhouse breakfasts have home-made jams and home-baked bread. 4½ miles E of Cirencester. BEDROOMS 6. OPEN All year. FACILITIES Bar, restaurant, free Wi-Fi, in-room TV (Freeview). BACKGROUND MUSIC In bar and restaurant. CHILDREN All ages welcomed. DOGS Allowed. PRICES Per room B&B from £104, D,B&B from £164. À la carte £30.

BARNSTAPLE Devon
Map 1:B4
BROOMHILL ART HOTEL, Muddiford Road, EX31 4EX. Tel 01271 850262, www.broomhillart.co.uk. Rinus and

Aniet van de Sande have created a much-praised meeting point for art, culture and hospitality at their 'quirky' late-Victorian hotel in a wooded Devon valley. It is surrounded by one of the largest permanent collections of contemporary sculpture in southwest England. Inside, 'interesting paintings' occupy every wall; an art gallery (open to the public) demands exploration. Spacious modern bedrooms have views over the sculptures in the grounds. At lunch and dinner, sample Mediterranean 'slow food' and tapas in the award-winning Terra Madre restaurant. 4 miles N of Barnstaple. BEDROOMS 6. OPEN All year except mid-Dec–mid-Jan. FACILITIES Bar, restaurant (closed Sun–Tues; 2-course dinner for hotel guests 6 pm–7.30 pm Mon/Tues), library, free Wi-Fi, in-room TV, civil wedding licence, art gallery, 10-acre grounds with sculpture park. BACKGROUND MUSIC None. CHILDREN All ages welcomed. DOGS Allowed in garden by arrangement. PRICES Per room B&B £75–£135, D,B&B (Wed–Sat) £135–£175.

BATH Somerset
Map 2:D1
DORIAN HOUSE, 1 Upper Oldfield Park, BA2 3JX. Tel 01225 426336, www.dorianhouse.co.uk. Away from the hordes of the city centre, retreat to this quiet, contemporary B&B owned by cellist Timothy Hugh and his wife, Kathryn. Robert and Lize Briers are the managers. An eclectic mix of Asian antiques, contemporary art and artefacts catches the eye in this Victorian stone house; there's seating in the garden for a sunny day. Modern bedrooms, named after the Hughs' favourite composers,

have a marble bathroom and plenty of inviting touches – a faux-fur throw or velour cushions, for instance, plus a capsule coffee machine in superior rooms. Some rooms, too, have 'fabulous views' over the Royal Crescent. Freshly baked croissants are among the options at breakfast. 10 mins' walk from the Roman Baths. BEDROOMS 13. 1 on ground floor. FACILITIES Lounge (open fire), conservatory breakfast room/music library, small, hilly garden, free Wi-Fi, in-room TV (Freeview), parking. BACKGROUND MUSIC Classical in breakfast room and lounge. CHILDREN All ages welcomed. PRICES Per room B&B £65–£195.

GRAYS, 9 Upper Oldfield Park, BA2 3JX. Tel 01225 403020, www.graysbath.co.uk. Wake to garden or city skyline views at this modern B&B in the Oldfield Park neighbourhood, a 15-minute uphill walk from the city centre. There's a peaceful atmosphere in the large Victorian villa, its airy rooms decorated in soothing shades. Each tasteful bedroom is well equipped with towelling robes and high-end bath products; the hospitality tray holds chocolate bars and cafetière coffee. Pick a room to suit: a spacious, light-filled ground-floor room has views across to the Royal Crescent; a cool and quirky attic room is styled in breezy blues. Breakfast in the conservatory has commendable provenance: bacon and sausages from Wiltshire pigs; eggs from a farm just outside the city. Help yourself to cereals, yogurts, fresh and dried fruit; meaty and vegetarian options are cooked to order. BEDROOMS 12. 4 on ground floor. OPEN All year except

Christmas. FACILITIES Lounge, breakfast room, small garden, free Wi-Fi, in-room TV (Freeview), parking. BACKGROUND MUSIC None. CHILDREN Not under 12. PRICES Per room B&B £110–£245. 2-night min. stay at weekends preferred.

HARINGTON'S HOTEL, 8–10 Queen Street, BA1 1HE. Tel 01225 461728, www.haringtonshotel.co.uk. A hotel with wit and character, this boutique pick is on a cobbled side street steps from the city's sights and shops. A trove of quirky touches (a stag-head wall hook, a rotary telephone) leads the way to cheerfully appointed bedrooms on the three upper floors. There's no lift, but friendly staff are on hand to help with luggage. Some rooms may be snug, but all are well equipped with bottled water, tea- and coffee-making facilities, oversized towels; a power shower. The coffee lounge has light meals and hot drinks; Bath ales are pulled and cocktails mixed in the bar. Escape the hustle by booking the private hot tub (extra charge) in the secluded courtyard. At breakfast, there are leaf teas and freshly squeezed orange juice; hot dishes include sausage and bacon butties and a stack of buttermilk pancakes. BEDROOMS 13, plus self-catering town house and apartments. FACILITIES Lounge, breakfast room, café/bar, free Wi-Fi, in-room TV, conference room, small courtyard, room service, secure parking nearby (£11 for 24 hours, advance booking required). BACKGROUND MUSIC In public areas. CHILDREN All ages welcomed in some rooms, by arrangement. PRICES Per room B&B £80–£218. 2-night min. stay on some weekends.

PARADISE HOUSE, 86–88 Holloway, BA2 4PX. Tel 01225 317723, www.paradise-house.co.uk. 'A good address', David and Annie Lanz's B&B stands in large gardens, a ten-minute walk, across the River Avon, from the city. It is liked for its 'charming, willing staff' and 'world-class breakfasts'. Floor-to-ceiling windows in the Georgian drawing room reveal views of the garden and the city beyond – admire the sights over afternoon tea or a pre-prandial drink. Bedrooms are individually decorated in period or modern style. Each has a 'most comfortable bed' and a 'powerful shower'; many have 'fine views' over the city. Breakfast includes vegetarian and vegan options. BEDROOMS 12. 4 on ground floor, 3 in annexe. OPEN All year except Christmas. FACILITIES Drawing room, breakfast room, free Wi-Fi, in-room TV (Freeview), ½-acre garden, parking. BACKGROUND MUSIC None. CHILDREN All ages welcomed. PRICES Per room B&B £150–£260. 2-night min. stay at weekends.

TASBURGH HOUSE, Warminster Road, BA2 6SH. Tel 01225 425096, www.tasburghhouse.co.uk. Susan Keeling's hilltop B&B stands above an expanse of terraced gardens leading down to the canal, with 'lovely views' over the city. It is managed by Grant Atkinson. The red-brick Victorian house has 'luxurious-feeling bedrooms' (some snug) stocked with biscuits, tea and coffee; good toiletries and large bath towels. Two are accessed via French doors off the garden terrace. 'Our first-floor room had windows on both sides – helpful and necessary, as we opened them to create a through draft during a warm spell.' An early supper menu is available most evenings; breakfast is taken in the 'pretty conservatory'. Follow the canal towpath into town – a 20-minute walk. 'I appreciated their directions to avoid traffic jams on the main road into Bath by taking a picturesque route via Bathampton and a toll bridge over the Avon.' BEDROOMS 15. OPEN All year except Christmas. FACILITIES Bar, dining room, conservatory, free Wi-Fi, in-room TV, 7-acre garden. BACKGROUND MUSIC All day in bar, dining room and conservatory. CHILDREN Not under 6. PRICES Per room B&B (continental) single £105, double from £149, D,B&B single £135, double from £209. Supper (6 pm–7.30 pm, Tues–Sat) £30, cooked breakfast from £7.50. 1-night bookings sometimes refused Sat.
25% DISCOUNT VOUCHERS

THREE ABBEY GREEN, 3 Abbey Green, BA1 1NW. Tel 01225 428558, www.threeabbeygreen.com. On a cobbled Georgian square as central as it gets, Nici and Alan Jones's prime-location B&B stretches across two town houses, with period features and well-considered touches in each. Every room is different: a small second-floor room has a window seat overlooking the courtyard; a spacious suite – the finest in the main house – has a four-poster bed and huge windows peering into the old plane tree in the square. Narrow, winding stairs lead to three more bedrooms in the Jane Austen wing. Sample home-made jams, marmalades and compotes at breakfast, along with plenty of cooked options. The friendly hosts are fonts of local information – starting, perhaps, with the monthly Sunday market of local growers, artisanal producers, makers and crafters on the doorstep. BEDROOMS 10. 3 in adjoining building, 2 on ground floor suitable for disabled, plus 1-bedroom apartment. OPEN All year except 24–26 Dec. FACILITIES Dining room, free Wi-Fi (computer and printer available), in-room TV (Freeview). BACKGROUND MUSIC In breakfast room. CHILDREN All ages welcomed. PRICES Per room B&B £90–£240. 2-night min. stay at weekends.

VILLA AT HENRIETTA PARK, Henrietta Road, BA2 6LX. Tel 01225 466329, www.villahenriettapark.co.uk. 'All very welcoming', the former Villa Magdala is today a 'nearly faultless' B&B where guests are greeted with a 'generous tea' on arrival. It is managed by 'delightful, obliging' Caroline Browning and Jean-Luc Bouchereau (with four-legged friend, Muttley) for Ian and Christa Taylor. Well-chosen antiques and interesting prints fill the Victorian villa; there's home-made shortbread and a flask of fresh milk in each of the individually decorated bedrooms. Afternoon tea may be taken in the 'pretty garden' in fine weather; for dinner, stroll to the Taylors' Abbey Hotel or No. 15 Great Pulteney (see main entries) – this 'quiet, leafy setting' is 'within walking distance of everything'. At breakfast: 'proper kippers' and locally sourced meats, plus freshly squeezed orange juice and complimentary Buck's Fizz for a morning treat. BEDROOMS 21. 2-room suite on lower ground floor. OPEN All year. FACILITIES Breakfast room, free Wi-Fi, in-room TV, small garden, terrace, parking ('a big plus'). BACKGROUND MUSIC 'Soft' radio in breakfast room.

CHILDREN All ages welcomed in some rooms. DOGS Allowed. PRICES Per room B&B from £140.

BAUGHURST Hampshire
Map 2:D2

THE WELLINGTON ARMS, Baughurst Road, RG26 5LP. Tel 0118 982 0110, www.thewellingtonarms.com. 'Bring any member of your family here and they would enjoy it.' Jason King and Simon Page's pub-with-rooms occupies an 18th-century former hunting lodge in the North Wessex Downs. Locals and visitors – and their family – come for the 'low-key', country-cosy atmosphere and Jason King's 'extraordinarily good' cooking. 'The sourcing is carefully done' in 'unfussy dishes' such as twice-baked Westcombe Cheddar soufflé, braised young leeks; Baughurst House roe deer and root vegetable pie. Simply stylish bedrooms have pleasing amenities: waffle bathrobes, a coffee machine, home-made biscuits. 'Our Cart House room had a vast bed. In the morning, we opened the curtains to quiet fields of grazing horses.' Breakfast, a 'comfortable, leisurely affair', includes fresh-laid eggs from the pub's free-range hens. BEDROOMS 4. 3 in converted outbuildings. FACILITIES Bar, restaurant (closed Sun eve), free Wi-Fi, in-room TV (Freeview), garden, parking. BACKGROUND MUSIC In bar and restaurant. CHILDREN All ages welcomed. DOGS Allowed. PRICES Per room B&B £110–£200. À la carte £35.

BEESANDS Devon
Map 1:E5

THE CRICKET INN, Kingsbridge, TQ7 2EN. Tel 01548 580215, www.thecricketinn.com. Well placed for walkers on the South West Coast Path, this 19th-century fisherman's inn faces the beach on Start Bay. 'Rightly popular' for its 'excellent pub grub' and comfy accommodation, it is run by Rachel and Nigel Heath, the owners, with a can-do attitude. 'It's a splendid place that caters for all – families, dogs, more sedate folk,' say Guide inspectors in 2017. Most of the simply decorated bedrooms have ocean views; all have tea- and coffee-making facilities and biscuits. Old photos of the area and its people hang in the bar. Sit here, in the large dining area or, in fine weather, by the sea wall for informal meals of 'wonderfully fresh sea bream, lemon sole and lobster'. Walk for miles from the door, towards Dartmouth or Salcombe. BEDROOMS 7. 4 in extension. FACILITIES Bar, restaurant (alfresco dining), private dining facilities, free Wi-Fi, in-room TV, parking. BACKGROUND MUSIC None. CHILDREN All ages welcomed. DOGS Allowed in bar. PRICES Per room B&B £110–£150, D,B&B £150–£190. 2-night min. stay preferred at weekends.

BELPER Derbyshire
Map 2:A2

DANNAH FARM, Bowmans Lane, Shottle, DE56 2DR. Tel 01773 550273, www.dannah.co.uk. Busy hens and the occasional tractor are as much traffic as there is to be found at this 'lovely', rustic B&B, on a 150-acre working farm in the Derbyshire Dales. Joan and Martin Slack are the 'charming, welcoming' owners. 'Spacious, beautifully clean bedrooms' each have their own style and character. There are split-level suites, four-poster rooms, a cottagey space for a family; if the fancy strikes for a spa bath on a private terrace, you have only to

ask. The Slacks can help with restaurant recommendations for dinner (and can arrange transport as well); alternatively, supper platters of meats, cheeses, fish, salads, home-made bread and puddings may be ordered in advance. 'Breakfast is delicious': 'plentiful' award-winning black pudding, locally made sausages, grilled Manx kippers, eggs from the farm's hens. 2 miles from town. BEDROOMS 8. 4 in adjoining converted barn, 3 on ground floor. OPEN All year except Christmas. FACILITIES 2 sitting rooms, dining room, meeting room, free Wi-Fi, in-room TV (Freeview), large walled garden, parking. BACKGROUND MUSIC None. CHILDREN All ages welcomed. PRICES Per room B&B £150–£295. Supper platter £18.95. 2-night min. stay on Fri, Sat.

BERWICK Sussex
Map 2:E4

GREEN OAK BARN, The English Wine Centre, Alfriston Road, BN26 5QS. Tel 01323 870164, www. englishwinecentre.co.uk. Connoisseurs and amateurs of every vintage find modern accommodation in Christine and Colin Munday's impressively reconstructed traditional Sussex barn, part of a complex including a restaurant and a wine shop. Mix and mingle, perhaps play a tune on the baby grand piano, in the open-plan lounge on the ground floor before heading to one of the smart bedrooms on the upper level. Comfortable, and hung with original art, rooms vary in size; one with a wet room is adapted for a wheelchair user. Order off the seasonal menu in the thatched Flint Barn restaurant; next day, ask the 'knowledgeable, helpful staff' for a recommendation in the wine

centre stocked with more than 150
English labels. Regular wine tastings.
5 miles from Glyndebourne. BEDROOMS
5. 1 suitable for disabled. OPEN All year
except Christmas, New Year. FACILITIES
Lift, bar/lounge, terrace, restaurant
(open lunch Tues–Sun, dinner Fri, Sat),
free Wi-Fi, in-room TV (Freeview),
civil wedding licence, function facilities,
wine shop, 3-acre garden with water
features. BACKGROUND MUSIC None.
CHILDREN All ages welcomed. PRICES Per
room B&B £140–£175. À la carte £28.

BEXHILL-ON-SEA Sussex
Map 2:E4
COAST, 58 Sea Road, TN40 1JP. Tel
01424 225260, www.coastbexhill.co.uk.
Guests receive a 'warm and friendly'
welcome from Piero and Lucia Mazzoni
at their 'impeccably decorated' B&B,
in an Edwardian villa close to the
sea. The house has a fresh, cool feel:
handsome wood floors, deep-red
wingback chairs against an otherwise-
minimalist palette. Some of the neat,
contemporary bedrooms may be snug,
but all have pampering touches such as
biscuits and a capsule coffee machine;
good toiletries; fluffy towels on a heated
towel rail; underfloor heating in the
bathroom. One room has a table and
chairs on its own balcony; another,
with light streaming in the large bay
window, is suitable for a family. There's
home-baked bread in the morning,
plus a choice of hot dishes including
pancakes with crème fraîche and maple
syrup. Convenient for shops, restaurants
and the station. BEDROOMS 5. FACILITIES
Lounge, breakfast room, free Wi-Fi,
in-room TV (Freeview), secure bicycle
storage. BACKGROUND MUSIC In breakfast
room. CHILDREN Not under 5. PRICES

Per room B&B single from £75, double
from £90.

BIBURY Gloucestershire
Map 3:E6
THE SWAN, GL7 5NW. Tel 01285
740695, www.cotswold-inns-hotels.
co.uk. Soak up the country calm on the
banks of the River Coln, where stands
this stylishly updated 17th-century
former coaching inn (Cotswold Inns
and Hotels). Perhaps the most beautiful
part of England – according to William
Morris – it's an ideal setting for gentle
rustic pursuits: gazing over gardens
and meadows, bird spotting, taking
afternoon tea by the river, perhaps a
spot of fishing at the local trout farm.
Well-appointed bedrooms, some ideal
for a family, may have a roll-top bath
or four-poster bed; standard amenities
include high-quality toiletries and a
capsule coffee machine. Cottage suites,
a short walk from the inn, have a
sitting room and a private garden.
Eat modern European dishes in the
brasserie; dine alfresco in fine weather.
BEDROOMS 22. Some on ground floor,
4 in garden cottages. OPEN All year.
FACILITIES Lift, lounge, bar (wood-
burning stove), brasserie, free Wi-Fi,
in-room TV (Freeview), ½-acre garden,
civil wedding licence, functions.
BACKGROUND MUSIC None. CHILDREN
All ages welcomed. DOGS Well-behaved
dogs allowed in bar, lounge, garden,
some bedrooms. PRICES Per room B&B
£190–£390. À la carte (brasserie) £35.

BILDESTON Suffolk
Map 2:C5
THE BILDESTON CROWN, 104 High
Street, IP7 7EB. Tel 01449 740510,
www.thebildestoncrown.com. Chef/

patron Chris Lee and his wife, Hayley, have returned to this 'handsomely restored' old coaching inn, this time as owners. The ochre-washed 15th-century building, on the main street of a lovely Suffolk village close to Lavenham, is brimming with colour and character inside. There are wonky beams, stripped floorboards, brick walls, massive fireplaces, and comfy seating in which to take it all in. The courtyard is ideal for alfresco food and drinks. There's a choice of regularly changing menus, each with 'high-standard cooking' in tune with the seasons: a Classic menu features pub favourites; the Select menu has more adventurous plates (perhaps fillet of hake, confit chicken wings, white asparagus, wild garlic, morels). Bedrooms veer between country simplicity and 'statement' decadence, but the amenities are well considered across the board: bathrobes, botanical-extract toiletries, a portable fan, a wide-screen TV. BEDROOMS 12. OPEN All year, no accommodation on Christmas Day. FACILITIES Lift, bar, lounge, restaurant, free Wi-Fi, in-room TV, courtyard, parking. BACKGROUND MUSIC In restaurant in evening. CHILDREN All ages welcomed. PRICES Per room B&B from £90. À la carte £32.

BIRMINGHAM Warwickshire
Map 2:B2
THE HIGH FIELD TOWN HOUSE, 23 Highfield Road, Edgbaston, B15 3DP. Tel 0121 647 6466, www.highfieldtownhouse.co.uk. In foodie Edgbaston – Michelin-starred Simpsons is a minute down the road – this Victorian villa has been voguishly refurbished with a 'boutique country house' feel. Well-chosen antiques and retro furnishings fill the creatively decorated bedrooms (some large enough to suit a family). Complimentary coffees and newspapers are available in the ground-floor sitting room; pour yourself something stronger from the honesty bar if you fancy. Next door, the sister gastropub has a wide selection of real ales, cocktails and wines to match its seasonal British menu. Breakfast has plenty of interesting choices, including coconut milk porridge, American pancakes and veggie options. Five mins from the city centre; on-street parking is by the garden and suntrap terrace. BEDROOMS 12. Some suitable for disabled. OPEN All year except 24–25 Dec. FACILITIES Sitting room, bar and restaurant in adjacent building, free Wi-Fi, in-room TV (Freeview), private dining, terrace, garden, parking. BACKGROUND MUSIC In sitting room. CHILDREN All ages welcomed. PRICES Per room B&B £120–£160. À la carte £35.

BISHOP'S CASTLE Shropshire
Map 3:C4
THE CASTLE HOTEL, Market Square, SY9 5BN. Tel 01588 638403, www.thecastlehotelbishopscastle.co.uk. Built on a castle bailey, this 'superbly located', good-value hotel is liked for its 'delightful staff', 'well-appointed rooms', 'first-rate food' and 'easy access' to walking routes. 'Our dog was given the loveliest of welcomes, too,' says a guest in 2017. In an 'interesting town' surrounded by hill-walking country, the 300-year-old building is run with 'genuine warmth' by Henry and Rebecca Hunter. (It is joint-owned with Henry Hunter's parents, who own Pen-y-Dyffryn, Oswestry – see main entry.) Individually styled bedrooms

of various sizes are up a Georgian staircase. 'The box of goodies and other necessities in the room was a really nice touch.' Order bistro-style dishes in the bar or 'handsome' oak-panelled restaurant; eat in the enclosed garden on a fine day. Breakfast is 'particularly good'. BEDROOMS 13. OPEN All year except Christmas Day. FACILITIES 3 bar areas, dining room, free Wi-Fi, in-room TV (Freeview), in-room spa treatments, patio, terrace, garden with fish pond, parking, bicycle storage, mud room. BACKGROUND MUSIC In bar area. CHILDREN All ages welcomed. DOGS Allowed in bedrooms, bar, not in restaurant. PRICES Per room B&B £105–£170, D,B&B £160–£225.

25% DISCOUNT VOUCHERS

BISHOP'S TACHBROOK
Warwickshire
Map 2:B2

MALLORY COURT, Harbury Lane, CV33 9QB. Tel 01926 330214, www.mallory.co.uk. In 'lovely, well-manicured gardens' with a zigzagging mini-maze, this 'luxurious' English manor house hotel has a reputation for its 'relaxing atmosphere' and 'willing staff'. Sarah Barker is the long-serving manager. A guest this year praised the 'constant facelifts': a garden-view spa has been added, plus several modern bedrooms in the newly refurbished Orchard House. These rooms, along with ones in the main house and Knights Suite annexe, are 'well equipped' with bathrobes and fine toiletries; beds are turned down in the evening. There's a choice of eating options: an 'excellent' daily-changing menu in the oak-panelled restaurant; 'perfectly cooked' informal fare in the 'light, stylish' brasserie. 'Beautifully situated' for Warwick Castle and Stratford-upon-Avon. BEDROOMS 43. 11 in Knight's Suite, 12 in Orchard House, some suitable for disabled. FACILITIES Lift, 2 lounges, brasserie (Thurs jazz nights, closed Sun eve), restaurant, free Wi-Fi, in-room TV, civil wedding licence, function facilities, spa (indoor and outdoor swimming pools, fitness suite, treatment rooms), terrace, garden, tennis court, croquet. BACKGROUND MUSIC In public rooms. CHILDREN All ages welcomed. PRICES Per room B&B from £189. Set dinner £49.50.

BISHOPSTONE Wiltshire
Map 3:E6

HELEN BROWNING'S ROYAL OAK, Cues Lane, SN6 8PP. Tel 01793 790481, helenbrowningsorganic.co.uk. 'Pigs, pies, pints and pillows' – find it all at this village dining pub-with-rooms, on a working organic farm run by food ethics pioneer Helen Browning. The well-established pub, managed by Tim Finney for Arkell's Brewery, is a quirky, affable spot (the annual International Pig Racing Festival is held here). It is well liked for the real ales, organic wines and cordials, and daily-changing menus using meat from the farm and produce from local villagers. Check in here, then stroll through the garden to recently refurbished bedrooms set around a sunny courtyard. Each is made inviting with a woollen throw on the bed, a coffee machine, maybe a double-ended bath. Walk the Ridgeway, then return to 'wallow in' the residents' lounge stocked with books, music and hot drinks. 7 miles E of Swindon. BEDROOMS 12. All in annexe, 100 metres from pub. OPEN All year. FACILITIES Lounge, pub, meeting/function room, free Wi-Fi, in-room TV

(Freeview), ½-acre garden (rope swing, Wendy house, 'flighty hens'), parking. BACKGROUND MUSIC None. CHILDREN All ages welcomed. DOGS Allowed in 2 bedrooms, public rooms. PRICES Per room B&B £85–£150. À la carte £29. **25% DISCOUNT VOUCHERS**

BLACKBURN Lancashire
Map 4:D3

MILLSTONE AT MELLOR, Church Lane, Mellor, BB2 7JR. Tel 01254 813333, www.millstonehotel.co.uk. 'A lively spot', this 'friendly' stone-built pub-with-rooms (Thwaites Inns of Character) sits in a rural village in the Ribble valley. 'Confident, well-prepared' dishes, perhaps maple-glazed crispy belly pork, spiced red cabbage, Lancashire cheese potato, cider and sage, are 'clearly the pub's main attraction' – ask for a tasting board of cask ales to match. Country-style bedrooms are all different, but each is provided with fresh milk, tea- and coffee-making facilities, home-made biscuits, 'fleecy bathrobes and a good shower'. 'Our reasonably sized room faced the road, but it wasn't too noisy.' Breakfast is served till 10 am at the weekend. BEDROOMS 23. FACILITIES Residents' lounge, bar, restaurant, free Wi-Fi, in-room TV, terrace, parking. BACKGROUND MUSIC Radio at breakfast 'but we were able to turn it down'. CHILDREN All ages welcomed. PRICES Per room B&B single £69–£109, double £75–£115. À la carte £30.

BLACKPOOL Lancashire
Map 4:D2

NUMBER ONE ST LUKE'S, 1 St Luke's Road, South Shore, FY4 2EL. Tel 01253 343901, www.numberoneblackpool.com.

Mark and Claire Smith's South Shore B&B is within easy reach of the promenade in this popular seaside resort. Contemporary bedrooms, each with a king-size bed, are kitted out with up-to-date technology including a large TV screen and a video games console. Roam Blackpool's streets, then come back to a relaxing spa bath; bathrooms also have a power shower, wall-mounted TV and music system. Lighter dishes at breakfast are an alternative to the 'full Blackpool'. A large conservatory overlooks the garden. 2 miles from town centre. The Smiths also own Number One South Beach (see next entry). BEDROOMS 3. FACILITIES Dining room, conservatory, free Wi-Fi, in-room TV (Freeview), garden (putting green, hot tub), parking, free POD Point for charging electric vehicles. BACKGROUND MUSIC None. CHILDREN Not under 4. PRICES Per room B&B from £110.

NUMBER ONE SOUTH BEACH, 4 Harrowside West, FY4 1NW. Tel 01253 343900, www.numberonesouthbeach. com. Minutes from Blackpool's Pleasure Beach, this modern hotel is owned by Janet and Graham Oxley and Claire and Mark Smith (see Number One St Luke's, previous entry). Individually decorated bedrooms – some with a seaview balcony – are bang up to date with technological touches: remote-controlled lighting; a waterproof TV by the spa bath. In the games room, an indoor golf simulator lets guests practise their swing. Local produce leads the way on the breakfast menu. Ask the clued-in owners for tips about the town. BEDROOMS 14. Some suitable for disabled. OPEN All year except 26–31 Dec. FACILITIES Lift, lounge (oversized plasma

TV), bar, restaurant, games room, free Wi-Fi, in-room TV (Freeview), meeting/conference facilities, parking. BACKGROUND MUSIC Quiet classical music in bar and lounge. CHILDREN Not under 5. PRICES Per room B&B £139–£175. À la carte £28. 2-night min. stay at weekends in high season.

BOURNEMOUTH Dorset
Map 2:E2
THE GREEN HOUSE, 4 Grove Road, BH1 3AX. Tel 01202 498900, www. thegreenhousehotel.com. Close to the seafront, this handsome Victorian villa takes a practise-what-you-preach approach to environmental consciousness. Rescued from dereliction, the hotel was restored with an eye on green issues: sustainability inspires everything from the eco paints and organic bedlinen to the solar panels and rooftop beehives. The result is cool and contemporary. Neat bedrooms vary in size and facilities; the best have a reclaimed Victorian roll-top bath, robes and slippers. In the Arbor restaurant, and on the terrace in clement weather, chef Andy Hilton's unfussy modern dishes prioritise organic, Fairtrade and locally sourced ingredients. Typical offerings: south coast crab tortellini, cauliflower 'couscous'; slow-roasted Wiltshire pork ribeye, warm potato salad, fennel slaw. BEDROOMS 32. 1 suitable for disabled, 5 master doubles have an open-plan bathroom. FACILITIES Lift, bar, restaurant, free Wi-Fi, in-room TV (Freeview), civil wedding licence, terrace, parking. BACKGROUND MUSIC In public areas. CHILDREN All ages welcomed. PRICES Per room B&B from £129, D,B&B from £159.

URBAN BEACH, 23 Argyll Road, BH5 1EB. Tel 01202 301509, www. urbanbeach.co.uk. There's a relaxed atmosphere at Mark Cribb's friendly small hotel, within a saunter of the beach and Boscombe Pier. Modern bedrooms come in a variety of configurations: choose among snug singles, roomy doubles and a spacious bay-windowed room that can accommodate a family. Each room has tea- and coffee-making facilities and good toiletries. A thoughtful bonus: helpful amenities – umbrellas, wellies, phone chargers – are available to borrow. Food is available from noon till late in the bar/bistro; lively sister restaurant, Urban Reef, on the promenade, is a fun alternative. Breakfast, as laid-back as a beach holiday, is served until 11.30 am – take that breakfast marmalade martini out on the terrace while the sun creeps into the sky. 1 mile E of the town centre. BEDROOMS 12. FACILITIES Bar/bistro, free Wi-Fi, in-room TV, heated covered deck, complimentary use of local leisure club, limited on-site parking, free street parking. BACKGROUND MUSIC In public areas, occasional live guitar music. CHILDREN All ages welcomed (toys, activities). PRICES Per room B&B single £72, double £100–£180. À la carte £32. 2-night min. stay at weekends.

BOWNESS-ON-WINDERMERE
Cumbria
Map 4: inset C2
LINDETH HOWE, Lindeth Drive, Longtail Hill, LA23 3JF. Tel 01539 445759, www.lindeth-howe.co.uk. Let the hillside setting and leafy copses around this Victorian country house capture the imagination – they inspired

Beatrice Potter to pen the adventures of her many woodland creatures. Some of the well-appointed bedrooms have views of Lake Windermere past the trees and sweeping lawns; two, on the ground floor, have direct access to the garden. Books and board games in the sitting room are just the ticket on rainy days. In good weather, take afternoon tea on the sun terrace or strike out further afield: good walks start from the door. Come evening, modern British dishes in the candlelit dining room might include salad of goat's cheese pearls, beetroot, granola; lamb cutlet and rump, wild forest mushrooms, smoked celery cream fondant. BEDROOMS 34. 2 suitable for disabled. OPEN All year. FACILITIES Sitting room, library, lounge bar, restaurant, free Wi-Fi, in-room TV (Freeview), civil wedding licence, sun terrace, 6-acre grounds, indoor swimming pool, sauna, fitness room, treatment room, electric car charging point, electric bicycles for hire. BACKGROUND MUSIC In bar and restaurant, live piano music Sat eve. CHILDREN All ages welcomed, no under-7s in restaurant at night (children's high tea 5 pm–6.30 pm). DOGS Allowed in some bedrooms, not in public rooms. PRICES Per room B&B from £180, D,B&B from £276. À la carte £35–£55.

THE RYEBECK, Lyth Valley Road, LA23 3JP. Tel 015394 88195, www.ryebeck. com. There's a 'homely atmosphere' and 'a sense of cosy welcome' at this unpretentious, gabled Edwardian country house overlooking Lake Windermere and Coniston Fells. The former Fayrer Garden hotel, it is today owned by Andrew Wildsmith, whose Hipping Hall, Cowan Bridge,

and Forest Side, Grasmere (see main entries), are well liked by Guide readers. Ask for one of the refurbished bedrooms; some have a private patio or glorious lake views. All rooms come equipped with home-made biscuits, tea and coffee from a local merchant, natural Cumbria-made toiletries. Lakeland produce informs the 'adventurous, well-presented dishes', served in a modern, glass-walled restaurant – try for a table overlooking the lake. Relax on the garden terrace on fine days, or borrow OS maps for walks from the door. 1 mile from town. BEDROOMS 24. OPEN All year. FACILITIES Bar, lounge, restaurant, free Wi-Fi, in-room TV (Freeview), civil wedding licence, 5-acre garden and grounds, croquet, terrace, parking, bicycle storage. BACKGROUND MUSIC None. CHILDREN All ages welcomed (games). DOGS Allowed in 4 bedrooms with garden access, public rooms 'as long as no food is being served'. PRICES Per room B&B £135–£275, D,B&B £210–£350. À la carte £40.

BRADFORD-ON-AVON Wiltshire Map 2:D1

TIMBRELL'S YARD, 49 Saint Margaret's Street, BA15 1DE. Tel 01225 869492, www.timbrellsyard.com. 'Ideal for the young and the young at heart', this riverside bar/restaurant-with-rooms near the medieval bridge is a popular spot in a 'delightful little town'. The wine bar has a 'great selection' of drinks and 'interesting tapas'. In the dining areas ('the converted-warehouse style gives it a fun feel'), 'adventurous items' on the menu ('perhaps a little too adventurous') might include smoked lamb scrumpets, spring remoulade, radish. Each of the modish bedrooms has its own character: choose between contemporary split-level suites with 'steep, polished steps', or cosy beamed bedrooms in the oldest part of the Grade II listed building. Toast your own bread and boil your own eggs off the rustic breakfast buffet. Part of the small Stay Original Company; see also The Swan, Wedmore, and The White Hart, Somerton (Shortlist entries). BEDROOMS 17. OPEN All year. FACILITIES Bar, restaurant, private dining room, free Wi-Fi, in-room TV (Freeview), terrace, train station close by. BACKGROUND MUSIC 'To suit time and ambience'. CHILDREN All ages welcomed. DOGS Allowed in some bedrooms. PRICES Per room B&B from £95, D,B&B from £127. À la carte £30.

WIDBROOK GRANGE, Widbrook, BA15 1UH. Tel 01225 864750, www. widbrookgrange.com. Stay on an original Georgian model farm in extensive grounds and gardens strewn with milk churns, a vintage tractor and a hay cart. This recently restored farmhouse on the outskirts of the town embraces its rustic roots: the hotel is playfully decorated with interesting objects and antiques; there are mismatched wingback armchairs and oriental rugs in the cosy, stone-floored snug. Individually decorated bedrooms in the main house and converted stable block have a contemporary country feel in their distressed-wood furnishings and botanical prints. Pick a pre-prandial drink from a collection of 50 gins and whiskies in the bar before sitting down to a modern farmhouse dinner in the restaurant. The Boathouse, a sister pub, is a stroll across the road.

BEDROOMS 19. Some in courtyard, some suitable for disabled. FACILITIES Bar, snug, restaurant, free Wi-Fi, in-room TV (Freeview), civil wedding licence, function facilities, 11-acre grounds, 11-metre indoor heated swimming pool, gym, giant chess, parking. CHILDREN All ages welcomed. DOGS Allowed in courtyard bedrooms. PRICES Per room B&B from £185. À la carte £32.

BRANSCOMBE Devon
Map 1:C5
THE MASON'S ARMS, EX12 3DJ. Tel 01297 680300, www.masonsarms.co.uk. In a village on the Jurassic coast, step through the ivy-wrapped threshold of this 14th-century former cider house and into a popular pub-with-rooms. Alison Ede manages for St Austell Brewery Hotels & Inns. The pub's real ales and 'cosy bar' (slate floors, stone walls, huge log fireplace) attract visitors to the 'delightful spot'; walkers off the South West Coast Path fuel up on the 'fresh, excellent cooking' – home-made chicken liver pâté, red onion marmalade, perhaps, or St Austell ale–battered fish, chunky chips, mushy peas. 'Comfortable bedrooms' in modern country style are in the main building and thatch-roofed garden cottages. Kick-start the day with the inn's custom blend of Fairtrade coffee at breakfast. 10 mins' walk to a secluded shingle beach. BEDROOMS 27. 14 in cottages, some suitable for disabled. FACILITIES Bar, restaurant, free Wi-Fi (in main bar), in-room TV, garden with outdoor seating. BACKGROUND MUSIC None. CHILDREN All ages welcomed. DOGS Allowed in some cottages (£10 per night). PRICES Per room B&B from £90. À la carte £30.

BRIGHTON Sussex
Map 2:E4

FIVE, 5 New Steine, BN2 1PB. Tel
01273 686547, www.fivehotel.com.
Caroline and Simon Heath's modern
B&B occupies a handsome Regency
town house on a garden square, ideally
located for exploring the beach and
the famous pier. Many of the bright,
well-equipped bedrooms (some snug)
have sea views through sash windows;
all are supplied with toiletries, and
tea- and coffee-making facilities. Pick
the hour and a breakfast picnic hamper
containing muffins, cereal, yogurts,
fruit and juice appears at the door. For
a special occasion, request extras such
as champagne and breakfast cakes – the
hosts are happy to oblige. Alternatively,
opt for a room-only rate and sample
breakfast or brunch in one of the many
cafés nearby. BEDROOMS 9. FACILITIES
Free Wi-Fi, in-room TV (Freeview),
DVD library, bicycle storage. CHILDREN
Not under 5. PRICES Per person B&B
£45–£70. 2-night min. stay at weekends.

PASKINS, 18–19 Charlotte Street, BN2
1AG. Tel 01273 601203, www.paskins.
co.uk. Susan and Roger Marlowe
pioneered sustainability practices
at their twin 19th-century stucco
houses in Kemp Town long before
such things became trendy. Check
in at the Art Nouveau reception of
this characterful B&B within the East
Cliff conservation area: upstairs are
'comfortable', colourful, eclectically
decorated bedrooms, their bathroom
stocked with certified cruelty-free
toiletries. In the morning, breakfast
in the Art Deco dining room has an
imaginative, international flair. Try
Cajun vegan sausages; fritters with

mango sauce; simple duck eggs with
soldiers; Sussex-landed fishy specials –
all made with organic, locally sourced
produce. BEDROOMS 19. FACILITIES
Lounge, breakfast room, free Wi-Fi,
parking vouchers (£10 for 24 hours).
BACKGROUND MUSIC None. CHILDREN
All ages welcomed. DOGS Allowed
(not unattended) in some bedrooms by
arrangement. PRICES Per person B&B
£50–£75. Discounts for Vegetarian
Society, Vegan Society and Amnesty
International members.

A ROOM WITH A VIEW, 41 Marine
Parade, BN2 1PE. Tel 01273 682885,
www.aroomwithaviewbrighton.com.
'Small but so comfortable', Stephen
Bull's 'cheerful, friendly' Kemp Town
B&B is steps from the beach. The style
is pleasingly modern: pared-down,
unfussy, with pictures of the town by
local artists. Almost every bedroom at
the 'immaculately presented' Regency
house looks over the sea and down
to Palace Pier. 'Light, airy and clean',
each room has a 'comfy bed' and many
'thoughtful touches' (ear plugs in the
bedside drawer, biscuits and a capsule
coffee machine, 'fluffy towels and
dressing gowns'). Some rooms have a
walk-in wet room, others, a freestanding
bath in the bathroom. Pick from an
'excellent' breakfast menu: blueberry
pancakes; 'highly recommended
double eggs Benedict'. All diets are
catered for. The Lanes, restaurants
and shops are within walking distance.
On-site parking is a bonus. BEDROOMS
9. FACILITIES Lounge, breakfast room,
free Wi-Fi, in-room TV, parking.
BACKGROUND MUSIC 'Gentle' in breakfast
room. CHILDREN Older children, able to
take their own room, welcomed. PRICES

Per room B&B single from £79, double
£135–£295.

BRISTOL
Map 1:B6
BACKWELL HOUSE, Farleigh Road,
BS48 3QA. Tel 0117 325 1110, www.
backwellhouse.co.uk. Reclaimed
timber, vintage finds and clever design
reinventions complement existing
grand features at Guy Williams's wittily
revamped Georgian mellow stone
mansion, a 15-minute drive from the
city. Distinctive bedrooms, handsome in
their eclectic country-house style, have
views of woodland or rolling hills. One
room has a bathroom sink made from
an old suitcase; another, a reconditioned
copper or enamel bathtub on a dais in
the room. A succinct modern British
menu in the restaurant makes use of
produce from the surrounding area, as
well as honey from the house's bees, and
home-grown vegetables and herbs. Soak
in the outdoor hot tub; roam the walled
gardens and 19th-century greenhouse.
A heated outdoor swimming pool
was in the works as the Guide went
to press. 8 miles from Bristol; well
located for the airport. BEDROOMS
9. OPEN All year except Christmas.
FACILITIES Bar, lounge, breakfast room,
restaurant (closed Sun eve, Mon, Tues),
conservatory, meeting room/snug,
free Wi-Fi, in-room TV (Freeview),
civil wedding licence, cinema room,
ornamental walled garden, heated
outdoor swimming pool, parking.
BACKGROUND MUSIC In public areas.
CHILDREN Not under 12. DOGS Allowed
in public rooms, not in bedrooms
(kennel accommodation provided).
PRICES Per room B&B £95–£245. Set
dinner £24.50–£30.

BROADWAY Worcestershire
Map 3:D6
THE OLIVE BRANCH, 78 High Street,
WR12 7AJ. Tel 01386 853440, www.
theolivebranch-broadway.com. 'I cannot
think how this beautifully appointed
and run B&B could be bettered,' says a
Guide reader in 2017. 'Helpful owners'
Pam and David Talboys – 'hospitality
itself' – have welcomed guests to this
stone house overlooking the High
Street of the Cotswold village since
1961. Traditional, country cottage-
style bedrooms have 'a comfy bed,
beautiful linen and towels, decent
cupboard space and a small but lavishly
provisioned bathroom'; some rooms
can accommodate a family. The 'large,
comfortable', homely sitting room has
an honesty bar – carry a drink into
the garden in good weather. 'First-
rate breakfasts', with home-made
breads, jams and cakes, and much
local produce, are taken in the stone-
flagged front parlour facing the street.
'Astonishingly affordable for the area.'
BEDROOMS 8. Some on ground floor.
FACILITIES Lounge, breakfast room,
free Wi-Fi, in-room TV, garden, 'easy
parking'. CHILDREN All ages welcomed.
PRICES Per room B&B single from £75,
double from £104. 2-night min. stay
at weekends.

BROCKENHURST Hampshire
Map 2:E2
DAISYBANK COTTAGE, Sway Road,
The New Forest, SO42 7SG. Tel
01590 622086, www.bedandbreakfast-
newforest.co.uk. 'Perfect hosts' Ciaran
and Cheryl Maher make things personal
at their Arts and Crafts B&B in the New
Forest. Enjoy home-made cupcakes on
arrival, wellingtons for muddy walks,

pick-me-ups from a well-stocked honesty bar, DVDs for a quiet night in. Spread across the main house and a prettily converted garden cottage, the 'spacious, beautifully decorated' bedrooms have a wide bed, plantation shutters and a well-designed bathroom or wet room. Each room is 'fully equipped with everything you could possibly want', from a capsule coffee machine to local bath products. Some cottage suites have their own patio with access to the garden. Before retiring for the night, place your breakfast order in the flowerpot outside your room; awake to a 'fantastic' Aga-fresh full Irish or New Forest breakfast. 10 mins' walk from the village. BEDROOMS 8. All on ground floor, plus 1-bed shepherd's hut available Apr–Sept. OPEN All year except 1 week over Christmas. FACILITIES 2 sitting rooms, breakfast room, free Wi-Fi, in-room TV (Freeview), ½-acre garden, secure parking. BACKGROUND MUSIC None. CHILDREN Not under 10. PRICES Per room B&B £110–£150. 2-night min. stay preferred.
25% DISCOUNT VOUCHERS

BROOK Hampshire
Map 2:E2
THE BELL INN, Roger Penny Way, nr Lyndhurst, SO43 7HE. Tel 023 8081 2214, www.bellinn-newforest.co.uk. Wild horses and donkeys nose around on the road outside this 18th-century coaching inn, in a quiet hamlet within the New Forest. The red-brick building has been in owner Robert Crosthwaite Eyre's family since 1782; today, updated in modern rustic style, it is 'great for a relaxed weekend away'. The flagstoned bar has an inglenook fireplace and cosy

corners with comfy sofas. 'Simply, but nicely, decorated bedrooms' vary in size and character; some may have a lounge area, beams or a sloping ceiling. (Some, too, may have road noise when the windows are open.) Eat in the bar – find a table by the large windows overlooking 'nice flowerbeds' – or in the farmhouse-style dining room. Served by 'friendly staff', pub classics and 'more gourmet dishes' use ingredients from local suppliers and wild food foraged from the forest. Ideal for golfers, who come for the 18-hole course next door. BEDROOMS 28. 8 on ground floor. OPEN All year. FACILITIES Bar (local gins), lounge, dining room, free Wi-Fi, in-room TV (Freeview), civil wedding licence, meeting rooms, garden (tables and seating, boules, giant Connect 4 and chess), patio, parking. BACKGROUND MUSIC 'Subtle' in public areas. CHILDREN All ages welcomed. DOGS Allowed in some bedrooms, bar, not in dining room. PRICES Per room B&B single from £79, double £99–£179, D,B&B £109–£229. À la carte £32.

BUCKDEN Cambridgeshire
Map 2:B4
THE GEORGE, High Street, PE19 5XA. Tel 01480 812300, www.thegeorgebuckden.com. Locals and visitors flock to the 'popular, buzzing restaurant' of this 19th-century coaching inn in a 'quaint village' – 'it's a real highlight'. Owned by Anne and Richard Furbank, the hotel has 'obliging staff', traditional bedrooms, and a 'family-friendly brasserie' where chef El Akil Benaissa turns out 'superb' modern British dishes. Typical offerings: smoked chicken and walnut terrine, pickled vegetables; pan-fried

Gressingham duck breast, potato and carrot rösti. Each bedroom ('a little old fashioned') is named after a famous George – Eliot, Gershwin, Stephenson etc. 'My room had a clean, modern bathroom and a comfortable bed; I had a nice night's sleep.' An appreciated touch: a help-yourself bowl of fresh fruit in the corridor. Try 'perfectly poached eggs' at breakfast; the coffee is 'excellent'. BEDROOMS 12. 3 suitable for disabled. OPEN All year except 25–26 Dec evenings, 1 Jan. FACILITIES Lift, bar, lounge, restaurant, private dining rooms, free Wi-Fi, in-room TV (Freeview), civil wedding licence, courtyard. BACKGROUND MUSIC In public areas. CHILDREN All ages welcomed. PRICES Per room B&B £95–£150, D,B&B £155–£180. À la carte £35.

BUCKFASTLEIGH Devon
Map 1:D4
KILBURY MANOR, Colston Road, TQ11 0LN. Tel 01364 644079, www.kilburymanor.co.uk. A characterful 17th-century longhouse in the Devonshire countryside is home to Julia and Martin Blundell's tranquil B&B. In the main house and converted barn, homely bedrooms, some traditionally decorated, look out over acres of gardens and pasture. Each room is provided with Fairtrade tea, coffee and hot chocolate. Greet the day with an interesting breakfast menu that includes home-made marmalade, conserves and compotes (specify dietary requirements when booking), then wander across the meadow to the River Dart. The hosts have dining recommendations in the evening. 1 mile from town; the tumbling rivers, open moorland and wooded gorges of Dartmoor national

park are within easy reach. BEDROOMS 4. 2 in converted stone barn across the courtyard, plus one 1-bedroom cottage. OPEN All year. FACILITIES Breakfast room (wood-burning stove), free Wi-Fi, in-room TV (Freeview), garden, courtyard (outdoor seating), bicycle and canoe storage. BACKGROUND MUSIC None. CHILDREN Not under 8. PRICES Per room B&B single from £65, double £80–£99. 2-night min. Apr–Sept. Credit cards not accepted.

BURFORD Oxfordshire
Map 3:D6
BAY TREE HOTEL, Sheep Street, OX18 4LW. Tel 01993 822791, www.cotswold-inns-hotels.co.uk/the-bay-tree-hotel. In a Cotswold town on the River Windrush, duck under the wisteria-draped arch of this well-updated hotel and enter a building rife with history. Formed from a row of 17th-century honey-stone houses, the hotel has restored flagstone floors, ancient beams, deep armchairs and big open fireplaces just right for taking afternoon tea by. It is managed by Mark Jelinek for Cotswold Inns and Hotels. Up the galleried staircase, colourful checks and jaunty tweeds give the variously sized bedrooms plenty of contemporary country charm. Two of the best rooms have a log burner or open fire; pooch-friendly rooms have direct outdoor access. There are board games, local ales and ciders and a menu of nibbles and light meals in the bar. In the restaurant, settle into sunlit lunches and dinners by candlelight. BEDROOMS 21. 2 adjoining garden rooms on ground floor. OPEN All year. FACILITIES Library, bar, restaurant, free Wi-Fi, in-room TV (Freeview), civil wedding licence,

function facilities, patio (alfresco dining), walled garden (croquet). BACKGROUND MUSIC None. CHILDREN All ages welcomed. DOGS Well-behaved dogs allowed in bedrooms and public rooms. PRICES Per room B&B from £149, D,B&B from £213.

BURY ST EDMUNDS Suffolk
Map 2:B5

THE NORTHGATE, Northgate Street, IP33 1HP. Tel 01284 339604, www. thenorthgate.com. An overhaul in 2016 by the small Chestnut Inns group has re-energised this large, red-brick Victorian hotel on a road leading to town. Spacious bedrooms are well decorated in a soothing, muted palette; modern bathrooms have stylishly retro fittings. Each room is different: one has a sofa in a bay window overlooking the garden; another has a walk-in wardrobe; yet another, a family suite, sleeps four. Rooms facing the garden are quietest. Order a cocktail in the fashionably moody bar before sitting down to ambitious offerings (perhaps sea trout, crispy grapes, razor clams) in the handsome restaurant. To watch the kitchen team at work, book the backstage Chef's Table for a tasting menu. In good weather, the large, south-facing terrace is the place to eat, drink and make merry. Sister outfit The Packhorse Inn is in Newmarket (see main entry). BEDROOMS 9. FACILITIES Bar, restaurant, private function room, free Wi-Fi, in-room TV (Freeview), garden, terrace, parking. BACKGROUND MUSIC In public areas. CHILDREN All ages welcomed. DOGS Allowed on terrace, not in house. PRICES Per room B&B from £150. Tasting menu £75, à la carte £40.

CAMBRIDGE Cambridgeshire
Map 2:B4

THE GONVILLE HOTEL, Gonville Place, CB1 1LY. Tel 01223 366611, www. gonvillehotel.co.uk. Colleges, shops and the Fitzwilliam Museum are all within easy reach of this large, family-owned hotel overlooking the green space of Parker's Piece. Cheerfully decorated public spaces and willing staff create a zesty ambience. There are 'fresh and tasty' snacks and meals to be had in the smart Atrium brasserie; in Cotto, the modern restaurant next door, fine dining menus are cooked by chef Hans Schweitzer (advance booking essential). Sleek, air-conditioned bedrooms ('our bathroom was compact') are equipped with tea- and coffee-making facilities, all-natural toiletries and an iPad for accessing hotel information; beds are turned down in the evening. (Rooms at the rear are quietest.) Breakfast brings an 'enormous buffet' and hot dishes cooked to order. On-site parking (charged) is a bonus. BEDROOMS 84. Some on ground floor. OPEN All year. FACILITIES Bar, lounge, 2 restaurants (Cotto open Tues eve–Sat eve), free Wi-Fi, in-room TV (Freeview), bicycles to borrow. BACKGROUND MUSIC In public areas. CHILDREN All ages welcomed. DOGS Allowed in reception area, some bedrooms. PRICES Per room B&B from £200. Set dinner (Cotto) £70–£75, à la carte (Atrium brasserie) £50.

QUY MILL HOTEL & SPA, Church Road, Stow-cum-Quy, CB25 9AF. Tel 01223 293383, www.cambridgequymill. co.uk. Within a 20-minute drive of the city centre, this modern spa hotel occupies a 19th-century water mill in large, landscaped gardens. Most of the contemporary bedrooms (some with a private patio) are in converted barns across the courtyard; snugger rooms are in the original mill building, with views over the grounds or river. Some rooms can accommodate an extra bed for a child. In the garden-facing Mill House restaurant, or on the patio in good weather, locally sourced ingredients are put to good use in such modern British and European dishes as soy-glazed chicken, sautéed curly kale, roast carrots, fondant potato. Lighter meals and sandwiches are available all day in the lounge/bar – plus a selection of more than 50 malt whiskies to round off the evening. 5 miles NE of city centre, off the A14; handy for the airport. BEDROOMS 51. Many on ground floor, 1 suitable for disabled. OPEN All year except Christmas Day. FACILITIES Bar/lounge, restaurant, free Wi-Fi, in-room TV (Freeview), civil wedding licence, conference facilities, leisure centre (gym, sauna, steam room, 12-metre heated indoor swimming pool), 2-acre grounds (garden, woodland walk), parking. BACKGROUND MUSIC In public areas. CHILDREN All ages welcomed (extra bed £20 per night). PRICES Per room B&B £175–£255, D,B&B £230–£275. **25% DISCOUNT VOUCHERS**

THE VARSITY HOTEL & SPA, 24 Thompson's Lane, off Bridge Street, CB5 8AQ. Tel 01223 306030, www. thevarsityhotel.co.uk. 'Helpful staff' stand out at this modern hotel, in a 'very convenient location' on the River Cam. The university's presence is felt throughout: graduating categories of rooms are named after the different colleges; portraits of famed alumni gaze down at visitors. Order a cocktail on the roof terrace and enjoy 'wonderful views' of Jesus Green and the five spires that dominate the nearby campuses. The views are shared by the cool bedrooms, some with extra seating and a large four-poster bed. Find a classic surf and turf menu in the River Bar steakhouse and grill; in the sixth-floor brasserie, take in the shifting panoramic vista over brunch, lunch, afternoon tea or dinner. 'Really good breakfasts' have much choice. 'The valet parking works well.' BEDROOMS 48. 3 suitable for disabled. FACILITIES Lift, bar, 2 restaurants, roof terrace (barbecue in season), Glassworks health club and spa, free Wi-Fi, in-room TV, civil wedding licence, room service, conference facilities, valet parking service (charge). BACKGROUND MUSIC In restaurants. CHILDREN All ages welcomed. PRICES Per room B&B (continental) from £255.

CANTERBURY Kent
Map 2:D5

CANTERBURY CATHEDRAL LODGE, The Precincts, CT1 2EH. Tel 01227 865350, www.canterburycathedrallodge.org. In the 'tranquil grounds' of the UNESCO-designated World Heritage site, this hotel, part of a modern complex, 'fits in well' with the medieval cathedral and its surroundings. The 'cheerful staff' and 'prime position' combine to make it a 'very special place', Guide readers say. 'It was a singular privilege to wander round the precincts late in the evening, after the day visitors had left.' Bedrooms are simply furnished but are 'comfortable and well-equipped, with an efficient shower room' ('shame about the captive hangers and poor bedside lighting, however'). Ask for a cathedral-view room and wake to the sight of the ecclesiastical building – 'bliss'. Breakfast has a 'small buffet'; hot dishes are 'well served in the busy refectory'. Eat alfresco on the terrace when weather permits. At dinner, guests have discounts at several local eateries, 'many within easy walking distance'. BEDROOMS 35. 1 suitable for disabled. FACILITIES Lift, sitting room (newspapers, 'packed bookshelves', 'comfortable sofas'), breakfast room, free Wi-Fi, in-room TV (Freeview), Campanile garden, meeting/function facilities, limited parking (pre-booking required). BACKGROUND MUSIC None. PRICES Per room B&B £92–£169.

CHATTON Northumberland
Map 4:A3
CHATTON PARK HOUSE, New Road, nr Alnwick, NE66 5RA. Tel 01668 215507, www.chattonpark.com. In peaceful countryside, Paul and Michelle Mattinson's Georgian house is run as a 'most welcoming', child-free B&B. Spacious, garden-facing bedrooms are provided with tea- and coffee-making facilities, a mini-fridge, bathrobes, slippers and good toiletries; two also have a separate lounge. There are books and newspapers to browse in the large sitting room; in good weather, stroll through the manicured grounds, where the loudest noise is the chatter of birds. Generous breakfasts, including hot toasted crumpets, oak-smoked local kippers and locally made jams, are ordered in advance. The Mattinsons are on hand with restaurant recommendations and plenty of local information to plan your day. In between the coast and the Cheviot Hills; Bamburgh Castle and Holy Island are within easy reach. ½ mile from Chatton. BEDROOMS 4. Plus 2-bed

self-catering lodge with private garden. OPEN Mar–Nov. FACILITIES Sitting room, breakfast room, free Wi-Fi, in-room TV (Freeview), weak mobile telephone signal, 4-acre grounds, grass tennis courts (June–Sept), parking. BACKGROUND MUSIC None. PRICES Per person B&B from £65.

CHELTENHAM Gloucestershire
Map 3:D5
BEAUMONT HOUSE, 56 Shurdington Road, GL53 0JE. Tel 01242 223311, www.bhhotel.co.uk. Fan and Alan Bishop's smart B&B occupies a Victorian merchant's house close to the centre. Bedrooms vary in size from compact doubles on the lower ground floor to spacious feature suites with a spa bath in the bathroom; all are equipped with tea- and coffee-making facilities, bottled water and biscuits. Carry a drink from the honesty bar on to the neat, pretty lawn – in fine weather, the small garden is a pleasing sun trap. Start a leisurely day with breakfast in bed, or go down to the breakfast room for smoked fish, local sausages or American-style pancakes. Regular buses nearby head for the shops, restaurants and cafés of the buzzy Montpellier quarter. The Bishops, self-proclaimed food lovers, have dinner recommendations to share. 1 mile S of town centre. BEDROOMS 16. OPEN All year. FACILITIES Lounge, breakfast room, free Wi-Fi, in-room TV (Sky, Freeview), garden, parking. BACKGROUND MUSIC In breakfast room. CHILDREN All ages welcomed (£30 per night charge for over-3s). PRICES Per room B&B single from £85, double £90–£220. 2-night min. stay on Sat night, and for Festivals and Cheltenham Gold Cup.

BUTLERS, Western Road, GL50 3RN. Tel 01242 570771, www.butlers-hotel. co.uk. 'An enjoyable, good-value option', this quirky B&B is in a 'quiet, well-located spot' within an 'easy 15-minute walk' of the town centre and the railway station. Paul Smyth and Shaun Bailey are the new owners; the 'exceptional service' remains. The 19th-century gentlemen's residence has been tastefully decorated with Edwardian paraphernalia ('we do have a bit of a theme, but nothing to scare the horses,' the owners say); the book-packed lounge is 'a tempting place to spend an hour browsing'. 'Well-appointed bedrooms', each with a candlestick telephone, bear the name of a famous butler (Jeeves, Hudson, Brabinger, etc). 'My elegant room had a comfortable bed with an antique bedstead; a gleaming bathroom.' Breakfast is 'perfectly tasty'. The hotel is 'handy for Cheltenham and Gloucester.' BEDROOMS 8. OPEN All year except Christmas. FACILITIES Drawing room, breakfast room, free Wi-Fi, in-room TV (Freeview), ¼-acre garden, parking. BACKGROUND MUSIC Quiet radio in the morning. CHILDREN Not under 10. PRICES Per room B&B single £80–£95, double £95–£180. 2-night min. stay during weekends and festivals.

THE CHELTENHAM TOWNHOUSE, 12–14 Pittville Lawn, GL52 2BD. Tel 01242 221922, www.cheltenhamtownhouse. com. Around the corner from Pittville Park, this contemporary B&B stands on a tree-lined street, a stroll from the town centre. It is managed by Nathaniel Leitch for the owners, Adam and Jayne Lillywhite. Borrow a book to read by the open fire in cool weather,

or, on a warm day, mix a drink at the honesty bar for sipping on the deck. In any season, choose one of the smart bedrooms in which to lay your head. The rooms vary in size, but all are well equipped with tea- and coffee-making facilities, biscuits and complimentary toiletries. A short walk away, studio apartments (some to suit a family) each have their own kitchen. There's hot chocolate on the breakfast menu, along with a fresh buffet, the usual cooked options and interesting daily specials (kedgeree, kippers, eggs Benedict). Leave the car: two bicycles and helmets are available to borrow. BEDROOMS 26. 5 studio apartments, 4 in separate building. OPEN All year, room-only rate for 4 days around Christmas. FACILITIES Lift, lounge, breakfast room, free Wi-Fi, in-room TV (Freeview), sun deck, DVD library, limited on-site parking (permits supplied for street). BACKGROUND MUSIC None. CHILDREN All ages welcomed. PRICES Per room B&B £78–£140.

No. 131, 131 The Promenade, GL50 1NW. Tel 01242 822939, theluckyonion. com/property/no-131. Decorated with flair, this grand Georgian villa across the road from the Imperial Gardens has bold bedrooms, modern artworks, a buzzy restaurant, and a 'nice atmosphere' throughout. It is part of Sam and Georgie Pearman's small, Cotswolds-based Lucky Onion group (see next entry). Modish bedrooms are stocked with a capsule coffee machine and locally made minibar snacks (plus, perhaps, an original David Hockney or William Kentridge). With a 'great bed' to boot, they're 'very comfortable indeed'. Merry-making locals gather in the Crazy Eights bar for cocktails; in the restaurant, local-ingredient-inspired menus might include wild garlic soup, crème fraîche; flat-iron Cotswold chicken, smoked bacon, baby onions, shiitake. An admirable breakfast menu includes all-butter croissants. BEDROOMS 11. OPEN All year. FACILITIES Drawing room, lounge, bar, restaurant, private dining rooms, games room, free Wi-Fi, in-room Apple TV (Sky), terrace (alfresco dining), 'very convenient' parking. BACKGROUND MUSIC All day in public areas. CHILDREN All ages welcomed (extra bed for under-12s £25 per night). PRICES Per room B&B (continental) £110–£400. À la carte £35.

NO. 38 THE PARK, 38 Evesham Road, GL52 2AH. Tel 01242 822929, theluckyonion.com/property/no-38-the-park. Rustic chic – and the laid-back atmosphere to match – fills this Georgian town house B&B, across the wide, leafy street from Pittville Park. Lee-Anna Rennie manages for Sam and Georgie Pearman (see previous entry). There are fresh flowers, art books, contemporary works on the walls; the walk-in drinks cabinet houses a remarkable honesty bar. Spread over three floors, the stylish bedrooms are all different – some have a claw-footed bath in the room; others have space for an additional child bed; another has twin walk-in showers. Sister restaurant The Tavern, a ten-minute walk away, is an easy dinner option, but the staff have plenty of other suggestions. Help yourself to a farmhouse buffet in the beamed breakfast room. 15 mins' walk from centre; on the A435 towards Evesham (front windows double glazed). BEDROOMS 13. 1, on ground floor, suitable for disabled. OPEN All year. FACILITIES Sitting room, open-plan dining area, private dining room (a chef can be arranged), free Wi-Fi, in-room Apple TV (Sky), small courtyard garden, limited parking. BACKGROUND MUSIC All day in public areas. CHILDREN All ages welcomed (extra bed £25 per night, childcare by arrangement). DOGS Allowed in bedrooms and public rooms. PRICES Per room B&B (continental) £110–£400.

CHESTER Cheshire
Map 3:A4

THE CHESTER GROSVENOR, Eastgate, CH1 1LT. Tel 01244 324024, www.chestergrosvenor.com. 'A good place to stay.' In a central location close to the cathedral and the ancient city walls, this 'very smart' Grade II listed hotel (Bespoke Hotels) has luxury to spare. 'Even walking down the wide staircase past the huge chandelier is itself rather dramatic.' Choose a bedroom decorated in modern or traditional style: each has air conditioning, double glazing, a marble bathroom. 'Our room, overlooking Eastgate, had a huge bed and every amenity. Piping hot water, too, in the bathroom.' Eat Josper-grilled meats and other classic dishes under the skylight in the 'attractive' brasserie; in chef Simon Radley's Michelin-starred restaurant, 'the superb food and splendid service put the place in a different class entirely'. 'Excellent breakfasts' with 'ample choice' are served at the table. BEDROOMS 80. 1 suitable for disabled. FACILITIES Lift, drawing room, gallery lounge, bar, brasserie, restaurant (closed

Sun, Mon), meeting/private dining rooms, free Wi-Fi, in-room TV, civil wedding licence, function facilities, spa, valet parking service, multi-storey car park. BACKGROUND MUSIC In public areas. CHILDREN All ages welcomed, no under-12s in restaurant. PRICES Per room B&B (continental) from £155. Tasting menu (restaurant) £69 or £99, à la carte (brasserie) £42.

ODDFELLOWS, 20 Lower Bridge Street, CH1 1RS. Tel 01244 345454, www. oddfellowschester.com. 'A great, quirky hotel.' Believed to be the former meeting spot of an altruistic society of misfits and artists (the Odd Fellows), this listed neoclassical mansion today embraces the eccentric. Typewriters climb the hotel's reception area; hand-painted birds and foxes eye one another across oak panelling in the restaurant. In the main house and a modern annexe, bedrooms have the same quirky character: twin roll-top baths or a circular bed here, Randolph Caldecott illustrations there. Sip cocktails in the 'secret garden' or the flamboyant lounge bar before sampling new chef Daniel Beech's imaginative, uncomplicated dishes (perhaps red mullet, brown shrimp linguine, broccoli pollen, romanesco). A bagged breakfast (croissant, natural yogurt, fresh orange juice, fruit) may be magicked to the bedroom door. BEDROOMS 18. 14 in annexe, 1 suitable for disabled. OPEN All year except Christmas Day. FACILITIES Lobby, bar, restaurant, private dining room, free Wi-Fi, in-room TV, civil wedding licence, terrace, garden. BACKGROUND MUSIC In public areas. CHILDREN All ages welcomed (extra bed £30 per night). PRICES Per room B&B from £129.

CHICHESTER Sussex
Map 2:E3
CHICHESTER HARBOUR HOTEL, North Street, PO19 1NH. Tel 01243 778000, www.chichester-harbour-hotel.co.uk. Within the city's Roman walls, this modern hotel occupies the former Ship, a Grade II* listed Georgian building steps from Priory Park. It was acquired by the Harbour Hotels group in 2016 (a sister hotel is in Salcombe, see Shortlist entry). Individually decorated bedrooms, including family rooms, have lively design touches (jewel-toned velvet cushions, an oversized headboard, quirky wallpaper) and views over the park or the town centre. Perch at the marble-topped bar for pre-dinner drinks – '15-mile cocktails', made with locally grown ingredients, are a draw – then choose from the brasserie-style menu (crab and avocado on toast, pickled pear and fennel; a 'catch of the day') in the cheery restaurant. A two-course set menu is available weekdays at lunch and early dinner. Chichester Cathedral is a stroll away. BEDROOMS 36. Plus cottage with outdoor seating and heaters. OPEN All year. FACILITIES Bar, restaurant, private dining room, free Wi-Fi, in-room TV, civil wedding licence, business facilities, limited parking. BACKGROUND MUSIC In public areas. CHILDREN All ages welcomed. PRICES Per room B&B from £145, D,B&B from £185. Set dinner £12.75, à la carte £30. 2-night min. stay preferred.

ROOKS HILL, Lavant Road, Mid Lavant, PO18 0BQ. Tel 01243 528400, www. rookshill.co.uk. Erling Sorensen runs this stylish B&B in an 18th-century farmhouse, in a rural village ten minutes' drive from the city centre. Rest on feather pillows and crisp bedlinen in the comfortable bedrooms (good double glazing keeps out noise from the road out front). Each room is supplied with good toiletries, bottled water, a hospitality tray with hot chocolate; a power shower in the bathroom. Take tea in the wisteria-hung patio when the weather cooperates; in colder months, a crackling fire warms the drawing room. There's a 'good selection' of fruit at breakfast in the 'bright, airy' dining room, plus home-made jams and home-made bread; the full English is 'beautifully cooked'. Local eateries are easily reached; a Michelin-mentioned gastropub is steps away. Regular buses (the stop is across the road) whiz you to the city. BEDROOMS 4. 1 suitable for disabled. OPEN All year. FACILITIES Drawing room, breakfast room, free Wi-Fi, in-room TV (Freeview), courtyard, parking. BACKGROUND MUSIC In breakfast room and drawing room at breakfast. CHILDREN Not under 14. PRICES Per room B&B £125–£175.

CHIDDINGFOLD Surrey
Map 2:D3

THE CROWN INN, The Green, Petworth Road, GU8 4TX. Tel 01428 682255, www.thecrownchiddingfold.com. 'Attentive service' and 'delicious pub grub' attract locals and visitors to Daniel and Hannah Hall's 'lovely' thatch-roofed 16th-century country inn, across the road from the village church. (The monthly pub quiz is an attraction, too.) 'We like the fact that it sticks to its traditional character.' Sip a local ale in the popular bar amid medieval carvings, 'massive beams' and

inglenook fireplaces; order off a 'really inviting menu' in the oak-panelled restaurant. 'Well-equipped bedrooms' have character in their sloping floors and antique furnishings, but it's not all olde-worlde: chic toiletries and a digital radio are among the amenities. Two rooms across the courtyard have French doors opening on to a private garden. Good choice at breakfast. 8 miles SW of Peterborough. BEDROOMS 8. 2 on ground floor. OPEN All year. FACILITIES Bar (open fire), snug, restaurant, free Wi-Fi, in-room TV (Freeview), 2 small courtyard gardens, large terrace, parking. BACKGROUND MUSIC In public areas. CHILDREN All ages welcomed. DOGS Allowed in bar and lounge, not in bedrooms. PRICES Per room B&B £95–£210, D,B&B £175–£200.

CHILGROVE Sussex
Map 2:E3

THE WHITE HORSE, 1 High Street, PO18 9HX. Tel 01243 519444, www.thewhitehorse.co.uk. 'Simply lovely.' In the foothills of the South Downs, this white-painted, rustic-chic inn is firmly rooted in the countryside. Sit on yak-hide banquettes for chef Rob Armstrong's 'simple but satisfying meals' in the 'lovely restaurant' – much of the produce, including trout from nearby rivers and pigeon from local estates, is freshly caught or foraged. A typical dish: chicken, leek and shiitake mushroom terrine, prosciutto and tarragon mayonnaise, toasted sourdough. 'Comfortable bedrooms' have quirky touches: steamer trunks, wool blankets, sheepskin rugs and the occasional copper bathtub. All rooms face a courtyard with views of the surrounding South Downs, but ask for a room with a private patio, and enjoy the vista from an outdoor hot tub. 10 mins' drive from Chichester. BEDROOMS 15. All on ground floor, 13 in rear annexe. FACILITIES Bar, restaurant, private dining room, free Wi-Fi, in-room TV, function facilities, 2 patios, garden, croquet, parking, helipad. BACKGROUND MUSIC 'Soft' in public areas, live jazz on Sun afternoons. CHILDREN All ages welcomed (cot, no bedding supplied, charge for extra bed). DOGS Allowed (£15 per night). PRICES Per room B&B from £99. À la carte £30.

CHURCH STRETTON Shropshire
Map 3:C4

VICTORIA HOUSE, 48 High Street, SY6 6BX. Tel 01694 723823, www.victoriahouse-shropshire.co.uk. 'Diane Chadwick maintains high standards' at her B&B, café and tea room in a 'splendid' Victorian house in the town centre, reports a returning visitor this year. 'The place meets all our needs: it's well priced, comfortable and convenient, with superb breakfasts.' 'Capable and wonderfully energetic', the hostess greets guests with afternoon tea. The treats continue in the homely bedrooms: each, hung with original artwork, is supplied with biscuits, hot chocolate and complimentary sherry. In the garden-facing breakfast room, a buffet holds fruit compotes, organic yogurt, and organic muesli from a nearby farm; hot dishes include French toast with Shrewsbury bacon, caramelised bananas and crème fraîche. Trek across the Shropshire hills, then return for home-baked cakes and scones in Jemima's Kitchen. BEDROOMS 6. 1 with private bathroom and dressing room.

FACILITIES Seating area, breakfast room, café/tea room (Wed–Sun), free Wi-Fi, in-room TV (Freeview), walled garden, pay-and-display parking (deducted from hotel bill or permits supplied). BACKGROUND MUSIC None. CHILDREN All ages welcomed. PRICES Per room B&B £60–£96.

CLEY-NEXT-THE-SEA Norfolk
Map 2:A5

CLEY WINDMILL, The Quay, NR25 7RP. Tel 01263 740209, www.cleywindmill.co.uk. There are inspiring views over salt marsh and sea from Julian and Carolyn Godlee's characterful B&B and restaurant on the north Norfolk coast – but you'll have to climb to the top of the 19th-century grinding mill to see them in their full glory. The top-floor Wheel Room is accessed via a ladder; for guests keen to stay grounded, other bedrooms, which overlook the reed beds or the charming village, are in the former store rooms and miller's accommodation. A daily-changing set supper menu (Cromer crab and chilli fish cakes; pan-seared rack of Norfolk lamb) is served at a candlelit communal dinner. The mill stands next to a bird sanctuary; regular birdwatching events are organised. After breakfast, follow the coastal path to the pebble and shingle beach. BEDROOMS 9. 3 in converted boathouse and granary. OPEN All year, self-catering only over Christmas and New Year. FACILITIES 2 lounges, restaurant, Wi-Fi, in-room TV (Freeview), civil wedding licence, ¼-acre garden. CHILDREN All ages welcomed (in some rooms, early supper by arrangement). PRICES Per room B&B £159–£225, D,B&B £224–£290. Set menu £32.50. 2-night min. stay on Fri and Sat nights.

COLWALL Worcestershire
Map 3:D5

COLWALL PARK HOTEL, Walwyn Road, WR13 6QG. Tel 01684 540000, www. colwall.com. A garden path from this Edwardian country house leads to the Malvern hills – and the 'friendly, helpful, efficient staff' are happy to send you off with a packed lunch and a walking map. With 'a charm all of its own', the hotel, in a village on the Herefordshire–Worcestershire border, has 'well-furnished bedrooms', 'excellent dinners' and a special welcome for canine companions. Lynsey Kettlewell is the manager. Bedrooms of various sizes include suites to suit a family; every room is equipped with good toiletries, home-made biscuits, even a treat for Fido. Order local ales and gastropubby meals in the bar (find a spot by the log fire in chilly weather). In the restaurant, modern British dishes use much seasonal Vale of Evesham produce. 'Plenty of variety' at breakfast. BEDROOMS 22. FACILITIES 2 lounges (1 with TV), library, bar, restaurant (closed Sun–Wed, Oct–Mar), free Wi-Fi, in-room TV (Freeview), civil wedding licence, conference facilities, 2-acre garden. BACKGROUND MUSIC None. CHILDREN All ages welcomed (extra bed £35 per night). DOGS Allowed in bedrooms, bar, garden. PRICES Per room B&B from £95, D,B&B from £145.

CONSTANTINE Cornwall
Map 1:E2

TRENGILLY WARTHA, Nancenoy, TR11 5RP. Tel 01326 340332, www.trengilly. co.uk. Down 'the narrowest of Cornish lanes', find a picture of jolly rusticity at Will and Lisa Lea's family-friendly pub-with-rooms, near-hidden in a secluded wooded valley. The lively bar is popular with locals for its well-selected list of wines, real ales and ciders, its hearty British cooking and its congenial folk music evenings. Local fishermen and farmers supply Nick Tyler's classic dishes (perhaps local mussels and chips; chicken and leek pie 'with veg and pots'), served in the bar, bistro or conservatory. Wake to garden or valley views in the country-style bedrooms. A well-stocked hospitality tray and DVD library encourage duvet days. Award-winning breakfasts include a filling full Cornish. On a fine day, take a turn in the lush garden, which slopes down to a sheltered pond. BEDROOMS 11. 2 in garden annexe. OPEN All year except Christmas. FACILITIES Bar, restaurant, conservatory, private dining room, free Wi-Fi, in-room TV, games room, terrace (alfresco dining), 6-acre garden (sheltered pond). BACKGROUND MUSIC Live music in bar Sun night. CHILDREN All ages welcomed. DOGS Allowed. PRICES Per person B&B single from £77, double from £84.

CONSTANTINE BAY Cornwall
Map 1:D2

TREGLOS HOTEL, Beach Road, St Merryn, nr Padstow, PL28 8JH. Tel 01841 520727, www.tregloshotel.com. 'Friendly, smiley staff' contribute to the 'extremely enjoyable' atmosphere of this traditional hotel overlooking the sea. It has been owned and run by the Barlow family for more than 40 years. From the golf course to the swimming pool, spa and play areas, there's entertainment for all ages. 'Our time there was a lovely mixture of walks, outings and competitive bridge after dinner,' says a Guide reader this year. Many of the

'beautiful, well-appointed' bedrooms have fine coastal views; some have a balcony. 'Imaginative' daily-changing menus and 'very good breakfasts' are served in the award-winning restaurant. 'There was good choice at dinner. The first and last courses were especially delicious.' 3 miles W of Padstow. BEDROOMS 42. 1 on ground floor, 2 suitable for disabled, plus self-catering apartments in grounds. OPEN Mar–Nov. FACILITIES Lift, 2 lounges, bar, conservatory, restaurant (smart/casual attire after 7 pm), children's den, games room, free Wi-Fi (variable signal), in-room TV (Freeview), 1-acre grounds, sunken garden, indoor swimming pool, Glo spa, parking. BACKGROUND MUSIC In bar and restaurant 'but guests may ask to turn it off anytime'. CHILDREN All ages welcomed. DOGS Allowed in some bedrooms, not in public rooms, on lead in grounds. PRICES Per room B&B from £150. Set dinner £38. 2-night min. stay during peak periods.
25% DISCOUNT VOUCHERS

CORNWORTHY Devon
Map 1:D4
KERSWELL FARMHOUSE, nr Totnes, TQ9 7HH. Tel 01803 732013, www. kerswellfarmhouse.co.uk. Pigs, lambs and chickens are the nearest neighbours at Nichola and Graham Hawkins's B&B on a small working farm between Totnes and Dartmouth. The renovated 400-year-old longhouse is surrounded by woodland trails and riverside footpaths; in the old milking parlour, a mini-gallery/honesty bar exhibits the work of contemporary ceramicists, glassmakers, painters and photographers. English oak, farmhouse furnishings and antiques fill the comfortable bedrooms,

while fresh-cut flowers bring the gardens indoors. All rooms have teas and ground coffee, fluffy bathrobes, novels and magazines. Farm-fresh produce features at breakfast: sausages and bacon from home-reared pigs; eggs Royale and Benedict from the free-range hens. 4 miles from Totnes. BEDROOMS 5. 1 in adjacent barn with private garden, 1 on ground floor. OPEN May–Oct. FACILITIES 2 dining rooms, sitting room, free Wi-Fi, in-room TV, art gallery, 14-acre grounds, parking, kayaking (1 kayak available to loan). BACKGROUND MUSIC None. CHILDREN Not under 12. PRICES Per room B&B single £90–£150, double £115–£150. 2-night min. stay preferred. Credit cards not accepted.

CORSHAM Wiltshire
Map 2:D1
THE METHUEN ARMS, 2 High Street, SN13 0HB. Tel 01249 717060, www. themethuenarms.com. In a historic market town – so picture-perfect it stood in for 18th-century Truro in the BBC's Poldark adaptation – this restored Georgian coaching inn is down the High Street from stately Corsham Court. It is now owned by Butcombe Brewery; Ashley Harlow and Abigail Vince are the managers. Locals and visitors drop in for craft brews and (ex-Royal Crescent Hotel in Bath) chef Leigh Evans's Italian-inspired cooking, perhaps including lamb short rib, peas, raw radicchio, morels. Guests from further afield stay in handsome heritage-hued bedrooms (some snug) kitted out with a Roberts radio, a mini-fridge and tea- and coffee-making facilities. At breakfast, there are freshly baked pastries, home-made granola,

and Wiltshire honey on the buffet; interesting cooked options. 8 miles NE of Bath. BEDROOMS 14. 1 in annexe. OPEN All year. FACILITIES Bar, restaurant, private dining rooms, free Wi-Fi, in-room TV (Freeview), garden, courtyard (alfresco dining), parking. BACKGROUND MUSIC In private dining areas and bar. CHILDREN All ages welcomed. DOGS Allowed in some bedrooms, bars, courtyard (£15 per night). PRICES Per room B&B £140–£240. À la carte £35. **25% DISCOUNT VOUCHERS**

COVENTRY Warwickshire
Map 2:B2

BARNACLE HALL, Shilton Lane, Shilton, CV7 9LH. Tel 02476 612629, www. barnaclehall.co.uk. Rose Grindal's centuries-old farmhouse is a rustic refuge 20 minutes by car from the city centre. Enter by the old oak door: the house has much character in its low doorways, nooks and crannies, and steps of varying heights. B&B accommodation is in spacious, traditionally decorated bedrooms with dark beams and fresh flowers. There's fresh fruit and cereal at breakfast, plus hot dishes cooked to order. Dietary requirements can be catered for, with advance notice. The garden comes into full bloom in the spring and summer – ask to take a cup of tea in the country calm. The M6 motorway is within easy reach. BEDROOMS 3. OPEN All year except Christmas. FACILITIES Sitting room (wood-burning stove), dining room, free Wi-Fi, in-room TV, patio, garden. BACKGROUND MUSIC None. CHILDREN All ages welcomed (rates based on age, no special facilities). PRICES Per person B&B single £45–£55, double £75–£85. Credit cards not accepted.

COOMBE ABBEY, Brinklow Road, Binley, CV3 2AB. Tel 02476 450450, www. coombeabbey.com. Steeped in 'character, eccentricity and individuality', this atmospheric, history-rich hotel retains many traces of its past as a 12th-century Cistercian abbey. Watch for deer as you approach through a 'well-maintained' country park; cross a bridge into 'superb' formal gardens. Inside the 'stunning' building, there are wrought-iron chandeliers, a carved stone pulpit, antique armchairs in the high-vaulted reception. Long corridors displaying 'magnificent' antiquities and china lead to the sumptuous 'bed chambers'. Rooms may have a canopy bed, original moulding or leaded windows; bathrooms, some hidden behind a bookcase, have a Victorian bath or a richly tiled waterfall shower. Modern dishes (crispy lamb shoulder bon bon and breast noisette, sweetbread, wild garlic mash, spring greens) are served in the conservatory dining room, candlelit at night. BEDROOMS 119. FACILITIES Bar, restaurant, private dining rooms, free Wi-Fi, in-room TV, wedding/conference facilities, room service, medieval banquets, terrace, 500-acre grounds (formal gardens, parkland, lake, walking trails, wildlife), parking (£5 per day). BACKGROUND MUSIC In public areas. CHILDREN All ages welcomed. PRICES Per room B&B from £89, D,B&B from £159.

COVERACK Cornwall
Map 1:E2

THE BAY HOTEL, North Corner, nr Helston, TR12 6TF. Tel 01326 280464, www.thebayhotel.co.uk. Almost all the incoming calls come from the birds at Victoria and Nicholas Sanders's 'welcoming hotel' on the Lizard peninsula. Forgo mobile reception; never mind the lack of landline. Instead, enjoy uninterrupted sea views from virtually every room in the house. Nearly all the bedrooms look across Coverack Bay; the best have a balcony, or French doors that open on to a private terrace. Some rooms may be snug, but all are decorated in a pleasing palette of Cornish seaside hues. Cross the tiered gardens to get to the beach, or head further afield: a coastal path starts at the foot of the drive. Fresh lobster and seasonal fare are served in the candlelit restaurant at dinner, chefs Ric House and Chris Conboye's menus change daily, according to the catch of the bay. Full Cornish breakfasts. BEDROOMS 14. 1, on ground floor, suitable for disabled. OPEN Mid-Mar–end Oct. FACILITIES Lounge, bar/restaurant, conservatory, free Wi-Fi in public areas, in-room TV (Freeview), 2 tiered gardens, large sun terrace, parking. BACKGROUND MUSIC Quiet classical music or blues in bar and restaurant. CHILDREN All ages welcomed, but only by arrangement for under-4s. DOGS Small to medium-size dogs allowed in bedrooms and on lead in grounds, not in public rooms, dog-friendly beach nearby. PRICES Per room B&B £140–£290, D,B&B £180–£330. Set dinner £35.

COWLEY Gloucestershire
Map 3:D5

COWLEY MANOR, GL53 9NL. Tel 01242 870900, www.cowleymanor.com. 'We had a great time.' Fifteen minutes' drive from Cheltenham, this contemporary country house and spa stands in acres of parkland, woods and meadows, a laid-back atmosphere all around. It is part of A Curious Group of Hotels, whose London sibling, The Portobello (see main entry), oozes city style. Exuberant decoration and furnishings bring flourish to the fine Italianate building. In the main house and converted stable block, bright, spacious bedrooms have a large bed and good amenities: a coffee machine, natural bath products, a wireless music system. Discover springs, lakes and Victorian cascades in the 'beautifully natural gardens'; another day, while away the hours in the glass-fronted C-Side spa, sunk into the hillside. Morning and night, the food is 'fabulous'. BEDROOMS 30. 15 in converted stables. OPEN All year. FACILITIES Bar, sitting room, billiard room, garden room, restaurant, private sitting room, private dining room, civil wedding licence, spa (17-metre indoor pool, 15-metre heated outdoor pool, sun loungers, sauna, steam room, gym, 4 treatment rooms), free Wi-Fi, in-room TV (Sky), 55-acre grounds (Grade II listed gardens), parking. BACKGROUND MUSIC In public areas. CHILDREN All ages welcomed (everything 'from bibs to babysitters' provided, holiday activities). DOGS Allowed in 2 bedrooms, not in public rooms. PRICES Per room B&B from £195, D,B&B from £255. À la carte £35.

CRAYKE Yorkshire
Map 4:D4

THE DURHAM OX, Westway, YO61 4TE. Tel 01347 821506, www.thedurhamox. com. Michael and Sasha Ibbotson carry on a 300-year history of hosting at this characterful country pub-with-rooms, on an ancient Celtic track-way to York. The village pub is all preserved flagstone floors, wood panelling, log fires and well-pulled pints; an 'interesting and varied' blackboard menu lists 'excellent' pub classics and daily specials (including vegetarian and gluten-free options). All but one of the country-style bedrooms are in converted farm buildings. Each has a large bed, space to sit, a tea and coffee tray and good toiletries. On a clear day, take in panoramic views across the Vale of York, all the way to the towers of York Minster. Walks from the door; walking guides available. 3 miles E of Easingwold. Convenient for Park-and-Ride into York. BEDROOMS 6. 1 suite accessed via external stairs, plus 3-bed self-catering cottage in village. OPEN All year. FACILITIES 3 bars, restaurant, private dining room, free Wi-Fi, in-room TV (Freeview), function facilities, 2-acre grounds, parking. BACKGROUND MUSIC In pub and restaurant. CHILDREN All ages welcomed. DOGS Allowed in public areas, some bedrooms. PRICES Per room B&B from £120. À la carte £30.

CROSTHWAITE Cumbria
Map 4: inset C2
THE PUNCH BOWL INN, Lyth Valley, nr Kendal, LA8 8HR. Tel 01539 568237, www.the-punchbowl.co.uk. 'Good beer', 'excellent food', 'nice bedrooms' and a 'relaxing ambience' win admirers at Richard Rose's 'fantastic' 300-year-old inn in the bucolic Lyth valley. The setting is textbook countryside: next to a stone church, the building overlooks a spread of rolling green; inside, there are thick wooden beams, a slate-topped bar, a hard-working wood-burner. Each bedroom, named after a former vicar of the parish church, has an upmarket country feel in its

hand-blocked wallpaper or comely floral prints; each, too, has a freestanding roll-top bath in a bathroom with underfloor heating. In the restaurant, new chef Arthur Bridgeman Quin cooks 'imaginative' gastropub dishes. Morning tea or coffee is brought to the room on request; a cream tea is offered every afternoon. 5 miles E of Bowness-on-Windermere. BEDROOMS 9. FACILITIES 2 bars, restaurant, free Wi-Fi in bar, in-room TV (Freeview), civil wedding licence, 2 terraces, parking. BACKGROUND MUSIC In public areas. CHILDREN All ages welcomed. DOGS Allowed in bar, not in bedrooms. PRICES Per room B&B £110–£310. À la carte £35.

DARLINGTON Co. Durham
Map 4:C4
HEADLAM HALL, nr Gainford, DL2 3HA. Tel 01325 730238, www. headlamhall.co.uk. A 'country house feel' imbues the Robinson family's stately Jacobean manor, which stands in walled gardens, with farmland sprawling beyond. All is smart and contemporary: there are deep armchairs, wide sofas and paintings of rustic scenes in a panelled sitting room; an open fire in the plaid-carpeted library bar. Throughout, housekeeping is 'exemplary'. Elegant bedrooms in the main house vary in size and character; more contemporary spa rooms have lovely views over the grounds. At mealtimes, modern British dishes use soft fruits and vegetables from the garden. Typical dishes: smoked salmon mousse, textures of beetroot, micro herbs; pan-roasted chicken breast, mushroom duxelle, pommes Anna, charred leeks. Extra de-stressing takes

place in the well-equipped spa. 8 miles W of Darlington. BEDROOMS 38. 9 in coach house, 6 in mews, 7 in spa, 2 suitable for disabled. OPEN All year except 24–27 Dec. FACILITIES Lift, bar, brasserie, lounge, drawing room, library, private dining rooms, free Wi-Fi, in-room TV (Freeview), civil wedding licence/function facilities, 4-acre garden (croquet, lake, ornamental canal), spa (15 by 6 metre heated indoor swimming pool), tennis, 9-hole golf course, parking. BACKGROUND MUSIC All day in lounge, bar and restaurant. CHILDREN All ages welcomed. DOGS Allowed in bedrooms and public rooms. PRICES Per room B&B single £110–£160, double £140–£200, D,B&B from £220. À la carte £35.

25% DISCOUNT VOUCHERS

HOUNDGATE TOWNHOUSE, 11 Houndgate, DL1 5RF. Tel 01325 486011, www.houndgatetownhouse.co.uk. Humour and heritage are the order of the day at Natalie Cooper's delightfully droll guest house and restaurant close to the town's iconic clock tower. A felt moose's head greets visitors to the restored 18th-century town house; eye-catching wallpaper and bespoke furniture make a stylish mix. Smart, modern bedrooms are individually decorated – go for one of the best, with a huge four-poster bed and a freestanding bath. Snacks, sandwiches and uncomplicated fare (spiced chicken and halloumi salad; Cumberland sausage and mash) are served all day till 8 pm; three nights a week, dinner from the bistro-style menu might include pork belly, mashed potato, pork beignets, savoy cabbage. Breakfast, served till noon, has plenty of choice. BEDROOMS

8. 1 suitable for disabled. OPEN All year except Sun, 25–26 Dec. FACILITIES Lift, lounge, bar (occasional jazz nights), restaurant (dinner Thurs–Sat), free Wi-Fi, in-room TV (Freeview), room service, terrace, use of local pool across the road. BACKGROUND MUSIC In reception, bar and restaurant. CHILDREN All ages welcomed. PRICES Per room B&B from £90. À la carte £25.

DARTMOUTH Devon
Map 1:D4
STRETE BARTON HOUSE, Totnes Road, Strete, TQ6 0RU. Tel 01803 770364, www.stretebarton.co.uk. In a village on the South West Coast Path, Stuart Litster and Kevin Hooper run their modern B&B in a 16th-century manor house, with a welcome slice of home-made cake at the ready. Many of the bedrooms have an Eastern influence in their decor (silks, tassels, Buddha sculptures); all have fresh flowers, magazines, biscuits and a beverage tray. Most rooms have views across the garden to the sea. Sink into squashy sofas in the drawing room (a fire is lit in cool weather); step on to the terrace when the sun's out. At breakfast: fresh fruit, local farm yogurts, Devon sausages. Blackpool Sands, set in a sheltered bay, is a 20-minute walk away. Ask to borrow a local guide book or walking map – the hosts are happy to provide. 5 miles SW of Dartmouth. BEDROOMS 6. 1 in cottage annexe. OPEN All year. FACILITIES Sitting room, breakfast room, free Wi-Fi, in-room TV, $^1/_3$-acre garden. BACKGROUND MUSIC None. CHILDREN Not under 8. DOGS Allowed in cottage suite. PRICES Per person B&B £40. 2-night min. stay preferred on Fri, Sat in peak season.

DELPH Greater Manchester
Map 4:E3
THE OLD BELL INN, Huddersfield
Road, nr Oldham, OL3 5EG. Tel 01457
870130, www.theoldbellinn.co.uk.
'Clearly popular', Philip Whiteman's
18th-century coaching inn, in a village
30 minutes' drive from Manchester,
attracts locals and visitors who crowd
the 'friendly' bar and restaurant.
'Enjoyable food' (perhaps pollock and
spinach fishcakes; 'tasty' steak and ale
pie) is served in the modern restaurant;
sandwiches and snacks are available
in the cosy brasserie. If gin's your
thing, choose from over 600 bottles
stocked in the emporium, a Guinness
World Record holder. 'The good-value
bedrooms aren't luxurious, but they're
clean and have a comfortable bed.'
Overnight guests have use of a first-floor
conservatory lounge in which to escape
the bustle below. Breakfast, with freshly
squeezed orange juice, is 'prompt to
arrive'. 5 miles from Oldham. BEDROOMS
18. FACILITIES Bar, lounge, brasserie,
restaurant, free Wi-Fi, in-room TV,
gin master classes, function facilities,
parking. BACKGROUND MUSIC In public
areas. CHILDREN All ages welcomed
(extra bed £25). PRICES Per room B&B
single £59.50–£69.50, double £95–£125.

DONNINGTON Sussex
Map 2:E3
THE BLACKSMITHS, Selsey Road, nr
Chichester, PO20 7PR. Tel 01243
785578, the-blacksmiths.co.uk. Near the
Chichester canal towpath, Mariella and
William Fleming's village pub-with-
rooms has been rejuvenated with a fresh
Scandinavian vibe. A fire is lit in the
bar on cold days; in sunshine and rain,
choose from a good selection of local

ales, organic wines, and bubbly from
the nearby vineyard at Tinwood Estate.
Upstairs, minimalist bedrooms in grey
and white share a small seating area
(books, hospitality tray, a bright orange
fridge for guests' use). Each room has a
large bed, plump armchairs and country
views; two, remarkably spacious, have
an original fireplace and a roll-top
bathtub. Eat in the snug, elegant
dining room or the walled terrace
(full use is made of the herb garden
and chicken flock): the mix of pub
classics and more modern dishes
might include slow-roasted sticky beef
brisket, French fries, roasted marrow
bone. BEDROOMS 3. OPEN All year except
Christmas, New Year's Eve. FACILITIES
Bar, restaurant, free Wi-Fi, in-room
TV, patio garden, parking. BACKGROUND
MUSIC In public areas, occasional
live music events. CHILDREN All ages
welcomed. DOGS Allowed. PRICES Per
room B&B £120–£150.

DULVERTON Somerset
Map 1:B5
THREE ACRES COUNTRY HOUSE,
Ellersdown Lane, Brushford, TA22
9AR. Tel 01398 323730, www.
threeacresexmoor.co.uk. 'A special
place', Julie and Edward Christian's
B&B is in a 'beautifully furnished'
1930s house in secluded grounds
overlooking Exmoor countryside.
Come up the curving, tree-lined lane;
arrive to hospitality that's 'second to
none'. The traditional bar/lounge is
stocked with local beers and gins; light
suppers of home-made soups, pâtés and
sandwiches, ordered in advance, may
be taken here. Individually decorated
bedrooms have thoughtful extras:
ground coffee, fresh milk, Exmoor

spring water. Wake to birdsong and a West Country breakfast – perhaps home-made cheese-and-leek sausages, or Exe valley cold-smoked trout and scrambled eggs. Hampers and packed lunches are available; ask the hosts where to find the county's best picnic spots. 2 miles S of Dulverton. BEDROOMS 6. 1 on ground floor, 1 family suite with extra beds in small annexe. OPEN All year. FACILITIES Bar, sitting room, breakfast room, free Wi-Fi, in-room TV (Freeview), sun terrace, 2-acre grounds. BACKGROUND MUSIC None. CHILDREN All ages welcomed (toys, play equipment in garden). PRICES Per person B&B £45–£60. 2-night min. stay preferred.

DUNWICH Suffolk
Map 2:B6
THE SHIP AT DUNWICH, St James Street, IP17 3DT. Tel 01728 648219, www. shipatdunwich.co.uk. A good base for outdoorsy sorts, and the dogs that accompany them, this 'unpretentious, friendly' inn (Agellus Hotels) is close to the beach and the RSPB reserves at Dingle Marshes and Minsmere. There are 'great walks from the door'. Real ales and 'very large portions' of pub favourites attract locals and visitors to the creeper-covered, red-brick building. On a warm day, find a spot in the sheltered courtyard or the 'lovely garden'. Each bedroom is different, and some are snug; the best have views over the marshes. (Some rooms, in the converted outbuildings, open directly on to the garden – 'perfect for the dogs'.) Discuss rooms before booking: some have night-time noise from the kitchen extractor fan. 'Excellent choices at breakfast', plus 'tasty' granary toast. BEDROOMS 16. 4 on ground floor in converted stables, 1 suitable for disabled. OPEN All year. FACILITIES Restaurant, bar, courtyard (alfresco dining), free Wi-Fi, in-room TV (Freeview, smart TV in family rooms), garden. BACKGROUND MUSIC None. CHILDREN All ages welcomed. DOGS 'Warmly welcomed inside and out.' PRICES Per room B&B £120–£145. À la carte £25.
25% DISCOUNT VOUCHERS

EAST WITTON Yorkshire
Map 4:C4
THE BLUE LION, nr Leyburn, DL8 4SN. Tel 01969 624273, www.thebluelion. co.uk. 'There's nothing "faux"' about Paul and Helen Klein's 'lovely, good-value' coaching inn, down the road from the village church. The scent of wood smoke hangs about the place; inside, bask in the 'good atmosphere' and 'outstanding service' from the 'pleasant, knowledgeable staff'. 'The inn gives little away to the 21st century' – real ales and 'well-executed British comfort food' are the order of the day – but the country-style bedrooms are 'spotlessly clean and comfortable (even if slightly dated)'. 'Our room in the converted outbuildings was large and quiet. But an umbrella would have been nice for the walk to the main house.' At breakfast, there's 'cool, fresh orange juice' and 'deep, dark coffee'; 'smoked haddock and poached eggs set us up for the day'. BEDROOMS 15. 9 in courtyard annexe. OPEN All year. FACILITIES 2 bars, 2 dining areas, private dining room, free Wi-Fi, in-room TV (Freeview), 1-acre garden, parking. BACKGROUND MUSIC None. CHILDREN All ages welcomed. DOGS Allowed in bar, some bedrooms. PRICES Per room B&B £94–£129, D,B&B £135–£169. À la carte £29.

EASTON GREY Wiltshire
Map 2:E5
WHATLEY MANOR, SN16 0RB. Tel 01666 822 888, www.whatleymanor.com. The lush grounds surrounding this luxury hotel and spa incorporate secluded arbours, outdoor sculptures, woodland trails and wild flower meadows, ideal for a picnic on a summer's day. Inside the Grade II listed 18th-century house, original artworks hang in the individually decorated bedrooms; many rooms overlook the gardens. New chef Niall Keating serves modern menus (regular, pescatarian or vegetarian) in the Dining Room; in the informal, newly refurbished Grey's brasserie, and on the garden terrace, a menu of comfort food might include prawn cocktail; Wiltshire spring lamb, crushed olive new potatoes, green beans, salsa verde. Breakfast has a 'very good' buffet. Borrow a bicycle for a spin around the grounds, or take it easy in the amenity-packed spa. BEDROOMS 23. Some on ground floor, 1 suitable for disabled. FACILITIES 3 lounges, 2 bars, brasserie, restaurant (Wed–Sun, 7 pm–10 pm), cinema, gym, spa (hydrotherapy pool, mud chamber, salt scrub shower, Iyashi Dome), free Wi-Fi, in-room TV, civil wedding licence, conference facilities, 12-acre garden. BACKGROUND MUSIC In public areas. CHILDREN Not under 12. DOGS Allowed in some rooms (treats and toys, £30 per night). PRICES Per room B&B from £190. Tasting menu (Dining Room) £99, à la carte (brasserie) £35.

EDENBRIDGE Kent
Map 2:D4
HEVER CASTLE B&B, Hever, TN8 7NG. Tel 01732 861800, www.hevercastle. co.uk. Connect with the past in this sumptuous B&B, which occupies two Edwardian additions to 13th-century Hever Castle. Moulded ceilings, grand chimney pieces, and corridors lined with paintings heighten the sense of grandeur; in the Astor and Anne Boleyn wings, individually decorated bedrooms, each with a bathroom of limestone or marble, are full of character. A blend of Tudor-inspired features and modern-day comfort, they may have a golden chaise longue, a four-poster bed, a glimpse of the castle through leaded windows. Residents have complimentary access to the castle and grounds during opening hours; parts of the peaceful gardens are yours to wander in after the public has left for the day. 2 mins' walk to village pub; 1½ miles from Hever station. BEDROOMS 28. Some on ground floor, some suitable for disabled, plus self-catering Medley Court cottage. OPEN All year except 25–27 Dec. FACILITIES Lounge, billiards room, free Wi-Fi, in-room TV (Sky), 680-acre gardens and grounds, parking. BACKGROUND MUSIC None. CHILDREN All ages welcomed. PRICES Per room B&B single £105, double from £125.

EDINGTON Wiltshire
Map 2:D1
THE THREE DAGGERS, 47 Westbury Road, nr Westbury, BA13 4PG. Tel 01380 830 940, www.threedaggers.co.uk. In a village at the foot of Salisbury Plain, this 'impressive' pub-with-rooms attracts all sorts. Craft-beer lovers come for the artisanal brews from the on-site microbrewery; foodies flock to the well-stocked farm shop and 'well-populated' dining room; travellers check in to one of the 'splendid' bedrooms, each supplied with fresh flowers and

fluffy towels, and styled with a cool, modern-rustic feel. Sample new chef Matt Gillard's seasonal produce–inspired modern dishes (cooked using ingredients grown in the pub's own Priory Farm, nearby), or order a pizza from the wood-fired oven in the garden. Afterwards, escape the buzz of the bar in the comfy residents' lounge, stocked with tea, coffee, biscuits, and – should the countryside beckon – wellies to borrow. BEDROOMS 3. FACILITIES Bar, dining area, private dining room, free Wi-Fi, in-room TV (Freeview), civil wedding licence, garden (pizza shack, benches), microbrewery, farm shop. BACKGROUND MUSIC In public areas. CHILDREN All ages welcomed (colouring sets, adjacent public play area). PRICES Per room B&B from £85. À la carte £25.

ELTERWATER Cumbria
Map 4: inset C2
THE ELTERMERE INN, LA22 9HY. Tel 015394 37207, www.eltermere. co.uk. In the Langdale valley, Mark and Ruth Jones's country hotel is a family affair: daughter Aimee is the 'charming' manager; son Edward cooks 'delicious' modern European recipes in the restaurant. The 18th-century house stands in green grounds with 'stunning views' over Elter Water. Within, there is a 'traditional country atmosphere' from the 'comfortable' public rooms to the individually decorated bedrooms. Plenty of walks start from the front door – with the promise of tea and cake in the bar or garden when you return. 2 miles from Grasmere; the Langdale Pikes rise in the distance. BEDROOMS 12. OPEN All year except Christmas and New Year (restaurant open New Year's Eve). FACILITIES 2 lounges, bar, restaurant

(closed Sun eve, Mon), terrace, free Wi-Fi (in public areas), 3-acre garden, complimentary passes for Langdale Hotel spa (pool, hot tub, steam room), 10 mins' walk away. BACKGROUND MUSIC Contemporary in public areas. DOGS Allowed in 1 bedroom, bar and garden. PRICES Per room B&B £149–£295. À la carte £30. 2-night min. stay at weekends.

ELTON Cambridgeshire
Map 2:B4
THE CROWN INN, 8 Duck Street, nr Peterborough, PE8 6RQ. Tel 01832 280 232, www.crowninnelton.co.uk. Under the shade of a leafy horse chestnut tree stands this pretty, thatch-roofed country inn. Locals and visitors come for chef/patron Marcus Lamb's wholesome pub classics and hearty Sunday roasts, eaten in sunny weather on the front terrace or in the rear garden. Neighbouring villages and landmarks give the 'well-equipped' modern bedrooms their name. All are supplied with bottled water, fresh milk and a tea and coffee tray; Burghley and Wadenhoe, across the courtyard, have French windows that open on to a private garden. Peterborough and its Norman cathedral are within reach; closer by, there are countryside walks aplenty – ask for a packed lunch to keep you going. 8 miles SW of Peterborough. BEDROOMS 8. 2 on ground floor. OPEN All year. FACILITIES Bar (local ales, open fire), snug, restaurant, free Wi-Fi, in-room TV (Freeview), parking. BACKGROUND MUSIC In bar and restaurant. CHILDREN All ages welcomed. DOGS Allowed in bar. PRICES Per room B&B single from £80, double from £140, D,B&B single from £105, double from £200. À la carte £28.

EXETER Devon
Map 1:C5

CITY GATE, Iron Bridge, Lower North Street, EX4 3RB. Tel 01392 495811, www.citygatehotel.com. At the gate of an ancient Roman wall, this old inn (Young's Brewery) close to the cathedral was given a stylish makeover in 2017. Lively with interesting curios and splashes of colour, it's a popular place with locals, who come for the cocktails and craft beers, and the pub food served all day. Eat in the buzzy restaurant (half-panelled walls, banquettes, mismatched chairs) or spill on to the large beer garden in balmy weather – pergolas and parasols provide shade. 'Boutiquey', air-conditioned bedrooms vary in size and style; some, with a sofabed, can accommodate a family. All are supplied with a capsule coffee machine, a selection of teas, complimentary port and Devon fudge. Interesting options at breakfast: 'doorstop' sandwiches, Brixham crab cakes. Train stations are within walking distance. BEDROOMS 14. FACILITIES Bar, restaurant, free Wi-Fi, in-room TV (Sky), function facilities, large beer garden, limited parking. BACKGROUND MUSIC Occasional live music events. CHILDREN All ages welcomed. PRICES Per room B&B from £105. À la carte £28.

FALMOUTH Cornwall
Map 1:E2

HIGHCLIFFE, 22 Melvill Road, TR11 4AR. Tel 01326 314466, www.highcliffefalmouth.com. Between the sea and the town, Vanessa and Simon Clark's B&B is a cheery spot filled with lively colours, imaginative design touches, and a friendly, personable feel. High-ceilinged bedrooms in the Victorian town house are each different, though all share a cool, 'boutiquey' feel and well-considered amenities: robes, large towels, high-end toiletries, a powerful shower. Ask for a room with sweeping views over the harbour and estuary – it's a fine sight to wake to. At breakfast, freshly squeezed orange juice and freshly pressed apple juice accompany the daily specials: an American pancake stack; wilted spinach and garlic mushrooms on organic bread; home-made rösti with a poached egg, dry-cured streaky bacon and seaweed. A breakfast basket delivered to the room door may be pre-ordered by guests keen on a lie-in. BEDROOMS 8. OPEN All year except 27 Nov–11 Jan. FACILITIES Lounge, breakfast room, free Wi-Fi, in-room TV (Freeview), parking. BACKGROUND MUSIC None. CHILDREN Not under 8. PRICES Per room B&B single from £50, double £80–£160.

THE ROSEMARY, 22 Gyllyngvase Terrace, TR11 4DL. Tel 01326 314669, www.therosemary.co.uk. A two-minute stroll from Gyllyngvase beach, Lynda and Malcolm Cook's 'delightful' B&B occupies an Edwardian town house with 'fantastic views' across the garden towards Falmouth Bay. 'Clean and comfortable', the homely bedrooms are individually styled; the best look towards the sea. All rooms are supplied with tea, coffee, bottled water and bathrobes. Sit in the lounge for a Cornish cream tea, or ask for a picnic hamper with fortifying slabs of home-baked cake, before setting off on a coastal ramble. 'Good-quality' breakfasts have home-made preserves, Cornish honey, plenty of fresh fruit (all diets may be catered for). 10 mins' walk to town. BEDROOMS 8. Two 2-bed suites. OPEN Generally Feb–end Oct, 'but call for availability over the winter'. FACILITIES Lounge, bar, dining room, free Wi-Fi, in-room TV, south-facing garden, sun deck. BACKGROUND MUSIC None. CHILDREN All ages welcomed. DOGS Allowed in some bedrooms by arrangement. PRICES Per room B&B single £50–£75, double £79–£162. 2-night min. stay preferred.

FAR SAWREY Cumbria
Map 4: inset C2
CUCKOO BROW INN, LA22 0LQ. Tel 015394 43425, www.cuckoobrow.co.uk. Dogs and muddy boots are welcome at this fuss-free, family-friendly pub-with-rooms in a village between Lake Windermere and Hawkshead. The convivial 18th-century inn has plenty of country character, not least in the local real ales and hearty dishes (duck confit terrine, pear and date chutney; hunter's hot pot) served in the bar, the dining room or the garden. Most of the modern, simply decorated bedrooms are in an annexe attached to the main building. They vary in size and facilities: family rooms have a bed for the children; superior rooms have a roll-top bath in the smartly refurbished bathroom. Interesting choices at breakfast: eggy brioche with a berry compote; eggs Hemingway. Well situated for the ferry to Bowness-on-Windermere. BEDROOMS 14. Some on ground floor. OPEN All year. FACILITIES Bar, lobby, dining room, lounge/games room, free Wi-Fi, in-room TV (Freeview), gravelled terrace, small garden. BACKGROUND MUSIC In bar and lounge. CHILDREN All ages welcomed. DOGS 'More than welcome' in bedrooms

and public rooms (£10 per night, biscuits, breakfast sausage). PRICES Per room B&B from £130, D,B&B from £170.

FERRENSBY Yorkshire
Map 4:D4
THE GENERAL TARLETON, Boroughbridge Road, nr Knaresborough, HG5 0PZ. Tel 01423 340284, www.generaltarleton.co.uk. A handy stopover for trips to and from Scotland, this restaurant-with-rooms is liked for its 'fantastic service', 'excellent food', 'well-equipped, modern bedrooms' and 'great value for money'. It is owned by chef/patron John Topham and his wife, Claire. After a drink by the fire in the cocktail lounge, sit in the stylishly updated restaurant (low beams, stone walls, leather chairs) for a 'first-rate' meal, perhaps including slowly braised sticky pig's cheek, pulled ham hock, pea velouté; Yorkshire fish pie with a Wensleydale crust. Head to one of the 'comfortable' bedrooms afterwards – each has home-made biscuits and high-end toiletries. The medieval ruins of Knaresborough Castle are close by. BEDROOMS 13. OPEN All year, no accommodation 24–26 Dec, 1 Jan. FACILITIES Bar, cocktail lounge, atrium, restaurant, private dining room, free Wi-Fi, in-room TV (Freeview), parking. BACKGROUND MUSIC In public areas. CHILDREN All ages welcomed. PRICES Per room B&B from £129. À la carte £35.

FOLKESTONE Kent
Map 2:E5
ROCKSALT, 4–5 Fish Market, CT19 6AA. Tel 01303 212070, www. rocksaltfolkestone.co.uk. All dark

timber, glass and striking sea views, this sleek restaurant-with-rooms brings a fresh perspective to the traditional English seaside. It is owned by Mark Sargeant and Josh de Haan. The stylish, purpose-built bar and dining room are cantilevered over the harbour, their vista stretching to the Channel. Find a seat on a leather banquette, or on the terrace in fine weather, to sample dishes off the 'imaginative', wide-ranging menu, which uses fish caught by local day boats off the southeast coastline. Typical offerings: lobster and salmon pasty, pickled cucumber; pan-fried whole lemon sole, brown caper butter. Bedrooms are across a cobbled street. Here, walls of stripped-back stone frame an outlook on the water (binoculars are provided); in the morning, a continental breakfast hamper is delivered to the room. BEDROOMS 4. FACILITIES Bar, restaurant (last orders by 5 pm in winter), terrace, free Wi-Fi, in-room TV, on-street parking. CHILDREN All ages welcomed. PRICES Per room B&B from £85. À la carte £30.

FONTMELL MAGNA Dorset
Map 2:E1

THE FONTMELL, SP7 0PA. Tel 01747 811441, thefontmell.com. Imaginative pub food and wood-fired summertime pizzas combine with upmarket country comforts at this quirkily renovated roadside inn. The village stream separates the smart dining room from the buzzy bar – pick a side. Here: home-made sausage rolls; mussels and chips; a selection of natural wines and guest ales. There: chef Tom Shaw's daily-changing menu, perhaps including seared hake, crushed Jersey Royals, wild garlic, potted shrimp butter, samphire.

Upstairs, colourful modern bedrooms may have exposed beams or a bay-window reading nook, plus a goose-down duvet, a powerful shower, perhaps a roll-top bath. Summer weekends, join hungry locals for alfresco pizzas in the garden. 4 miles from Shaftesbury. BEDROOMS 6. FACILITIES Bar, restaurant (closed Mon, Tues), large garden, free Wi-Fi, in-room TV (Freeview), DVD library. BACKGROUND MUSIC In public areas. CHILDREN All ages welcomed (extra bed £20 per night). DOGS Allowed in 1 bedroom. PRICES Per room B&B £85–£145. À la carte £30.

FOWEY Cornwall
Map 1:D3

THE OLD QUAY HOUSE, 28 Fore Street, PL23 1AQ. Tel 01726 833302, www. theoldquayhouse.com. Let the sound of seagulls and views of sand and surf introduce the day: most of the 'clean, fresh, contemporary' bedrooms in this 'marvellously situated' quayside hotel have views over the estuary. Each room in the former Victorian seamen's mission has thoughtful touches: biscuits and bottled water, books and DVDs, local guides, earplugs, umbrellas and raincoats. 'I liked the fridge on the landing with little jugs of fresh milk.' Relax in the 'tastefully rejuvenated' public areas – 'exceptionally friendly and helpful' staff are on hand for any request – then move to the informal restaurant and 'beautiful terrace', where new chef Richard Massey cooks classic French dishes with a Cornish twist. 'The sun streams into the restaurant at breakfast time.' BEDROOMS 11. OPEN All year. FACILITIES Open-plan lounge, bar, restaurant (closed for lunch Mon, Tues Easter–Sept), free

Wi-Fi, in-room TV, civil wedding licence, waterside terrace (alfresco dining), parking permits supplied. CHILDREN Not under 12. PRICES Per room B&B £190–£335, D,B&B £265–£410. Set dinner £30–£37.50.

GATESHEAD Tyne and Wear
Map 4:B4

ESLINGTON VILLA, 8 Station Road, Low Fell, NE9 6DR. Tel 01914 876017, www. eslingtonvilla.co.uk. Two Victorian villas stand amid mature trees and shrubs on the city outskirts, forming a 'pleasant' hotel, 'well located for "doing" Newcastle'. It is owned by Nick and Melanie Tulip. Individually decorated bedrooms range from traditional rooms, perhaps with a four-poster bed, to brightly coloured, more modern accommodation. (A programme of refurbishment is underway.) 'Ours was spacious and comfortable, with new carpeting and good views over the garden. Some gripes: captive coat hangers; no bathrobes or slippers; sash windows we couldn't open.' Modern British dishes are served by 'cheerful staff' in the dining room or conservatory; sharing platters (from midday) and a good-value early-bird menu (on weekdays) are also available. 2 miles S of city centre. BEDROOMS 18. 3 on ground floor in annexe. OPEN All year except 25–26 Dec. FACILITIES Bar/lounge, dining room, conservatory, private dining room, free Wi-Fi, in-room TV (Freeview), 2-acre garden, parking. BACKGROUND MUSIC In public rooms. CHILDREN All ages welcomed. PRICES Per room B&B £84.50–£140, D,B&B £105–£175. À la carte £28.50.
25% DISCOUNT VOUCHERS

GATWICK Sussex
Map 2:D4

LANGSHOTT MANOR, Ladbroke Road, Langshott, Horley, RH6 9LN. Tel 01293 786680, www.langshottmanor. com. Whether for a fly-by visit or an extended stay, this Elizabethan manor house (Alexander Hotels) is liked for its 'friendly staff' and 'well-presented meals'. The smartly decorated bedrooms are all different – some have an antique bathtub, others a four-poster bed, yet others a private patio garden. All are provided with tea- and coffee-making facilities, bathrobes and slippers. (Light sleepers, discuss rooms before booking: guests this year reported noise from neighbouring rooms and corridors.) Casual meals and afternoon teas may be taken in the lounges or on the terrace. In the elegant restaurant, chef Phil Dixon's modern European dishes use produce from the kitchen garden. Imaginative breakfasts start the day. Convenient for Gatwick airport. BEDROOMS 22. 15 in mews, a short walk across hotel grounds. FACILITIES 3 lounges, bar, restaurant, private dining room, free Wi-Fi, in-room TV (Freeview), civil wedding licence, conference facilities, terrace (alfresco dining), 3-acre garden. BACKGROUND MUSIC In lounges and restaurant. CHILDREN All ages welcomed. DOGS Allowed in 2 rooms, by arrangement. PRICES Per person B&B from £69.50, D,B&B from £99. À la carte £49.50, tasting menu £70. 2-night min. stay preferred.

GILSLAND Cumbria
Map 4:B3

THE HILL ON THE WALL, Brampton, CA8 7DA. Tel 01697 747214, www. hillonthewall.co.uk. 'Elaine Packer has thought of every comfort' at her 'superb' Georgian farmhouse overlooking Hadrian's Wall, near Birdoswald. Sit down to tea and home-made cake beside the drawing room fire or in the 'beautiful' walled garden when you arrive at the B&B. Afterward, unpack in one of the traditionally decorated bedrooms, each 'sumptuously styled' and stocked with glossy magazines, cafetière coffee, a biscuit barrel and chocolates. 'Shutters closed, I slept in perfect peace.' 'Delicious' home-cooked Northumbrian breakfasts, ordered the night before, are served in 'gigantic portions' – ideal fuel for hikers and bikers of any stripe. Packed lunches available (£6). 1 mile W of Gilsland on the B6318. BEDROOMS 3. 1 on ground floor. OPEN Mar–Oct. FACILITIES Lounge (library, wood-burning stove), breakfast room, free Wi-Fi, in-room TV (Freeview), 1-acre garden, terrace, parking, secure bicycle storage. BACKGROUND MUSIC None. CHILDREN Not under 10. PRICES Per room B&B £80–£90. Credit cards not accepted.

WILLOWFORD FARM, CA8 7AA. Tel 01697 747962, www.willowford. co.uk. National Trail-blazers find cosy accommodation and a hearty breakfast at Liam McNulty and Lauren Harrison's rustic B&B. The longest-running stretch of uninterrupted Hadrian's Wall wends through the yard of their 100-acre organic sheep and cattle farm; from the bedrooms in the converted byre, peer out at the remains of a bridge and two turrets. The characterful, energy-efficient rooms have exposed wood beams, antique furniture and a heated floor of local Westmorland slate; each is

supplied with Fairtrade tea, coffee and hot chocolate. At dinner, head to the Samson Inn in the village, under the same management (lifts are cheerfully offered); lamb from the farm appears on the menu. Packed lunches available (£6). ½ mile W of Gilsland, between Gilsland village and Birdoswald Roman fort. BEDROOMS 5. All on ground floor. OPEN Mar–Nov. FACILITIES Lounge/ breakfast room, free Wi-Fi, in-room TV (Freeview). BACKGROUND MUSIC None. CHILDREN All ages welcomed. DOGS Well-behaved dogs allowed by arrangement in bedrooms, not in public rooms (£5 charge, chickens and sheep on farm). PRICES Per room B&B £88–£95.

GRAFFHAM Sussex
Map 2:E3
WILLOW BARNS, nr Petworth, GU28 0NT. Tel 01798 867493, www. willowbarns.co.uk. In a 'stunning' location on the edge of a village in the South Downs, Amanda and William Godman's 'stylish' B&B occupies two handsomely rough-hewn, flint-and-brick buildings on a tranquil courtyard. Modern, country-cottage bedrooms are made homely with fresh flowers, dressing gowns and home-baked treats; two can accommodate an extra bed for a child. Head to the owners' White Horse pub next door for classic British dishes cooked with modern flair (perhaps lamb kebab, tzatziki; Selsey crab risotto). In the morning, 'there's every variation of cooked breakfast that you could want'. Many footpaths and cycle routes nearby; cyclists and walkers are warmly welcomed. 5 miles from Petworth. BEDROOMS 6. All on ground floor. OPEN All year, room-only rates over Christmas and New Year.

FACILITIES Sitting room with log fire in the pub (restaurant closed Sun eve, and Mon in Jan, Feb), free Wi-Fi, in-room TV (Freeview), large courtyard, pub garden, parking. BACKGROUND MUSIC None. CHILDREN Not under 12. PRICES Per room B&B from £110. 2-night min. stay at peak weekends. À la carte £25.

GRANGE-OVER-SANDS Cumbria
Map 4: inset C2

CLARE HOUSE, Park Road, LA11 7HQ. Tel 01539 533026, www. clarehousehotel.co.uk. 'Old fashioned, but none the worse for that', the Read family's traditional hotel enjoys a loyal following. Especially liked by Guide readers this year: the 'friendly, efficient staff'; the 'cosy, welcoming atmosphere'; the 'outstanding food'. Log fires blaze in the comfortable sitting rooms of the Victorian house; most of the 'well-maintained bedrooms', two with a balcony, look to the sea. 'Our superior room had wonderful uninterrupted views of the hotel garden and Morecambe Bay.' Take morning coffee and afternoon tea in the lounges or under a parasol in the garden. In the evening, Andrew Read and Mark Johnston cook 'excellent, beautifully presented' classic English and French dishes 'with good choice' (served between 6.30 pm and 7.30 pm). BEDROOMS 18. 1 on ground floor suitable for disabled. OPEN Mid-Mar–mid-Dec. FACILITIES 2 lounges, dining room, free Wi-Fi, in-room TV, ¾-acre grounds, 1-mile promenade at the bottom of the garden, parking. BACKGROUND MUSIC None, brass band concerts on the bandstand throughout the summer. CHILDREN All ages welcomed. PRICES Per person D,B&B £96–£104.

GRASSINGTON Yorkshire
Map 4:D3

GRASSINGTON HOUSE, 5 The Square, nr Skipton, BD23 5AQ. Tel 01756 752406, www.grassingtonhouse. co.uk. Contemporary flair and classic English cuisine mix at this restaurant-with-rooms on the cobbled square of a Dales village. It is owned by chef/patron John Rudden and his wife, Sue. The Grade II listed Georgian house has many glamorous touches: cascading chandeliers, bold brass sculptures, ornate fireplaces. Some of the individually decorated bedrooms have a balcony or window seat; all are provided with Fairtrade tea and coffee, home-made flapjacks, waffle bathrobes, organic toiletries. Sit in the smart restaurant and fireside bar for 'enjoyable' dinners using much locally sourced produce; in fine weather, go alfresco and dine on the terrace. The hosts' rare-breed pigs provide the restaurant with bacon, sausages and plenty of crackling. 'We were pleased with it in every way.' BEDROOMS 9. OPEN All year except Christmas Day. FACILITIES Lounge, bar, restaurant, free Wi-Fi, in-room TV, civil wedding licence, function facilities, terrace, cookery master classes, horse riding, cycle hire, fly fishing and shooting can be arranged, parking. BACKGROUND MUSIC In public areas. CHILDREN All ages welcomed. PRICES Per room B&B £125–£145, D,B&B £195–£235. Set dinner £35–£49.50.

GREAT LANGDALE Cumbria
Map 4: inset C2

THE OLD DUNGEON GHYLL, LA22 9JY. Tel 01539 437272, www.odg.co.uk. 'What a glorious setting.' For more than

300 years, fell walkers and climbers have sought the views and comforts from this unpretentious, dog-friendly inn at the head of the Great Langdale valley. It is managed by Jane and Neil Walmsley for the National Trust. 'It's not the height of elegance, but it's very reasonably priced, and the staff are willing and helpful.' Most of the 'basic', country-style rooms (some suitable for a family) have views of the surrounding fells. Eat 'straightforward pub food' in the lively Hikers' Bar (one-time cow stalls); the residents' lounge is just the spot for morning coffee, afternoon tea and a home-baked treat or two. Walking routes and packed lunches available. BEDROOMS 12. OPEN All year except 23–27 Dec. FACILITIES Residents' bar and lounge, dining room, Hikers' bar (open to public), beer garden, free Wi-Fi in public areas and some bedrooms, 1-acre garden, drying room, parking. BACKGROUND MUSIC None, live music on first Wed of every month. CHILDREN All ages welcomed (special rates for over-5s). DOGS Allowed (£5 per night). PRICES Per room B&B from £62.50. À la carte £25. 2-night min. stay at weekends.

GURNARD Isle of Wight
Map 2:E2
THE LITTLE GLOSTER, 31 Marsh Road, PO31 8JQ. Tel 01983 298776, www.thelittlegloster.com. Scandinavian flair and seaside charm are found at this much-praised restaurant-with-rooms on a small bay just west of Cowes. It is owned by chef/patron Ben Cooke and his wife, Holly, 'a likeable pair'. The glass-fronted dining room takes in the spread of the Solent – a fitting setting for the modern dishes that use heaps of Isle of Wight produce. Typical offerings:

Bembridge Ledge crab cakes, crab bisque, lemon mayonnaise; chargrilled Isle of Wight sirloin steak, garlic local mushrooms, watercress. Sharing menus, served family style, are just right for large groups. Coastal-themed bedrooms (stripes, scrubbed wood) are in a separate wing, with their own entrance; binoculars are provided to enjoy the view. Lots of choice at breakfast: 'super' juices, home-made marmalade, home-cured gravadlax, eggs all ways. BEDROOMS 3. All in adjoining building. OPEN All year except Christmas, Jan–second week Feb. FACILITIES Bar, restaurant (closed Sun eve, Mon–Wed, Oct–Apr), free Wi-Fi, in-room TV (Freeview), function facilities, garden, petanque court. BACKGROUND MUSIC In dining room. CHILDREN All ages welcomed. PRICES Per room B&B £115–£245. À la carte £45.

HALIFAX Yorkshire
Map 4:D3
SHIBDEN MILL INN, Shibden Mill Fold, HX3 7UL. Tel 01422 365840, www.shibdenmillinn.com. Simon and Caitlin Heaton's refurbished 17th-century inn stands on a bend of a quiet country lane in the wooded Shibden valley. Cheery bedrooms mix original features with updated style: pick a room with a wall of windows, perhaps, or another with a standalone bath through a stone archway. All rooms are supplied with teas and coffees, towelling robes, a DVD-player (and access to a DVD library). Chef Darren Parkinson specialises in Yorkshire steaks grilled in the charcoal oven, but there's much more to please: early-bird menus, Friday 'fizz and chip' nights, summertime seafood and burgers in

the 'posh shed' on the terrace. Shibden Mill's own brew is a must-have in the 'bustling' oak-beamed bar. 2 miles NE of Halifax. BEDROOMS 11. OPEN All year except 25–26 Dec, 1 Jan. FACILITIES Bar, restaurant, private dining room, free Wi-Fi, in-room TV (Freeview), small conference facilities, patio (alfresco dining), parking, complimentary access to health club, 6 mins' drive away. BACKGROUND MUSIC In main bar and restaurant. CHILDREN All ages welcomed. DOGS Allowed in bar. PRICES Per room B&B from £130, D,B&B from £182. À la carte £35.

HARROGATE Yorkshire
Map 4:D4
THE WEST PARK HOTEL, 19 West Park, HG1 1BJ. Tel 01423 524471, thewestparkhotel.com. On a smart parade facing the leafy Stray, this modern town-centre hotel has been slickly converted from a Victorian coach house. Nathan George manages for Provenance Inns & Hotels. Food is served all day in the lively brasserie (zinc-topped bar, sea-green leather banquettes, wood flooring, designer lighting); in good weather, eat and drink alfresco in the courtyard. Smart, individually decorated bedrooms (quieter at the back) have a large bed, a coffee machine, treats to nibble on and fine toiletries; bathrooms are fitted with underfloor heating and speakers. Live the high life in one of the two penthouse duplexes, which have a lounge, dining area and access to a roof terrace. The extensive breakfast menu has leaf teas, smoothies, many interesting cooked options. BEDROOMS 25. OPEN All year. FACILITIES Bar, brasserie, meeting/private dining rooms, free Wi-Fi, in-room

TV (Freeview), large walled terrace. BACKGROUND MUSIC In public areas. CHILDREN All ages welcomed. DOGS Allowed in bedrooms, public rooms. PRICES Room from £125. À la carte £30.

HEACHAM Norfolk
Map 2:A4
HEACHAM HOUSE, 18 Staithe Road, PE31 7ED. Tel 01485 579529, www. heachamhouse.com. Overlooking the village duck pond, Rebecca and Robert Bradley's smart B&B is a fine base for local exploration; the sandy beaches and salt marshes of the north Norfolk coast are within easy reach. Enter the red-brick Victorian house mid-afternoon to be greeted with tea and home-made cake in the lounge (a log fire is lit here when the weather turns chilly). Well-equipped bedrooms, each different, have fresh flowers, home-baked biscuits, bathrobes and slippers; there are fluffy towels and face cloths in the bathrooms. Breakfast brings home-baked bread, home-made preserves and award-winning sausages – good fuel for a day of tackling any of the walking and cycling routes from the door. A drying room is much appreciated on wet days. 3 miles from Hunstanton. BEDROOMS 3. OPEN All year. FACILITIES Sitting room, breakfast room, free Wi-Fi, in-room TV (Freeview), small front garden, parking, bicycle storage. BACKGROUND MUSIC None. CHILDREN Not under 14. PRICES Per room B&B £85–£95. Credit cards not accepted.

HERTFORD Hertfordshire
Map 2:C4
NUMBER ONE PORT HILL, 1 Port Hill, SG14 1PJ. Tel 01992 587350, www.numberoneporthill.co.uk.

Get delightfully lost amid the treasure trove of Annie Rowley's artfully styled Georgian town house B&B: 'an unbelievable collection' of vintage glassware, sculptures and objects fills the 'immaculately kept' rooms. (Admire it all while savouring the home-made sloe gin.) Belgian hot chocolate, plentiful snacks, bathrobes and 'eclectic' reading material make the top-floor bedrooms cosy (two are petite); 'very good' double glazing keeps out traffic noise, though there may be occasional creaks and bumps from other rooms. Wake to a 'superb' breakfast, with freshly ground coffee and home-made preserves, at an elegantly laid communal table. On a fine day, ask to have it under the ancient wisteria in the walled garden. Look out for regular supper club events. 5 mins' walk from town centre. BEDROOMS 3. OPEN All year except Christmas. FACILITIES Drawing room, free Wi-Fi, in-room TV (Sky, Freeview), front and back gardens, limited street parking. BACKGROUND MUSIC At breakfast (radio). CHILDREN Not under 12 ('though exemptions may be made, if discussed, for younger children'). PRICES Per room B&B £120–£150.

HEXHAM Northumberland
Map 4:B3
THE HERMITAGE, Swinburne, NE48 4DG. Tel 01434 681248, www. thehermitagebedandbreakfast.co.uk. 'Just lovely.' Arrive to a welcoming pot of tea and home-baked cake at Catherine Stewart's B&B. Fans like the traditional atmosphere, in a 'beautiful house' built with the same type of stone that makes up Hadrian's Wall nearby. There are antiques and old family photographs; the large lounge has a TV

and a small library of books to browse. Sun yourself in the spacious garden one day, or play tennis another. Upstairs, fresh flowers brighten the peaceful, 'very comfortable' bedrooms. The hostess is on hand with advice about nearby eateries and easily accessible circular walks. 'Excellent' communal breakfasts. 7 miles N of Corbridge (ask for directions). BEDROOMS 3. OPEN Mar–Oct. FACILITIES Drawing room, breakfast room, free Wi-Fi, 2-acre grounds, terrace, tennis court. CHILDREN Babes in arms, and children over 6 welcomed. PRICES Per room B&B single £56–£62, double £95–£99. Credit cards not accepted.

HOLT Norfolk
Map 2:A5
BYFORDS, 1–3 Shirehall Plain, NR25 6BG. Tel 01263 711400, www.byfords. org.uk. 'Friendly staff' extend a 'great welcome' at this laid-back operation, an all-day café, store and B&B in the oldest house in a Georgian market town. Owners Clair and Iain Wilson also own The Dial House, Reepham (see main entry). Enter through the deli; individually decorated bedrooms, full of character, some snug, are at the back, up a winding staircase. They have stripped wood flooring, vintage furnishings, a plate of home-made biscuits; a shared fridge on the landing supplies fresh milk and water. Straightforward dishes, such as slow-cooked lamb, sweet-and-spicy chicken, pastas and pizzas, are served in the 'rustic' restaurant, candlelit at night. At breakfast, order 'whatever hot dishes you like' from the café menu. Set off with a picnic from the deli. BEDROOMS 16, plus self-catering apartment.

FACILITIES Café, deli, free Wi-Fi, in-room TV (Sky), terrace, parking. BACKGROUND MUSIC In café. CHILDREN All ages welcomed. PRICES Per room B&B £165–£215, D,B&B £205–£255.

HOOK Hampshire
Map 2:D3
TYLNEY HALL, Ridge Lane, Rotherwick, RG27 9AZ. Tel 01256 764881, www.tylneyhall.co.uk. Sweep up the tree-lined avenue to this Victorian mansion standing in 'fantastic' Gertrude Jekyll-designed gardens; when you arrive, take in the far-reaching views of 'lovely, peaceful' countryside. The staff at this luxury hotel are 'welcoming and always helpful' – even Fido gets a warm greeting, with bowls, a bed and 'high-quality dog food'. 'Well-furnished bedrooms' are conservative and elegant; golf carts ('always swift') ferry guests from the main house to cottage rooms in the grounds. 'We were happy in our ground-floor garden room as we could let the dog out in the morning and at night.' In the wood-panelled restaurant, chef Stephen Hine cooks 'good' modern British dishes; informal meals are taken in the lounge or on the garden-facing terrace. BEDROOMS 112. Some in cottages in the grounds, some suitable for disabled. FACILITIES 2 lounges, bar, restaurant, private dining rooms, free Wi-Fi, in-room TV (Freeview), civil wedding licence, conference/function facilities, spa (indoor and outdoor swimming pools, gym, tennis, treatment rooms), 66-acre grounds. CHILDREN All ages welcomed (goody bags, exploration trails, ducks to feed). DOGS Allowed in some rooms (£25 per night). PRICES Per room B&B from £250. À la carte £45.

HUDDERSFIELD Yorkshire
Map 4:E3
THE THREE ACRES INN & RESTAURANT, Roydhouse, HD8 8LR. Tel 01484 602606, www.3acres.com. 'The food is worth the detour' at this 'friendly' roadside drovers' inn set 'high on the hills' near Huddersfield, with 'tremendous views to all sides'. Brian Orme and Neil Truelove opened their pub-with-rooms some 40 years ago; today, Neil's son, Tom, makes up the trio. Bedrooms are in the main building and garden cottages. Discuss rooms at booking: a single room this year was found 'comfortable, clean and functional, with an agreeable bed', though there was some noise from a neighbouring room. In the 'civilised' dining room, 'high-quality' modern British dishes are 'clearly popular locally'. Breakfast has home-made muesli, local bacon and sausage, porridge with cream and golden syrup. Popular Sunday lunches. 6 miles from town centre (busy morning traffic). BEDROOMS 17. 1 suitable for disabled, 8 in adjacent cottages. OPEN All year except evenings 25–26 Dec, midday 31 Dec, evening 1 Jan. FACILITIES Bar, restaurant, free Wi-Fi, in-room TV (Freeview), civil wedding licence, small function/private dining facilities, terraced garden. BACKGROUND MUSIC In bar and restaurant. CHILDREN Well-behaved children welcomed. PRICES Per room B&B from £100. À la carte £45.

HURLEY Berkshire
Map 2:D3
HURLEY HOUSE, Henley Road, SL6 5LH. Tel 01628 568500, hurleyhouse.co.uk. Where an 18th-century pub once stood, this privately owned,

rebuilt-from-the-ground-up roadside hotel today has understated rooms, a traditionally styled bar, and an 'excellent restaurant' headed by award-winning chef Michael Chapman. 'Nice, local staff' welcome guests to the characterful pub (granite, limestone and oak; rustic furnishings; wood-burning stoves); above are modern bedrooms, handsome in cream and grey. Each has comforts such as underfloor heating, air conditioning, and a smart bathroom with a 'good, strong shower'. 'Efficient double-glazing keeps out traffic noise from the busy road', but this is not for walkers from the door (no pavement). Eat inside or on the rear terrace: the locally sourced, seasonal menus are enjoyed. 'Good choice' at breakfast. Close to Marlow and Henley-on-Thames. BEDROOMS 10. OPEN All year. FACILITIES Bar, snug, restaurant (closed Sun eve), private dining room, free Wi-Fi, in-room TV (Freeview), function facilities, massage and beauty treatment room, terrace, barbecue lawn, parking. BACKGROUND MUSIC In public areas 'but they turned it off when we asked'. CHILDREN All ages welcomed. PRICES Per room B&B £170–£295. À la carte £45.

ILSINGTON Devon
Map 1:D4

ILSINGTON COUNTRY HOUSE, nr Newton Abbot, Dartmoor National Park, TQ13 9RR. Tel 01364 661452, www.ilsington. co.uk. 'It's a pleasure to stay here.' In a 'beautiful location with stunning views of Hay Tor and Dartmoor', the Hassell family's 'delightful' hotel has 'a lot going for it': 'friendly, helpful and efficient staff'; 'good-quality food'; the 'quiet surroundings'. ('A little tricky to find' – 'but worth finding!') Take in 'lovely' moorland views from any of the traditionally furnished bedrooms. 'We thought our room could have used some updating, but we appreciated the big, comfortable bed, the heaps of storage space, and the modern bathroom, which had a good shower over the bath.' Bistro food and snacks are served in the Blue Tiger Inn; in the dining room, chef Mike O'Donnell's 'excellently presented' British dishes might include 'perfect smoked haddock risotto' or 'commendable guinea fowl confit'. 4 miles NE of Ashburton. BEDROOMS 25. 8 on ground floor. OPEN All year. FACILITIES Lift, 2 lounges, bar, restaurant, pub, conservatory, spa (fitness suite, sauna, steam room, heated indoor swimming pool, hydrotherapy pool), free Wi-Fi, in-room TV (Freeview), civil wedding licence, conference facilities, 10-acre grounds. BACKGROUND MUSIC All day in bar, in restaurant in the evening. CHILDREN All ages welcomed. DOGS Allowed in ground-floor bedrooms, bar, conservatory, on lead in garden. PRICES Per room B&B from £130, D,B&B from £197. Set dinner £33.50–£39.50.

IRONBRIDGE Shropshire
Map 2:A1

THE LIBRARY HOUSE, 11 Severn Bank, TF8 7AN. Tel 01952 432299, www. libraryhouse.com. Once the village library, this 'beautifully decorated' Grade II listed Georgian building near the River Severn is today a cheerful B&B run by Sarah and Tim Davis. The book-lined sitting room retains the original library shelves; in chilly weather, a fire in the log burner makes this a cosy spot. Bedrooms are each named after a writer. Choose Chaucer for its private garden terrace, or high-ceilinged Eliot for its views towards the river. All rooms are well equipped with waffle dressing gowns, fresh milk, and a hot-water bottle on a cool night. Well placed for visiting the UNESCO World Heritage site of Ironbridge Gorge and its museums. Restaurants and pubs nearby. 3 miles from Telford. BEDROOMS 3. 1 with private terrace. FACILITIES Sitting room, breakfast room, free Wi-Fi, in-room TV (Freeview), courtyard, mature garden, parking passes for local car parks. BACKGROUND MUSIC None. CHILDREN Not under 16. PRICES Per person B&B £75–£120.

KESWICK Cumbria
Map 4: inset C2

DALEGARTH HOUSE, Portinscale, CA12 5RQ. Tel 01768 772817, www.dalegarth-house.co.uk. Choose a room, then pick your route: Craig and Clare Dalton's friendly, good-value guest house is surrounded by walks for all levels. Each restful bedroom is supplied with a hospitality tray and a flat-screen TV; nearly every room of the Edwardian house looks out on to spectacular vistas of Derwentwater and the northern fells. Hearty Cumbrian breakfasts and home-baked cakes at teatime keep you going all day. Ask in advance about the hostess's local-produce-packed four-course dinners, served by arrangement at 7 pm. (Dietary requirements may be catered for, with notice.) BEDROOMS 10. 2 on ground floor in annexe. OPEN Mar–mid-Dec. FACILITIES Lounge, bar, dining room, free Wi-Fi, in-room TV (Freeview), garden, parking, bicycle storage. BACKGROUND MUSIC Occasional radio at breakfast, classical/'easy listening' at dinner. CHILDREN Not under

12. PRICES Per person B&B £45–£55, D,B&B £69–£79. 2-night min. stay preferred.

LYZZICK HALL, Underskiddaw, CA12 4PY. Tel 01768 772277, www.lyzzickhall.co.uk. Families are 'warmly welcomed' at this early Victorian country house, 'ideally positioned' for exploring the Catbells and Borrowdale valley. The hotel is owned by the Fernandez and Lake families. Gaze at 'glorious views' of the Lakeland fells from the 'well-equipped' bedrooms, or step into the 'stunning scenery' via good walking and cycling routes from the door. Return to relax in the lounge, where a toasty fire is lit when the weather turns cool; in balmy weather, an icy drink in the garden is just the ticket. 'Excellent' British dishes are served in the elegant dining room; the chef will whip up 'whatever the children fancy', depending on the ingredients at hand. Save room for the 'fine desserts'. No buffet at breakfast, but 'plenty of choice'. 2 miles N of Keswick. BEDROOMS 30. 1 on ground floor. OPEN Feb–Dec except Christmas. FACILITIES 2 lounges, bar, orangery, restaurant, free Wi-Fi, in-room TV, heated indoor swimming pool, sauna, spa bath, 4-acre landscaped grounds. BACKGROUND MUSIC In public areas. CHILDREN All ages welcomed (toys, books, play area). PRICES Per person B&B from £79, D,B&B from £104.

KINGHAM Oxfordshire
Map 3:D6

MILL HOUSE HOTEL, OX7 6UH. Tel 01608 658 188, www.millhousehotel.co.uk. 'A warm, family-friendly atmosphere' fills Paul and Maria

Drinkwater's 'lovely old building', a one-time flour mill, now a bustling hotel on the River Everlode. 'Good-value' accommodation is in bedrooms supplied with complimentary toiletries and home-made biscuits. There's plenty of space to play in the 'well-kept gardens', and a lounge to be cosy in – by the fireplace in wintery weather. Order light bites here, or on the terrace overlooking the trout stream; drink real ales in the bar. 'Well-presented, well-cooked' dishes are 'promptly and courteously served' in the traditional restaurant. 6 miles from Stow-on-the-Wold, complimentary collection/drop-off service to and from Kingham Station. BEDROOMS 21. FACILITIES Bar, restaurant, free Wi-Fi, in-room TV (Freeview), terrace, 10-acre landscaped gardens, parking. BACKGROUND MUSIC In public areas (live music performed 4 pm–7 pm on the first Sunday of every month). CHILDREN All ages welcomed. DOGS Allowed. PRICES Per room B&B from £120, D,B&B from £165.

KINGSBRIDGE Devon
Map 1:D4

THURLESTONE HOTEL, Thurlestone, TQ7 3NN. Tel 01548 560382, www.thurlestone.co.uk. 'The Grose family maintains its excellent tradition' of providing first-class hospitality near the rugged Devon coastline, where consecutive generations have run the family-friendly hotel for more than 120 years. Well-equipped (if 'a bit old-fashioned') bedrooms have 'mesmerising views' of the subtropical gardens and the coast; larger family rooms have bunk beds for the children, or space to accommodate a cot or extra bed.

Consume crab sandwiches, seafood platters and real ales in the 16th-century village inn or the terrace bar; dress up for dinner in the newly refurbished Trevilder restaurant. Stroll five minutes to the sea or choose one of the diversions available in the grounds: croquet lawns, sun terraces, sports facilities, a spa; a children's club during the school holidays. 4 miles SW of Kingsbridge. BEDROOMS 65. 2 suitable for disabled. FACILITIES Lift, lounges, bar, restaurant, bistro (May–Sept), village pub, free Wi-Fi, in-room TV (Sky), civil wedding licence, function facilities, terrace, spa, outdoor heated swimming pool (May–Sept), tennis, squash, badminton, croquet, 9-hole golf course. CHILDREN All ages welcomed. DOGS Allowed in some bedrooms, not in public rooms. PRICES Per room B&B from £180. À la carte £40. 2-night min. stay.

KINGSWEAR Devon
Map 1:D4

KAYWANA HALL, Higher Contour Road, nr Dartmouth, TQ6 0AY. Tel 01803 752200, kaywanahall.co.uk. In acres of mature woodland, Tony Pithers and Gordon Craig's uber-modern home (one of five 'butterfly' houses in Devon) is all curving stairways, unexpected angles and walls of glass. Each light-filled bedroom at the adults-only B&B has its own entrance and private decking area reached via steep steps. Inside, a cool modern aesthetic takes hold, with abstract art on the walls. Thoughtful extras: a mini-fridge, iPod docking station, espresso machine, fudge and home-made biscuits. Breakfast at a time to suit in the airy, open-plan dining room/kitchen overlooking the swimming pool. The menu includes freshly squeezed juices, locally baked bread, fruit compote, summer berries in season, and plenty of cooked options. ½ mile from Kingswear. BEDROOMS 4. OPEN Apr–Sept. FACILITIES Breakfast room, free Wi-Fi in bedrooms, in-room TV (Freeview), 12-acre grounds, 9-metre heated outdoor swimming pool, parking. BACKGROUND MUSIC None. CHILDREN Not accepted. PRICES Per room B&B £165–£210.

KIRKBY LONSDALE Cumbria
Map 4: inset C2
SUN INN, 6 Market Street, LA6 2AU. Tel 015242 71965, www.sun-inn.info. A meander from the River Lune, this 17th-century inn by the old churchyard in the historic market town reserves a special welcome for walkers and their dogs. Iain and Jenny Black took over ownership in 2017; the real ales, log fires, wonky beams and 'friendly atmosphere' remain. There's modern country cooking in the restaurant and bar (perhaps rosemary and garlic hogget, crapaudine beetroot, creamed potato); and your dog can also look forward to a treat. Bedrooms have a carpet of Swaledale wool, and nice amenities: fresh milk, Cumbrian biscuits, bottled water. Breakfast includes home-made granola, pastries, and fresh and poached fruit on the buffet. BEDROOMS 11. OPEN All year except Christmas Day. FACILITIES Bar, restaurant, free Wi-Fi, in-room TV (Freeview), parking (permits supplied). BACKGROUND MUSIC In bar. CHILDREN All ages welcomed. DOGS Allowed in bedrooms, public rooms (separate dog-friendly area in restaurant). PRICES

Per room B&B £115–£190, D,B&B £179–£258. À la carte £34.

KNARESBOROUGH Yorkshire
Map 4:D4
NEWTON HOUSE, 5–7 York Place, HG5 0AD. Tel 01423 863539, www. newtonhouseyorkshire.com. Denise Carter's 'good-value' B&B is an 'enjoyable spot', say Guide readers this year. In the 'fascinating' 300-year-old house at the centre of a 'lovely' market town, traditional bedrooms are 'spacious, comfortable and well appointed', with thoughtful extras – books, magazines, filtered water, a hospitality tray. There are treats in the honesty bar in the sitting room, too: local beers, soft drinks, aperitifs and nightcaps. Ask the hostess for recommendations of nearby eateries at dinnertime, or stay in for a light bite – soup, an omelette or a sandwich may be 'rustled up'. Start the day with home-baked sourdough bread; jams and compotes made on the Aga; locally sourced eggs, milk, smoked fish, bacon and sausages. 'The organic breakfasts deserve their excellent reputation.' On-site parking is a bonus. 4 miles from Harrogate. BEDROOMS 12. 2 on ground floor suitable for disabled, 2 in converted stables. FACILITIES Sitting room (books, magazines, newspapers, games), dining room, conservatory, free Wi-Fi, in-room TV (Freeview), small courtyard garden, 'wildlife area' with bird feeders, parking. BACKGROUND MUSIC Classic FM at breakfast. CHILDREN All ages welcomed (books, games, toys). DOGS Allowed in 2 stable block rooms with outside access (home-made treats). PRICES Per room B&B single £60–£100, double £85–£125.

LANCASTER Lancashire
Map 4:D2

THE ASHTON, Well House, Wyresdale Road, LA1 3JJ. Tel 01524 684600, www.theashtonlancaster.com. James Gray, a former TV set dresser, wins praise for the 'high standards and superb attention to detail' at his stylish, modern B&B, in a Georgian mansion down the road from Williamson Park. Arrive to drinks and home-baked nibbles, then explore the house: there are homely touches (and clever style ideas to borrow) throughout. Bedrooms have individual charm – perhaps tall wooden shutters or an enormous roll-top bath; each has a bathroom with underfloor heating, bathrobes and chic toiletries. Simple, deli-style suppers (locally sourced meat, fish, cheese, chutneys, home-baked bread; order in advance) may be taken in the dining room or bedroom. Breakfast has a generous supply of fresh muffins and fruit salad; the garden hens provide the eggs. 1 mile E of city centre. BEDROOMS 5. 1 on ground floor. OPEN All year except 24–26 Dec, 31 Dec, 1 Jan. FACILITIES Lounge, dining room, free Wi-Fi, in-room TV (Freeview), 1-acre garden, parking. BACKGROUND MUSIC In dining room. CHILDREN Not under 6. DOGS Allowed in 1 bedroom, public rooms. PRICES Per room B&B £110–£180.

GREENBANK FARMHOUSE, Abbeystead, LA2 9BA. Tel 01524 792063, www.greenbankfarmhouse.co.uk. 'Wonderful moorland views' surround Sally and Simon Tait's 'well-appointed', 'very affordable' B&B, on a former cheese-making farm on the edge of the Forest of Bowland. 'It's a good centre for exploring the area,' say guests in 2017 – and a 'haven' for birdwatchers: many bird species can be spotted from the comfort of the conservatory lounge. Arrive to a 'warm welcome', then settle in to one of the 'spacious', country-style bedrooms: each has 'ample storage', 'adequate lighting', and panoramic views of the surrounding fells ('even from the loo!'). Wake to an 'excellent', freshly cooked breakfast (ordered the night before) of farm-fresh eggs, home-made bread, loose-leaf tea and local bacon and sausages. 8 miles from the city. Dinner in neighbouring Dolphinholme gets a thumbs-up. BEDROOMS 4. 1 on ground floor. OPEN All year. FACILITIES Conservatory breakfast room/sitting area, free Wi-Fi, in-room TV (Freeview), ½-acre lawned garden on 6-acre grounds (some working farmland), parking. BACKGROUND MUSIC None. PRICES Per person B&B single £50, double £65. Credit cards not accepted.

LECHLADE Gloucestershire
Map 3:E6

THE FIVE ALLS, Filkins, GL7 3JQ. Tel 01367 860875, www.thefiveallsfilkins.co.uk. Flagstone floors, stone walls and a huge fireplace are expected of an 18th-century coaching inn in the Cotswolds. Unexpected, and wholly welcome, is the quirky sophistication that owners Lana and Sebastian Snow have brought to their dining pub-with-rooms. There are colourful textiles, Bill Brandt prints and playful wallpapers; leather chesterfield sofas by the log fire. Pubby informality reigns in the buzzing bar and stylish dining area, where Sebastian Snow's modern plates might include cracked Kelmscott pork, caramelised apples, white bean and sage cassoulet. On a sunny day, picnic tables are set out in the garden for alfresco dining.

Upstairs, cosy, pale-hued bedrooms have a comfortable bed, a smart bathroom, local artwork on the walls. The Snows also own The Plough, Kelmscott (see main entry), nearby. BEDROOMS 9. 5 in annexe. OPEN All year. FACILITIES Snug, bar, restaurant (closed Sun eve), free Wi-Fi, in-room TV (Freeview), garden, parking. BACKGROUND MUSIC In public areas. CHILDREN All ages welcomed. DOGS Allowed in public rooms, not in bedrooms. PRICES Per room B&B £95–£180. À la carte £30.

LEICESTER Leicestershire
Map 2:B3
HOTEL MAIYANGO, 13–21 St Nicholas Place, LE1 4LD. Tel 01162 518898, www.maiyango.com. Bespoke wood furnishings, original artwork and bold colours have transformed this one-time shoe factory near the historic centre into a modern, style-led hotel. Head to the top for city-skyline views and pre-dinner drinks in the Glass bar or on the wraparound roof terrace, then swing down to the informal, lantern-lit restaurant, to sample the menu of fusion dishes. A typical option: steamed wild sea bass, spiced coconut laksa, bok choi, chilli, coriander. Bedrooms of varying sizes are colourful and contemporary; each is supplied with bottled water, organic tea and coffee, fresh milk, fine toiletries and a choice of pillows. 15 mins' walk to train station. BEDROOMS 14. 1 suitable for disabled. OPEN All year except Christmas, New Year. FACILITIES Lift, bar, restaurant (closed for lunch Sun–Tues), free Wi-Fi, in-room TV (Freeview), function facilities, 24-hour room service, roof terrace, paid public parking nearby. BACKGROUND MUSIC In public areas. CHILDREN All ages

welcomed. PRICES Per person B&B from £79, D,B&B from £111.

LEVENS Cumbria
Map 4: inset C2
HARE AND HOUNDS, LA8 8PN. Tel 015395 60004, www.hareandhoundslevens.co.uk. Becky and Ash Dewar's popular village pub 'with a modern twist' is in a 16th-century coaching inn in the Lyth valley. Join locals in the beamed, slate-floored bar for cask ales, craft beers or a cocktail made with locally produced spirits. At any time of day, choose from a menu of burgers, pizzas and comfort food in the light-filled dining room. On a sunny day, the beer garden's the place to be. Upstairs, smart, contemporary bedrooms have lovely extras: home-made brownies, freshly ground coffee and fresh milk, a digital radio, Cumbrian-made toiletries. There are fresh fruit, cereals, yogurt and locally baked bread at breakfast; cooked dishes include smoked salmon and scrambled eggs, and a full English. BEDROOMS 4. OPEN All year, no accommodation 24–25 Dec. FACILITIES Bar, lounge, restaurant, free Wi-Fi, in-room TV (Freeview), beer garden, parking. BACKGROUND MUSIC In bar and restaurant. CHILDREN All ages welcomed. DOGS Allowed in pub and garden. PRICES Per room B&B £85–£145, D,B&B £135–£195. 2-night min. stay at weekends.

LEWANNICK Cornwall
Map 1:D3
COOMBESHEAD FARM, PL15 7QQ. Tel 01566 782 009, www.coombesheadfarm.co.uk. A farmhouse retreat for foodies, this informal B&B, in a rural setting of meadows, woodland and oak-lined

streams, mixes handsomely rustic bedrooms with convivial feasts rustled up in an open kitchen. It was set up by two chefs – April Bloomfield, of New York's Spotted Pig, and Tom Adams, of London's Pitt Cue. Four nights a week, crowd around the ten-seater table for the single-sitting set dinner, cooked using home-smoked, -cured and -pickled ingredients, local produce and wild food foraged from the surrounding estate. Uncluttered bedrooms are countryside fresh, with views of Dartmoor on the horizon. Breakfast, naturally, is a feast: home-made yogurts, home-baked breads, freshly milled oats and grains, and much more home-cooking besides. A restaurant is planned; cooking workshops are regularly organised. 6 miles from Launceston. BEDROOMS 5. 1 with adjoining bunk-bedroom. OPEN Thurs–Sun Feb–Dec. FACILITIES Living room, library, dining room, kitchen, bakery, free Wi-Fi, 66-acre grounds, parking. BACKGROUND MUSIC In evening in living room, dining room and kitchen. CHILDREN Not under 16. DOGS Not allowed in bedrooms. PRICES Per room B&B £175, D,B&B £275. Set menu £50.

LICHFIELD Staffordshire
Map 2:A2

SWINFEN HALL, Swinfen, WS14 9RE. Tel 01543 481494, www. swinfenhallhotel.co.uk. 'I was greeted at the door when I arrived; the attention to detail continued throughout my stay.' Praise this year from a Guide reader for this 'superb' Georgian manor in extensive, 'well-maintained grounds'. The house is 'very grand' – even the entrance lobby has a balustraded minstrel's gallery – but 'friendly staff' create a 'relaxing experience'. Stuart Kennedy manages for the owners, Helen and Vic Wiser. Choose among spacious, well-appointed bedrooms decorated in traditional or modern style – each looks over formal gardens or parkland. Evenings, sip pre- and post-prandial cocktails in the clubby lounge or the wood-panelled Edwardian bar. In between, dine in the award-winning restaurant on estate-reared venison and lamb, and produce from the Victorian walled garden and orchard. 2 miles S of Lichfield. BEDROOMS 17. OPEN All year except Christmas Day evening, Boxing Day. FACILITIES Bar, lounge, cocktail lounge, restaurant (closed Sun, Mon eve, bar and terrace menu available), function/private dining rooms, free Wi-Fi, in-room TV (Sky), civil wedding licence, 100-acre grounds (formal gardens, woodlands, parkland, wild hay meadows, 45-acre deer park), regular events (weddings, concerts, wine and jazz suppers, gourmet nights), parking. BACKGROUND MUSIC 'As appropriate' in cocktail lounge, bar, restaurant. CHILDREN All ages welcomed. PRICES Per room B&B single from £140, double from £170. À la carte £50, tasting menus £59–£75.

LINCOLN Lincolnshire
Map 4:E5

THE CASTLE HOTEL, Westgate, LN1 3AS. Tel 01522 538801, www. castlehotel.net. On the site of Lincoln's Roman Forum, this smartly refurbished hotel in the historic Bailgate area is an excellent base from which to explore the city. The 'extremely pleasant' staff are praised. Choose a view: 'comfortable' contemporary bedrooms (some small) in the main building overlook the castle walls or the medieval cathedral. Courtyard rooms in the peaceful, 250-year-old coach house may lack the city scenery, but they're all conveniently on the ground floor, with parking just outside. At mealtimes, 'beautifully presented' modern European dishes might include English asparagus, fried duck egg, Old Winchester, watercress gremolata; braised blade of beef, hispi cabbage, champ mash, seared scallops. Lighter, bistro-style options may be taken in the elegant bar. BEDROOMS 18. Some in attic, some in courtyard, 1 suitable for disabled, plus 1 apartment, and 2-bed Castle Mews (available for self-catering). FACILITIES 2 small lounges, bar, restaurant (closed Sun eve), free Wi-Fi, in-room TV, wedding/ function facilities, massage and beauty treatments, parking. BACKGROUND MUSIC In public areas. CHILDREN All ages welcomed. PRICES Per room B&B single £90–£130, double £110–£150, D,B&B single £120–£165, double £170–£220. Set menus £30–£35, à la carte £34.

LITTLE ECCLESTON Lancashire
Map 4:D2

THE CARTFORD INN, Cartford Lane, PR3 0YP. Tel 01995 670166, www. thecartfordinn.co.uk. On the banks of the River Wyre, Julie and Patrick Beaumé's refurbished 17th-century coaching inn surprises with its voguish bedrooms and imaginative, French-inflected cooking. Locals and visitors eat informally in the convivial bar (with its roster of regional cask ales and its own brew, it's also a happy spot for beer lovers). In the restaurant, seasonal Lancashire produce is showcased on the menu and the daily specials board.

Each of the eclectically styled bedrooms is different: some have a Juliet balcony with river views; a penthouse suite takes in a panorama of the Bowland Fells. Two uber-modern studio lodges overlooking the water were added in 2017. Don't leave without calling in at the deli, TOTI, for sweet and savoury takeaway treats from the inn's kitchen. BEDROOMS 17. Some in riverside annexe, 1 suitable for disabled, 2 lodges in grounds. OPEN All year except Christmas Day. FACILITIES Bar, restaurant, delicatessen, free Wi-Fi, in-room TV (Freeview), riverside terrace, garden, parking. BACKGROUND MUSIC In public areas. CHILDREN All ages welcomed. PRICES Per room B&B single from £90, double £125–£230.

LIVERPOOL Merseyside
Map 4:E2

HARD DAYS NIGHT, Central Buildings, North John Street, L2 6RR. Tel 01512 361964, www.harddaysnighthotel.com. Close to the famous Cavern Club, this Beatles-themed hotel is a must for fans of the Fab Four. The grand Victorian building has 'a strong dash of personality', with original art and cleverly incorporated references to the Liverpool band here, there and everywhere. Shout if you need somebody – 'friendly staff' are on hand to help. Discuss bedroom choices when booking: some rooms have a private balcony; the quietest rooms overlook the rear. Each individually decorated bedroom has a large bed, 'good fittings', a well-equipped bathroom. Shake it up with dinner in the restaurant (decorated with Sir Peter Blake's iconic artwork), where traditional British dishes have a contemporary twist. BEDROOMS 110. 1 suitable for disabled. OPEN All year.

FACILITIES Lift, lounge/bar, cocktail bar, restaurant (closed for lunch Sun and Mon), art gallery, free Wi-Fi, in-room TV (Sky), civil wedding licence, function facilities, parking discounts. BACKGROUND MUSIC All day in public areas, live music on Fri and Sat nights in bar. CHILDREN All ages welcomed. PRICES Per room B&B from £135. À la carte £25.

HOPE STREET HOTEL, 40 Hope Street, L1 9DA. Tel 0151 709 3000, www. hopestreethotel.co.uk. 'Well located for exploring the city', this contemporary hotel opposite the Philharmonic Hall basks in the buzz of the vibrant cultural quarter. 'Light, airy' public areas showcase the history of the former Victorian coach factory – exposed brick walls, vintage metal supports and old beams have been retained. Smart, stripped-back bedrooms (white walls, uncovered wood floors) vary in size and aspect. Those at the top have 'wonderful views' of the river or city landmarks; others have a less inspiring outlook. Order sharing platters and cocktails in the bar; in the London Carriage Works restaurant, 'delicious' modern dishes use plenty of regional produce. At breakfast, a guest this year found the continental selection lacking imagination, though 'the cooked dishes, off a varied menu, are generous'. 25 mins' downhill walk to Lime Street Station. BEDROOMS 89. Some interconnecting, 2 suitable for disabled. FACILITIES Lift, lounge, bar, restaurant, private dining rooms, free Wi-Fi, in-room TV (Sky, Freeview), civil wedding licence, functions, 24-hour room service, gym, treatment rooms, limited parking nearby (£10 charge). BACKGROUND MUSIC In public areas. CHILDREN All

ages welcomed. DOGS Allowed (£15 per night). PRICES Per room B&B from £89.

THE NADLER LIVERPOOL, 29 Seel Street, L1 4AU. Tel 0151 705 2626, www. thenadler.com. In a handsome former printworks, this 'practical, efficient' hotel has good-value accommodation in the lively Ropewalks area. It is part of a small chain specialising in 'affordable luxury' (see The Nadler Kensington, London, Shortlist entry). Air-conditioned bedrooms vary in size, from a snug double to a two-level suite with a private courtyard. All have triple-glazed windows. Travellers with a DIY spirit appreciate the mini-kitchen in each room, equipped with tea, coffee, a microwave, a fridge, crockery and cutlery. There's no bar or restaurant, but guests receive a discount at a slew of neighbourhood eateries, bars and clubs. A continental breakfast (ordered in advance) is taken in the lounge. BEDROOMS 106. Some suitable for disabled. FACILITIES Lift, lounge, meeting room, free Wi-Fi, in-room TV, 30 mins of free local and national landline calls per day, vending machines, parking discounts. BACKGROUND MUSIC In public areas. CHILDREN All ages welcomed. PRICES Room from £62. Breakfast £7.

LOOE Cornwall
Map 1:D3
THE BEACH HOUSE, Marine Drive, Hannafore, PL13 2DH. Tel 01503 262598, www.thebeachhouselooe.co.uk. Coastal trails, fishing villages, rock pools and sandy beaches are within reach of this 'ideally located' seafront B&B, up the riverside road from the centre. Rosie and David Reeve are the 'superb

hosts'. Take in super views over tea and home-made cake in the garden room when you arrive. Homely bedrooms are 'spotlessly clean' and stocked with tea- and coffee-making facilities, a fridge with fresh milk, 'regularly replenished' bottles of Cornish water. Three rooms are sea-facing; two have garden access. At breakfast, help yourself to fresh fruit, home-made muffins and yogurt; good hot options are cooked to order. The South West Coast Path runs past the front gate; the Reeves have advice on day-trips to Polperro. ½ mile from town centre. BEDROOMS 5. OPEN All year except Christmas. FACILITIES Garden room, breakfast room, free Wi-Fi, terrace, ½-acre garden, beach opposite. BACKGROUND MUSIC In breakfast room. CHILDREN Not under 16. PRICES Per room B&B £100–£130.

LUDLOW Shropshire
Map 3:C4

SHROPSHIRE HILLS, Aston Munslow, SY7 9ER. Tel 01584 841565, www. shropshirehillsbedandbreakfast.co.uk. Chris and Linda Baker live up to their name at their country B&B, welcoming guests with home-baked cake and tea. 'Linda made sure I was never short of her delicious gluten-free cakes and biscuits,' says one well-fed Guide reader. Each 'spacious, spotless' bedroom has its own entrance and is well equipped with fresh milk, teas, ground coffee and a locally hand-woven wool throw. Start the day with a visit to the alpacas grazing in the paddock, then come back for a home-grown breakfast with greenhouse-fresh produce, home-made jams and compotes made from garden fruit, eggs from the Bakers' chickens. Drying facilities and a boot room are

ideal for walkers and cyclists. Well positioned for walking the Shropshire Way along the slopes of Wenlock Edge. 8 miles NE of Ludlow. BEDROOMS 3. All with separate entrance from main house. OPEN Easter–Nov. FACILITIES Lounge/dining room, free Wi-Fi, in-room TV (Freeview), 2-acre garden, terrace (outdoor seating). BACKGROUND MUSIC None. CHILDREN Not under 16. PRICES Per room B&B £98–£125. 2-night min. stay preferred.

LUPTON Cumbria
Map 4: inset C2

THE PLOUGH, Cow Brow, LA6 1PJ. Tel 01539 567700, www.theploughatlupton. co.uk. Laid-back and friendly, with a side of sweet potato fries, this refurbished 18th-century roadside inn is liked for its superior pub grub and handsome accommodation. The pub and dining areas have an updated rustic look: wide wooden tables and mismatched chairs; leather sofas under old oak beams; sheepskin-covered bar stools; a busy wood-burning stove in cold weather. At lunch and dinner, consider potted Ravenglass crab or a bavette steak grilled over barbecue coals. (Good vegetarian options, too.) Smart bedrooms vary in size and decor. One room has a working record player; another, clear views over Farleton Knott; yet another, squashy armchairs in a generous seating area. Light sleepers might ask for a room away from the road. 5 mins' drive from M6 junction 36. BEDROOMS 6. OPEN All year, no accommodation 24–25 Dec. FACILITIES Lounge, bar, restaurant, free Wi-Fi (signal variable), in-room TV (Freeview), civil wedding licence, terrace, garden, parking. BACKGROUND

MUSIC In reception, bar and restaurant. CHILDREN All ages welcomed. DOGS Allowed in bar, 1 bedroom. PRICES Per room B&B from £85. À la carte £30.

LYME REGIS Dorset
Map 1:C6

DORSET HOUSE, Pound Road, DT7 3HX. Tel 01297 442055, www. dorsethouselyme.com. The interior of this refurbished Regency house has much that is eye-catching, but the views out the sash windows are more than a match – the best bedrooms look along the coast. Lyn and Jason Martin's B&B is a short walk from the historic Cobb. Pour a complimentary hot drink, or an aperitif from the well-stocked honesty bar (the locally produced Castlewood bubbly is worth a try); there are newspapers and magazines in the fire-warmed snug to browse. Fresh and modern, bedrooms have a burnished wood floor and plenty of extras: thick bathrobes, natural toiletries, artisan teas, locally baked treats. Aga-cooked breakfasts, with much organic produce, are eaten communally. On a fine morning, ask to eat on the veranda – 'if you stand on tiptoe, you can even see the sea!' BEDROOMS 5. OPEN All year except Christmas. FACILITIES Snug, breakfast room, free Wi-Fi, in-room TV (Freeview), veranda, drying facilities, paid parking nearby. BACKGROUND MUSIC In breakfast room. CHILDREN All ages welcomed. PRICES Per room B&B £95–£170. 2-night min. stay.

LYTHAM Lancashire
Map 4:D2

THE ROOMS, 35 Church Road, FY8 5LL. Tel 01253 736000, www. theroomslytham.com. Andy Baker's modern B&B on the Fylde coast stands within walking distance of shops, restaurants and the sea. Well-fitted bedrooms might have a sloping ceiling, a skylight, a staircase leading to the bathroom; all have up-to-date technology (digital radio, iPod docking station, flat-screen TV), plus underfloor heating and a rain shower in the stylish bathroom. Breakfast on freshly blended smoothies, locally baked bread, perhaps a Buck's Fizz; cooked dishes include local sausages, smoked haddock, waffles and pancakes. The morning sun's the best side order: when weather permits, eat in the walled garden. The helpful host has plenty of local tips to share, including where to find the best pizza-and-jazz combos in town. BEDROOMS 5 ('lots of stairs'), plus 2-bed serviced apartment. FACILITIES Breakfast room, free Wi-Fi, in-room TV (Freeview), meeting facilities, decked garden. BACKGROUND MUSIC In breakfast room. CHILDREN All ages welcomed. PRICES Per room B&B single £90–£110, double £110–£140.

MALVERN WELLS Worcestershire
Map 3:D5

THE COTTAGE IN THE WOOD, Holywell Road, WR14 4LG. Tel 01684 588860, www.cottageinthewood.co.uk. Julia and Nick Davies are bringing a breath of fresh air – and a few 'tastefully flamboyant touches' – to their 18th-century dower house high on the east side of the Malvern hills. The 'stunning setting' remains, of course: 'You'd be hard pressed to find a hotel with a more impressive view.' The staff, many long-serving, continue to be 'friendly, helpful and attentive'. The 'modern makeover' ('along the grey-walls-and-hardwood-floors theme') has introduced a stylish restaurant and bar – a fine background for the 'excellent food and drink' at mealtimes. Further refurbishment is planned for the bedrooms, each varying in size, character and aspect. Breakfast is 'commendable', with 'delicious, and novel, dishes': avocado, poached eggs and bacon; assorted wild mushrooms on toast; home-made baked beans. 'We enjoyed our stay, and the enthusiasm of the staff.' BEDROOMS 30. 4 in Beech Cottage, 19 in Coach House; 10 on ground floor; 1 suitable for disabled. OPEN All year. FACILITIES Bar, restaurant, meeting room, free Wi-Fi, in-room TV (Freeview), 8-acre grounds, parking. BACKGROUND MUSIC 'Quiet, relaxing music' in restaurant and bar. CHILDREN All ages welcomed (cot £15, extra bed £25). DOGS Allowed in some bedrooms (£10 per night), not in public rooms. PRICES Per person B&B from £50, D,B&B from £90. À la carte £40.

MANCHESTER Greater Manchester Map 4:E3

DIDSBURY HOUSE, Didsbury Park, Didsbury Village, M20 5LJ. Tel 0161 448 2200, www.didsburyhouse.co.uk. A home-away-from-home, this Victorian villa is in a leafy urban village not far from the city centre. The style-conscious 'boutique B&B' (part of the Eclectic Hotels group; see Eleven Didsbury Park, next entry) is stocked with fresh flowers and books to borrow; there are open fires, and sofas to sink into. Prints and statement wallpaper blend well with original features (high windows, delicate cornices) in the individually styled bedrooms; many rooms have a freestanding roll-top bath. Weekends are made for lying in: breakfast is served until noon. At dusk, take aperitifs alfresco on the walled terrace (heated in cool weather). Quick trains take you to the city centre; late at night, a taxi does the job. 4 miles from the airport. BEDROOMS 27. FACILITIES 2 lounges, bar, breakfast room, free Wi-Fi, in-room TV (Sky), civil wedding licence, meeting room, walled terrace with water feature, exclusive use for weddings/functions. BACKGROUND MUSIC 'Chill-out' music in public areas. CHILDREN All ages welcomed. PRICES Room £135–£270. Breakfast £14–£16.

ELEVEN DIDSBURY PARK, 11 Didsbury Park, Didsbury Village, M20 5LH. Tel 0161 448 7711, www.elevendidsburypark.com. There are sun loungers and a hammock in the walled garden of this suburban Victorian town house, plus many other peaceful spots to sit and relax in. The modern hotel (part of the Eclectic Hotels group, see Didsbury House, previous entry) has large, airy sitting rooms, and handsome bedrooms spread over three floors, each stylishly homely and comfortable. Some rooms may be snug; the best have a private balcony or canopied terrace. All have good toiletries, a minibar and a butler tray with fresh milk. Breakfast may be taken in the bright conservatory. The city centre is a short train journey away. 15 mins by car to the airport. BEDROOMS 20. 1 on ground floor, suitable for disabled. FACILITIES 2 lounge/bars, free Wi-Fi, in-room TV (Sky), veranda, large walled garden, wedding/conference facilities, parking. BACKGROUND MUSIC All day in public areas. CHILDREN All ages welcomed. DOGS 'Well-behaved' dogs allowed. PRICES Room from £150.

MARAZION Cornwall
Map 1:E1
GODOLPHIN ARMS, West End, TR17
0EN. Tel 01736 888510, www.
godolphinarms.co.uk. Admire St
Michael's Mount across the sandy
causeway from this 'unpretentious',
'superbly located' beachside inn. It is
owned by James and Mary St Levan;
Bev Worth manages 'obliging, efficient
staff'. Coastal colours and local artwork
give the light-filled bedrooms a by-
the-seaside personality; bathrobes
and high-quality toiletries are in the
bathroom. Ring to discuss room choices:
many have sea views; some have a
balcony; others are accessed via 'steep
stairs'. Connecting doors create a family
suite. Take a drink to an easy chair or
comfy sofa before the log-burner in the
informal drinking and dining areas,
or carry it through the glass-and-zinc
extension to the beach bar and terrace.
All-day menus draw inspiration from
the day's catch. 4 miles E of Penzance.
BEDROOMS 10. OPEN All year. FACILITIES 2
bars, split-level dining area, free Wi-Fi,
in-room TV (Sky), wedding/function
facilities, 2 terraces, buckets, spades
and fishing nets available to borrow,
parking. BACKGROUND MUSIC In public
areas, occasional live acoustic music.
CHILDREN All ages welcomed. DOGS
Allowed in 2 bedrooms, designated
dining area, on terrace. PRICES Per room
B&B £70–£280. À la carte £28.

MARCHAM Oxfordshire
Map 2:C2
B&B RAFTERS, Abingdon Road,
OX13 6NU. Tel 01865 391298, www.
bnb-rafters.co.uk. On the edge of the
village, 20 minutes by car from Oxford,
Sigrid Grawert's B&B has stylish

modern bedrooms and a breakfast
porridge selection that's hard to beat.
Bedrooms, including two single
rooms, are provided with thoughtful
amenities: fluffy robes; a welcome
tray with coffee, teas and a cool
drink. The best room has a private
balcony, and a freestanding bath in
the bathroom. Sit in the sun if the
weather cooperates: an outdoor
seating area has been newly created.
Communal breakfasts include
freshly squeezed orange juice, home-
baked bread, home-made jams and
marmalade; whisky porridge is a
speciality. Vegetarian and special
diets are catered for. 3 miles W of
Abingdon. BEDROOMS 4. OPEN All year
except Christmas, New Year. FACILITIES
Lounge, breakfast room, free Wi-Fi, in-
room TV (Freeview), garden, parking.
BACKGROUND MUSIC None. CHILDREN Not
under 12. PRICES Per room B&B single
from £57, double from £99. 2-night min.
stay on bank holiday weekends.

MARGATE Kent
Map 2:D5
THE READING ROOMS, 31 Hawley
Square, CT9 1PH. Tel 01843 225166,
www.thereadingroomsmargate.co.uk.
Louise Oldfield and Liam Nabb artfully
restored their 200-year-old town house
with an eye to preserving its history
while updating it for the modern guest.
Styled with a casual elegance, their
B&B stands on a Georgian square,
a ten-minute walk from the Turner
Contemporary gallery. There are
stripped wooden floors, enormous sash
windows, original shutters and vintage
plasterwork. Bright, airy bedrooms
each take up an entire floor. Each room
has a large French-style bed, seasonal

blooms, vintage books; a 'cavernous' bathroom with a freestanding roll-top bath. 'You don't have to face the world before breakfast,' the owners say; have a leisurely start with a much-praised windowside spread 'beautifully served' in the bedroom at a time of your choosing. BEDROOMS 3. FACILITIES Free Wi-Fi, in-room TV, parking vouchers available. BACKGROUND MUSIC None. PRICES Per room B&B £150–£180. 2-night min. stay at weekends and bank holidays.

MATLOCK Derbyshire
Map 3:A6

THE MANOR FARMHOUSE, Manor Farm, Dethick, DE4 5GG. Tel 01629 534302, www.manorfarmdethick.co.uk. The pace slows at Gilly and Simon Groom's 'wonderfully quiet' 16th-century stone house. On a sheep farm between two dales, the 'excellent, very comfortable' B&B has associations with Mary, Queen of Scots. Choose between the large, traditionally furnished bedrooms: two are in the beamed hayloft; another, on the ground floor of the main house, has direct access to the garden. Breakfast is taken around the large refectory table in the original Elizabethan kitchen. Here, the Grooms whip up dishes to suit all diets, using fresh local ingredients and home-grown produce. Chatsworth House, Hardwick Hall and Haddon Hall are within easy reach (book early for accommodation during the RHS Chatsworth Flower Show). 2 miles E of Matlock; collection from railway/ bus station can be arranged. BEDROOMS 4. FACILITIES Sitting rooms (TV, games), breakfast room, free Wi-Fi, in-room TV, 1-acre grounds, drying facilities, parking, bicycle/motorcycle storage.

CHILDREN Not under 5. PRICES Per room B&B £80–£95. 2-night min. stay on Sat, Apr–Oct.

MATLOCK BATH Derbyshire
Map 3:B6

HODGKINSON'S HOTEL, 150 South Parade, nr Matlock, DE4 3NR. Tel 01629 582170, www.hodgkinsons-hotel. co.uk. Take in 'superb views' over the valley from Chris and Zoe Hipwell's 'very special' Georgian town house hotel. The quirky Victorian house (tiled entrance hall, ornate glasswork, the original wood-and-glass bar) has a rich history – ask to explore the atmospheric cellars. Traditionally furnished bedrooms may have river views or a four-poster bed; the walnut-trimmed bathrooms have a roll-top bath or an Edwardian-style walk-in shower. Leigh Matthews's 'excellent' modern British menus are served in the restaurant; breakfast has lots of choice, including omelettes, kedgeree and a full vegetarian. A large terraced garden has views stretching to the granite cliffs and the River Derwent beyond. 'Challenging walks' nearby. BEDROOMS 8. OPEN All year except Christmas week. FACILITIES Sitting room, bar, restaurant (closed Sun eve except bank holiday Sun), free Wi-Fi, in-room TV, terraced garden, limited on-site parking (additional parking nearby). BACKGROUND MUSIC Radio (daytime) and 'mix of classic lounge and easy listening' (evening) in bar and restaurant. CHILDREN All ages welcomed. DOGS Allowed in lounge, some bedrooms, not in bar or restaurant. PRICES Per room B&B single from £55, double £77–£155. Set dinner £26–£29. 2-night min. stay on Sat.

MEVAGISSEY Cornwall
Map 1:D2

PEBBLE HOUSE, Polkirt Hill, PL26 6UX. Tel 01726 844466, www.pebblehousecornwall.co.uk. At the top of a steep lane leading from the 14th-century fishing village, Andrea and Simon Copper's sleekly designed B&B above Mevagissey Bay takes in panoramic views that make the climb worthwhile. Mount the 34 steps between the parking bay and the house: all but one of the modern bedrooms look towards the water; most have floor-to-ceiling windows to take in the spread of the sea. Marvel at the vista stretching across the bay to historic Chapel Point and beyond from the front terrace, where generous breakfasts, Cornish cream teas, snacks and drinks are served in fine weather. The South West Coast Path is steps away; order a picnic before stepping out. Later, take a piece of your holiday home – everything you see in the house is available to buy. BEDROOMS 6. 1 on ground floor with private terrace. OPEN Feb–Nov, 4 nights over New Year. FACILITIES Breakfast room, free Wi-Fi, in-room TV (Freeview, Sky in some rooms), terrace, small functions, parking. BACKGROUND MUSIC In breakfast room. CHILDREN Not under 16. PRICES Per room B&B £135–£220.

MIDHURST Sussex
Map 2:E3

THE CHURCH HOUSE, Church Hill, GU29 9NX. Tel 01730 812990, www.churchhousemidhurst.com. 'The feeling of a private home' infuses Fina Jurado's relaxed, elegant B&B in a medieval market town within the South Downs national park. The house sprawls, genteelly, across what was once four 13th-century cottages. There are polished oak floors, oriental carpets, period features and vintage finds. Guests are greeted with tea and home-baked cake. Most of the bedrooms are up the handsome curving staircase. All, cheery with fresh flowers, are stylishly rustic: one has a soaring beamed ceiling; another, a mezzanine and velvet chaise longue; yet another, a study overlooking the garden. Breakfast, taken communally at a large oak table, is served at a time to suit. Start the day with organic yogurts, home-made jams and marmalades, locally sourced bacon and sausages. BEDROOMS 5. 1 on ground floor. OPEN All year except Christmas. FACILITIES Sitting room/dining room, conservatory with TV, free Wi-Fi, in-room TV (Sky, Freeview), garden. CHILDREN All ages welcomed. PRICES Per room B&B single from £70, double £140–£165.

MILLOM Cumbria
Map 4: inset C2

BROADGATE HOUSE, Broadgate, Thwaites, LA18 5JZ. Tel 01229 716295, www.broadgate-house.co.uk. Past fields grazed by Hardwick sheep, Diana Lewthwaite's guest house stands against the dramatic backdrop of the Lakeland fells. The white-painted Georgian house has been home to the Lewthwaite family for almost 200 years. Grand public rooms are filled with antique furniture and sumptuous fabrics, and have an original fireplace. Colour and pattern lend country character to the spacious, traditionally furnished bedrooms. Each has a separate, private bathroom with a throne loo and freestanding bath. Venture into the large grounds, designed as a series of

'garden rooms' in bloom throughout the year: there are terraces, a croquet lawn, a walled garden and an 'oasis' with a palm tree. 4 miles from town; beaches nearby. BEDROOMS 5. OPEN All year except 1–23 Dec. FACILITIES Sitting room (wood-burning stove), dining room, breakfast room, free Wi-Fi in reception. BACKGROUND MUSIC None. CHILDREN Not under 12. PRICES Per room B&B single £55, double £95. Dinner (by arrangement) £30. Credit cards not accepted.
25% DISCOUNT VOUCHERS

MISTLEY Essex
Map 2:C5
THE MISTLEY THORN, High Street, CO11 1HE. Tel 01206 392821, www.mistleythorn.co.uk. Chef Sherri Singleton and her husband, David McKay, run their affable restaurant-with-rooms in a coastal village (noted for its swans) close to Constable country. Seafood is a speciality in the relaxed, beamed drinking and dining areas (smart tongue-and-groove panelling, a wood-burning stove), where the 'unpretentious' menus list Mersea oysters and other locally landed seafood, plus meats from nearby Sutton Hoo. Interesting vegetarian options might include asparagus and artichoke pearl barley 'risotto', Lyburn Gold cheddar, crispy nettles. Cosy bedrooms decorated in a soothing palette have nice extras (dressing gowns, luxury toiletries, home-made biscuits); four have views down the Stour estuary. Light sleepers, ask for a room away from traffic noise. 3 mins' walk from train station. BEDROOMS 12. 3 with separate entrance, 1 suite in Little Thorn Cottage. OPEN All year except Christmas Day. FACILITIES Bar,

restaurant, free Wi-Fi, in-room TV (Freeview), outdoor seating, cookery workshops at the Mistley Kitchen, next door (special room rates for attendees). BACKGROUND MUSIC In restaurant during mealtimes. CHILDREN All ages welcomed. DOGS Small/medium dogs allowed in 3 rooms and in 'quiet part' of restaurant. PRICES Per room B&B (Tues–Sat) £105–£170, D,B&B £120–£220.

MORETON-IN-MARSH
Gloucestershire
Map 3:D6
THE OLD SCHOOL, Newtown, Little Compton, GL56 0SL. Tel 01608 674588, www.theoldschoolbedandbreakfast.com. Wendy Vale receives top marks for the warm welcome to her B&B in a converted Victorian schoolhouse in a north Cotswold village. Arrive to tea and home-made cake, then unpack in one of the country-style bedrooms, each with a super-king-size bed, thick towels and fluffy bathrobes. Extra touches: biscuits and fresh blooms. A food writer and stylist, the hostess prepares tasty breakfasts including 'eggs in all guises'. Freshly ground coffee, fruit, compotes, granola and local honey complete the meal. A light supper tray (smoked salmon sandwiches or a tart and salad, plus a sweet treat) may be ordered in advance; picnic hampers include a rug and a brolly. 3 miles E of Moreton-in-Marsh. BEDROOMS 4. 1 on ground floor. OPEN All year. FACILITIES 2 sitting rooms, dining room, free Wi-Fi (computer available), in-room TV (BT), 1-acre garden (pergolas, patios, fish pond, orchard), laundry room, parking. BACKGROUND MUSIC None. CHILDREN Not under 14 (in own room). PRICES

Per room B&B £130–£150. 2-night min. stay at weekends. 4-course dinner (for 4 or more guests staying 2 or more nights) £32.

MULLION Cornwall
Map 1:E2
POLURRIAN BAY HOTEL, Polurrian Road, TR12 7EN. Tel 01326 240421, www.polurrianhotel.com. Whether junior swimming enthusiast or mini film fanatic, pint-sized gourmand or budding artist, there's a pursuit to suit children at this family-friendly clifftop hotel (Luxury Family Hotels). Yvonne Colgan is the manager. Standing above a sandy bay on the Lizard peninsula, the revamped Edwardian building has stunning coast views from its 'well-appointed, comfortable' bedrooms. Many have space for an extra bed or cot; some rooms interconnect to accommodate a larger family. Choose a spot to feast: the 'impressive' Vista lounge has freshly cooked food all day; the terrace is the place for an alfresco lunch on a balmy afternoon; more sophisticated meals, once the children have been put to bed, are taken in the restaurant. The beach is a short stroll away. BEDROOMS 41. Some on ground floor, 1 suitable for disabled. FACILITIES Lift, lounge, snug, dining room, cinema, Den (nursery for children 6 months–8 years old), Blue Room (older children; video games, pool, table football), spa (9-metre pool), free Wi-Fi, in-room TV, civil wedding licence, function facilities, 12-acre grounds, terrace. BACKGROUND MUSIC In dining areas. CHILDREN All ages welcomed. DOGS Allowed in some bedrooms, not in restaurant or part of lounge. PRICES Per room B&B from £120, D,B&B from £190. À la carte £38. 2-night min. stay in peak season.

NEWBY BRIDGE Cumbria
Map 4: inset C2
THE SWAN HOTEL & SPA, The Colonnade, LA12 8NB. Tel 015395 31681, www.swanhotel.com. A lively spot, this family-friendly hotel on the banks of the River Leven stands in sweeping gardens, and has a cheery mix of colours and prints inside. It is owned by Sharon and Audrey Bardsley. Ongoing refurbishment has given the 17th-century former coaching house its playful public areas (parrot-print wallpaper, up-to-date florals, pompom-fringed lampshades), cool, contemporary spa and modern country-style bedrooms. Accommodation comes in a host of options: choose from top-floor adult-only suites, interconnecting family rooms, and others in between. Visit the atmospheric pub for classic dishes; check out the River Room restaurant for chef Claire Asbury's modern menu. A marbled-topped juice bar has smoothies, ice creams, juices and light lunches. Breakfasts are ample. BEDROOMS 54. Some suitable for disabled, plus 5 self-catering cottages. FACILITIES Sitting room, library, Swan Inn, restaurant, juice bar, free Wi-Fi, in-room TV (Sky), civil wedding licence, function facilities, spa (treatments), indoor pool, gym, terrace, 10-acre grounds, parking, mooring. BACKGROUND MUSIC In public areas. CHILDREN All ages welcomed (adventure playground, nature trail, milk and cookies before bed). DOGS Allowed in pub, not in bedrooms. PRICES Per room B&B from £142. À la carte £32. 2-night min. stay on bank holiday weekends.

NEWMARKET Suffolk
Map 2:B4

BEDFORD LODGE, Bury Road, CB8 7BX. Tel 01638 663175, www. bedfordlodgehotel.co.uk. In large grounds beside the stables and training gallops in this horseracing town, this family-run hotel is liked for its 'superb service', 'lovely gardens' and 'excellent breakfasts'. Originally a Georgian hunting lodge built for the sixth Duke of Bedford, it is today a 'delightful' place whose decor recalls the town's racing heritage – look out for the display of racing silks. 'Well-maintained' bedrooms (some small) are provided with bottled water, tea- and coffee-making facilities and posh toiletries; one of the best has a balcony, ideal for breakfast in morning sunshine. A straightforward menu (sharing platters, sandwiches, chargrilled meats) is served in the restaurant; in good weather, spill on to the terrace for alfresco dining. BEDROOMS 77. Some suitable for disabled. FACILITIES Bar, sitting room, library, restaurant, private dining room, free Wi-Fi, in-room TV (Sky, Freeview), civil wedding licence, function facilities, 3-acre grounds, spa (treatments, tanning), gym (indoor pool, sauna, steam room, hot tub), parking. BACKGROUND MUSIC In public areas. CHILDREN All ages welcomed. PRICES Per room B&B from £180. 2-night min. stay on bank holiday weekends.

NEWQUAY Cornwall
Map 1:D2

THE HEADLAND HOTEL, Headland Road, TR7 1EW. Tel 01637 872211, www.headlandhotel.co.uk. Make waves at the Armstrong family's imposing red-brick Victorian hotel, which gazes seaward above the end of sandy Fistral beach. In a renowned surfers' hotspot, the large, family-friendly hotel has its own surf academy to take advantage of the 12-foot swells that break from autumn to spring. Coastal views and hues are found in most of the modern bedrooms – ask for one with a private balcony. Children have buckets and spades to borrow for trips to the beach; for indoor time, there are plenty of games, books and DVDs. (Grown-ups could book a session at the cool, contemporary spa.) Informal meals may be taken in the beach-facing Terrace restaurant; white-tablecloth Samphire has sophisticated modern menus. BEDROOMS 96. 1 suitable for disabled, plus 39 self-catering cottages in the grounds. FACILITIES Lounges, bar, 2 restaurants, free Wi-Fi, in-room TV, civil wedding licence, conference/ event facilities, veranda, 10-acre grounds, indoor and outdoor heated swimming pools, tennis courts, croquet, putting, boules, surf school, spa, gym. BACKGROUND MUSIC In restaurant. CHILDREN All ages welcomed. DOGS Allowed (£24 per night). PRICES Per room B&B from £110, D,B&B from £170.

LEWINNICK LODGE, Pentire Headland, TR7 1QD. Tel 01637 878117, www. lewinnicklodge.co.uk. The setting is rugged – the building stands on the edge of a rocky headland – but, inside, everything is sleek and stylish at this laid-back modern hotel. It is owned by Pete and Jacqui Fair. Ask for a bedroom looking over the water – the exhilarating views (even from the bathtub, in some rooms) stretch towards Towan Head and the expanse of Fistral beach. Each of the minimalist bedrooms has a comfy bed and home-made biscuits; a power shower and slipper bath. New ocean-view rooms were under construction as the Guide went to press. In the 'busy, informal' open-plan restaurant and bar, 'uncomplicated but sufficiently tasty' Cornish feasts follow the daily catch, with specials changing twice a day. Eat while admiring the view through floor-to-ceiling windows, or sit on the large decked terrace that juts over the sea. Good walks from the door. 2½ miles from town centre. BEDROOMS 11. Some suitable for disabled. FACILITIES Lift, bar, restaurant, free Wi-Fi, in-room TV, in-room treatments, parking. BACKGROUND MUSIC In public areas. CHILDREN All ages welcomed. DOGS Allowed in some bedrooms, not in restaurant. PRICES Per room B&B from £147.25. À la carte £30.

NORTHALLERTON Yorkshire
Map 4:C4

CLEVELAND TONTINE, Staddlebridge, DL6 3JB. Tel 01609 882671, www.theclevelandtontine.com. Once a travellers' inn, this Victorian house between Yarm and Thirsk is today a modern hotel liked for its 'quirky accommodation' and 'delicious food'. It is part of the Provenance Inns group (see The Carpenters Arms, Felixkirk, main entry). Arrive to a 'warm welcome' – head straight for afternoon tea, perhaps, in the 'splendid, light-filled' drawing room. 'Dramatic decor' (bold wallpaper, colourful bed coverings) adds character to the individually styled bedrooms; good amenities – magazines, a well-stocked hospitality tray, efficient secondary glazing – contribute to their comfort. In the candlelit dining room,

bistro favourites are cooked 'with flair'. A substantial breakfast includes toast 'thickly sliced from a proper loaf'. 8 miles NE of Northallerton. BEDROOMS 7. OPEN All year. FACILITIES Lounge, bar, bistro, free Wi-Fi, in-room TV (Freeview), room service, function facilities, garden, parking. BACKGROUND MUSIC In public areas. CHILDREN All ages welcomed. DOGS Allowed in bar and lounge. PRICES Per room B&B from £130, D,B&B from £210. Set menu £21.95, à la carte £45.

NORWICH Norfolk
Map 2:B5

NORFOLK MEAD, Church Loke, Coltishall, NR12 7DN. Tel 01603 737531, www.norfolkmead.co.uk. 'Lush grounds' lead from James Holliday and Anna Duttson's 'stylish', wisteria-hung Georgian house down to the River Bure. 'We found perfect peace and quiet,' says a Guide reader this year. 'Informal, attentive, helpful staff' create a 'homely atmosphere'. Individually decorated bedrooms of various sizes are comfortable, though guests are advised to choose wisely – gripes include a too-snug bathroom; noise from kitchen extractor ducts. Some rooms in the cottage and summer houses in the grounds are ideal for larger groups. Modern British dishes are 'satisfactorily cooked and elaborately presented' in the 'pleasant' dining room ('pity about the vocal muzak'). In the morning, breakfast is 'so good': home-made cereals, 'perfect scrambled eggs'. On fine days, relax in the pretty walled garden or pack a picnic for a potter along the Norfolk Broads. 7 miles NE of Norwich. BEDROOMS 15. 2 in cottage, 3 in summer houses. OPEN All year.

FACILITIES Lounge, bar, snug, restaurant, private dining, 2 beauty treatment rooms, free Wi-Fi, in-room TV (Freeview), civil wedding licence, walled garden, fishing lake. BACKGROUND MUSIC In public areas. CHILDREN All ages welcomed (£35 per night). DOGS Allowed in some outside rooms (£20 per night). PRICES Per room B&B from £135. Set menus £30.50–£38.50.

OUNDLE Northamptonshire
Map 2:B3

LOWER FARM, Main Street, Barnwell, PE8 5PU. Tel 01832 273220, www.lower-farm.co.uk. Homely accommodation, wholesome food and fresh air by the lungful are on offer at this B&B on the Marriott family's small arable farm. 'Friendly, accommodating' Caroline Marriott takes care of guests; her husband, Robert, and his brother, John, look after the farm. Modest bedrooms in the converted milking parlour and stables are arranged around a central courtyard; some may be connected to suit a family. Make yourself blissfully unreachable: Wi-Fi is limited, as is a mobile signal. Turn to the land instead – there are walking and cycling tracks from the door, including the Nene Way footpath which runs through the farm. Breakfast has farmhouse fare; steak and eggs are a speciality. 3 miles from Oundle. BEDROOMS 10. All on ground floor, 1 suitable for disabled. OPEN All year. FACILITIES Breakfast room (fridge, microwave for guests' use), free Wi-Fi, in-room TV (Freeview), courtyard garden with seating, parking. BACKGROUND MUSIC Radio 'if guests wish' in breakfast room. CHILDREN All ages welcomed. DOGS Allowed in 2

bedrooms, not in public rooms. PRICES Per person B&B £50.
25% DISCOUNT VOUCHERS

OXFORD Oxfordshire
Map 2:C2

THE BELL AT HAMPTON POYLE, 11 Oxford Road, Hampton Poyle, OX5 2QD. Tel 01865 376242, www.thebelloxford.co.uk. Come for the pizzas, stay for the pause – in one of the bright, contemporary bedrooms at this refurbished honey-stone inn, eight miles from Oxford city centre. Owner George Dailey turned around the fortunes of this roadside pub when he bought it in 2009. Today, it is a popular place, liked by locals for its steaks, pub classics and more modern additions (gin, dill and coriander-cured sea trout, cucumber salad; linguine, toasted hazelnuts, piquillo pepper, morel mushrooms, shaved asparagus). Flagstone floors and 18th-century beams have been preserved; deep leather chairs and a large log fire add character. Each bedroom is provided with tea- and coffee-making facilities and posh toiletries; a bath or a monsoon shower. Blenheim Palace is not far. BEDROOMS 9. 1 on ground floor. FACILITIES 2 bars, library (private parties), restaurant, free Wi-Fi, in-room TV (Freeview), function facilities, terrace, parking. BACKGROUND MUSIC In bar. CHILDREN All ages welcomed. DOGS Allowed in bar, not in bedrooms. PRICES Per room B&B (continental) single £95–£130, double £120–£175. À la carte £35 (£15 3-course set menu Mon–Thurs, 6 pm–7.30 pm).

BURLINGTON HOUSE, 374 Banbury Road, OX2 7PP. Tel 01865 513513, www.burlington-hotel-oxford.co.uk.

A ten-minute bus ride from the centre, this friendly B&B in a leafy suburb has breakfasts worth waking up for. The spread includes freshly squeezed orange juice and freshly ground coffee, home-made granola and yogurt, and home-baked bread. Hot dishes range from gruyère cheese omelettes or field mushrooms on toast to the house speciality – a marmalade omelette. Some of the 'cheerfully decorated' bedrooms (in the main house and set around the courtyard) may be snug, but all have a comprehensive refreshment tray with fruit teas and home-made biscuits. Frequent buses into the city; the bus stop is a minute down the road. BEDROOMS 12. 4 on ground floor, 2 in courtyard. OPEN All year except Christmas, New Year. FACILITIES Sitting room, breakfast room, free Wi-Fi, in-room TV, small Japanese garden, limited parking. CHILDREN Not under 12. PRICES Per room B&B from £70.

VANBRUGH HOUSE HOTEL, 20–24 St Michael's Street, OX1 2EB. Tel 01865 244622, www.vanbrughhousehotel. co.uk. 'Friendly staff', thoughtfully equipped bedrooms and a convenient location make this 'boutique B&B' a fine choice for visitors to the historic city. David Robinson is the manager. Spread over conjoined 17th- and 18th-century buildings, handsome, heritage-hued bedrooms vary in size. 'Our top-floor room overlooking the Oxford Union was well furnished, though the shower-only bathroom was small. A well-stocked hospitality tray had complimentary bottled water, crisps and Kit Kats – a nice touch.' In good weather, you may breakfast on the rear patio: there are seasonal fruits

and home-made jams; Cumberland or veggie sausages; 'nicely cooked eggs Benedict'. Light lunches are available, though dinner isn't served – 'but, as the hotel is so central, this isn't an issue'. 7 mins' walk from rail station. BEDROOMS 22. 1 suitable for disabled. OPEN All year. FACILITIES Breakfast room, free Wi-Fi, in-room TV (Freeview), small terrace, Park-and-Ride recommended. BACKGROUND MUSIC None. CHILDREN All ages welcomed. PRICES Per room B&B from £165. 2-night min. stay at weekends.

PENZANCE Cornwall
Map 1:E1

ARTIST RESIDENCE CORNWALL, 20 Chapel Street, TR18 4AW. Tel 01736 365664, www.artistresidence.co.uk. 'Achingly cool yet comfortable', this youthful hotel receives praise for its 'very nice staff', 'well-appointed bedrooms' and 'great breakfasts'. (The 'first-rate' orange juice is worthy of mention, too.) It is part of Justin and Charlotte Salisbury's eclectic collection (see main entries in London and Brighton; Shortlist entry in South Leigh). The Georgian house is chock full of 'intriguing' artworks, eccentricity and vintage flourishes, from the popular restaurant to the highly individual bedrooms. It's not to all tastes – 'one man's quirky/funky/ fun could be another man's odd/weird/ peculiar,' a Guide inspector says – but the staff are roundly 'eager, pleasant and obliging', and do what they can to help. Meals in the informal restaurant/ bar/smokehouse draw hungry locals ('the beer-can-smoked chicken is truly stupendous'); a terrace and beer garden are ideal on a sunny day. 10 mins' walk from railway station; 5 mins' walk from seafront. BEDROOMS 21. 4 self-contained apartments next door. OPEN All year. FACILITIES Bar/lounge, restaurant, free Wi-Fi, in-room TV (Freeview), small courtyard garden with bar, table tennis and table football, meeting/function facilities. BACKGROUND MUSIC In public spaces. CHILDREN All ages welcomed. DOGS Allowed in 2 ground-floor bedrooms (£10 charge). PRICES Per room/apartment B&B £79–£450. À la carte £30.

VENTON VEAN, Trewithen Road, TR18 4LS. Tel 01736 351294, www.ventonvean.co.uk. There's a bijou feel at Philippa McKnight and David Hoyes's stone-built B&B, close to the seafront and the town. Original Victorian features (stained-glass panels, original cornices, fireplaces) sit comfortably alongside arresting colours, vintage furnishings and artistic touches. Relax over a welcoming afternoon tea, then stroll through the garden or borrow a book from the collection in the sitting room. Spacious bedrooms have a king-size bed and plenty of pleasing amenities: a digital radio, tea and coffee tray, bathrobes and eco-friendly toiletries. No wardrobe in most rooms – wall hooks do the job instead. Breakfast is packed with locally sourced and produced ingredients; imaginative options include Mexican and Spanish dishes and imaginative vegetarian and vegan choices. BEDROOMS 5. 1 with adjoining single room, suitable for a family. OPEN All year except 25–26 Dec, 4 Jan–4 Feb. FACILITIES Sitting room, dining room, free Wi-Fi, in-room smart TV, garden. BACKGROUND MUSIC At breakfast in dining room. CHILDREN Not

under 5. PRICES Per room B&B single £71–£87, double £81–£97.

PRESTON Lancashire
Map 4:D2
BARTON GRANGE HOTEL, 746–768 Garstang Road, Barton, PR3 5AA. Tel 01772 862551, www.bartongrangehotel.co.uk. The 'enthusiastic, helpful staff' stand out at the Topping family's hotel, the one-time country abode of a cotton mill owner. With easy access to the M6, it is an 'excellent stop-over spot', a Guide reader reports in 2017. A recent makeover has resulted in the large, comfortable lounge and well-appointed bedrooms. 'Our compact room, with a good walk-in shower, had been well designed to maximise space.' Hunker down in the sauna, soak in the swimming pool or stroll through the 'pleasant garden' ('partially overlooked by bordering houses'). When hunger strikes, pull up a seat in the Walled Garden restaurant. 'We enjoyed pork rillettes with apricot; fillets of plaice with prawns, potato rösti and fennel.' Breakfast by buffet or order a 'grab-and-go' breakfast bag. 6 miles from Preston city centre. BEDROOMS 51. 8 in Garden House in the grounds, 1 suitable for disabled. FACILITIES Lift, lounge, snug, bistro/wine bar, meeting/private dining room, free Wi-Fi, in-room TV (Sky), civil wedding licence, leisure centre (swimming pool, sauna), pool/bar billiards, parking. BACKGROUND MUSIC None. CHILDREN All ages welcomed. PRICES Per room B&B from £90.

RAMSGATE Kent
Map 2:D6
THE FALSTAFF, 16–18 Addington Street, CT11 9JJ. Tel 01843 482600,

www.thefalstafframsgate.com. 'Always buzzy and friendly', this pub-with-rooms in two 'tastefully refurbished' Regency town houses near the harbour is a good-natured place, liked by locals and visitors in equal measure. Service is 'efficient and personable'; a wood-burning stove is lit in cool weather; 'there might be a couple of obviously home-made cakes on the counter on any given day – a nice sort of unpredictability'. 'On a festive Sunday, the genial ambience was enhanced by live piano music,' guests report in 2017. There are heritage shades and vintage furnishings, oriental rugs and fine prints. Bedrooms, each with a large bed, are all different. 'Good breakfasts' and informal lunches are served in the bar and restaurant; four nights a week, sample the 'varied, interesting menu' at dinner. BEDROOMS 8. Plus 2 self-catering apartments. FACILITIES Bar, restaurant (no dinner Sun–Tues), deli, free Wi-Fi, in-room TV (Freeview), garden with seating (summer barbecues), parking, bicycle storage. BACKGROUND MUSIC In restaurant. CHILDREN All ages welcomed. DOGS Allowed in 1 bedroom with garden access. PRICES Per room B&B £89–£139.

RICHMOND Yorkshire
Map 4:C3
EASBY HALL, Easby, DL10 7EU. Tel 01748 826066, www.easbyhall.com. Karen and John Clarke's Georgian country house stands on a rustic lane outside the town, with views over the ruins of Easby Abbey from its large garden. B&B accommodation is in spacious suites in a dedicated wing of the house. Each lavishly decorated room has a huge bed dressed with a

velvet coverlet, throws and heaps of cushions; each, too, has a log-burner or open fire – even a champagne fridge, should the mood strike. The gardens are flanked by a short woodland walk, an orchard and a paddock – head out for a wander before returning to afternoon tea in the drawing room. Breakfast at a time to suit: there are home-made preserves with fruit from the kitchen garden; poached pears from the orchard; local bacon; eggs from resident hens. Stroll along the banks of the Swale into Richmond. BEDROOMS 3. 1, on ground floor, has easy access for disabled guests, plus 2-bed self-catering cottage. FACILITIES Drawing room, dining room, free Wi-Fi, in-room TV (Freeview), gardens, paddocks, loose boxes and stables for horses. BACKGROUND MUSIC None. CHILDREN All ages welcomed. DOGS 'Obedient, house-trained dogs' allowed. PRICES Per room B&B £180. Credit cards not accepted.

RIPLEY Surrey
Map 2:D3
BROADWAY BARN, High Street, nr Woking, GU23 6AQ. Tel 01483 223200, www.broadwaybarn.com. Mindi McLean's B&B is in a refurbished 200-year-old barn in the centre of a historic Surrey village, ten minutes' drive from RHS Wisley. Creatively decorated bedrooms are supplied with fresh flowers, dressing gowns, slippers, chocolates and home-made shortbread; bathrooms, with underfloor heating, are stocked with complimentary toiletries. A fine breakfast with plenty of choice is taken in a light-filled conservatory overlooking the walled garden. Sit down to fresh fruit, home-baked bread, home-made granola and

preserves, village honey; daily specials might include Belgian waffles with strawberries and maple syrup. There's no shortage of local eating places at dinnertime; the Clock House, a modern, fine-dining restaurant, is steps away. BEDROOMS 4. Plus self-catering flat and cottages. FACILITIES Conservatory sitting room/breakfast room, free Wi-Fi, in-room TV (Freeview), small garden. BACKGROUND MUSIC Soft music during breakfast. CHILDREN Not under 12. PRICES Per room B&B £120.

RYE Sussex
Map 2:E5
THE HOPE ANCHOR, Watchbell Street, TN31 7HA. Tel 01797 222216, www. thehopeanchor.co.uk. Guests at this privately owned hotel join a tradition begun by the rowdy bunch of sailors, shipbuilders and smugglers who once crowded the 18th-century watering hole. The nooks, crannies and secret passages remain, but the experience today, at the end of a cobbled street, is a much more tranquil one. Many of the bedrooms have views across the quayside, the Romney Marshes and Camber Castle. The rooms may be old-fashioned, but they're 'warm and comfortable', and are supplied with basic comforts: a hospitality tray, a clock radio, slippers. In the restaurant, the menu of traditional English dishes includes a catch of the day, straight from Rye Bay. BEDROOMS 16. 3 in cottage and apartments, 10 yards away, 1 on ground floor with patio. OPEN All year. FACILITIES Lounge, bar (snack menu), restaurant, private dining room, free Wi-Fi, in-room TV (Freeview), wedding facilities, room

service, parking permits supplied. BACKGROUND MUSIC In public areas. CHILDREN All ages welcomed. DOGS Allowed in some bedrooms, not in restaurant. PRICES Per room B&B £95–£185, D,B&B £140–£200.
25% DISCOUNT VOUCHERS

THE SHIP INN, The Strand, TN31 7DB. Tel 01797 222233, www.theshipinnrye. co.uk. A jolly place, Karen Northcote's 'charming' pub-with-rooms pleases with its 'really delicious food' and 'welcoming staff'. 'We were not disappointed,' say regular Guide readers this year. Locals and visitors pack the buzzy bar and restaurant; upstairs, quirky bedrooms have mismatched furniture on uneven wooden floors. 'The accommodation isn't large, but the beds are comfy and the bathrooms reasonable. Despite the youthful revellers in the bar, the noise didn't reach our rooms.' Help yourself to 'anything and everything' at the breakfast buffet; interesting cooked dishes include scrambled eggs, green chilli and chorizo; French toast, berries and bacon; grilled kippers. (On a dog day, your pet might even get a sausage.) Close to Rye Harbour nature reserve and Camber Sands. BEDROOMS 10. OPEN All year except Christmas Day. FACILITIES Residents' lounge (board games, books, DVDs), bar, restaurant, function/private dining room, free Wi-Fi, in-room TV (Freeview), small terrace with picnic benches, pay-and-display parking nearby. BACKGROUND MUSIC In bar and restaurant. CHILDREN All ages welcomed. DOGS Allowed in bedrooms and public rooms. PRICES Per room B&B £110–£125. À la carte £26. 2-night min. stay on Sat.

ST EWE Cornwall
Map 1:D2

LOWER BARNS, Bosue, nr St Austell, PL26 6EU. Tel 01726 844881, www. lowerbarns.co.uk. Janie and Mike Cooksley have brought a riotous combination of colour and eye-catching features to the Cornish countryside. Their faintly bohemian B&B on the Roseland peninsula, in extensive grounds, has indulgent bedrooms in the main house and in quirky buildings accessed through the garden. Each is as different as can be – one suite has its own stone-built sauna; another, a gypsy caravan parked outside the front door. Well equipped, all have plenty of space, a Roberts radio, a TV/DVD and much else. An informal three-course set dinner may be served, by arrangement, in the 'party shed' in the wild flower garden (special diets catered for). Guests in three garden suites have breakfast delivered to the room; for the others, the morning meal is taken communally in the conservatory: fresh fruit compotes, warm muffins, local smoked fish, farm sausages, eggs 'any way you like'. BEDROOMS 8. 4 in the grounds, 1 suitable for disabled. OPEN All year. FACILITIES Conservatory breakfast room, dining room, free Wi-Fi, in-room TV, civil wedding licence, small function facilities, garden, gym, therapy room (treatments), outdoor hot tub, parking. BACKGROUND MUSIC Wireless speaker and record player in dining room 'so guests can play their own music'. CHILDREN All ages welcomed. DOGS Allowed in 2 suites, with own bedding. PRICES Per room B&B £100–£225. Set dinner £50 (BYO). 2-night min. stay at weekends.
25% DISCOUNT VOUCHERS

ST IVES Cornwall
Map 1:D1

BLUE HAYES, Trelyon Avenue, TR26 2AD. Tel 01736 797129, www.bluehayes. co.uk. Malcolm Herring's small hotel stands high above Porthminster beach, with sweeping views towards Godrevy lighthouse. There's a laid-back, home-away-from-home feel about the 1920s house – its exotic palms, seascapes, squashy sofas and airy, clotted-cream-coloured interiors. Take in the views from each of the simply furnished bedrooms, some with a balcony, terrace or private patio. Light suppers (salads, dressed crab, a lobster platter) may be eaten in the dining room or on the terrace; in clement weather, breakfast by the balustrade to take in the vista. Just past the garden gate, a coastal path meanders to the beach. BEDROOMS 6. OPEN Mar–Oct. FACILITIES 2 lounges, bar, dining room, free Wi-Fi, in-room TV (Freeview), small functions, room service, terrace, garden, parking. BACKGROUND MUSIC None. CHILDREN Not under 10. PRICES Per room B&B £130–£280. Supper from £17.

HEADLAND HOUSE, Headland Road, Carbis Bay, TR26 2NS. Tel 01736 796647, www.headlandhousehotel. co.uk. Coastal colours and a breezy style fill this chic Edwardian house above the sandy beach at Carbis Bay. The B&B is owned by Mark and Fenella Thomas, who have created a tranquil retreat from the bustle of St Ives proper. Decorated in marine hues, inviting bedrooms are set over three floors. Each has its own character and special touches: a garden room has outdoor seating on a private deck; an upper-floor seaview room has a window seat from which to watch the waves on the beach below. All rooms are exceedingly well equipped, down to the home-made cake that appears in the room each afternoon. Borrow a book to read in the garden hammock; evenings, a complimentary drink is on offer. Breakfast brings organic Cornish fare and a broad vista across the bay. 1½ miles from St Ives. BEDROOMS 9. 3 off the courtyard garden at the rear. OPEN Mid-Mar–Oct. FACILITIES Snug lounge (bar, board games, magazines), conservatory breakfast room, free Wi-Fi, in-room TV (Freeview), large front garden, terrace, parking. BACKGROUND MUSIC None. CHILDREN Not under 16. PRICES Per room B&B £95–£170. 2-night min. stay preferred.

TREVOSE HARBOUR HOUSE, 22 The Warren, TR26 2EA. Tel 01736 793267, www.trevosehouse.co.uk. Angela and Olivier Noverraz's 'beautifully appointed' 1850s mid-terrace house is a B&B with pizzazz. Vintage furnishings mix easily with the latest technology; all around is design-conscious decor in whites and blues. Deep-cushioned chairs in the cosy lounge call for a captivating book, or a cocktail from the honesty bar. Each individually styled bedroom has a large bed and organic toiletries; most have views over the harbour and the bay. Alfresco breakfasts may be taken on the terrace overlooking the Warren, or in the bright breakfast room, when cool air blows in. Whatever the weather, the imaginative organic feast includes home-made preserves, granola-yogurt-and-fruit parfaits, 'smoothie shots' and veggie-friendly cooked choices. BEDROOMS 6. 1 in rear annexe. OPEN Mar–Oct. FACILITIES

Snug (newspapers, magazines, books, honesty bar), breakfast room, free Wi-Fi, in-room TV (Freeview), in-room treatments, picnic hampers, terrace, limited parking close by. BACKGROUND MUSIC In snug. CHILDREN Not under 12. PRICES Per room B&B £160–£275.

ST MAWES Cornwall
Map 1:E2

THE ST MAWES HOTEL, 2 Marine Parade, TR2 5DW. Tel 01326 270 170, www.stmaweshotel.com. Seaside style and modern Cornish plates attract locals and passers-by to this casual, buzzy hotel, bar and restaurant on the quay. It is owned by David and Karen Richards. Public rooms have jauntily striped seating, local art and seafaring paraphernalia (look out for the crab cages). Join the crew over cocktails and nibbles in the lively bar, or pull up a seat in the Upper Deck restaurant, where the wide view is of boats in the bay. Bedrooms are chic and comfortable, with cheery marine stripes, and underfloor heating in the bathroom. Some suit a family; the best have views stretching over the harbour to St Anthony's Head. Big-sister hotel Idle Rocks is up the street (see main entry). BEDROOMS 7. 4 in annexe around the corner. FACILITIES Bar, lounge, restaurant, cinema, function/private dining room, free Wi-Fi, in-room TV (Freeview). BACKGROUND MUSIC All day in public areas, occasional live music in bar. CHILDREN All ages welcomed. DOGS Allowed in bar, 2 bedrooms (bed, towel, bowl, treats, maps of local walks, £30 per stay). PRICES Per room B&B £185–£285. 2-night min. stay at weekends.

ST MELLION Cornwall
Map 1:D3
PENTILLIE CASTLE, PL12 6QD. Tel
01579 350044, www.pentillie.co.uk.
At the end of a long driveway, this
'magnificent, lovingly restored'
castellated mansion is now a grand
country B&B surrounded by extensive
grounds on the banks of the River
Tamar. Steeped in history, the house
has belonged to the Coryton family for
nearly 300 years. Take afternoon tea
or pre-dinner drinks by an open fire
in one of the sitting rooms furnished
with antiques, old mirrors and original
artwork, or sit on the terrace on a
sunny day. Spacious bedrooms have
glorious countryside or valley views. At
breakfast, jams, honey, apple juice and
eggs all come from the estate. Formal
three-course dinners are occasionally
organised; 'DIY' picnics and suppers,
ready for heating up in the Aga, can
be arranged. Free access to the historic
gardens. BEDROOMS 9. 1 on ground floor,
suitable for disabled. OPEN All year,
exclusive use Christmas and New Year.
FACILITIES Morning room, drawing
room (honesty bar), dining room,
guest kitchen, free Wi-Fi, in-room TV
(Freeview), civil wedding licence, 55-
acre grounds, terrace, heated outdoor
swimming pool (Apr–Sept), croquet,
boules, parking. CHILDREN All ages
welcomed. DOGS Allowed in heated
boot room, on lead in garden. PRICES Per
room B&B £145–£230.

SALCOMBE Devon
Map 1:E4
SALCOMBE HARBOUR HOTEL, Cliff Road,
TQ8 8JH. Tel 01548 844444, www.
salcombe-harbour-hotel.co.uk. On the
Salcombe estuary, this Victorian hotel
makes the most of the panoramic vista
across the water, with wide terraces,
huge windows and binoculars in
the bedrooms to take in the views.
Decorated in maritime stripes and
shades of blue, bedrooms are nicely
nautical. Book a room with a private
balcony, then watch the sunset with a
drink rustled up from the decanters of
gin or sherry provided – ice and lemon
slices are delivered to the room each
evening. There's a 'good ambience' in
the Jetty restaurant and on the sunny
terraces, where you'll tuck in to Devon
produce and freshly landed fish and
seafood (seared scallops, bacon, cider-
pickled cockles, smoked cauliflower
purée, say) from a choice of two menus.
For complete relaxation, a modern
spa is set over two levels. A sister hotel
is in Chichester (see Shortlist entry).
BEDROOMS 50. 2 suitable for disabled.
FACILITIES Bar/lounge, restaurant, free
Wi-Fi, in-room TV, civil wedding
licence, mini-cinema, spa (fitness suite,
15-metre indoor pool, hot tub, steam
room, sauna, treatments), terraces, valet
parking. BACKGROUND MUSIC In public
areas. CHILDREN All ages welcomed.
DOGS Allowed in some bedrooms. PRICES
Per room B&B from £145. À la carte
£45. 2-night min. stay preferred.

SOUTH SANDS, Bolt Head, TQ8 8LL.
Tel 01548 845 900, www.southsands.
com. At high tide, the waves come
up to the wraparound terrace of this
'beautifully designed' beachside hotel,
sheltered in a pretty cove. Inside, a dash
of New England charm infuses the
'relaxed, informal' lounge and beachy
bedrooms. Each room, styled in coastal
colours, has seasidey touches (seascape
paintings; a seagull sculpture); those at

the front have magnificent views. (Some rear rooms might have traffic noise.) Guests travelling with family might consider a beach suite with a separate living and dining area. Sip cocktails on the terrace before dinner in the airy restaurant: there could be chargrilled squid, chilli; pan-fried monkfish, caramelised cabbage purée, pickled vegetables. Beaches and coastal paths await. BEDROOMS 27. Some on ground floor, 2 suitable for disabled. OPEN All year. FACILITIES Lounge, bar, restaurant, free Wi-Fi, in-room TV (Freeview), civil wedding licence, terrace, parking. BACKGROUND MUSIC In public areas. CHILDREN All ages welcomed. DOGS Allowed in some bedrooms, on lead in lounge, bar and terrace. PRICES Per room B&B £215–£595. 3-course set menu £45. 2-night min. stay at weekends.
25% DISCOUNT VOUCHERS

SALISBURY Wiltshire
Map 2:D2
LEENA'S GUEST HOUSE, 50 Castle Road, SP1 3RL. Tel 07814 897907, www. leenasguesthouse.co.uk. 'One of the best small guest houses I have stayed in,' reports a regular Guide reader in 2017. The Street family's good-value B&B is conveniently located for exploring the medieval city. It may be modest but it's 'immaculate, well decorated and comfortably appointed'. Traditionally styled bedrooms in the Edwardian house are supplied with chocolates and biscuits on the hospitality tray. A bonus: multilingual guests welcome the opportunity to practise their French, German and Suomi with the 'helpful, informative' hosts. In any language, breakfast is 'excellent'. Hot dishes are cooked to order and served on pretty

blue-and-white crockery; there may be seasonal berries from the garden. On a busy junction; down the road, a riverside footpath leads to the city centre, 15 mins' walk away. BEDROOMS 6. 1 on ground floor. OPEN All year except Christmas, New Year. FACILITIES Lounge, breakfast room, free Wi-Fi, in-room TV (Freeview), garden, parking. CHILDREN All ages welcomed. PRICES Per room B&B £75–£110. Credit cards not accepted.

SPIRE HOUSE, 84 Exeter Street, SP1 2SE. Tel 01722 339213, www.salisbury-bedandbreakfast.com. Handy for the cathedral, which is steps away, Lois and John Faulkner's 'very nice' B&B is a 'friendly' place, and a good base for exploring the city. The 18th-century town house has traditionally decorated bedrooms ('pleasant to be in'); two overlook the quiet walled garden. A continental breakfast is delivered to the room: fresh juice and fruit, plus locally baked treats such as warm croissants, pain au chocolat and granola slices. The hosts have heaps of local recommendations, including 'great places to eat' nearby. Free parking, though it can be 'a bit tricky, on this busy street'. BEDROOMS 3. OPEN All year except Christmas, New Year. FACILITIES Free Wi-Fi, in-room TV, garden. CHILDREN Not under 11. PRICES Per room B&B £100.

SCARBOROUGH Yorkshire
Map 4:C5
PHOENIX COURT, 8–9 Rutland Terrace, Queens Parade, YO12 7JB. Tel 01723 501150, www.hotel-phoenix.co.uk. Alison and Bryan Edwards extend a 'warm welcome' to guests at their

unassuming guest house overlooking North Bay and the beach. It is liked for its 'good central position'; the private car park is a bonus. Bedrooms may be 'plain', but they're spacious, clean and comfortable, and many have sea views. 'We slept well.' A 'great breakfast' is cooked to order in the morning: home-baked bread, home-made jams and marmalade, Yorkshire smoked kippers, tofu-and-mushroom sausages, bacon from local farms. A continental breakfast may be taken in the bedroom. For amblers and ramblers, the hosts have route information and car-free itineraries to recommend; ask for a packed lunch, with home-baked rolls and cakes, to take with you (£6 per person). 10 mins' walk from the town centre. BEDROOMS 13. 1 on ground floor. OPEN New Year, Feb–Nov. FACILITIES Lounge (bar area), breakfast room, free Wi-Fi, in-room TV (Freeview), drying facilities, parking. BACKGROUND MUSIC Local radio in breakfast room. CHILDREN All ages welcomed. PRICES Per room B&B single £36–£40, double £50–£66. **25% DISCOUNT VOUCHERS**

SEDBERGH Cumbria
Map 4:C3
THE MALABAR, Garths, Marthwaite, LA10 5ED. Tel 015396 20200, www.themalabar.co.uk. In open farmland in the Yorkshire Dales national park, Graham and Fiona Lappin's luxurious B&B in a massively restored cattle barn is a haven for walkers and devotees of a good cuppa. Arrive to an afternoon feast of sandwiches, scones, pastries and cakes, plus a choice of 12 types of tea. Spacious, thoughtfully equipped bedrooms feature original stone walls and oak beams; warm colours and block-print fabrics (inspired by the years the owners spent in India and Southeast Asia) add personality. Wake to a leisurely breakfast, taken at a communal table or in the garden, at a time of your choosing. There's freshly ground coffee, home-baked bread, seasonal juices, and a Cumbrian Fell special of wild boar bacon, venison sausages and freshly laid eggs. The Dales Way footpath is a field away. 2 miles W of Sedbergh. BEDROOMS 6. 1 family suite with private entrance. OPEN All year. FACILITIES Sitting room (wood-burning stove, honesty bar), dining room, free Wi-Fi, in-room TV (Freeview), $1/3$-acre garden, parking. BACKGROUND MUSIC None. CHILDREN All ages welcomed. PRICES Per room B&B £160–£240.

SEDGEFORD Norfolk
Map 2:A5
MAGAZINE WOOD, Peddars Way, nr Hunstanton, PE36 5LW. Tel 01485 750740, www.magazinewood.co.uk. Pip and Jonathan Barber's chic, rural retreat is surrounded by countryside close to the north Norfolk coast. Luxurious and cocooning, self-contained B&B suites each have their own entrance and terrace; boutique hotel-inspired interiors include a large bed, mood lighting and a bathroom with a deep bath and separate shower. Plenty of thoughtful extras, too: books, DVDs, binoculars; a tablet computer that serves as online concierge – use it to summon breakfast, download a newspaper, make plans for the day. 'Anytime' breakfasts are taken in the room: a well-stocked cupboard contains muesli, cereals, fruits and croissants; milk and organic yogurts are in the fridge. Order cooked breakfasts the night before (charged extra). 5 miles

from Hunstanton. BEDROOMS 3. All on ground floor, 2 in converted barn. OPEN All year except Christmas. FACILITIES Free Wi-Fi, in-room TV (on-demand movies), garden, parking. CHILDREN Infants welcomed. DOGS Allowed (not unattended) in 1 bedroom. PRICES Per room B&B (continental) £115–£129. Cooked breakfast £5–£7. 2-night min. stay most weekends.

SETTLE Yorkshire
Map 4:D3
SETTLE LODGE, Duke Street, BD24 9AS. Tel 01729 823258, www.settlelodge. co.uk. Within easy reach of the Three Peaks and the Dales, Amanda and Eduardo Martinez's B&B has 'comfortable accommodation' in a 'peaceful location'. Guests arrive at the Victorian house to find a welcoming spread of tea and cake. Beyond, there are 'spacious, beautiful' bedrooms, each with views of the surrounding landscape. Start the day with a 'delicious breakfast' served in 'generous portions' – award-winning sausages, say, or scrambled eggs and salmon. Walks in the fells start from the door; the amenable hosts can direct you to the best walking routes (maps are gladly provided) and local eating places. 5 mins' walk from the town centre and train station. BEDROOMS 7. FACILITIES Sitting room, dining room, free Wi-Fi, in-room TV, terrace, garden, parking. PRICES Per room B&B £75–£99.

SHANKLIN Isle of Wight
Map 2:E2
RYLSTONE MANOR, Rylstone Gardens, Popham Road, PO37 6RG. Tel 01983 862806, www.rylstonemanor.co.uk. 'Delightfully relaxing', Mike and Carole Hailston's small Isle of Wight hotel is in a 'lovely' clifftop setting, surrounded by a public park with steps leading down to Sandown Bay. The 19th-century gentleman's residence has plenty of space to relax in sitting rooms decorated with period furnishings; upstairs, some of the traditionally styled bedrooms have glimpses of the sea through trees. In the evening, the host's short, daily-changing menu of modern and classic dishes is served in the chandelier-lit dining room. 'The fish – so fresh – was perfect every night.' Take pause in the secluded private garden – it's 'a pleasant place to sip wine'. Long-time Isle of Wight residents, the Hailstons have plenty of local information to share. Direct access to sand/shingle beach. BEDROOMS 9. OPEN Feb–Nov. FACILITIES Drawing room (books, games), bar/lounge, dining room, free Wi-Fi, in-room TV (Freeview), terrace, ¼-acre garden in 4-acre public gardens. BACKGROUND MUSIC None. CHILDREN Not under 16. PRICES Per room B&B from £140, D,B&B from £198. 2-night min. stay in peak season.
25% DISCOUNT VOUCHERS

SHERBORNE Dorset
Map 2:E1
THE EASTBURY HOTEL, Long Street, DT9 3BY. Tel 01935 813131, www. theeastburyhotel.co.uk. 'A little oasis' in the market town, this 'pleasant' hotel stands in a 'lovely' walled garden ideal for an alfresco drink or two. It is owned by Nicky and Paul King. 'Comfortable, well-furnished' bedrooms are decorated in modern or traditional style. Ask for one with a private garden, and receive extra space in which to stretch out. Afternoon teas, snacks, sandwiches

and light meals may be taken in the bar and lounge; in the restaurant, 'tasty' seasonal menus might include Devon crab, cucumber and horseradish, green apple, sea purslane; confit duck, parsley gnocchi. Eat on the terrace in good weather. Sherborne Abbey is close by. BEDROOMS 23. 3 with external access, 1 suitable for disabled. OPEN All year. FACILITIES Drawing room, lounge, bar, library, conservatory restaurant, private dining room, free Wi-Fi, in-room TV (Freeview), wedding/function facilities, terrace, garden. BACKGROUND MUSIC In bar and restaurant. CHILDREN All ages welcomed (cots £8.50, extra beds £20). DOGS Allowed in bedrooms and lounge, not in bar or restaurant (£10 per night). PRICES Per room B&B single £85–£165, double £155–£205, D,B&B single £105–£185, double £195–£245. Tasting menu £55.
25% DISCOUNT VOUCHERS

THE KINGS ARMS, North Street, Charlton Horethorne, DT9 4NL. Tel 01963 220281, www.thekingsarms. co.uk. In a pretty village five miles from Sherborne, chef/patron Sarah Lethbridge and her husband, Anthony, are the hands-on hosts at the country pub they restored nearly ten years ago. Colourful, individually styled bedrooms are provided with towelling bathrobes and tea- and coffee-making facilities; some rooms look over the croquet lawn. There are newspapers to browse in the snug, and broad countryside views from the terrace; in cool weather, the wood-burning stove is lit. Sample the varied menu in the restaurant at lunch or dinner. Typical dishes: goats' cheese fritters, wild garlic salsa verde; roasted lamb rump, honey roast parsnips, spring cabbage; meats cooked in the Josper charcoal oven. BEDROOMS 10. 1 suitable for disabled. OPEN All year, limited service over Christmas, New Year. FACILITIES Lift, snug, bar, restaurant, free Wi-Fi, in-room TV (Freeview), terrace, garden, croquet lawn, shooting parties, free use of sports centre in Sherborne, discounts at Sherborne Golf Club, parking. BACKGROUND MUSIC None. CHILDREN All ages welcomed. DOGS Allowed in bar. PRICES Per room B&B from £145. À la carte £26–£30.

SHREWSBURY Shropshire
Map 3:B4

CHATFORD HOUSE, Chatford, Bayston Hill, SY3 0AY. Tel 01743 718301, www. chatfordhouse.co.uk. The hospitality is 'first class' at Christine and Rupert Farmer's B&B close to the Shropshire Way. Visitors to the 18th-century farmhouse are 'warmly greeted' with tea and home-made cake – 'we felt so spoiled,' Guide readers say. Traditional, cottage-style bedrooms are on the first floor, with views across the garden or towards the Wrekin. Nice touches: fresh flowers, magazines and a regularly topped-up hospitality tray. In the morning, Aga-cooked breakfasts use produce from the Farmers' organic smallholding; home-made jams and local honey sweeten the feast. On a fine day, explore the pretty garden and orchard, fitting in a visit to the farm animals. 5 miles S of Shrewsbury; within walking distance of Lyth Hill. BEDROOMS 3. FACILITIES Sitting room, breakfast room (open fire), free Wi-Fi, in-room TV, garden, orchard, parking. CHILDREN All ages welcomed. PRICES Per room B&B single £60, double £80–£90. Credit cards not accepted.

GROVE FARM HOUSE, Condover, SY5 7BH. Tel 01743 718544, www. grovefarmhouse.com. Liz Farrow's peaceful B&B offers plenty of pampering: the third-generation owner of the Georgian house bids guests welcome with tea and cake, and stocks the pretty bedrooms with home-made shortbread and garden blooms. Rooms, on the first and second floors, have countryside charm in their tongue-and-groove panelling and graceful florals; a digital radio, DVD-player and bathrobes are supplied. Breakfast brings home-baked bread and muffins and home-made granola; plentiful cooked options use eggs from the garden hens and meats from nearby farms. Parkland and woodland walks are nearby, as are many restaurants – ask for recommendations. 6 miles S of Shrewsbury. BEDROOMS 4. Plus 2 self-catering suites with log burner, private courtyard, optional food hamper. OPEN All year except Christmas, New Year. FACILITIES Lounge, dining room, free Wi-Fi, in-room TV (Freeview), ½-acre garden, parking. BACKGROUND MUSIC None. CHILDREN All ages welcomed. PRICES Per room B&B single £75, double £100. 2-night min. stay Apr–Sept.

LION AND PHEASANT, 49–50 Wyle Cop, SY1 1XJ. Tel 01743 770345, www. lionandpheasant.co.uk. The 'friendly staff' are praised at this modernised 16th-century coaching inn, in a city-centre location 'with easy access to all parts'. Join locals in the popular local-ale-stocked bar or the split-level restaurant ('the upper level is the quieter and nicer place to eat'). The modern dishes, using plenty of Shropshire produce, are 'well cooked', report

Guide readers in 2017. Varying in size, uncluttered bedrooms ('a little basic,' one guest thought) are up the stairs and down beamed corridors. Some overlook the river. 'Our room was light and airy, for its size, with a comfortable bed and a roomy shower in the bathroom. Shame about the UHT cartons – but they supplied us with fresh milk from the bar.' Rooms at the front have traffic noise (earplugs are provided); light sleepers should ask for a rear room. 'There's a good selection at breakfast, and plenty of it.' BEDROOMS 22. OPEN All year except 25–26 Dec. FACILITIES 2 bars, restaurant, function room, free Wi-Fi, in-room TV (Freeview), room service, garden terrace (alfresco dining), parking (narrow entrance). BACKGROUND MUSIC In public areas, occasional live music in bar. CHILDREN All ages welcomed. PRICES Per room B&B £99–£225. À la carte £38.

SIDMOUTH Devon
Map 1:D5

VICTORIA HOTEL, The Esplanade, EX10 8RY. Tel 01395 512651, www. victoriahotel.co.uk. Overlooking the bay, this large, traditional hotel is 'old-fashioned in the best sense of the word'. It attracts regular returnees, who like the 'immaculate bedrooms' and 'delightful gardens', the Saturday-night dinner dances and the cohort of amiable staff. Sofas by the bay windows in the sun lounge give the best views of the esplanade; in the garden, benches are set among the flowerbeds. Most of the bedrooms, conservative and comfortable, have views over the sea; some have French windows opening on to a private balcony. Evening turn-down leaves a chocolate on the pillow. Dress up for dinner in the Jubilee restaurant, where a live band plays every night; in the informal White Room restaurant, sample chef Stuart White's modern, French-inflected menu. BEDROOMS 61. 3 poolside suites. FACILITIES Sun lounge, lounge bar, 2 restaurants, free Wi-Fi, in-room TV (Sky, Freeview), spa (sauna, treatments), garden, outdoor and indoor swimming pools, tennis court, putting, gift shop, parking. BACKGROUND MUSIC In public areas. CHILDREN All ages welcomed. PRICES Room from £180. Breakfast £18, set dinner (Jubilee restaurant) £42, à la carte (White Room restaurant) £48. 2-night min. stay.

SISSINGHURST Kent
Map 2:D5
THE MILK HOUSE, The Street, TN17 2JG. Tel 01580 720200, www.themilkhouse.co.uk. An 'enjoyable' pub-with-rooms, this 16th-century hall house has been updated with stylish, unfussy bedrooms and a buzzy, village-hub feel. It is owned by Dane and Sarah Allchorne. Come in to timber beams and a Tudor fireplace; cask ales alongside local beers and wines. Wood-fired pizzas and uncomplicated pub food may be eaten on the terrace or in the large garden; more creative, modern plates are served in the rustic dining room. 'The food was good, from a small, unchanging menu; one night we had bar snacks – just as tasty, despite the owners being away,' reports a Guide reader in 2017. Bedrooms upstairs are 'very comfortable', with 'a good bed'. (Front rooms may have road noise.) Hearty breakfasts kick off the day. Sissinghurst Castle Garden is a mile up the road. BEDROOMS 4. FACILITIES Bar, restaurant (closed Sun eve), private dining room, free Wi-Fi, in-room TV (Freeview), sun terrace, large garden (pond, play area), parking. BACKGROUND MUSIC In bar and restaurant. CHILDREN All ages welcomed. DOGS Allowed in bar and garden, not in bedrooms or restaurant. PRICES Per room B&B £80–£140. 2-night min. stay at weekends.

SISSINGHURST CASTLE FARMHOUSE, nr Cranbrook, TN17 2AB. Tel 01580 720992, www.sissinghurstcastlefarmhouse.com. Within a National Trust estate of ancient woodland and farmland stands Sue and Frazer Thompson's tranquil Victorian farmhouse B&B. Country-style bedrooms are decorated with pictures and a mix of contemporary and period furniture; each room has views across the estate or towards Sissinghurst Castle's Elizabethan tower. Arrive to welcoming tea and home-baked cake, served in the sitting room or on the sunny, south-facing lawn; later, explore Vita Sackville-West's historic gardens, just yards away. In the morning, breakfast is a spread of Kentish apples and pears, locally smoked bacon and salmon, and hearty sausages. Picnic lunches can be arranged. BEDROOMS 7. 1 suitable for disabled. OPEN Mar–Nov. FACILITIES Lift, sitting room, dining room, free Wi-Fi, in-room TV, small functions, ¾-acre garden. BACKGROUND MUSIC None. CHILDREN All ages welcomed. PRICES Per room B&B £150–£200. 2-night min. stay at weekends, Easter–Sept.

SOMERTON Somerset
Map 1:C6
THE WHITE HART, Market Place, TA11 7LX. Tel 01458 272273, www.whitehartsomerton.com. The 'superb

meals' at this revamped pub-with-rooms on the edge of the Somerset Levels are 'up there with the best', report Guide readers in 2017. Locals and visitors gather in the jolly bar and conservatory dining room, or go alfresco in the courtyard. Upstairs, most of the well-equipped bedrooms overlook the 13th-century church and the market square, or the pretty rear garden. Each room has a large bed with crisp linen; deep-pile towels and natural bath and body products. Breakfast, served till 11 am, has plenty of interesting choices: soy porridge, summer berries; smoky beans, bubble and squeak cake, roast tomatoes. Part of the small Stay Original Company; see also Timbrell's Yard, Bradford-on-Avon, and The Swan, Wedmore (Shortlist entries). BEDROOMS 8. FACILITIES Bar, restaurant (3 dining areas), free Wi-Fi, in-room smart TV, large courtyard garden, secure bicycle storage. BACKGROUND MUSIC In bar. CHILDREN All ages welcomed. DOGS Allowed in 1 room. PRICES Per room B&B from £75.

SOUTH ALKHAM Kent
Map 2:D5

ALKHAM COURT, Meggett Lane, nr Dover, CT15 7DG. Tel 01303 892056, www.alkhamcourt.co.uk. Watch the sun set over the Alkham valley from Wendy and Neil Burrows's farmhouse B&B in the Kent Downs. Green countryside stretches out in front of the house – it's an ideal setting for a welcome drink in the garden. (On cool days, a seat by the log-burner in the sitting room is just as nice.) Country-style bedrooms, each with a private entrance, have fresh flowers, a coffee machine and complimentary sherry; alternatively, a restored shepherd's hut in the grounds, cosy with a wood-burning stove and electric heating, makes a quirky 'glamping' option. A bonus, for utter relaxation: a sauna and indoor hot tub. Hearty breakfasts have freshly baked muffins, local pressed apple juice, eggs from the house's free-range hens. 15 mins' drive from the Eurotunnel and the port of Dover; pubs and restaurants nearby. BEDROOMS 4. 3 on ground floor, plus shepherd's hut. OPEN All year except 24–25 Dec. FACILITIES Sitting/breakfast room, free Wi-Fi, in-room TV (Freeview), spa barn, large garden with wild flower paddock, 60-acre grassland, parking. BACKGROUND MUSIC None. CHILDREN All ages welcomed. PRICES Per room B&B £140–£170. Picnic lunch £7.50, soup and rolls £5.50.

SOUTH BRENT Devon
Map 1:D4

GLAZEBROOK HOUSE, Glazebrook, TQ10 9JE. Tel 01364 73322, www.glazebrookhouse.com. 'All rather fun', Fran and Pieter Hamman's 19th-century manor house on the edge of Dartmoor national park teems with curiosities and vintage pieces. Drums, hats and old street signs adorn the walls; chandeliers and a stuffed flamingo decorate the hall. 'Zany' bedrooms take style inspiration from Alice in Wonderland: Mad Hatter has a display of antique plates; Tweedle Deez has twin four-poster beds. Amenities are taken seriously: a luxurious bathroom; plenty of complimentary extras, such as chocolates and mini-bottles of wine. Sample local beers and speciality cocktails in the glamorous bar. The 'pleasant, airy' dining room has imaginative modern dishes and eight-course tasting menus. Guided walking tours on Dartmoor. 1 mile SW of town centre. BEDROOMS 9. 1 on ground floor, 1 suitable for disabled. OPEN All year except 2 weeks Jan. FACILITIES Bar, drawing room, library, restaurant, Chef's Kitchen patio, free Wi-Fi, in-room TV (Freeview), civil wedding licence, wine, whisky and gin tasting room, 3½-acre mature garden, parking. BACKGROUND MUSIC In public areas, except library and tasting room. CHILDREN Not under 16. PRICES Per room B&B from £199. À la carte £40. **25% DISCOUNT VOUCHERS**

SOUTH LEIGH Oxfordshire
Map 3:E6

ARTIST RESIDENCE OXFORDSHIRE, The Mason Arms, Station Road, OX29 6XN. Tel 0203 198 1066, artistresidenceoxford. co.uk. As rural as its sister hotels are coolly urban, this thatch-roofed farmhouse is now home to the newest of Justin and Charlotte Salisbury's Artist Residences. The 16th-century building has been refurbished and revamped in the duo's now-signature style: bohemian flourishes, reclaimed pieces and modern luxuries are placed against a backdrop of original features (flagstone floors, exposed brickwork, a huge fireplace). Chef Leon Smith serves a seasonal, 'low-mileage' menu, using foraged or home-grown ingredients, in the cosy dining areas; the pub has a short menu of sophisticated snacks and bar classics. Quirky bedrooms are upstairs: beams, wooden floorboards, eclectic artwork, organic toiletries; a mini-fridge stocked with local goodies. 10 miles from Oxford. BEDROOMS 5. OPEN All year. FACILITIES Bar, restaurant (2 dining areas, closed Sun eve), free

Wi-Fi, in-room TV (Freeview), large garden. BACKGROUND MUSIC In public areas. CHILDREN All ages welcomed, no under-10s in restaurant after 6 pm. DOGS Allowed in 1 bedroom, public rooms (treats, bowls; £20 per dog per night). PRICES Per room B&B from £130, D,B&B (Mon–Thurs) from £270. À la carte £50. 2-night min. stay preferred.

SOUTH MOLTON Devon
Map 1:C4

ASHLEY HOUSE, 3 Paradise Lawn, EX36 3DJ. Tel 01769 573444, www. ashleyhousebedandbreakfast.com. A former gentleman's residence is today Nicky Robbins's welcoming B&B, in the centre of this market town close to Exmoor national park. Fans of historical trivia, take note: the blue plaque out front honours Lord Samuel Widgery, a former Lord Chief Justice of England, who was born in the house. High-ceilinged bedrooms in the Victorian villa are decorated with a mix of antiques, contemporary pieces, original photography and artwork; a well-stocked tea tray is provided. Breakfast well: there are home-made jams and marmalades, locally sourced bacon and sausages, eggs from the house's hens. BEDROOMS 3. OPEN All year. FACILITIES Breakfast/sitting room (wood-burning stove), free Wi-Fi, in-room TV (Freeview), large garden, parking. BACKGROUND MUSIC Classic FM in breakfast room. CHILDREN Not under 14. PRICES Per room B&B £75–£105.

SOUTHAMPTON Hampshire
Map 2:E2

WOODLANDS LODGE HOTEL, Bartley Road, SO40 7GN. Tel 02380 292257, www.woodlands-lodge.co.uk. 'A perfect little dog-friendly hotel.' Imogene and Robert Anglaret ensure that travelling pets and their human companions are well taken care of at their country hotel in the New Forest. Dogs receive a treat, a blanket and a towel in several of the spacious bedrooms, but there's more to please their owners: the smart, modern country style; the garden and woodland views; even a working gas fireplace in some bedrooms. Snacks are available all day in the conservatory, lounge or bedrooms; at mealtimes, eat in Hunters restaurant – the walled garden provides the kitchen with fruit and vegetables in season. 1 mile from train station; 15 mins' drive from Southampton. BEDROOMS 17. 2 with garden access, 1 suitable for disabled. FACILITIES Lounge, bar, conservatory, restaurant, free Wi-Fi in public areas, in-room TV (Freeview), civil wedding licence, business facilities, 3-acre garden. BACKGROUND MUSIC Radio or 'easy listening' in bar and restaurant. CHILDREN All ages welcomed. DOGS Allowed in some bedrooms, bar, lounge. PRICES Per room B&B from £79, D,B&B from £139.

SOUTHWOLD Suffolk
Map 2:B6
SUTHERLAND HOUSE, 56 High Street, IP18 6DN. Tel 01502 724 544, www. sutherlandhouse.co.uk. Andy and Kinga Rudd's modern restaurant-with-rooms occupies a fine 15th-century building in this popular seaside resort. Rich with period charm and history – the Duke of York (later James II) visited frequently when he was High Admiral of the English navy during the Anglo-Dutch war – the Grade II* listed building is filled with modern fabrics, and contemporary and vintage furnishings

against handsome old beams, wide elm floorboards and medieval windows. Harbour-fresh fish features in the popular restaurant, in dishes such as pan-fried sea bream, potato and emmental soufflé, pistachio pesto. Most of the characterful bedrooms are up a narrow staircase. Each is different: one has a glorious pargetted ceiling; another has a double-ended slipper bath in front of an original fireplace. BEDROOMS 4. 1 on ground floor. FACILITIES Bar, restaurant (closed Mon, reservations recommended), free Wi-Fi, in-room TV, garden (alfresco eating and drinking). PRICES Per room B&B £185. Check-in from 1 pm–3 pm and 6 pm–9 pm.

STAMFORD Lincolnshire
Map 2:B3
THE BULL AND SWAN AT BURGHLEY, High Street, St Martins, PE9 2LJ. Tel 01780 766412, www.thebullandswan. co.uk. Allegedly the one-time meeting place of a raucous coterie of 17th-century gentlemen – the Honourable Order of Little Bedlam – this refurbished coaching inn now attracts a more honourable order of regulars and visitors to its inviting pub. It is part of the small Hillbrooke Hotels group (see The Master Builder's, Beaulieu, main entry). Hungry diners tuck in to modern pub grub in one of the lively dining areas or, on warm-weather weekends, by the new 'pizza potting shed' in the garden. Bedrooms have character in their exposed stone walls or feature wallpaper, their mix of vintage furnishings and modern comforts. Among the well-considered extras: fancy tea, 'proper coffee', biscuits, a mini-bottle of organic vodka. Burghley

House is not far. BEDROOMS 9. FACILITIES Bar with 3 dining areas, private dining/meeting room, free Wi-Fi, in-room TV (Freeview), courtyard garden with seating, outdoor cinema, parking (narrow entrance). BACKGROUND MUSIC In bar. CHILDREN All ages welcomed. DOGS Allowed in 3 bedrooms (dog bed, bowls, special treats, room-service menu, £20). PRICES Per room B&B £87–£180, D,B&B £162–£220.

STOKE BY NAYLAND Suffolk
Map 2:C5

THE CROWN, Park Street, CO6 4SE. Tel 01206 262001, www.crowninn.net. In a Suffolk village on the Stour Valley Path, Richard Sunderland's 'delightful' pub and hotel are liked for the 'characterful' restaurant and 'smart, modern' bedrooms. Pull up a seat in the beamed dining area or eat under a parasol on the sunny terrace, where the views are of rolling countryside and Constable skies. A wide selection of brasserie-style food, including interesting vegetarian options, is served all day. Real ales and an 'outstanding choice' of wines come from the glass-walled shop on site; bottles can be purchased to take home. In a separate clapboard building, generously sized, well-equipped bedrooms (some with a private terrace) are decorated in country or contemporary style, and have a 'very smart bathroom'. Excellent walking nearby. BEDROOMS 11. Some on ground floor, 1 suitable for disabled. OPEN All year except 25–26 Dec. FACILITIES Bar, restaurant, terrace, wine shop, free Wi-Fi, in-room TV, garden, parking. BACKGROUND MUSIC None. CHILDREN All ages welcomed, not in restaurant after 8 pm. PRICES Per room B&B from £145. À la carte £35.

STOWMARKET Suffolk
Map 2:C5

BAYS FARM, Forward Green, Earl Stonham, IP14 5HU. Tel 441449711286, www.baysfarmsuffolk.co.uk. Amid rolling countryside, Stephanie and Richard Challinor's restored 17th-century farmhouse B&B stands in award-winning gardens just right for a wander and quiet contemplation. Individually decorated bedrooms have a country feel and views over the landscaped garden. Each is provided with bottled water, an espresso machine and DVDs. A shepherd's hut in the wild flower garden makes a quirky choice – it has adjustable heating and a traditional wood burner, plus all the extras, including organic toiletries for the oversized shower. Tasty breakfasts, served in the former dairy (the oldest part of the house), have home-made bread, marmalade and jams; dry-cured Suffolk bacon. Simple suppers (fish pie; pâté and Suffolk chutney) may be served, by arrangement. 4 miles E of Stowmarket. BEDROOMS 5. 1 in adjacent building, 1 in shepherd's hut. OPEN All year. FACILITIES Reception hall, drawing room, dining room, free Wi-Fi, in-room TV (Freeview), 4-acre garden (heated pavilion). BACKGROUND MUSIC In drawing room and dining room, 'but we will turn it off if asked'. CHILDREN Not under 12. PRICES Per room B&B £85–£130. À la carte £25. 2-night min. stay on summer weekends.

STRATFORD-UPON-AVON
Warwickshire
Map 3:D6

WHITE SAILS, 85 Evesham Road, CV37 9BE. Tel 01789 550469, www.white-sails.co.uk. Experience the Bard from

Tim and Denise Perkin's comfortable B&B on the outskirts of Stratford – the RSC theatres in town are within a 20-minute stroll. Little extras make guests feel at home: help yourself to complimentary sherry, espresso coffee and home-made treats in the lounge. 'Clean, comfy bedrooms' are supplied with bathrobes, a digital radio/iPod docking station, home-baked cake and a silent fridge with chilled water and fresh milk. Breakfast on home-made granola, bread and cakes; hot dishes, such as eggs Benedict or smoked haddock with poached eggs, are cooked to order. 1 mile W of centre; within walking distance of Anne Hathaway's cottage and garden. Stratford racecourse is nearby. BEDROOMS 5. 1 on ground floor. OPEN All year except Christmas Day, New Year's Day. FACILITIES Small lounge, dining room, free Wi-Fi, in-room TV (Freeview), garden, parking, bicycle storage. CHILDREN Not under 12. PRICES Per room B&B £105–£130. 2-night min. stay preferred at weekends.

TAVISTOCK Devon
Map 1:D4

TAVISTOCK HOUSE HOTEL, 50 Plymouth Road, PL19 8BU. Tel 01822 481 627, www.tavistockhousehotel.co.uk. Five minutes' walk from the town square, Brad and Gill Walker have refurbished this Victorian town house, creating a clutch of well-appointed bedrooms within. The small hotel is pristine throughout, from its gleaming marble-floored entrance hall to its bright, elegant lounge. Chic, modern bedrooms in varying sizes have luxury bedding, a capsule coffee machine, dressing gowns and slippers, plus a tablet computer to access free online newspapers; the bath-

and shower rooms have underfloor heating. Generous breakfasts, light lunches, sandwiches and clotted cream teas please peckish guests; restaurants and bars are a saunter away. The Meadowlands tennis courts are just across the road; bring a racket, or borrow one from the hosts. BEDROOMS 6. OPEN All year except 25–26 Dec, 31 Dec, 1 Jan. FACILITIES Breakfast room/lounge with honesty bar, free Wi-Fi, in-room TV (Freeview, Netflix), front garden. BACKGROUND MUSIC None. CHILDREN Not under 10. PRICES Per room B&B £104–£144.

TENBURY WELLS Worcestershire
Map 3:C5

THE TALBOT INN, Newnham Bridge, WR15 8JF. Tel 01584 781941, www. talbotinnnewnhambridge.co.uk. In the Teme valley, an area abundant with hops and mistletoe, this refurbished red-brick Victorian coaching inn has 'plenty of character'. It is run by Barnaby Williams, the 'hard-working, ever-present' owner, with 'friendly, efficient staff'. At once contemporary and rustic, the wood burner-warmed pub has hops hanging from the ceiling, and photographs of its brewing heritage on the walls – join locals here for a pint of real ale or cider. When hunger strikes, sample chef Jacob Vaughan's inspired dishes, many cooked in the Josper charcoal oven. His imaginative pub grub, served on scrubbed pine tables, might include such dishes as Springfield chicken breast, pear, cider fondant potato. Well-proportioned bedrooms are 'modern, bright and immaculately kept'. 4 miles from Tenbury Wells. BEDROOMS 7. OPEN All year except 2–12 Jan, no accommodation Christmas Day.

FACILITIES Bar, snug, 2 dining areas, free Wi-Fi, in-room TV (Freeview), garden, parking. BACKGROUND MUSIC In dining areas 'but we can turn it off if asked'. CHILDREN All ages welcomed. DOGS Allowed in 3 bedrooms, bar. PRICES Per room B&B £70–£110. À la carte £30. 2-night min. stay preferred at weekends May–Sept.

TETBURY Gloucestershire
Map 3:E5

THE ROYAL OAK, 1 Cirencester Road, GL8 8EY. Tel 01666 500021, www.theroyaloaktetbury.co.uk. In a Cotswold village, this 18th-century stone-built pub-with-rooms is a lively community hub. Dog-friendly, family-friendly, all-round inviting, it is owned by husband-and-wife team Chris York and Kate Lewis. There are real ales and a reconditioned jukebox in the buzzy bar; at mealtimes, feast on seasonal fare, including a noteworthy vegan menu, that uses the best of 'superb' Cotswold produce. In the summer months, the restaurant goes retro, with food served from a vintage Airstream trailer on the terrace. Cross the courtyard to get to modern rustic bedrooms. Top-floor rooms have views across the valley; families may opt for the spacious mezzanine suite, which has leather armchairs and a wood-burner in a comfy living area. BEDROOMS 6. 1 suitable for disabled. OPEN All year except 1 week Jan. FACILITIES Bar, restaurant (closed Sun eve), private dining/meeting room, free Wi-Fi, in-room TV (Freeview), large garden (boules pitch), parking, bike shed. BACKGROUND MUSIC In bar and restaurant, monthly live music sessions. CHILDREN All ages welcomed, not after 8 pm in restaurant.

DOGS Allowed in ground-floor rooms, bar and garden, not in restaurant. PRICES Per room B&B £85–£170. À la carte £25. 2-night min. bookings preferred.
25% DISCOUNT VOUCHERS

THORNHAM Norfolk
Map 2:A5

THE LIFEBOAT INN, Ship Lane, PE36 6LT. Tel 01485 512236, www.lifeboatinnthornham.com. With nothing between it and the salt marshes, this atmospheric 16th-century inn is just the place for beach walks and the fireside drinks that follow them. Sit in the oak-beamed bar or the cosy lounge; eat in the modern dining room or under a 200-year-old vine spreading over the conservatory. In good weather, find a seat on the terrace or in the sheltered beer garden. The menu might include such dishes as a smoked fish and shellfish platter, warm caper bread; crispy garlic and herb polenta, smoked bean chilli. Most of the smart, rustic bedrooms have views over the sea and the salt marshes – perhaps even the sounds of the sea breeze coming in over the coast. Breakfast is fine fuel for coastal strolls: local ham, home-made jams, kippers and grilled tomatoes. Even Fido gets a sausage. BEDROOMS 13. 1, on ground floor, in adjacent cottage. OPEN All year. FACILITIES Bar, 2 lounge areas, conservatory, restaurant, private dining pavilions, free Wi-Fi, in-room smart TV, terrace, garden, parking. BACKGROUND MUSIC All day in public areas. CHILDREN All ages welcomed. DOGS Allowed in bedrooms, public rooms (£10 per stay). PRICES Per room B&B £140–£190. À la carte £28. 2-night min. stay preferred.
25% DISCOUNT VOUCHERS

THORNTON HOUGH Merseyside
Map 4:E2

MERE BROOK HOUSE, Thornton Common Road, Wirral, CH63 0LU. Tel 07713 189949, www.merebrookhouse. co.uk. On the Wirral peninsula, Lorna Tyson and her husband, Donald, a farmer, have transformed an Edwardian country house into a relaxed B&B – 'no notices/rules anywhere!' It stands in mature grounds that reach, through paddocks and woodland, to the Mere Brook. Individually decorated bedrooms are in the original building and a converted coach house; most have garden or countryside views. Both buildings have their own lounge and kitchen for guests' use, plus complimentary home-made cakes, snacks and hot drinks for whenever hunger strikes. Breakfast is in the conservatory. Super-local ingredients include honey from the garden beehives; milk from the Tysons' dairy cows; apple juice made using fruit from the orchard. 20 mins' drive from Liverpool and Chester. BEDROOMS 8. 4 in coach house, 3 on ground floor, 1 suitable for disabled. OPEN All year, limited availability over Christmas, New Year. FACILITIES 3 lounges, conservatory, dining room, guest kitchens, free Wi-Fi, in-room TV (Freeview), wedding/function facilities, 1-acre garden (benches, gazebo) in 4-acre grounds (pond, paddocks). BACKGROUND MUSIC None. CHILDREN All ages welcomed. PRICES Per room B&B £75–£130.

THORPE MARKET Norfolk
Map 2:A5

THE GUNTON ARMS, Cromer Road, NR11 8TZ. Tel 01263 832010, www. theguntonarms.co.uk. Artful surprises await around every corner at art dealer Ivor Braka's sophisticated yet 'relaxed' pub-with-rooms: find Stubbs engravings above crackling fires, a Damien Hirst painting in the ladies' loo. Tracey Manning is the manager. On the edge of a historic deer park, the flint-stoned, red-gabled inn has 'lovely' country-house bedrooms lavishly adorned with handmade wallpaper, Turkish rugs and antique furniture. Broad windows give on to views over the estate. (Raid a downstairs pantry for juice, tea and coffee.) At mealtimes, chef Stuart Tattersall cooks modern rustic dishes (perhaps pea and lovage soup; Blythburgh pork belly, Bramley apple); most nights, steaks, Barnsley chops and estate-reared venison are cooked, 'as if in a medieval banqueting hall', over an open fire in the Elk dining room. 5 miles from Cromer. BEDROOMS 12. 4 in coach house. OPEN All year except Christmas Day. FACILITIES 2 restaurants (closed Sun), lounge, bar, free Wi-Fi. BACKGROUND MUSIC In public areas. CHILDREN All ages welcomed. DOGS Allowed in bar, 1 restaurant, some bedrooms. PRICES Per room B&B £95–£250. À la carte from £35. 2-night min. stay at weekends.

THURNHAM Kent
Map 2:D4

THURNHAM KEEP, Castle Hill, nr Maidstone, ME14 3LE. Tel 01622 734149, www.thurnhamkeep.co.uk. 'We enjoyed it all.' 'Charming host' Amanda Lane greets guests with home-baked treats – perhaps 'the best shortbread ever' – at her 'impressive' Edwardian B&B in acres of landscaped gardens on the crest of the North Downs. Built from the ruins of Thurnham Castle, the 'magnificent place' has traditionally furnished bedrooms up an oak staircase. Each has its own elegant personality; two have a huge, original Edwardian bath in the bathroom. A spacious self-contained suite, suitable for a family, is in the newly converted stables. Greet the day over a communal breakfast, with home-made jams, honey from the garden's bees and eggs from resident hens. Arrange supper in advance or venture out to one of the many pubs nearby. 3 miles from Maidstone. BEDROOMS 3, plus self-contained suite in grounds. OPEN Mar–mid-Dec. FACILITIES Sitting room, dining room, conservatory, billiard room (in the old chapel), free Wi-Fi, in-room TV (Freeview), 7-acre terraced garden, pond, kitchen garden, dovecote, summer house, terrace, heated outdoor swimming pool (June–early Sept), tennis, croquet, parking. BACKGROUND MUSIC None. CHILDREN Not under 12. PRICES Per room B&B £130–£160.

TILLINGTON Sussex
Map 2:E3

THE HORSE GUARDS INN, Upperton Road, nr Petworth, GU28 9AF. Tel 01798 342332, www.thehorseguardsinn. co.uk. A 19th-century resting place for the Household Cavalry as its soldiers made their way to Portsmouth, this 350-year-old inn remains a relaxing refuge for today's travellers. It stands opposite the church of a quintessentially English village overlooking the rolling South Downs. Restored and refreshed, the rambling interior has crooked oak beams, stripped floorboards and a trove of eye-catching curiosities. A short daily-changing menu, well in tune with the seasons and the serendipitous

availability of foraged wild foods, is served in the restaurant, along with home-made sloe gin, farm fruit juices, real ales and an eclectic wine list. On a sunny day, retreat to the 'hidden' garden strewn with hammocks, deckchairs and straw-bale seats. The bedrooms are stylishly simple: pretty florals add country charm. BEDROOMS 3. 1 in cottage. FACILITIES Bar, restaurant, free Wi-Fi, in-room TV (Freeview), garden, secure bicycle storage. CHILDREN All ages welcomed. DOGS Well-behaved dogs allowed. PRICES Per room B&B £110.

TISBURY Wiltshire
Map 2:D1

THE COMPASSES INN, Lower Chicksgrove, nr Salisbury, SP3 6NB. Tel 01722 714318, www.thecompassesinn. com. Come down a quiet country lane to this thatch-roofed 14th-century inn 'in the middle of nowhere': there are flagstone floors, ancient beams, nooks and crannies, an inglenook fireplace. There's a new owner, too – Ben Maschler, who has retained the inn's unpretentious atmosphere and period charm while updating the sophisticated pubby menu and country-cosy bedrooms. The daily-changing selection of uncomplicated dishes uses the best available produce in season; cocktails, local ales and European wines make good accompaniment. Above the pub, simply furnished bedrooms are cheery and cottagey, with a Roberts radio and a clutch of Penguin Classics. Walks from the door; the Nadder valley is all around. 2 miles E of Tisbury. BEDROOMS 4. Plus 2-bed self-catering cottage. OPEN All year except 25–26 Dec. FACILITIES Bar, restaurant, free Wi-Fi, in-room TV (Freeview), ¼-acre garden. BACKGROUND

MUSIC None, occasional live music events. CHILDREN All ages welcomed. DOGS Allowed. PRICES Per room B&B from £95. À la carte £26. 2-night min. stay on summer and bank holiday weekends.

TIVERTON Devon
Map 1:C5

HARTNOLL HOTEL, Bolham, EX16 7RA. Tel 01884 252777, www.hartnollhotel. co.uk. 'Warm and familiar', this country hotel, in 'a chocolate-box-perfect part of Exmoor', has been refurbished in a 'luxurious, contemporary' style by its owner, Claire Carter. 'It is wonderfully clean and new inside,' say Guide inspectors in 2017. 'And the friendly, welcoming staff really make the place.' Modern bedrooms vary in size, but all have plush bedlinens and fluffy dressing gowns; a marble bathroom. 'Our Gatehouse room had a cosy, country-chic feel and all the necessary conveniences. But the loo had a glass door, which we thought rather too intimate.' The conservatory restaurant is a 'lovely' place to sample meals cooked with much Devon produce. Take a wander in the grounds after breakfast: 'I loved strolling along the banks of the babbling brook, past quirky sculptures and water features, then sitting at one of the outdoor tables to read the complimentary newspapers and drink coffee in the sunshine.' 2 miles from town centre. BEDROOMS 18. 5 in Gatehouse. OPEN All year. FACILITIES Bar, 2 sitting rooms, conservatory restaurant, free Wi-Fi, in-room TV (Freeview), civil wedding licence, garden, shooting parties, parking. BACKGROUND MUSIC In reception, bar and sitting room. CHILDREN All ages welcomed (extra bed

£25). DOGS Allowed in some bedrooms and public rooms, not in conservatory (£10 per night). PRICES Per room B&B single (Sun–Thurs) £115–£165, double £140–£190. À la carte £35.

TOLLARD ROYAL Wiltshire
Map 2:E1

KING JOHN INN, SP5 5PS. Tel 01725 516207, www.kingjohninn.co.uk. In a village on the edge of Cranborne Chase, this sophisticated yet unpretentious pub-with-rooms provides 'enticing' British meals, and the country chic bedrooms in which to sleep them off. There's a 'good atmosphere' in the 'simply set' dining room within the ivy-wrapped Victorian inn – a convivial setting for the modern, farm-to-fork dishes rich in locally sourced produce (say best end of lamb, fondant potato, ratatouille). In fine weather, eaters and drinkers spill on to the terraced garden. 'Pleasing, restful bedrooms' (some up 'steep, narrow stairs') have a rustic feel with their pale colours, antiques, home-made shortbread and books; nice extras include all-natural toiletries, fancy teas and an espresso machine. 6 miles W of Shaftesbury. BEDROOMS 8. Some on ground floor, 3 in coach house. OPEN All year. FACILITIES Lounge, bar, restaurant, free Wi-Fi, in-room TV, garden (outdoor functions), shooting parties, parking. BACKGROUND MUSIC None. CHILDREN All ages welcomed. DOGS Allowed by prior arrangement. PRICES Per room B&B from £90. À la carte £35.

TOPSHAM Devon
Map 1:C5

THE SALUTATION INN, 68 Fore Street, EX3 0HL. Tel 01392 873060, www. salutationtopsham.co.uk. An inn since the 1720s, this characterful place rich in maritime history continues to welcome weary travellers to the old port and ship-building town. It is owned by the Williams-Hawkes family; Tom Williams-Hawkes heads the much-praised kitchen. Dashing events punctuate the inn's long history, from regatta balls in the former assembly rooms to a horse-leaping stunt over a dining-room table. Today's attractions are more delicious: afternoon teas and light lunches in the airy café; weekly-changing tasting menus in the restaurant. Accommodation is in restrained modern bedrooms; a shared galley kitchen has help-yourself hot drinks, fruit and home-made biscuits. The staff have local recommendations to share; the RSPB Bowling Green Marsh nature reserve is nearby. 5 miles from Exeter. BEDROOMS 6. 2 suites, accommodating up to 4 people. OPEN All year except 25 Dec evening, 26 Dec, 1 Jan. FACILITIES 2 lounges, restaurant (closed Sun eve), café, meeting/function room, free Wi-Fi, in-room TV (Freeview), walled seating area, parking. BACKGROUND MUSIC In public areas. CHILDREN All ages welcomed. PRICES Per room B&B £135–£225, D,B&B (Mon–Thurs) £200–£295. Set menus £42.50–£85. 2-night min. stay at weekends May–Oct.

TORQUAY Devon
Map 1:D5

ORESTONE MANOR, Rockhouse Lane, Maidencombe, TQ1 4SX. Tel 01803 328098, www.orestonemanor.com. Narrow country lanes lead to the D'Allen family's hotel in sub-tropical gardens overlooking Lyme Bay. Within the Georgian manor house, comfortable leather settees sit on colourful Persian-style carpets amid 'an eclectic assortment of artefacts': Victorian paintings in heavy gold frames, sculpted elephants and rabbits, a classical Greek statue. Most striking of all: the 'impressive view' from the terrace and gardens, over the trees to the sea, say Guide inspectors in 2017. Bedrooms vary in size and decor; most have views of the bay. Some have a private outdoor hot tub; all have a 'state-of-the-art bathroom' stocked with 'generous towels and first-class goodies'. Dinner is 'delicious': 'perfectly cooked' scallops and lobster Thermidor, perhaps, or monkfish and pancetta to 'go into raptures over'. 'Delightful desserts', too. 4½ miles N of Torquay. BEDROOMS 14. 3 in grounds. OPEN All year except Jan. FACILITIES Bar, 2 lounges, 2 dining rooms, free Wi-Fi, in-room TV (Sky), patio, 2-acre grounds, parking. BACKGROUND MUSIC In public areas. CHILDREN All ages welcomed, no under-10s in main restaurant at dinner. PRICES Per room B&B £110–£300, D,B&B £180–£370. Table d'hôte menus £21–£27, à la carte £35.

THE 25, 25 Avenue Road, TQ2 5LB. Tel 01803 297517, www.the25.uk. 'Personable hosts' Andy and Julian Banner-Price run their award-winning B&B in a zestfully refurbished, 'meticulously maintained' Edwardian villa near Torre Abbey. 'The decor is edgy but comfortably short of giddy,' say guests in 2017. 'And the amenities, including lavish in-room tea- and coffee-making facilities and daily fresh-baked treats, are commendable.' Arrive to a welcoming drink and cake in the drawing room, then unpack in one of the modern, remarkably well-equipped

bedrooms, each as different as can be. In the morning, fruit smoothie shots kick off breakfast; fruit salad, home-made yogurt and granola, and a choice of hot dishes follow. Walk through gardens towards the seafront, and the shops, restaurants and bars on the main harbour. BEDROOMS 6. OPEN Feb–Oct. FACILITIES Drawing room, dining room, free Wi-Fi, in-room smart TV (movies on demand), patio, parking. BACKGROUND MUSIC At breakfast. CHILDREN Not accepted. PRICES Per room B&B £99–£159.
25% DISCOUNT VOUCHERS

TRESCO Isles of Scilly
Map 1: inset C1
THE NEW INN, New Grimsby, TR24 0QG. Tel 01720 422849, www.tresco.co.uk. Locals and holiday-makers mingle at this 'relaxed' inn, the only pub on Robert Dorrien-Smith's private, car-free island. 'Deliberately unchanged', the characterful place has a wood-burning stove and a 'well-stocked bar', plus a Michelin-approved menu that showcases the best local produce from land and sea. Try a Tresco partridge sausage roll, perhaps, or go for a full surf and turf with Bryher lobster and chargrilled Tresco beef steak. Hope for good weather: the canopied garden is a 'very pretty' spot in which to eat. Bed down in simple yet 'lovely' bedrooms recently updated with a beachy palette. Some may be snug; those in the modern annexe are more spacious. All have welcome treats: freshly ground coffee, home-made biscuits, high-end toiletries. 10 mins' walk from 'amazing' Abbey Garden. BEDROOMS 16. Some on ground floor. OPEN All year. FACILITIES Bar, residents' lounge, restaurant, free Wi-Fi,

in-room TV (Freeview), patio, garden, pavilion (alfresco dining), heated outdoor swimming pool, annual music, beer and cider festivals. BACKGROUND MUSIC In pub and restaurant, occasional live music events. CHILDREN All ages welcomed. PRICES Per person B&B £65–£110, D,B&B £100–£160. À la carte £35.

TROUTBECK Cumbria
Map 4: inset C2
BROADOAKS, Bridge Lane, LA23 1LA. Tel 01539 445566, www.broadoakscountryhouse.co.uk. 'Helpful, charming, welcoming staff' make a stay at this 'beautiful' 19th-century stone-and-slate country house a 'relaxing experience'. The Lake District hotel is owned by Tracey Robinson and Joanna Harbottle. Slumber in one of the 'gorgeous bedrooms' styled with bold wallpaper and antique furnishings; there might be a roll-top bath or a sunken spa bath in the bathroom. Ideal for a family, a suite in the grounds has two bedrooms, a lounge and a private patio. Pre-dinner canapés are served in the panelled sitting room; in the Oaks brasserie, sample chef Sharon Elders's 'excellent' French-inflected Cumbrian dishes. (Good vegetarian options.) Breakfast has plenty of choice: griddled pancakes, beech-smoked Cartmel valley kippers, porridge with Lakeland heather honey. 2 miles N of Bowness-on-Windermere. BEDROOMS 20. Some on ground floor, 5 in coach house, 3 detached garden suites, 5 mins' walk from house. FACILITIES Sitting room, bar, restaurant, orangery private dining room, free Wi-Fi, in-room TV (Freeview), civil wedding licence, 8-acre grounds, stream, complimentary access to nearby spa (swimming pool).

BACKGROUND MUSIC 'On low volume' in public areas. CHILDREN Not under 5. DOGS Allowed in some bedrooms, on lead in garden, bar and lounge. PRICES Per room B&B £155–£335, D,B&B £185–£375.

TUNBRIDGE WELLS Kent
Map 2:D4

HOTEL DU VIN TUNBRIDGE WELLS, Crescent Road, TN1 2LY. Tel 08447 489266, www.hotelduvin.com. Within walking distance of the Pantiles, this 'excellent' hotel, an outpost of the du Vin group, makes a fine base for the Georgian spa town. Sink into comfortable seating in the lounges, which have 'the genteel air of an 18th-century manor house'. Board games are supplied; a clubby bar provides the drinks. Modern bedrooms have a 'luxurious bathroom' and plenty of perks: a capsule coffee machine, fluffy bathrobes, chic toiletries. Some rooms look over Calverley Park. 'Delicious' bistro dishes may be eaten in the informal restaurant or alfresco on the terrace; inside or out, the staff are 'very friendly and extraordinarily efficient'. Close to the station. BEDROOMS 34. 4 in annexe. FACILITIES Bar, bistro, lounge, private dining room, free Wi-Fi, in-room TV (Sky), terrace, 1-acre garden (boules), vineyard, limited parking. CHILDREN All ages welcomed. DOGS Allowed in some bedrooms, not in food service areas. PRICES Per room B&B from £130, D,B&B from £176.

ULVERSTON Cumbria
Map 4: inset C2

THE BAY HORSE, Canal Foot, LA12 9EL. Tel 01229 583972, www. thebayhorsehotel.co.uk. 'We love the wonderful views and the air of tranquillity.' Watch the tide race in from this pub-with-rooms at the water's edge, across from Morecambe Bay. Much loved by its many regular returnees, it is a laid-back, low-key place, where owners Robert Lyons and Lesley Wheeler have been making guests 'feel very welcome' for 30 years. Public spaces are warm and cosy (though guests this year thought some upkeep wouldn't go misplaced). Afternoon tea here is 'a home-made treat'. Six of the traditional bedrooms have French doors opening on to a terrace; all have board games, books and magazines. Some rooms may be snug, but 'those views make up for the size of the room'. Book ahead for Robert Lyons's 'consistently sound' cooking at dinner – there's a single 7.30 pm sitting in the candlelit conservatory. Cooked breakfasts are 'exceptional'. 1½ miles from town centre. BEDROOMS 9. OPEN All year. FACILITIES Bar/lounge, restaurant (closed Mon lunch), free Wi-Fi, in-room TV (Freeview), picnic area, parking. BACKGROUND MUSIC In bar and restaurant. CHILDREN Not under 9. DOGS Allowed in bedroom (2 dogs max.), not in restaurant. PRICES Per room B&B £95–£120. À la carte £40. 2-night min. stay preferred.

UPTON MAGNA Shropshire
Map 3:B5

THE HAUGHMOND, Pelham Road, nr Shrewsbury, SY4 4TZ. Tel 01743 709918, www.thehaughmond.co.uk. The remarkable restaurant draws hungry diners to Mel and Martin Board's modern inn, in a village seven miles east of Shrewsbury. The host, a self-taught cook, devises informal meals and fine seven-course tasting menus using Shropshire produce wherever possible. Typical offerings: English asparagus, pink grapefruit, almonds, scallop; new-season lamb rump, faggot, goat's cheese croquette, fresh peas. Simply decorated bedrooms are above the bar. Each is supplied with a hospitality tray and a smart TV with on-demand movies; one, in the eaves, has a Juliet balcony with views across the fields. Stop in at the rustic coffee shop, where passing walkers and cyclists take a break, before heading out; the deli/farm shop has picnic hampers and takeaway lunches. BEDROOMS 5. OPEN All year except Christmas Day, New Year's Day. FACILITIES Bar/brasserie, breakfast room, conservatory, free Wi-Fi, in-room smart TV, terrace, ½-acre garden, parking. CHILDREN All ages welcomed. DOGS Allowed (not unattended) in bedrooms, on lead in public areas (£10 per night, own bed required). PRICES Per room B&B £90–£120. À la carte £27, tasting menu £40.

WADDESDON Buckinghamshire
Map 2:C3

THE FIVE ARROWS, High Street, HP18 0JE. Tel 01296 651727, www. fivearrowshotel.co.uk. Originally built to house the architects and craftsmen working on nearby Waddesdon Manor, this half-timbered, ornately patterned Grade II listed building is today a 'comfortable' hotel run by the Rothschild family trust in conjunction with the National Trust. (Hotel guests receive complimentary tickets to visit the manor house.) Recent refurbishment has resulted in modern country-style bedrooms, well appointed in soothing natural hues. Ring to discuss room choices: some guests report noise from

the 'busy' A road; others are untroubled by it. In the smart restaurant ('spruced up and in good shape'), 'the cooking is excellent': 'flavourful' lime and lemongrass-crusted smoked salmon, perhaps, or loin of pork served with 'tasty deep-fried black pudding balls and an interesting parsnip gratin'. 'Good service, too – we were left to sit and chat until we were ready to leave.' BEDROOMS 16. 5 in Old Coach House, 3 on ground floor in courtyard. OPEN All year. FACILITIES Bar, restaurant, free Wi-Fi, in-room smart TV (Freeview), civil wedding licence, 1-acre garden. BACKGROUND MUSIC In restaurant. CHILDREN All ages welcomed. PRICES Per room B&B single from £95, double from £145, D,B&B single from £125, double from £205.

WARTLING Sussex
Map 2:E4

WARTLING PLACE, Herstmonceux, nr Hailsham, BN27 1RY. Tel 01323 832590, www.wartlingplace.co.uk. The 'wonderful atmosphere' makes this 'delightful' B&B popular with visitors to nearby Glyndebourne. 'Warm hosts' Rowena and Barry Gittoes have filled their Grade II listed Georgian former rectory with interesting prints and comfortable spots to relax in. Well-appointed bedrooms have 'real coffee' and Fairtrade teas; a DVD library provides entertainment for guests looking for a quiet night in. Breakfast in bed or in the spacious dining room: an 'excellent spread' includes fresh fruit, cereals, honey from local bees; home-grown salads; smoked salmon from a fishery half an hour away. Explore the 'well-kept' sub-tropical gardens before striking out to visit beaches nearby.

Evening suppers and picnic hampers can be arranged. 5 miles E of Hailsham. BEDROOMS 4. Plus 2-bed self-catering cottage suitable for disabled. OPEN All year. FACILITIES Drawing room, dining room (honesty bar, CD player), free Wi-Fi in main house, in-room TV (Freeview), 3-acre garden, parking. BACKGROUND MUSIC None. CHILDREN All ages welcomed. DOGS Allowed in cottage. PRICES Per room B&B £130–£165.

WARWICK Warwickshire
Map 3:C6
PARK COTTAGE, 113 West Street, CV34 6AH. Tel 01926 410319, www. parkcottagewarwick.co.uk. At the entrance to Warwick Castle, Janet and Stuart Baldry's 'good-value' B&B is fronted with hanging baskets of colourful blooms. Inside the 15th-century timber-framed building, find oak beams and sloping floors – evidence of its long history. Climb a steep staircase to most of the traditionally decorated bedrooms on the first floor. Each is different: one has a 300-year-old four-poster bed, another has a king-size spa bath. A ground-floor room has access to the pretty patio garden. Breakfast is taken in the former castle dairy (the original sandstone floor has been retained). Start the day with cereals, yogurts, fruit and juices; a 'perfectly cooked' full English; cafetière coffee or a pot of Yorkshire tea. A good base for the town; further afield, Stratford-upon-Avon and Leamington Spa are within a 20-minute drive. BEDROOMS 7. 2 on ground floor. OPEN All year except Christmas, New Year. FACILITIES Reception/sitting area, breakfast room, free Wi-Fi, in-room TV (Freeview), small garden (patio, tables and seating), parking. BACKGROUND MUSIC None. CHILDREN All ages welcomed. PRICES Per room B&B single £55–£80, double £80–£99.

WATCHET Somerset
Map 1:B5
SWAIN HOUSE, 48 Swain Street, TA23 0AG. Tel 01984 631038, www.swain-house.com. In an ancient harbour town watched over by a 150-year-old lighthouse, Jason Robinson's chic B&B is steps away from the coastal spot that inspired Coleridge. Stylishly converted, the 18th-century town house and shop are today an inviting mix of slate floors, soft velvet and warm wood. Each of the modern bedrooms has a mural of an Old Master painting, plus a king-size bed and plenty of perks: waffle bathrobes, fluffy towels, chic toiletries; a roll-top slipper bath and separate walk-in shower in the bathroom. In the evening, ask the host for restaurant recommendations, or stay in: charcuterie or cheese boards may be arranged. Home-cooked breakfasts include a full veggie option, and American-style pancakes with fruit, yogurt and maple syrup. 7 miles from Dunster Castle. BEDROOMS 4. OPEN All year except Christmas, New Year. FACILITIES Lounge, dining room, free Wi-Fi, in-room TV (Freeview). BACKGROUND MUSIC None. CHILDREN Not under 12. PRICES Per room B&B £135.

WATERGATE BAY Cornwall
Map 1:D2
WATERGATE BAY, On the beach, TR8 4AA. Tel 01637 860543, www. watergatebay.co.uk. From water sports to yoga to simply sprawling in the sun,

this 'great' modern hotel on a stretch of sandy beach has something for everyone. It is owned by Will Ashworth; Mark Williams is the long-serving manager. The on-site Extreme Academy specialises in such adrenalin-driven activities as kitesurfing, wave skiing and stand-up paddleboarding; the sleek Swim Club has an ocean-view infinity pool, a hot tub and a series of treatment rooms. Young visitors have the run of three play areas in the Kids Zone. Plenty of choice at mealtimes, too: modern American-style dishes at Zacry's; seasonal fare in the Living Space; classic surf 'n' turf at the Beach Hut. You'll need a lie-down after it all: head for one of the 'super-clean' bedrooms (many with sea views), each contemporary, with a cheering coastal feel. 5 miles from Newquay. BEDROOMS 71. 2 suitable for disabled. OPEN All year. FACILITIES Lounge/bar, 3 restaurants, free Wi-Fi, in-room TV (Freeview), civil wedding licence, terrace, sun deck, indoor/outdoor swimming pool, surf school, treatment rooms. BACKGROUND MUSIC All day in public areas. CHILDREN All ages welcomed. DOGS Allowed in some bedrooms, 2 restaurants (£15 per night, dog-friendly beach). PRICES Per room B&B from £160, D,B&B from £210. À la carte (Zacry's restaurant) £38.

WEDMORE Somerset
Map 1:B6

THE SWAN, Cheddar Road, BS28 4EQ. Tel 01934 710337, www.theswanwedmore.com. There's a 'lovely, informal atmosphere' at this 'friendly' pub-with-rooms, down the street from the old, stone-built village church. The agreeably updated 18th-century beer house has stripped wooden floors, comfy seats, local ales and newspapers; a sunny terrace is just the ticket on a warm day. 'Smart' modern bedrooms on the first and second floors are well stocked with ground coffee for the cafetière, old-fashioned sweets, 'super toiletries'. Quirky touches lend personality: a pink-painted claw-foot bath; a vintage shipping trunk serving as a coffee table. At mealtimes, choose from the simple-yet-sophisticated gastropub menu, and ask to eat inside or out. 'Breakfast is a real treat with lots of options', including home-cured bacon and freshly baked bread. Part of the small Stay Original Company; see also Timbrell's Yard, Bradford-on-Avon, and The White Hart, Somerton (Shortlist entries). BEDROOMS 7. OPEN All year. FACILITIES Bar (wood-burning stove), restaurant (closed Sun eve), free Wi-Fi, in-room TV, function facilities, terrace, garden (wood-fired oven and barbecue), parking. BACKGROUND MUSIC In bar. CHILDREN All ages welcomed. DOGS Allowed in bar and garden. PRICES Per room B&B £85–£125. À la carte £28.

WESTBROOK Herefordshire
Map 3:D4

WESTBROOK COURT B&B, nr Hay-on-Wye, HR3 5SY. Tel 01497 831752, www.westbrookcourtbandb.co.uk. Sleek design transformed a timber-clad stable into five voguish B&B suites, set behind Kari and Chris Morgan's rambling 17th-century farmhouse. The spacious, light-filled rooms are styled with pops of colour and some quirky flourishes (a bird-cage lampshade; trompe l'oeil book-lined wallpaper), but the most eye-catching feature may be the uninterrupted vista stretching over the Wye valley. Each suite has a lounge

area and a private sun-trap deck; four
have a mezzanine bedroom with views
of Merbach hill. Weekday breakfasts
of pastries, smoked salmon, fruit and
yogurt are brought to the door; on the
weekend, the Morgans host a communal
breakfast in the farmhouse kitchen,
with home-baked bread, local meats and
garden-fresh eggs. 'Speedy suppers' can
be arranged. 3 miles E of Hay-on-Wye.
BEDROOMS 5. 1 suitable for disabled.
FACILITIES Communal breakfast room/
kitchen, free Wi-Fi ('slow – welcome
to rural life!'), in-room TV (Freeview),
5-acre grounds, terrace, cycle and kayak
storage. BACKGROUND MUSIC None.
CHILDREN All ages welcomed (cot –
linen not provided, extra bed £15 per
night). PRICES Per room B&B from £95.

WESTLETON Suffolk
Map 2:B6
THE WESTLETON CROWN, The Street,
nr Southwold, IP17 3AD. Tel 01728
648777, www.westletoncrown.co.uk.
Dogs visiting this Fido-friendly, 12th-
century coaching inn receive biscuits,
a bowl and a blanket, plus a sausage
at breakfast. Their owners have much
more that's agreeable: space to sit before
the huge fireplace in the traditional bar,
and a menu of 'hearty yet sophisticated'
dishes at mealtimes. On a sunny day,
the terraced garden is ideal for alfresco
dining for all. In the country-style
bedrooms (most are in converted stables
or cottages by the garden), thoughtful
amenities – good toiletries, local
magazines, ground cafetière coffee,
home-made biscuits – come as standard.
At breakfast, mix and match sausages,
Suffolk bacon, sautéed mushrooms,
grilled tomatoes and locally laid eggs for
a custom cooked dish. Sister hotel The

Ship at Dunwich (see Shortlist entry)
is close to the coast; maps are available
for circular walks through Suffolk
countryside. 2 miles from the RSPB
nature reserve at Minsmere. BEDROOMS
34. 1 suitable for disabled. OPEN All
year. FACILITIES Bar, snug, lounge,
2 dining areas, free Wi-Fi, in-room
TV (Freeview), civil wedding licence,
terraced garden. BACKGROUND MUSIC All
day in dining areas. CHILDREN All ages
welcomed. DOGS Allowed in bedrooms
and public rooms (£7.50 per night,
outdoor dog wash for muddy paws,
towels provided). PRICES Per room B&B
from £130. À la carte £30.
25% DISCOUNT VOUCHERS

WHEATHILL Shropshire
Map 3:C5
THE OLD RECTORY, nr Ludlow,
WV16 6QT. Tel 01746 787209, www.
theoldrectorywheathill.com. Homely
touches and a welcoming spirit
create a cheerful atmosphere at Izzy
Barnard's Georgian B&B in Shropshire
countryside. There are wild flowers
throughout the house and knitted cosies
on the boiled eggs at breakfast; guests
are treated to home-made treats on
arrival. Sit by the fire in cool weather,
or stroll in the acres of garden when
it's fine. A four-course dinner may be
served (by arrangement) by candlelight;
light supper trays are an alternative.
At bedtime, retire to one of the
country-cosy bedrooms, each home-
away-from-home comfortable with
antique furnishings, books and biscuits.
Breakfast has home-grown, home-
made preserves; home-cured bacon;
orange-yolked duck eggs from the
resident flock. Horses and hounds are
well looked after – ask for guides and

route cards detailing nearby bridleways. 7 miles E of Ludlow. BEDROOMS 3. OPEN All year except Christmas, Jan. FACILITIES Drawing room, dining room, sauna (in cellar), free Wi-Fi, in-room TV (Freeview), in-room treatments by arrangement, 7-acre gardens, boot room, tack room, loose boxes for horses staying over. BACKGROUND MUSIC None. CHILDREN All ages welcomed, by arrangement. DOGS Allowed (£10 per night in boot room). PRICES Per room single B&B from £75, double £90–£130. Set dinner £35, supper tray £10. 2-night min. stay preferred.

WINCHESTER Hampshire
Map 2:D2

HANNAH'S, 16a Parchment Street, SO23 8AZ. Tel 01962 840623, www. hannahsbedandbreakfast.co.uk. Sweet hospitality is par for the course at Hannah McIntyre's B&B off the High Street: mid-afternoons, the hostess supplies a spread of freshly baked treats for guests to help themselves to. On a cool day, make a spot for yourself on one of the squashy sofas by the wood-burning stove; in good weather, the picture-perfect terrace is the place to be. Push through heavy timber doors into the chic, country bedrooms – split-level suites, really – each filled with flowers and lined with books to borrow. Breakfast in the spacious, beamed breakfast room: there are home-made jams and granola, home-baked seeded loaves, specially blended teas and coffees, a changing weekend special. BEDROOMS 3. OPEN Thurs–Sun, Feb–mid-Dec. FACILITIES Breakfast room, library (honesty bar), free Wi-Fi, in-room TV (Freeview), terrace with seating. BACKGROUND MUSIC In communal areas. CHILDREN Not under 12. PRICES Per room B&B from £155.

THE WYKEHAM ARMS, 75 Kingsgate Street, SO23 9PE. Tel 01962 853834, www.wykehamarmswinchester.co.uk. Come in to log fires and local ales at this 18th-century coaching inn (Fuller's Hotels and Inns) between the cathedral and the medieval college. A warm, characterful place, it is a 'top-rate example of a pub-with-rooms'. The walls in the bar are lined with pictures, ale mugs and kitschy breweriana; old school desks, tucked into nooks, create cosiness. Jon Howard manages 'helpful, friendly staff'. Feast on modern British dishes and pub classics in the wood-panelled dining room, then retire to one of the well-equipped, individually decorated bedrooms (some up a narrow staircase). 'Perfectly bearable' chatter from the pub stops around 11 pm, but light (and early) sleepers may wish to discuss room options. An 'excellent' breakfast includes 'outstanding' local black pudding. BEDROOMS 14. 7 in adjacent building. OPEN All year. FACILITIES Bar, 2 restaurants, 2 function rooms, free Wi-Fi (in public areas), in-room TV, small patio with seating, parking. BACKGROUND MUSIC None. CHILDREN Not under 12. DOGS Allowed in 2 bedrooms, not in restaurant (£7.50 per night). PRICES Per room B&B from £149, D,B&B from £189. À la carte £32. **25% DISCOUNT VOUCHERS**

WOODBRIDGE Suffolk
Map 2:C5

THE CROWN, The Thoroughfare, IP12 1AD. Tel 01394 384242, www. thecrownatwoodbridge.co.uk. In the centre of a market town near the Deben estuary, this 16th-century coaching inn has been given a chic revamp. It is a 'comfortable, welcoming' spot, liked for its modern design, 'excellent food' and smart bedrooms. A wooden sailing skiff is suspended over the long, polished bar; locals and tourists mingle here over cocktails and Suffolk ales. 'Enjoyable' brasserie-style dishes are served in the buzzy restaurant and on the new decked terrace. Soothing bedrooms are stylish in neutral tones and smoky shades. Biscuits, books and local magazines are supplied; bathrooms have underfloor heating and top-end toiletries. Reach the coast within a 20-minute drive, but start with the town's own attractions: the fascinating Tide Mill living museum is a five-minute walk away. BEDROOMS 10. OPEN All year. FACILITIES 4 dining areas, bar, private dining room, free Wi-Fi, in-room TV (Sky), terrace (alfresco drinking and eating), parking. BACKGROUND MUSIC In public areas, plus monthly jazz evenings. CHILDREN All ages welcomed. DOGS Allowed in bar. PRICES Per room B&B from £100, D,B&B from £150. À la carte £34.

WOODSTOCK Oxfordshire
Map 2:C2

THE FEATHERS, 16–20 Market Street, OX20 1SX. Tel 01993 812291, www.feathers.co.uk. 'We wanted old-world charm with modern facilities, and we got it – down to the cosy bar and the slightly sloping wooden floors.' A Guide reader in 2017 found this characterful, child-friendly hotel, in the centre of the Cotswold town, 'perfect on all levels'. Formed from an 'interesting collection' of buildings, the hotel has boldly styled bedrooms reached via winding staircases. The well-equipped rooms vary in size and style, with playful touches to add personality – 'ours had a jar of Jelly Babies to greet us'. Afternoon tea is 'taken seriously', as is apertif hour – the bar has more than 400 gins from around the world. The relaunched restaurant is now under the direction of Dominic Chapman (formerly of Heston Blumenthal's Hind's Head), whose unfussy modern menu might include wild rabbit and foie gras lasagne, wild mushrooms, chervil. Blenheim Palace is a stroll away. Sister hotel Lords of the Manor is in Upper Slaughter (see main entry). BEDROOMS 21. 1 suitable for disabled, 5 in adjacent town house. OPEN All year. FACILITIES Study, bar, restaurant, free Wi-Fi, in-room TV (Freeview), function facilities, courtyard (alfresco meals), free long-term parking within walking distance. BACKGROUND MUSIC None. CHILDREN All ages welcomed. DOGS Allowed in some bedrooms, public rooms, not in restaurant. PRICES Per room B&B from £159, D,B&B from £239. À la carte £40.

WOOLACOMBE Devon
Map 1:B4

WATERSMEET, EX34 7EB. Tel 01271 870333, www.watersmeethotel.co.uk. Above Woolacombe Bay, this former Edwardian gentleman's retreat is today a 'comfortable, relaxed' hotel owned by Amanda James. The 'professional staff' are 'friendly and helpful at all times'. Recently refurbished bedrooms are supplied with bottled water, upmarket toiletries, bathrobes and a season-appropriate duvet; all but three have 'fantastic' sea views; some have a balcony or garden terrace. ('A grumble: our bathroom didn't reflect the quality of the handsome bedroom.')

Afternoon tea, with a cake of the day, may be taken on the sea-facing terrace in good weather. When the evening draws in, 'well-cooked' British dishes are served in the informal bistro and candlelit restaurant. 'Excellent' walks on the Coastal Path nearby; private steps lead to the sandy beach. BEDROOMS 29. 3 on ground floor, 1 suitable for disabled. OPEN All year. FACILITIES Lift, lounge, snug, bar, restaurant, bistro, free Wi-Fi, in-room TV (Freeview), terrace (alfresco meals and drinks), civil wedding licence, function facilities, room service, ½-acre garden, heated outdoor swimming pool, treatment room. BACKGROUND MUSIC In public areas. CHILDREN All ages welcomed. PRICES Per room B&B from £125, D,B&B from £220. Set dinner (restaurant) £37–£45, à la carte (bistro) £30.

YELVERTON Devon
Map 1:D4

CIDER HOUSE, Buckland Abbey, PL20 6EZ. Tel 01822 259062, www.cider-house.co.uk. Wake to birdsong at this mellow stone building in secluded gardens – Bertie and Bryony Hancock's sophisticated B&B is surrounded by the National Trust's Buckland Abbey estate, and the 700 acres of grounds that come with it. (B&B guests receive complimentary passes for the abbey, the home of Sir Francis Drake, and may freely explore the gorgeous gardens and sprawl of wooded valley.) The former brew house has been impeccably designed in contemporary country-house style. An elegant drawing room has an open fire and fresh flowers; maps and guide books for browsing. Mullioned windows in the pretty first-floor bedrooms

give on to glorious views; glamorous bathrooms have a roll-top bath. At the freshest of breakfasts, sample heaps of home-grown, home-reared produce, plus honey from the bees on the estate. BEDROOMS 4. Plus 2 adult-only luxury self-catering shepherd's huts. OPEN Mar–Oct, shepherd's huts all year except Feb. FACILITIES Drawing room, free Wi-Fi, in-room TV (Freeview), civil wedding licence, terrace, garden, parking. 1 mile from village, a 15-minute walk to pubs with food. BACKGROUND MUSIC None. CHILDREN Not under 12. PRICES Per room B&B from £135. 2-night min. stay preferred.

YORK Yorkshire
Map 4:D4

BAR CONVENT, 17 Blossom Street, YO24 1AQ. Tel 01904 643238, www.bar-convent.org.uk. Home to England's oldest active convent, this unusual Grade I listed Georgian building by the medieval city wall also houses a café, and good-value B&B accommodation. Lesley Baines is the manager. Past the 'magnificent' glass-roofed entrance hall, the 'living heritage centre' includes an 18th-century domed chapel and a library of antique Catholic texts. Immaculate bedrooms – some spacious, some with a shared bathroom – may be simply decorated, but they're peaceful, and have a 'wickedly comfortable' bed, biscuits and tea- and coffee-making facilities. A communal, fully equipped kitchen is useful for rustling up evening snacks. Breakfast is served in the newly refurbished café; at dinner, head to any of the many eating places within walking distance. BEDROOMS 20. Some suitable for disabled, 12 with nearby bathroom facilities. OPEN All year except

Easter, some days over Christmas.
FACILITIES Lift (to 1st and 2nd floors),
sitting room, kitchen, licensed café,
meeting rooms, free Wi-Fi, in-room TV
(Freeview), ½-acre garden, museum,
shop, chapel. PRICES Per room B&B
(continental) single £42–£67, double
£80–£120.

THE BLOOMSBURY, 127 Clifton,
YO30 6BL. Tel 01904 634031, www.
thebloomsburyguesthouse.com. Guests
are greeted with a hot drink and 'a slice
of something sweet' at this Victorian
town house B&B within easy reach of
the city centre. It is run by 'charming
hosts' Matthew Townsley and Paul
Johnson, who make a remarkable
lemon drizzle cake. Most of the 'lovely'
bedrooms are up the original staircase.
Some may seem old-fashioned (gentle
refurbishments are underway), but
all are comfortable, well maintained,
and supplied with tea- and coffee-
making facilities. Breakfast has plenty
of locally sourced fare: sausages and
thick-cut bacon from the butcher 200
yards away; locally roasted and ground
coffee from an independent coffee
merchant. The scenic route into the city
follows the bank of the River Ouse. 1
mile to city centre. BEDROOMS 7. 1 on
ground floor. OPEN All year except 23
Dec–New Year. FACILITIES Sitting room,
dining room, free Wi-Fi, in-room TV
(Freeview), terrace, 'secret' courtyard
garden, parking. BACKGROUND MUSIC
'Relaxing hits from the 1950s to the
present day' in dining room at breakfast.
CHILDREN Not under 12. PRICES Per
room B&B £80–£90. 2-night min. stay
at weekends in summer. Credit cards
not accepted.
25% DISCOUNT VOUCHERS

SCOTLAND

ABERDEEN
Map 5:C3
ATHOLL HOTEL, 54 King's Gate, AB15
4YN. Tel 01224 323505, www.atholl-
aberdeen.co.uk. In a Victorian Gothic
Revival building, this traditional hotel
within reach of the city centre is popular
with business travellers. Straightforward
bedrooms are cheered up by tartan
bedcovers and cushions, and have the
necessary amenities: a tea and coffee
tray, hair dryer, iron and ironing board.
Family rooms are available – ring to
discuss. Hearty Scottish dishes are
served in the restaurant, bar or lounge.
At breakfast, try tattie scones, Finnan
haddies or Scottish buttery. Regular
buses go straight into town; the airport
is a 15-minute drive away. Golf courses
are close by. 1½ miles W of the city
centre. BEDROOMS 34. 2 suitable for
disabled. FACILITIES Lift (to 1st floor),
lounge, bar, restaurant, patio, free Wi-
Fi, in-room TV (Sky Sports), weddings,
functions, parking. BACKGROUND
MUSIC In restaurant. CHILDREN All ages
welcomed. PRICES Per room B&B single
£65–£70, double £80–£95. À la carte £30.

ALLANTON Scottish Borders
Map 5:E3
ALLANTON INN, nr Duns, TD11 3JZ.
Tel 01890 818260, www.allantoninn.
co.uk. Katrina and William Reynolds
run their 'good-value' restaurant-with-
rooms in a rural village by the River
Whiteadder. The 'good ambience' and
'first-class food and service' attract locals
to the stone-built 18th-century coaching
inn; visitors stay for the comfortable
accommodation. In warm weather,
all are drawn to the picnic tables in

the rear garden, and the wide views over open fields. Chef Lee Cessford's local-ingredient-inspired modern and classic dishes are served in the informal restaurant or bar, washed down, perhaps, with a glass of home-made ginger beer. Bedrooms, decorated with local artwork, are supplied with Scottish-produced biscuits and toiletries. Breakfast on home-made granola, home-baked bread, Eyemouth kippers and the hostess's jams and marmalade. Day permits for trout and salmon fishing are available. BEDROOMS 6. OPEN All year except 25–26 Dec. FACILITIES Bar (over 30 gins), 2 restaurant areas, free Wi-Fi, in-room TV (Freeview), large garden, parking. BACKGROUND MUSIC In bar and restaurant. CHILDREN All ages welcomed. PRICES Per room B&B £80–£95, D,B&B £120–£150.

ALYTH Perth and Kinross
Map 5:D2

TIGH NA LEIGH, 22–24 Airlie Street, PH11 8AJ. Tel 01828 632372, www. tighnaleigh.com. In a stone-built Victorian villa close to the town centre, Chris and Bettina Black run this modern guest house with a 'friendly, welcoming feel'. It sits in a 'pretty, surprisingly large garden'. There are 'sizeable' lounges with maps, books and guides to borrow, and 'well-appointed' contemporary bedrooms of different sizes. 'Our suite had a pleasant sitting room with a sofa and two comfortable chairs; DVDs, books and magazines were supplied. The spacious bathroom, with its own window, had a spa bath.' 'Good dinners', ordered in advance, may be served by arrangement; award-winning breakfasts, eaten in the lawn-facing dining room, have

tomatoes and peppers from the garden, and wild mushrooms foraged locally. The hosts have plenty of advice for distillery and castle visits, and nature and heritage trails. BEDROOMS 6. 1 on ground floor, 1 via steep stairs. OPEN Feb–Nov. FACILITIES Lounge (log fire), TV room, reading room, conservatory dining room, free Wi-Fi, in-room TV (Freeview), ½-acre landscaped garden with pond, parking. BACKGROUND MUSIC In dining room and main lounge during meal service. CHILDREN Not under 12. DOGS Allowed, not in dining room (small cleaning charge). PRICES Per room B&B single £55, double £110–£133. À la carte £25. 2-night min. stay at weekends.

APPLECROSS Highland
Map 5:C1

APPLECROSS INN, Shore Street, IV54 8LR. Tel 01520 744262, www.applecross. uk.com/inn. Resilience pays off at Judith Fish's near-legendary, white-painted hostelry on the shores of the Applecross peninsula. At the end of an 11-mile stretch of winding single-track road, visitors are rewarded with superlative views over the Inner Sound of Raasay, and a feast of just-landed seafood. Sample the large selection of Scottish gins and malt whiskies in the buzzy, wood fire-warmed bar (their own Applecross ale is in the works), then make your choice from the daily-changing blackboard menu in the small dining room. In spring and summer, a retro food truck on the shore sells ice creams, cakes and coffees. Clean, comfortable bedrooms have all the essentials, plus sea views; there may be some pub noise. Cyclists, walkers, kayakers and campers are welcomed. BEDROOMS 7. 1 on ground floor. OPEN All year, no accommodation for 2 weeks over Christmas, New Year. FACILITIES Bar, dining room, free Wi-Fi, beer garden, bicycle storage. BACKGROUND MUSIC In bar. CHILDREN All ages welcomed, not in bar after 8.30 pm. DOGS Allowed in 2 bedrooms, on lead in bar (£15 per stay). PRICES Per person B&B £70. À la carte £35.

ARINAGOUR Argyll and Bute
Map 5:C1
COLL HOTEL, Isle of Coll, PA78 6SZ. Tel 01879 230334, www.collhotel. com. Overlooking Inner Hebridean islands, Kevin and Julie Oliphant's small hotel is the lively hub of the only village on the Isle of Coll. It is managed by the Oliphants' daughter, Laura. Understated modern bedrooms have welcoming extras such as home-made biscuits, rainy-day board games and Scottish-made toiletries. Most, too, have views down the bay to Mull, Staffa, Iona and Jura. An unpretentious menu, dictated by the catch of the day, is served in the bar and restaurant, or in the garden in fine weather. After sunset, glow-in-the-dark skyscopes let guests take advantage of Coll's Dark Sky status (the island has no artificial light pollution) – borrow a celestial map and trace the skies. Complimentary pick-up from and drop-off to the ferry pier. 1 mile from the ferry pier; 3-hour ferry journey from Oban. BEDROOMS 6. OPEN All year except Christmas, house parties only at New Year. FACILITIES Lounge, 2 bars (darts, pool table, open fires), restaurant, residents' lounge and dining room, free Wi-Fi, in-room TV (Freeview), garden (pétanque), helipad, bicycles and helmets to borrow. BACKGROUND MUSIC None. CHILDREN All

ages welcomed. DOGS Allowed in public bar. PRICES Per room B&B single £70, double £120–£150. À la carte £26.
25% DISCOUNT VOUCHERS

ARISAIG Highland
Map 5:C1
THE OLD LIBRARY LODGE AND RESTAURANT, PH39 4NH. Tel 01687 450651, www.oldlibrary.co.uk. Across the road from the sheltered harbour in this Highland village, Mags and Allan Ritchie's modest restaurant-with-rooms is a 'friendly, casual' spot. The 'smart, bistro-style restaurant' has a daily specials board of modern Scottish dishes cooked with a French touch – loin of venison, red onion tarte Tatin, perhaps, or Cullen skink 'to rave about'. Bedrooms at the front have a 'wonderful view' across the bay, but most of the simply decorated rooms are in converted 200-year-old stables at the back – look out for the garden gnomes on the way over. 'Our large annexe room had a newish bed and a spacious, airy bathroom, but more modernisation would be welcome.' 'Well-cooked Scottish breakfasts' have black pudding and haggis. 10 mins' drive from the ferry. BEDROOMS 6. 4 in annexe. OPEN All year except Jan. FACILITIES Residents' lounge, restaurant, free Wi-Fi, terraced garden. BACKGROUND MUSIC Traditional in restaurant. CHILDREN All ages welcomed. DOGS Allowed. PRICES Per room B&B single £75, double £120.

AUCHENCAIRN Dumfries and Galloway
Map 5:E2
HAZLEFIELD HOUSE, nr Castle Douglas, DG7 1RF. Tel 01556 640597, www. hazlefieldhouse.co.uk. 'Generous hosts'

Moyra and Rod Davidson 'warmly welcome' guests to their 'relaxing' Georgian B&B, in lawns and wooded grounds close to the coast. 'The hosts make it special.' The 'comfortably furnished' living room has a wood-burner and 'books everywhere, which we loved'. Large, 'well-appointed' bedrooms are provided with a hot-water bottle and a choice of bedding. An 'excellent' home-cooked dinner of local and home-grown produce (typically hot-smoked Scottish salmon; citrus and herb pork tenderloin) may be served, by arrangement. Bring a bottle – there's no corkage charge. Breakfast is 'ample and beautifully arranged', and includes home-made marmalade, and honey from hives in the garden. Eat well, then step out to impressive views across the Solway Firth. 2 miles from village. BEDROOMS 3. 1 on ground floor. OPEN All year except Christmas, New Year. FACILITIES Sitting room/study, dining room, free Wi-Fi, in-room TV (Freeview), 4-acre grounds, drying and storage facilities, parking. BACKGROUND MUSIC None. PRICES Per room B&B £80–£90. Set dinner £16.50–£19.50.

BALLYGRANT Argyll and Bute
Map 5:D1

KILMENY COUNTRY HOUSE, Isle of Islay, PA45 7QW. Tel 01496 840668, www.kilmeny.co.uk. Tea and home-baked cake welcome guests to this 'superb' B&B, in a handsomely furnished 19th-century house surrounded by acres of farmland on the Isle of Islay. Margaret and Blair Rozga are the 'fabulous hosts'. Each of the traditionally furnished bedrooms has its own style, with country house decor, antiques aplenty

and 'spectacular views' over hills, glen and wide countryside. A complimentary dram of whisky makes a thoughtful nightcap. Some rooms are particularly spacious: two access a sheltered garden; a suite with a separate entrance has a kitchen, and an extra-large bathroom with twin basins, a slipper bath and a walk-in shower. Breakfast brings home-made bread, oatcakes and preserves. 'Nothing short of excellent.' ½ mile S of Ballygrant; 10 mins' drive to Port Askaig. BEDROOMS 5. 2 on ground floor. OPEN Mar–Oct. FACILITIES Drawing room, dining room, sun lounge, free Wi-Fi, in-room TV (Freeview), ½-acre garden. CHILDREN Not under 6. DOGS Allowed in some bedrooms. PRICES Per room B&B £140–£170. Credit cards not accepted.

BARCALDINE Argyll and Bute
Map 5:D1

ARDTORNA, The Mill Farm, PA37 1SE. Tel 01631 720125, www.ardtorna.co.uk. Sea views and sleek, Scandi-style appeal bring travellers to Sean and Karen O'Byrne's super-modern, eco-friendly house overlooking Loch Creran. Floor-to-ceiling windows let in the light and the surrounding scenery; the decor is coolly comfortable. Neat bedrooms have a king-size bed and underfloor heating, plus little extras: high-end toiletries, hand-made chocolates, complimentary treats in the fridge. Arrive to sweet pastries at teatime; help yourself to coffee and home-made whisky cream liqueur whenever the desire strikes. In the morning, wake to home-baked soda bread or a Scottish platter with Stornoway black pudding and tattie scones, served in the glass-fronted dining room. The hosts can suggest local itineraries; alternatively, stay on site and take a traditional longbow lesson: Sean O'Byrne is a former world champion. 12 miles N of Oban. BEDROOMS 4. OPEN Mar–Nov. FACILITIES Dining room, free Wi-Fi, in-room TV (Freeview), 1-acre farmland (archery range), parking. CHILDREN Not under 12. PRICES Per person B&B £60–£90.

BORVE Isle of Harris
Map 5:B1

PAIRC AN T-SRATH, HS3 3HT. Tel 01859 550386, www.pairc-srath. co.uk. Lena and Richard MacLennan's modest guest house on the Isle of Harris stands on a working croft by Borve's golden sand beach, with 'superb views' over the sound of Taransay. This is a 'lovely, comfortable' place in rugged surroundings: simply furnished, wood-floored bedrooms have blankets of Harris tweed; the peat fire-warmed sitting room has shelves of books to borrow. After a day of hill walking, golfing, cycling, beachcombing or kiting, ease tired muscles in the sauna. 'Exceptionally good, well-presented' home-cooked dinners of locally sourced produce (Uist scallops, Stornoway black pudding) are served by candlelight in the dining room overlooking the sea. Substantial Scottish breakfasts. 10 mins' drive from Tarbert ferry terminal. BEDROOMS 4. OPEN All year except Christmas, New Year. FACILITIES Sitting room, dining room (no dinners served Sat, May–Sept), free Wi-Fi, sauna. BACKGROUND MUSIC None. CHILDREN All ages welcomed. DOGS Allowed in 1 bedroom, by arrangement. PRICES Per person B&B £54. Set 3-course dinner £38.

BRAE Shetland
Map 5: inset A2

BUSTA HOUSE, ZE2 9QN. Tel 01806 522506, www.bustahouse.com. Island-hopping is made easy at this small hotel on the sheltered shore of Busta Voe – each bedroom in the 18th-century house is named after a Shetland island. Parts of the house date back to 1588; the result is a quirky layout, with creaky floors, lots of stairs, an open peat fire and a friendly ghost. Welcoming staff are managed by Joe and Veronica Rocks. A homely lounge has colourful carpets on wood floors, and wingback armchairs by the window; on the first and second floors, traditionally furnished bedrooms (some snug) have views of the gardens or harbour. Choose from an extensive menu of malt whiskies in the bar, then tuck in to unfussy, generously portioned dishes in the restaurant or lounges. BEDROOMS 22. OPEN All year except 2 weeks over Christmas and New Year. FACILITIES 2 lounges, bar/dining area, restaurant, free Wi-Fi, in-room TV, wedding facilities, garden, computer for guests' use. BACKGROUND MUSIC In restaurant. CHILDREN All ages welcomed. PRICES Per room B&B £115–£160. À la carte £35.

BRAEMAR Aberdeenshire
Map 5:C2

CALLATER LODGE, 9 Glenshee Road, AB35 5YQ. Tel 01339 741275, www.callaterlodge.co.uk. A hammer throw from the annual Highland Games, 'impressive, charming hosts' Julian and Katy Fennema provide 'pleasingly unfussy' accommodation and a treat for whisky lovers at their granite-built Victorian shooting lodge in the Cairngorms. (Ask about their whisky-sampling packages.) 'Good-looking', comfortable bedrooms in the 'immaculate, sympathetically refurbished' guest house have local guidebooks and pleasing touches: a tweed blanket, Scottish toiletries, 'delicious home-made lemon drizzle cake on the coffee tray'. The hosts provide hill walkers and ramblers with good route information, substantial packed lunches and a flask of tea; a tot of whisky in the sitting room upon their return. 'At breakfast, we enjoyed home-made French toast with maple syrup; good and plentiful coffee; warm, fresh brown toast with whisky marmalade.' 'A memorable stay.' 9 miles S of Braemar. BEDROOMS 6. OPEN All year. FACILITIES Sitting room, dining room, free Wi-Fi, in-room TV (Freeview), 1-acre grounds (mature Scots pine trees, red squirrels, free-range hens), drying room. BACKGROUND MUSIC None. CHILDREN Not under 8. PRICES Per person B&B from £42.

BRIDGEND Argyll and Bute
Map 5:D1
BRIDGEND HOTEL, PA44 7PJ. Tel 01496 810212, www.bridgend-hotel.com. Whisky-sampling opportunities at Islay's distilleries are within easy reach of this homely small hotel in a tranquil village. Lorna McKechnie manages for the Islay Estates Company. Tea and home-baked treats, plus local ales and Islay malts, may be taken in the tartan-carpeted lounge. Well-equipped, warmly decorated bedrooms are stocked with Islay tablet fudge and locally made toiletries. Come dinnertime, choose between traditional dishes in the cosy, garden-facing restaurant, and classic pub grub in Katie's Bar. At breakfast:

potato scones, Loch Fyne kippers, eggs 'cooked how you like'. The hotel has complimentary access to bank fishing, and preferential rates for boats on the estate's trout-fishing lochs. Walkers and cyclists are welcomed. BEDROOMS 11. 1 family room with bunk bed. OPEN All year except Feb. FACILITIES Lounge, bar, restaurant, free Wi-Fi, in-room TV (Freeview), wedding facilities, terrace, garden, drying room, parking. BACKGROUND MUSIC In public areas. CHILDREN All ages welcomed (extra bed £20 per night). DOGS Well-behaved dogs allowed in bedrooms, bar. PRICES Per room B&B single £95–£100, double £110–£170.

BROADFORD Highland
Map 5:C1
TIGH AN DOCHAIS, 13 Harrapool, Isle of Skye, IV49 9AQ. Tel 01471 820022, www.skyebedbreakfast.co.uk. Every room at Neil Hope and Lesley Unwin's modern, architect-designed B&B has 'glorious views' of Broadford Bay and the Cuillin mountains. Cross a galvanised footbridge to get to the bright, open-plan lounge and dining areas; there are plump sofas, a log-burning stove and a wall of books to browse. Tartan-accented bedrooms, each with sliding doors leading to larch decking, are on the floor below. In the morning, Neil Hope cooks a 'delicious breakfast', taken communally. There's plenty of local produce to sample: sausages from a Skye farmstead; cheeses from the Isle of Lewis; home-made bread, muffins and yogurt. An evening meal can be arranged in advance; restaurants are within walking distance. The 'friendly hosts' provide 'helpful information' on local walks,

beachcombing and kayaking. 1 mile
E of Broadford. BEDROOMS 3. All on
ground floor. OPEN Mar–Nov. FACILITIES
Lounge/dining area, free Wi-Fi,
in-room TV (Freesat). BACKGROUND
MUSIC Traditional, occasionally,
during breakfast. CHILDREN All ages
welcomed (in own room, no special
facilities). PRICES Per room B&B £105.
Set menu £25.

BRODICK Ayrshire
Map 5:E1

AUCHRANNIE HOUSE HOTEL,
Auchrannie Road, Isle of Arran,
KA27 8BZ. Tel 01770 302234, www.
auchrannie.co.uk. Choose your own
adventure at the Johnston family's
large, child-friendly resort on the Isle of
Arran. The 19th-century country house
is one of two hotels on the extensive
estate. There are modern bedrooms
and 'plush lounges' to relax in; a spa,
swimming pools and a well-stocked
library. Three restaurants offer plenty of
choice at mealtimes: informal Brambles
is liked for its sharing platters, grilled
meats and West Coast seafood; family-
friendly Cruize has pizzas and pastas
alongside brasserie classics; conservatory
restaurant eighteen69 serves Scottish-
themed tapas (open for dinner Thurs–
Mon). If ever you decide to leave the
resort, the island is ripe for discovery,
on foot, bicycle and pony. 5 miles from
town. BEDROOMS 28. Some suitable for
disabled, plus Spa Resort rooms and
30 self-catering lodges. OPEN All year.
FACILITIES Bar, lounges, 3 restaurants,
spa (20-metre heated indoor pool,
steam room, spa bath, gym), free Wi-Fi,
in-room TV (Freeview), wedding/
function facilities, 60-acre grounds,
snooker room, tennis, badminton,

bowls, parking, complimentary bus
service to and from the ferry terminal 1
mile away. BACKGROUND MUSIC In public
areas. CHILDREN All ages welcomed
(play barn, outdoor play/picnic area,
children's swimming pool, library). DOGS
Allowed in some bedrooms, some public
rooms. PRICES Per room B&B from £99,
D,B&B from £139.

BRUICHLADDICH Argyll and Bute
Map 5:D1

LOCH GORM HOUSE, Isle of Islay,
PA49 7UN. Tel 01496 850139, www.
lochgormhouse.com. Warm, welcoming
Fiona Doyle runs her B&B in this
'charming, beautifully appointed'
stone-built house on the northern shore
of Islay, with 'amazing views over the
bay'. 'The place is spotlessly clean, and
the bedrooms and bathrooms are just
lovely,' says a Guide reader this year.
The hostess, a florist, fills the house
with 'magnificent' flower arrangements.
Enjoy drinks by the fire in the large
drawing room; take it outside when
the sun shines. Bedrooms (two with
sea views) are 'cosy, comfortable, bright
and airy'. A 'scrumptious breakfast' –
'such a feast' – provides fuel for the
half-mile coastal walk to the village
distillery, sandy beaches and historic
sites. Wellies, coats and beach towels
are provided. A thoughtful touch:
'Fiona booked us into a nearby
restaurant for dinner, which we
really appreciated.' BEDROOMS 3. OPEN
Mar–Dec. FACILITIES Drawing room,
dining room, free Wi-Fi, in-room
TV (Freeview), 1-acre garden, drying
facilities. BACKGROUND MUSIC None.
CHILDREN All ages welcomed. PRICES
Per room B&B from £135.
25% DISCOUNT VOUCHERS

CRINAN Argyll and Bute
Map 5:D1

CRINAN HOTEL, PA31 8SR. Tel 01546
830261, crinanhotel.com. Seafood is an
art at this 'friendly, informal' hotel in a
'spectacular position' overlooking the
sea and a canal lock. It has been owned
and run by artist Frances Macdonald
and her husband, Nick Ryan, for nearly
half a century. Watch the daily catch
of langoustines being landed just in
time for dinner, then pull up a seat at
a table in the lively Seafood bar, the
loch-facing Westward restaurant or the
summertime rooftop restaurant, Lock
16. 'It was lovely to know our meal
had been caught hours before eating.'
Simply furnished bedrooms have views
of the canal basin or over Loch Crinan
towards the islands of Scarba and Mull.
'Our room was of a good size, with
lovely linen on the large double bed.
The decor was fresh but plain; a big
picture window opened on to a balcony
overlooking the lock.' Art lovers, check
out the 'wonderful contemporary art'
in the top-floor gallery. Painting trips
on the hotel's 40-foot motor boat can be
arranged. 6 miles from Lochgilphead.
BEDROOMS 21. OPEN New Year, Mar–
Christmas. FACILITIES Lift, 2 lounges,
bar/bistro, 3 restaurants, coffee shop,
art gallery, free Wi-Fi, in-room TV,
¼-acre garden (sheltered spots), patio,
wedding/function facilities, health and
beauty treatment room. BACKGROUND
MUSIC None. CHILDREN All ages
welcomed (£35 per night). DOGS Well-
behaved dogs allowed by arrangement,
not in Westward restaurant (£10 per
night, own bedding required). PRICES
Per room B&B from £110. Set dinner
(Westward) £45, à la carte (Seafood
bar) £26.

CUMNOCK Ayrshire
Map 5:E2

DUMFRIES HOUSE LODGE, Dumfries
House Estate, KA18 2NJ. Tel 01290
429920, www.dumfrieshouselodge.
com. Guests at this historic 18th-century
factor's house are 'encouraged to treat
the place as their own'. 'Luxurious and
beautifully furnished', the guest house
stands on the edge of the 2,000-acre
Dumfries House estate. It is owned
by the Prince's Trust. Past the cosy
drawing rooms and open log fires,
characterful bedrooms (some compact)
are traditionally styled with antiques,
period prints and pictures. Each room
is different: some have a country
cottage feel, while others are grander;
one has patio doors that open on to
the courtyard garden. (Discuss room
choices before booking: previous visitors
discovered three sets of stairs between
the front door and their ground-floor
room.) Breakfast is served till 10 am.
Book a private tour of Dumfries
House (£25) – 'a must'. BEDROOMS 22.
Some on ground floor, 13 in courtyard
gardens, 1 suitable for disabled, plus
2 self-catering cottages. OPEN All year
except Christmas, New Year. FACILITIES
Lounge, snug, study, breakfast room,
private function room, free Wi-Fi, in-
room TV (Freeview), courtyard gardens
in 2,000-acre estate. BACKGROUND MUSIC
None. CHILDREN All ages welcomed.
PRICES Per room B&B £90–£160.

DALKEITH Midlothian
Map 5:D2

THE SUN INN, Lothianbridge, EH22
4TR. Tel 0131 663 2456, www.
thesuninnedinburgh.co.uk. A humble,
white-painted frontage gives way
to handsome interiors at the Minto

family's 'down-to-earth' roadside pub-with-rooms on the Edinburgh approach. The setting – facing a railway viaduct – could be more charming, but inside has all the pizzazz you'll need. Stylish wallpaper, tweed scatter pillows and cheeky bibelots complement the original fireplace and old beams. Tuck in to updated pub classics (confit pheasant Caesar salad, white anchovies, crispy bacon, perhaps) in the popular dining room; in the summertime, enjoy barbecues and spritzers in the covered courtyard. Well-designed bedrooms (bold prints, handcrafted furniture) are stocked with home-made biscuits, a Roberts radio and a DVD library; the lavish suite has a copper bath, built for two, at the foot of the modern four-poster bed. Light sleepers might wish to ask for a room that faces away from the street. 7 miles S of Edinburgh. BEDROOMS 5. FACILITIES Bar, restaurant, free Wi-Fi, in-room TV (Sky), garden, parking. BACKGROUND MUSIC In restaurant. CHILDREN All ages welcomed. PRICES Per room B&B £95–£150. À la carte £30.

DORNOCH Highland
Map 5:B2

2 QUAIL, Castle Street, IV25 3SN. Tel 01862 811811, www.2quail.com. Close to the cathedral and the Royal Dornoch Golf Club, this 'comfortable, very pleasant' guest house is run by 'helpful hosts' Kerensa and Michael Carr. A homely place, the late-Victorian town house has a wood-burning stove in the lounge, plus a library to browse, and antiques that have been in the family for years. Up tartan-carpeted stairs, traditionally decorated bedrooms have a well-equipped hospitality tray, and a

power shower in the bathroom. Stay in for a supper tailored to suit – the host plans the evening's set menu taking into account guests' allergies, intolerances or dislikes. A 'delicious breakfast' is served from 7 am. The sandy beaches of the Dornoch Firth are nearby. BEDROOMS 3. OPEN All year except Christmas. FACILITIES Lounge/library, dining room, free Wi-Fi, in-room TV (Freeview). BACKGROUND MUSIC None. CHILDREN 'Babes in arms' and children over 10 welcomed. PRICES Per room B&B £80–£120, D,B&B (double) £130–£170. Set dinners £20–£25.

DULNAIN BRIDGE Highland
Map 5:C2

MUCKRACH COUNTRY HOUSE HOTEL, nr Grantown-on-Spey, PH26 3LY. Tel 01479 851227, www.muckrach.com. There's a jaunty, contemporary feel to the Cowap family's restored Victorian shooting lodge in the Cairngorms national park. Wood-panelled public areas are decorated with local artwork, bright modern furnishings and Scottish flourishes; on fine days, stroll across the slated terrace overlooking pond and pastureland. Cheerfully designed bedrooms have fluffy bathrobes and the latest gadgetry (smart TV, iPod dock, ceiling speakers); the views are of surrounding scenery. Cake, coffees and a grazing menu are served all day, but leave room for dinner: the candlelit conservatory restaurant serves 'home-style cooking with a twist', perhaps Balliefurth sticky pork belly, smoked polenta, apple mirin sauce. Whisky is taken seriously: there are more than 70 choices to sample – perhaps with a haggis bon-bon or two. 5 miles from Grantown-on-Spey. BEDROOMS 13. Some in garden annexe, 2 interconnecting rooms suitable for a family. OPEN All year. FACILITIES Drawing room, library, bar, conservatory restaurant/coffee shop, private dining room, free Wi-Fi, in-room TV (Freeview), 1-acre garden, terraced patio, weddings, meetings, drying room. BACKGROUND MUSIC In public areas. CHILDREN All ages welcomed. DOGS Well-behaved dogs allowed in some bedrooms, on lead in library. PRICES Per room B&B from £99, D,B&B from £159. À la carte £27.

EDINBURGH
Map 5:D2

THE BALMORAL, 1 Princes Street, EH2 2EQ. Tel 0131 556 2414, www.roccofortehotels.com/the-balmoral-hotel. A kilted doorman ushers guests into this city-centre landmark, one of the great Victorian railway stopovers, today a luxury hotel (Rocco Forte Hotels). Guests come to be impressed: there are grand public spaces, sleek, modern bedrooms, a Michelin-starred restaurant and an award-winning spa. Most of the bedrooms have views of Edinburgh Castle; all have a bathroom of Italian marble. Indulge in afternoon tea under the glass dome of the Palm Court or choose from more than 400 whiskies in the bar. Eat an informal meal in buzzy Hadrian's brasserie. In Number One, Scottish dishes are cooked with a French twist. Set out for a day of exploring in good time: the hotel's iconic clock has been set three minutes fast since 1902, to ensure no one misses their train. BEDROOMS 188. 3 suitable for disabled. FACILITIES Drawing room, 3 bars, restaurant, brasserie, free Wi-Fi, in-room TV, civil wedding licence, conferences, 15-metre indoor swimming pool, spa (treatment rooms, sauna, gym, exercise studio), room service, 24-hour concierge, valet parking. CHILDREN All ages welcomed. PRICES Per room B&B from £224. 7-course set menu £89, 10-course set menu £120.

BROOKS HOTEL EDINBURGH, 70–72 Grove Street, EH3 8AP. Tel 0131 228 2323, www.brooksedinburgh.com. Vintage style and a cool, contemporary air mix at this recently revamped 1840s West End hotel within easy reach of the city's landmarks. It is owned by Andrew and Carla Brooks (see Brooks Guesthouse, Bristol, main entry). The elegant, clubby lounge has deep leather seating, a stash of periodicals, board games and an honesty bar; a DVD library provides entertainment for guests who want a quiet night in. Well-appointed, good-value bedrooms, some suitable for a family, have flashes of personality in an antique desk or dressing table, say, or a vintage lamp or designer chair. Lie in at the weekends, when Scottish breakfasts are served until 11 am. There's no restaurant, but a room-service menu of easy dishes (fish pie, roasted vegetable lasagne, Kerala prawn curry, each £10) is available till 10 pm. 10 mins' walk to the Edinburgh International Conference Centre. BEDROOMS 46. Some in annexe, 1 suitable for disabled. OPEN All year except 23–27 Dec. FACILITIES Lounge (honesty bar), breakfast room, free Wi-Fi, in-room TV, courtyard garden, small conferences, paid parking nearby (£12 per day). BACKGROUND MUSIC In lounge (jazz/contemporary). CHILDREN All ages welcomed. PRICES Per room B&B £49–£169.

CITYROOMZ EDINBURGH, 25–33 Shandwick Place, EH2 4RG. Tel 0131 229 6871, cityroomz.com. No frills, but there's plenty to fancy at this budget-friendly hotel within walking distance of both Old Town and New Town. Bright, modern decor lends cheer to the bedrooms and common areas. Rooms may be boxy, but they're practical and well thought out: each is outfitted with blackout curtains or blinds, and supplied with an iron and ironing board, a laptop safe and a bedside nook for a cup of tea. They vary in size, too, from compact to capacious, and guests may choose to have a bath or a shower. A wealth of eateries is close by; takeaway meals may be eaten in the communal dining area (crockery and cutlery provided). A continental breakfast buffet or a grab bag of coffee and pastries is available at extra charge. BEDROOMS 45. 9 family rooms with bunk bed. FACILITIES Lift, dining room, free Wi-Fi, in-room TV, discounts for parking at Castle Terrace car park, close by. BACKGROUND MUSIC In public areas. CHILDREN All ages welcomed. PRICES Room from £63. Breakfast £7.95.

94DR, 94 Dalkeith Road, EH16 5AF. Tel 0131 662 9265, www.94dr.com. Five minutes' walk from Holyrood Park, Paul Lightfoot's stylish Victorian town house is a Southside escape from the bustling centre. Neat bedrooms mix contemporary and traditional furniture and modern Scottish artwork; each has a bathroom with underfloor heating and good toiletries. Rooms at the front have views of Salisbury Crags and Arthur's Seat; rear rooms overlooking the garden are well protected from noise from the busy road. Families are welcomed: a suite connects a double room with a bunk-bed room to sleep four; books, DVDs, games and an Xbox are available. Home-cooked organic breakfasts include daily special. Enthusiastic about the city, the host has heaps of local tips. 10 mins by bus from the centre. BEDROOMS 6. OPEN All year except Christmas Day, Jan. FACILITIES Lounge (honesty bar), drawing room, breakfast room, free Wi-Fi, in-room TV (Freeview, Netflix), walled garden, bicycles available to borrow, pop-up dining event twice a month. BACKGROUND MUSIC None. CHILDREN Not under 3. PRICES Per room B&B £100–£225. 2-night min. stay preferred.

THE RAEBURN, 112 Raeburn Place, Stockbridge, EH4 1HG. Tel 0131 332 7000, www.theraeburn.com. The classy revamp of this elegant Georgian house has made it a go-to spot in Stockbridge, a vibrant area north of the centre. Handsome, and very smart, the hotel, pub and brasserie are modern, while retaining a heritage style in their wooden floors, muted tartans and tweedy accents. Generously sized bedrooms have a large Victorian-style bathroom; one room has a walk-in wardrobe. Among the much-appreciated extras: an iPod dock, coffee machine, hair straightener and disguised minibar. Head to the popular bar, with its outdoor terrace; claim a spot on a leather chesterfield in the clubby library lounge. Classic dishes and steaks are served in the smart brasserie. The Royal Botanical Gardens are a stroll away. BEDROOMS 10. 1 suitable for disabled. OPEN All year except Christmas Day. FACILITIES Bar, restaurant, library/function room, private dining area, conference room, free Wi-Fi, in-room TV (Freeview), terrace. BACKGROUND MUSIC In public areas. CHILDREN All ages welcomed. DOGS Allowed in bar. PRICES Per room B&B from £135.

THE RUTLAND HOTEL, 1–3 Rutland Street, EH1 2AE. Tel 0131 229 3402, www.therutlandhotel.com. The former home of medical pioneer Sir Joseph Lister is anything but clinical today: the modern hotel occupying this 19th-century building, steps from the top of Princes Street, is awash in rich fabrics, bold patterns and ornate mirrors. Individually styled bedrooms have useful extras: bathrobes, Scottish toiletries, home-baked shortbread, a fully stocked minibar. People-watch over hotdogs and small plates in the informal Huxley bar; prime Scottish steaks are a speciality in the smart Kyloe restaurant. Visit the gin stills and sign up for a tour or tasting in the basement Edinburgh Gin Distillery by day – the space morphs into the popular Heads and Tales bar most evenings, with custom cocktails and small bites. BEDROOMS 11. Plus 5 serviced apartments in adjacent buildings. OPEN All year except 24–25 Dec. FACILITIES Lift, 2 bars, restaurant, private dining room, free Wi-Fi, in-room TV (Freeview), discounted parking at Castle Terrace car park. BACKGROUND MUSIC In public areas. CHILDREN All ages welcomed. DOGS Assistance dogs allowed in hotel, all dogs allowed in apartments. PRICES Per room B&B from £140.
25% DISCOUNT VOUCHERS

SOUTHSIDE GUEST HOUSE, 8 Newington Road, EH9 1QS. Tel 0131 668 4422, www.southsideguesthouse.co.uk. The well-planted front courtyard marks out this friendly B&B, an easy walk, past the Meadows, to the university. Owners Franco and Lynne Galgani have restored many of the original features in their Victorian terraced house, including the tall windows in most of the bedrooms. The best rooms have a four-poster bed, a sofa and an espresso machine, but all accommodation is homely and comfortable, with oriental rugs on wood floors, perhaps, and artwork on the walls. A whisky nightcap is offered before bedtime. 'Proper breakfasts' are served on crisp white linen. Vegetarian and vegan options are available, plus a daily special – venison sausages, French toast, haggis. Frequent bus service to most destinations in the city. BEDROOMS 8. OPEN All year except Christmas. FACILITIES Breakfast room, free Wi-Fi, in-room TV, limited free parking nearby, by prior arrangement. BACKGROUND MUSIC 'Mainly Bach' at breakfast. CHILDREN Not under 10. PRICES Per room B&B single £90–£100, double £100–£180. 2-night min. stay preferred.
25% DISCOUNT VOUCHERS

TIGERLILY, 125 George Street, EH2 4JN. Tel 0131 225 5005, www. tigerlilyedinburgh.co.uk. Sassy interiors unfurl behind the restrained Georgian exterior of this playful hotel in New Town. A sense of fun and opulence fills the place: there are spirited prints, jewel tones and mirror-ball surfaces; oversized velvet armchairs and a lushly growing green wall. Recently refreshed bedrooms are more restrained (though there remain some design flourishes); most attention-grabbing are the amenities they're packed with: fluffy bathrobes, slippers, a stash of DVDs, a pre-loaded iPod, and wireless speakers so you can play your own tunes. Join locals on a night out in the popular, cocktail-dispensing bars or buzzy restaurant: steaks, sharing platters and a menu of modern dishes offer good choice. Next morning, detox juices and breakfast baps kick-start the day. BEDROOMS 33. Some smoking. OPEN All year except 24–25 Dec. FACILITIES Lift, 2 bars (resident DJs), restaurant, free Wi-Fi, in-room TV (Freeview). BACKGROUND MUSIC In bar and restaurant. CHILDREN All ages welcomed (babysitting by arrangement). PRICES Per room B&B from £250, D,B&B from £310. À la carte £30.

23 MAYFIELD, 23 Mayfield Gardens, EH9 2BX. Tel 0131 667 5806, www.23mayfield.co.uk. In a three-storey Victorian house a mile from the city centre, Ross Birnie's 'lovely' B&B has 'all the modern features one needs when away from home'. Smart, rather masculine, bedrooms have handcrafted mahogany furniture, quality linen, high-end toiletries and fresh coffee for the cafetière; a shower in the bathroom. A family 'observatory' with views towards Arthur's Seat is provided with a telescope. Downstairs, original stained-glass windows, leather sofas and heavy drapes make the panelled lounge a soothing place to relax. Help yourself to a drink from the honesty bar or browse a rare tome from the library shelves (some works date back to the 1740s); pit your skills on the oversized ConnectFour. 'Fabulous', hearty breakfasts and daily specials are served in the morning. Buses to the centre

stop frequently just outside. BEDROOMS 7. 1 on ground floor. OPEN All year except Christmas. FACILITIES Club room, breakfast room, free Wi-Fi, in-room TV (Freeview), terrace, garden, parking. BACKGROUND MUSIC At breakfast. CHILDREN Not under 3. PRICES Per room B&B £80–£170.

21212, 3 Royal Terrace, EH7 5AB. Tel 0345 22 21212, www.21212restaurant. co.uk. Come for the Michelin-starred cooking, stay for the well-appointed rooms and excellent location. Chef/patron Paul Kitching and his partner, Katie O'Brien, run their restaurant-with-rooms in a Georgian town house facing the Royal Terrace Gardens. Accommodation is in large bedrooms, each with ample seating, and city or garden views through tall windows. Look across the gardens to the Firth of Forth while sipping an aperitif in the handsome first-floor drawing room; three-, four- and five-course dinners are from a limited-choice, weekly-changing menu of intriguing modern dishes: chicken curry, peas, pines; pintade, bacon, mustard, bread sauce. BEDROOMS 4. OPEN All year except 12 days Jan, 12 days Sept, 25–26 Dec, New Year. FACILITIES Drawing room, restaurant (closed Sun, Mon), private dining rooms, free Wi-Fi, in-room TV (Freeview). BACKGROUND MUSIC None. CHILDREN Not under 5. PRICES Per room B&B £95–£295. Set menus £70–£85. 2-night min. stay preferred.

THE WITCHERY BY THE CASTLE, Castlehill, The Royal Mile, EH1 2NF. Tel 0131 225 5613, www.thewitchery. com. The candlelit rooms, secret doors, and nooks and crannies of these conjoined 16th- and 17th-century buildings overlooking the Royal Mile weave a spell over charmed guests. This dramatic restaurant-with-suites, by the gates of Edinburgh Castle, is owned by James Thomson, whose rococo Prestonfield stands next to Holyrood Park (see main entry). Swathed in tapestries and fine carvings, the two dining rooms are a theatrical serving ground (take your eye off the food to admire the painted ceiling). Indulge in the modern Scottish menu, then retreat to one of the Gothic-style bedrooms, each more extravagant than the other. A bottle of champagne is presented on arrival; in the morning, a breakfast hamper may be delivered to the room. **BEDROOMS** 9 suites. **FACILITIES** 2 dining rooms, free Wi-Fi, terrace. **BACKGROUND MUSIC** In public areas. **PRICES** Per room B&B from £345. 3-course set menu £38.

FORT WILLIAM Highland
Map 5:C1

THE LIME TREE, Achintore Road, PH33 6RQ. Tel 01397 701806, www.limetreefortwilliam.co.uk. The 'original, imaginative food' and 'wonderfully thoughtful staff' keep guests coming back to this small hotel, restaurant and modern art gallery overlooking the loch in the Highland town. Owner David Wilson, a visual artist, displays his and others' work throughout the building. Stay in one of the 'well-designed bedrooms' – they were all renovated in 2017. 'We slept well in our comfortable, well-equipped loch-facing room.' Dishes off the modern Scottish menu in the 'warm, cosy' dining room are 'all tasty, and served in generous portions'. 'The next morning, the chef made us a perfect off-menu breakfast because he'd

heard us talking about how much we liked eggs Benedict and smoked salmon – that's what we call true hospitality.' 5 mins' walk to town centre. **BEDROOMS** 9. Some in modern extension. **OPEN** All year except Christmas. **FACILITIES** 3 lounges (map room with maps and guides), restaurant, gallery, free Wi-Fi, in-room TV (Freeview), garden with seating area, drying room, bicycle storage, parking. **BACKGROUND MUSIC** None. **CHILDREN** All ages welcomed. **DOGS** Allowed, not in restaurant (£5, separate dining area). **PRICES** Per room B&B £125–£135. À la carte £50.

GLASGOW
Map 5:D2

BLYTHSWOOD SQUARE HOTEL, 11 Blythswood Square, G2 4AD. Tel 0141 248 8888, www.blythswoodsquare.com. 'A lovely building in a beautiful square', this style-conscious hotel is liked for its 'charming, quietly efficient staff' and its modish bedrooms – 'comfortable, with a touch of luxury'. Modern tweedy touches sit against glamorous marble in the spacious reception hall and salon; a state-of-the-art spa is the ideal place to recuperate from the busy city. Sweep up the grand staircase (or take the lift) to smart bedrooms of various sizes. The smallest may be compact – go for one of the suites with original Georgian features for something more special. Well-executed meals are served in the popular restaurant – start here, and end with a cocktail in the buzzy bar. 'Great breakfasts' include a Bloody Mary station. 10 mins' walk to Buchanan Street. Part of the Principal Hotels group; The Bonham, Edinburgh (see main entry), is under the same ownership. **BEDROOMS** 100. Some suitable for disabled.

FACILITIES Lift, 3 bars, salon, restaurant, private screening room, free Wi-Fi, in-room TV (Sky), civil wedding licence, spa (2 relaxation pools, treatment rooms, rasul mud chamber), valet parking (from £27.50 for 24 hours). BACKGROUND MUSIC In public areas. CHILDREN All ages welcomed (6–12s £30 per night). DOGS Allowed in some bedrooms (£30). PRICES Room from £130. Breakfast £12, market menu £18.50–£22.

15GLASGOW, 15 Woodside Place, G3 7QL. Tel 0141 332 1263, www.15glasgow.com. 'Well located' in a leafy neighbourhood a short walk from the West End, Lorraine Gibson's modern town house B&B is a tranquil base. The Victorian house has been elegantly restored: original fireplaces and intricate cornicing remain. Spacious, high-ceilinged bedrooms have a super-king-size bed and mood lighting; two suites, positively vast, have huge windows overlooking gardens to the front or rear. Breakfast, ordered the night before, may be brought to the room at a time to suit, or eaten communally in the lounge. Guests are given access to the private garden across the road; pretty Kelvingrove Park is just steps further. BEDROOMS 5. OPEN All year. FACILITIES Lounge, free Wi-Fi, in-room TV (Freeview), small garden, parking. BACKGROUND MUSIC None. CHILDREN Not under 5 (extra bed £20). DOGS Allowed in bedrooms, not in public spaces. PRICES Per room B&B £130–£165.

GLENEGEDALE Argyll and Bute
Map 5:D1

GLENEGEDALE HOUSE, Isle of Islay, PA42 7AS. Tel 01496 300 400, www. glenegedalehouse.co.uk. Midway between Port Ellen and Bowmore, Graeme and Emma Clark dispense freshly baked cakes and a wealth of local knowledge to appreciative B&B guests. Their white-painted house on the Isle of Islay is in a prominent position surrounded by large gardens; the views stretch over the Mull of Oa to the Atlantic beyond. Bedrooms are smartly decorated with antiques and plaid, and are supplied with well-considered perks: good toiletries, Scottish-blended teas, chocolates from a Highland chocolatier. At breakfast, help yourself from a sideboard laden with jugs of juice, and poached and fresh fruit; wholesome cooked dishes include porridge laced with whisky. Glorious scenery, beaches and archaeological sites are within easy reach. Close to the small island airfield; ferry terminals are a short drive away. BEDROOMS 4. Plus 4-bed self-catering house. OPEN Feb–Nov. FACILITIES Morning room, drawing room, dining room, music room, free Wi-Fi, in-room TV (Freeview), garden, parking. BACKGROUND MUSIC None. CHILDREN Not under 12. PRICES Per room B&B £140–£160.

GRANTOWN-ON-SPEY Highland
Map 5:C2

THE DULAIG, Seafield Avenue, PH26 3JF. Tel 01479 872065, www.thedulaig. com. Liked for its 'unfussy atmosphere', 'warm hospitality' and home-made Seville orange marmalade, this 'friendly' B&B occupies a 'gorgeous' Edwardian country house, ten minutes' walk from town. Carol and Gordon Bulloch, the owners, are 'simply wonderful'. They have furnished their house with a mix of Arts and Crafts antiques and contemporary pieces;

the drawing room has an open log fire in cool weather. Touches of whimsy are much appreciated: the 'cake fairy' leaves freshly baked sweet treats in the spacious, tastefully decorated bedrooms each day. Generous Scottish breakfasts include haggis, home-made potato scones, whisky- and cream-laced porridge, and eggs from the resident Black Rock hens. Packed lunches are available for a day of walks, fishing or sampling vintages at the nearby distillery. **BEDROOMS** 3. **OPEN** All year except Christmas, New Year. **FACILITIES** Drawing room, dining room, free Wi-Fi, computer available, in-room TV (Freesat), 1½-acre garden (pond, summer house), veranda, parking (garage for motorbikes and bicycles). **BACKGROUND MUSIC** Quiet Scottish music at breakfast 'with guests' permission'. **CHILDREN** Not under 12. **PRICES** Per room B&B £165–£180.

GULLANE East Lothian
Map 5:D3

GREYWALLS, Muirfield, EH31 2EG. Tel 01620 842144, www.greywalls. co.uk. A golfer's paradise near the sea, the Weaver family's 'well-located' luxury hotel stands on the edge of Muirfield golf course, with nine other courses nearby. Duncan Fraser is the manager. The Edwardian honey stone house was designed by Sir Edwin Lutyens as a 'dignified holiday home'; today, it retains a plush, home-away-from-home feel in its antique-filled bedrooms, well-maintained walled gardens (attributed to Gertrude Jekyll) and civilised afternoon teas of loose-leaf blends, finger sandwiches, sweet treats and champagne. Classic French dishes cooked with plenty of locally sourced produce are served in the restaurant, Chez Roux; lighter meals may be eaten in the bar/lounge. Wake to nature: the traditionally styled bedrooms have long views to the Firth of Forth, or across fields of green to the Lammermuir hills. 15 mins' walk to sea. **BEDROOMS** 23. 4 on ground floor, 6 in lodges nearby. **OPEN** All year. **FACILITIES** Bar/lounge, drawing room, library, restaurant, free Wi-Fi, in-room TV (Freeview), weddings/function facilities, spa treatments, 6-acre garden, tennis court. **CHILDREN** All ages welcomed. **DOGS** Allowed in cottage bedrooms, not in public rooms. **PRICES** Per room B&B single from £93.50, double from £269.50. Set dinner £37, à la carte £45.
25% DISCOUNT VOUCHERS

INNERLEITHEN Scottish Borders
Map 5:E2

CADDON VIEW, 14 Pirn Road, EH44 6HH. Tel 01896 830208, www. caddonview.co.uk. Ideal for the outdoorsy traveller – and with plenty to please indoorsy types – Stephen and Lisa Davies's 'good-value' Victorian guest house in the Tweed valley is a 'highly recommended' base for travellers exploring the Scottish Borders. Guests in 2017 praised the 'excellent food', 'good-sized bedrooms', and 'friendly welcome, with tea and home-baked treats'. There are books, games and a blazing fire in the drawing room; bedrooms are 'rustic but nice' ('though we thought our bathroom needed a little updating,' one Guide reader said). Stephen Davies serves seasonal Scottish cuisine in the candlelit dining room, five nights a week. (Room snacks are available when the restaurant is closed; alternatively, restaurants in town are a short walk away.) Breakfast ('exceptional') is served until 10 am. **BEDROOMS** 8. **OPEN** All year except Christmas. **FACILITIES** Drawing room (books, guides, games), dining room (no dinner Sun, Mon), free Wi-Fi, in-room TV (Freeview), ½-acre mature garden, storage for bicycles and fishing gear, picnics available, parking. **BACKGROUND MUSIC** In dining room. **CHILDREN** Well-behaved children of all ages welcomed. **DOGS** Allowed in 1 bedroom, drawing room 'if no other guests object' (£5 per night). **PRICES** Per room B&B £70–£115, D,B&B £130–£170.

INVERNESS Highland
Map 5:C2

MOYNESS HOUSE, 6 Bruce Gardens, IV3 5EN. Tel 01463 236624, www. moyness.co.uk. Close to the city's attractions, Wilma and John Martin's B&B stands just apart from the bustle on a quiet residential street. It's a modest, restful place, in its own pretty garden; restaurants and the riverside are a stroll away. The Victorian villa was once home to the novelist Neil M Gunn, the Highland literary hero. Browse the collection of his books in the sitting room before heading to one of the comfortable bedrooms – each is named after one of Gunn's works. Individually styled, rooms are supplied with bathrobes, toiletries, a hospitality tray. 'Good breakfasts' include eggs from the garden hens. Consummate hosts, the Martins are happy to provide local recommendations, and can help arrange tours of the city and surrounding area. **BEDROOMS** 7. **OPEN** Feb–Dec. **FACILITIES** Sitting room, dining room, free Wi-Fi, in-room TV, ¼-acre garden, parking. **BACKGROUND MUSIC** At breakfast.

CHILDREN All ages welcomed. **PRICES** Per room B&B £80–£125.

TRAFFORD BANK GUEST HOUSE, 96 Fairfield Road, IV3 5LL. Tel 01463 241414, www.traffordbankguesthouse. co.uk. 'Helpful and very friendly', Lorraine Pun has 'put much thought' into her 'beautifully decorated' B&B near the Caledonian Canal. The bay-windowed, sandstone Victorian house has a casual elegance – tartan rugs on polished wood floors; paintings and objets d'art from a local gallery – plus space to sit, shaded by wide parasols, in the pretty garden. Bright, homely bedrooms are equipped with useful amenities including an espresso machine, a silent mini-fridge and an iPod dock. Start the day with a 'great breakfast' (ordered the night before), served in the conservatory. 10 mins' walk from the centre; well located for exploring local attractions and the loch. **BEDROOMS** 5. **OPEN** Mar–Nov. **FACILITIES** 2 lounges, conservatory breakfast room, free Wi-Fi, in-room TV (Freeview), ½-acre garden, parking. **BACKGROUND MUSIC** None. **CHILDREN** Not under 5. **PRICES** Per room B&B £110–£150.

KIPPEN Stirlingshire
Map 5:D2

THE CROSS KEYS, Main Street, FK8 3DN. Tel 01786 870293, www. kippencrosskeys.com. Soups and sirloins, pies and puddings, perhaps even a Highland venison stew with herby dumplings – the refined pub grub attracts crowds and wins awards at Debby McGregor and Brian Horsburgh's lively, unassuming inn. In a village on the edge of the Loch Lomond and the Trossachs national park, the pub is one of Scotland's oldest – it's served as a gateway to the north for the past 300 years. Join locals, walkers, families and dogs in the beer garden while admiring views of the Gargunnock and Fintry hills; in winter, get cosy by a fire in the rustic bar. There's a wide selection of whiskies and real ales to choose from. Good-value bedrooms are neat, modern and straightforward: oak furnishings, crisp linens, a small selection of DVDs; underfloor heating in the bathroom. 10 miles W of Stirling. BEDROOMS 3. OPEN All year except Christmas Day, New Year's Day. FACILITIES Bar/dining areas, private dining room, free Wi-Fi, in-room TV (Freeview), civil wedding licence, terrace, beer garden. BACKGROUND MUSIC In bar. CHILDREN All ages welcomed (extra bed £10 per night). DOGS Allowed (£10 per night). PRICES Per room B&B single £55, double £70–£90. À la carte £25.

LOCHMADDY Western Isles
Map 5: inset A1
HAMERSAY HOUSE HOTEL, Isle of North Uist, HS6 5AE. Tel 01876 500 700, www.hamersayhouse.co.uk. A cheering sight in blue and white, this laid-back modern hotel is in a small village on North Uist, a paradise for wildlife and beach lovers. Owned by Amanda and Niall Leveson Gower, it is run with the 'same high standards and very good food' as sister hotel Langass Lodge, Locheport (see main entry). A nautical theme runs through the light-filled lounge and contemporary brasserie, where the imaginative menus use local game, the freshest of seafood, and garden vegetables and herbs. 'Well-equipped bedrooms' are made cosy with tweedy fabrics; four rooms open on to the garden. Surrounded by a rugged beauty, the landscaped grounds contain a decked area with views over the bay. Excellent walks; a village shop and pub are close by. Well placed for the ferries. BEDROOMS 12. 6 in extension. FACILITIES Bar, lounge, restaurant, free Wi-Fi, in-room TV, gym, garden, parking. BACKGROUND MUSIC At low volume in restaurant in evening. CHILDREN All ages welcomed (early suppers). PRICES Per room B&B single £100, double £140. À la carte £35.

LOCHRANZA Ayrshire
Map 5:D1
APPLE LODGE, Isle of Arran, KA27 8HJ. Tel 01770 830229, www.applelodgearran.co.uk. Binoculars and a guide to local fauna are a must when staying at Jeannie and John Boyd's welcoming B&B in Isle of Arran countryside – red deer and eagles are regularly spotted from every window. Decorated with retro flair, the white-painted Edwardian manse brims with embroidery, paintings, ruffles and swagged valances; the hallways are wallpapered in pink. Traditionally furnished bedrooms are supplied with a hot drinks tray, books and plenty of local information. A self-contained suite with a kitchen and sitting room has French doors opening on to the garden. Good walks from the door. The Kintyre ferry docks at the pier 1 mile away. BEDROOMS 4. 1 suite on ground floor. OPEN Mid-Jan–mid-Dec. FACILITIES Lounge, dining room, free Wi-Fi, in-room TV (Freeview), ¼-acre mature garden, parking. BACKGROUND MUSIC None. CHILDREN Not under 12. PRICES Per person B&B from £39. 3-night min. stay.

MELROSE Scottish Borders
Map 5:E3

BURTS, Market Square, TD6 9PL. Tel 01896 822285, www.burtshotel.co.uk. In the centre of a pretty Borders town, this 'excellent', well-established hotel near the banks of the River Tweed has been run by the Henderson family for 46 years. The 18th-century building on the High Street is a low-key, welcoming place, with smartly styled bedrooms (good Scottish toiletries, too) and a locally well-regarded restaurant. Spend the day fishing, golfing or walking, then return for chef Trevor Williams's modern Scottish dishes at dinner. Lunches and casual suppers may be taken in the bar, where a whisky menu has more than 90 single malts. The Hendersons also own The Townhouse, across the street (see main entry). Handy for the historic Borders Railway – the Tweedbank station is a five-minute drive away. BEDROOMS 20. OPEN All year, no accommodation 24–26 Dec. FACILITIES Lobby lounge, residents' lounge, bistro bar, restaurant (closed for lunch Mon–Sat), private dining room, free Wi-Fi, in-room TV (Freeview), wedding/function facilities, ½-acre garden, parking. BACKGROUND MUSIC None. CHILDREN All ages welcomed, not under 8 in restaurant. DOGS Allowed in some bedrooms, bar, not in restaurant. PRICES Per room B&B from £70, D,B&B from £95. À la carte £39.

MOFFAT Dumfries and Galloway
Map 5:E2

HARTFELL HOUSE & THE LIMETREE RESTAURANT, Hartfell Crescent, DG10 9AL. Tel 01683 220153, www.hartfellhouse.co.uk. In a 'pleasant town' close to the scenic Southern Upland Way, Robert and Mhairi Ash's 'lovely house' is praised for its 'well-appointed rooms' and 'fantastic cooking'. 'The views and the food are to die for,' says a Guide reader this year. The 'very good-value' Victorian guest house has 'comfortable bedrooms' supplied with a memory foam mattress on the bed, and nice extras – Scottish biscuits, fine toiletries. In the restaurant, chef Matt Seddon's modern Scottish dishes, from a short and frequently changing menu, might include loin of Annanwater hogget lamb and crispy confit shoulder, dauphinoise potato, sautéed kale. 'After that delicious dinner, it was a challenge to do justice to the equally excellent breakfast – but we managed.' Easy access to the M74. 5 mins' walk to the town centre. BEDROOMS 7. Plus self-catering cottage in the grounds. OPEN All year except Mon, Christmas. FACILITIES Lounge, restaurant (closed Sun, Mon), free Wi-Fi, in-room TV (Freeview), garden, cooking classes, bicycle storage, parking. BACKGROUND MUSIC In restaurant. CHILDREN All ages welcomed. PRICES Per room B&B from £75, D,B&B from £133. Set menu £29.

NAIRN Highland
Map 5:C2

SUNNY BRAE, Marine Road, IV12 4EA. Tel 01667 452309, www.sunnybraehotel.com. In a seaside town that's one of the sunniest in Scotland, John Bochel and Rachel Philipsen's 'good-value' small hotel is minutes from the beach. The glass-fronted building overlooks the green, the promenade and 'the panorama of the sea'. 'Light, cheerfully decorated bedrooms' are provided with bottled water and bathrobes; four have views over the Moray Firth. At dinner, the host's 'homely' Scottish dishes are 'competently cooked' with a European twist: Nairnshire steak tartare; Scrabster halibut, prawns, asparagus, baby potatoes, leek cream. There's a 'good choice of wine' and more than 100 malt whiskies on the menu. Good variety, too, at breakfast. **BEDROOMS** 8. 1 suitable for disabled. **OPEN** Mid-Mar–end Oct. **FACILITIES** Lounge, dining room, free Wi-Fi, in-room TV (Freeview), terrace, front and rear gardens, parking. **BACKGROUND MUSIC** None. **CHILDREN** All ages welcomed. **PRICES** Per room B&B from £85. À la carte £35.

OBAN Argyll and Bute
Map 5:D1
GREYSTONES, 1 Dalriach Road, PA34 5EQ. Tel 01631 358653, www.greystonesoban.co.uk. The views stretch across Oban Bay from Mark and Suzanne McPhillips's hillside B&B. The thoughtfully restored baronial mansion retains stained-glass windows, moulded ceilings and a fine wooden staircase; understated furnishings and contemporary art keep things fresh. Chic, uncluttered bedrooms, each with a spacious bathroom, have all the necessities: fluffy bathrobes and Scottish toiletries, tea-making facilities, wine glasses and a corkscrew. Most rooms look towards the water. Breakfast in the turreted dining room may bring raspberry cranachan or a cheesy spinach frittata. Days out are easy – just ask the obliging hosts for an itinerary of their favourite trips around the Inner Hebrides. The town centre, harbour and seafood restaurants are within walking distance. **BEDROOMS** 5. **OPEN** Feb–Nov. **FACILITIES** Sitting room, dining room, free Wi-Fi, in-room TV (Freeview),

½-acre garden, parking. **BACKGROUND MUSIC** None. **PRICES** Per room B&B £120–£175. 2-night min. stay preferred.

PEEBLES Scottish Borders
Map 5:E2
CRINGLETIE HOUSE, off Edinburgh Road, EH45 8PL. Tel 01721 725750, www.cringletie.com. Glimpse the turrets of this small baronial mansion through acres of mature woodland, in a secluded setting north of the country town. Standing in sweeping, manicured lawns, the country house hotel is managed by Jeremy Osborne for the owners, Jacob and Johanna van Houdt. Each bedroom has its own charm – some are unfussy and modern, others lean towards the traditional – but all look over the grounds and surrounding hillside. Tasting and à la carte menus in the lawn-facing restaurant highlight Scottish produce and vegetables from the kitchen garden. A log fire in the lounge creates a cosy atmosphere, but go outside (wellies and umbrellas are provided): the extensive grounds stretch to a river and waterfall, an ancient dovecote and back-to-nature woodland trails. 2 miles N of Peebles. **BEDROOMS** 13. 1 suitable for disabled, 2-bed family cottage in grounds. **OPEN** All year except 2–3 weeks Jan. **FACILITIES** Lift, bar, lounge, conservatory, garden room, restaurant, free Wi-Fi, in-room TV (Freeview), wedding facilities, 28-acre fully accessible grounds (sculptures, walled garden, pitch-and-putt, croquet, boules), parking. **BACKGROUND MUSIC** In public areas. **CHILDREN** All ages welcomed (play area, trampoline). **DOGS** Allowed in bedrooms, garden room. **PRICES** Per room B&B from £114, D,B&B from £189. À la carte £37.50.

THE HORSESHOE RESTAURANT,
Eddleston, EH45 8QP. Tel 01721
730225, www.horseshoeinn.co.uk.
'Keep it small and do it well' – that's
the philosophy at this surprisingly
sophisticated restaurant-with-rooms in a
quiet village four miles north of Peebles.
Within the squat, white-painted,
roadside building, chef Alistair Craig's
modern menus showcase Scottish
produce, and vegetables and herbs from
the kitchen garden: poached trout,
buttermilk, pickled cucumber, green
beans; duck breast, carrots, hash brown,
chard. Cross the rear courtyard to a
converted Victorian schoolhouse where
the 'modest bedrooms' (some compact)
are supplied with bathrobes and organic
toiletries; a hospitality tray with fruit,
home-baked cake and fresh milk.
Sweet treats at breakfast: local honey;
home-made jams and marmalade.
Mark Slaney, the personable manager,
has a wealth of local knowledge: ask
him about the excellent rambling in the
area. BEDROOMS 8. FACILITIES Lounge,
restaurant, private dining room, free
Wi-Fi, in-room TV (Freeview), small
kitchen garden, parking. BACKGROUND
MUSIC In restaurant, occasional live jazz.
CHILDREN All ages welcomed, no under-
5s in restaurant. DOGS Well-behaved
dogs allowed in some bedrooms (£10 per
night). PRICES Per room B&B from £100,
D,B&B from £140. À la carte £50, tasting
menu £60.

THE TONTINE, High Street, EH45 8AJ.
Tel 01721 720 892, www.tontinehotel.
com. Kate and Gordon Innes's town-
centre hotel is a welcome retreat for
outdoorsy types in the Tweed valley, an
area rich in opportunities for walking,
golfing, fishing, cycling, mountain
biking and high-stakes garden-visiting.
The early-19th-century building on the
High Street is popular for afternoon
teas and cocktail evenings. Mingle
with locals and tourists over real ales
and lagers, then choose to eat seasonal
Scottish food in the informal bistro
or the high-ceilinged, chandelier-lit
restaurant. Modern bedrooms, some
overlooking the River Tweed, are in
the main building and a rear extension
connected by a glass-sided corridor.
Some are neat and straightforward,
with plaid accessories adding charm,
but go for a feature room, perhaps
with a handsome four-poster bed.
BEDROOMS 36. 20 in annexe. FACILITIES
Bar, lounge, bistro, restaurant, private
dining/meeting room, free Wi-Fi, in-
room TV (Freeview), 2 garden areas
(alfresco dining), drying room, secure
bicycle and motorcycle storage, parking.
BACKGROUND MUSIC In public rooms.
CHILDREN All ages welcomed. DOGS
Allowed in annexe bedrooms, bar,
bistro, garden, not in restaurant (£10 per
dog). PRICES Per room B&B from £70,
D,B&B from £130. À la carte £25.

PERTH Perth and Kinross
Map 5:D2

SUNBANK HOUSE, 50 Dundee Road,
PH2 7BA. Tel 01738 624882, www.
sunbankhouse.com. Remigio and
Georgina Zane's unpretentious
Victorian house in mature gardens
makes a tranquil base for exploring the
city's nightlife and café culture – the
centre is an easy walk away. Spacious
bedrooms in the traditionally furnished
house are homely and comfortable, with
a charming, faintly old-fashioned air.
One is suitable for a family; those at the
back are quietest. Gather with fellow

guests for pre-dinner drinks in the fire-lit lounge before sitting down to 'Remo' Zane's uncomplicated, Italian-inflected dinners (booking advised). Light bites may be taken in the lounge. Generous breakfasts; special diets are catered for. Ask the hosts for their tips about the surrounding area, then request a picnic before heading out. ½ mile NE of town centre. BEDROOMS 10. Some on ground floor, 2 suitable for disabled. FACILITIES Lounge/bar, restaurant, free Wi-Fi, in-room TV (Freeview), wedding/function facilities, terrace, ½-acre garden, parking. BACKGROUND MUSIC In restaurant. CHILDREN All ages welcomed. DOGS Allowed (£15 charge). PRICES Per person B&B from £50, D,B&B from £65.

PITLOCHRY Perth and Kinross
Map 5:D2

EAST HAUGH HOUSE, by Pitlochry, PH16 5TE. Tel 01796 473121, www.easthaugh.co.uk. Tramp along the banks of nearby rivers Tummel and Tay, then back through woodland towards the McGown family's friendly country hotel in a 17th-century turreted stone house just outside the town. Cheery modern bedrooms are decked in tartan and toile de Jouy, and are thoughtfully stocked with home-baked shortbread and fresh milk. Each room is different: one has a four-poster bed; a new suite has a cinema room, open fire and spa bath. Seasonal seafood and game are the highlights on Neil McGown's much-praised modern menus. Outdoorsy guests have use of the fishing lodge, with barbecue and cooking facilities, on the River Tay; hunting excursions on nearby estates are regularly arranged. 1½ miles S of

town centre. BEDROOMS 12. 1 suitable for disabled, 5 in converted 'bothy' adjacent to hotel, plus 2-bed cottage. OPEN All year except 1 week over Christmas. FACILITIES Lounge, bar, restaurant (closed for lunch Mon–Fri), free Wi-Fi, in-room TV (Freeview), wedding/function facilities, patio, 3-acre grounds, river beat, parking. BACKGROUND MUSIC In bar and restaurant. CHILDREN All ages welcomed. DOGS Allowed in some bedrooms. PRICES Per room B&B £80–£220, D,B&B £130–£270. À la carte £30.

25% DISCOUNT VOUCHERS

PINE TREES, Strathview Terrace, PH16 5QR. Tel 01796 472121, www.pinetreeshotel.co.uk. The extensive grounds of Valerie and Robert Kerr's 'warm and welcoming' hotel on the outskirts of town are just the place to watch for roe deer and red squirrels. A 'quiet, friendly' place, the Victorian mansion stands in well-maintained gardens surrounded by woodland; inside, cosy lounges are just right for a good book and a tot of whisky. 'Very comfortable', traditionally decorated bedrooms are individually styled, but each has sweets, bottled water, tea- and coffee-making facilities and a radio. (Some have a shower room – ask for a room with a bath if you'd like a soak.) Sample Scottish-influenced dishes in the garden-facing restaurant – roast saddle of Perthshire venison, red cabbage, aubergine purée, perhaps. Fishing trips and theatre packages appeal to outdoorsy and indoorsy folk. ¼ mile N of town. BEDROOMS 29. 3 in annexe, 6 in coach house; 7 on ground floor. FACILITIES 3 lounges (log fire), bar, restaurant, free Wi-Fi (in lounge), in-room TV (Freeview), 7-acre grounds, parking. BACKGROUND MUSIC In bar and restaurant. CHILDREN All ages welcomed in coach house (charge for extra bed). DOGS Well-behaved dogs allowed (£7.50 per night). PRICES Per person B&B from £54, D,B&B from £74. À la carte £25.50.

ST ANDREWS Fife
Map 5:D3
RUFFLETS, Strathkinness Low Road, KY16 9TX. Tel 01334 472594, www. rufflets.co.uk. 'The elegance of the beautiful birdsong and gardens' characterises this turreted 1920s mansion, an 'extremely welcoming' country hotel in large grounds outside the town. Family owned for 66 years, it is managed by Stephen Owen; the 'helpful staff' are 'excellent'. 'Superb bedrooms' are well supplied with bathrobes, top-end toiletries and home-made shortbread; a hot-water bottle is tucked under the covers on a cool night. At lunch and dinner, find a seat overlooking the award-winning gardens in the restaurant, where a modern Scottish menu of home-grown produce is served on bare wooden tables. ('The food looked good, but we wished the menu had changed during our three-night stay,' a guest said this year.) Never changing: the popularity of afternoon tea on the terrace on a balmy day, with finger sandwiches, sweet cakes and a mini sausage roll or two. 1½ miles W of town. BEDROOMS 24. 5, on ground floor, in gatehouse and lodge, 1 suitable for disabled, plus 3 self-catering cottages in gardens. OPEN All year. FACILITIES Drawing room (open fire), library, bar, restaurant, free Wi-Fi, in-room TV (Freeview), wedding/function facilities,

10-acre grounds. BACKGROUND MUSIC In bar and restaurant. CHILDREN All ages welcomed. DOGS Allowed in some bedrooms. PRICES Per room B&B from £150, D,B&B from £220. À la carte £38.50.

SANQUHAR Dumfries and Galloway
Map 5:E2
BLACKADDIE HOUSE, Blackaddie Road, DG4 6JJ. Tel 01659 50270, www. blackaddiehotel.co.uk. On the banks of the River Nith, near the Southern Upland Way, this restaurant-with-rooms with a 'welcoming atmosphere' and a 'restful ambience' is 'well worth a detour for the food alone'. Chef/patron Ian McAndrew is praised for his 'imaginative yet unpretentious menus' and 'elegant, inspired cooking'; his wife, Jane, runs the 'beautiful' 16th-century stone-built manse with 'care and attention'. Recently refurbished bedrooms now have an up-to-date bathroom with a spa bath and a monsoon shower. Each room is different, so discuss choices when booking – the River Suite (adjacent to the hotel) has magnificent views from a private patio; a small double room was less liked by guests this year. 'Plenty of choice' at a 'well-cooked breakfast'. BEDROOMS 7. Plus two 2-bed self-catering cottages. OPEN All year. FACILITIES Bar, restaurant, breakfast/function room, library, conservatory, free Wi-Fi (can be limited), in-room TV (Freeview), wedding/function facilities, 2-acre grounds, cookery school, fishing, shooting, parking. BACKGROUND MUSIC In public areas. CHILDREN All ages welcomed (over-5s £20 per night). DOGS Allowed in some bedrooms, £10 per night). PRICES Per room B&B from £125,

D,B&B from £245. Set menu £62.50, tasting menu £80.

25% DISCOUNT VOUCHERS

SCOURIE Highland
Map 5:B2
EDDRACHILLES HOTEL, Badcall Bay, Lairg, IV27 4TH. Tel 01971 502080, www.eddrachilles.com. At the head of Badcall Bay, this 18th-century manse is in a 'splendid location' – look through a gap in the trees towards a 'tranquil scene' of fishing boats on the water. Fiona and Richard Trevor, the new owners, are hands-on and motivated – 'just great', says a regular Guide correspondent this year. The Trevors have been refurbishing the old house and replanting the gardens; a 'glorious wood burner-warmed lounge' and 'well-appointed bar' are welcome additions. Arrive at teatime to be welcomed with a hot drink and home-baked cake, then head to one of the modest bedrooms (most look towards the sea). 'Ours was a tad small, but it had all the facilities you could want: sumptuous bedlinens, lovely soaps, a great selection of teas.' Stay in for dinner: chef Per Soderberg's Scottish-Nordic dishes are 'superb'. 'Excellent breakfast – and the coffee was equally good.' 2 miles S of village. BEDROOMS 10. Some suitable for disabled. OPEN Apr–Oct, exclusive use over Christmas and New Year, winter openings by arrangement. FACILITIES Large reception (maps, information), bar/lounge (complimentary afternoon pots of tea or coffee), sun lounge, restaurant, free Wi-Fi in reception, in-room TV (Freeview), 3-acre grounds with seating, laundry service, parking. BACKGROUND MUSIC In public areas. CHILDREN All ages welcomed. DOGS Well-behaved dogs allowed. PRICES Per room B&B single £90–£115, double £125–£150. Set dinner £30–£36, 7-course tasting menu £45.

SLEAT Highland
Map 5:C1
DUISDALE HOUSE, Isle of Skye, IV43 8QW. Tel 01471 833202, www.duisdale.com. Highland heritage is brought well up to date at this stylishly refurbished Victorian hunting lodge on the Isle of Skye. Owners Anne Gracie and Ken Gunn have filled their modern hotel with bold colours and plush fabrics. Sip afternoon tea by the log fire in the lounge or outside on the south-facing deck; take pre-dinner drinks in the Chart Room. In the restaurant, daily-changing modern Scottish menus feature plenty of island produce in season. Bedrooms with views towards mountains or water are all different: some, rather dramatic, have a four-poster bed; others, unfussy, are sleeker. From April to September, book a day of whale spotting on the hotel's luxury yacht. Sister Skye hotels are in Skeabost Bridge and close by on the Sleat peninsula (see main entries). 7 miles from Broadford. BEDROOMS 18. 1 suite in garden annexe, suitable for disabled. OPEN All year. FACILITIES Lounge, bar, restaurant, conservatory, free Wi-Fi, in-room TV (Sky), wedding facilities, 35-acre grounds (10-person garden hot tub), parking. BACKGROUND MUSIC None. CHILDREN All ages welcomed. PRICES Per person B&B £89–£179. Set menu £55, à la carte £33.

SPEAN BRIDGE Highland
Map 5:C2
SMIDDY HOUSE, Roy Bridge Road, nr Fort William, PH34 4EU. Tel 01397

712335, www.smiddyhouse.com. Guests receive 'the warmest of welcomes' from Robert Bryson and Glen Russell at their 'lovely' restaurant-with-rooms on the scenic West Highland rail route. Arrive to afternoon tea in the garden room; in the evening, the welcome turns to sherry and home-made shortbread. 'Very comfortable' bedrooms are 'beautifully decorated', and provided with bottled water, tea- and coffee-making facilities, good toiletries. A 'spacious, comfortable' cottage is suitable for a family: 'It has a nice lounge area and patio.' Dine on fresh shellfish and local, organic produce in the award-winning restaurant; 'excellent' vegetarian options. Good variety at breakfast. 'Robert and Glen had very good advice about the local area.' 9 miles N of Fort William. BEDROOMS 5. 1 suite in adjacent building. OPEN All year except 25–26 Dec, 31 Jan, restricted opening Nov–Mar. FACILITIES Garden room, restaurant (booking essential, open for dinner Thurs–Sun Nov–Mar, Wed–Sun Mar–Apr, Tues–Sun May–Oct), free Wi-Fi, in-room TV (Freeview), golf, mountain bike trails nearby, parking. BACKGROUND MUSIC In restaurant. PRICES Per room B&B £120–£150, D,B&B £185–£390. À la carte £38.50.
25% DISCOUNT VOUCHERS

STIRLING Stirlingshire
Map 5:D2
POWIS HOUSE, FK9 5PS. Tel 01786 460231, www.powishouse.co.uk. Beneath the Ochil hills, Jane and Colin Kilgour's secluded Georgian mansion is approached up a long driveway flanked by trees and fields, ten minutes' drive from the city. The carefully restored home (well documented, too, with records of everyone who has lived in it since it was built in 1746) has polished wood-floored bedrooms made homely with a bowl of fresh fruit and a handmade Harris tweed bed throw. There are board games and DVDs to borrow in the fire-warmed lounge; in the vast grounds, look out for rabbits, squirrels or pheasants taking their morning hop, scamper or stroll. An ample breakfast, served in the sunny dining room, includes eggs from the Kilgours' hens. 3 miles E of town. BEDROOMS 3. OPEN Mar–Christmas. FACILITIES Lounge, dining room, free Wi-Fi, in-room TV (Freeview), terrace, 9-acre garden and grounds (ha-ha, listed shafted stone sundial), parking. BACKGROUND MUSIC None. CHILDREN All ages welcomed (over-2s £10 per night). PRICES Per room B&B £110.

VICTORIA SQUARE, 12 Victoria Square, FK8 2QZ. Tel 01786 473920, www.victoriasquareguesthouse.com. Kari and Phillip Couser's guest house, in the leafy King's Park conservation area, is an easy stroll from many of the city's attractions. The tree-lined neighbourhood is a peaceful retreat from the centre; the wide expanse of the Stirling Golf Club is just up the street. Sip a welcome drink in the 'lovely' double-fronted Victorian house and admire the view over the square through big windows. Tastefully decorated bedrooms are supplied with bathrobes, Scottish toiletries, a hot drinks tray and bottled water; each, too, has space to sit. Breakfast well on a generous buffet; cooked dishes include pancakes with home-made fruit compote, and poached eggs with haggis. ½ mile to city centre and Stirling Castle. BEDROOMS 10. 1 on ground floor. OPEN

All year except Christmas. FACILITIES Lounge, breakfast room, free Wi-Fi, in-room smart TV (Freeview), garden, parking. BACKGROUND MUSIC None. CHILDREN Not under 12. PRICES Per room B&B £70–£140.

TARBERT Argyll and Bute
Map 5:B1

WEST LOCH HOTEL, Campbeltown Road (A83), PA29 6YF. Tel 01880 820283, www.westlochhotel.com. 'Outstanding cooking' and an impressive collection of rare whiskies attract visitors to Andrew and Rosaline Ryan's 'hospitable' small hotel at the top of the Kintyre peninsula. The 18th-century coaching inn overlooks the loch from which it takes its name; many of the simple bedrooms have views across the water. 'Ours, at the front with a road and loch view (and some night-time traffic noise), was small and straightforward, with a comfortable bed and a tiny but clean bathroom. All right for an overnight stop,' report trusted Guide correspondents this year. The decor in the public areas may be 'a step back in time', but the food cooked by chef Ross Payne – 'a fine chef' – is wholly of the moment: langoustines with the 'tastiest' black pudding; 'superlative' sea bass and spicy rice. Close to the ferry dock. 1 mile from village. BEDROOMS 8. OPEN All year. FACILITIES 2 lounges, bar (log fire), restaurant, free Wi-Fi, in-room TV (Freeview), functions, parking. BACKGROUND MUSIC In public areas. CHILDREN All ages welcomed. DOGS Allowed, not in restaurant (£4.50 per night). PRICES Per room B&B single from £59.50, double from £89.50. À la carte £24.

TAYNUILT Argyll and Bute
Map 5:D1

ROINEABHAL COUNTRY HOUSE, Kilchrenan, PA35 1HD. Tel 01866 833207, www.roineabhal.com. In the wild glens of Argyll, Roger and Maria Soep's rustic guest house is a haven for walkers, anglers, birders and stargazers. It is surrounded by peaceful gardens next to a tumbling stream, and little else for miles. Home-away-from-home bedrooms have fresh flowers and shortbread; stunning views from the windows. (Bird books and binoculars are supplied for guests keen on spotting visitors to the bird feeders and fruited shrubs.) A supper platter of smoked fish, venison, cheese and oatcakes, salads, home-made conserves and desserts may be served, by request. In the morning, breakfast heartily on locally smoked kippers, porridge and home-baked bread. Ask the obliging hosts for advice on day trips to Inveraray, Glencoe, Fort William and Kintyre; ferries dock at the nearby port of Oban. BEDROOMS 3. 1 on ground floor, suitable for disabled. OPEN Apr–Nov. FACILITIES Lounge, dining room, free Wi-Fi, in-room TV (Sky, Freeview), covered veranda, 1½-acre garden, bicycle storage. BACKGROUND MUSIC None. CHILDREN All ages welcomed (over-3s half price). DOGS Well-behaved dogs allowed (must have own bedding). PRICES Per room B&B single from £85, double from £120. 2-night min. stay preferred.

TONGUE Highland
Map 5:B2

THE TONGUE HOTEL, IV27 4XD. Tel 01847 611206, www.tonguehotel.co.uk. 'Wonderfully remote', Lorraine and

David Hook's small hotel is in a sleepy village reached via miles of single-track road. The Victorian sporting lodge is in a 'spectacular area' ideal for watching or stalking local fauna. This is a 'homely, characterful' place, with cosy tweeds and tartan fabrics; individually styled bedrooms, each supplied with fruit, sweets and sherry, may have dark, polished furnishings, an original fireplace or a marble washstand. The views are atmospheric: over to the ruins of Castle Varrich, or towards Ben Loyal. Simple Scottish fare is served in the restaurant, beside a warming fire. Breakfast, ordered the night before, has home-made compotes and a hearty porridge. BEDROOMS 19. OPEN All year except Christmas, New Year. FACILITIES Lounge, 2 bars, restaurant (closed Mon, Oct–Mar), free Wi-Fi in public areas, in-room TV (Freeview), civil wedding licence, therapy room, small garden. BACKGROUND MUSIC In public areas. CHILDREN All ages welcomed (6–13s £20). PRICES Per person B&B £45–£65, D,B&B £82–£92.

ULLAPOOL Highland
Map 5:B2

THE SHEILING, Garve Road, IV26 2SX. Tel 01854 612947, www. thesheilingullapool.co.uk. Lesley and Iain MacDonald run their B&B on the outskirts of the village, where the 'spectacular views' stretch over Loch Broom and the mountains beyond. Bedrooms are simple, but well equipped with all the necessities, plus a few extras: tea- and coffee-making facilities, a clock radio, sherry and sweets. On a chilly day, play a board game in the lounge or curl up before the open fire with a book

or magazine off the shelves; in balmy weather, sit in the garden to soak in the vista. Served in a bright, split-level room overlooking the loch, breakfast has smoked fish, and porridge with cream (ordered the night before). 10 mins' walk to town centre; 5 mins' walk to ferry for the Hebrides. BEDROOMS 6. 2 on ground floor. OPEN Easter–end Oct. FACILITIES Sitting room, dining room, Sportsman's Lodge (guest laundry, drying room, sauna, shower), free Wi-Fi, in-room TV (Freeview), 1-acre garden, lochside patio, bicycle storage, fishing permits, parking. BACKGROUND MUSIC None. CHILDREN All ages welcomed (cot with bedding £10 per night). DOGS Allowed in ground-floor rooms, by arrangement (£10 per night). PRICES Per room B&B £85–£90.

WALKERBURN Scottish Borders
Map 5:E2

WINDLESTRAW, Galashiels Road, EH43 6AA. Tel 01896 870636, www. windlestraw.co.uk. In walking country, this Edwardian stone house, originally built for a mill owner's bride, is today a fine small hotel owned by Sylvia and John Matthews. Elegantly updated bedrooms with Tweed valley views are fresh and bright in a modern country style; each is supplied with biscuits, bathrobes, a capsule coffee machine. For a soak of historic proportions, book the room with the original Edwardian bath in the bathroom. An open fire in the sitting room is just right for pre-dinner drinks and home-made canapés; in the wood-panelled dining room, John Matthews's seasonal modern Scottish cooking uses home-grown vegetables from the kitchen garden and restored greenhouse. Ruined abbeys and storeyed mansions are within reach; the Southern Upland Way is barely further afield. BEDROOMS 6. OPEN Mid-Feb–mid-Dec. FACILITIES Bar, lounge, sun room, restaurant, free Wi-Fi in reception, in-room TV, 2-acre garden, parking. BACKGROUND MUSIC None. CHILDREN All ages welcomed, not under 10 in restaurant. DOGS Allowed in bedroom, public rooms, in travel cot while owners dine. PRICES Per room B&B £175–£250, D,B&B £285–£360. À la carte £35, 5-course set menu £55.

WALES

ABERGELE Conwy
Map 3:A3

THE KINMEL ARMS, The Village, St George, LL22 9BP. Tel 01745 832207, www.thekinmelarms.co.uk. Lynn Cunnah-Watson and Tim Watson's handsomely refurbished sandstone inn in the Elwy valley is a 'delightful, relaxed hideaway'. Home-baked cakes and loose-leaf tea are served on charmingly mismatched fine bone china in the tea rooms; in the buzzy bar, choose from a menu of real ales, Welsh ciders and wines. Seasonal brasserie-style lunches and dinners are taken in the well-regarded conservatory restaurant. 'Beautifully appointed bedrooms', with Tim Watson's artwork on the walls, might have a huge slipper bath, a decked balcony or patio. A generous continental breakfast is magicked to the room by the 'Room Fairy' each evening: cereals, pastries and croissants; juices, natural yogurt, home-made chutney and local cheeses and ham in the fridge. Good walks;

golf nearby. BEDROOMS 4. 2 on ground floor. OPEN All year except Christmas, New Year. FACILITIES Bar (wood-burning stove), restaurant (closed Sun, Mon), deli/shop, tea rooms, free Wi-Fi, in-room TV (Freeview), small rear garden, seating area at front, parking. BACKGROUND MUSIC In public areas. CHILDREN Not under 13. PRICES Per room B&B £135–£175, D,B&B from £195.

AMROTH Pembrokeshire
Map 3:D2

MELLIEHA GUEST HOUSE, SA67 8NA. Tel 01834 811581, www.mellieha. co.uk. On the edge of the National Trust's Colby Woodland Garden, outside popular Saundersfoot, Julia and Stuart Adams's peaceful B&B makes a change from the resort town. Their ranch-style house, in a wooded valley close to the sea, is an ideal base for seekers of the quiet life. Sit down to a 'generous welcome' of tea and home-baked cake, then settle in to one of the pretty bedrooms, where wide views cross the garden to the sea. Thoughtful extras include bathrobes, and a torch for dark nights. A Welsh breakfast is replete with laver bread and cockles. Easy access to the beach and the Pembrokeshire Coastal Path; pubs, restaurants and shops are nearby. 2 miles E of Saundersfoot. BEDROOMS 5. OPEN All year except 21 Dec–3 Jan. FACILITIES Lounge (log-burning stove), dining room, free Wi-Fi, in-room TV, 1-acre garden with pond, parking. BACKGROUND MUSIC None. CHILDREN Not under 10. PRICES Per room B&B £80–£103. 2-night min. stay at weekends preferred May–Sept. 25% DISCOUNT VOUCHERS

BALA Gwynedd
Map 3:B3
PALÉ HALL, Palé Estate, Llandderfel, LL23 7PS. Tel 01678 530285, www.palehall.co.uk. On the edge of Snowdonia national park, this historic mansion, lavishly refurbished, is today a sumptuous country house hotel rich in antiques, plush fabrics, fine wood panelling and painted ceilings. (The Biedermeier divans are just right for swooning into.) Spacious bedrooms retain original features such as a marble fireplace, and add modern luxuries: towelling bathrobes, a complimentary decanter of sherry, a gilt-framed mirror that transforms into a television screen. Two suites are in a turret. Under the mentorship of Michelin-recognised chef Michael Caines, Gareth Stevenson cooks seasonal fine-dining menus in the formal restaurant. The pampering extends to the luckiest dogs, who receive food, a comfy dog bed and a doggy robe. 2 miles from town. BEDROOMS 18. OPEN All year. FACILITIES Grand Hall, 2 drawing rooms, library (family games), 3 private dining rooms, free Wi-Fi, in-room TV (Freeview), civil wedding licence, 50-acre grounds (croquet, boules, petting zoo), parking. BACKGROUND MUSIC In public areas. CHILDREN All ages welcomed, not in dining room after 8.30 pm. DOGS Allowed in 5 bedrooms, Grand Hall, library (£25 per dog). PRICES Per room B&B from £190, D,B&B from £310. À la carte £60, 8-course taster menu £85.

CAERNARFON Gwynedd
Map 3:A2
PLAS DINAS COUNTRY HOUSE, Bontnewydd, LL54 7YF. Tel 01286 830214, www.plasdinas.co.uk. Between the mountains and the sea, the former country home of the Armstrong-Jones family is today a luxurious B&B run by 'delightful owners' Neil and Marco Soares-Baines. Vintage and modern pieces mix and mingle in the individually styled bedrooms, each supplied with 'all the things you might have forgotten to pack'. Among the perks: high-end toiletries, up-to-date magazines. Find a spot before a log fire in the drawing room, or take a drink out to the terrace in warm weather. Most evenings, stay in for drinks and nibbles followed by a traditional country-house dinner in the new, elegantly decorated restaurant (wood floors, white tablecloths, gilt-framed portraits). 'Breakfast was great.' 2 miles from Caernarfon. BEDROOMS 10. 1 on ground floor. OPEN All year except Christmas. FACILITIES Drawing room, restaurant (closed Sun, Mon), private dining room, free Wi-Fi, in-room TV (Freeview), civil wedding licence, 15-acre grounds, parking. BACKGROUND MUSIC In drawing room and dining room. CHILDREN Not under 14. DOGS Small, well-behaved dogs allowed in 2 bedrooms, by arrangement (£10 per night). PRICES Per room B&B from £109. 4-course set menu £35. 2-night min. stay at weekends.
25% DISCOUNT VOUCHERS

CARDIFF
Map 3:E4
CATHEDRAL 73, 73 Cathedral Road, CF11 9HE. Tel 02920 235005, www.cathedral73.com. Across the park and the River Taff from Cardiff Castle, the service guests receive at this stylishly refurbished Victorian town house hotel is positively royal: a butler, a

personal chef and a chauffeur-driven vintage Rolls-Royce are at the ready. Choose between a smart bedroom and a sleek, modern apartment with a fully equipped kitchen; wherever you lay your head, the amenities are top of the line: high-quality bedlinen, a smart TV, good toiletries, fresh milk for the tea and coffee tray. Light lunches and afternoon tea with home-made cakes are served in the tea room; in the evening (Thurs–Sat), the space transforms into a cosy wine bar with live piano music. ½ mile from city centre. BEDROOMS 12. 1 on ground floor, suitable for disabled, 3 apartment suites, 2-bed coach house behind the hotel. OPEN All year, minimum housekeeping and no breakfast 25–26 Dec, 1 Jan. FACILITIES Sitting room, bar/tea room, free Wi-Fi, in-room TV (Freeview), civil wedding licence, terrace, limited parking. BACKGROUND MUSIC In public areas. CHILDREN All ages welcomed. DOGS Allowed in ground-floor room. PRICES Per room B&B from £150.

COWBRIDGE Vale of Glamorgan
Map 3:E3

THE BEAR, 63 High Street, CF71 7AF. Tel 01446 774814, www.townandcountrycollective.co.uk/thebear. On the High Street of a fashionable market town in the Vale of Glamorgan, this well-located hotel has been a lively hub for centuries. It was once a stopover for mail coaches running between Swansea and Cardiff; today, it remains popular with locals and tourists who drop in for its real ales, hale-and-hearty pub food and well-appointed bedrooms. Modern rooms vary in size (some suit a family), but all have tea, coffee, Welsh toiletries

and individual charm. Eat wherever you fancy: in the bar, lounge, courtyard or Cellars dining room, there's much choice on the local-produce-packed menu. Buffet breakfasts. BEDROOMS 33. Some suitable for disabled, some in annexe, plus 1- and 2-bed self-catering apartments a short way away. OPEN All year. FACILITIES Lounge, restaurant, grill/bar, free Wi-Fi, in-room TV, wedding/conference facilities, courtyard, parking. BACKGROUND MUSIC In restaurant. CHILDREN All ages welcomed. DOGS Allowed in Stockwood cottage. PRICES Per room B&B from £177. À la carte £30.

EGLWYSFACH Powys
Map 3:C3

YNYSHIR, Eglwysfach, Machynlleth, SY20 8TA. Tel 01654 781209, www.ynyshir.co.uk. In beautiful grounds near the Dyfi estuary, this chic restaurant-with-rooms occupies a 16th-century manor house once owned by Queen Victoria. Owners John and Jennifer Talbot took over the much-loved country house hotel after the death of its matriarch, Joan Reen. Today, it is a dining destination where guests 'murmur in delight' over chef Gareth Ward's 'superlative' Michelin-starred tasting menus. Slow Food–inspired dishes fully embrace the foodie philosophy: in the evening, multi-course dinner menus are served over four hours. Linger, then lay your head in one of the individually styled mountain- or garden-view bedrooms, some seductive, some sleek, some with a soupçon of fun, all cosseting in their own way. BEDROOMS 10. 3 in annexe with wood-burning stove and outdoor seating area. OPEN Tues–Sat all year, 3-night packages

over Christmas, New Year. FACILITIES
Drawing room, bar, restaurant, free
Wi-Fi, in-room TV (Freeview), civil
wedding licence, 14-acre gardens in
1,000-acre bird reserve. BACKGROUND
MUSIC In bar and restaurant. CHILDREN
All ages welcomed, not under 10 in
restaurant in evening. DOGS Allowed
in some bedrooms, not in public rooms
(£25 per night). PRICES Per person B&B
£85–£225, D,B&B £195–£350. Tasting
menu £110.
25% DISCOUNT VOUCHERS

HAY-ON-WYE Powys
Map 3:D4
THE BEAR, 2 Bear Street, HR3 5AN. Tel
01497 821302, www.thebearhay.com.
Bright and bookish, David Gibbon's
urbane B&B embraces the wonky angles
and rough-hewn stone of the 16th-
century coaching house it occupies. In
the heart of a literary town, this is a
chic retreat, with quirky artwork and
modern accessories that complement
old beams and vintage furniture. The
airy bedrooms are comfortably styled; a
supply of home-made biscuits sweetens
the deal. Catch up on reading in the
book-strewn sitting room, where a huge
squashy sofa sits before a wood-fired
stove. In the morning, breakfast on
tasty vegetarian options, home-made
fruit salads and compotes, and locally
baked bread. A wealth of walks and
river-based activities (canoeing, fishing)
are within easy reach. BEDROOMS 3. OPEN
All year except Christmas, New Year.
FACILITIES Sitting/dining room, reading
room, free Wi-Fi, in-room smart TV
(Freeview), walled patio garden, small
car park. BACKGROUND MUSIC None.
PRICES Per room B&B £80–£100. Credit
cards not accepted.

LLANARTHNE Carmarthenshire
Map 3:D2
LLWYN HELYG, SA32 8HJ. Tel 01558
668778, www.llwynhelygcountryhouse.
co.uk. 'Stunning', 'superb', 'absolute
bliss'… Guide readers' praise must be
music to the ears of owners Fiona and
Caron Jones – and these two are big on
music. In 'magnificent countryside', the
'glossy luxury B&B' has an acoustically
designed, vaulted listening room
equipped with a sound system 'that's
the best we've heard since the Royal
Albert Hall'. Settle into one of the
squashy sofas, with tea and shortbread,
to be blown away by the works of the
great composers ('truly amazing').
Upstairs bedrooms have a 'very
comfortable' bed and a 'luxurious'
marble bathroom. Readers write of
the Joneses 'genuine kindness'. 'Caron
recommended a restaurant for dinner,
booked us in, then ferried us to and
fro.' BEDROOMS 3. OPEN All year except
10 days over Christmas. FACILITIES 4
lounges, listening room, breakfast room,
free Wi-Fi, in-room TV (Freeview),
3-acre garden. BACKGROUND MUSIC
None. CHILDREN Not under 16. PRICES
Per room B&B £135–£155.

LLANDUDNO Conwy
Map 3:A3
ESCAPE, 48 Church Walks, LL30 2HL.
Tel 01492 877776, www.escapebandb.
co.uk. Fun, contemporary and cool,
Sam Nayar and Gaenor Loftus's style-
conscious B&B occupies a white-stucco
Victorian villa on the gentle slopes of
the Great Orme in this seaside resort.
Modern and vintage furnishings
and fabrics sit against oak panelling,
stained glass and period fireplaces.
Each bedroom is different – one has a

copper bath, another, a pair of Eames-style swivel chairs in the bay window. Whether decked out in coastal stripes or crystal-encrusted wallpaper, every room has high-end toiletries and up-to-date technology. Comfort reigns: on a stay-in evening, borrow a DVD and curl up under a wool throw or a crocheted granny-square blanket. Generous breakfasts. The beach is within walking distance. BEDROOMS 9. OPEN All year except 18–26 Dec. FACILITIES Lounge (honesty bar), breakfast room, free Wi-Fi, in-room TV, front garden 'of moderate size', limited parking. BACKGROUND MUSIC At breakfast. CHILDREN Not under 10. PRICES Per room B&B £99–£149.

LLANDYRNOG Denbighshire
Map 3:A4
PENTRE MAWR, nr Denbigh, LL16 4LA. Tel 01824 790732, www.pentremawrcountryhouse.co.uk. In parkland, woods and meadows below Offa's Dyke, Bre and Graham Carrington-Sykes cater for all sorts. They run their ancestral country house with a sense of fun, and some unusual touches – 'daft ideas,' the owners say. There's a wide choice of accommodation, each complete with a spa bath: spacious bedrooms in the old farmhouse, done in period style; contemporary cottage suites in the grounds; canvas safari 'lodges' with a sitting room, and a freestanding bath in the bathroom. Bread and cakes are baked daily; on Friday and Saturday evenings, a limited-choice menu (perhaps including salmon pâté, salad; confit duck leg and duck shepherd's pie) is served in the restaurant. The

village and pubs are close by. 3 miles from Denbigh. BEDROOMS 12. 2 cottage suites, 6 safari lodges. OPEN All year except Christmas, New Year. FACILITIES 2 sitting rooms, 2 dining rooms, gallery for parties/functions, free Wi-Fi in main house, in-room TV (Freeview), civil wedding licence, 6-acre grounds (walled garden, small heated outdoor swimming pool), tennis, croquet, golf-buggy lifts for the mobility impaired. BACKGROUND MUSIC Pianola in restaurant. CHILDREN Not under 10. DOGS Allowed. PRICES Per person B&B £90–£120, D,B&B (weekends) £110–£140. 5-course dinner £37.50. 2-night min. stay.

LLANGAFFO Isle of Anglesey
Map 3:A2
THE OUTBUILDINGS, Bodowyr Farmhouse, LL60 6NH. Tel 01248 430132, www.theoutbuildings.co.uk. In sheep-grazed countryside on the Isle of Anglesey, this quirky, 'much-enjoyed' restaurant-with-rooms is in a converted stone-built barn and granary, with glorious views to Snowdonia. Jack Matthews and Millie Mantle manage for Judith 'Bun' Matthews. Cheery modern bedrooms each have a good-humoured name (Pink Spotty Jug, Button's Room) and plenty of serious extras: a hot drinks tray, home-baked treats, a quality music system. No less well equipped, a pink-painted shepherd's hut in the grounds has a wood-burning stove. In good weather, eat lunch outside; evenings, an 'excellent' set menu (discussed with guests in the morning) is cooked using local produce and foraged ingredients. Breakfast is a communal affair. 25 mins' drive to the ferry terminal at Holyhead; Llanddwyn beach is not far. BEDROOMS 5. 1 on ground floor, 1 in garden.

FACILITIES 2 sitting rooms, restaurant with sitting area, free Wi-Fi, in-room TV (Freeview), civil wedding licence, private dining/function facilities, holistic treatments, garden, tennis court (racquets and balls provided), parking. BACKGROUND MUSIC In sitting room and dining room, 'but we're happy to turn it off'. CHILDREN Babes-in-arms and over-12s welcomed. DOGS Small, well-behaved dogs allowed in 1 bedroom (surrounding farmland has livestock). PRICES Per room B&B £90–£110. Set dinner £35.

LLANSTEFFAN Carmarthenshire
Map 3:D2
MANSION HOUSE LLANSTEFFAN, Pantyrathro, nr Carmarthen, SA33 5AJ. Tel 01267 241515, www. mansionhousellansteffan.co.uk. The views stretch over the Tywi estuary and Carmarthen Bay from the well-maintained grounds that surround David and Wendy Beaney's stylish restaurant-with-rooms. Tastefully refurbished, the Georgian mansion retains many original features: a marble-tiled entrance hall, grand staircase, stained glass and ornate plasterwork. Modern, individually styled bedrooms are comfortably plush, and supplied with fluffy bathrobes and Welsh toiletries. Rooms vary in size and shape: two interconnecting ground-floor rooms are suitable for a family; others, under the eaves, are up narrow stairs. In the garden-facing restaurant, chef Paul Owen's contemporary cooking distils the taste of Welsh land and sea in such dishes as line-caught local bass fillet, Tenby asparagus, heritage baby tomatoes, mussels, pesto. 5 miles SW of Carmarthen. BEDROOMS 8. 2 on ground

floor, 1 suitable for disabled. OPEN All year. FACILITIES Large open-plan bar/reception area, lounge, restaurant (closed Sun eve for non-residents, Mon, Nov–Feb), free Wi-Fi, in-room TV (Freeview), civil wedding licence, conference facilities, 5-acre garden, parking. BACKGROUND MUSIC In public areas. CHILDREN All ages welcomed (extra bed £25). DOGS Small dogs allowed in garden room (£25). PRICES Per room B&B from £109, D,B&B from £142. À la carte £40, market menu £13.95–£17.95.
25% DISCOUNT VOUCHERS

LLANWRTYD WELLS Powys
Map 3:D3
LASSWADE COUNTRY HOUSE, Station Road, LD5 4RW. Tel 01591 610515, www.lasswadehotel.co.uk. In an unspoilt setting on the edge of the town, Roger and Emma Stevens fill their traditional restaurant-with-rooms with homely charm. ('Boutique and high luxury we are not,' they say.) There are squashy sofas, books and a log fire in the sitting room; upstairs, bedrooms take in 'superb views' of the Brecon Beacons. In the conservatory dining room, the host's hearty breakfasts and daily-changing dinner menus are 'exceptional'. Helpful and informative, the Stevenses have plenty of advice on exploring old market towns, ruined castles and National Trust country houses in the area. Go green: an electric vehicle charging point is available for guests; incentives are offered to visitors who arrive by public transport. BEDROOMS 8. OPEN All year except Christmas Day. FACILITIES Drawing room, restaurant (booking essential), conservatory, free Wi-Fi, in-room TV

(Freeview), function room, patio, small garden, parking. CHILDREN All ages welcomed, not under 8 in restaurant. DOGS Allowed by arrangement. PRICES Per room B&B £90–£135, D,B&B £160–£230, except during Royal Welsh Show week.

MONTGOMERY Powys
Map 3:C4

THE CHECKERS, Broad Street, SY15 6PN. Tel 01686 669822, www. checkerswales.co.uk. Step through low doorways and along sloping floors at this historic coaching inn on the square, today a 'charming' restaurant-with-rooms in a perfectly preserved mid-Wales town. It is owned by sisters Kathryn and Sarah Francis, and Sarah's husband, Stéphane Borie, a Michelin-starred chef. Refined tasting menus (perhaps including crab-stuffed courgette flower, cauliflower purée, sauce Nantua) are served in the elegant, rustic dining room; vegetarian and pescatarian menus are 'no problem'. Country-style bedrooms are supplied with home-baked biscuits. For breakfast there'll be home-made brioche toast, fresh fruit, yogurts, a full cooked plate with local sausages and bacon. 1 mile from Offa's Dyke; 'epic' walks from the front door. BEDROOMS 5. 1, in annexe, accessed via roof terrace. OPEN All year except Christmas, 2 weeks Jan, 1 week in late summer. FACILITIES Lounge/bar (wood-burning stove), restaurant (closed Sun, Mon), free Wi-Fi, in-room TV, small terrace, cooking masterclasses. BACKGROUND MUSIC None. CHILDREN All ages welcomed, not under 8 in restaurant in evening. PRICES Per room D,B&B from £275. 6-course tasting menu (Tues–Sat) £65.

MUMBLES Swansea
Map 3:E3

PATRICKS WITH ROOMS, 638 Mumbles Road, SA3 4EA. Tel 01792 360199, www.patrickswithrooms.com. 'The cucumber gin and tonic is a triumph' at this long-established, family-friendly restaurant-with-rooms in a pretty village near Swansea – but there's much more besides that receives admiration, including the 'excellent' cooking. The enterprise is run with generosity by two husband-and-wife teams, Sally and Dean Fuller and Catherine and Patrick Walsh ('such friendly people'). Individually decorated bedrooms (some interconnecting) are spread between a converted pub and boathouse. 'Ours was huge and bright, with a colossal shower and a big bath in the spacious bathroom.' At lunch and dinner, sample a 'superb' leek and asparagus soup or 'the best rack of Welsh lamb ever'. Mornings, a 'very good' breakfast has interesting choices: a spicy kedgeree; a full Welsh with cockles and laver bread. BEDROOMS 16. 1 suitable for disabled, 6 in converted boathouse. FACILITIES Lift, lounge/bar, restaurant, free Wi-Fi, in-room TV, civil wedding licence, meeting room, gym, on-street parking (can be difficult at peak times). BACKGROUND MUSIC In public areas. CHILDREN All ages welcomed. PRICES Per room B&B £125–£185. À la carte £30.

NARBERTH Pembrokeshire
Map 3:D2

CANASTON OAKS, Canaston Bridge, SA67 8DE. Tel 01437 541254, www. canastonoaks.co.uk. Five minutes' drive from the likeable market town, this 'very good' B&B has peaceful accommodation and a fine breakfast to fuel exploration in countryside and along the coast. The Pembrokeshire longhouse is owned and run by attentive hosts Eleanor and David Lewis and their daughter, Emma Millership. Bedrooms in converted barns each have their own entrance; within, thoughtful extras are provided: dressing gowns, candles, a fridge with milk and water. Three first-floor rooms in a lodge have lake views; a suite of interconnecting rooms with a terrace overlooking vast countryside is ideal for a family. Plentiful choice at breakfast, including smoked haddock fishcakes and Welsh cheese omelettes. 2 miles W of Narberth. BEDROOMS 10. 3 in lodge, 2 suitable for disabled, plus 1-bed self-catering apartment. OPEN All year. FACILITIES Lounge, dining rooms, free Wi-Fi, in-room TV (Freeview), 1-acre grounds, parking. BACKGROUND MUSIC None. CHILDREN All ages welcomed. PRICES Per room B&B £95–£170.

NEWTOWN Powys
Map 3:C4
THE FOREST COUNTRY GUEST HOUSE, Gilfach Lane, Kerry, SY16 4DW. Tel 01686 621821, www. bedandbreakfastnewtown.co.uk. This family-friendly B&B in undulating countryside has plenty to raise a smile. Owners Paul and Michelle Martin have filled their traditional Victorian country house with books, maps and games, plus an antique Bechstein grand piano, and a suit of armour with a sword that children are allowed to brandish. Up the 19th-century oak staircase, bedrooms may be old fashioned, but they're peaceful, and have lovely views over the large garden – look out for the herd of rare-breed

sheep just beyond. A kitchenette is useful for DIY meals and snacks; in the morning, organic breakfasts use eggs from the Martins' free-range hens. 1 mile from Kerry village; 3 miles SE of Newtown. BEDROOMS 5. Plus 4 self-catering cottages. OPEN All year except Christmas, New Year; self-catering cottages open all year. FACILITIES Sitting room, dining room, kitchenette, games room (toy box), free Wi-Fi, in-room TV (Freeview), 4-acre garden, play area (swings, house, timber fort), tennis court, parking, secure bicycle storage. BACKGROUND MUSIC None. CHILDREN All ages welcomed (over-2s £15). DOGS Allowed in kennels in the grounds, and in cottages. PRICES Per room B&B £80–£115.

PORTMEIRION Gwynedd
Map 3:B3
HOTEL PORTMEIRION, Minffordd, Penrhyndeudraeth, LL48 6ER. Tel 01766 770000, www.portmeirion-village. com. Built over 50 years, from 1925, by Sir Bertram Clough Williams-Ellis, Portmeirion, the Italianate village, grew up behind this Victorian mansion, now a hotel that 'combines old-world touches with stylish modernity'. Choose between traditionally decorated bedrooms in the main hotel; contemporary rooms with views of estuary, countryside and gardens in Castell Deudraeth; and brightly coloured village buildings inspired by the architecture of the Italian Riviera. For meals there is the informal brasserie, or the curvilinear Art Deco hotel dining room for modern cooking ('very good, but rather elaborately presented,' said a guest this year). Go exploring: there's a shell grotto, a bell tower, a dog cemetery, a

pantiled temple and more besides.
2 miles SE of Porthmadog. BEDROOMS
57. 14 in hotel, some on ground floor,
1 suitable for disabled, 11 in Castell
Deudraeth, 32 in village. FACILITIES Lift,
3 lounges, bar, restaurant, brasserie in
Castell, free Wi-Fi, in-room TV, civil
wedding licence, function facilities,
beauty salon, 170-acre grounds, heated
swimming pool (May–Sept). CHILDREN
All ages welcomed. PRICES Per room
B&B from £154, D,B&B from £219. Set
menu (restaurant) £40–£55, à la carte
£50. 2-night min. stay preferred.

ST DAVID'S Pembrokeshire
Map 3:D1
CRUG-GLÂS, Abereiddy, Haverfordwest,
SA62 6XX. Tel 01348 831302, www.
crug-glas.co.uk. Laid-back and rustic,
the Evans family's restaurant-with-
rooms stands in the midst of north
Pembrokeshire farmland. The Georgian
house is a family home, filled with
photographs and inherited artefacts –
the honesty bar occupies a handsome,
generations-old dresser. Spread across
the main building, a converted milk
parlour and a coach house, country
cottage bedrooms differ in size and style:
one has a king-size four-poster bed and
a double-ended copper bath; another,
with a Victorian-style bathroom, has a
separate sitting room. In the evening,
Janet Evans's praiseworthy home-
cooked dinners include such dishes as
twice-cooked Caerfai cheese soufflé,
roasted mushrooms. An 'excellent
breakfast' has a 'superb selection' of
cooked dishes. The coast is close.
3½ miles NE of St David's. BEDROOMS
7. 2 in outbuildings, 1 on ground
floor. OPEN All year except 24–26 Dec.
FACILITIES Drawing room, dining room,

free Wi-Fi, in-room TV (Freeview),
civil wedding licence, 1-acre garden
on 600-acre farm. BACKGROUND MUSIC
Classical. CHILDREN Not under 12.
PRICES Per room B&B £150–£190.
À la carte £35.

CHANNEL ISLANDS

ST BRELADE Jersey
Map 1: inset E6
LA HAULE MANOR, La Neuve Route,
JE3 8BS. Tel 01534 741426, www.
lahaulemanor.com. Something of the
French country abode characterises
this Georgian manor house across the
road from St Aubin's Bay – starting
from the complimentary glass of
bubbly offered on arrival. It is run
by Ola Przyjemska with 'helpful and
efficient' staff. The high-ceilinged
sitting room has chandeliers and ornate
furnishings; B&B accommodation is in
traditionally decorated bedrooms, each
different, some with a wide view over
the water. In sunshine, find a lounger
under a parasol by the swimming pool.
Sandwiches and drinks are available
all day in the bar. No dinner is served,
but free transport can be arranged to
the restaurant at sister hotel La Place;
other eateries are a short walk away.
10 mins' drive from the airport;
complimentary transfers from airport
and harbour. BEDROOMS 16. Some
on ground floor, plus 2 self-catering
apartments. FACILITIES Sitting room, bar,
TV room, breakfast room, free Wi-Fi,
in-room TV (Freeview), terrace, garden,
15-metre outdoor swimming pool
(heated Apr–Oct), hot tub, parking.
CHILDREN All ages welcomed (3–11s
£30 per night). PRICES Per room B&B
£98–£217.

ST MARTIN Guernsey
Map 1: inset E5
BELLA LUCE HOTEL, La Fosse, GY4 6EB. Tel 01481 238764, www.bellalucehotel.com. The 'delightful staff', 'comfortable bedrooms' and 'outstanding food' draw visitors to this luxury small hotel, in an extended Norman manor house above Moulin Huet bay. In an area that inspired Renoir's Guernsey paintings, the house has been handsomely restored by its owners, the Wheadon family. Tastefully decorated bedrooms might have a modern four-poster bed; spacious loft and garden suites have a separate lounge area. Candles are lit in the garden-facing restaurant at dinner; Simon McKenzie cooks modern European dishes with much fresh seafood. 'The chef is a man of genius,' said a Guide reader this year. ('The muzak was a real shame, however.') Evenings, linger over small-batch gin traditionally distilled in the atmospheric cellar bar. A rock beach is five mins' walk away. 2 miles from St Peter Port and airport. BEDROOMS 23. 2 on ground floor. OPEN All year except Jan. FACILITIES Snug, bar, restaurant, cellar lounge (tasting room), free Wi-Fi, in-room TV (Freeview), civil wedding licence, function facilities, 2-acre garden, courtyard, outdoor swimming pool (loungers, sofas), spa, parking. BACKGROUND MUSIC In public areas. CHILDREN All ages welcomed. PRICES Per room B&B from £124.

ST PETER PORT Guernsey
Map 1: inset E5
LA COLLINETTE HOTEL, St Jacques, GY1 1SN. Tel 01481 710331, www.lacollinette.com. There's a friendly atmosphere at this white-painted Georgian mansion, its window boxes lushly green. A relaxed, unpretentious place not far from the waterfront, the hotel has been owned by the Chambers family for more than 50 years. Cyril Fortier is the long-serving manager. Overlooking the gardens and grounds, bedrooms are supplied with coffee, teas and biscuits; bottled water and fruit are available on request. At lunch and dinner, a straightforward menu (prawn cocktail; seafood linguine; grilled steak and chips) is served in the informal restaurant. Lounge by the swimming pool or go exploring – Candie Gardens, nearby, leads to cobbled streets, shops and the harbour. Island-hop to Sark and Herm from the pretty port. 1 mile W of town centre. BEDROOMS 22. Some suitable for disabled, plus 15 self-catering cottages and apartments. OPEN All year. FACILITIES Lounge, bar, restaurant, free Wi-Fi, in-room TV (Sky, Freeview), 2-acre garden, heated outdoor swimming pool, gym, massages. BACKGROUND MUSIC In bar and restaurant. CHILDREN All ages welcomed (baby-listening, children's pool, play area). PRICES Per person B&B from £60. À la carte £20.
25% DISCOUNT VOUCHERS

THE DUKE OF RICHMOND, Cambridge Park, GY1 1UY. Tel 01481 726221, www.dukeofrichmond.com. The gleaming black-and-white reception hall of this refined hotel (Red Carnation Hotels) makes a striking sight, but there's more to draw guests' attention – not least the spread of complimentary fruit, sweets and freshly baked treats that appears throughout the day. The 19th-century building is an easy stroll to the harbour; immaculate bedrooms, some modern, others elegantly traditional, have views over the town towards the sea. Freshly caught local seafood features on the menu and daily specials board in the restaurant. In good weather, find a seat on the terrace and take in the vista over Victorian Candie Gardens, the sea and the islands beyond. BEDROOMS 73. FACILITIES Lounge, bar, restaurant, free Wi-Fi, in-room TV, room service, wedding/function facilities, terrace, heated outdoor swimming pool. CHILDREN All ages welcomed (games, toys, DVDs). DOGS Allowed in 2 bedrooms, not in restaurant. PRICES Per room B&B from £159.

IRELAND

BALLINTOY Co. Antrim
Map 6:A6
WHITEPARK HOUSE, 150 Whitepark Road, nr Ballycastle, BT54 6NH. Tel 028 2073 1482, www.whiteparkhouse.com. Bob Isles's 'exemplary' B&B stands above the sandy beach of Whitepark Bay. A traveller himself, he has filled his crenellated 18th-century house with art, artefacts and souvenirs from his adventures in Asia and Africa. The collection provides a feast for the eyes in the 'delightful' lounge, where afternoon tea, with home-baked biscuits, may be taken. Spacious, traditionally decorated bedrooms – 'ours was more like a suite,' a Guide reader reports – have many nice touches: fluffy bathrobes, a hot-water bottle, 'a face cloth tied with a red ribbon'; sea or garden views. The host has plenty of advice on restaurants and places to visit. Full Irish breakfasts (vegetarians catered for). 5 miles E of Bushmills. BEDROOMS 4. OPEN Mar–Nov.

FACILITIES Sitting room (peat fire), conservatory, free Wi-Fi, 1-acre garden. BACKGROUND MUSIC None. CHILDREN Not under 10 (must be able to take separate room). PRICES Per room B&B single £80, double £130.

BALLYGALLY Co. Antrim
Map 6:B6
BALLYGALLY CASTLE, Coast Road, BT40 2QZ. Tel 028 2858 1066, www.hastingshotels.com/ballygally-castle. On the scenic Antrim Coast Road, this 'excellently located' hotel, in a 17th-century castle, is set in 'well-kept grounds' overlooking the beach. It is part of the Hastings Hotels group. Each room in the extended building is different: some are shaped by the castle's original architecture, others are more modern, but all are well equipped, down to the rubber duck in the bathroom. Many, too, have broad views across the water all the way to Scotland. (And one, in the tower, has a ghost.) Classic Irish dishes are served in the restaurant. Mornings, take breakfast in a 'pretty, well-lit' room with a view of the grounds. 10 mins' drive from the Larne ferry terminal. BEDROOMS 54. Some suitable for disabled. OPEN All year. FACILITIES Lounge, bar, restaurant, free Wi-Fi, in-room TV (Freeview), wedding/function facilities, 1½-acre walled gardens with stream. BACKGROUND MUSIC None. CHILDREN All ages welcomed (charge for over-4s). PRICES Per person B&B from £60, D,B&B from £80. À la carte £28.

BALLYLICKEY Co. Cork
Map 6:D4
SEAVIEW HOUSE. Tel 00 353 27 50073, www.seaviewhousehotel.com. A

'country way of life' is preserved at this traditional hotel on the edge of a village on the west Cork coast. Kathleen O'Sullivan, who welcomed newcomers and regular returnees for many years, has now retired; her nephew, Ronan O'Sullivan, has taken over stewardship of this popular place. In private grounds overlooking Bantry Bay, the house is filled with family heirlooms, ornaments and objets d'art; there are books to borrow in the cosy library. Tea can be taken in the garden on a sunny day. Bedrooms of various sizes have fine furniture and art on the walls. When cool evenings draw in, gather for an aperitif by the fire in the lounge before sitting down to a dinner of home-cooked country food, served in the garden-facing restaurant. 4 km N of Bantry town. BEDROOMS 25. 2 on ground floor, suitable for disabled. OPEN Mid-Mar–mid-Nov. FACILITIES Bar/lounge, residents' lounge, library, restaurant, free Wi-Fi in reception, in-room TV (Ericom), wedding facilities, 4-acre garden, parking. BACKGROUND MUSIC None. CHILDREN All ages welcomed. DOGS Allowed in bedrooms, not in public rooms. PRICES Per room B&B €140, D,B&B €240.

BELFAST
Map 6:B6

THE OLD RECTORY, 148 Malone Road, BT9 5LH. Tel 028 9066 7882, www.anoldrectory.co.uk. In a well-maintained Victorian villa in a leafy residential suburb, Mary Callan's homely guest house is a good-value base for the city centre and university. There are books and board games in the drawing room; a complimentary hot whiskey warms the cockles on cool

days. Bedrooms (some with views of the Belfast mountains) are supplied with biscuits and reading material. In the morning, wake to an award-winning feast, with home-made raspberry jam, and home-baked soda and wheaten breads. Hot choices include a full Ulster, a veggie fry-up, and porridge with a dash of whiskey. A small supper menu is available Mon–Fri (£20). 1¾ miles to city centre; regular buses stop opposite. 10 mins' walk to Lagan Meadows (river walks). BEDROOMS 6. 1 on ground floor. OPEN All year except Christmas, New Year, 2 weeks mid-July. FACILITIES Drawing room, dining room, free Wi-Fi, in-room TV, garden, parking. BACKGROUND MUSIC 'Quiet' at breakfast. CHILDREN All ages welcomed. PRICES Per room B&B single from £52, double from £80. 2-night min. stay May–Sept. Credit cards not accepted.

RAVENHILL HOUSE, 690 Ravenhill Road, BT6 0BZ. Tel 028 9020 7444, www.ravenhillhouse.com. Within easy access of the centre, Olive and Roger Nicholson's restored Victorian house is close to popular neighbourhood restaurants, independent shops and a park. The red-brick house is set back from the road in a residential area. Tea and oven-fresh treats greet arriving B&B guests. Pretty bedrooms have two armchairs and a writing desk, plus some lovely touches: home-baked shortbread; a vintage Hacker radio. Lie in at the weekend, when breakfast is served till 10 am. The generous buffet has home-made marmalades and jellies, spiced fruit compote, freshly baked banana bread; cooked dishes include good vegetarian options. 2 miles S of the

city. BEDROOMS 4. OPEN Feb–mid-Dec.
FACILITIES Sitting room, dining room,
free Wi-Fi, in-room TV (Freeview),
small garden, parking. BACKGROUND
MUSIC Radio 3 at breakfast. CHILDREN
Not under 12. PRICES Per room B&B
£95–£130. 2-night min. stay preferred on
busy weekends.

BUSHMILLS Co. Antrim
Map 6:A6
BUSHMILLS INN, 9 Dunluce Road,
BT57 8QG. Tel 028 2073 3000, www.
bushmillsinn.com. The turf fire is
always lit at this friendly old coaching
inn, in a village on the Causeway
Coastal Route. Come in to a characterful
jumble of ancient wooden booths,
interconnecting snugs and a 'secret'
library. On the banks of the River
Bush, spacious bedrooms in the mill
house each have their own sitting
area. Split-level suites are ideal for a
family. Whiskey cocktails and Irish
music seem made for each other in
the gaslight-lit bar. In the restaurant,
modern Irish dishes include fish caught
in local waters – perhaps Greencastle sea
trout, buttered leeks, broccoli, shellfish
velouté. Plan days out and in using
well-thought-out top-10 lists ('10 things
to do when it's raining', '…without
a car', '…as a family', etc). 2 miles
from the Giant's Causeway. BEDROOMS
41. Some on ground floor, some
suitable for disabled. OPEN All year, no
accommodation 24–25 Dec. FACILITIES
Lift, lounge, restaurant, bar, gallery,
oak-beamed loft, free Wi-Fi, in-room
TV, conference facilities, treatment
room, 30-seat cinema, patio, 2-acre
garden, parking. BACKGROUND MUSIC In
public areas, live traditional Irish music
sessions every Sat in bar. CHILDREN All

ages welcomed. PRICES Per room B&B
£120–£210. À la carte £40.

CALLAN Co. Kilkenny
Map 6:D5
BALLAGHTOBIN COUNTRY HOUSE,
Ballaghtobin. Tel 00 353 56 772 5227,
www.ballaghtobin.com. Laid-back
and low-key, this rural B&B occupies
an 18th-century farmhouse that 14
generations of the Gabbett family have
called home. Catherine and Mickey
Gabbett are the warm, easy-going
owners. The house stands in 'informal
gardens' within 450 acres of woodland
and working farmland. (Wood chips
from their Christmas tree crop power
the boiler for heating and hot water.)
Sleep well in one of the country-style
bedrooms, surrounded by paintings
and antiques passed down through
the generations. The Barrack Room,
'where drunken visitors were once
sent to sleep', accommodates four.
Gather for a generous breakfast in the
morning, served at a large table in the
dining room. A fine base for touring
the Kilkenny area. 4 km E of Callan.
BEDROOMS 3. OPEN Mar–Oct. FACILITIES
Drawing room, dining room, study,
conservatory, free Wi-Fi, garden, tennis,
croquet, clock golf, parking. CHILDREN
All ages welcomed. DOGS Allowed.
PRICES Per person B&B €50 (based on
2 people sharing). Credit cards not
accepted.

CARLINGFORD Co. Louth
Map 6:B6
GHAN HOUSE. Tel 00 353 42 937 3682,
www.ghanhouse.com. In large gardens,
behind lovely old stone walls, this
pretty Georgian house – with its family
photographs, squashy sofas, antique

French beds and claw-footed baths – is steps from medieval Carlingford's old town gate. It has been in the Carroll family for 27 years. Paul Carroll now runs the hotel; his mother, Joyce, tends the herb garden and fills the rooms with freshly cut flowers. Spread across the main house and a garden annexe, traditionally decorated bedrooms have views of Carlingford Lough or the mountains beyond. In the drawing room or 'elegant' dining room, 'excellent' dinner menus include mountain-reared meat, lough shellfish and home-grown produce. At breakfast: Cooley sausages, Irish cheeses, home-made jams and marmalades. The house recipe for molasses soda bread is readily shared. A popular venue for weddings and private parties. BEDROOMS 12. 8 in annexe. OPEN All year except 24–26 Dec, 31 Dec, 1 Jan. FACILITIES Bar, lounge, restaurant (pre-booking advised), 2 private dining rooms, free Wi-Fi, in-room TV (Freeview), wedding facilities, 3-acre garden, parking, charging point for electric cars. CHILDREN All ages welcomed. DOGS Allowed in kennels in stables. PRICES Per room B&B from €80, D,B&B from €120. 4-course menu €45, 6-course midweek tasting menu €38.

CLIFDEN Co. Galway
Map 6:C4

BLUE QUAY ROOMS, Seaview. Tel 00 353 095 21369, www.bluequayrooms.com. Painted an unmissable blue, Paddy and Julia Foyle's new Connemara venture is this playfully styled, good-value option, minutes from the town centre. Managed by Toby, the Foyles' son, the B&B is sister to The Quay House on the harbour (see main entry). The 200-year-old building has been brought up to date with eclectic decor: white-painted antlers hang on the wall across from gilt-framed portraits and unusual mirrors; bold black-and-white flooring lies beneath a ceiling of blue. All but one of the pretty, modern bedrooms has a view of the harbour. In the morning, the host cooks an imaginative, well-prepared breakfast. An ideal base for walkers and cyclists. BEDROOMS 8. Plus 2-bed self-catering apartment. OPEN Apr–Oct. FACILITIES Sitting area (wood-burning stove), breakfast room, free Wi-Fi, in-room TV, garden. BACKGROUND MUSIC None. CHILDREN Not under 12. PRICES Per room B&B (light breakfast) €80.

COBH Co. Cork
Map 6:D5

KNOCKEVEN HOUSE, Rushbrooke. Tel 00 353 21 481 1778, www.knockevenhouse. com. On the outskirts of a historic seaport town, Pam Mulhaire's friendly B&B, in a double-fronted Victorian house, stands in a garden with cheerful displays of magnolias, azaleas and camellias in spring. Guests are welcomed with hot drinks and home-baked scones in the traditionally furnished drawing room, where a fire is lit in cool weather. Spacious, high-ceilinged bedrooms are fittingly furnished with period pieces, and provided with terry cloth robes and high-end toiletries. Mornings start at a shared mahogany table with a generous breakfast including seasonal fruits, preserves and home-baked brown bread. Helpful and informative, the hostess has plenty of advice on exploring the town and surrounds. 1 mile W of town; 3 mins' drive from Rushbrooke

railway station. BEDROOMS 5. OPEN
All year except Christmas. FACILITIES
Drawing room, dining room, free
Wi-Fi, in-room TV, 2-acre grounds.
BACKGROUND MUSIC At breakfast.
CHILDREN All ages welcomed. PRICES Per
room B&B single €90, double €120.

COLLON Co. Louth
Map 6:C6

COLLON HOUSE, Ardee Street, A92
YT29. Tel 00 353 87 235 5645, www.
collonhouse.com. 'A fascinating
historical experience.' Michael
McMahon and John Bentley-Dunn's
authentically restored and painstakingly
maintained house in the Boyne valley
'exudes class from bedroom to table'.
Built in 1740, it was once the home of
John Foster, the last Speaker of the Irish
House of Commons. There's exploration
to be done inside and out: the house is
filled with period-appropriate antiques,
paintings and furnishings; the enclosed
gardens, with an intricate sunken box
parterre and Greek-style summerhouse,
are surrounded by mature trees, shrubs
and a ten-foot laurel hedge. Toast the
past in a former ballroom, then dine
'sumptuously' in the panelled dining
room (dinners by arrangement for
groups of six or more). Later, retire to
one of the well-dressed bedrooms, each
equipped with modern comforts and a
subtly disguised bathroom. BEDROOMS
4. Plus 2-room suite in adjacent mews
house. OPEN New Year, Feb–Dec.
FACILITIES 2 reception rooms, dining
room, free Wi-Fi, TV in mews house,
¾-acre garden. BACKGROUND MUSIC
None. CHILDREN Not under 14. PRICES
Per room B&B €160, D,B&B €215. Set
dinner €55. Credit cards not accepted.
25% DISCOUNT VOUCHERS

DONEGAL TOWN Co. Donegal
Map 6:B5

HARVEY'S POINT, Lough Eske. Tel 00
353 74 972 2208, www.harveypoint.
com. Between Lough Eske and the
foothills of the Blue Stack mountains,
Deirdre McGlone and Marc Gysling's
traditional hotel is run with heart. Its
fans love the old-fashioned care and
attention to detail – plus the rare Irish
whiskeys ready for sipping by a peat fire.
Spacious bedrooms are stocked daily
with fresh milk, fruit and biscuits; each
lakeshore suite has its own entrance and
a lough-facing terrace. In the restaurant
overlooking the water, modern Irish
dishes might include smoked lamb
loin, confit shoulder, wild garlic, white
asparagus, anchovy. Breakfast has
buttermilk pancakes, Donegal bacon, a
daily fish special. There's much to do:
active pursuits (archery, canoeing, golf),
leisurely walking routes, loughside
picnics. 4 miles from town. BEDROOMS
64. Some suitable for disabled, plus 13
in Lodge for group bookings. FACILITIES
Lift, drawing room, bar, restaurant
(cabaret dinners June–Oct, closed Mon,
Tues Nov–Mar), ballroom, free Wi-Fi,
in-room TV (Sky), wedding/conference
facilities, 20-acre grounds, stabling and
grazing for visiting horses. BACKGROUND
MUSIC Resident pianist, Irish/classical
music in ballroom. CHILDREN All ages
welcomed. DOGS Allowed. PRICES Per
room B&B from €199. Set dinner €55,
tasting menu €65. 2-night min. stay at
weekends.

DUBLIN
Map 6:C6

ARIEL HOUSE, 50–54 Lansdowne Road,
Ballsbridge. Tel 00 353 1 668 5512,
www.ariel-house.net. The 'helpful

staff' encourage the home-away-from-home feeling at Jennie McKeown's 'warmly welcoming' guest house near Ballsbridge village. 'Our friends arrived in the morning, after an overnight flight from the States. Cecilia, one of the reception staff, fed them breakfast and invited them to check into their room as soon as it was ready,' reports a Guide reader this year. Up the external stone staircase, the three sympathetically restored Victorian town houses retain plenty of original features; the best bedrooms are particularly handsomely furnished with antiques. Join fellow guests around the grand piano in the 'comfortable lounge' for complimentary afternoon tea. In the morning, an 'excellent breakfast' includes 'divine pancakes'; 'perfectly poached eggs'. 2 km from the city centre. BEDROOMS 37. 8 in mews. OPEN All year except 2 weeks over Christmas and New Year. FACILITIES Drawing room, dining room, free Wi-Fi, in-room TV, front and back garden, limited parking. BACKGROUND MUSIC At breakfast. CHILDREN All ages welcomed. PRICES Per room B&B from €99.

NUMBER 31, 31 Leeson Close. Tel 00 3531 676 5011, www.number31.ie. Close to St Stephen's Green, this style-conscious B&B occupies two buildings, linked by an orderly town house garden, in a quiet city-centre location. It is owned by Noel Comer. Enter via the Sam Stephenson-designed mews house: its sunken lounge, centred on an open fireplace, is stocked with guides and contemporary literature. Modern bedrooms here and in the Georgian house across the garden have crisp bedlinen and comfy seating. Discuss

room choices before booking: those in the terraced house tend to be quieter and larger (good family options). A generous organic breakfast is taken communally in the mews building: fresh fruits, home-made granola, a famed cranberry-walnut loaf, a full Irish. Sit outdoors on fine-weather days. BEDROOMS 21. 15 in terraced house. OPEN All year. FACILITIES Sitting room, breakfast room, free Wi-Fi, in-room TV, courtyard garden. BACKGROUND MUSIC None. CHILDREN All ages welcomed. PRICES Per person B&B from €95.

WATERLOO HOUSE, 8–10 Waterloo Road, Ballsbridge. Tel 00 353 1 660 1888, www.waterloohouse.ie. Two 'elegant houses' with twin red doors make one 'usefully located' B&B within walking distance of St Stephen's Green and many of the city's landmarks. Evelyn Corcoran is the 'high-profile and very helpful' owner. Traditionally furnished bedrooms (some compact) have 'everything one might require'. 'My room faced the street, but noise was not a problem.' Mornings begin with an 'extensive breakfast', served in the dining room or the adjoining conservatory: perhaps cold cuts, an omelette, a full Irish breakfast or 'catch of the day'; the muesli and Irish soda bread are home made. The hostess has plenty of local recommendations. A computer is available for guest use. 1 mile from city centre. BEDROOMS 19. Some suitable for disabled. OPEN All year. FACILITIES Lift, lounge, dining room, conservatory, free Wi-Fi, in-room TV, garden, parking. BACKGROUND MUSIC All day in lounge, at breakfast in eating areas. CHILDREN All ages

welcomed. PRICES Per room B&B
€99–€199. 2-night min. stay preferred on
peak weekends.

DUNFANAGHY Co. Donegal
Map 6:A5

THE MILL, Figart. Tel 00 353 74 913
6985, www.themillrestaurant.com.
Susan and Derek Alcorn's friendly
restaurant-with-rooms occupies a
19th-century flax mill in a small resort
town on the Wild Atlantic Way. Guide
readers this year thought it 'exceptional'.
'The food is delicious, the rooms are
modern and comfortable, and the
staff are genial and well presented.
The kitchen readily catered for a food
allergy – "not a problem," they said.'
The popular restaurant ('well supported
by the community') serves seasonal
fare with an emphasis on local seafood;
a range of local craft beers is good
accompaniment. Homely bedrooms,
including a spacious suite, have 'all
the accoutrements one needs', plus
home-baked oatmeal cookies. 'Excellent
breakfasts.' ½ mile W of town.
BEDROOMS 7. OPEN Mid-Mar–mid-Dec.
FACILITIES Drawing room, restaurant
(closed Mon all year, various other times
throughout the year, booking advisable),
conservatory, free Wi-Fi, in-room TV,
garden. BACKGROUND MUSIC In public
areas. CHILDREN All ages welcomed.
PRICES Per person B&B €50–€75.

GALWAY Co. Galway
Map 6:C5

THE G HOTEL, Old Dublin Road. Tel
00 353 91 865200, www.theghotel.ie.
Milliner extraordinaire Philip Treacy,
a son of Galway, designed this modern
hotel with more than a touch of
glamour. (It's a feather in the cap of the
Edward Hotels group.) Vibrant public
spaces mix antique and contemporary
furniture; there are prints, interesting
ceramics, a mirrored wall, a dramatic
light installation. Bedrooms are
soothing: styled in oyster shades (a nod
to the city's maritime heritage), they
have pleasing views over the city or
the hotel's bamboo terrace; some suit
a family. Dine on European-inspired
dishes and Irish steaks in the velvety
restaurant; lighter menus and afternoon
tea are served in the lounges. The city
centre and airport are within easy
reach. BEDROOMS 101. Some suitable for
disabled. OPEN All year except 23–26
Dec. FACILITIES Lift, 3 lounges, cocktail
bar, restaurant, free Wi-Fi, in-room
smart TV (Sky), wedding/function
facilities, spa (hydro pool, sauna, steam
room, treatments), indoor swimming
pool, gym, bamboo 'Zen' garden,
parking. BACKGROUND MUSIC In public
areas. CHILDREN All ages welcomed
(milk and cookies on arrival, DVDs,
babysitting). PRICES Per room B&B from
€135, D,B&B from €175. À la carte €43.

GLASHABEG Co. Kerry
Map 6:D4

GORMAN'S CLIFFTOP HOUSE, Ballydavid.
Tel 00 353 66 915 5162, www.
gormans-clifftophouse.com. 'The
warm hospitality of this family-run
outfit made this one of our favourite
places on an Irish tour,' reports a
regular Guide correspondent this year.
Sheelagh and Vincent Ó Gormáin
– 'fantastic, informative hosts' – are
the seventh generation to live in
this 'wonderful spot' on the Dingle
peninsula. Their 'great-value' guest
house is an unpretentious place where
guests can count on 'excellent service',

'commendable meals' and 'beautiful views' of the sea. Homely bedrooms have a selection of local-interest books, and views over mountains or water. (Rooms on the top floor may be under a sloping ceiling.) In the evening, the host's home-cooked dinners (for residents only) may include just-landed fish and garden-fresh produce ('great vegetarian choices, too'). 'Generous breakfasts.' 12½ km W of Dingle. BEDROOMS 8. OPEN Mar–Oct. FACILITIES Lounge, library, dining room (closed Sun, light meals available for residents), free Wi-Fi, in-room TV, 3-acre grounds. BACKGROUND MUSIC Irish or classical music in reception and dining room. CHILDREN All ages welcomed. PRICES Per room B&B from €150, D,B&B from €220.

INIS MEÁIN Co. Galway
Map 6:C4

INIS MEÁIN RESTAURANT AND SUITES, Aran Islands. Tel 00 353 86 826 6026, www.inismeain.com. On the most remote of the Aran Islands, a stronghold of Irish culture, Ruairí and Marie-Thérèse de Blacam's sustainably run stone-and-glass restaurant-with-suites blends into the landscape, revealing 'stunning views' to Galway Bay and the Connemara mountains. A stay here is as much about the keenly considered meals – cooked using ingredients from the island and surrounding waters – as it is an appreciation of the extraordinary setting. Design-led bedrooms have panoramic views from vast windows, and a private outdoor seating area. Guests are encouraged to explore: the room rate includes walking sticks, bicycles, a fishing rod, swimming towels, wildlife binoculars, nature guides and maps, and a daily hotpot lunch in a backpack. A breakfast box delivered to the door includes a sweet for elevenses. 45-min. ferry from Ros a' Mhíl; 7-min. flight from Connemara airport. BEDROOMS 5 suites. OPEN Apr–Sept. FACILITIES Restaurant (dinner served at 8 pm; closed Sun nights), free Wi-Fi, 3-acre grounds. PRICES Per suite B&B from €265. Set dinner €70. 2-night min. stay.

KANTURK Co. Cork
Map 6:D5

GLENLOHANE HOUSE. Tel 00 353 29 50014, www.glenlohane.com. The Sharp Bolster family invite visitors to stay 'as if with friends' at their ivy-draped Georgian country house in the Blackwater valley. The house is surrounded by acres of landscaped gardens, meadows and fields; within, rooms brim with heirlooms and memorabilia collected by the seven generations who have made it their home. The book-lined study, with its open fire and deep armchairs, is a place to while away the day. (Break for tea in the airy drawing room.) Spacious, traditionally furnished bedrooms have a pleasingly old-fashioned country-house feel. Ask for recommendations for eateries in town, or arrange to dine with the family. The hosts can help with organising vintage motorcycle or classic car tours. 1½ miles E of town. BEDROOMS 3. Plus 2-bed self-catering cottage nearby, suitable for disabled. FACILITIES Drawing room, library, dining room, free Wi-Fi, 250-acre gardens and parkland (chickens, fantail pigeons, sheep, horses). CHILDREN Not under 12. PRICES Per room B&B single €120–€135, double €220–€235. Dinner €50.

KENMARE Co. Kerry
Map 6:D4

SHEEN FALLS LODGE. Tel 00 353 64 6641600, www.sheenfallslodge.ie. Cast your sights across the suspension bridge from the heritage town, towards this much-refurbished 17th-century fishing lodge. The luxury hotel (Palladian Hotels) overlooking Kenmare Bay and the Sheen waterfalls has plush bedrooms, fine meals, a serene spa, a host of entertainments, and a three-tier afternoon tea. Tastefully decorated, modern bedrooms are in the main building, or in cottages or villas in the grounds. Some are spacious enough to accommodate a family. Daily-changing modern Irish menus are served in the well-regarded restaurant. Head out to play golf or tennis, ride a bicycle or horse, fish for salmon or discover the 19th-century plantation; return for tea or Irish whiskeys in the sun lounge and cocktail bar. BEDROOMS 68. Some suitable for disabled, plus 5 villas available for self-catering. OPEN All year except Jan (open New Year), mid-week Feb–Mar and Nov–Dec. FACILITIES 2 lounges, drawing room, library, study, bar, restaurant, free Wi-Fi, in-room TV (Sky), wedding/function facilities, spa (sauna, steam room, beauty/holistic therapies), indoor heated pool, terrace, 300-acre grounds. BACKGROUND MUSIC In public areas. CHILDREN All ages welcomed. DOGS Allowed in heated stables (£25). PRICES Per room B&B from €180, D,B&B from €290. À la carte €65.

KILKENNY Co. Kilkenny
Map 6:D5

ROSQUIL HOUSE, Castlecomer Road. Tel 00 353 56 772 1419, www.rosquilhouse. com. A fine base for exploring the medieval town, Phil and Rhoda Nolan's good-value B&B is a 20-minute stroll, or quick taxi ride, across the River Nore to the castle. The friendly hosts make the place: well informed and eager to help, the Nolans have ready advice on local restaurants and goings-on, and day trips further afield. Straightforward bedrooms, each with a hot drinks tray, vary in size; a family room with two king-size beds sleeps four. Wholesome breakfasts of home-baked bread, fruit compotes, organic yogurt, granola, hams and local cheeses have some treats, too – scones, perhaps, or tasty cakes. Kilkenny Golf Club is close by. BEDROOMS 7. 1 suitable for disabled, plus a self-catering apartment. FACILITIES Lounge, free Wi-Fi, in-room TV, smoking patio, small garden. CHILDREN All ages welcomed. DOGS Allowed. PRICES Per room B&B from €80.

KILLARNEY Co. Kerry
Map 6:D4

THE BREHON, Muckross Road. Tel 00 353 64 663 0700, www.thebrehon.com. Outside the centre, this large spa hotel has great green views over Killarney national park and the mountains beyond. It is convenient for the town and for events at INEC, just down the road. Understated modern bedrooms with a marble bathroom vary in size; book one with a bay window or balcony to fully take in the vista. Interconnecting rooms and open-plan suites comfortably accommodate a family. Head to the bar for informal light bites; traditional dishes are cooked with a modern twist in the restaurant, Danú. Younger travellers are well taken care of: child-friendly activities include a fairy trail and a junior afternoon tea, plus a play centre and more at sister hotel The Gleneagle, next door. ½ mile from town centre. BEDROOMS 125. Some suitable for disabled. FACILITIES Lift, lounge, bar, restaurant, private dining room, free Wi-Fi, in-room TV, wedding/function facilities, seasonal playroom, Angsana spa (12-metre indoor Vitality pool, steam room, herb sauna, spa bath, fitness centre, massage, treatments), parking. BACKGROUND MUSIC In public areas. CHILDREN All ages welcomed. PRICES Per room B&B from €115. À la carte €42.

LAHINCH Co. Clare
Map 6:C4
MOY HOUSE. Tel 00 353 65 708 2800, www.moyhouse.com. Take in 'great Atlantic views' from Antoin O'Looney's 'fabulously located' 19th-century house standing in large grounds above Lahinch Bay. Sympathetically restored with much personality, the small hotel is 'hospitably run' with a country house feel. Handcrafted furnishings lend charm and warmth to the comfortable bedrooms. Each room is different – one has a turf-burning fireplace, another a canopy bed. A neat, modern suite has its own conservatory lounge with panoramic ocean views. Settle before the fire with a drink from the honesty bar, then sample the 'excellent' daily-changing menu of home-grown produce and locally landed seafood. Extraordinary walks from the front door: a path leads from the lawns through woodland and on to the stony beach. Breakfast brings home-made bread and granola. 2 miles outside Lahinch; golf course nearby. BEDROOMS 9. 4 on ground floor. OPEN Apr–Oct. FACILITIES Drawing room, library, restaurant (closed Sun, Mon),

free Wi-Fi, computer provided, in-room TV (Sky), 15-acre grounds, drying room. BACKGROUND MUSIC In restaurant at mealtimes. CHILDREN All ages welcomed. PRICES Per room B&B from €165, D,B&B from €185.

MAGHERAFELT Co. Londonderry
Map 6:B6
LAUREL VILLA TOWNHOUSE, 60 Church Street, BT45 6AW. Tel 028 7930 1459, www.laurel-villa.com. A rich collection of the late poet-playwright Seamus Heaney's books and memorabilia is displayed at Eugene and Gerardine Kielt's elegant town-centre B&B in the heart of Heaney country. Follow the poetry trail in the large garden, or enjoy tours of the area by Eugene Kielt, a Blue Badge guide. Return for the hostess's home-baked treats at afternoon tea. Each bedroom is named after one of the great Ulster poets, and decorated with pictures, paintings and poems. Breakfast well on fresh fruit salad and an Ulster fry-up in the panelled dining room. The Kielts have a large collection of local genealogical and historical materials; their ancestry-tracing service helps guests to trace their Northern Irish roots. Arts and literary centre Seamus Heaney HomePlace, which opened in September 2016, is an easy ten-minute drive away. BEDROOMS 4. OPEN All year except Christmas, New Year. FACILITIES 2 lounges, dining room, patio, free Wi-Fi, in-room TV, parking. CHILDREN All ages welcomed. PRICES Per person B&B £45 (based on two people sharing).

MOUNTRATH Co. Laois
Map 6:C5
ROUNDWOOD HOUSE. Tel 00 353 57 873 2120, www.roundwoodhouse.com. The

vista stretches over open pastures from Paddy and Hannah Flynn's Georgian mansion, standing in extensive grounds below the Slieve Bloom mountains. A family-run, family-style place, the house has an informal atmosphere that allows for a 'warts-and-all Irish experience', say Guide inspectors in 2017. 'Lovely people', the hosts lay out hot drinks and home-baked biscuits when guests arrive. Traditionally furnished bedrooms ('in need of a little TLC') have a 'comfortable bed' and gracious views over the grounds. In the evening, Paddy Flynn cooks an 'excellent dinner' of local meat and produce in season – perhaps 'perfectly pink' strip loin of beef. (Served in the small dining room, the no-choice menu takes guests' dislikes and dietary restrictions into account.) At breakfast: fresh juices and a 'first-rate' hot dish. Glorious nature is all around; a fascinating 'library of civilisation' appeals on an indoor day. 3 miles N of village. BEDROOMS 10. 4 in garden building. OPEN All year except 24–26 Dec. FACILITIES Drawing room, study, dining room, playroom, library, free Wi-Fi, wedding facilities, 18-acre grounds, parking. BACKGROUND MUSIC None. CHILDREN All ages welcomed. PRICES Per room B&B €150, D,B&B €260. 3-course set dinner (Sun–Thurs) €40, 5-course set dinner €55.
25% DISCOUNT VOUCHERS

MOYARD Co. Galway
Map 6:C4
CROCNARAW COUNTRY HOUSE. Tel 00 353 95 41068, www.crocnaraw.ie. The 'terrific hospitality' stands out at Lucy Fretwell's Georgian guest house close to Ballinakill Bay. Old trees lean over the rustic stone wall at the bottom of the driveway. Come up the path: a modest, homely place, the house has a lived-in feel, with flowers, pictures and ornaments filling the rooms. Upstairs, light-filled, country-style bedrooms have broad views of the surrounding acres of gardens and rugged meadowland; one has a claw-footed bath in the bathroom. Afternoons, the hostess serves tea with Aga-fresh cakes or scones by a peat fire in the drawing room. A generous breakfast has home-baked soda bread, and produce from the kitchen garden and orchard. Private parties with a chef can be arranged. Outdoor pursuits nearby. 2 miles from Letterfrack. BEDROOMS 4. OPEN May– Oct. FACILITIES Dining room, drawing room, snug, free Wi-Fi, 2-acre garden in 20-acre grounds (orchard, donkeys), fishing, angling, pony trekking and golf can be arranged. CHILDREN All ages welcomed (under 6 months by arrangement). PRICES Per person B&B €35–€58.
25% DISCOUNT VOUCHERS

NEWPORT Co. Mayo
Map 6:B4
NEWPORT HOUSE. Tel 00 353 98 41222, www.newporthouse.ie. A traditional Irish country house atmosphere fills this creeper-clad Georgian mansion overlooking the quay of a heritage town on the shores of Clew Bay. It has been owned, and impeccably maintained, by Kieran Thompson since 1985. High-ceilinged public rooms are hung with artworks; there are plenty of books to browse, and the 'lived-in' fireside sofas on which to read them. Traditional bedrooms are spread across the main house and two smaller courtyard

buildings (one of which was the holiday home of the late Seán Lemass, former taoiseach of Ireland). In the gracious dining room, French-influenced dishes are cooked using local produce – fish and shellfish from the bay; Irish beef and farmhouse cheeses. A special place for fisherfolk, the house has extensive fishing rights on the river; basket lunches and, later, freezing and smoking facilities can be arranged. 7 miles N of Westport. BEDROOMS 14. 4 in courtyard, 2 on ground floor. OPEN 19 Mar–end Oct. FACILITIES Drawing room, sitting room, bar, dining room, free Wi-Fi (in public areas and some bedrooms), in-room TV, 15-acre grounds, walled garden, private fishery, bicycle hire. BACKGROUND MUSIC None. CHILDREN All ages welcomed. DOGS Allowed in courtyard bedrooms. PRICES Per person B&B €110–€145, D,B&B €175–€210. 5-course dinner €58.
25% DISCOUNT VOUCHERS

RAMELTON Co. Donegal
Map 6:B5

FREWIN, Rectory Road. Tel 00 353 74 915 1246, www.frewinhouse.com. Regina Gibson and Thomas Coyle's creeper-covered Victorian house is a warm and welcoming place on the outskirts of a heritage town at the mouth of the River Lennon. The owners have run their B&B for nearly 20 years. A labour of love, the family home has been refurbished 'with flair' – Thomas Coyle, an antiques collector and restorer, has returned the stained-glass windows and elegant staircase to their original splendour, adding a collection of antiques, squashy sofas and candle-holding chandeliers. Sleep in one of the spacious country house-style bedrooms, each with a compact bathroom and woodland views. Book lovers, ask for the suite with its own library. Sit down to a praiseworthy communal breakfast in the morning, then take a stroll through the town to the water's edge. BEDROOMS 3. Plus 1-bed cottage in the grounds. OPEN Apr–Oct, by special arrangement for groups of 4–6 in Feb, Mar, Nov. FACILITIES Sitting room, library, dining room, free Wi-Fi, 2-acre mature garden, golf, horse-riding. BACKGROUND MUSIC None. CHILDREN Not under 10. PRICES Per person (sharing) B&B €75–€85.

RATHNEW Co. Wicklow
Map 6:C6

HUNTER'S HOTEL, Newrath Bridge. Tel 00 353 404 40106, www.hunters.ie. In the spring and summer, a riot of colour bursts from the gardens and flowerbeds surrounding this rambling riverside coaching inn, said to be the longest-running in Ireland. Owned by the same family for 200 years, the characterful building is today under the stewardship of brothers Richard and Tom Gelletlie. Spacious bedrooms, many overlooking the gardens, have old-world charm in their chintz and creaking floorboards, well-chosen antiques and prints. Traditional Irish dishes are served on crisp tablecloths in the dining room; Sunday luncheon is a feast. Sit outside on a sunny day: you're on the banks of the River Vartry, a delightful spot for a picnic or an alfresco G&T. 2 km SE of Ashford. BEDROOMS 16. 1 on ground floor. OPEN All year except 24–26 Dec. FACILITIES Drawing room, lounge, bar, dining room, private dining room, free Wi-Fi, in-room TV (Freeview), 2-acre

garden in 5-acre grounds (river walks), golf, tennis, riding, sandy beach, fishing nearby. BACKGROUND MUSIC None. CHILDREN All ages welcomed. DOGS Allowed by arrangement. PRICES Per person B&B from €65, D,B&B from €95. Set dinner €29.50–€48, Sunday lunch from €33.50.
25% DISCOUNT VOUCHERS

RECESS Co. Galway
Map 6:C4
LOUGH INAGH LODGE, Inagh Valley. Tel 00 353 95 34706, www. loughinaghlodgehotel.ie. A 'lovely, peaceful spot' embraced on all sides by spectacular mountains, the lake here offers unhurried respite – as fishing enthusiasts have known since the 1880s. On its shore, this 19th-century fishing lodge has been owned by the O'Connor family for nearly 30 years. Alternate days by the lake with days out on the river on one of the hotel's boats, accompanied by an experienced ghillie. Return to tea in the well-appointed sitting room, where a log fire burns. At dinner, tuck in to seafood and Connemara produce cooked with French flair, or order a simpler dish in the oak-panelled bar. Later, fall asleep in one of the comfortable, traditionally furnished bedrooms, each different, all charming in their way. BEDROOMS 13. 4 on ground floor. OPEN Mar–Dec. FACILITIES Sitting room, bar, library, dining room, free Wi-Fi, in-room TV (Freeview), 14-acre grounds, wedding facilities. BACKGROUND MUSIC None. CHILDREN All ages welcomed. DOGS Allowed, on lead in grounds. PRICES Per room B&B €155–€220, D,B&B €250–€320. À la carte €50.
25% DISCOUNT VOUCHERS

STRANGFORD Co. Down
Map 6:B6
THE CUAN, 6–10 The Square, BT30 7ND. Tel 028 4488 1222, www.thecuan. com. Liked for its laid-back, village-hub atmosphere, Peter and Caroline McErlean's lively 200-year-old inn is in a conservation area on the shores of Strangford Lough. Rub shoulders with locals in the pub; at mealtimes, feast on traditional roasts and local seafood, perhaps award-winning smoked haddock, or langoustines freshly caught in the lough. Bed down, afterwards, in one of the comfortable, simply furnished bedrooms. The McErleans have anticipated many niche tastes and put together packages to suit, from sporty breaks to winning Winterfell experiences inspired by the Game of Thrones TV series, which films nearby. BEDROOMS 9. 1 suitable for disabled, plus 2-bed self-catering cottage. FACILITIES 2 lounges, bar, restaurant, free Wi-Fi, wedding/function facilities. BACKGROUND MUSIC Traditional music in bar and restaurant, live music events in the summer. CHILDREN All ages welcomed. PRICES Per person B&B single £59.50–£67, double £44.50–£49.50, D,B&B single £75–£82, double £60–£65.

THOMASTOWN Co. Kilkenny
Map 6:D5
BALLYDUFF HOUSE. Tel 00 353 56 775 8488, www.ballyduffhouse.ie. In a Georgian country house beside the River Nore, Brede Thomas runs her elegant B&B with 'real style and friendliness'. Fresh flowers fill the public rooms; there are oil paintings, book-lined shelves and open fires. Every window takes in wide views of farmland and gardens. Upstairs, with plaid or chintz or a

colourful rug, spacious bedrooms have plenty of country charm, plus heaps of natural light through tall windows. Spend an afternoon fishing on the Nore, or trailing country and riverside paths – tranquillity suffuses the air. The hostess has local recommendations at dinnertime. Full Irish breakfasts are served in the dining room. 1 hour from Dublin. BEDROOMS 6. FACILITIES Drawing room, library, dining room, free Wi-Fi, garden, fishing, canoeing. CHILDREN All ages welcomed. DOGS Allowed by arrangement. PRICES Per person B&B €50.

WATERFORD Co. Waterford
Map 6:D5
FOXMOUNT COUNTRY HOUSE, Passage East Road. Tel 00 353 51 874308, www. foxmountcountryhouse.com. Fall into the relaxed pace of country life here: green fields on the horizon, Margaret and David Kent's ivy-clad Georgian house stands amid large, well-kept gardens on the owners' working dairy farm. In a sitting room decorated with antiques and family photographs, the grand marble fireplace is just right for a fireside afternoon tea with buttered scones. (Guests are welcome to bring their own wine and aperitifs if they fancy something stronger.) Homely, traditionally furnished bedrooms overlook the garden; a spacious room is suitable for a family. Breakfast is a generous array of home-baked breads, freshly laid eggs, compotes and preserves made from home-grown fruit. 3 miles SW of the city. BEDROOMS 4. OPEN Mar–Sept. FACILITIES Dining room, drawing room, free Wi-Fi, 4-acre grounds. BACKGROUND MUSIC None. CHILDREN All ages welcomed. DOGS Allowed in private kennels in the grounds. PRICES Per person B&B €50–€60 (sharing).

WATERVILLE Co. Kerry
Map 6:D4
BUTLER ARMS. Tel 00 353 66 947 4144, www.butlerarms.com. In a village on the Wild Atlantic Way, this 'friendly, well-run' Victorian hotel has been owned by the Huggard family since 1915. Gazing across the ocean as it has done since it first opened, it is today a welcoming spot with roaring fires, and plenty of seating to take in the glorious views. 'Excellent' Irish cooking is on the menu in Charlie's restaurant; the bar, adorned with fishing memorabilia, is the place for an informal pub dish, a Guinness and some local gossip. Most of the unfussy bedrooms have broad views over the water; some, on the ground floor, have a sitting area, a fireplace and direct access to the garden. BEDROOMS 36. 10 on ground floor. OPEN Mar–Nov. FACILITIES Lounge, bar, restaurant, coffee shop, free Wi-Fi, in-room TV (Sky), garden, wedding/function facilities, parking. BACKGROUND MUSIC None. CHILDREN All ages welcomed. DOGS Allowed. PRICES Per room B&B from €110, D,B&B from €209.

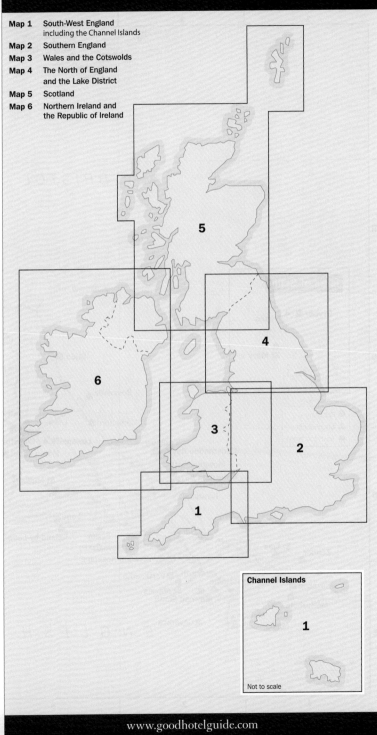

5

4

6

3

2

1

Channel Islands

1

Not to scale

MAP 1 • SOUTH-WEST ENGLAND

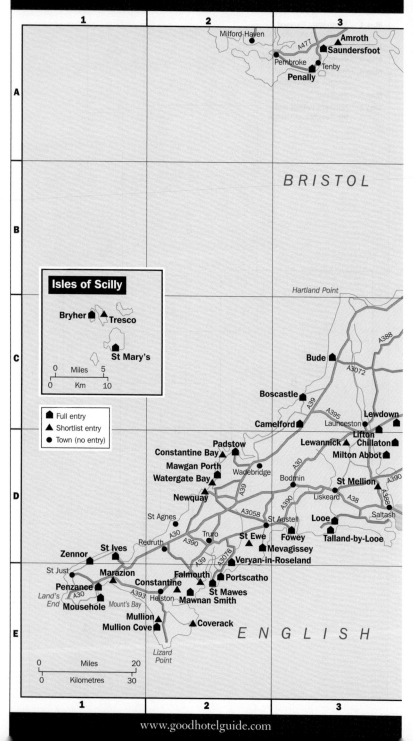

BRISTOL

Milford Haven
A477
Amroth
Saundersfoot
Pembroke
Penally
Tenby

Isles of Scilly

Bryher
Tresco

St Mary's

0 Miles 5
0 Km 10

■ Full entry
▲ Shortlist entry
● Town (no entry)

Hartland Point

A388

Bude
A3072
Boscastle
A39
A395
Lewdown
Camelford
Launceston
Lewannick
Lifton
Chillaton
Padstow
Milton Abbot
Constantine Bay
Mawgan Porth
Watergate Bay
Wadebridge
A30
Bodmin
St Mellion
A390
Newquay
A39
A390
Liskeard
A38
A3058
St Austell
Saltash
St Agnes
Truro
St Ewe
Looe
Redruth
A30
A390
Fowey
Talland-by-Looe
Zennor
St Ives
A39
A3078
Mevagissey
St Just
Marazion
Veryan-in-Roseland
Penzance
Constantine
Falmouth
Portscatho
Land's
End
A30
A393
Helston
St Mawes
Mousehole
Mount's Bay
Mawnan Smith
Mullion
Coverack
Mullion Cove
ENGLISH
Lizard
Point

0 Miles 20
0 Kilometres 30

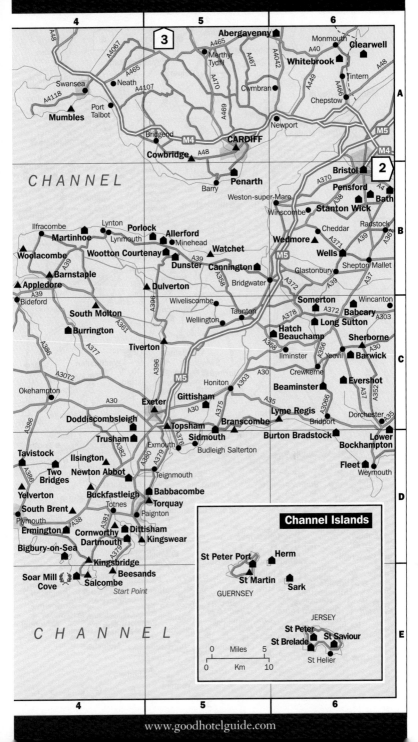

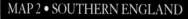

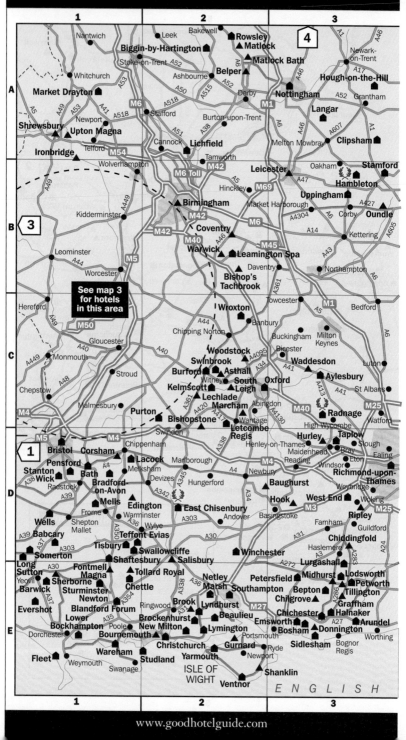

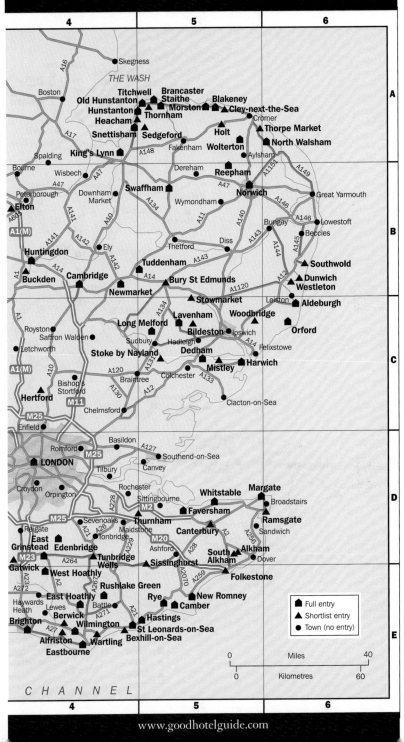

4 **5** **6**

THE WASH

Skegness

Boston

A16

A17

Old Hunstanton
Hunstanton
Heacham
Snettisham
Titchwell
Brancaster
Staithe
Thornham
Morston
Sedgeford
Blakeney
Cley-next-the-Sea
Cromer
Thorpe Market
North Walsham
Holt
Wolterton
Fakenham
Aylsham

King's Lynn
A148

Spalding

Bourne

Wisbech

A47

Peterborough
Downham
Market
Dereham

Elton
A605

A1(M)

A141
A142
A10
A142

Huntingdon
A14

Buckden
A1

Cambridge

Newmarket

Ely

Thetford

Swaffham
A134

Reepham

Norwich

Wymondham

A11

A140

A47

Bungay

A146

Great Yarmouth

Lowestoft

A146

Beccles

A145

Diss

A143

Tuddenham

Bury St Edmunds
A143

A1120

Southwold

Dunwich
Westleton

A12

A144

Stowmarket

Lavenham

Long Melford

Bildeston

Woodbridge

Leiston

Aldeburgh

Ipswich

Orford

Royston

Saffron Walden

Letchworth

A1

Sudbury

Hadleigh

Dedham

A14

Felixstowe

Stoke by Nayland

A131

Mistley

Harwich

A1(M)

A10

Bishop's
Stortford

Hertford

M11

Braintree

A120

Colchester

A133

A130

A12

Chelmsford

Clacton-on-Sea

M25

Enfield

Romford

Basildon

A127

Southend-on-Sea

M25

LONDON

Tilbury

Canvey

Croydon

Orpington

Rochester

Sittingbourne

Whitstable

Margate

Broadstairs

Faversham

Ramsgate

M2

M25

Sevenoaks

Thurnham

Maidstone

Canterbury

A2

Sandwich

A21
A26

Tonbridge

M20

A229

Ashford

A28

A256

South
Alkham

Alkham

Dover

Reigate

East
Grinstead

Edenbridge

Tunbridge
Wells

Sissinghurst

A2070

A259

Folkestone

M23

Gatwick

A264

A23

West Hoathly

A2272

A2

A26

Rushlake Green

Haywards
Heath

East Hoathly

Battle

Rye

New Romney

Lewes

Berwick

A271

Camber

Brighton

Wilmington

A27

A21

Hastings

Alfriston

Wartling

St Leonards-on-Sea

Bexhill-on-Sea

Eastbourne

Legend:
■ Full entry
▲ Shortlist entry
● Town (no entry)

0   Miles   40

0   Kilometres   60

C H A N N E L

4 **5** **6**

MAP 3 • WALES AND THE COTSWOLDS

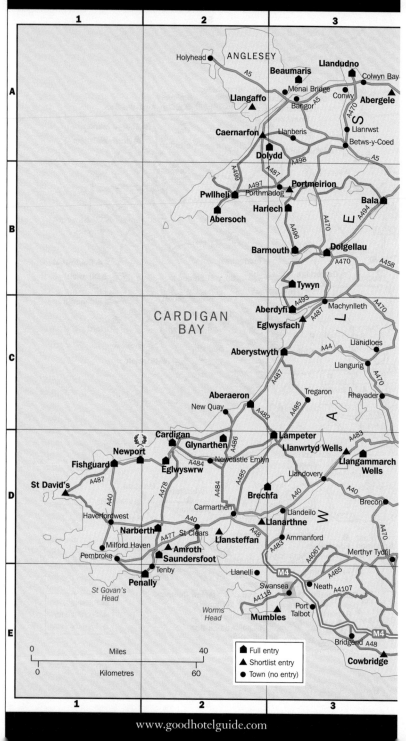

1 **2** **3**

Holyhead

ANGLESEY

A5

Beaumaris

Llandudno
Colwyn Bay

A Menai Bridge
Conwy
Llangaffo
Bangor A5
Llanrwst
Abergele

Caernarfon Llanberis
Betws-y-Coed
Dolydd
A498 A5

A499 A497 A487

Portmeirion

Pwllheli Porthmadog
Bala
A470
Harlech
A494
Abersoch

B A496

Barmouth
Dolgellau
A470 A458

Tywyn

A493

CARDIGAN
Aberdyfi Machynlleth A470
BAY
Eglwysfach

Llanidloes

Aberystwyth A44

A487 Llangurig

C A470

Aberaeron Tregaron
New Quay
A482 A485 Rhayader

Cardigan **Lampeter**
Glynarthen A486 **Llanwrtyd Wells** A483
Newport
Fishguard Newcastle Emlyn
A484 **Llangammarch
Eglwyswrw** Wells

St David's A487 Llandovery
A40 A478 A484 A485 A40 A40
Brechfa
Haverfordwest Llandeilo Brecon

D Carmarthen A40
Narberth **Llanarthne**
St Clears A483
Milford Haven A477 **Llansteffan** Ammanford
Pembroke **Amroth** A483 A4067 Merthyr Tydfil
Saundersfoot
Tenby Llanelli M4 A465
Penally
St Govan's Swansea Neath A4107
Head
Worms A4118 Port
Head **Mumbles** Talbot
M4
E Bridgend A48

0 Miles 40 **Cowbridge**

0 Kilometres 60

■ Full entry
▲ Shortlist entry
● Town (no entry)

1 **2** **3**

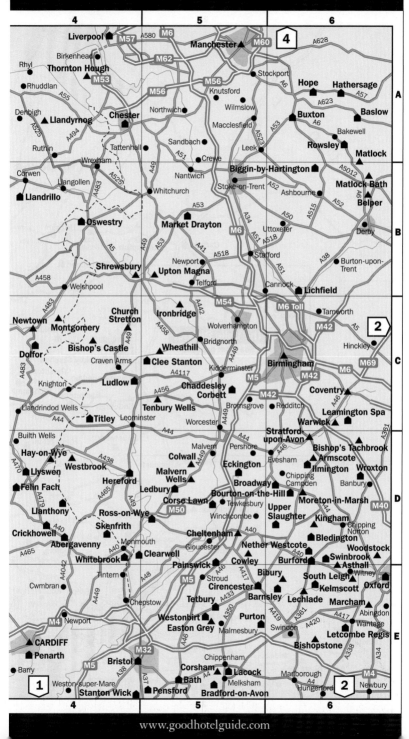

MAP 4 • THE NORTH OF ENGLAND AND THE LAKE DISTRICT

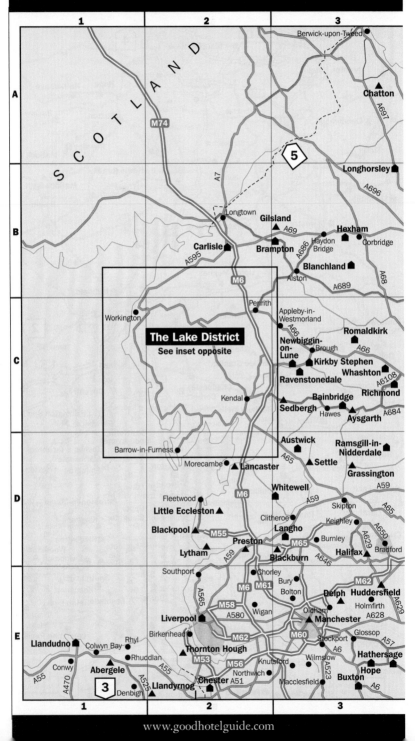

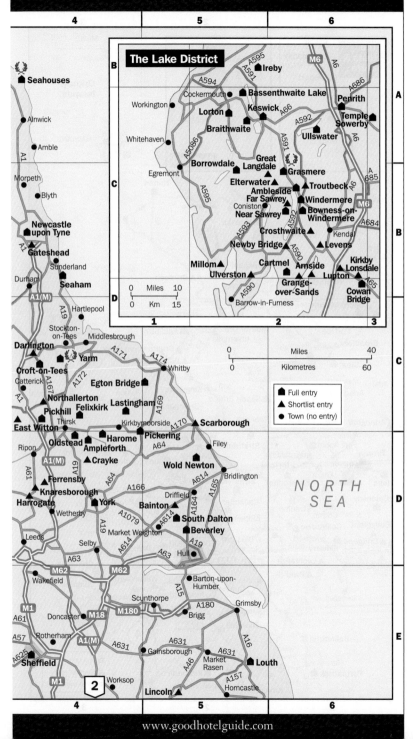

The Lake District

Seahouses
Alnwick
Amble
Morpeth
Blyth
Newcastle upon Tyne
Gateshead
Sunderland
Durham
Seaham
Hartlepool
Stockton-on-Tees
Middlesbrough
Darlington
Yarm
Croft-on-Tees
Catterick
Egton Bridge
Whitby
Northallerton
Felixkirk
Lastingham
Pickhill
Thirsk
Kirkbymoorside
Scarborough
East Witton
Oldstead
Harome
Pickering
Filey
Ripon
Ampleforth
Wold Newton
Crayke
Bridlington
Ferrensby
A166
Driffield
Knaresborough
Harrogate
York
Bainton
Wetherby
South Dalton
Market Weighton
Beverley
Leeds
Selby
Hull
Wakefield
Barton-upon-Humber
Scunthorpe
Grimsby
Doncaster
Brigg
Rotherham
Gainsborough
Market Rasen
Louth
Sheffield
Worksop
Lincoln
Horncastle

Workington
Cockermouth
Ireby
Bassenthwaite Lake
Lorton
Keswick
Penrith
Braithwaite
Temple Sowerby
Whitehaven
Ullswater
Borrowdale
Great Langdale
Egremont
Elterwater
Grasmere
Ambleside
Troutbeck
Far Sawrey
Windermere
Coniston
Near Sawrey
Bowness-on-Windermere
Kendal
Crosthwaite
Newby Bridge
Levens
Millom
Cartmel
Kirkby Lonsdale
Ulverston
Arnside
Lupton
Grange-over-Sands
Cowan Bridge
Barrow-in-Furness

0 Miles 10
0 Km 15

NORTH SEA

0 Miles 40
0 Kilometres 60

- ■ Full entry
- ▲ Shortlist entry
- ● Town (no entry)

MAP 5 • SCOTLAND

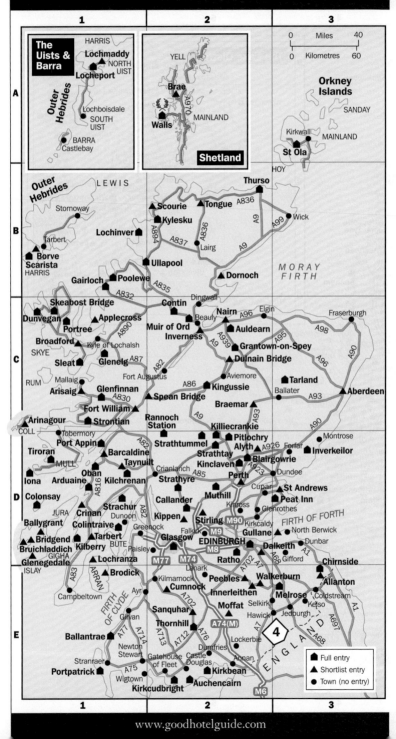

The Uists & Barra

HARRIS

Lochmaddy
NORTH UIST
Locheport

Outer Hebrides

Lochboisdale
SOUTH UIST

BARRA
Castlebay

Shetland

YELL

Brae

A970

MAINLAND

Walls

Orkney Islands

SANDAY

Kirkwall
MAINLAND

St Ola

0   Miles   40
0   Kilometres   60

Outer Hebrides

LEWIS

HOY

Stornoway

Tarbert

Borve
Scarista
HARRIS

Lochinver

Scourie

Kylesku

Tongue   A836

Thurso

A99   Wick

A836

A894

A837

Lairg

A9

MORAY FIRTH

Gairloch   Poolewe

Ullapool

Dornoch

A835

Skeabost Bridge

Dunvegan   Applecross

Portree

Broadford

SKYE

Sleat   Glenelg

Contin

A832

Dingwall

Muir of Ord

Inverness

Beauly

A96

Nairn   Elgin

Auldearn

A95

Fraserburgh

A98

A90

Kyle of Lochalsh

A890

A87

A82

Grantown-on-Spey

A939

A9

Dulnain Bridge

A96

RUM   Mallaig

Arisaig   Glenfinnan

A830

Fort Augustus

Aviemore

A86

Kingussie

Tarland

Ballater

Aberdeen

Spean Bridge

Braemar

A93

Fort William

Strontian

A9

Killiecrankie

A93

Arinagour

COLL

Port Appin

Tobermory

Barcaldine

Taynuilt

TIRORAN

MULL

Oban

Arduaine

Kilchrenan

Rannoch Station

Strathtummel

Pitlochry

Alyth   A926   Forfar

Inverkeilor

Strathtay

Kinclaven   Blairgowrie

A823

Dundee

A90

Montrose

Crianlarich

A85

Strathyre

Perth

Cupar

St Andrews

Iona

Arduaine

A816

Callander

Muthill

Peat Inn

Kinross

Kirkcaldy

FIRTH OF FORTH

Colonsay

JURA

Strachur

Dunoon

Kippen

Stirling

M90

North Berwick

Gullane

Crinan

Colintraive

Greenock

Falkirk

M9

Ballygrant

Tarbert
BUTE

Paisley

Glasgow

M8

EDINBURGH

Dalkeith

Dunbar

A1

Gifford

Bruichladdich
GIGHA

Kilberry

Lochranza

Ratho

A702

A7

A68

Chirnside

Glenegedale

ISLAY

ARRAN

Brodick

Lanark

Peebles

Walkerburn

Allanton

Bridgend

A83

Kilmarnock

Cumnock

Innerleithen

Melrose

Coldstream

Campbeltown

FIRTH OF CLYDE

Ayr

Sanquhar

Moffat

Selkirk

Kelso

A1

Girvan

A77

Thornhill

A74(M)

Hawick

Jedburgh

A697

Ballantrae

A714

A713

A712

A76

Lockerbie

4

ENGLAND

A68

Newton Stewart

Dumfries

Annan

A75

Portpatrick

Stranraer

Gatehouse of Fleet

Castle Douglas

Kirkbean

Wigtown

Kirkcudbright

Auchencairn

M6

■ Full entry
▲ Shortlist entry
● Town (no entry)

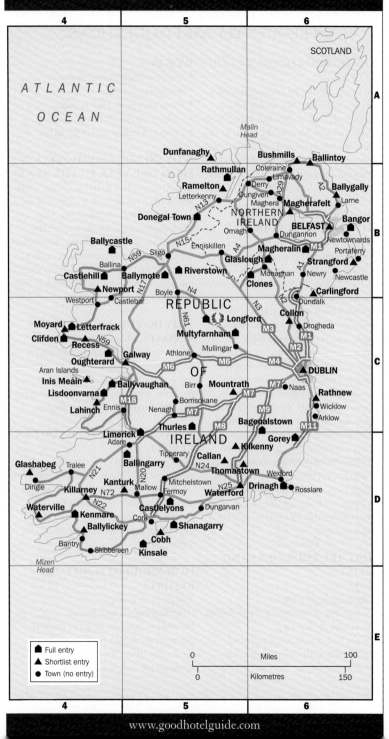

SCOTLAND

ATLANTIC

OCEAN

Malin
Head

Dunfanaghy

Bushmills   Ballintoy

Rathmullan
Coleraine
Limavady
Ramelton   Derry   Ballygally
Letterkenny   Dungiven   Larne
N13   Maghera   Magherafelt
Donegal Town   NORTHERN   Bangor
IRELAND
Omagh   BELFAST
Dungannon   Newtownards
N15   Enniskillen   A4   Portaferry
Ballycastle   Magheralin   M1   Strangford
N59   Sligo   Glaslough   A1
Ballina   Riverstown   Newry   Newcastle
Castlehill   Ballymote   Monaghan
Newport   Clones   Carlingford
Westport   Boyle   N4   Dundalk
Castlebar
REPUBLIC   Collon
Moyard   Letterfrack   Longford   M3   Drogheda
N61
Clifden   Multyfarnham   M1
Recess   N59   M2
Oughterard   Galway   Mullingar   M4
Aran Islands   Athlone   M6   DUBLIN
Inis Meáin   OF   Naas
Ballyvaughan   Birr   Mountrath   M7
Lisdoonvarna   Borrisokane   M7   Rathnew
Lahinch   M18   Nenagh   M7   M9   Wicklow
Ennis   Thurles   Bagenalstown   Arklow
Limerick   M8   M11
Adare   IRELAND   Gorey
Ballingarry   Tipperary   Kilkenny
Glashabeg   Tralee   Callan
N21   N24   Thomastown   Wexford
Dingle   Kanturk   Mitchelstown   N25   Drinagh
Killarney   Mallow   Fermoy   Waterford   Rosslare
N72   Castlelyons   Dungarvan
Waterville   N22   Cork   Shanagarry
Kenmare   Cobh
Ballilickey   Kinsale
Bantry   Skibbereen
Mizen
Head

Full entry
Shortlist entry
Town (no entry)

0   Miles   100
0   Kilometres   150

FREQUENTLY ASKED QUESTIONS

HOW DO YOU CHOOSE A GOOD HOTEL?

The hotels we like are relaxed, unstuffy and personally run. We do not have a specific template: our choices vary greatly in style and size. Most of the hotels in the Guide are family owned and family run. These are places where the needs and comfort of the guest are put ahead of the convenience of the management.

YOU ARE A HOTEL GUIDE – WHY DO YOU INCLUDE SO MANY PUBS AND B&BS?

Attitudes and expectations have changed considerably since the Guide was founded in the 1970s. Today's guests expect more informality, less deference. There has been a noticeable rise in the standards of food and accommodation in pubs and restaurants. This is demonstrated by the number of such places suggested to us by our readers. While pubs may have a more relaxed attitude than some traditional hotels, we ensure that only those that maintain high standards of service are included in our selections. The best B&Bs have always combined a high standard of accommodation with excellent value for money. Expect the bedrooms in a pub or B&B listed in the Guide to be well equipped, with thoughtful extras. B&B owners invariably know how to serve a good breakfast.

WHAT ARE YOUR LIKES AND DISLIKES?

We like

* Flexible times for meals.
* Two decent armchairs in the bedroom.
* Good bedside lighting.
* Proper hangers in the wardrobe.
* Fresh milk with the tea tray in the room.

We dislike

* Intrusive background music.
* Stuffy dress codes.
* Bossy notices and house rules.
* Hidden service charges.
* Packaged fruit juices at breakfast.

WHY DO YOU DROP HOTELS FROM ONE YEAR TO THE NEXT?

Readers are quick to tell us if they think standards have slipped at a hotel. If the evidence is overwhelming, we drop the hotel from the Guide or perhaps downgrade it to the Shortlist. Sometimes we send inspectors just to be sure. When a hotel is sold, we look for reports since the new owners took over, otherwise we inspect or omit it.

WHY DO YOU ASK FOR 'MORE REPORTS, PLEASE'?

When we have not heard about a hotel for several years, we ask readers for more reports. Sometimes readers returning to a favourite hotel may not send a fresh report. Readers often respond to our request.

WHAT SHOULD I TELL YOU IN A REPORT?

How you enjoyed your stay. We welcome reports of any length. We want to know what you think about the welcome, the service, the building and the facilities. Even a short report can tell us a great deal about the owners, the staff and the atmosphere.

HOW SHOULD I SEND YOU A REPORT?

You can email us at editor@goodhotelguide.com. Or you can write to us at the address given on the report form opposite, or send a report via the GHG's website: www.goodhotelguide.com.

Please send your reports to:
The Good Hotel Guide, 50 Addison Avenue, London W11 4QP, England.

Unless asked not to, we assume that we may publish your name. If you would like more report forms please tick ☐ Alternatively, you can either photostat this form or submit a review on our website: www.goodhotelguide.com

NAME OF HOTEL: _____
ADDRESS: _____
_____

Date of most recent visit: _____ Duration of stay: _____

☐ New recommendation   ☐ Comment on existing entry

Report:

Please continue overleaf

I am not connected directly or indirectly with the management or proprietors

Signed: _____

Name: (CAPITALS PLEASE) _____

Address: _____

_____

Email address: _____

INDEX OF HOTELS BY COUNTY
(S) indicates a Shortlist entry

ALPHABETICAL LIST OF HOTELS
(S) indicates a Shortlist entry

Fischer's at Baslow Hall Baslow 85

Five Brighton (S) 519

Five Alls Lechlade (S) 555

Five Arrows Waddesdon (S) 596

Fleur de Lys Shaftesbury 286

Fontmell Fontmell Magna (S) 543

Forest Country Guest House Newtown (S) 637

Forest Side Grasmere 168

Forss House Thurso 403

41 London (S) 491

Foveran St Ola 392

Fowey Hall Fowey 166

Foxmount Country House Waterford (S) 653

Frégate St Peter Port 451

Frewin Ramelton (S) 651

Frog Street Farmhouse Hatch Beauchamp 178

Fuzzy Duck Armscote (S) 504

G

g Galway (S) 646

Gallivant Camber 127

General Tarleton Ferrensby (S) 542

George Buckden (S) 521

George Hathersage 179

George Stamford 295

George Yarmouth 339

George in Rye Rye 277

Ghan House Carlingford (S) 642

Gilpin Hotel and Lake House Windermere 332

Glazebrook House South Brent (S) 584

Glenapp Castle Ballantrae 347

Glenegedale House Glenegedale (S) 617

Glenelg Inn Glenelg 360

Glenfinnan House Glenfinnan 361

Glenholme Country House Kirkcudbright 372

Glenlohane House Kanturk (S) 647

Gliffaes Crickhowell 420

Godolphin Arms Marazion (S) 563

Goldstone Hall Market Drayton 219

Gonville Cambridge (S) 523

Good London (S) 492

Gordon's Inverkeilor 364

Goring London 55

Gorman's Clifftop House Glashabeg (S) 646

Grand Eastbourne 156

Grasmere Grasmere 169

Grasshoppers Glasgow 359

Grassington House Grassington (S) 546

Gravetye Manor East Grinstead 153

Grays Bath (S) 508

Grazing Goat London 56

Great House Lavenham 197

Great Northern London (S) 492

Green House Bournemouth (S) 516

Green Oak Barn Berwick (S) 511

Green Park Pitlochry 383

Greenbank Farmhouse Lancaster (S) 555

Greenhills St Peter 450

Gregans Castle Ballyvaughan 460

Greyhound Inn Letcombe Regis 200

Greystones Oban (S) 622

Greywalls Gullane (S) 618

Grove Narberth 436

Grove Farm House Shrewsbury (S) 582

Gunton Arms Thorpe Market (S) 590

Gurnard's Head Zennor 341

Gwesty Cymru Aberystwyth 413

H

Hack & Spade Whashton 326

Halfway Bridge Lodsworth 205

Ham Yard London (S) 492

K

Kaywana Hall Kingswear (S) 553

Kensington London (S) 495

Kerswell Farmhouse Cornworthy (S) 532

Kilberry Inn Kilberry 366

Kilbury Manor Buckfastleigh (S) 522

Kilcamb Lodge Strontian 400

Killiane Castle Drinagh 468

Killiecrankie Killiecrankie 368

Kilmeny Country House Ballygrant (S) 606

King John Inn Tollard Royal (S) 592

Kings Arms Sherborne (S) 581

King's Head Inn Bledington 103

Kings Head Cirencester 139

Kinloch House Blairgowrie 348

Kinmel Arms Abergele (S) 630

Knightsbridge London (S) 495

Knockendarroch Pitlochry 384

Knockeven House Cobh (S) 643

Knockinaam Lodge Portpatrick 388

Kylesku Kylesku 373

L

La Collinette St Peter Port (S) 639

Lake Llangammarch Wells 433

Lake Isle Uppingham 317

Lamb Inn Burford 123

Langar Hall Langar 194

Langass Lodge Locheport 374

Langshott Manor Gatwick (S) 544

Laslett London (S) 496

Lasswade Country House Llanwrtyd Wells (S) 635

Lastingham Grange Lastingham 196

Laurel Villa Townhouse Magherafelt (S) 649

Leathes Head Borrowdale 104

Leena's Guest House Salisbury (S) 578

Levin London 58

Lewinnick Lodge Newquay (S) 568

Lewtrenchard Manor Lewdown 201

Library House Ironbridge (S) 551

Lifeboat Inn Thornham (S) 589

Lime Tree Fort William (S) 616

Lime Tree London (S) 496

Lime Wood Lyndhurst 217

Lindeth Fell Bowness-on-Windermere 108

Lindeth Howe Bowness-on-Windermere (S) 516

Lion and Pheasant Shrewsbury (S) 582

Little Barwick House Barwick 83

Little Gloster Gurnard (S) 547

Llangoed Hall Llyswen 435

Llanthony Priory Llanthony 434

Llwyn Helyg Llanarthne (S) 633

Llwyndu Farmhouse Barmouth 416

Llys Meddyg Newport 438

Loch Gorm House Bruichladdich (S) 609

Loch Melfort Arduaine 344

Long Melford Swan Long Melford 206

Longueville Manor St Saviour 452

Lord Crewe Arms Blanchland 101

Lords of the Manor Upper Slaughter 316

Lorum Old Rectory Bagenalstown 456

Lough Inagh Lodge Recess (S) 652

Low Mill Guest House Bainbridge 81

Lower Barns St Ewe (S) 575

Lower Farm Oundle (S) 570

Luttrell Arms Dunster 151

Lynch Country House Somerton 292

Lyzzick Hall Keswick (S) 552

M

Magazine Wood Sedgeford (S) 579

Main House London (S) 496